TV SEASON
77-78

ORYX PRESS

Operation Oryx, started more than 15 years ago at the Phoenix Zoo to save the rare white antelope—believed to have inspired the unicorn of mythology—has apparently succeeded. The operation was launched in 1962 when it became evident that the animals were facing extinction in their native habitat of the Arabian peninsula.

An original herd of nine, put together through *Operation Oryx* by five world organizations now number 47 in Phoenix with another 38 at the San Diego Wild Game Farm, four others have recently been sent to live in their natural habitat in Jordan, and 26 have been shipped to new breeding grounds in Israel, Rotterdam and Stockholm.

Also, in what has come to be known as "The Second Law of Return," rare biblical animals are being collected from many countries to roam freely at the Hai Bar Biblical Wildlife Nature Reserve in the Negev, in Israel, the most recent addition being a breeding herd of eight Arabian Oryx. With the addition of these Oryx, their collection of rare biblical animals is complete.

Copyright © 1979 by Nina David
Published by The Oryx Press
3930 East Camelback Road
Phoenix, Arizona 85018

Published simultaneously in Canada

Printed and Bound in the United States of America

Library of Congress Card No. 77-94093

ISBN 0-912700-23-8

Contents

Introduction

TV Season is an annual reference work of current and future value to researchers interested in the history of the medium, to television viewers, and to librarians and their patrons. The 1977–78 edition is the fourth of the series to be issued.

Information on each national TV program presented by the networks—ABC, CBS, NBC, and PBS—as well as currently produced syndicated shows with national distribution, is given in the "TV Programs 1977–78" section. The listings are alphabetic by program name. Reruns in syndication are not listed. "See" references are used when a title is unclear.

Information on each regularly scheduled show includes name, network, type of show, descriptive material, and credits, such as executive producer, producer, director, writer, host, announcer, and the stars and the characters they portray. For specials, e.g., variety shows, awards shows, parades, pageants, sports events, and interviews, guests are noted; other specials, such as made-for-television movies, include cast names whenever possible. Feature films originally made for theater distribution do not list cast and credits. All individuals listed are included in the "Who's Who in TV" section.

Syndicated shows and shows on Public Television Stations (PBS) air on different dates in different locations. For these, the first day or date a show is televised is noted. Preview shows for the 1978–79 season have been omitted. Presidential newscasts are not specifically included.

This volume covers shows originating between September 12, 1977 (the date chosen as the first day of the 1977–78 season) and the date each network decided to begin the 1978–79 season: ABC, September 11, 1978; CBS, September 23, 1978; and NBC, September 18, 1978. This marks a change from previous editions, in which an arbitrary cut-off date had been selected. Since PBS has no official season, September 11, 1978, was chosen as the last day of the 1977–78 season. Some PBS programs which are a part of a series may have been shown after September 11, 1978. For example, the "Cleo Laine and John Dankworth" program in the series "In Performance at Wolftrap," was shown on September 14, 1978. Therefore, *TV Season 77-78* covers at least a calendar year of programming for each network.

The special lists encompass new shows, cancelled shows, new and cancelled shows, summer series, and a list of shows captioned or translated for the hearing impaired. As in previous years, PBS series (which are usually of limited duration) and special shows are not found in these lists. The only exceptions are programs captioned for the hearing-impaired.

Emmy-award winning shows cover the period March 4, 1977–June 30, 1978. Daytime Emmy-award winning shows cover the period March 14, 1977–March 28, 1978. All Emmy nominees are included; winners are noted with a star. The 1977 George Foster Peabody Broadcasting Awards for Television have also been listed.

The editor and publishers have tried to include all programs telecast in 1977–78 and to list all individuals connected to these programs, but they have no legal responsibility for any omissions or errors. We will be grateful for any comments or suggestions, whether favorable or critical, for use in future editions.

Shows by Program Type

xi

Shows Captioned or Translated for the Hearing Impaired

Cancelled Shows 1977-78

New Shows 1977-78

New and Cancelled Shows 1977-78

Summer Shows 1977-78

Emmy Awards

Presented by the Academy of Television Arts and Sciences for programs shown March 14, 1977-June 30, 1978

Outstanding Comedy Series [award(s) to executive producer(s) and/or producer(s)]
* *All in the Family* Mort Lachman, Executive Producer; Milt Josefsberg, Producer (CBS)
  Barney Miller Danny Arnold, Executive Producer; Tony Sheehan, Producer (ABC)
  *M*A*S*H* Burt Metcalfe, Producer (CBS)
  Soap Paul Junger Witt, Tony Thomas, Executive Producers; Susan Harris, Producer (ABC)
  Three's Company Don Nicholl, Michael Ross, Bernie West, Producers (ABC)

Outstanding Writing in a Comedy Series [for episode(s) of a regular or limited series with continuing characters and/or theme]
* Bob Weiskopf, Bob Schiller, Teleplay; Barry Harman, Harve Brosten, Story *Cousin Liz*, All in the Family. Shown October 9, 1977 (CBS)
  Alan Alda *Fallen Idol*, M*A*S*H. Shown September 27, 1977 (CBS)
  Mel Tolkin, Larry Rhine, Teleplay; Erik Tarloff, Story *Edith's Crisis of Faith-Part II*, All in the Family. Shown December 25, 1977 (CBS)
  Bob Weiskopf, Bob Schiller *Edith's 50th Birthday*, All in the Family. Shown October 16, 1977 (CBS)

Outstanding Directing in a Comedy Series [for episode(s) of a regular or limited series with continuing characters and/or theme]
* Paul Bogart *Edith's 50th Birthday*, All in the Family. Shown October 16, 1977 (CBS)

Hal Cooper *Vivian's Decision*, Maude. Shown February 18, 1978 (CBS)
Burt Metcalfe, Alan Alda *Comrades in Arms-Part I*, M*A*S*H. Shown December 6, 1977 (CBS)
Jerry Paris *Richie Almost Dies*, Happy Days. Shown January 31, 1978 (ABC)
Jay Sandrich *#24*, Soap. Shown March 21, 1978 (ABC)

Outstanding Continuing Performance by a Supporting Actor in a Comedy Series [for a regular or limited series]
* Rob Reiner *All in the Family* (CBS)
  Tom Bosley *Happy Days* (ABC)
  Gary Burghoff *M*A*S*H* (CBS)
  Harry Morgan *M*A*S*H* (CBS)
  Vic Tayback *Alice* (CBS)

Outstanding Continuing Performance by a Supporting Actress in a Comedy Series [for a regular or limited series]
* Julie Kavner *Rhoda* (CBS)
  Polly Holliday *Alice* (CBS)
  Sally Struthers *All in the Family* (CBS)
  Loretta Swit *M*A*S*H* (CBS)
  Nancy Walker *Rhoda* (CBS)

Outstanding Lead Actress in a Comedy Series
* Jean Stapleton *All in the Family* (CBS)
  Beatrice Arthur *Maude* (CBS)
  Cathryn Damon *Soap* (ABC)
  Valerie Harper *Rhoda* (CBS)
  Katherine Helmond *Soap* (ABC)
  Suzanne Pleshette *The Bob Newhart Show* (CBS)

Outstanding Lead Actor in a Comedy Series
* Carroll O'Connor *All in the Family* (CBS)
  Alan Alda *M*A*S*H* (CBS)
  Hal Linden *Barney Miller* (ABC)
  John Ritter *Three's Company* (ABC)
  Henry Winkler *Happy Days* (ABC)

Outstanding Drama Series [award(s) to executive producer(s) and/or producer(s)]
* *The Rockford Files* Meta Rosenberg, Executive Producer; Stephen J. Cannell, Supervising Producer; David Chase, Charles F. Johnson, Producers (NBC)
  Columbo Richard Alan Simmons, Executive Producer (NBC)
  Family Aaron Spelling, Leonard Goldberg, Executive Producers; Nigel McKeand, Producer (ABC)
  Lou Grant James L. Brooks, Allan Burns and Gene Reynolds, Executive Producers; Gene Reynolds, Producer (CBS)
  Quincy Glen A. Larson, Jud Kinberg and Richard Irving, Executive Producers; B. W. Sandefur, Supervising Producer; Chris Morgan, Peter J. Thompson, Edward J. Montagne and Robert F. O'Neill, Producers; Michael Sloan, Associate Executive Producer (NBC)

Outstanding Writing in a Drama Series [for episode(s) of a regular or limited series with continuing characters and/or theme]
* Gerald Green *Holocaust*, entire series. Shown April 16-19, 1978 (NBC)
  Steve Allen *Meeting of Minds*, entire series (PBS)
  Alan Ayckbourn *The Norman Conquests*, entire series. Shown June 14, 21, 28, 1978 (PBS)
  Robert W. Lenski *The Dain Curse*, entire series. Shown May 22-24, 1978 (CBS)
  Abby Mann *King*, entire series. Shown February 12-14, 1978 (NBC)

Outstanding Directing in a Drama Series [for episode(s) of a regular or limited series with continuing characters and/or theme]
* Marvin J. Chomsky *Holocaust*, entire series. Shown April 16-19, 1978 (NBC)
  Abby Mann *King*, entire series. Shown February 12-14, 1978 (NBC)
  Gary Nelson, *Washington: Behind Closed Doors*, entire series. Shown September 6-11, 1977 (ABC)

E. W. Swackhamer *The Dain Curse*, entire series. Shown May 22-24, 1978 (CBS)
Herbert Wise *I, Claudius*, entire series, Masterpiece Theatre (PBS)

Outstanding Continuing Performance by a Supporting Actor in a Drama Series [for a regular or limited series]
* Robert Vaughn *Washington: Behind Closed Doors* (ABC)
  Ossie Davis *King* (NBC)
  Will Geer *The Waltons* (CBS)
  Sam Wanamaker *Holocaust* (NBC)
  David Warner *Holocaust* (NBC)

Outstanding Continuing Performance by a Supporting Actress in a Drama Series [for a regular or limited series]
* Nancy Marchand *Lou Grant* (CBS)
  Meredith Baxter Birney *Family* (ABC)
  Tovah Feldshuh *Holocaust* (NBC)
  Linda Kelsey *Lou Grant* (CBS)
  Kristy McNichol *Family* (ABC)

Outstanding Lead Actress in a Drama Series
* Sada Thompson *Family* (ABC)
  Melissa Sue Anderson *Little House on the Prairie* (NBC)
  Fionnula Flanagan *How the West Was Won* (ABC)
  Kate Jackson *Charlie's Angels* (ABC)
  Michael Learned *The Waltons* (CBS)
  Susan Sullivan *Julie Farr, M.D.* (ABC)

Outstanding Lead Actor in a Drama Series
* Edward Asner, *Lou Grant* (CBS)
  James Broderick *Family* (ABC)
  Peter Falk *Columbo* (NBC)
  James Garner *Rockford Files* (NBC)
  Jack Klugman *Quincy* (NBC)
  Ralph Waite *The Waltons* (CBS)

Outstanding Children's Special [for specials which were broadcast in the evening. Award(s) to executive producer(s) and/or producer(s)]
* *Halloween is Grinch Night* David H. DePatie, Friz Freleng, Executive Producers; Ted Geisel, Producer. Shown October 29, 1977 (ABC)
  A Connecticut Yankee in King Arthur's Court Jay Rayvid, Executive Producer; Jay Rayvid, Chiz Schultz and Shep Green, Producers. Shown May 23, 1977 (PBS)

The Fat Albert Christmas Special Lou Scheimer, Norm Prescott, Producers. Shown December 18, 1977 (CBS)
Once Upon a Brothers Grimm Bernard Rothman, Jack Wohl, Producers. Shown November 23, 1977 (CBS)
Peter Lundy and the Medicine Hat Stallion Ed Friendly, Producer. Shown November 6, 1977 (NBC)

Outstanding Limited Series [award(s) to executive producer(s) and/or producer(s)]
* *Holocaust* Herbert Brodkin, Executive Producer; Robert Beger, Producer (NBC)
King Edward S. Feldman, Executive Producer; Paul Maslansky, Producer; William Finnegan, Supervising Producer (NBC)
Washington: Behind Closed Doors Stanley Kallis, Executive Producer; Eric Bercovici, David W. Rintels, Supervising Producers; Norman Powell, Producer (ABC)
Anna Karenina, Masterpiece Theatre. Ken Riddington, Executive Producer; Donald Wilson, Producer; Joan Sullivan, Series Producer (PBS)
I, Claudius, Masterpiece Theatre. Joan Sullivan, Series Producer; Martin Lisemore, Producer (PBS)

Outstanding Lead Actress in a Limited Series
* Meryl Streep *Holocaust* (NBC)
Rosemary Harris *Holocaust* (NBC)
Elizabeth Montgomery *The Awakening Land* (NBC)
Lee Remick *Wheels* (NBC)
Cicely Tyson *King* (NBC)

Outstanding Lead Actor in a Limited Series
* Michael Moriarty *Holocaust* (NBC)
Hal Holbrook *The Awakening Land* (NBC)
Jason Robards, Jr. *Washington: Behind Closed Doors* (ABC)
Fritz Weaver *Holocaust* (NBC)
Paul Winfield *King* (NBC)

Outstanding Informational Series [award(s) to executive producer(s) and/or producer(s)]
* *The Body Human* Thomas W. Moore, Executive Producer; Alfred R. Kelman, Producer (CBS)
Between the Wars Alan Landsburg, Executive Producer; Anthony Potter, Series Producer (SYN)

Cousteau Oasis in Space Philippe Cousteau, Executive Producer; Andrew Solt, Producer (PBS)
Mutual of Omaha's Wild Kingdom Don Meier, Producer (SYN)
Nova John Angier, Executive Producer (PBS)

Outstanding Continuing or Single Performance by a Supporting Actor in Variety or Music [for a continuing role in a regular or limited series, or a one-time appearance in a series or a special]
* Tim Conway *The Carol Burnett Show.* Series (CBS)
Dan Aykroyd *NBC's Saturday Night Live.* Series (NBC)
John Belushi *NBC's Saturday Night Live.* Series (NBC)
Louis Gossett, Jr. *The Sentry Collection Presents Ben Vereen-His Roots.* Shown March 2, 1978 (ABC)
Peter Sellers *The Muppet Show* (SYN)

Outstanding Continuing or Single Performance by a Supporting Actress in Variety or Music [for a continuing role in a regular or limited series, or for a one-time appearance in a series or a special]
* Gilda Radner *NBC's Saturday Night Live.* Series (NBC)
Beatric Arthur *Laugh-In.* Shown October 25, 1977 (NBC)
Jane Curtin *NBC's Saturday Night Live.* Series (NBC)
Dolly Parton *Cher. . . Special.* Shown April 3, 1978 (ABC)
Bernadette Peters *The Muppet Show* (SYN)

Outstanding Writing in a Comedy-Variety or Music Series [for episode(s) of a regular or limited series]
* Ed Simmons, Roger Beatty, Rick Hawkins, Liz Sage, Robert Illes, James Stein, Franelle Silver, Larry Siegel, Tim Conway, Bill Richmond, Gene Perret, Dick Clair and Jenna McMahon *The Carol Burnett Show with Steve Martin, Betty White.* Shown March 5, 1978 (CBS)
Ed Simmons, Roger Beatty, Elias Davis, David Pollock, Rick Hawkins, Liz Sage, Adele Styler, Burt Styler, Tim Conway, Bill Richmond, Gene Perret, Dick Clair and Jenna McMahon *The Carol Burnett Show with Ken Berry.* Shown March 26, 1977 (CBS)

Jerry Juhl, Don Hinkley, Joseph Bailey and Jim Henson *The Muppet Show with Dom De Luise* (SYN)

Alan Thicke, John Boni, Norman Stiles, Jeremy Stevens, Tom Moore, Robert Illes, James Stein, Harry Shearer, Tom Dunsmuir and Dan Wilcox *America 2Night with Carol Burnett* (SYN)

Dan Aykroyd, Anne Beatts, Tom Davis, James Downey, Brian Doyle-Murray, Al Franken, Lorne Michaels, Marilyn Suzanne Miller, Don Novello, Michael O'Donoghue, Herb Sargent, Tom Schiler, Rosie Shuster and Alan Zweibel *NBC's Saturday Night Live, Host: Steve Martin*. Shown April 22, 1978 (NBC)

Outstanding Directing in a Comedy-Variety or Music Series [for episode(s) of a regular or limited series]

* Dave Powers *The Carol Burnett Show with Steve Martin, Betty White*. Shown March 5, 1978 (CBS)

Steve Binder *Shields and Yarnell with John Aylesworth*. Shown February 21, 1978 (CBS)

Peter Harris *The Muppet Show with Elton John* (SYN)

John C. Moffitt *The Richard Pryor Show with Paula Kelly*. Shown September 13, 1977 (NBC)

Dave Wilson *NBC's Saturday Night Live with Steve Martin*. Shown April 22, 1978 (NBC)

Outstanding Comedy-Variety or Music Series [award(s) to executive producer(s) and/or producer(s) and star(s), if applicable]

* *The Muppet Show* David Lazer, Executive Producer; Jim Henson, Producer; The Muppets-Frank Oz, Jerry Nelson, Richard Hunt, David Goelz and Jim Henson,Stars (SYN)

America 2Night Alan Thicke, Producer (SYN)

The Carol Burnett Show Joe Hamilton, Executive Producer; Ed Simmons, Producer; Carol Burnett, Star (CBS)

Evening at Pops Bill Cosel, Producer; Arthur Fiedler, Star (PBS)

NBC's Saturday Night Live Lorne Michaels, Producer (NBC)

Outstanding Classical Program in the Performing Arts [for a special program, or for a series (excluding drama). Award(s) to executive producer(s) and/or producer(s) and star(s), if applicable]

* *American Ballet Theatre's "Giselle"* -Live from Lincoln Center. John Goberman, Producer. Shown June 2, 1977 (PBS)

American Ballet Theatre-Live from Lincoln Center. John Goberman, Executive producer; Emile Ardolino, Producer. Shown May 17, 1978 (PBS)

Dance in America: Choreography by Balanchine Jac Venza, Executive Producer; Emile Ardolino, Merrill Brockway, Producers. Shown December 14 & 21, 1977 (PBS)

La Boheme-Live from the Met. Michael Bronson, Executive Producer; John Goberman, Producer. Shown March 15, 1977 (PBS)

The Nutcracker (Baryshnikov) Herman Krawitz, Executive Producer; Yanna Kroyt Brandt, Producer. Shown December 16, 1977 (CBS)

Outstanding Single Performance by a Supporting Actress in a Comedy or Drama Series [for a one-time appearance in a regular or limited series]

* Blanche Baker *Holocaust Part I*. Shown April 16, 1978 (NBC)

Ellen Corby *Grandma Comes Home*, The Waltons. Shown March 30, 1978 (CBS)

Jeanette Nolan *The Awakening Land Part I*. Shown February 19, 1978 (NBC)

Beulah Quo *Douglas, Tz'u-Hsi, Beccaria, de Sade*, Meeting of Minds. Shown March 20, 1978 (PBS)

Beatrice Straight *The Dain Curse Part I*. Shown May 22, 1978 (CBS)

Outstanding Single Performance by a Supporting Actor in a Comedy or Drama Series [for a one-time appearance in a regular or limited series]

* Ricardo Montalban *How the West Was Won-Part II*. Shown February 19, 1978 (ABC)

Will Geer *Yes, Nicholas. . . There is a Santa Claus*, Eight is Enough. Shown December 14, 1977 (ABC)

Larry Gelman *Goodbye Mr. Fish-Part II*. Barney Miller. Shown September 22, 1977 (ABC)

Harold Gould *Happy Anniversary,* Rhoda.
Shown January 29, 1978 (CBS)
Abe Vigoda *Goodbye Mr. Fish-Part II,*
Barney Miller. Shown September 22,
1977 (ABC)

**Outstanding Lead Actress for a Single
Appearance in a Drama or Comedy Series**
* Rita Moreno *The Paper Palace,* The
Rockford Files. Shown January 20, 1978
(ABC)
Patty Duke Astin *Having Babies, III,* Having
Babies. Shown March 3, 1978 (ABC)
Kate Jackson *James at 15,* James at 15/16.
Shown September 5, 1977 (NBC)
Jayne Meadows *Luther, Voltaire, Plato,
Nightingale,* Meeting of Minds. Shown
March 6, 1978 (PBS)
Irene Tedrow *Ducks,* James at 15/16. Shown
June 22, 1978 (NBC)

**Outstanding Lead Actor for a Single
Appearance in a Drama or Comedy Series**
* Barnard Hughes, *Judge,* Lou Grant. Shown
November 15, 1977 (CBS)
David Cassidy *A Chance to Live,* Police
Story. Shown May 28, 1978 (NBC)
Will Geer *The Old Man and the Runaway,*
The Love Boat. Shown December 24,
1977 (ABC)
Judd Hirsch *Rhoda Likes Mike,* Rhoda.
Shown November 6, 1977 (CBS)
John Rubinstein *And Baby Makes Three,*
Family. Shown February 7, 1978 (ABC)
Keenan Wynn *Good Old Uncle Ben,* Police
Woman. Shown March 29, 1978 (NBC)

First Annual ATAS Governors' Award
* To William S. Paley, Chairman of the Board,
CBS

**Outstanding Informational Special [award(s)
to executive producer(s) and/or producer(s)]**
* *The Great Whales,* National Geographic.
Thomas Skinner, Dennis B. Kane,
Executive Producers; Nicholas Noxon,
Producer. Shown February 16, 1978
(PBS)
Bing Crosby: His Life and Legend Franklin
Konigsberg, Executive Producer;
Marshall Flaum, Producer. Shown May
25, 1978 (ABC)
Calypso's Search for Atlantic, Cousteau
Odyssey. Jacques Cousteau, Philippe

Cousteau, Executive Producers; Andrew
Solt, Producer. Shown May 1 & 2, 1978
(PBS)
The Treasures of Tutankhamun Donald Knox,
Executive Producer; Valerie Gentile,
Producer. Shown November 1, 1977
(PBS)
Tut: The Boy King George A. Heinemann,
Executive Producer. Shown July 27, 1977
(NBC)

**Outstanding Writing in a Comedy-Variety or
Music Special**
* Lorne Michaels, Paul Simon, Chevy Chase,
Tom Davis, Al Franken, Charles Grodin,
Lily Tomlin and Alan Zweibel *The Paul
Simon Special.* Shown December 8, 1977
(NBC)
Alan Buz Kohan, Rod Warren, Pat
McCormick, Tom Eyen, Jerry Blatt, Bette
Midler and Bruce Vilance *Bette
Midler-Ol' Red Hair is Back.* Shown
December 7, 1977 (NBC)
Elon Packard, Fred Fox and Seaman Jacobs
The George Burns One-Man Show.
Shown November 23, 1977 (CBS)
Ernest Chambers, Barry Manilow *The Second
Barry Manilow Special.* Shown February
24, 1978 (ABC)
Michale H. Kagan *The Sentry Collection
Presents Ben Vereen-His Roots.* Shown
March 2, 1978 (ABC)

**Outstanding Directing in a Comedy-Variety
or Music Special**
* Dwight Hemion *The Sentry Collection
Presents Ben Vereen-His Roots.* Shown
March 2, 1978 (ABC)
Tony Charmoli *Mitzi. . . Zings into Spring.*
Shown March 29, 1977 (CBS)
Walter C. Miller *Doug Henning's World of
Magic.* Shown December 15, 1977 (NBC)
George Schaefer *The Second Barry Manilow
Special.* Shown February 24, 1978 (ABC)
Dave Wilson *The Paul Simon Special.* Shown
December 8, 1977 (NBC)

**Outstanding Special—Comedy-Variety or
Music [award(s) to executive producer(s)
and/or producer(s) and star(s) if applicable]**
* *Bette Midler—Ol' Red Hair is Back* Aaron
Russo, Executive Producer; Gary Smith,
Dwight Hemion, Producers; Bette Midler,
Star. Shown December 7, 1977 (NBC)

Doug Henning's World of Magic Jerry
Goldstein, Executive Producer; Walter C.
Miller, Producer; Doug Henning, Star.
Shown December 15, 1977 (NBC)
The George Burns One-Man Show Irving
Fein, Executive Producer; Stan Harris,
Producer; George Burns, Star. Shown
November 23, 1977 (CBS)
*Neil Diamond: I'm Glad You're Here with Me
Tonight* Jerry Weintraub, Executive
Producer; Art Fisher, Producer; Neil
Diamond, Star. Shown November 17,
1977 (NBC)
The Second Barry Manilow Special Miles J.
Lourie, Executive Producer; Ernest
Chambers, Barry Manilow, Producers;
Barry Manilow, Star. Shown February 24,
1978 (ABC)

**Outstanding Writing in a Special
Program—Drama or Comedy—Adaptation**
* Caryl Ledner *Mary White*. Shown November
18, 1978 (ABC)
Blanche Hanalis *A Love Affair: The Eleanor
and Lou Gehrig Story*. Shown January 15,
1978 (NBC)
Albert Innaurato *Verna: USO Girl*, Great
Performances. Shown January 25, 1978
(PBS)
Jerome Lawrence, Robert E. Lee *Actor*,
Hollywood Television Theatre. Shown
February 21, 1978 (PBS)
Barbara Turner *The War Between the Tates*.
Shown June 13, 1977 (NBC)

**Outstanding Writing in a Special
Program—Drama or Comedy—Original
Teleplay**
* George Rubino *The Last Tenant*. Shown June
25, 1978 (ABC)
Bruce Feldman *The Defection of Simas
Kudirka*. Shown January 23, 1978 (CBS)
Richard Levinson, William Link *The
Storyteller*. Shown December 5, 1977
(NBC)
Loring Mandel *Breaking Up*. Shown January
2, 1978 (ABC)
Jerry McNeely *Something for Joey*. Shown
April 6, 1977 (CBS)
James Poe *The Gathering*. Shown December
4, 1977 (ABC)

**Outstanding Directing in a Special
Program—Drama or Comedy**
* David Lowell Rich *The Defection of Simas
Kudirka*. Shown January 23, 1978 (CBS)

Lou Antonio *Something for Joey*. Shown
April 6, 1977 (CBS)
Randal Kleiser *The Gathering*. Shown
December 4, 1977 (ABC)
Delbert Mann *Breaking Up*. Shown January
2, 1978 (ABC)
Ronald Maxwell *Verna: USO Girl*, Great
Performances. Shown January 25, 1978
(PBS)
George Schaefer *Our Town*, Bell System.
Shown May 30, 1977 (NBC)

**Outstanding Performance by a Supporting
Actress in a Drama or Comedy Special**
* Eva La Gallienne *The Royal Family*. Shown
November 9, 1977 (PBS)
Patty Duke Astin *A Family Upside Down*.
Shown April 9, 1978 (NBC)
Tyne Daly *Intimate Strangers*. Shown
November 11, 1977 (ABC)
Mariette Hartley *The Last Hurrah*, Hallmark
Hall of Fame. Shown November 16, 1977
(NBC)
Cloris Leachman *It Happened One
Christmas*. Shown December 11, 1977
(ABC)
Viveca Lindfors *A Question of Guilt*. Shown
February 21, 1978 (CBS)

**Outstanding Performance by a Supporting
Actor in a Comedy or Drama Special**
* Howard Da Silva *Verna: USO Girl*, Great
Performances. Shown January 25, 1978
(PBS)
James Farentino *Jesus of Nazareth*. Shown
April 3 & 10, 1977 (NBC)
Burgess Meredith *The Last Hurrah*, Hallmark
Hall of Fame. Shown November 16, 1977
(NBC)
Donald Pleasance *The Defection of Simas
Kudirka*. Shown January 23, 1978 (CBS)
Efrem Zimbalist, Jr. *A Family Upside Down*.
Shown April 9, 1978 (NBC)

**Outstanding Lead Actress in a Drama or
Comedy Special**
* Joanne Woodward *See How She Runs*, GE
Theater. Shown February 1, 1978 (CBS)
Helen Hayes *A Family Upside Down*. Shown
April 9, 1978 (NBC)
Eva Marie Saint *Taxi!!!*, Hallmark Hall of
Fame. Shown February 2, 1978 (NBC)
Maureen Stapleton *The Gathering*. Shown
December 4, 1977 (ABC)
Sada Thompson *Our Town*, Bell System.
Shown May 30, 1977 (NBC)

Outstanding Lead Actor in a Drama or Comedy Special
* Fred Astaire *A Family Upside Down*. Shown April 9, 1978 (NBC)
  Alan Alda *Kill Me If You Can*. Shown September 25, 1977 (NBC)
  Hal Holbrook *Our Town*, Bell System. Shown May 30, 1977 (NBC)
  Martin Sheen *Taxi!!!*, Hallmark Hall of Fame. Shown February 2, 1978 (NBC)
  James Stacy *Just a Little Inconvenience*. Shown October 2, 1977 (NBC)

Outstanding Special—Drama or Comedy [award(s) to executive producer(s) and/or producer(s)]
* *The Gathering* Joseph Barbera, Executive Producer; Harry R. Sherman, Producer. Shown December 4, 1977 (ABC)
  A Death in Canaan Robert W. Christiansen and Rick Rosenberg, Producers. Shown March 1, 1978 (CBS)
  Jesus of Nazareth Bernard J. Kingham, Executive Producer; Vincenzo Labella, Producer. Shown April 3 & 10, 1977 (NBC)
  Our Town, Bell System Special. Saul Jaffe, Executive Producer; George Schaefer, Producer. Shown May 30, 1977 (NBC)
  Young Joe, The Forgotten Kennedy William McCutchen, Producer. Shown September 18, 1977 (ABC)

Creative Arts in Entertainment Areas [possibility of one award, more than one award or no award]

Outstanding Achievement in Special Musical Material [for a song (which must have both music and lyrics), a theme for a series, or special material for a variety program providing that the first usage of this material was written expressly for television]
  Stan Freeman, Arthur Malvin, Music and Lyrics *The Carol Burnett Show*, Mini Musical: "Hi-Hat." Shown January 8, 1978 (CBS)
  Ken Welch, Mitzie Welch, Music and Lyrics *The Sentry Collection Presents Ben Vereen-His Roots*, Song: "See You Tomorrow In Class." Shown March 2, 1978 (ABC)

Outstanding Achievement in Any Area of Creative Technical Crafts [an award for individual technical craft achievement which does not fall into a specific category, and is not otherwise recognized]
  William F. Brownell, John H. Kantrowe, Jr., Sound Effects, *Our Town*, Bell System. Shown May 30, 1977 (NBC)

Special Classification of Outstanding Individual Achievement [an award for unique individual achievement, which does not fall into a specific category, or is not otherwise recognized]
  William Pitkin, Costume Designer,*Romeo and Juliet*. Shown June 7, 1978 (PBS)

Outstanding Individual Achievement in Children's Programming [for a single episode of a series or for a special program]
  Once Upon a Brothers Grimm Ken Johnson, Art Director, Robert Checchi, Set Director. Shown November 23, 1977 (CBS)
  Once Upon a Brothers Grimm Bill Hargate, Costume Designer. Shown November 23, 1977 (CBS)

Special Classification of Outstanding Program Achievement [an award for unique program achievement, which does not fall into a specific category, or is not otherwise recognized (possibility of one award, more than one award or no award)
* *The Tonight Show Starring Johnny Carson* (Series) Fred De Cordova, Producer; Johnny Carson, Star (NBC)

Outstanding Art Direction for a Comedy Series [for a single episode of a regular or limited series]
* Ed Stephenson, Production Designer; Robert Checchi, Set Decorator *Episode #1, Soap*. Shown September 13, 1977 (ABC)
  Thomas E. Azzari *In the Black*, A.E.S. Hudson Street. Shown March 30, 1978 (ABC)
  Roy Christopher, Art Director; James Shanahan, Art Director *Barbarino in Love, Part I*, Welcome Back, Kotter. Shown November 3, 1977 (ABC)

Eugene H. Harris, Paul Sylos, Art Directors; John McCarthy, Robert Signorelli, Set Decorators, entire series, The Love Boat (ABC)

C. Murawski *The Wake*, Maude. Shown April 15, 1978 (CBS)

Outstanding Art Direction for a Drama Series [for a single episode of a regular or limited series]

* Tim Harvey, Art Director *I, Claudius*. Masterpiece Theatre-Episode #1. Shown November 6, 1977 (PBS)

Jack De Shields, Production Designer; James F. Claytor, Art Director; Barbara Kreiger, Set Decorator, *Washington: Behind Closed Doors*-Episode #3. Shown September 8, 1977 (ABC)

Derek Dodd *Anna Karenina*, Masterpiece Theatre-Episode #1. Shown February 5, 1978 (PBS)

Wilfred J. Shingleton, Production Designer; Theo Harisch, Art Director; Jurgen Kiebach, Art Director; Maxi Hareiter, Set Decorator *Holocaust*-entire series. Shown April 16-19, 1978 (NBC)

Outstanding Art Direction for a Comedy-Variety or Music Series [for a single episode of a regular or limited series]

* Roy Christopher *The Richard Pryor Show*. Shown September 20, 1977 (NBC)

Bob Sansom, Art Director; Paul Barnes, Art Director; Bill Harp, Set Decorator *The Final Show*, The Carol Burnett Show. Shown March 29, 1978 (CBS)

Bill Bohnert, Art Director; Arlene Alen, Set Decorator *Opening Show*, Donny and Marie. Shown September 23, 1977 (ABC)

Romain Johnston *Captain and Tenille*. Shown March 14, 1977 (ABC)

Eugene Lee, Leo Yoshimura, Art Directors; Franne Lee, Lee Mayman, Set Decorators *NBC's Saturday Night Live with Host Steve Martin*. Shown April 22, 1978 (NBC)

Outstanding Art Direction for a Dramatic Special

* John De Cuir, Production Designer/Art Director; Richard C. Goddard, Set Decorator *Ziegfeld: The Man and His Women*. Shown May 21, 1978 (NBC)

Roy Christopher, Production Designer; James Shanahan, Set Decorator *Our Town*, Bell System. Shown May 30, 1977 (NBC)

John J. Lloyd, Art Director; Hal Gausman, Set Decorator *It Happened One Christmas*. Shown December 11, 1977 (ABC)

Loyd S. Papez, Art Director; Richard Friedman, Set Decorator *The Bastard* (SYN)

Jan Scott, Art Director; Anne D. McCulley, Set Decorator *The Gathering*. Shown December 4, 1977 (ABC)

Outstanding Art Direction for a Comedy-Variety or Music Special

* Romain Johnston, Art Director; Kerry Joyce, Set Decorator *The Sentry Collection Presents Ben Vereen-His Roots*. Shown March 2, 1978 (ABC)

Brian C. Bartholomew, Art Director *Cher . . . Special*. Shown April 3, 1978 (ABC)

Roy Christopher, Art Director; Don Remacle, Set Decorator *How to Survive the 70s and Maybe Even Bump into Happiness*. Shown February 22, 1978 (CBS)

Romain Johnston, John Dapper, Art Directors; Robert Checchi, Set Decorator *They Said It With Music: Yankee Doodle to Ragtime*. Shown July 4, 1977 (CBS)

Robert Kelly *Mitzi . . . Zings into Spring*. Shown March 29, 1977 (CBS)

Outstanding Achievement in Film Sound Editing for a Series [for a single episode of a regular or limited series]

* Douglas H. Grindstaff, Hank Salerno, Larry Singer, Christopher Chulack, Richard Raderman, Don Crosby, H. Lee Chaney, Mark Dennis and Don V. Issacs *River of Promises*, Police Story. Shown January 14, 1978 (NBC)

Larry Carow, David Pettijohn, Don Warner, Colin Mouat, Chuck Moran and Peter Hubbard *The Hawk Flies on Sunday*, Baa Baa Black Sheep/Black Sheep Squadron. Shown December 28, 1977 (NBC)

Tony Garber, Dale Johnston and Ron Clark *Nazi*, Lou Grant. Shown October 18, 1977 (CBS)

Douglas H. Grindstaff, Larry Singer, Hank Salerno, Christopher Chulack, Luke Wolfram, Al Kajita, Dwayne Avery, Richard Friedman and Don V. Isaacs *Racer and Lady of the Evening*, Fantasy Island. Shown February 25, 1978 (ABC)

William Stevenson, Richard Raderman *Roll of Thunder, Hear My Cry*. Shown June 2-4, 1978 (ABC)

Outstanding Achievement in Film Sound Editing for a Special

* Jerry Rosenthal, Michael Corrigan, Jerry Pirozzi, William Jackson, James Yant, Richard Le Grand, Donald Higgins and John Strauss *The Amazing Howard Hughes*. Shown April 13-14, 1977 (CBS)

Douglas H. Grindstaff, H. Lee Chaney, Don V. Isaacs, Larry Kaufman, Steve Olson, Don Crosby, Al Kajita, Bob Human, Hank Salerno and Larry Singer *The Last Hurrah*, Hallmark Hall of Fame. Shown November 16, 1977 (NBC)

Douglas H. Grindstaff, Hank Salerno, Larry Singer, Christopher Chulack, Mark Dennis, Don Crosby, H. Lee Chaney and Don V. Isaacs *To Kill a Cop-Part I*. Shown April 10, 1978 (NBC)

Don Hall, Dwayne Avery, Tom Burke and Chick Camera *Standing Tall*. Shown January 21, 1978 (NBC)

Bernard F. Pincus, Patrick R. Somerset, Jeffrey Bushelman, A. Jeremy Hoenack, John Bushelman, Edward L. Sandlin, Robert A. Biggart and Jerry Rosenthal *The Dark Secret of Harvest Home*. Shown January 23-24, 1978 (NBC)

Donald L. Warner, Jr., Larry Carow, Colin Mouat, David Pettijohn, Gary Vaughan, Chuck Moran, Peter Hubbard and Fred Stafford *Tarantulas: The Deadly Cargo*. Shown December 28, 1977 (CBS)

Outstanding Achievement in Film Sound Mixing [for a single episode of a regular or limited series, or for a special program]

* William Teague, George E. Porter, Eddie J. Nelson and Robert L. Harman *Young Joe, The Forgotten Kennedy*. Shown September 18, 1977 (ABC)

Alan Bernard, George E. Porter, Eddie J. Nelson and Hoppy Mehterian *Having Babies*. Shown October 28, 1977 (ABC)

Eddie Knowles, George E. Porter, Eddie J. Nelson and J. Robert Pettis *Tarantulas: The Deadly Cargo*. Shown December 28, 1977 (CBS)

Hoppy Mehterian, George E. Porter, Eddie J. Nelson and Dean Hodges *A Sensitive, Passionate Man*. Shown June 6, 1977 (NBC)

J. Robert Pettis, George E. Porter, Eddie J. Nelson and Cabell Smith *See How She Runs*, GE Theater. Shown February 1, 1978 (CBS)

Tommy Thompson, George E. Porter, Eddie J. Nelson and Hoppy Mehterian *In the Matter of Karen Ann Quinlan*. Shown September 26, 1977 (NBC)

Outstanding Achievement in Music Composition for a Series (Dramatic Underscore)[for a single episode of a regular or limited series]

* Billy Goldenberg *King*. Shown February 12-14, 1978 (NBC)

Morton Gould *Holocaust*. Shown April 16-19, 1978 (NBC)

Fred Karlin *The Awakening Land*. Shown February 19-21, 1978 (NBC)

Morton Stevens *Wheels*. Shown May 9-15, 1978 (NBC)

Patrick Williams *Try and Catch Me*, Columbo. Shown November 21, 1977 (NBC)

Outstanding Achievement in Music Composition for a Special (Dramatic Underscore)

* Jimmie Haskell *See How She Runs*, GE Theater. Shown February 1, 1978 (CBS)

Dick De Benedictis *Ziegfeld: The Man and His Women*. Shown May 21, 1978 (NBC)

Billy Goldenberg *Actor*, Hollywood Television Theatre. Shown February 21, 1978 (PBS)

David Shire *The Defection of Simas Kudirka*. Shown January 23, 1978 (CBS)

Outstanding Achievement in Music Direction [for a single episode of a series, or a special program, whether it be variety or music]

* Ian Fraser *The Sentry Collection Presents Ben Vereen-His Roots*. Shown March 2, 1978 (ABC)

Jimmie Haskell *The Second Barry Manilow Special*. Shown February 24, 1978 (ABC)

Zubin Mehta *The New York Philharmonic/ Mehta Live from Lincoln Center*. Shown September 24, 1977 (PBS)

Andre Previn *Previn and the Pittsburgh, The Music that Made the Movies*. Shown March 26, 1978 (PBS)

Outstanding Film Editing in a Comedy Series [for a single episode of a regular or limited series]

* Ed Cotter *Richie Almost Dies*, Happy Days. Shown January 31, 1978 (ABC)

M. Pam Blumenthal *A Jackie Story*. The Bob Newhart Show. Shown October 8, 1977 (CBS)

Stanford Tischler, Larry L. Mills *Fade Out, Fade In*, M*A*S*H. Shown September 20, 1977 (CBS)

Norman Wallerstein, A.C.E., Bob Moore, A.C.E. *(Masquerade; The Caper; Eyes of Love; Hollywood Royalty)*, Love Boat. Shown January 21, 1978 (ABC)

Outstanding Film Editing in a Drama Series [for a single episode of a regular or limited series]

* Stephen A. Rotter, Robert M. Reitan, Craig McKay, Alan Heim and Brian Smedley-Aston *Holocaust*. Series (NBC)

David G. Blangsted, A.C.E., Howard Terrill, A.C.E. *Yes, Nicholas ... There Is a Santa Clause*, Eight is Enough. Shown December 14, 1977 (ABC)

Byron "Buzz" Brandt, A.C.E., Richard Meyer and David Berlatsky *King*. Series (NBC)

Jim Faris *Acts of Love-Part I*, Family. Shown September 13, 1978 (ABC)

Bill Mosher *Grandma Comes Home*, The Waltons. Shown March 30, 1978 (CBS)

Robert Watts *How to Dial a Murder*, Columbo. Shown April 15, 1978 (NBC)

Outstanding Film Editing for a Special [for a drama, comedy or music-variety special or film made for television]

* John A. Martinelli, A.C.E. *The Defection of Simas Kudirka*. Shown January 23, 1978 (CBS)

Ronald J. Fagan, A.C.E. *Young Joe, The Forgotten Kennedy*. Shown September 18, 1977 (ABC)

Leslie L. Green *Ziegfeld: The Man and His Women*. Shown May 21, 1978 (NBC)

Harry Kaye, A.C.E., Donald Rode *To Kill a Cop*. Shown April 10 & 11, 1978 (NBC)

Kenneth R. Koch *Mary Jane Harper Cried Last Night*. Shown October 5, 1977 (CBS)

Bernard J. Small *Just a Little Inconvenience*. Shown October 2, 1977 (NBC)

Ken Zemke *A Killing Affair*. Shown September 21, 1977 (CBS)

Outstanding Achievement in Tape Sound Mixing [for a single episode of a regular or limited series or for a special program]

* Thomas J. Huth, Edward J. Greene and Ron Bryan *Bette Midle-Ol' Red Hair Is Back*. Shown December 7, 1977 (NBC)

Ron Estes *Our Town*, Bell System. Shown May 30, 1977 (NBC)

Phillip J. Seretti, Bob Gaudio, Val Garay, Rick Ruggieri and John Walker *The Neil Diamond Special: I'm Glad You're Here with Me Tonight*. Shown November 17, 1977 (NBC)

Larry Stephens, Tomas J. Huth, Ron Bryan, Eric Levinson and Grover Helsley *Perry Como's Easter by the Sea*. Shown March 22, 1978 (ABC)

Dick Wilson *The Lawrence Welk Show with Roger Williams at the Piano* (SYN)

Outstanding Achievement in Video Tape Editing for a Series

* Tucker Wiard *The Final Show*, The Carol Burnett Show. Shown March 29, 1978 (CBS)

Gary H. Anderson *Episode #2*, Soap. Shown September 20, 1977 (ABC)

Ed. J. Brennan *Show #6*, Laugh-In. Shown Febrary 8, 1978 (NBC)

Chip Brooks *Pilot*, The Betty White Show. Shown September 12, 1977 (CBS)

Jerry Davis *Chrissy, Come Home*, Three's Company. Shown February 28, 1978 (ABC)

Marco Zappia *The One Where Everybody is Looking for a Little Action*, Husbands, Wives & Lovers. Shown April 7, 1978 (CBS)

Outstanding Achievement in Video Tape Editing for a Special

* Pam Marshall, Andy Zall *The Sentry Collection Presents Ben Vereen-His Roots*. Shown March 2, 1978 (ABC)

Ed J. Brennan *The Goldie Hawn Special*. Shown March 1, 1978 (CBS)

Chip Brooks, Hal Collins *Texaco Presents Bob Hope in a Very Special Special-On the Road with Bing*. Shown October 28, 1977 (NBC)

Jimmy B. Frazier *The Carpenters-Space Encounters*. Shown May 17, 1978 (ABC)

Marco Zappia, Terry Greene, Harvey Berger and Jimmy B. Frazier *Superstunt*. Shown November 17, 1977 (NBC)

Outstanding Achievement in Costume Design for a Drama Special

* Noel Taylor *Actor*, Hollywood Television Theatre. Shown February 21, 1978 (PBS)

Jean-Pierre Dorleac *The Bastard* (SYN)

Grady Hunt *Ziegfeld: The Man and His Women*. Shown May 21, 1978 (NBC)

Bill Jobe *The Dark Secret of Harvest Home.* Shown January 24, 1978 (NBC)
Olga Lehmann *The Four Feathers,* Bell System. Shown January 1, 1978 (NBC)

Outstanding Achievement in Costume Design for Music-Variety [for a single episode of a series or for a special program]
* Bob Mackie, Ret Turner *Mitzi . . . Zings into Spring.* Shown March 29, 1977 (CBS)
David Doucette *Dorothy Hamill Presents Winners.* Shown April 28, 1978 (ABC)
Bill Hargate *Doug Henning's World of Magic.* Shown December 15, 1977 (NBC)
Warden Neil *The John Davidson Christmas Special.* Shown December 9, 1977 (ABC)
Sandra Stewart *Cindy.* Shown March 24, 1978 (ABC)

Outstanding Achievement in Costume Design for a Drama or Comedy Series [for a single episode of a regular or limited series]
* Peggy Farrell, Edith Almoslino *Holocaust.* Shown April 16-19, 1978 (NBC)
Don Feld *Anschlus' 77,* The New Adventures of Wonder Woman. Shown September 23, 1977 (CBS)
Grady Hunt *The Emperor's Quasi Norms-Part I* Quark. Shown March 31, 1978 (NBC)
Bill Jobe *Testimony of Two Men-Part III* (SYN)
Yvonne Wood *79 Park Avenue.* Shown October 16-18, 1977 (NBC)

Outstanding Cinematography in Entertainment Programming for a Series [for a single episode of a regular or limited series]
* Ted Voigtlander, ASC *The Fighter,* Little House on the Prairie. Shown November 21, 1977 (NBC)
Lloyd Ahern *(The Inspector; A Very Special Girl; Until the Last Goodbye),* The Love Boat. Shown February 11, 1978 (ABC)
Joseph Biroc, ASC *Washington: Behind Closed Doors-Part I.* Shown September 6, 1977 (ABC)
Robert Hauser *Roll of Thunder, Hear My Cry.* Shown June 2-4, 1978 (ABC)
Michel Hugo, ASC *The Awakening Land.* Shown February 19-21, 1978 (NBC)

Outstanding Cinematography in Entertainment Programming for a Special [for a special or feature length program made for television]
* Gerald Perry Finnerman, ASC *Ziegfeld: The Man and His Women.* Shown May 21, 1978 (NBC)

Joseph Biroc, ASC *A Family Upside Down.* Shown April 9, 1978 (NBC)
Sol Negrin, ASC *The Last Tenant.* Shown June 25, 1978 (ABC)
Howard Schwartz, ASC *The Ghost of Flight 401.* Shown February 18, 1978 (NBC)
Richard Waite *The Life and Assasination of the Kingfish.* Shown March 21, 1977 (NBC)

Outstanding Achievement in Make-Up [for a single episode of a series, or for a special program]
* Richard Cobos, Walter Schenck *How the West Was Won-Part II.* Shown February 19, 1978 (ABC)
Hank Edds, Allan "Whitey" Snyder *The Fighter,* Little House On The Prairie. Shown November 21, 1977 (NBC)
Christina Smith *King*-entire series. February 12-14, 1978 (NBC)
Frank C. Westmore, Michael G. Westmore *A Love Affair: The Eleanor and Lou Gehrig Story.* Shown January 15, 1978 (NBC)
Michael G. Westmore, Henry Edds and Lynn Reynolds *The Amazing Howard Hughes.* Shown April 13 & 14, 1977 (CBS)

Outstanding Achievement in Lighting Direction [for a single episode of a regular or limited series or for a special program]
* Greg Brunton *Cher . . . Special.* Shown April 3, 1978 (ABC)
Leard Davis, Lighting Designer; Ken Dettling, Lighting Director *You Can Run But You Can't Hide,* Visions. Shown November 13, 1977 (PBS)
Imero Fiorentino *The Neil Diamond Special: I'm Glad You're Here with Me Tonight.* Shown November 17, 1977 (NBC)
Fred McKinnon, Carl J. Vitelli, Jr. *Happy Birthday, Las Vegas.* Shown October 23, 1977 (ABC)
Alan K. Walker, Bill Klages *Olivia.* Shown May 17, 1978 (ABC)
George Riesenberger *The Great Trolley Strike of 1895,* Best of Families. Shown October 27, 1977 (PBS)

Outstanding Achievement in Technical Direction and Electronic Camerawork [for a single episode of a regular or limited series or for a special program]
* Gene Crowe, TD, Wayne Orr, Larry Heider, Dave Hilmer and Bob Keys, Cameramen *The Sentry Collection Presents Ben Vereen-His Roots.* March 2, 1978 (ABC)

Charles Franklin, TD, Steve Cunningham, TD, Harry Tatarian, TD, Mark Miller, TD, Gorman Erickson, John Aguirre, Stanley Zitnick, David Finch, Richard Nelson, Hector Ramirez, Louis Shore, Ben Wolf, Thomas Brown, Gordon Sweeney, Robert Welsh and Brian Cunneen, Cameramen *CBS: On the Air*. Shown March 26-April 1, 1978 (CBS)

Louis Fusari, TD, Roger Harbaugh, Roy Holm, Rick Lombardo and Peggy Mahoney, Cameramen *Mitzi . . . What's Hot, What's Not*. Shown April 6, 1978 (CBS)

Karl Messerschmidt, TD, Jon Olson, Mike Stramisky, George Loomis, George Falandeau, Mike Higuera and Jim Dodge, Cameramen *Doug Henning's World of Magic*. Shown December 15, 1977 (NBC)

O. Tamburri, TD, Jon Olson, Roy Holm and Reed Howard, Cameramen *Our Town*, Bell System. Shown May 30, 1977 (NBC)

Outstanding Achievement in Graphic Design and Title Sequences [for a single episode of a series or for a special program. This includes animation only when created for use in titling]
* Bill Davis, Bob Fletcher and Bill Melendez *NBC: The First Fifty Years-A Closer Look*, Variety. Shown October 23, 1977 (NBC)

Eytan Keller, Stewart Bernstein *50th Annual Awards of the Academy of Motion Picture Arts and Sciences*. Shown April 3, 1978 (ABC)

Maury Nemoy, Robert Branham and John De Cuir *Ziegfeld: The Man and His Women*. Shown May 21, 1978 (NBC)

Phil Norman *Washington: Behind Closed Doors*. Shown September 6-11, 1977 (ABC)

Outstanding Achievement in Choreography [for episode(s) of a series or for a special program]
* Ron Field *The Sentry Collection Presents Ben Vereen-His Roots*. Shown March 2, 1978 (ABC)

George Balanchine, Alexandra Danilova *New York City Ballet: Coppelia-Live from Lincoln Center*. Shown January 31, 1978 (PBS)

Tony Charmoli *Mitzi . . . Zings into Spring*. Shown March 29, 1977 (CBS)

Ernest O. Flatt *The Final Show*, The Carol Burnett Show. Shown March 29, 1978 (CBS)

Mariam Nelson *Ziegfeld: The Man and His Women*. Shown May 21, 1978 (NBC)

Daytime Emmy Awards

Presented by the National Academy of Television Arts and Sciences for programs shown March 14, 1977-March 28, 1978

Outstanding Daytime Drama Series [emmy(s) to executive producer(s) and producers(s)]
* *Days of Our Lives* Betty Corday, Wesley Kenny, Executive Producers; Jack Herzberg, Producer (NBC)
All My Children Bud Kloss, Agnes Nixon, Producers (ABC)
Ryan's Hope Claire Labine, Paul A. Mayer, Executive Producers; Robert Costello, Producer (ABC)
The Young and the Restless John Conboy, Executive Producer; Patricia Wenig, Producer (CBS)

Outstanding Game or Audience Participation Show [emmy(s) to executive producer(s) and producer(s)]
* *Hollywood Squares* Merrill Heatter, Bob Quigley, Executive Producers; Jay Redack, Producer (NBC)
Family Feud Howard Felsher, Producer (ABC)
The $20,000 Pyramid Bob Stewart, Executive Producer; Ann Marie Schmitt, Producer (ABC)

Outstanding Talk, Service, or Variety Series [emmy(s) to executive producer(s) and producer(s)]
* *Donahue* Richard Mincer, Executive Producer; Patricia McMillen, Producer (SYN)
Dinah! Henry Jaffe, Executive Producer; Fred Tatashore, Producer (SYN)
Merv Griffin Show Bob Murphy, Producer (SYN)

The Mike Douglas Show Frank Miller, Executive Producer; Brad Lachman, Producer (SYN)

Outstanding Actor in a Daytime Drama Series
* James Pritchett *The Doctors* (Role: Dr. Matt Powers)(NBC)
Matthew Cowles *All My Children* (Role: Billy Clyde)(ABC)
Larry Keith *All My Children* (Role: Nick Davis)(ABC)
Michael Levin *Ryan's Hope* (Role: Jack Fenelli)(ABC)
Andrew Robinson *Ryan's Hope* (Role: Frank Ryan)(ABC)
Michael Storm *One Life to Live* (Role: Dr. Larry Wolek)(ABC)

Outstanding Actress in a Daytime Drama Series
* Laurie Heineman *Another World* (Role: Charlene Frame Matthews)(NBC)
Mary Fickett *All My Children* (Role: Ruth Martin)(ABC)
Susan Seaforth Hayes *Days of Our Lives* (Role: Julie Williams)(NBC)
Jennifer Harmon *One Life to Live* (Role: Cathy Lord)(ABC)
Susan Lucci *All My Children* (Role: Erica Kane)(ABC)
Beverlee McKinsey *Another World* (Role: Iris Bancroft)(NBC)
Victoria Wyndham *Another World* (Role: Rachel Corey)(NBC)

Outstanding Host or Hostess in a Game or Audience Participation Show
* Richard Dawson *Family Feud* (ABC)
  Dick Clark *The $20,000 Pyramid* (ABC)
  Gene Rayburn *Match Game* (CBS)
  Chuck Woolery, Host; Susan Stafford, Hostess *Wheel of Fortune* (NBC)

Outstanding Host or Hostess in a Talk, Service, or Variety Series
* Phil Donahue *Donahue* (SYN)
  James Crockett *Crockett's Victory Garden* (PBS)
  Jim Nabors *The Jim Nabors Show* (SYN)
  Dinah Shore *Dinah!* (SYN)

Outstanding Individual Director for a Daytime Drama Series [for a single episode]
* Richard Dunlap *The Young and the Restless*. Shown March 3, 1978 (CBS)
  Ira Cirker *Another World*. Shown December 20, 1977 (NBC)
  Richard T. McCue *As the World Turns*. Shown April 29, 1977 (CBS)
  Robert Myhrum *Love of Life*. Shown August 31, 1977 (CBS)
  Al Rabin *Days of Our Lives (Julie's Rape)*. Shown February 21, 1978 (NBC)
  Lela Swift *Ryan's Hope*. Shown November 3, 1977 (ABC)

Outstanding Individual Director for a Daytime Game or Audience Participation Show [for a single episode]
* Mike Gargiulo *The $20,000 Pyramid*. Shown June 20, 1977 (ABC)
  Paul Alter *Family Feud*, Valentine's Day Celebration Special. Shown February 14, 1978 (ABC)

Outstanding Individual Director for a Variety Program [for a single episode]
* Martin Haig Mackey *Over Easy*. Shown March 20, 1978 (PBS)
  Donald R. King *Mike in Hollywood*, The Mike Douglas Show. Shown February 9, 1978 (SYN)
  Glen Swanson *Dinah Salutes Philadelphia*, Dinah! Shown February 28, 1978 (SYN)

Outstanding Writing for a Daytime Drama Series [for a single episode of a series; or for the entire series]
* Claire Labine, Paul Avila Mayer, Mary Munisteri, Allan Leicht and Judith Pinsker *Ryan's Hope* (ABC)

William J. Bell, Kay Lenard, Bill Rega, Pat Falken Smith and Margaret Stewart *Days of Our Lives*. Shown April 18, 1977 (NBC)
Jerome & Bridget Dobson, Nancy Ford, Jean Ruvernol and Robert & Phyllis White *The Guiding Light* (CBS)
Agnes Nixon, Cathy Chicos, Doris Frankel, Ken Harvey, Kathryn McCabe, Wisner Washam, Mary K. Wells and Jack Wood *All My Children* (ABC)

Outstanding Children's Entertainment Special [emmy(s) to executive producer(s) and producer(s)]
* *Hewitt's Just Different*, ABC Afterschool Special. Daniel Wilson, Executive Producer; Fran Seras, Producer (ABC)
  A Piece of Cake, Special Treat. Marilyn Olin, Lee Polk, Producers (NBC)
  How the Beatles Changed the World, Special Treat. Charles E. Andrews, Ken Greengrass, Executive Producers (NBC)
  I Can, The Winners. Robert Guenette, Executive Producer; Paul Asselin, Diane Asselin, Producers (CBS)
  Journey Together. The Winners. Robert Guenette, Executive Producer; Paul Asselin, Diane Asselin, Producers (CBS)
  Man from Nowhere, Once Upon a Classic. George Gallico, Executive Producer; Jay Rayvid, Producer (PBS)
  The Pinballs, ABC Afterschool Special. Martin Tahse, Producer (ABC)

Outstanding Children's Entertainment Series [emmy(s) to executive producer(s) and producer(s)]
* *Captain Kangaroo* Jim Hirschfeld, Producer (CBS)
  Robin Hood, Once Upon a Classic. George Gallico, Executive Producer; Jay Rayvid, Producer (PBS)
  Zoom Terri Payne Francis, Executive Producer; Bob Glover, Producer (PBS)

Outstanding Children's Informational Series [emmy(s) to executive producer(s) and producer(s)]
* *Animals Animals Animals* Lester Cooper, Executive Producer; Peter Weinberg, Producer (ABC)
  ABC Minute Magazine Tom Wolf, Executive Producer (ABC)
  Villa Alegre Claudio Guzman, Executive Producer; Larry Gotlieb, Producer (PBS)

**Outstanding Children's Information Special
[emmy(s) to executive producer(s) and
producer(s)]**
* *Very Good Friends,* ABC Afterschool
  Special. Martin Tahse, Producer (ABC)
  Henry Winkler Meets William Shakespeare.
  Festival of Lively Arts for Young People.
  Daniel Wilson, Producer (CBS)

**Outstanding Children's Instructional Series
[emmy(s) to executive producer(s) and
producer(s)]**
* *Schoolhouse Rock* Tom Yohe, Executive
  Producer; Radford Stone, George Newall,
  Producers (ABC)
  Grammar Rock, Schoolhouse Rock. Tom
  Yohe, Executive Producer; Radford
  Stone, Producer (ABC)
  Sesame Street Al Hyflop, Producer (PBS)

**Outstanding Achievement in Religious
Programming [an award for programs—
series and specials (possibility of one award,
more than one award, or no award)]**
  Directions Series Sid Darion, Executive
  Producer (ABC)
  Francis of Assissi: A Search, The Man and
  His Meaning. Doris Ann, Executive
  Producer; Martin Hoade, Producer.
  Shown December 11, 1977 (NBC)
  Woman of Valor Doris Ann, Executive
  Producer; Martin Hoade, Producer.
  Shown March 20, 1977 (NBC)

**Special Classification of Outstanding
Program Achievement [an award for unique
program achievements, which do not fall into
a specific category, or are not otherwise
recognized (possibility of one award, more
than one award, or no award)]**
* *Live from Lincoln Center: Recital of Tenor
  Luciano Pavarotti from the Met* John
  Goberman, Executive Producer (PBS)
  Camera Three John Musilli, Executive
  Producer; John Musilli, Roger Englander,
  Producers (CBS)
  Good Morning America Series Woody
  Fraser, Executive Producer; George
  Merlis, Merrill Mazuer and Bob Blum,
  Producers (ABC)
  Mutual of Omaha's Wild Kingdom Don
  Meier, Executive Producer (SYN)

**Outstanding Achievement in Coverage of
Special Events [an award for program and
individual achievements. A special event is a
single program presented as live coverage; i.e.
parades, pageants, awards presentations,
salutes and coverage of other live events which
were not covered by the news division
(possibility of one award, more than one
award, or no award)]**
* *The Great English Garden Party—Peter
  Ustinov Looks at 100 Years of Wimbledon*
  Ken Ashton, Allison Hawkes and Pamela
  Moncur, Producers. Shown June 18, 1977
  (NBC)
  All-American Thanksgiving Day Parade Mike
  Gargiulo, Executive Producer; Vern
  Diamon, Clarence Schimmel, Jim
  Hirschfeld, Wilfred Fielding and Malachy
  Wiengers, Producers. Shown November
  24, 1977 (CBS)
  Tournament of Roses Parade & Pageant Mike
  Gargiulo, Executive Producer; Vern
  Diamon, Producer. Shown January 2,
  1978 (CBS)
  Fourth Annual Daytime Emmy Awards Walter
  Miller, Producer. Shown May 12, 1977
  (NBC)
  *Macy's 51st Annual Thanksgiving Day
  Parade* Dick Schneider, Producer. Shown
  November 24, 1977 (NBC)

**Creative Arts in Entertainment Areas
[possibility of one award, more than one
award or no award]**

**Outstanding Individual Achievement in
Children's Programming**
* Tom Aldredge, Actor *Henry Winkler Meets
  William Shakespeare,* CBS Festival of
  Lively Arts for Young People. Shown
  March 20, 1977 (CBS)
* Jan Hartman, Writer *Hewitt's Just Different,*
  ABC Weekend Specials. Shown October
  12, 1977 (ABC)
* David Wolf, Writer *The Magic Hat.* Unicorn
  Tales. Shown December 5, 1977 (SYN)
* Tony DiGirolamo, Lighting Director *Henry
  Winkler Meets William Shakespeare,* CBS
  Lively Arts for Young People. Shown
  March 20, 1978 (CBS)
* Vince Humphrey, Film Editor *Very Good
  Friends,* ABC Afterschool Special.
  Shown April 6, 1977 (ABC)

* Bonnie Karrin, Film Editor *Big Apple Birthday,* Unicorn Tales. Shown February 7, 1978 (SYN)
* Brianne Murphy, Cinematographer *Five Finger Discount,* Special Treat. Shown November 1, 1977 (NBC)

Outstanding Individual Achievement in Daytime Programming in Any Area of Creative Technical Crafts [an award for individual technical craft achievement which does not fall into a specific category, and is not otherwise recognized]
* Connie Wexler, Costume Design *Search for Tomorrow.* Shown February 14, 1978 (CBS)
* Steve Cunningham, Technical Director; Hector Ramirez, Cameraman; Sheldon Mooney, Cameraman; Martin Wagner, Cameraman; Dave Finch, Cameraman

After Hours: Singin', Swingin' & All That Jazz. Shown December 6, 1977 (CBS)
* David M. Clark, Lighting Director *The Mike Douglas Show* (The New York Remotes). Shown November 8, 1977 (SYN)
* Joyce Tamara Grossman, Video Tape Editing *Family Feud* (Valentine's Day Special). Shown February 14, 1978 (ABC)

Outstanding Individual Achievement in Religious Programming
* Carolee Campbell, Performer *This is My Son.* Shown June 19, 1977 (NBC)
* Douglass Watson, Narrator *Continuing Creation.* Shown February 19, 1978 (NBC)
* Joseph Vadala, Cinematographer *Continuing Creation.* Shown February 19, 1978 (NBC)

The 1977 George Foster Peabody Broadcasting Awards

KABC-TV, Los Angeles, California, for *Police Accountability,* a part of *Eyewitness News.*

KCMO-TV, Kansas City, Missouri, for *Where Have All the Flood Cars Gone?* a part of *Eyewitness News.*

WNBC-TV, New York, New York, for *F.I.N.D. Investigative Reports,* a part of *Newscenter 4.*

WNET/13, New York, New York and WETA, Arlington, Virginia, for *The MacNeil/Lehrer Report.*

WBTV, Charlotte, North Carolina, for *The Rowe String Quartet Plays on Your Imagination.*

LORIMAR PRODUCTIONS, Los Angeles, California, for the ABC Theatre presentation of *Green Eyes.*

DAVID WOLPER AND ABC-TV, for the ABC Novel for Television presentation of *Roots.*

NORMAN LEAR, for *All in the Family.*

LONDON WEEKEND TELEVISION, London, England, for *Upstairs Downstairs.*

MTM PRODUCTIONS, Los Angeles, California, for *The Mary Tyler Moore Show.*

Steve Allen of KCET, Los Angeles, California, for *Meeting of Minds.*

NBC-TV, New York, New York, for *Tut: The Boy King.*

METROPOLITAN OPERA ASSOCIATION, New York, New York, for *Live from the Met,* as exemplified by performances of *La Boheme* and *Rigoletto.*

WNET/13, New York, New York, for *A Good Dissonance Like a Man.*

MULTIMEDIA PROGRAM PRODUCTIONS, Cincinnati, Ohio, for *Joshua's Confusion.*

NBC-TV, Arthur Rankin and Jules Bass, for *The Hobbit.*

WCBS-TV, New York, New York, for *Camera Three.*

WPIX, New York, New York, for *The Lifer's Group—I Am My Brother's Keeper,* a part of WPIX Editorial Report.

WNBC-TV, New York, New York, for *Buyline: Betty Furness.*

WNET/13, New York, New York, for *Police Tapes.*

TV Programs 1977-1978

1 A.E.S. Hudson St.   ABC
Program Type Comedy Series
30 minutes. Thursdays. Premiere date: 3/23/78.
Last show: 4/20/78. Comedy set in a city hospital emergency ward. Created by Tony Sheehan;
Danny Arnold; and Chris Hayward.
Executive Producer Danny Arnold
Producer Roland Kibbee
Company Triseme Corporation
Director Noam Pitlik
Writers Roland Kibbee, Bob Colleary, Tom
   Reeder, Tony Sheehan
Music Jack Elliott, Allyn Ferguson
Art Director Thomas E. Azzari
CAST

Dr. Antonio "Tony" Menzies .... Gregory Sierra
Nurse Rosa Santiago .... Rosana Soto
J. Powell Karbo ....Stefan Gierasch
Foshko .... Susan Peretz
Stanke .... Ralph Manza
Newton .... Ray Stewart
Dr. Mackler .... Bill Cort
Dr. Glick .... Allan Miller
Dr. Gloria Manners .... Barrie Youngfellow

**2 AAU Junior Olympic National
Multi-Sports Championships**   NBC
Program Type Sports Special
90 minutes each day. Coverage of the AAU Junior Olympics from the University of Nebraska
at Lincoln 8/12/78 and 8/13/78.
Executive Producer Don Ohlmeyer
Producer Mike Weisman
Company NBC sports
Director Ken Fouts
Commentators Mike Adamle, Donna de Varona,
   Micki King Hogue, Charlie Jones, Frank
   Shorter, Jim Simpson, Nancy Theis

3 ABC Afterschool Specials   ABC
Program Type Children's Series
60 minutes. Wednesdays. Premiere date: 10/72.
Sixth season premiere: 10/12/77. Young people's specials presented during the school year.
13 shows aired during the 1977–78 season:
"Francesca, Baby," "Hewitt's Just Different,"
"The Horrible Honchos," "It Isn't Easy Being a
Teenage Millionaire," "It's a Mile from Here to
Glory," "Michel's Mixed-Up Musical Bird,"

"Mighty Moose and the Quarterback Kid,"
"Mom and Dad Can't Hear Me," "My Mom's
Having a Baby," "The Pinballs," "P.J. & the
President's Son," "The Rag Tag Champs,"
"Very Good Friends." (*See* individual titles for
credits.)

**4 The ABC All-Star Thanksgiving
Special**   ABC
Program Type Children's Special
3-1/2 hours. 11/24/77. A holiday package from
the "ABC All-Star Saturday" children's programs.
Producers Sid Krofft, Marty Krofft

ABC Captioned News *See* Captioned
ABC Evening News

5 ABC Children's Novel for Television   ABC
Program Type Children's Series
30 minutes. Season premiere: 9/10/77. Four stories aired during the 1977–78 season: "The Escape of a One-Ton Pet," "The Nunundaga,"
"Trouble River," "The Winged Colt." (*See* individual titles for credit.)

**6 ABC Evening News with Harry
Reasoner and Barbara Walters**   ABC
Program Type News Series
30 minutes. Mondays-Fridays. Season premiere:
9/16/77. Last show: 7/28/78.
Executive Producer Av Westin
Senior Producer Jeff Gralnick
Company ABC News
Anchors Harry Reasoner, Barbara Walters
Commentator Howard K. Smith

7 The ABC Friday Night Movie
Program Type Feature Film Series – TV
   Movie Series   ABC
2 hours. Fridays. Season premiere: 9/16/77. A
combination of made-for-television films and
theatrically released motion pictures. The TV
films are: "Black Market Baby" (formerly titled

The ABC Friday Night Movie *Continued*
"A Dangerous Love"), "The Boy in the Plastic
Bubble," "Cindy," "Cruise into Terror," "Curse
of the Black Widow," "Dr. Scorpion," "Eleanor
and Franklin—Part I," "The Great Houdinis,"
"Having Babies II," "Having Babies III," "Inti-
mate Strangers," "It Happened at Lakewood
Manor," "Kate Bliss and the Ticker Tape Kid,"
"The Last Dinosaur," "Murder at the World
Series," "Return to Fantasy Island," "Secrets,"
"Stickin' Together," "Telethon," "Three on a
Date," "The Trial of Lee Harvey Oswald,"
"True Grit (A Further Adventure)," "The Two-
Five," "With This Ring," and "Young Joe, The
Forgotten Kennedy." (*See* titles for credits.) The
feature films are: "At the Earth's Core" (1976)
shown 9/1/78, "Beautiful But Deadly" (1973—
theatrically released as "The Don Is Dead")
shown 7/28/78, "Beneath the Planet of the
Apes" (1970) shown 1/9/78, "The Bermuda
Depths" (1978) shown 1/27/78, "Buster and Billie" (1974) shown 3/17/78, "Dirty Mary Crazy
Larry" (1974) shown 3/31/78, "Fat City" (1972)
shown 7/7/78, "Forty Carats" (1973) shown
6/23/78, "Freebie and the Bean" (1974) shown
2/10/78, "Futureworld" (1976) shown 5/12/78,
"The Golden Voyage of Sinbad" (1974) shown
12/16/77, "Play Misty for Me" (1971) shown
4/28/78, "The Return of the Pink Panther"
(1975) shown 9/23/77, "Take the Money and
Run" (1969) shown 8/4/78, "Terror in the Wax
Museum" (1973) shown 6/16/78, "W.W. and
the Dixie Dancekings" (1974) shown 10/21/77,
"Walking Tall, Part 2" (1975) shown 1/6/78,
"You Can't Steal Love" (1974—released theatrically as "Live a Little, Steal a Lot") shown
1/13/78."

8   ABC Holiday Weekend Specials ABC
Program Type Children's Series
30 minutes. Two shows shown on 12/24/77:
"Blind Sunday," and "The Haunted Trailer."
(*See* individual titles for credits.)

9   ABC Minute Magazine ABC
Program Type Children's Special
60 seconds. Sundays. Premiere date: 1/30/77.
Season premiere: 9/11/77. Evening series for
young people on world news events.
Executive Producer Thomas H. Wolf
Producer Thomas H. Wolf
Company ABC News
Hosts Various

10   The ABC Monday Night Movie ABC
Program Type Feature Film Series – TV
   Movie Series
2 hours (generally). Mondays. Season premiere:
2/6/78. A combination of made-for-TV movies

and theatrically released feature films. The
made-for-TV movies are: "Doctors' Private
Lives," "The Initiation of Sarah," "Little Ladies
of the Night," and "Wild and Wooly." (*See* individual titles for credits.) The films are: "The Adventures of the Wilderness Family" (1975)
shown 5/15/78, "The Laughing Policeman"
(1973) shown 3/13/78, "The Seven-Ups" (1974)
shown 3/6/78, and "Such Good Friends" (1971)
shown 2/27/78.

11   ABC News Brief ABC
Program Type News Series
60 seconds. Daily. Premiere date: 3/14/77. Season premiere: 9/11/78. Anchored by Tom Jarriel
to 7/24/78.
Company ABC News
Anchor Max Robinson

12   ABC News Brief (Daytime) ABC
Program Type News Series
60 seconds. Mondays-Fridays. Premiere date:
4/25/77. Season premiere: 9/12/77. Afternoon
report from Washington, DC, covering late-
breaking news.
Company ABC News

13   ABC News Closeup ABC
Program Type Documentary/Informational
   Series
60 minutes each. Premiere date: 10/18/73. Fifth
season premiere: 10/27/77. Eight documentary
specials shown during the 1977–78 season:
"ABC News Closeup—The American Army: 'A
Shocking State of Readiness,' " "ABC News
Closeup—Arson: Fire for Hire!" "ABC News
Closeup—Asbestos: The Way to Dusty Death,"
"ABC News Closeup: The Class That Went to
War," "ABC News Closeup: Hostage!" "ABC
News Closeup: The Police Tapes," "ABC News
Closeup—Teenage Turn-on: Drinking and
Drugs," "ABC News Closeup—Youth Terror:
The View From Behind the Gun." (*See* individ-
ual titles for credits.)

**14   ABC News Closeup: The American
Army: 'A Shocking State of Readiness'**
   ABC
Program Type Documentary/Informational
   Special
60 minutes. Premiere date: 4/20/78. Documents
the U.S. Army's readiness since the end of the
draft in 1973. Music, "Two Thousand Miles
From Home," by Fletcher Dubois.
Executive Producer Pamela Hill
Senior Producer Richard Richter
Producer Tony Batten
Company ABC News

Director Tony Batten
Writers Bill Wordham, Tony Batten, Christopher Koch
Cinematographers Erik Durschmied, Chuck Levy, Dick Roy, Jorg Weiland
Film Editors Nils Rasmussen, Walter Essenfeld
Reporter Bill Wordham

15 ABC News Closeup—Arson: Fire for Hire! ABC

Program Type Documentary/Informational Special
60 minutes. Premiere date: 8/3/78. Investigation of arson.
Executive Producer Pamela Hill
Senior Producer Richard Richter
Producer Richard Gerdau
Company ABC News
Writers Brit Hume, Richard Gerdau
Narrator Brit Hume
Reporter Mike Connors

16 ABC News Closeup—Asbestos: The Way to Dusty Death ABC

Program Type Documentary/Informational Special
60 minutes. Premiere date: 7/14/78. Investigative documentary on asbestos.
Executive Producer Pamela Hill
Senior Producer Richard Richter
Producer Phil Lewis
Company ABC News
Director Tom Priestley
Writers Phil Lewis, Jules Bergman
Cinematographers Terry Morrison, Don Guy, Mirek Snopek
Film Editors Henriette Huehne, Nils Rasmussen
Correspondent Jules Bergman

17 ABC News Closeup: The Class That Went to War ABC

Program Type Documentary/Informational Special
60 minutes. Premiere date: 12/1/77. An examination of the people of the Vietnam era tracing the lives of some of the members of the Chatham, New Jersey, High School Class of 1964.
Producer Richard Gerdau
Company ABC News
Director Richard Gerdau
Writer Richard Gerdau
Cinematographer Dick Roy
Film Editor James Flanagan
Host Steve Bell

18 ABC News Closeup: Hostage! ABC

Program Type Documentary/Informational Special
60 minutes. Premiere date: 1/30/78. An examination of the seizure of hostages by political terrorists.
Executive Producer William Peters
Producers Ene Riisna, Robert Richter, Aram Boyajian
Company ABC News
Directors Ene Riisna, Aram Boyajian, William Peters
Writer William Peters
Cinematographers William Brayne, Michael Doods, Sid Reichman, Mike Hoover, Peter Dunnigan, Tony Foresta, Ross Lowell
Film Editors Gerard Klein, Nicolas Kaufman, Ara Chekmayan, Nancy Cook
Correspondent Peter Jennings

19 ABC News Closeup: The Police Tapes ABC

Program Type Documentary/Informational Special
60 minutes. Premiere date: 8/3/78 (PBS). Repeat date: 8/17/78. Documentary about the daily life of policemen in New York's 44th Precinct.
Executive Producer Pamela Hill
Senior Producer Richard Richter
Producers Alan Raymond, Susan Raymond
Company ABC News

20 ABC News Closeup—Teenage Turn-on: Drinking and Drugs ABC

Program Type Documentary/Informational Special
60 minutes. Premiere date: 10/27/77. An examination of drinking and drug abuse among today's teenagers. Recommended for viewing by the National Education Association.
Producer Tom Bywaters
Company ABC News
Director Tom Bywaters
Writer Tom Bywaters
Cinematographers Chuck Barbee, Larry Mitchell, Dan O'Reilly
Film Editor Walter Essenfeld
Host Tom Jarriel

21 ABC News Closeup—Youth Terror: The View From Behind The Gun ABC

Program Type Documentary/Informational Special
60 minutes. Premiere date: 6/28/78. Non-narrative documentary film report on youth crime allows youth offenders themselves to tell their story.
Executive Producer Pamela Hill

ABC News Closeup—Youth Terror: The View From Behind The Gun *Continued*
Senior Producer Richard Richter
Producer Helen Whitney
Company ABC News
Director Helen Whitney
Writer Helen Whitney
Cinematographers Don Guy; Bryan Anderson
Film Editors Pat Cook; James Flanagan

22   ABC News' World News Tonight
ABC
Program Type News Series
30 minutes. Mondays–Fridays. Premiere date: 7/10/78.
Executive Producer Av Westin
Company ABC News
Anchors Max Robinson in Chicago, Frank Reynolds in Washington, Peter Jennings in London, Barbara Walters in New York

23   ABC Out-of School Specials/ABC Weekend Specials   ABC
Program Type Children's Series
30 minutes. Season premiere: 9/10/77. Seventeen stories aired during the 1977–78 season: "The Amazing Cosmic Awareness of Duffy Moon," "Dear Lovey Hart (I Am Desperate!)," "The Escape of a One-Ton Pet," "Homer and the Wacky Doughnut Machine," "It Must Be Love ('Cause I Feel So Dumb!)," "The Magical Mystery Trip through Little Red's Head," "Portrait of Grandpa Doc," "Pssst! Hammerman's After You!" "The Puppy Who Wanted a Boy," "The Ransom of Red Chief," "Rookie of the Year," "Sara's Summer of the Swans," "The Secret Life of T. K. Dearing," "The Skating Rink," "Soup and Me," "Trouble River," "The Winged Colt." (*See* individual titles for credits.)

24   ABC Presents Tomorrow's Stars
ABC
Program Type Music/Comedy/Variety Special
2 hours. Premiere date: 6/17/78. Audience at home and in the studio vote for the best of talented new performers.
Executive Producers Dan Lewis; Marty Pasetta
Producer Eric Lieber
Company Photoplay Magazine Television and Pasetta Productions
Director Marty Pasetta
Host John Ritter
Guest Stars Cheryl Tiegs, Norm Crosby, Joan Rivers, Captain and Tennille, Big Bird, Dick Van Patten, Charles Nelson Reilly, Florence Henderson

25   ABC Saturday Comedy Special ABC
Program Type Limited Series
30 minutes (generally). Premiere date: 6/24/78. Last show: 8/25/78. Series of pilots. Shows are: "The Archie Situation Comedy Musical Variety Show," "Harvey Korman Show," "Jackie & Darlene," "The Krofft Comedy Hour," "The Rag Business," and "Snavely." (*See* individual titles for credits.)

26   ABC Saturday News with Ted Koppel   ABC
Program Type News Series
30 minutes. Saturdays. Last show: 9/24/77.
Senior Producer Phil Bergman
Company ABC News
Anchor Ted Koppel

27   ABC Saturday News with Tom Jarriel and Sylvia Chase ABC
Program Type News Series
30 minutes. Saturdays. Premiere date: 10/1/77. Retitled 7/17/78 to "ABC News' World News Tonight—Saturday Report."
Senior Producer Jeff Gralnick
Company ABC News
Anchors Sylvia Chase, Tom Jarriel

28   ABC Short Story Specials   ABC
Program Type Children's Series
30 minutes. Saturdays. Premiere date: 1/29/77. Season premiere: 10/15/77. Adaptations of short stories for young people. Four stories aired during the 1977–78 season: "Homer and the Wacky Doughnut Machine," "My Dear Uncle Sherlock," "Portrait of Grandpa Doc," "Ransom of Red Chief." (*See* individual titles for credits.)

29   ABC Sports Magazine   ABC
Program Type News Magazine Series
15 minutes. Sundays. Premiere date: 1/8/78. Sports issues and news with commentary by ABC sportscasters.
Executive Producer Roone Arledge
Producer Terry O'Neil
Company ABC Sports
Director Joe Aceti

30   The ABC Summer Movie
Program Type Feature Film Series – TV Movie Series   ABC
90 minutes. Thursdays. Premiere date: 6/15/78. A combination of made-for-TV movies and theatrically released films shown during the summer months. The TV movies are: "Phase IV," and "Vega$." (*See* individual titles for credits.) The feature films are "Ash Wednesday" (1973)

shown 7/6/78, "Claudine" (1974) shown 7/27/78, "For Pete's Sake" (1974) shown 8/10/78, "The Lords of Flatbush" (1974) shown 6/15/78, "A Minute to Pray, a Second to Die" (1968) shown 7/20/78, "Return to Fantasy Island" (1978) shown 7/13/78, and "S*P*Y*S" (1974) shown 6/29/78.

31 The ABC Sunday Night Movie ABC
Program Type Feature Film Series – TV Movie Series
2 hours (generally). Sundays. Season premiere: 9/18/77. A combination of made-for-TV movies and theatrically released feature films. The TV-movies are: "It Happened One Christmas," "Leave Yesterday Behind," "Murder at the World Series," "The New Maverick," "Night Cries," "Return to Fantasy Island," "SST Disaster in the Sky" (originally broadcast 2/25/77 as "SST–Death Flight"), "Telethon," "The Trial of Lee Harvey Oswald," and "Young Joe, The Forgotten Kennedy." (*See* individual titles for credits.) The feature films are: "Anything for Love" (1974) shown 8/6/78, "Bite the Bullet" (1975) shown 11/20/77, "Custer of the West" (1967) shown 7/2/78, "Darling Lili" (1970) shown 7/9/78, "Deliverance" (1972) shown 12/18/77, "Diamonds Are Forever" (1971) shown 4/16/78, "The Friends of Eddie Coyle" (1973) shown 7/30/78, "Funny Girl" (1968) shown 12/25/77, "Gold" (1974) shown 7/23/78, "High Plains Drifter" (1973) shown 4/2/78, "Joe Kidd" (1972) shown 8/20/78, "The Lady and the Outlaw" (1974) shown 4/9/78, "Law and Disorder" (1974) shown 1/15/78, "Live and Let Die" (1973) shown 2/26/78, "The Longest Yard" (1974) shown 9/25/77, "The Man with the Golden Gun" (1974) shown 1/22/78, "Murder on the Orient Express" (1974) shown 10/9/77, "Nashville" (1975) shown 1/8/78, "Newman's Law" (1974) shown 8/13/78, "The Poseidon Adventure" (1972) shown 11/13/77, "Serpico" (1973) shown 1/1/78, "Sky Terror" (1972) shown 4/30/78, "Shoot Out" (1971) shown 6/11/78, "The Stepford Wives" (1975) shown 3/19/78, "The Take" (1974) shown 7/16/78, "Thunderbolt and Lightfoot" (1974) shown 10/30/77, "Walking Tall" (1973) shown 4/23/78, "The Way We Were" (1973) shown 3/5/78, and "White Line Fever" (1975) shown 10/16/77 and 6/18/78.

32 ABC Theatre ABC
Program Type Drama Series
Five specials seen during the 1977–78 season: "Breaking Up," "Eleanor and Franklin: The White House Years," "The Gathering," "The Last Tenant," and "Mary White." (*See* individual titles for credits.)

33 ABC Tuesday Movie of the Week ABC
Program Type Feature Film Series – TV Movie Series
Times vary. Tuesdays. Season premiere: 9/13/77. A combination of made-for-television films and theatrically released motion pictures repeated for late night viewing.

34 ABC Weekend News ABC
Program Type News Series
15 minutes. Saturdays and Sundays. Late night broadcasts anchored by Tom Jarriel and Sylvia Chase as of 10/23/77. New title as of 7/17/78 is "ABC News Weekend Report."
Executive Producer Robert Chenault
Senior Producer Ron Kershaw
Company ABC News
Anchors Bill Beutel, Tom Jarriel

35 ABC Weekend Specials ABC
Program Type Children's Series
30 minutes. Premiere date: 9/10/77. Multipart telecasts of novels adapted for television, short stories and encore presentations of "ABC Afterschool Specials" which are entitled, "ABC Out-of-School Specials." (*See* "ABC Out-of-School Specials.")

36 ABC's Championship Auto Racing ABC
Program Type Sports Special
Live coverage of four stock car races: the Daytona "500," the Atlanta "500," the Trenton "200," and "Bumping Day," final day of time trials for the Indy "500."

Daytona "500"
90 minutes. Live coverage of the 20th annual Daytona "500" 2/19/78.
Executive Producer Roone Arledge
Producer Chet Forte
Company ABC Sports
Director Larry Kamm
Announcer Jim McKay
Expert Commentators Jim McKay; Chris Economaki

Atlanta "500"
60 minutes. Live coverage of the 19th annual Atlanta "500" Stock Car Race 3/19/78.
Executive Producer Roone Arledge
Producer Dick Buffinton
Company ABC Sports
Director Chet Forte
Announcer Al Michaels
Expert Commentators Jackie Stewart, Chris Economaki

ABC's Championship Auto Racing
Continued
Trenton "200"
90 minutes. Live coverage of Trenton "200" Indianapolis Car Race 4/23/78.
Executive Producer Roone Arledge
Producer Bob Goodrich
Company ABC Sports
Director Chet Forte
Announcer Jim McKay
Expert Commentators Jackie Stewart, Chris Economaki

Bumping Day (Indy "500")
60 minutes. Live coverage of final day of time trials for the Indianapolis "500" 5/21/78.
Executive Producer Roone Arledge
Producer Bob Goodrich
Company ABC Sports
Director Chris Economaki

37   ABC's Monday Night Baseball   ABC
Program Type Limited Sports Series
18 live primary and secondary telecasts of major league baseball. Monday nights. Premiere date: 4/12/76. Third season premiere: 4/10/78. Produced through the end of the regular baseball season in September 1978.
Executive Producer Roone Arledge
Producers Chuck Howard, Dennis Lewin, Bob Goodrich, Terry O'Neil, Joe Aceti, Dick Buffinton, Ric LaCivita
Company ABC Sports
Directors Chet Forte, Joe Aceti, Lou Volpicelli, Craig Janoff
Announcers Jim Lampley, Al Michaels, Kieth Jackson, Sal Marchiano
Expert Commentators Don Drysdale, Bob Vecker, Bill White, Howard Cosell

38   ABC's Monday Night Football   ABC
Program Type Limited Sports Series
14-game schedule of National Football League. Premiere date: 9/21/70. Eighth season premiere: 9/19/77. Last game of season: 12/17/77.
Producer Dennis Lewin
Company ABC Sports
Director Chet Forte
Announcers Frank Gifford, Howard Cosell, Don Meredith

39   ABC's Silver Anniversary Celebration—25 and Still the One   ABC
Program Type Music/Comedy/Variety Special
4 hours. 2/5/78. Hundreds of ABC stars, past and present, gathered for a salute to ABC's 25th anniversary.
Executive Producer Dick Clark
Producer Bill Lee

Associate Producer Victor Kaplan
Company ABC in association with dick clark teleshows
Director Perry Rosemond
Head Writer Robert Arthur
Writers Bill Lee, Stuart Bloomberg, Phil Hahn
Musical Director Lenny Stack
Choreographers Ron Poindexter
Costume Designer Bill Bellew
Production Designers Ray Clausen, Brian Bartholomew
Sports Segments Produced by Ned Steckel
Exec. in Charge of Talent Gary L. Pudney
Stars Edie Adams, Sy Amlen, John Astin, Patty Duke Astin, Lenny Bari, Julie Barnathan, Rona Barrett, Dick Beesemyer, John Beradino, Ernest Borgnine, Tom Bosley, Todd Bridges, Paul Burke, Ron Carey, John Cassisi, Charo, Deborah Clinger, Mark Cohen, Dennis Cole, Michael Cole, Olivia Cole, Tina Cole, Chuck Conners, Robert Conrad, Howard Cosell, Johnny Crawford, Richard Crenna, Billy Crystal, Cathryn Damon, David Doyle, Daryl Dragon, Louise Duart, James Duffy, Barbara Eden, Vince Edwards, Lola Falana, Norman Fell, Fionnuala Flanagan, Ann Flood, Steve Forrest, John Forsythe, Redd Foxx, Gary Frank, Max Gail, Betty Garrett, Christopher George, Lynda Day George, Edmund Gilbert, Leonard Goldenson, Barry Gordon, Fred Grandy, Cathy Green, James Gregory, Robert Guillaume, Lloyd Haynes, David Hedison, Robert Hegyes, Katherine Helmond, Sandy Hill, Ron Howard, Kate Jackson, Keith Jackson, Lawrence-Hilton Jacobs, Rick Jason, Bruce Jenner, Gabriel Kaplan, Jack Kelly, Cissy King, Bernie Kopell, Cheryl Ladd, Ted Lange, Diane Lennon, Janet Lennon, Kathy Lennon, Peggy Lennon, Hal Linden, Audra Lindley, Paul Lynde, Gavin MacLeod, Fred MacMurray, Robert Mandan, Barry Manilow, Penny Marshall, Pamela Sue Martin, Paul Masterson, Kristy McNichol, Denise Miller, Nancy Morgan, Vic Morrow, Donny Most, Sarah Natoli, Melinda Naud, David Nelson, Harriet Nelson, Heywood Nelson, Rick Nelson, Kathleen Nolan, Hugh O'Brian, Dick O'Leary, Patti Page, Richard Paul, Arthur Peterson; Fred Pierce; Sarah Purcell; Donna Reed, Alejandro Rey, Kathryn Reynolds, Adam Rich, John Ritter, Caesar Romero, Elton Rule, Squire Rushnell, William Schallert, Chris Schenkel, Jeannie Sheffield, Fred Silverman, Madge Sinclair, Jaclyn Smith, Jack Soo, Jim Spence, Robert Stack, Florence Stanley, Parker Stevenson, Marcia Strassman, Toni Tennille, Danny Thomas, Ernest Thomas, Marlo Thomas, William Turner, Leslie Uggams, Robert Urich, Karen Valentine, Rudy Vallee, Ed Vane, Abe Vigoda, Marcy Vosburgh, Ted Wass, Vernee Watson,

John Wayne, Anson Williams, Clarence Williams III, Billy Dee Williams, Cindy Williams, Henry Winkler

40 ABC's Sportswatch   ABC
Program Type News Series
Times vary. Presents reports on the breaking news stories in the world of sports. Premiere date: 1/14/78.
Executive Producer Roone Arledge
Company ABC Sports

41 ABC's Wide World of Sports   ABC
Program Type Sports Special
90 minutes. Saturdays (year round)/Sundays (winter-spring). Saturday premiere date: 4/29/61. Continuous. Fifth Sunday premiere: 1/8/78. Last Sunday show: 5/21/78. Coverage of all types of sports events held throughout the world, including the "World Series of Auto Racing," the Little League Baseball World Series, the Hula Bowl Classic and the Pro Football Hall of Fame Game.
Executive Producer Roone Arledge
Coordinating Producer Dennis Lewin
Producers Various
Company ABC Sports
Directors Various
Host Jim McKay
Announcers Howard Cosell, Bill Flemming, Frank Gifford, Keith Jackson, Jim Lampley, Andrea Kirby, Jim McKay, Al Michaels, Bud Palmer, Chris Schenkel, Jackie Stewart, Bob Beattie

42 Abide with Me
Great Performances   PBS
Program Type Dramatic Special
60 minutes. Premiere date: 12/11/77. Drama based on "A Child in the Forest" by Winifred Foley about a 14-year-old girl who serves as housekeeper and maid for six months to a 90-year-old woman.
Executive Producer Jac Venza
Coordinating Producer Ann Blumenthal
Company WNET-TV/New York
Writer Julian Mitchell

CAST

Mrs. Hollins	Cathleen Nesbitt
Winnie Mason	Ann Francis
Iris Allen	Zena Walker
Joan Drummond	Phylleda Law
Robert Drummond	John Nettleton
Vicar	Geoffrey Bayldon
Mr. Spanier	Denis Carey
Anne Mason	Denise Haskins

43 Academy Awards   ABC
Program Type Parades/Pageants/Awards
Special
Live coverage of the 50th annual Awards of the Academy of Motion Picture Arts and Sciences 4/3/78 from the Dorothy Chandler Pavilion of the Los Angeles Music Center.
Producer Howard W. Koch
Company The Academy of Motion Picture Arts and Sciences
Director Marty Pasetta
Writers William Ludwig; Leonard Spigelgass
Musical Director Nelson Riddle
Choreographers Rob Iscove; Patricia Birch
Costume Designer Moss Mabry
Master of Ceremonies Bob Hope
Presenters Fred Astaire, Jacqueline Bisset, Ellen Burstyn, Michael Caine, Paddy Chayesfsky, Bette Davis, Olivia de Havilland, Kirk Douglas, Fay Dunaway, Joan Fontaine, Jodie Foster, Greer Garson, Janet Gaynor, John Green, Mark Hamill, Goldie Hawn, William Holden, Olivia Newton John, Farrah Fawcett Majors, Henry Mancini, James Mason, Marcello Mastroianni, Walter Matthau, Steve McQueen, Gregory Peck, Maggie Smith, Sylvester Stallone, Barbara Stanwyck, John Travolta, Cicely Tyson, Jack Valenti, King Vidor, Jon Voight, Raquel Welch, Billy Dee Williams, Henry Winkler, Natalie Wood, R2D2 (Kenny Baker), C3PO (Anthony Daniels).
Performers Sammy Davis, Jr., Marvin Hamlisch, Gene Kelly, Natalie Wood, Karen Black, Susan Blakely, Stockard Channing, Cyd Charisse, Joan Collins, Eleanor Parker, Camilla Sparv, Debby Boone, Aretha Franklin, Gloria Loring, Jane Powell, Starr Danais

44 Action: The October Crisis 1970 PBS
Program Type Public Affairs Special
90 minutes. Premiere date: 1/24/78. State of martial law temporarily imposed in Canada in response to terrorism examined. Film originally shown on "Verite" series, includes update. Program made possible in part by a grant from the Corporation for Public Broadcasting.
Producer Robin Spry
Company National Film Board of Canada

45 Actor
Hollywood Television Theatre   PBS
Program Type Dramatic Special
2 hours. Premiere date: 2/21/78. Original musical play for television based on the early years of actor Paul Muni. Teleplay and lyrics written by Jerome Lawrence and Robert E. Lee with music by Billy Goldenberg. Presented by KCET-TV Los Angeles. Program made possible by grants from the Corporation for Public Broadcasting and the Ford Foundation.

Actor *Continued*
Executive Producer Norman Lloyd
Producer Norman Lloyd
Company KCET-TV/Los Angeles
Director Norman Lloyd
Choreographer Michael Kidd
Costume Designer Noel Taylor
CAST
Paul Muni (adult) .... Michael Kidd
Favel Weisenfreund ....Herschel Bernardi
Salche Weisenfreund .... Georgia Brown
Boris Thomashevsky .... Walter Matthau
Winfield Sheehan .... Howard Duff
Sol Wurtzel .... Harold Gould
Paul Muni (child) .... Jeff Lynas
Paul Muni (young man) .... Barry Robins
Jacob Adler .... Robert Harris
Bella .... Hildy Brooks
Additional Cast Ezra Stone, Guy Raymond, Monica
Lewis, Alvin Hammer

Adam at 6 A.M. *See* NBC Monday
Night at the Movies

46   The Adams Chronicles   PBS
Program Type Limited Series
60 minutes. Premiere date: 1/20/76. Series
repeated: 1/4/78 and 10/6/77. 13-part series
dramatizing the Adams family from 1750–1900.
Conceived and created by Virginia Kassel with
the collaboration of The Adams Papers, the Mas-
sachusetts Historical Society and the Harvard
University Press. Series made possible by grants
from the National Endowment for the Humani-
ties, the Andrew W. Mellon Foundation and the
Atlantic Richfield Company. Captioned for the
hearing impaired. (Cast list in alphabetical or-
der.)
Executive Producer Jac Venza
Coordinating Producer Robert Costello
Producers Various
Company WNET-TV/New York
Directors Various
Story Editor Anne Howard Bailey
Writers Various
Script Consultant Jacqueline Babbin
CAST
Andrew Jackson ....Wesley Addy
Charles Francis Adams .... John Beal
John Quincy Adams (age 36–48) .... David Birney
Henry Adams ....Peter Brandon
Samuel Adams .... W. B. Brydon
Mrs. Charles Francis Adams .... Nancy Coleman
Abigail Adams (age 44–73) ....Leora Dana
John Quincy Adams (age 50–81) .... William Daniels
John Hancock .... Curt Dawson
John Adams ....George Grizzard
Henry Clay .... George Hearn
Jay Gould .... Paul Hecht
George Washington ....David Hooks
Jeremiah Gridley .... John Houseman
Tsar Alexander I .... Christopher Lloyd
Abigail Adams II ....Lisa Lucas

Mrs. Smith .... Nancy Marchand
Mrs. Henry Adams .... Gilmer McCormick
Abraham Lincoln .... Stephen D. Newman
Mrs. John Quincy Adams ...... Pamela Payton-Wright
John Quincy Adams II .... Nicholas Pryor
Charles Francis Adams II .... Charles Siebert
Thomas Jefferson .... Albert Stratton
Alexander Hamilton .... Jeremiah Sullivan
Benjamin Franklin .... Robert Symonds
Brooks Adams ....Charles Tenney
King George III .... John Tillinger
Abigail Adams (age 18–44) .... Kathryn Walker

Adventures of Frontier Freemont *See*
NBC Wednesday Night at the Movies

47   The Advocates   PBS
Program Type Public Affairs Series
60 minutes. Alternate Thursdays. Return after
4-year absence on 1/26/78. Topical issues de-
bated in a mock courtroom trial. Series made
possible by grants from the Charles Stewart Mott
Foundation; Merrill, Lynch, Pierce, Fenner, and
Smith, Inc.; the Polaroid Corporation; the John
M. Olin Foundation, Inc.
Executive Producer Peter Cook
Company WGBH-TV/Boston
Moderator Marilyn Berger

48   Aeromeds   Syndicated
Program Type Dramatic Special
30 minutes. Premiere date: 1/17/78. Pilot about
a trio of U.S. Air Force medical technicians on
airlift assignments.
Company Bruce Lansbury Productions and Co-
lumbia Pictures TV
Executive Producer Bruce Lansbury
Producer Leonard Katzman
Director Leonard Katzman
Writer Laurence Heath
CAST
Jenny .... Lauren Tewes
Mich .... John Bennett Perry
Toby .... Carl Anderson
Missy .... Sherry Lynne Hummer
Major Oberlin .... Elinor Donahue
Ken Pierce ....Sanford Gibbons

49   Aetna World Cup Tennis
Festival '78   PBS
Program Type Sports Special
7 hours. Taped coverage of championship tennis
3/11/78 and 3/12/78 at Hartford, CT.
Executive Producer Al Binford
Producers Ken Horseman, Greg Harney
Company Connecticut Public Television
Director Greg Harney
Commentators Bud Collins, Donald Dell

50 AFC Championship Game NBC
Program Type Sports Special
Live coverage of the American Football Conference championship between The Denver Broncos and the Oakland Raiders from Denver's Mile High Stadium 1/1/78.
Executive Producer Scotty Connal
Producers Ted Nathanson, George Finkel
Company NBC Sports
Director Ted Nathanson
Announcers Dick Enberg, Len Dawson

51 AFC Play-Offs (Game I) NBC
Program Type Sports Special
Live coverage of the play-off game between the Oakland Raiders and the Baltimore Colts from Baltimore, MD 12/24/77.
Executive Producer Scotty Connal
Company NBC Sports

52 AFC Play-Offs (Game II) NBC
Program Type Sports Special
Live coverage of the play-off game between the Pittsburgh Steelers and the Denver Broncos in Denver 12/24/77.
Executive Producer Scotty Connal
Company NBC Sports

53 Affair in the Air PBS
Program Type Documentary/Informational Special
60 minutes. Premiere date: 6/6/78. Special on aerobatic flying. Program made possible by grants from Miles Kimball Company; Wisconsin National Life Insurance Company; KWSU-TV/Pullman, Washington; the Wisconsin Educational Communications Board.
Producer Rudi Goldman
Company WHA-TV/Madison, Wisconsin
Director Rudi Goldman

54 After Hours: Singin', Swingin' and All that Jazz CBS
Program Type Music/Comedy/Variety Special
60 minutes. Premiere date: 12/6/77. Third annual musical special with daytime television stars. Special musical material by Billy Barnes.
Producer John Conboy
Company CBS TV
Director Bill Glenn
Musical Director Marvin Laird
Choreographer Carl Jablonski
Costume Designer Pete Menefee
Art Director James J. Agazzi
Stars Keith Charles, Don Hastings, Beau Kayzer, Victoria Mallory, John McCook

Against a Crooked Sky *See* NBC Movie of the Week

55 The Age of Uncertainty PBS
Program Type Educational/Cultural Series
60 minutes. Premiere date: 5/19/77. Series repeated: 9/19/77. 13-part series exploring 200 years of political economics and social thought. Regular feature: rebuttal essay called "Another View" seen at the conclusion of each episode. Programs made possible by grants from Public Television Stations, the Ford Foundation and the Corporation for Public Broadcasting.
Executive Producer Adrian Malone
Senior Producer Dick Gilling
Producers David Kennard; Mick Jackson
Company The British Broadcasting Corporation, KCET-TV/Los Angeles, the Canadian Broadcasting Corporation and the Ontario Educational Communications Authority
Writer John Kenneth Galbraith
Narrator John Kenneth Galbraith
Project Coordinator Greg Andorfer

56 Alambrista! PBS
Visions
Program Type Dramatic Special
2 hours. Premiere date: 10/16/77. Story of a young man's journey from Michoacan, Mexico, to the agricultural fields of California. Original music composed and arranged by Michael Martin
Producers Michael Hausman; Irwin Young
Company KCET-TV/Los Angeles
Director Robert M. Young
Writer Robert M. Young
Art Director Lilly Kilvert
Film Editor Edward Beyer
CAST
Roberto .... Domingo Ambriz
Joe .... Trinidad Silva
Sharon (waitress) .... Linda Gillin
Roberto's wife .... Ludevina Mendez Salazar
Roberto's mother .... Maria Guadalupe Chavez
Cook in cafe .... George Smith
Sharon's brother .... Dennis Harris
First drunk .... Edward Olmos
Second drunk .... Julius Harris
Man in cafe .... Jerry Hardin
Revival Preacher .... Reverend J. D. Hurt
Anglo Coyote .... Ned Beatty
Mexican Coyote .... Salvador Martinez
Junkyard cook .... Felix Jose Alvarez
Pregnant woman .... Lily Alvarez

The Alamo *See* The CBS Tuesday Night Movies

57   Alan King Tennis Classic at Caesars Palace   ABC
Program Type Sports Special
Live coverage of the tournament from Caesars Palace in Las Vegas 4/29/78 and 4/30/78.
Executive Producer Roone Arledge
Producer Terry Jastrow
Company ABC Sports
Director Andy Sidaris
Commentator Howard Cosell
Expert Commentator Arthur Ashe
Interviewer Cheryl Tiegs

58   Alan King's Second Annual Final Warning   ABC
Program Type Comedy Special
60 minutes. Premiere date: 5/13/78. Comedian Alan King in a comedic look at modern man's battle for survival. Music by Elliot Lawrence.
Executive Producers Alan King; Rupert Hitzig
Producer Rocco Urbisci
Company A King-Hitzig Production
Writers Harry Crane, Jeffrey Barron, Rick Kellard, Bob Comfort, Chris Cluess, Stu Kreismen, Rocco Urbisci, Alan King
Costume Designer Bill Hargate
Art Director Charles Lisanby

59   Alaska: The American Child   ABC
Program Type Music/Comedy/Variety Special
2 hours. Premiere date: 9/3/78. Special wilderness adventure film of America's 49th state. Three original songs composed by John Denver and Joe Henry; arranged by Jerry Holdridge.
Executive Producers Roone Arledge; Jerry Weintraub
Producer John Wilcox
Company ABC Sports in cooperation with John-Jer Productions
Director John Wilcox
Writer Pat Smith
Directors of Photography Peter R. Henning; D'Arcy Marsh
Host John Denver

60   Alaska Oil: America's Pipe Dream?   PBS
Program Type Public Affairs Special
60 minutes. 3/2/78. Examines industry/government energy planning. Program made possible by grants from the National Science Foundation and Sigma Xi, The Scientific Research Society of North America.
Executive Producer Jeffrey Kirsch
Producer Susan Pollock
Company KPBS-TV/San Diego
Director Ryall Wilson

61   Albert Herring
Opera Theater   PBS
Program Type Music/Dance Special
2-1/2 hours. Premiere date: 8/7/78. Opera by Benjamin Britten performed by the Opera Theatre of St. Louis is based on a story by Guy De Maupassant titled "Le Risier de Mme. Husson"; libretto by Eric Crozier. Program made possible by grants from Monsanto Fund, PBS stations, The Nate B. and Frances Spingold Foundation, and the Missouri Arts Council.
Producer David Griffiths
Company WNET-TV/New York and BBC
Director Lou Galterio
Director for BBC Brian Large
Conductor John Moriarty
Orchestra St. Louis Symphony
CAST
Albert Herring ....James Hoback
Police Superintendent Budd .... David Ward
Additional Cast Stephen Dickson, Evelyn Petros, Mallory Walker, Joyce Gerber

62   Alcatraz   PBS
Program Type Documentary/Informational Special
60 minutes. Premiere date: 5/2/78. Documentary on island prison. Program made possible by a grant from the Corporation for Public Broadcasting.
Producer Tom Thayer
Company WNET-TV/New York
Director Tom Thayer
Cinematographer Michael Scott
Film Editor Michael Scott

63   The Alfred I. DuPont-Columbia University Awards for Journalism   PBS
Program Type Parades/Pageants/Awards Special
2 hours. Premiere date: 2/14/78. The 1976–77 Alfred I. duPont-Columbia University Awards. The presenters (all of whom are previous award recipients) include David Brinkley, Pauline Frederick, Edward P. Morgan, Howard K. Smith, and Mike Wallace. Program made possible by grants from the Ford Foundation and Atlantic Richfield Company. First time in 36-year history that awards are broadcast nationally.
Company WNET-TV/New York

64   Alice   CBS
Program Type Comedy Series
30 minutes. Sundays. Premiere date: 9/29/76. Second season premiere: 10/2/77. Comedy about a would-be-singer working as a waitress in Mel's Cafe outside Phoenix. Based on the 1974 film "Alice Doesn't Live Here Any More" by Robert Getchell.

Executive Producer Chris Hayward
Producers Madelyn Davis, Bob Carroll, Jr.
Company Warner Bros. Television.
Director Various
Executive Story Editor Tom Whedon
Writers Various
Art Director Thomas E. Azzari
CAST
Alice Hyatt .... Linda Lavin
Mel .... Vic Tayback
Flo ....Polly Holliday
Vera ....Beth Howland
Tommy Hyatt .... Philip McKeon

65 The Aliens
CBS Reports   CBS
Program Type Documentary/Informational
Special
60 minutes. Premiere date: 12/27/77. Documentary about the Mexican illegal aliens in California.
Executive Producer Howard Stringer
Producer Tom Spain
Company CBS News
Director Tom Spain
Writers Bill Moyers, Tom Spain
Cinematographer Dan Lerner
Film Editor Peter C. Frank
Researcher Peter Schweitzer
Translator Maruta Friedler
Correspondent Bill Moyers

66 All I Could See from Where I Stood
Visions   PBS
Program Type Dramatic Special
90 minutes. Premiere date: 11/10/77. Drama of a young girl's attempts to cope with her mother's alcoholism. Program made possible by grants from the Ford Foundation, Corporation for Public Broadcasting and the National Endowment for the Arts.
Executive Producer Barbara Schultz
Producer Barbara Schultz
Company KCET-TV/Los Angeles
Director Burt Brinckerhoff
Writer Elizabeth Clark
CAST
Sara Blakemore .... Season Hubley
Mary Blakemore .... Louise Latham
Mark Taylor .... Richard Gilliland
Mr. Blakemore .... Biff McGuire
Mr. Taylor ....Jack Murdock
Mrs. Taylor .... Phyllis Thaxter

67 All in the Family
                                                     CBS
Program Type Comedy Series
30 minutes. Sundays. Premiere date: 1/12/71.
Eighth season premiere: 10/2/77. (60-minute episode). Comedy about a working-class bigot set in Queens, NY. Based on "Till Death Do Us Part" created for the British Broadcasting Corporation

by Johnny Speight. Developed by Norman Lear. "Those Were the Days" by Lee Adams and Charles Strouse; "Remembering You" composed by Roger Kellaway with lyrics by Carroll O'Connor
Executive Producer Mort Lachman
Producer Milt Josefsberg
Company Tandem Productions, Inc.
Director Paul Bogart
Story Editors Mel Tolkin, Larry Rhine
Writers Various
CAST
Archie Bunker .... Carroll O'Connor
Edith Bunker ....Jean Stapleton
Mike Stivic .... Rob Reiner
Gloria Stivic .... Sally Struthers

68 All in the Family (Daytime)   CBS
Program Type Comedy Series
30 minutes. Mondays–Fridays. Premiere date: 12/1/75. Continuous. Afternoon reruns of evening series. For credit information, *see* "All in the Family."

69 All My Children   ABC
Program Type Daytime Drama Series
60 minutes. Mondays–Fridays. Premiere date: 1/5/70. Continuous. Created by Agnes Nixon. Set in Pine Valley, U.S.A.; story concentrates on the Martin and Tyler families. Rosemary Murphy appeared as Mark Dalton's mother in a limited number of episodes during 1977–78 season. Cast list is alphabetical.
Producer Bud Kloss
Company Creative Horizons
Directors Del Hughes, Henry Kaplan, Jack Coffey
Head Writer Agnes Nixon
Writers Wisner Washam, Kathryn McCabe, Mary K. Wells, Jack Wood, Cathy Chicos, Doris Frankel, William Delligan, Ken Harvey
CAST
Brooke English .... Julia Barr
Philip Brent ....Nick Benedict
Dottie Thornton .... Dawn Marie Boyle
Kate Martin ....Kay Campbell
Billy Clyde ....Matthew Cowles
Dr. Franklin Grant ....John Danelle
Estelle Latour ....Kathleen Dezina
Caroline Murray .... Pat Dixon
Tad Gardner ....John E. Dunn
Donna Beck .... Candice Early
Ruth Martin ....Mary Fickett
Benny Sago .... Larry Fleischman
Tara Brent .... Nancy Frangione
Dr. Charles Tyler .... Hugh Franklin
Edna Thornton ....Sandy Gabriel
Harlan Tucker .... William Griffis
Mona Kane .... Frances Heflin
Myrtle Lum .... Eileen Herlie
Kitty Tyler .... Francesca James
Nick Davis ....Larry Keith
Dan Kennicott .... Daren Kelly

All My Children Continued

Mark Dalton	Mark LaMura
Philip Tyler	Brian Lima
Erica Kane Brent	Susan Lucci
Dr. Joe Martin	Ray MacDonnell
Wally McFadden	Jeff Magee
Paul Martin	William Mooney
Ellen Shepherd	Kathleen Noone
Dr. Jeff Martin	James O'Sullivan
Claudette Montgomery	Susan Plantt-Winston
Eddie Dorrance	Ross Petty
Devon Shepherd	Tricia Pursley
Tom Cudahy	Richard Shoberg
Dr. Christina Karras	Robin Strasser
Maggie Flanagan	Paula Trueman
Chuck Tyler	Richard Van Vleet
Mel Jacobi	Chris Wallace
Phoebe Tyler	Ruth Warrick
Lincoln Tyler	Peter White
Nancy Grant	Lisa Wilkinson

70 All Over

Theatre in America/Great Performances PBS
Program Type Dramatic Special
2 hours. Premiere date: 4/12/78. Performed by the Hartford (Conn.) Stage Company. Program made possible by grants from Exxon Corporation and support from Public Television Stations.
Executive Producer Jac Venza
Producers Jac Venza, Phyllis Geller
Company WNET-TV/New York
Directors Paul Weidner, John Desmond
Writer Edward Albee

CAST

Wife	Anne Shropshire
Best Friend	William Prince
Son	Pirie MacDonald
Daughter	Anne Lynn
Mistress	Myra Carter

71 All You Need Is Cash

Program Type Music/Comedy/Variety Special
NBC
90 minutes. Premiere date: 3/22/78. A Beatles parody. Created by Eric Idle. Music and lyrics by Neil Innes.
Executive Producer Lorne Michaels
Producers Gary Weis, Craig Kellem
Company Rutles Corps Productions
Directors Gary Weis, Eric Idle
Writer Eric Idle

CAST

Dirk McQuickly	Eric Idle
Ron Nasty	Neil Innes
Stig O'Hara	Rikki Fataar
Barry Wom	John Halsey
Mick Jagger	Mick Jagger
Paul Simon	Paul Simon
Interviewer	George Harrison
Adrian Jones	Dan Aykroyd
Ron Decline	John Belushi
Bill Murray the K	Bill Murray
Passerby	Gilda Radner
Martini	Bianca Jagger

Chastity	Gwen Taylor
Bigamy Sisters	Carinthia West
Penelope	Penelope Tree
Hells Angel	Ron Wood
Queen Elizabeth	Jeanette Charles
Leggy Mountbatten	Terence Bayler
Eric Manchester	Michael Palin
Archie Macaw	Frank Williams
Dick Jaws	Barry Cryer
Decline's Henchmen	Al Franken; Tom Davis
Blind Lemon Pye	Jerome Green
Rambling Orange Peel	Bob Gibson
Mrs. Iris Mountbatten	Gwen Taylor
Mrs. Peel	Pat Perkins
Leppo	Ollie Halsall
Journalist	Bunny May
Roadie	Robert Putt

All-England Tennis Championship See Wimbledon

72 The All-New Superfriends Hour ABC

Program Type Animated Film Series
60 minutes. Saturdays. Premiere date: 9/10/77. An animated comedy-adventure series, featuring Superman, Batman and Robin, Wonder Woman, Aquaman and The Wonder Twins.
Executive Producers William Hanna, Joseph Barbera
Creative Producer Iwao Takamoto
Company Hanna-Barbera Productions
Director Charles A. Nichols
Story Editor Jeff Maurer
Writers Haskell Barkin, Kerry Cummings, Don Gut, Mark Jones, Norman Maurer, Janai Pringle, J. Kenneth Rotcop, Henry Sharp, Marshall L. Williams, Dick Conway, Willie Gilbert, Owen Harris, Elana Lesser, Duane Poole, Dick Robbins, Cliff Ruby, John Strong
Musical Direction Hoyt Curtin
Musical Supervision Paul DeKorte
Animation Supervision Bill Kail, Jay Srbry
Voices Jack Angel, Norman Alden, Michael Bell, Ted Cassidy, Danny Dark, Jane James, Joyce Mancini, Chuck McClennan, Barney Phillips, Olan Soule, William Woodson, Wally Burr, Regis Cordic, Shannon Farnon, Casey Kasem, Ross Martin, Richard Paul, Mike Road, Liberty Williams

73 All-Star Anything Goes Syndicated

Program Type Game/Audience Participation Series
30 minutes. Premiere date: 9/17/77. Pits show business teams against each other. Based on "Almost Anything Goes," 1/24/76–5/9/76.
Executive Producers Bob Banner, Beryl Vertue
Producer Sam Riddle
Company Bob Banner Associates and Robert Stigwood Organization

Director Louis Horwitz
Hosts Bill Boggs, Chuck Healy

74 All-Star Family Feud ABC
Program Type Game/Audience Participation
Special
60 minutes. Premiere date: 5/16/78. Cast members of "Eight Is Enough," "The Love Boat," "Soap," and "Three's Company," compete for cash in a celebrity charity competition.
Producer Howard Felsher
Company Goodson-Todman Productions, Inc.
Director Paul Alter
Host Richard Dawson
Guest Stars Dick Van Patten, Grant Goodeve, Lani O'Grady, Lauri Walters, Susan Richardson, Diana Canova, Jennifer Salt, Jay Johnson, Sal Viscuso, Dinah Manoff, Gavin MacLeod, Fred Grandy, Bernie Kopell, Ted Lange, Lauren Tewes, John Ritter, Joyce DeWitt, Norman Fell, Audra Lindley, Richard Kline

75 All-Star Game ABC
Program Type Sports Special
Live coverage of the 49th annual baseball all-star game from San Diego Stadium in San Diego 7/11/78.
Executive Producer Roone Arledge
Company ABC Sports
Announcers Keith Jackson, Howard Cosell, Don Drysdale

76 The All-Star Salute to Women's Sports ABC
Program Type Sports Special
90 minutes. 3/2/78. Entertainment salute to women in sports as well as an auction to implement the Women's Sports Foundation.
Executive Producer Carolyn Raskin
Host Billie Jean King
Performers Alan King, Bill Cosby, Helen Reddy, Harvey Korman, MacLean Stevenson, Phyllis Diller
Guest Athletes Margo Oberg, Paula Sperber, Donna De Varona, Micki King, Sheila Young, Cathy Rush, Karen Logan, Billie Moore, Mary Jo Peppler, Suzy Chaffee, Cathy Rigby.

77 An All-Star Tribute to Elizabeth Taylor CBS
Program Type Music/Comedy/Variety Special
60 minutes. Premiere date: 12/1/77. Celebrity party held in Sound Stage 5 of The Burbank Studios in honor of Elizabeth Taylor on behalf of the Variety Clubs International's children's charities.
Producer Paul W. Keyes
Director Dick McDonough

Writers Paul W. Keyes, Marc London, Bob Howard
Musical Director Nelson Riddle
Art Director E. Jay Krause
Guests Robert Blake, Debby Boone, Billy Carter, Tom Drake, Henry Fonda, Frank Gorshin, Monty Hall, Bob Hope, Rock Hudson, James Lydon, Roddy McDowall, Paul Newman, Carroll O'Connor, Dan Rowan, Dick Martin

78 Almaden Grand Masters
Program Type Sports Special PBS
2 hours. 11/6/77. Taped coverage of singles tennis finals from Seabrook Island, SC.
Company WGBH-TV/Boston
Announcers Jack Kramer, Frank Deford

79 Almaden Grand Masters Championships PBS
Program Type Sports Special
3 hours. 11/20/77. Live coverage of final-round tennis matches in the Almaden Grand Masters Tournament, taped at Greenbriar, WV.
Company WGBH-TV/Boston
Announcers Bud Collins, Jack Kramer

80 The Aman Folk Ensemble PBS
Program Type Music/Dance Special
60 minutes. Premiere date: 12/4/77. Ethnic dance group born and based in Los Angeles spotlighted.
Producer Loring d'Usseau
Company KCET-TV/Los Angeles
Director Bruce Franchini
Artistic Director Leona Wood
Host Marge Champion

81 The Amazing Cosmic Awareness of Duffy Moon
ABC Out-of-School Specials/ABC Weekend Specials
Program Type Children's Special ABC
60 minutes. Premiere date: 2/4/76. Repeat date: 1/28/78. Comedy adventure of sixth grader with unusual powers. Based on the novel "The Strange But Wonderful Cosmic Awareness of Duffy Moon" by Jean Robinson. Music by Joe Weber; lyrics by Zoey Wilson.
Producer Daniel Wilson
Company Daniel Wilson Productions, Inc.
Director Larry Elikann
Writer Thomas Baum
CAST
Peter Finley .... Lance Kerwin
Duffy Moon .... Ike Eisenmann
Dr. Flamel .... Jim Backus
Mr. Finley .... Jerry Van Dyke
Photographer .... Basil Hoffman
Aunt Peggy .... Jane Connell

The Amazing Cosmic Awareness of Duffy Moon *Continued*

Uncle Ralph ....Jack Collins
Old Lady ....Marie Earle
Mrs. Varner .... Carol Worthington
Brian Varner .... Sparky Marcus
Andrew Varner .... Tommy Crebbs
Mrs. Charles ....Peggy Rea
Mrs. Toby .... Dodo Denney
Boots McAfee .... Alexa Kenin

82   The Amazing Howard Hughes   CBS
Program Type Dramatic Special
4 hours. Premiere dates: 4/13/77 and 4/14/77 (two hours each). Repeat dates: 8/29/78 and 8/30/78. Biographical drama based on the book "Howard, the Amazing Mr. Hughes" by Noah Dietrich and Bob Thomas. Music by Laurence Rosenthal. Aviation coordination by Tallmantz Aviation.
Executive Producer Roger Gimbel
Producer Herbert Hirschman
Company A Roger Gimbel Production for EMI Television Programs, Inc.
Director William A. Graham
Writer John Gay
CAST
Howard Hughes .... Tommy Lee Jones
Noah Dietrich .... Ed Flanders
Wilbur Peterson .... James Hampton
Katharine Hepburn .... Tovah Feldshuh
Billie Dove .... Lee Purcell
George .... Jim Antonio
Mayor La Guardia .... Sorrell Booke
Jimmy .... Lee Jones-de Broux
Production Manager .... Roy Engel
Barnes .... Arthur Franz
Shirley ....Denise Galik
Jenks .... Howard Hesseman
Irene .... Tannis G. Montgomery
Henry Kaiser .... Garry Walberg
Jean Peters .... Carol Bagdasarian
Robert Maheu .... Bart Burns
Odlum .... Thayer David
Forbes ....Ray Ballard
Lewis .... Robert Baron
Asst. Cutter .... James Beach
Lewis Milestone .... Marty Brill
Ella Hughes ....Morgan Brittany
Jean Harlow .... Susan Buckner
P.R. Man .... Ray Buktenica
Gresham .... Sid Conrad
Chauffeur ....Jack Denbo
Cutter .... John Dennis
Harris ....Steve Doubet
Butler ....Shay Duffin
Doctor .... S. John Launer
M.C. ....Joel Lawrence
Major .... John Lupton
Graves .... Jim McKrell
Gen. Hap Arnold .... Walter O. Miles
Stunt Pilot ....Glenn Miller
Air Show Announcer .... Myron Natwick
Arlene .... Kim O'Brien
Roy Cruickshank .... Andy Romano
Greta Nissen ....Jette Seear

Sen. Brewster ....Barry Atwater
Jim Bacon .... Jim Bacon
Station Attendant ....John Bellah
Guard .... Thom Carey
DeMarco .... Peter Dane
Sen. Ferguson .... William Dozier
Reeves .... Hal England
Newsreel Announcer .... Art Gilmore
Dr. Palmer .... Ben Hammer
Gene Handsaker .... Gene Handsaker
Russ .... Ed Harris
Attorney ....Ted Hartley
Dr. Bergman .... Wayne Heffley
Sheriff .... Russ McGinn
Marvin Miles .... Marvin Miles
Saunders .... Barney Phillips
McKenna ....John S. Ragin
Hospital Administrator .... Ken Sansom
Vernon Scott .... Ken Scott
Government Official ....Dave Shelley
Wayne Thomis .... Wayne Thomis
Counsel .... Jerome Thor
Mr. Hardesty .... Bert Williams

83   The Amazing Spider-Man   CBS
Program Type Crime Drama Series
60 minutes. Wednesdays Premiere: 4/5/78. Based on the comic book hero created by Stan Lee for Marvel Comics Group. 90-minute movie for television, "Spider Man:" 9/14/77. Fights choreographed by Emil Farkas. Title changed to "Spider Man" 9/12/78.
Executive Producers Charles Fries; Daniel R. Goodman
Producers Robert Janes, Ron Satlof
Company Charles Fries Productions, Inc. in association with Dan Goodman Productions, Inc.
Directors Various
Writers Various
CAST
Spider-Man/Peter Parker .... Nicholas Hammond
Capt. Barbera .... Michael Pataki
F. Jonah Jameson ....Robert F. Simon
Rita .... Chip Fields

84   Amelia Earhart
The Big Event   NBC
Program Type Dramatic Special
3 hours. Premiere date: 10/25/76. Repeat date: 7/23/78. A biography of Amelia Earhart. Music composed by David Shire. Aerial sequences staged by Frank Tallman.
Producer George Eckstein
Company Universal Television in association with NBC-TV
Director George Schaefer
Writer Carol Sobieski
Costume Designer Edith Head
Art Director William H. Tuntke
CAST
Amelia Earhart ....Susan Clark
George Putnam ....John Forsythe

Paul Mantz	Stephen Macht
Snookie	Susan Oliver
Pidge	Catherine Burns
Amy	Jane Wyatt
Mr. Earhart	Charles Aidman
Radio Operator	David Huffman
Sid Isaacs	Ed Barth
Fred Noonan	Bill Vint
David	Lance Kerwin
Railey	Robert Ridgely
Bradford	Kip Niven
Stultz	Jack Colvin
Miss Perkins	Florida Friebus

85 America Alive!   NBC
Program Type Talk/Service/Variety Series
60 minutes. Monday-Friday. Premiere date: 7/24/78. Live series about real people and events.
Executive Producer Woody Fraser
Senior Producer Raysa Bonow
Producers Marty Berman, Bob Raser, Joan Auritt
Company Fraser-Greengrass
Directors Don King, Bob Loudin
Head Writer Bob Blum
Host Jack Linkletter
Traveling Co-Hosts Bruce Jenner, Janet Langhart, Pat Mitchell
Regulars David Sheehan (media critic), David Horowitz (consumer expert), Dick Orkin and Bert Berdis (comedy), Virginia Graham (gossip), Dr. William H. Masters and Virginia E. Johnson (experts on human sexual behavior).

86 America, America, America   PBS
Program Type Music/Dance Special
90 minutes. Premiere date: 7/4/76. Repeat date: 5/29/78. A bicentennial concert by the Mormon Youth Symphony and Chorus. Included: Aaron Copland's "A Lincoln Portrait." Chorus directed by Robert C. Bowden at the Mormon Tabernacle in Salt Lake City.
Company KUED-TV/Salt Lake City

87 America Salutes Richard Rodgers: The Sound of His Music   CBS
Program Type Music/Comedy/Variety Special
2 hours. Premiere date: 12/9/76. Repeat date: 6/3/78. A retrospective on the career of Richard Rodgers. Special musical material by Larry Grossman.
Executive Producers Jack Haley, Jr., David Susskind
Producers Gary Smith, Dwight Hemion
Company A 20th Century-Fox presentation in association with Talent Associates and Smith-Hemion Productions
Director Dwight Hemion
Writers Buz Kohan, Ted Strauss

Musical Director Ian Fraser
Choreographer Ron Field
Costume Designer Frank Thompson
Art Director Bob Kelly
Hosts Gene Kelly (as Oscar Hammerstein II), Henry Winkler (as Lorenz Hart)
Guest Stars Diahann Carroll, Vic Damone, Sammy Davis, Jr., Sandy Duncan, Lena Horne, Cloris Leachman, Peggy Lee, John Wayne

88 America Salutes the Queen   NBC
Program Type Music/Comedy/Variety Special
3 hours. Premiere date: 11/29/77. Event celebrating Queen Elizabeth's Silver Jubilee at the London Palladium. Music by the Jack Parnell Orchestra.
Producers Gary Smith, Dwight Hemion
Company ATV Presentation
Director Dwight Hemion
Writers Marty Farrell, Gig Henry, Charles Lee, Robert Mills, Gene Perret, Norman Sullivan, Bryant Blackburn
Host Bob Hope
Stars Julie Andrews, Paul Anka, Harry Belafonte, Alan King, Cleo Laine with the John Dankworth Orchestra, Rich Little, Shirley MacLaine, The Muppets, Rudolf Nureyev, Yoko Morishita, Tommy Cooper, The Brotherhood of Man

89 America 2-Night   Syndicated
Program Type Comedy Series
30 minutes. Premiere date: 9/77. Comedy-variety-talk show based on "Fernwood 2-Night," 7/4/77–9/30/77. Last Show 7/4/78.
Producer Alan Thicke
Company TAT Communications Co
Regulars Martin Mull, Fred Willard, Frank DeVol

90 American Ballet Theatre
Great Performances/Dance in America   PBS
Program Type Music/Dance Special
60 minutes. Premiere date: 12/15/76. Repeat date: 1/11/78. The American Ballet Theatre in two dances from their repertoire: "Billy the Kid" with music by Aaron Copland and "Les Patineurs" with music by Giacomo Meyerbeer. Program funded by grants from Exxon Corporation, the National Endowment for the Arts and the Corporation for Public Broadcasting.
Executive Producer Jac Venza
Producer Emile Ardolino
Company WNET-TV/New York
Director Merrill Brockway

Billy the Kid
Choreographer Eugene Loring

American Ballet Theatre *Continued*
Scenic Designer Jac Venza
Narrator Paul Newman
CAST
Billy .... Terry Orr
Pat Garrett .... Frank Smith
Alias .... Clark Tippet
Sweetheart/Mother .... Marianna Tcherkassky
Prospector .... Victor Barbee
Mailman ....Michael Owen
Dance Hall Girls Marie Johansson, Ruth Mayer,
                                                      Patricia Wesche
Cowboy in Red .... Kirk Peterson
Mexican Girls ....Francia Kovak, Christine Spizzo

Les Patineurs (The Skaters)
Choreographer Frederick Ashton
Scenic Designer William Mickley
CAST
The Girl in Pink .... Karena Brock
The Girl In Yellow .... Kristine Elliott
Skating Couples .... Elizabeth Ashton, Susan Jones
The Lovers .... Nanette Glushak, Charles Ward
The Friends .... Jolinda Menendez, Janet Shibata
   Cathryn Rhodes, Denise Warner, Warren Conover,
   Charles Maple, Richard Schafer, Michael Owen
The Boy in Green .... Fernando Bujones

91 American Ballet Theatre
Live from Lincoln Center/Great Performances
                                                                 PBS
Program Type Music/Dance Special
3 hours. Premiere date: 5/17/78. Four works
performed by the American Ballet Theatre.
"Don Quixote" music by Leon Minkus. "The
Firebird" music by I. Stravinsky. "Les Syl-
phides" music by F. Chopin. Program funded by
grants from Exxon Corporation, the Andrew W.
Mellon Foundation, the National Endowment
for the Arts and the Corporation for Public
Broadcasting.
Executive Producer John Goberman
Producer Emile Ardolino
Company Lincoln Center in collaboration with
   WNET-TV/New York
Directors Lucia Chase, Oliver Smith
Conductors Akira Endo, John Lanchbery
Host Robert Macneil

Theme and Variations
Choreographer George Balanchine
Dancers Mikhail Baryshnikov, Gelsey Kirkland

Don Quixote
Choreographer Marius Petipa
Dancers Natalia Makarova, Fernando Bujones

The Firebird
Choreographer Michel Fokine
Dancers Cynthia Gregory, Clark Tippet

Les Sylphides
Choreographer Michel Fokine

Dancers Marianna Tcherkassy, Karena Brock,
Rebecca Wright, John Meehan

92 American Bandstand   ABC
Program Type Music/Dance Series
60 minutes. Saturdays. Premiere date: 8/5/57.
Season premiere: 9/10/77. Weekly teen dance
program featuring top recording artists. Viewers
choose winners of annual dance contest.
Producers Barry Glazer; Larry Klein
Company dick clark teleshows, inc.
Director Barry Glazer
Host Dick Clark

**93 The American Film Institute Salute
to Henry Fonda**   CBS
Program Type Parades/Pageants/Awards
Special
2 hours. Premiere date: 3/15/78. Testimonial
dinner-program honoring Henry Fonda, includ-
ing presentation of the Sixth Annual American
Film Institute Life Achievement Award.
Executive Producer George Stevens, Jr.
Producers George Stevens, Jr.; Eric Lieber
Company The American Film Institute
Director Marty Pasetta
Writer Hal Kanter
Conductor Nelson Riddle
Art Director Ray Klausen
Guest Stars Jane Alexander, Lucille Ball, Rich-
ard Burton, Bette Davis, Kirk Douglas, Jane
Fonda, Peter Fonda, James Garner, Lillian
Gish, Charlton Heston, Ron Howard, Jack
Lemmon, Marsha Mason, Fred MacMurray,
Dorothy McGuire, Lloyd Nolan, Gregory
Peck, Barbara Stanwyck, James Stewart,
Richard Widmark, Billy Dee Williams

**94 The American Film Institute 10th
Anniversary Special**   CBS
Program Type Parades/Pageants/Awards
Special
90 minutes. Premiere date: 11/21/77. Scenes
from American motion pictures chosen by 35,-
000 members. Taped at the John F. Kennedy
Center for the Performing Arts, Washington,
DC. Music by Henry Mancini.
Executive Producer George Stevens, Jr.
Producer Marty Pasetta
Company AFI and Pasetta Productions
Director Marty Pasetta
Writers Larry McMurtry, Rod Warren
Host Charlton Heston
Guest Stars Lauren Bacall, Henry Fonda, Henry
Mancini, Lily Tomlin, Sidney Poitier

95 **American League Championship (Baseball)** ABC
Program Type Sports Special
Live coverage of the American League Championship games between the New York Yankees and Kansas City Royals beginning 10/5/77.
Executive Producer Roone Arledge
Producers Roy Hammerman, George Finkel
Company ABC Sports
Director Ken Fouts

96 **The American Music Awards** ABC
Program Type Parades/Pageants/Awards Special
2 hours. Live coverage of the fifth annual music awards from the Santa Monica (Calif.) Civic Auditorium 1/16/78.
Executive Producer Dick Clark
Producer Al Schwartz
Company dick clark teleshows, inc.
Director Tim Kiley
Musical Director George Wilde
Hosts Glen Campbell, Natalie Cole, David Soul
Performers The Commodores, Andy Gibb, Kiss, Loretta Lynn
Presenters Aretha Franklin, Crystal Gayle, Andy Gibb, Barry Manilow, Ronnie Milsap, Tony Orlando, Dolly Parton, Charley Pride, Kenny Rogers, Barry White

97 **The American Newsreel of Crime** Syndicated
Program Type Public Affairs Series
60 minutes. Premiere date: 10/29/77. Collection of news archives clips.
Producer Al Korn
Company RKO General Productions
Director Don Horan
Writer David Askling
Host Jimmy Breslin

98 **The American Short Story** PBS
Program Type Drama Series
60 minutes/90 minutes. Tuesdays. Premiere date: 4/5/77. Series repeated: 10/3/77. Six-part series dramatizing famous American short stories: "Bernice Bobs Her Hair/I'm a Fool," "The Blue Hotel," "The Displaced Person," "The Music School," (*See* individual titles for credits.) Programs presented by South Carolina Educational Television and made possible by a grant from the National Endowment for the Humanities.

99 **The American Sportsman** ABC
Program Type Limited Sports Series
60 minutes. Sunday afternoons. Show premiered in 1965. 14th season premiere: 4/2/78. Last

show of season: 6/25/78. Seven shows with celebrities and outdoor experts in varied nature programs.
Executive Producer Roone Arledge
Coordinating Producer Robert Duncan
Producer John Wilcox
Company ABC Sports
Directors Various
Writers Pat Smith and others
Host Curt Gowdy

100 **Americana** PBS
Program Type Documentary/Informational Series
30 minutes. Tuesdays. Premiere date: 12/3/76. Repeat date: 10/4/77. Documentaries produced by local PBS stations and some independent filmmakers. Programs seen during the 1977-78 season are: "Amiotte," "A Blind Teacher in a Public School," "Boley, Oklahoma—Alive and Well," "The Eleventh Year," "A Matter of Size," "A Storyteller's Town," (*See* individual titles for credits.)

101 **Americans All** ABC
Program Type Documentary/Informational Special
5 minutes each. Two mini-documentaries highlighting the achievements of minority group individuals. Shows aired on 10/21/77 and 3/27/78 following the "ABC Friday Night Movie." Series premiered during the 1973-74 season.
Executive Producers Marlene Sanders, Pamela Hill
Producer Ann S. Hayward
Company ABC News Television Documentaries
Director Ann S. Hayward
Writer Ann S. Hayward

102 **America's Bake-off Awards Presented by the Pillsbury Company** CBS
Program Type Parades/Pageants/Awards Special
30 minutes. Premiere date: 2/21/78. Announcement of prize winners and presentation of cash awards.
Executive Producer Bob Barker
Company Bob Barker Productions
Director Vern Diamond
Musical Director Bobby Walters
Host Bob Barker

103 **America's Junior Miss Pageant** CBS
Program Type Parades/Pageants/Awards Special
90 minutes. Premiere date: 5/8/78. Finale of pageant highlighted by announcement of new titleholder from Mobile, Ala.

America's Junior Miss Pageant
Continued
Executive Producers Saul Ilson, Ernest Chambers
Producer Harry Waterson
Director Jeff Margolis
Musical Director Bob Rosario
Costume Designer Bill Hargate
Art Director Rene Lagler
Hosts Hal Linden, Vicki Lawrence

104   AMF Grand Prix of Bowling   NBC
Program Type Sports Special
Live coverage of the finals of the second AMF Grand Prix of Bowling from the Thunderbowl Lanes in Allen Park, MI. 12/10/77.
Producer Larry Cirillo
Company NBC Sports
Director Harry Coyle
Announcer Jack Buck

105   Amiotte
Americana   PBS
Program Type Documentary/Informational Special
30 minutes. Premiere date: 6/10/77. Repeat date: 3/30/78. The story of Arthur Amiotte, a Sioux Indian artist, after his return to the Pine Ridge Reservation in western South Dakota. Program made possible by grants from the Jerome Hill Foundation and the Corporation for Public Broadcasting.
Producer Bruce Baird
Company South Dakota Public Television
Director Richard Muller
Cinematographer Richard Muller

106   The Amish: People of Preservation
Documentary Showcase   PBS
Program Type Documentary/Informational Special
60 minutes. Premiere date: 6/10/77. Repeat date: 10/22/77. A profile of the Amish community of Lancaster, Pennsylvania. Program presented by WITF-TV/Hershey, Pennsylvania and made possible by a grant from the Corporation for Public Broadcasting.
Producer John L. Ruth
Company Heritage Productions, Inc.
Cinematographer Burton Buller

107   Anatomy of a Scandal   CBS
Program Type News Special
60 minutes. Premiere date: 4/3/78. An investigation into the causes, events and five year cover-up of a conspiracy by Korea to influence the U.S. Congress.
Producer Jay L. McMullen

Director Jay L. McMullen
Writer Jay L. McMullen
Cinematographer Greg Cooke
Film Editor David Hanser
Researcher Mary Frances Lithak
Host Jay L. McMullen

108   And the Soul Shall Dance
Hollywood Television Theatre   PBS
Program Type Dramatic Special
90 minutes. Premiere date: 2/7/78. Repeat date: 7/15/78. Story of two Japanese-American families struggling for survival in pre-World War II rural California. Presented by KCET-TV/Los Angeles and made possible by grants from the Corporation for Public Broadcasting and the Ford Foundation. Performed by cast of original production at the East West Players Theater in Los Angeles.
Executive Producer Norman Lloyd
Company KCET-TV/Los Angeles
Director Paul Stanley
Writer Wakako Yamauchi
CAST
Murata .... Sab Shimono
Hana .... Pat Li
Masako .... Denise Kumagai
Oka .... Yuki Shimoda
Emiko .... Haunani Minn
Kiyoko .... Diane Takei

109   Andy Williams San Diego Open
                                            CBS
Program Type Sports Special
Coverage of the final two rounds from Torrey Pines Golf Club, La Jolla, Calif. Taped 1/28/78 and live 1/29/78.
Producer Frank Chirkinian
Company CBS Television Network Sports
Directors Bob Dailey, Frank Chirkinian
Commentators Vin Scully, Pat Summerall, Jack Whitaker, Ben Wright, Ken Venturi

110   Animal World   Syndicated
Program Type Science/Nature Series
30 minutes. Weekly. Premiered on NBC 6/68; went into syndication 1/73. Eleventh season premiere: 9/77. Animal life and survival.
Producer Betty Bettino
Company Bill Burrud Productions, Inc.
Distributor Les Wallwork & Associates
Writer Miriam Birch
Host Bill Burrud

111   Animals Animals Animals   ABC
Program Type Children's Series
30 minutes. Sunday mornings. Premiere date: 9/12/76. Second season premiere: 9/11/77. Magazine-format show focusing on a single ani-

mal in art, history, legend, music and religion plus film of the animal as it exists today. Music by Sandra Keenan, Michael Kamen, Stan Davis and Lester Cooper. Recommended by the National Education Association.
Executive Producer Lester Cooper
Producer Peter Weinberg
Company ABC News Public Affairs
Director Lester Cooper
Writer Lester Cooper
Musical Director Michael Kamen
Art Director Al Brodax
Cinematographer Al Niggemeyer
Film Editor Samuel Cohen
Host Hal Linden
Regulars Lynn Kellogg, Roger Caras
Voices Estelle Parsons, Mason Adams

112 The Animals Nobody Loved
National Geographic Special   PBS
Program Type Science/Nature Special
60 minutes. Premiere date: 2/10/76. Repeat date: 5/16/78. A look at the controversy surrounding coyotes, rattlesnakes and wild mustangs. Program funded by a grant from Gulf Oil Corporation and presented by WQED-TV/Pittsburgh.
Executive Producer Dennis B. Kane
Producer Christine Z. Wiser
Company National Geographic Society in association with Wolper Productions
Directors Christine Z. Wiser, Wolfgang Bayer
Writer Nicolas Noxon
Narrator Hal Holbrook

113 Anna Karenina
Masterpiece Theatre   PBS
Program Type Limited Series
60 minutes. Sundays. Premiere date: 2/5/78. 10-part dramatization of novel by Leo Tolstoy. Presented by WGBH-TV/Boston; produced by Joan Sullivan. Series made possible by a grant from Mobil Oil Corporation.
Executive Producer Ken Riddington
Producer Donald Wilson
Company BBC/London Films Production
Director Basil Coleman
Writer Donald Wilson
Costume Designer Joan Ellacott
Choreographer Geraldine Stephenson
Host Alistair Cooke
CAST
Anna Karenina .... Nicola Pagett
Count Vronsky .... Stuart Wilson
Karenin .... Eric Porter
Kitty .... Caroline Langrishe
Dolly .... Carole Nimmons
Levin .... Robert Swann
Stiva .... Davyd Harries
Annushka .... Marilyn Le Conte
Matvey .... Robert Russell

Seriozha .... Paul Spurrier
Betsy .... Sheila Gish
Nikolai .... Nicholas Jones
Countess Vronsky .... Mary Morris
Varya .... Norma Streader
Agafea .... Anna Wing
Lydia .... Margot Van Der Burgh

114 The 'Annie' Christmas Show
The Big Event   NBC
Program Type Music/Dance Special
60 minutes. Premiere date: 12/4/77. A musical with the cast of the Broadway show "Annie." Created by Charles Strouse; Martin Charnin; and Thomas Meehan. New song, "It's Christmas," written by Charles Strouse and Martin Charnin.
Executive Producer Mike Nichols
Company Martin Charnin Production
Musical Director Peter Howard
Choreographer Peter Gennaro
Stars Andrea McArdle, Dorothy Loudon

115 Annie Flynn
                    CBS
Program Type Comedy Special
30 minutes. Premiere date: 1/21/78. Pilot about a woman medical student. Music by Gene Page.
Producers Coleman Mitchell, Gregory Neigher
Company Uncle Toby Productions in association with Columbia Pictures Television
Director Robert Moore
Writers Coleman Mitchell, Geoffrey Neigher
CAST
Annie Flynn .... Barrie Youngfellow
C.C. .... Carol Potter
Mr. Kosloff .... Louis Guss
Elliot Hoag .... Harvey Lewis
Paul Lucas .... Charles Frank
Mr. Braden .... Jack Fletcher
Sherry .... Lisa Loring
Marty Trellis .... Josh Grenrock
Stephanie Pilzyck .... Renee Lippin

116 Another Day
                    CBS
Program Type Comedy Series
30 minutes. Saturdays. Premiere: 4/8/78. Last show: 4/29/78. Married couple faced with problems involving their jobs, growing children and mounting bills. Created by James Komack. Theme song "Just Another Day," written and performed by Paul Williams.
Executive Producer James Komack
Company The Komack Company
Directors Various
Writers Various
CAST
Don Gardner .... David Groh
Ginny Gardner .... Joan Hackett
Olive Gardner .... Hope Sommers
Kelly Gardner .... Lisa Lindgren
Mark Gardner .... Al Eisenmann

117 Another World   NBC
Program Type Daytime Drama Series
60 minutes. Mondays–Fridays. Premiere date:
5/4/64. Continuous. Became first regularly
scheduled 60-minute daytime drama on televi-
sion as of 1/6/75. Revolves around the Mat-
thews, Cory and Carrington families in Bay City,
U.S.A Cast listed alphabetically.
Executive Producer Paul Rauch
Producers Mary S. Bonner, Joseph Willmore
Company Proctor & Gamble Productions
Directors Ira Cirker, Melvin Bernhardt, Paul
  Lammers
Writers Harding Lemay, David Robinson
CAST
Clarice Hobson .... Gail Brown
Liz Matthews .... Irene Dailey
Eileen Simpson .... Vicki Dawson
Ada McGowan .... Constance Ford
Sally Frame .... Cathy Greene
Alice Frame .... Susan Harney
Charlene Frame Matthews .... Laurie Heineman
Jamie Frame .... Tim Holcum
Michael Randolph .... Lionel Johnston
Angela Perrini ....Maeve Kinkead
Olive Gordon .... Jennifer Leak
Joey Perrini ....Ray Liotta
Gwen Parrish .... Dorothy Lyman
Jim Matthews .... Hugh Marlowe
Iris Bancroft ....Beverlee McKinsey
Louise Goddard .... Anne Meacham
Linda Metcalf ....Vera Moore
Vince Frame .... Jay Morran
Susan Shearer .... Lynn Milgrim
Pat Randolph .... Beverly Penberthy
Elena ....Christina Pickles
Dennis Carrington .... Jim Poyner
Willis Frame .... Leon Russom
John Randolph .... Michael M. Ryan
Greg Barnard .... Ned Schmidtke
Charlie Hobson .... Fred Scollay
Brian Bancroft .... Paul Stevens
Brooks ....John Tilleger
Marianne Randolph .... Adrienne Wallace
Mackenzie Cory .... Douglass Watson
Rose Perrini .... Kathleen Widdoes
Rachel Cory .... Victoria Wyndham

118 Antonia: A Portrait of the Woman
                                                PBS
Program Type Documentary/Informational
  Special
60 minutes. Premiere date (on PBS): 4/20/76.
Repeat date: 9/5/78. The 1975 award-winning
documentary about Antonia Brico. Presented by
WNET-TV/New York through a grant from the
Corporation for Public Broadcasting and the Na-
tional Endowment for the Arts.
Producer Judy Collins
Company Rocky Mountain Productions, Inc.
Directors Judy Collins, Jill Godmilow

119 Anyone for Tennyson?   PBS
Program Type Educational/Cultural Series
30 minutes. Mondays. Premiere date: 1/5/76.
Third season premiere: 1/30/78. 15 programs of
dramatized poetry by The First Poetry Quartet:
George Backman, Cynthia Herman, Norman
Snow and Jill Tanner plus weekly guests. Pro-
grams made possible by grants from the Corpo-
ration for Public Broadcasting, the Ford Foun-
dation and Public Television Stations.
Executive Producer William Perry
Producer Marshall Jamison
Company Nebraska Educational Television Net-
  work in association with The Great Amwell
  Company, Inc.
Director Marshall Jamison
Writer Jane Iredale
Research Consultant Laurie Zwicky

Anything for Love *See* The ABC Sunday
  Night Movie

120 Arabs and Israelis   PBS
Program Type Limited Series
30 minutes. Premiere date: 2/5/75. Repeat dates:
4/6/78 and 7/4/78. Five up-dated programs
from a series about the Arab-Israeli dispute.
Executive Producer Peter S. McGhee
Producers Roger Fisher, Zvi Dor-Ner, Mo-
  hammed Salmawy
Company WGBH-TV/Boston
Correspondent Marilyn Berger

121 The Arcata Promise
Great Performances   PBS
Program Type Dramatic Special
90 minutes. Premiere date: 11/16/77. Repeat
date: 8/16/78. Drama about an actor and his
self-desctruction. Program made possible by
grants from the National Endowment for the
Arts, Corporation for Public Broadcasting,
member stations of PBS and Exxon Corporation.
Executive Producer Jac Venza
Producer Peter Willies
Company WNET-TV/New York
Director David Cunliffe
Writer David Mercer
CAST
Theo Gunge ....Anthony Hopkins
Laura .... Kate Nelligan
Hired Man ....John Fraser

122 The Archie Situation Comedy
Musical Variety Show
The ABC Saturday Comedy Special   ABC
Program Type Music/Comedy/Variety Special
60 minutes. 8/5/78. Archie Andrews, the comic
strip character, and his friends in a series of

comedy stories. Comic strip characters created by John L. Goldwater.
Executive Producer James Komack
Company The Komack Company, Inc.
Director Tom Trbovich
CAST
Archie Andrews ....Dennis Bowen
Betty ....Audrey Landers
Veronica ....Hilary Thompson
Reggie ....Mark Winkworth
Jughead ....Derrel Maury
Moose ....Jim Boelsen
Midge ....Susan Blu

123 An Architectural Odyssey With G. E. Kidder Smith   PBS
Program Type Documentary/Informational Special
60 minutes. Premiere date: 8/2/78. Chronicle of American architecture. Program made possible by a grant from the Robert Wood Johnson, Jr. Charitable Trust.
Producer Milton Hoffman
Company WNET-TV/New York
Host G. E. Kidder Smith

124 Are You a Missing Heir?   ABC
Program Type Documentary/Informational Special
60 minutes. Premiere date: 6/8/78. Dramatization of five true stories of unclaimed inheritances. Music composed and conducted by William Loose and Jack Tillar.
Executive Producer Alan Landsburg
Producer Robert Scheerer
Company Alan Landsburg Productions
Director Robert Scheerer
Writer Noreen Stone
Costume Designer Joseph Roveto
Art Director Keaton Walker
Host Hal Linden
Guest Stars Brooke Bundy, Toni Kalem, Joanna Kerns, Constance McCashin, Michael Williams

125 Art in Public Places   PBS
Program Type Documentary/Informational Special
30 minutes. Premiere date: 10/28/74. Repeat date: 9/21/77. Tour of outdoor art in New York City.
Producer Fred Barzyk
Company WGBH-TV/Boston and the Metropolitan Museum of Art
Director Fred Barzyk
Narrator Russell Connor

126 Arvilla   PBS
Program Type Documentary/Informational Special
30 minutes. Premiere date: 10/19/77. Repeat date: 3/23/78. Story of a 63-year-old woman dairy farmer, Arvilla Groesbeck, rapidly losing the struggle to a world not ready to accept her. Program made possible by a grant from the New York State Council on the Arts and the Corporation for Public Broadcasting.
Producer Michael Marton
Company WMHT-TV/Schenectady
Director Michael Marton
Narrator Arvilla Groesbeck

127 As the World Turns   CBS
Program Type Daytime Drama Series
60 minutes. Mondays–Fridays. Premiere date: 4/2/56. Continuous. Became 60-minute show 12/1/75. Drama of the closely-related Hughes, Lowell and Stewart families in Oakdale, U.S.A. Theme music by Charles Paul. Don MacLaughlin and Helen Wagner are original cast members. (Cast as of July 1978.)
Executive Producer Joe Rothenberger
Producer Arthur Richards
Company Proctor & Gamble Productions
Directors Leonard Valenta, Allen Fristoe, Heather Hill
Head Writers Robert Soderberg, Edith Sommer
Writers Ralph Ellis, Ted Apstein, Gillian Spencer, Eugenie Hunt
Announcer Dan McCullough
CAST
Teddy Ellison ....Tommy Baudo
Marion Connelly ....Clarice Blackburn
Alma Miller ....Dorothy Blackburn
Ellen Stewart ....Patricia Bruder
Dr. John Dixon ....Larry Bryggman
Ralph Mitchell ....Keith Charles
Teddy Ellison ....Joseph Christopher
Dr. Dan Stewart ....John Colenback
Jay Stallings ....Dennis Cooney
Dr. Alexander Keith ....Jon Cypher
Betsy Stewart ....Suzanne Davidson
Annie Spencer ....Martina Deignan
Laurie Keaton ....Laurel Delmar
Karen Parker ....Leslie Denniston
Grant Colman ....James Douglas
Andrew Dixon ....Robert Dwyer
Dr. David Stewart ....Henderson Forsythe
Don Hughes ....Conrad Fowkes
Lisa Shea Colman ....Eileen Fulton
Franny Hughes ....Maura Gilligan
Emmy Stewart ....Jenny Harris
Dr. Bob Hughes ....Don Hastings
Kim Stewart ....Kathryn Hays
Beau Spencer ....Wayne Hudgins
Jane Spencer ....Georgann Johnson
Judge Lowell ....William Johnston
Dick Martin ....Ed Kemmer
Chris Hughes ....Don MacLaughlin
Dr. Susan Stewart ....Marie Masters
Dee Stewart ....Marcia McClain

As the World Turns Continued

Valerie Conway ....Judith McConnell
Melinda Gray .... Ariane Munker
Kevin Thompson .... Michael Nader
Joyce Hughes .... Barbara Rodell
Sandy Thompson .... Barbara Rucker
Nick Conway .... Doug Travis
Nancy Hughes ....Helen Wagner
Carol Stallings ....Rita M. Walter
Mary Ellison .... Kelly Wood

128   As * We * See * It   PBS
Program Type Public Affairs Series
30 minutes. Premiere date: 9/19/77. High school
students from 16 cities examine effect of desegre-
gation in their schools. Program made possible
by a grant from the Department of Health, Education and Welfare.
Project Director Clarence McIntosh
Company WTTW-TV/Chicago
Producers Various
Directors Various

As You Like It See PBS Movie Theater

The Ascent of Mt. Fugi
Hollywood Television Theatre PBS –
                                    Dramatic Special
2 hours. Premiere date: 1/10/78. Contemporary
Soviet drama dealing with the issues of dissent
and human rights. Presented by KCET-TV/Los
Angeles and made possible by grants from the
Corporation for Public Broadcasting and the
Ford Foundation. Translated from the Russian
by Nicholas Bethell.
Producer Norman Lloyd
Company KCET-TV/Los Angeles
Director Norman Lloyd
Writers Chingiz Aitmatov, Kaltai Mukhamedz-
hanov
                           CAST
Dosbergen .... Avery Schreiber
Isabek ....Joseph Campanella
Mambet .... Michael Strong
Yosif ....Stefan Gierasch
Almagul .... Diane Shalet
Gulzhan ....Andrea Marcovicci
Anvar .... Joanne Linville
Aisha-Apa .... Jeanette Nolan

Ash Wednesday See The ABC Summer
Movie

129   Aspen
NBC Novel for Television/The Big
Event/NBC Monday/Saturday Night at the
Movies   NBC
Program Type Limited Series
6 hours. 11/5/77–11/7/77. Drama about ambi-
tious young lawyer, interspersed with real estate

interests trying to turn town into major ski re-
sort. Based on novels "Aspen" by Bert Hirsch-
field and "The Adversary" by Bart Spicer.
Executive Producer Michael Klein
Producer Jo Swerling, Jr.
Company Universal Studios
Director Douglas H. Heyes
Writer Douglas H. Heyes
Costume Designer Charles Waldo
Art Director John Corso
Film Editors Larry Lester, Edwin F. England
Director of Photography Isidore Mankofsky
                           CAST
Tom Keating .... Sam Elliott
Lee Bishop .... Perry King
Carl Osborne .... Gene Barry
Joan Carolinian ....Martine Beswick
Max Kendrick .... Roger Davis
Sheriff Dinehart .... Lee Jones-de Broux
Abe Singer ....George DiCenzo
Alex Budde ....Anthony Franciosa
Kit Pepe ....Jessica Harper
Jon Osborne .... Douglas Matthew Heyes
Joseph M. Drummond .... John Houseman
Budd Townsend ....Bo Hopkins
Owen Keating ....John McIntire
Gloria Osborne ....Michelle Phillips
Judge Kendrick .... William Prince
Angela Morelli ....Debi Richter
Harry Rodano ....Michael Carr
Miss Lavatta ....Leslie Simms
Horton Paine ....Joseph Cotten
Maralee Beck .... Maralee Beck
Matador ....Raoul Martinez
Jacqueline ....Connie Kreski
Len Ralston .... Angus Duncan
Vanessa Faye .... Stephanie Blackmore
Mrs. Morelli .... Corinne Michaels
John Oesterreich ....James Houghton
Glen Nelson .... Rod Haase
Coker ....Don Collier

At Long Last Love See ABC Tuesday
Movie of the Week

At the Earth's Core See The ABC
Friday Night Movie

130   Austin City Limits   PBS
Program Type Music/Dance Series
60 minutes. Mondays. Premiere date: 1/2/76.
Third season premiere: 2/17/78. Series repeats
began 4/21/78. Progressive country music series.
Program made possible by grants from the Cor-
poration for Public Broadcasting, the Ford
Foundation and Public Television Stations.
Executive Producers Howard Chalmers, Bill Ar-
hos
Producer Charles Vaughn
Company KLRN-TV/San Antonio-Austin
Director Charles Vaughn

131 **Autobiography of a Princess** PBS
Program Type Dramatic Special
60 minutes. Premiere date: 10/13/75. Repeat
date: 9/29/77. Part fiction, part documentary
about an exiled Indian princess. Uses footage
shot in India in the first half of this century.
Presented by WNET-TV/New York through a
grant from Volkswagon of America, Inc.
Producer Ismail Merchant
Company A Merchant-Ivory Production
Director James Ivory
Writer Ruth Prawer Jhabvala
CAST
Cyril Sahib .... James Mason
The Princess .... Madhur Jaffrey
Delivery Man .... Keith Varnier
Blackmailers .... Diane Fletcher, Timothy Bateson,
Johnny Stuart
Papa .... Nazruh Rahman

132 **Avalanche**
Once Upon a Classic PBS
Program Type Children's Special
60 minutes. Premiere date: 1/1/77. Repeat date:
9/14/78. Story about youngsters on a skiing holiday in the Austrian Tirol. Music by John Shakespeare and Derek Warne. Filmed on location.
Program captioned for the hearing-impaired.
Presented by WQED-TV/Pittsburgh and made
possible by grants from McDonald's Local Restaurants Association and McDonald's Corporation.
Coordinating Producer John Coney
Producer Harry Field
Company Telstar Specialized Productions, Ltd.
for Children's Film Foundation/London
Director Frederic Goode

133 **Avery Schreiber's Time Slot**
Syndicated
Program Type Comedy Special
30 minutes. Premiere date: 3/18/78. Pilot for a
comedy series starring Avery Schreiber.
Producer Alan Sloan
Company Columbia Pictures TV
Director Steve Katten
Writer E. Jack Kaplan

134 **The Awakening Land: The Saga of
an American Woman**
The Big Event/NBC World Premiere
Movie/NBC Monday Night at the Movies
NBC
Program Type Limited Series
7 hours. 2/19/78–2/21/78. Story of an American pioneer woman's courage and her love for
her family, her husband, and the land. Based on
the trilogy of novels, "The Trees," "The Fields,"
and "The Town" by Conrad Richter. Music
composed by Fred Karlin.

Executive Producers Harry Bernsen, Tom Kuhn
Producer Robert E. Relyea
Company Harry Bernsen—Tom Kuhn—Boris
Sagal Production in association with Warner
Bros. TV
Director Boris Sagal
Writers James Lee Barrett, Liam O'Brien
Director of Photography Michel Hugo
CAST
Sayward Luckett .... Elizabeth Montgomery
Portius Wheeler .... Hal Holbrook
Genny Luckett .... Jane Seymour
Jake Tench .... Steven Keats
Worth Sayward .... Tony Mockus
Ascha .... Derin Altay
Sulie .... Michelle Stacy
Jary .... Louise Latham
Lovie Scurrah .... Barney McFadden
Kinsie .... Johnny Timko
Hulda (as child) .... Pia Romans
Hulda (grown-up) .... Devon Ericson
Little Sulie .... Theresa Landreth
Mistress Bartram .... Dorrie Kavanaugh
Will Beagle .... W. H. Macy
Resolve .... Sean Frye
Chancey .... Dennis Dimster
Rosa .... Katy Kurtzman
Cornelia .... Joan Tompkins

135 **Baby, I'm Back** CBS
Program Type Comedy Series
30 minutes. Mondays/Saturdays (as of 6/3/78).
Premiere date: 1/30/78. Comedy about couple
who may or may not be married. Pilot for series
aired 10/22/77. Last show: 8/12/78.
Executive Producer Charles Fries
Producer Lila Garrett
Company Lila Garrett Productions in associa-
tion with Dewill Productions, Inc. and Charles
Fries Productions
Directors Various
Writers Various
CAST
Raymond Ellis .... Demond Wilson
Olivia Ellis .... Denise Nicholas
Luzelle Carter .... Helen Martin
Angie Ellis .... Kim Fields
Jordan Ellis .... Tony Holmes

136 **Backstage at the Met - Cavalleria
Rusticana/Pagliacci** PBS
Program Type Music/Dance Special
30 minutes. Premiere date: 3/21/78. Tony Ran-
dall inteviews Franco Zeffirelli who did the origi-
nal production. Francis Robinson talks about the
life of Enrico Caruso.
Executive Producer Michael Bronson
Producer Christopher Sarson
Company WNET-TV/New York
Director Christopher Sarson
Host Tony Randall

137   Backstage at the Met - Don Giovanni   PBS
Program Type Music/Dance Special
30 minutes. Premiere date: 3/14/78. Tony Randall provides background information on the opera Don Giovanni by Wolfgang Amadeus Mozart. Joan Sutherland and Richard Bonynge tell the story of Don Giovanni. Francis Robinson talks about Mozart's life and music. Also featured is a fencing session between James Morris and John Macurdy.
Company WNET-TV/New York
Producer Christopher Sarson
Director Christopher Sarson
Executive Producer Michael Bronson
Host Tony Randall

138   Baggy Pants and the Nitwits   NBC
Program Type Animated Film Series
30 minutes. Sunday mornings. Saturday mornings as of 10/8/77. Premiere: 9/11/77. Two shows in one: "Baggy Pants" is a silent movie; "The Nitwits" is an animated recreation of "Laugh-In" characters, Tyrone and Gladys.
Executive Producers David H. DePatie, Friz Freleng
Company DePatie-Freleng Enterprises, Inc. for NBC-TV
Directors Gerry Chiniquy, Bob McKimson, Sid Marcus
Head Writer Bob Ogle
VOICES
Gladys .... Ruth Buzzi
Tyrone .... Arte Johnson

139   Bakke Case
NBC News Special   NBC
Program Type News Special
30 minutes. 6/28/78. Live coverage of the Supreme Court's decision in favor of Allan Paul Bakke and interviews with William Taylor, Catholic University Law School, and John Kramer, Georgetown University Law School.
Company NBC News
Anchors John Chancellor, Douglas Kiker
Correspondents Carl Stern, Don Oliver, Carole Simpson, Rick Davis,Jack Perkins

Bang the Drum Slowly *See* ABC Tuesday Movie of the Week

140   Bar Mitzvah Boy   PBS
Program Type Dramatic Special
75 minutes. Premiere date: 3/77. Repeat date: 12/7/77. Original British television play about a Jewish boy reaching his 13th birthday. Originally shown on the BBC series "Play for Today."
Producer Graeme McDonald

Company British Broadcasting Corporation
Director Michael Tuchner
Writer Jack Rosenthal
CAST
Eliot Green ....Jeremy Steyn
Leslie Green .... Adrienne Posta
Mrs. Green .... Maria Charles
Mr. Green .... Bernard Spear
Rabbi Sherman .... Jack Lynn
Grandad .... Cyril Shaps

Bank Shot *See* CBS Special Movie Presentations
CAST
Boyfriend .... Jonathan Lynn

141   The Barbara Walters Special (First Special)   ABC
Program Type Documentary/Informational Special
60 minutes. Premiere date: 12/6/77. Interviews with Lucille Ball and Gary Morton, Dolly Parton, and Henry Winkler and Stacy Weitzman. Theme music by W. Michael Lewis and Jack Tillar.
Producers JoAnn Goldberg, Don Mischer
Company ABC News
Director Don Mischer
Interviewer Barbara Walters

142   The Barbara Walters Special (Second Special)   ABC
Program Type Documentary/Informational Special
60 minutes. Premiere date: 4/4/78. Interviews with Vice-President and Mrs. Walter Mondale, Reggie Jackson, Donny and Marie Osmond, and Mr. and Mrs. Walter Matthau and their son.
Producers Joann Goldberg, Don Mischer
Company ABC News
Director Don Mischer
Interviewer Barbara Walters

143   The Barbara Walters Special (Third Special)   ABC
Program Type Documentary/Informational Special
60 minutes. Premiere date: 5/30/78. Interviews with Burt Reynolds, Michael Landon, and Muhammad Ali.
Producers JoAnn Goldberg, Don Mischer
Company ABC News
Director Don Mischer
Interviewer Barbara Walters

144   The Barbara Walters Summer Special   ABC
Program Type Documentary/Informational

Special
60 minutes. Premiere date: 8/9/78. Interviews seen first on "The Barbara Walters Specials" during the year include Bing Crosby, Henry Winkler, Donny Osmond, and Dolly Parton.
Producers JoAnn Goldberg, Don Mischer
Company ABC News
Director Don Mischer
Interviewer Barbara Walters

145 Baretta   ABC
Program Type Crime Drama Series
60 minutes. Wednesdays. Thursdays as of 2/2/78. Premiere date: 1/17/75. Fourth season premiere: 9/28/77. Last show: 6/1/78. Adventures of undercover police detective with pet cockatoo, Fred. Series created by Stephen J. Cannell. Theme "Keep Your Eye on the Sparrow" with music by Dave Grusin, lyrics by Morgan Ames, sung by Sammy Davis, Jr.
Executive Producer Bernard L. Kowalski
Supervising Producer Ed Waters
Producers Alan Godfrey, Charles E. Dismukes, Ed Waters
Company Public Arts/Roy Huggins/Universal Production
Directors Various
Executive Story Consultant Sidney Ellis
Writers Various
Art Director John P. Bruce
Cinematographer Sherman Kunkel
Film Editor Donald Douglas
CAST
Tony Baretta ....Robert Blake
Billy Truman .... Tom Ewell
Lt. Hal Brubaker ....Ed Grover
Rooster .... Michael D. Roberts

146 Baretta (Late Night)   ABC
Program Type Crime Drama Series
60 minutes. Fridays. Premiere date: 4/22/77. Late-night repeat presentations of the primetime series. For credit information, *see* "Baretta."

147 Barnaby Jones   CBS
Program Type Crime Drama Series
60 minutes. Thursdays. Premiere date: 1/28/73. Sixth season premiere: 9/15/77. 2 hour special: 1/26/78. Crime drama of private investigator, daughter-in-law/girl Friday and nephew. Theme by Jerry Goldsmith.
Executive Producer Quinn Martin
Producer Philip Saltzman
Company Quinn Martin Productions
Directors Various
Writers Various
CAST
Barnaby Jones ....Buddy Ebsen
Betty Jones .... Lee Meriwether
J. R. Jones .... Mark Shera

148 Barney Miller   ABC
Program Type Comedy Series
30 minutes. Thursdays. Premiere date: 1/23/75. Fourth season premiere: 9/15/77. Comedy about detectives in New York City's 12th police precinct. Series created by Danny Arnold and Theodore J. Flicker. Music by Jack Elliott and Allyn Ferguson. February 1977 spinoff: "Fish."
Executive Producer Danny Arnold
Producer Tony Sheehan
Company Four D Productions
Director Danny Arnold
Exec. Script Consultant Reinhold Weege
Writers Various
Art Director Art Mula
CAST
Capt. Barney Miller .... Hal Linden
Det. Phil Fish ....Abe Vigoda
Det. Wojohowicz ....Max Gail
Det. Nick Yemana .... Jack Soo
Det. Harris .... Ron Glass
Insp. Luger .... James Gregory
Det. Arthur Dietrich .... Steve Landesberg
Officer Carl Levitt ....Ron Carey

Barrier *See* PBS Movie Theater

149 Bartleby, the Scrivener   PBS
Program Type Dramatic Special
60 minutes. Premiere date: 5/30/78. A play based on a short story by Herman Melville.
Executive Producer Michael B. Styer
Company MCPB-TV/Maryland
Writer Israel Horovitz
Dramatic Director Stan Wojewodski
Television Director Tom Barnett
CAST
Lawer ....Nicholas Kepros
Bartleby .... Joel Colodner
Nippers ....Robert Hitt
Turkey .... Patrick Hines
Ginger Nut .... Timothy Mark Zerkel

150 Baseball Game-of-the-Week   NBC
Program Type Limited Sports Series
Live coverage of 23 regular-season major league baseball games. Saturdays. 13th season premiere: 4/8/78.
Executive Producer Don Ohlmeyer
Company NBC Sports
Announcers Joe Garagiola, Tony Kubek (primary game), Monte Moore, Charlie Jones, or Wes Parker and Maury Wills (secondary game)

151 The Bastard   Syndicated
Program Type Dramatic Special
4 hours. Premiere date: 5/22/78. Second part shown 5/29/78. Dramatization of first novel in Bicentennial series by John Jakes about the ille-

The Bastard *Continued*
gitimate son of a French actress by an English
duke who emigrates to America.
Executive Producer John Wilder
Producer Joe Byrne
Company John Wilder Productions and Universal TV
Director Lee H. Katzin
Writer Guerdon Trueblood
Costume Designer Jean-Pierre Dorleac
Art Director Loyd S. Papez
Set Decorator Richard Friedman

CAST

Phillipe Charboneau	Andrew Stevens
Mother	Patricia Neal
Benjamin Franklin	Tom Bosley
Plummer	Cameron Mitchell
Lady Amberly	Eleanor Parker
Roger Amberly	Mark Neely
Sholto	Donald Pleasence
Emma Sholto	Elizabeth Shepherd
Alicia	Olivia Hussey
Caleb	Harry Morgan
Bishop Francis	Lorne Greene
Lucas	Herb Jefferson, Jr.
Edes	Buddy Ebsen
Anne	Kim Cattrall
Ware	Barry Sullivan
Samuel Adams	William Daniels
Campbell	James Gregory
O'Brien	Noah Beery
Paul Revere	William Shatner
Daisy	Carol Tru Foster
Lumden	Charles Haid

152   The Battle for South Africa
CBS Reports   CBS
Program Type Documentary/Informational
Special
60 minutes. Premiere date: 9/1/78. In-depth
look at the escalating terrorist war being waged
by the black underground against the white
South African government.
Executive Producer Howard Stringer
Producers Judy Chrichton, George Crile
Company CBS News
Anchor Bill Moyers

**153   Battle of the Network Stars:
Net-War IV**   ABC
Program Type Sports Special
2 hours. 5/7/78. Contest pitting teams of stars
from ABC, CBS, and NBC against each other in
athletic events.
Executive Producer Roone Arledge
Producer Doug Wilson
Director Larry Kamm
Stars from ABC Gabriel Kaplan (captain), Cheryl Tiegs, Debby Boone, Daryl Dragon, Toni Tennille, Parker Stevenson, Kene Holliday, Steve Landesberg.
Stars from CBS Tony Randall (captain), Kevin

Dobson, James MacArthur, Denise Nicholas,
Mackenzie Phillips, Victoria Principal, Bo
Svenson, Jimmie Walker.
Stars from NBC Dan Haggerty (captain),
Rhonda Bates, Dennis Dugan, Melissa Gilbert, Arte Johnson, Lance Kerwin, Larry Wilcox, Jane Curtin.
Special Guests Lou Goldstein, Ashley Whippet
Hosts Howard Cosell, Suzanne Somers
Commissioner Micki King
Commentator Bruce Jenner

154   Battle of the Network Stars '77
                                                   ABC
Program Type Sports Special
2 hours. Premiere date: 11/4/77. Second contest
pitting teams of stars from ABC, CBS, and NBC
against each other in the athletic events.
Executive Producer Roone Arledge
Company Candid Productions and Trans World
International in association with ABC Sports
Director Rodger Goodman
Stars from ABC Gabriel Kaplan (captain), Fred
Berry, Billy Crystal, Christopher De Rose,
Cheryl Ladd, Penny Marshall, Kristy McNichol, Parker Stevenson, Victor French, Suzanne Somers.
Stars from CBS Jimmie Walker (captain),
Adrienne Barbeau, Valerie Bertinelli, Kevin
Dobson, Jamie Farr, James MacArthur,
Loretta Swit, Lyle Waggoner, Caren Kaye,
James Vincent McNichol.
Stars from NBC Dan Haggerty (captain), Robert
Conrad, Elinor Donahue, Patrick Duffy, Peter
Isacksen, Michelle Phillips, Larry Wilcox,
Lance Kerwin, Belinda J. Montgomery.
Hosts Howard Cosell, Telly Savalas
Commissioner Frank Robinson
Reporters Bruce Jenner, Dave Marr

155   The Battle Over Panama
CBS Reports   CBS
Program Type Documentary/Informational
Special
60 minutes. Premiere date: 11/1/77. Explores
the debate over the ratification of the Panama
Canal Treaty.
Executive Producer Howard Stringer
Producers Judy Crichton, Janet Roach; Stephen
Glauber
Company CBS News
Reporter George Crile

**156   Be Glad Then America ... A
Documentary**   PBS
Program Type Documentary/Informational
Special
60 minutes. Premiere date: 7/4/77. Repeat date:
7/4/78. A behind-the-scenes look at the events

contributing to the world premiere of the Bicentennial opera, "Be Glad Then America: A Decent Entertainment from the Thirteen Colonies."
Producers Gary Perdue
Company WPSX-TV/University Park

157 **The Beach Girls** Syndicated
Program Type Comedy Special
30 minutes. Premiere date: 12/27/77. Pilot about three college girls anxious to break into show business.
Executive Producer Joseph Barbera
Producer Walt deFaria
Company Hanna-Barbera Productions
Director Stan Cherry
Writer Marian C. Freeman
Cast Ava Lazar, Kim O'Brien, Ria Wilson, Don Calfa, Frankie Avalon

158 **The Bear Who Slept through Christmas** NBC
Program Type Animated Film Special
30 minutes. Premiere date: 12/17/73. Repeat date: 12/25/77. Based on a story by John Barrett. Music and lyrics by Doug Goodwin.
Executive Producer Norman Sedawie
Producers David H. DePatie, Friz Freleng
Company Sed/Bar Production in association with DePatie-Freleng Enterprises
Directors Hawley Pratt, Gerry Chiniquy
Writers Larry Spiegel, John Barrett
VOICES
Bear .... Tommy Smothers
Patti Bear ....Barbara Feldon
Professor .... Arte Johnson
Santa Claus .... Robert Holt
Weather Bear .... Kelly Lange
Honey Bear .... Michael Bell
Additional Voices Casey Kasem, Caryn Paperny

159 **The Beasts Are in the Streets**
NBC Movie of the Week NBC
Program Type Dramatic Special
2 hours. Premiere date: 5/18/78. Repeat date: 8/16/78. Drama about a truck accident at a wildlife park that frees dozens of dangerous animals. Filmed in Grand Prairie, Texas. Based on a story by Frederic Louis Fox.
Director Peter H. Hunt
Company Hanna-Barbera
Writer Laurence Heath
CAST
Claire ....Carol Lynley
Kevin .... Dale Robinette
Jim .... Billy Green Bush
Eddie .... Philip Michael Thomas
Rick ....Casey Biggs
Al .... Burton Gilliam
Lucetta .... Sharon Ullrick
Lady in bed .... Anna Lee

160 **The Beatles Forever** NBC
Program Type Music/Dance Special
60 minutes. Premiere date: 11/24/77. Thanksgiving Day salute to the Beatles and their music by eight headliners from the U.S.A. and England.
Producer Syd Vinnedge
Company Syd Vinnedge Production in association with ATV for ITC Entertainment, Ltd.
Director Jon Scoffield
Writers Sheldon Keller, Richard Albrecht, Casey Keller
Musical Director Larry Grossman
Conductor Jack Parnell
Stars Diahann Carroll, Ray Charles, Anthony Dowell, Anthony Newley, Bernadette Peters, Tony Randall, Mel Tillis, Paul Williams

Beautiful but Deadly *See* The ABC Friday Night Movie

Beauty and the Beast *See* PBS Movie Theater

161 **Behind the Fence—Albert Paley: Metalsmith** PBS
Program Type Documentary/Informational Special
30 minutes. Premiere date: 2/23/77. Repeat date: 3/7/78. Documentary following the construction of an 80-foot iron fence for the Hunter Museum of Art in Chattanooga, Tenn. by Albert Paley.
Company KUED-TV/Salt Lake City
Cinematographer David Darby

162 **... Behold Wondrous Things** CBS
Program Type Religious/Cultural Series
60 minutes. Sunday mornings. Premiere date: 3/5/78. An anthology of drama, music, dance, poetry, art and documentaries presented on "Lamp Unto My Feet" and its sister broadcast "Look Up and Live," now in its 25th year, to celebrate the 30th anniversary year of "Lamp Unto My Feet." Weekly retrospective beginning with 1948.
Executive Producer Pamela Ilott
Company CBS News

163 **Bell System Family Theatre** NBC
Program Type Drama Series
Specials of various types. Premiere date: 9/12/70. Eighth season premiere: 1/1/78. Programs broadcast during the 1977–78 season are: "Captains Courageous," "Four Feathers," and "Our Town." (*See* individual titles for credits.)

164   The Belle of Amherst   PBS
Program Type Dramatic Special
90 minutes. Premiere date: 12/29/76. Repeat dates: 11/1/77, and 8/29/78. One-woman show about Emily Dickinson based on her poems, notes and letters. Recorded before a live audience. Program made possible by a grant from IBM.
Producers Mike Merrick, Don Gregory
Company A Dome/Creative Image Production in association with KCET-TV/Los Angeles
Director Charles S. Dubin
Writer William Luce
Production Designer H. R. Poindexter
Costume Designer Theoni V. Aldredge
Artistic Advisor Charles Nelson Reilly
Compiler Timothy Helgeson
CAST
Emily Dickinson .... Julie Harris

165   Ben Vereen—His Roots
The Sentry Collection Presents   ABC
Program Type Music/Comedy/Variety Special
60 minutes. Premiere date: 3/2/78. Singing, dancing and drama of Ben Vereen as he recalls his career.
Executive Producer Jerrold H. Kushnick
Producers Gary Smith, Dwight Hemion
Company Smith-Hemion Productions and Turtle IV Productions
Director Dwight Hemion
Writer Michael Kagan
Musical Director Ian Fraser
Choreographer Ron Field
Art Director Romain Johnston
Star Ben Vereen
Guest Stars Cheryl Ladd, Lou Gossett, Debbie Allen

Benny Goodman *See* King of Swing

The Bermuda Depths *See* The ABC Friday Night Movie

166   Bernice Bobs Her Hair/I'm a Fool
The American Short Story   PBS
Program Type Dramatic Special

Bernice Bobs Her Hair
45 minutes. Premiere date: 4/5/77. Repeat date: 10/3/77. Adaptation of the short story by F. Scott Fitzgerald set in the Midwest circa 1919. Music by Dick Hyman. Program funded by a grant from the National Endowment for the Humanities. Presented by South Carolina Educational Television.
Executive Producer Robert Geller
Producer Paul R. Gurian
Company Learning in Focus, Inc.

Director Joan Micklin Silver
Writer Joan Micklin Silver
Costume Designer Robert Pusilo
Scenic Designer Stuart Wurtzel
Host Colleen Dewhurst
CAST
Bernice .... Shelly Duvall
Marjorie .... Veronica Cartwright
Warren .... Bud Cort
Mrs. Harvey .... Polly Holliday
Additional Cast Dennis Christopher, Gary Springer, Lane Binkley, Mark LaMura, Murray Moston, Patrick Byrne, Mark Newkirk, Leslie Thorsen, Claudette Warlick

I'm a Fool
36 minutes. Adaptation of a short story by Sherwood Anderson set in the early 1900s. Music by Ed Bogas.
Executive Producer Robert Geller
Producer Dan McCann
Company Learning in Focus, Inc.
Director Noel Black
Writer Ron Cowen
Costume Designer Marianne DeFina
Scenic Designer Don DeFina
Host Colleen Newhurst
CAST
Andy .... Ron Howard
Lucy .... Amy Irving
Burt .... Santiago Gonzales
George .... John Tidwel
Wilbur .... John Light
Additional Cast Randi Kallan, Otis Calef

167   Bernstein Conducts Mahler
Fine Music Specials/Great Peformances   PBS
Program Type Music/Dance Special
90 minutes. Premiere date: 2/9/77. Repeat date: 8/23/78. The Israel Philharmonic taped at the Frederic Mann Auditorium in Tel Aviv, Israel in a peformance of "Das Lied von der Erde" ("The Song of the Earth") by Gustav Mahler. Program stereo-simulcast on local FM radio stations. Presented by WNET-TV/New York and made possible by grants from Exxon Corporation, the Corporation for Public Broadcasting, the Ford Foundation and Public Television Stations.
Executive Producer Fritz Buttenstedt
Producer David Griffiths
Company Unitel Production in association with Amberson Productions
Director Humphrey Burton
Conductor Leonard Bernstein
Featured Soloists Christa Ludwig, Rene Kollo

168   Bernstein 60/An Appreciation: Live from Wolf Trap   PBS
Program Type Music/Dance Special
2-1/2 hours. Premiere date: 8/25/78. Leonard Bernstein celebrates his 60th birthday with fellow conductor Mstislav Rostropovich and other

artists in a live performance from Wolf Trap Farm Park. Program made possible by grants from the Corporation for Public Broadcasting, PBS member stations and Allied Chemical Corporation.
Executive Producer David Griffiths
Producer Hal Hutkoff
Company WETA-TV/Washington

169 The Best of "All in the Family"
CBS
Program Type Comedy Special
60 minutes. Premiere date: 12/21/74. Repeat date: 9/18/77. Highlights of previous shows originally presented in celebration of the series' 100th broadcast.
Executive Producer Don Nicholl
Producers Michael Ross, Bernie West
Company Bud Yorkin-Norman Lear Tandem Productions
Director H. Wesley Kenney
Host Henry Fonda
CAST
Archie Bunker .... Carroll O'Connor
Edith Bunker ....Jean Stapleton
Mike Stivic .... Rob Reiner
Gloria Stivic .... Sally Struthers

170 The Best of Carson
NBC
Program Type Talk/Service/Variety Series
90 minutes. Tuesdays (intermittently) Premiere date: 3/21/78. (*See* "The Tonight Show Starring Johnny Carson" for credit information.)

171 The Best of Ernie Kovacs
PBS
Program Type Comedy Series
30 minutes. Thursdays. Premiere date: 4/12/77. Repeat dates: 3/18/78 and 10/6/77. Ten programs featuring black-and-white video-tape and kinescope footage from the "Ernie Kovacs" shows of the 1950s seen on NBC and ABC. Put together by John Lollos of the Video Tape Network. Programs made possible by grants from the Corporation for Public Broadcasting, the Ford Foundation and Public Television Stations.
Producer David Erdman
Company WTTW-TV/Chicago
Star Ernie Kovacs
Host Jack Lemmon

172 The Best of Families
PBS
Program Type Limited Series
60 minutes. Thursdays. Premiere date: 10/27/77. Drama set in late 19th century America of three fictionalized sets of families. Special two-hour premiere followed by seven subsequent one-hour episodes. Created by Naomi Foner. Series made possible by grants from the National Endowment for the Humanities, Mobil Corpora-

tion, Arthur Vining Davis Foundation, Corporation for Public Broadcasting, Ford Foundation and CTW.
Executive Producer Ethel Winant
Producer Gareth Davies
Company Children's Television Workshop
Directors Jack Hofsiss, Glenn Jordan, Peter Levin, Seymore Robbie, Robert Stevens
Head Writer Corinne Jacker
Writers Conrad Bromberg, David Epstein, Roger Hirson, Corinne Jacker, Ernest Kinoy, Loring Mandel
CAST
Stephen Rafferty .... Guy Boyd
Peter Rafferty .... William Carden
Frederick Coffin ....Matt Tilden
Mabel Baldwin .... Alice Drummond
Frederick Baldwin .... George Ede
Sarah Lathrop .... Jill Eikenberry
Wilbur Evans ....Peter Evans
Aline Rafferty .... Pauline Flanagan
Dan Fitzpatrick ....Clarence Felder
Teddy Wheeler .... Victor Garber
John Patrick Rafferty .... Sean Griffin
Rev. Dupee .... George Hearn
James Lathrop .... William Hurt
Maeve Rafferty ....Suzanne Lederer
Maureen Rafferty ....Julia McKenzie
Evelyn Stokes ....Kate McGregor-Stewart
Patrick Rafferty .... Milo O'Shea
Mary Margaret Rafferty .... Lisa Pelikan
Robert Wheeler .... William Prince
Jacob Riis .... Josef Sommer
Laura Wheeler ....Sigourney Weaver

173 The Best of "Little House on the Prairie"
NBC
Program Type Drama Series
60 minutes. Mondays. Premiere date: 8/14/78. Repeats of "Little House on the Prairie." (*See* "Little House on the Prairie" for credits.)

174 The Best of Rockford
NBC
Program Type Crime Drama Series
2 hours. Premiere date: 7/28/78. Fridays. Repeats of previous shows. (*See* "The Rockford Files" for credits.)

175 Bette Midler—Ol' Red Hair Is Back
NBC
Program Type Music/Comedy/Variety Special
60 minutes. Premiere date: 12/7/77. Singer Bette Midler in musical variety special.
Executive Producer Aaron Russo
Producers Gary Smith, Dwight Hemion
Company Divine Television Inc. in association with Smith-Hemion Productions
Director Dwight Hemion
Writers Buz Kohan, Jerry Blatt, Tom Eyen, Pat McCormick, Rod Warren, Bette Midler, Bruce Vilanch

Bette Midler—Ol' Red Hair Is Back
Continued
Star Bette Midler
Guest Stars Dustin Hoffman, Emmett Kelly, Harlettes

176   The Better Sex   ABC
Program Type Game/Audience Participation Series
30 minutes. Mondays-Fridays. Premiere date: 7/18/77. Last show of series: 1/13/78. A bluffing game between one team of six men and a second of six women.
Executive Producer Ira Skutch
Producer Robert Sherman
Company Goodson-Todman Productions
Director Paul Alter
Hosts Bill Anderson, Sarah Purcell

177   The Betty White Show   CBS
Program Type Comedy Series
30 minutes. Mondays. Premiere date: 9/12/77. Last show: 1/9/78. Comedy about an actress in a television series. Premiere episode produced by Bob Ellison with Ed. Weinberger and Stan Daniels as executive producers.
Executive Producer Bob Ellison
Producers Charles Raymond, Dale McRaven
Company MTM Enterprises, Inc.
Directors Various
Writers Various
CAST
Joyce Whitman ....Betty White
John Elliot ....John Hillerman
Mitzi Maloney ....Georgia Engel
Hugo .... Charles Cyphers
Doug Porterfield .... Alex Henteloff
Lisa Vincent .... Carla Borelli
Fletcher Huff .... Barney Phillips

178   Between the Wars   Syndicated
Program Type Documentary/Informational Series
30 minutes. Premiere date: 4/12/78. 16-part documentary explores the political and diplomatic upheavals of the years between the end of World War I and the beginning of World War II.
Executive Producer Alan Landsburg
Producer Anthony Potter
Company Mobil Oil and Alan Landsburg Productions
Writer Anthony Potter
Host Eric Sevareid

179   Beyond Niagara   NBC
Program Type Religious/Cultural Special
60 minutes. Premiere date: 2/20/77. Repeat date: 6/4/78. A look at Canada's historical, cultural and religious development. Filmed on location in various parts of Canada.
Producer Doris Ann
Company NBC Television Religious Programs Unit in association with the Southern Baptist Radio and Televison Commission
Director Joseph Vadala
Writer Philip Scharper
Film Editor Ed Williams
Host/Narrator Alexander Scourby

The Bible See The CBS Friday Night Movies

180   Big Band Bash
Festival '78   PBS
Program Type Music/Dance Special
2 hours. Premiere date: 3/18/78. Tribute to the popular bands and vocalists of the "swing" era in music (1935–45).
Executive Producer Jack Sameth
Producer John Adams
Company WNET-TV/New York

181   Big Blue Marble   Syndicated
Program Type Children's Series
30 minutes. Weekly. Premiere date: 9/74. Fourth season premiere: 9/77. Magazine format focusing on children from all over the world. Regular feature: "Dear Pen Pal." Show is a public service of I.T.T. Corporation.
Executive Producer Henry Fownes
Company Alphaventure
Distributor Vitt Media International
Directors Various
Writers Various
Musical Director Norman Paris
Animation Director Ron Campbell

182   Big Bob Johnson and His Fantastic Speed Circus
The Big Event   NBC
Program Type Dramatic Special
2 hours. Premiere date: 6/27/78. A stunt car racing team in a cross-country auto race.
Executive Producers Bob Goodwin, Edward L. Rissien
Producer Joe Gantman
Company Paramount Pictures production in association with Playboy Productions
Director Jack Starrett
Writers Bob Comfort, Rick Kellard
CAST
Bob Johnson .... Charles Napier
Vikki Lee Sanchez .... Maud Adams
Julie Hunsacker ....Connie Forslund
W. G. Blazer .... Robert Stoneman
Timothy Stepwell .... Rick Hurst

Lawrence Stepwell .... William Daniels
Half-Moon Muldoon .... Burton Gilliam

The Big Bus *See* The CBS Wednesday Night Movies

183 **Big City Boys**   CBS
Program Type Comedy Special
30 minutes. Premiere date: 4/11/78. Pilot about a New York bachelor and his nephew.
Executive Producer Frank Konigsberg
Producers Bruce Paltrow, Stephanie Sills
Company Silliphant-Konigsberg Co. in association with Warner Bros. Television
Director Bill Persky
Writer Bob De Laurentis
CAST
Harry .... Austin Pendleton
Peter .... Chris Barnes
Susan .... Francesca Bill
Emily .... Laurie Heineman
Pancho .... David Yanez

184 **The Big Event**   NBC
Program Type Miscellaneous Series
Times vary. Premiere date: 9/18/77. An array of special programs, including miniseries, made-for-TV movies, theatrical movies, comedy-variety specials, sports events and miscellaneous shows. The miniseries are: "The Awakening Land: The Saga of an American Woman," "Aspen," "Black Beauty," "Holocaust," "King," "Loose Change," "The Moneychangers," "Once an Eagle," "The Rhinemann Exchange" "Seventh Avenue," "79 Park Avenue," and "Wheels." The TV-movies are: "Amelia Earhart," "Big Bob Johnson and His Fantastic Speed Circus," "Contract on Cherry Street," "The Cops and Robin," "The Critical List," "The Deadly Game," "The Dark Secret of Harvest Home," "The Death of Ritchie," "Emergency!," "Father Knows Best Christmas Reunion," "Fire!," "Flood!," "The Great Wallendas," "Just a Little Inconvenience," "Kill Me If You Can," "Killing Stone," "Lacy and the Mississippi Queen," "Little Mo," "A Love Affair: The Eleanor and Lou Gehrig Story," "Love's Dark Ride," "The Other Side of Hell," "Police Story," "Raid on Entebbe," "Scott Joplin: King of Ragtime," "Sybil," "To Kill a Cop," "Top Secret," "Snowbeast," "When Every Day Was the Fourth of July," and "Ziegfield: The Man and his Women."(*See* individual titles for credits.) The theatrical movies are: "Big Jake" (1971) shown 3/13/78, "Darker Than Amber" (1970) shown 7/25/78, "Earthquake" (1974) shown 6/18/78, "Mario Puzo's 'The Godfather': The Complete Novel for Television" (1972, 1974—Godfather I, II) shown 11/12, 13, 14, 15/77, "The Lincoln Conspiracy" (1977)

shown 5/16/78, "Midway" (1961) shown 2/5–6/78, "Misty" (1961) shown 3/21/78, "My Name Is Nobody" (1974) shown 4/1/78 and repeated 8/15/78. Comedy-variety specials are: "Dick Clark's Good Ol' Days: From Bobby Sox to Bikinis." Sport event: Orange Bowl. Other items are "The Billboard #1 Music Awards," "50 Years of Country Music," "Halloween with the New Addams Family," "Hee Haw," "Hollywood Foreign Press Association's Golden Globe Awards," "Life Goes to War," "Memories of Elvis," "Nashville Remembers Elvis on His Birthday," "NBC: The First 50 Years—a Closer Look," "The 1977 Emmy Awards," "Exploring the Unknown," "Seventh Annual Las Vegas Entertainment Awards," and "Superstunt." (*See* individual titles for credits.)

185 **Big Hawaii**   NBC
Program Type Drama Series
60 minutes. Wednesdays. Premiere date: 9/21/77. Last show: 11/30/77. Contemporary series set in Hawaii. Created by William Wood.
Executive Producer Perry Lafferty
Supervising Producer William Finnegan
Producer William Wood
Company Finnegan and Associates and Filmways TV Productions, Inc. with NBC-TV
Directors Various
Story Consultant Ken Pettus
Writers Various
CAST
Mitch Fears .... Cliff Potts
Barrett Fears .... John Dehner
Oscar Kalahani .... Bill Lucking
Karen Fears .... Lucia Stralser
Lulu Kalahani .... Elizabeth Smith
Garfield Kalahani .... Moe Keale

186 **Big Henry and the Polka Dot Kid**
Special Treat   NBC
Program Type Children's Special
60 minutes. Premiere date: 11/9/76. Repeat date: 3/7/78. Dramatization based on the story "Luke Baldwin's Vow" by Morley Callaghan about a 10-year-old orphan and a blind dog. Music by Carl Davis.
Executive Producer George A. Heinemann
Producer Linda Gottlieb
Company Learning Corporation of America
Director Richard Marquand
Writer W. W. Lewis
Scenic Designer Robert Lachman
Dog Trainers Leonard Brook; Bunny Brook
CAST
Big Henry .... Ned Beatty
Luke Baldwin .... Chris Barnes
Edwina Kemp .... Estelle Parsons
Aunt Helen .... Estelle Omens
Conductor .... Robert Gerringer
Telegraph Man .... Paul Benedict
Stokey Andrews ....Barry Corbin

Big Henry and the Polka Dot Kid
Continued
Veterinarian .... Fred Stuthman
Sam Carter .... William Duell
Dan .... Wolfie

Big Jake *See* The Big Event

187　**Big Mo**
The CBS Friday Night Movies　　　　CBS
Program Type TV Movie
2 hours. Premiere date: 2/17/78. Drama based on the lives of basketball players Maurice Stokes and Jack Twyman. Music by Joe Raposo.
Producers Frank Ross, Douglas Morrow
Director Daniel Mann
Writer Douglas Morrow
CAST
Maurice Stokes .... Bernie Casey
Jack Twyman .... Bo Svenson
Dorothy Parsons .... Janet McLachlan
Carole Twyman .... Stephanie Edwards
Rosie Sanders .... Paulene Myers
Mr. Stokes .... Bill Walker
Mrs. Stokes .... Maidie Norman
Dr. Stewart .... Curt Conway
Oscar Robertson ....Ji-Tu Cumbuka
Lisa Twyman .... Lori Busk
Milton Kutsher .... Tol Avery
Chris Schenkel .... Chris Schenkel

188　**Bill Moyer's Journal: International Report**　　　　PBS
Program Type Public Affairs Series
60 minutes. Sundays. Premiere date: 1/16/75. Repeats of four programs shown in 1975. Repeat dates: 8/6-27/78. Series examining American life. Series funded by the Corporation for Public Broadcasting, the Ford Foundation, Public Television Stations, IBM, the Inter-American Foundation and the German Marshall Fund of the United States.
Executive Producer Jack Sameth
Company WNET-TV/New York
Host Bill Moyers

189　**The Billboard #1 Music Awards**
　　　　NBC
The Big Event
Program Type Parades/Pageants/Awards Special
2 hours. Premiere date: 12/11/77. First live televised annual presentation honoring recording artists who achieve excellence in all aspects of contemporary music as determined by Billboard magazine's audience surveys between 11/1/76 and 10/31/77 from the Santa Monica (Calif.) Civic Auditorium.
Executive Producer Burt Sugarman
Producers Ken Ehrlich, Bob Henry

Company NBC-TV
Director Bob Henry
Hosts Kris Kristofferson, The Bee Gees
Presenters Shaun Cassidy, Debby Boone, Peter Frampton, Glen Campbell, Donna Summer; Cat Sevens, Bay City Rollers
Performers Rita Coolidge, Steve Martin, Paul Simon, Leonard Bernstein, Patti Page, Frankie Laine, Marvin Hamlisch, Teresa Brewer; Four Preps

190　**Billion Dollar Bubble**　　　　NBC
Program Type Dramatic Special
60 minutes. Premiere date: 8/31/77. Dramatization based on the two billion dollar insurance embezzlement involving the Equity Funding Corporation of America. Filmed in London, England.
Producer Tom Clarke
Company A BBC-TV Production
Distributor Time-Life Television
Director Brian Gibson
Writer Tom Clarke
CAST
Art Lewis .... James Woods
Stanley Goldblum ....Sam Wanamaker
Lloyd Edens .... Bill Hootkins
Al Green .... Christopher Guest
Fred Levin .... Shane Rimmer
Joe Taubkin .... Lionel Murton

191　**Billy: Portrait of a Street Kid**
NBC Monday Night at the Movies/NBC World Premiere Movie　　　　NBC
Program Type Dramatic Special
2 hours. Premiere date: 9/12/77. Drama about a ghetto youth and his plans and obstacles in escaping from his dismal existence. Music by Fred Karlin. Based on the book, "Peoples," by Robert C. S. Downs.
Producer Mark Carliner
Company Mark Carliner Productions, Inc. in association with NBC-TV
Director Steve Gethers
Writer Steve Gethers
CAST
Billy Peoples .... LeVar Burton
Roseanne .... Tina Andrews
Dr. Silver ....Michael Constantine
Dr. Fredericks .... Ossie Davis

192　**Bing Crosby: His Life and Legend**
　　　　ABC
Program Type Documentary/Informational Special
2 hours. Premiere date: 5/25/78. Retrospective on Bing Crosby's life and career.
Executive Producer Frank Konigsberg
Producer Marshall Flaum
Company The Konigsberg Company
Director Marshall Flaum

Writer Marshall Flaum
Film Editor James Coblentz
Narrator William Holden

193 Bing Crosby National Pro-Am Golf Championship   ABC
Program Type Sports Special
Live coverage of the final two rounds from Pebble Beach (Calif.) Golf Links 1/21/78 and 1/22/78.
Executive Producer Roone Arledge
Producer Chuck Howard
Company ABC Sports
Directors Jim Jennett, Terry Jastrow
Hosts Phil Harris, Jim McKay
Anchor Jim McKay
Expert Commentators Peter Alliss, Dave Marr

194 Bing Crosby's Merrie Olde Christmas   CBS
Program Type Music/Comedy/Variety Special
60 minutes. Premiere date: 11/30/77. Christmas special taped in London. Special musical material by Larry Grossman.
Executive Producer Frank Konigsberg
Producers Gary Smith, Dwight Hemion
Company The Kinigsberg Company with Smith-Hemion Productions, Inc. for ITC Entertainments
Director Dwight Hemion
Writer Buz Kohan
Musical Director Ian Fraser
Choreographer Norman Maen
Art Director Henry Graveney
Star Bing Crosby with Kathryn, Mary Frances, Harry and Nathaniel Crosby.
Special Guest David Bowie
Guests Twiggy, Ron Moody, Stanley Baxter, the Trinity Boys Choir

195 The Bionic Woman   NBC
Program Type Crime Drama Series
60 minutes. Saturdays. Premiere date: 1/14/76 on ABC. Third season premiere: 9/10/77. Last show: 9/2/78. Spin-off from "The Six Million Dollar Man." Action adventure of bionic schoolteacher/Office of Scientific Information (OSI) agent. Created for television by Kenneth Johnson; based on the novel "Cyborg" by Martin Caidin. Music by Joseph Harnell.
Supervising Producer Kenneth Johnson
Producers Arthur Rowe, James D. Parriott
Company Universal Television in association with NBC-TV
Directors Various
Writers Various
CAST
Jaime Sommers .... Lindsay Wagner

Oscar Goldman .... Richard Anderson
Rudy Wells .... Martin E. Brooks

196 Birth and Death of a Star   PBS
Program Type Documentary/Informational Special
30 minutes. Premiere date: 1/29/73. Repeat date: 1/2/78. Documentary special on how stars are born, live and die. Program made possible by a grant from the National Science Foundation.
Executive Producer Richard S. Scott
Company KCET-TV/Los Angeles
Director Bert Shapiro
Writer Bert Shapiro
Host DR John A. Wheeler
Scientists participating are John A. Wheeler, Prof. of Physics, Princeton Univ.; Beverley T. Lynds and Don Hall, astronomers, Kitt Peak National Observatory; Jesse L. Greenstein, astronomer, Hale Observatories; John A. Ball, radio astronomer, Harvard Univ.; Frank D. Drake, astronomer, Cornell Univ.

197 Birthday Party for Josef Strauss
Festival '78   PBS
Program Type Music/Dance Special
60 minutes. Premiere date: 3/12/78. The 150th anniversary of composer Josef Strauss's birthday is honored. The Vienna Philharmonic is conducted by Willie Boskovsky. Also features the Vienna State Opera Corps de Ballet and Vienna Boys' Choir. Program made possible by a grant from Hyatt-Regency Corp.
Company WGBH-TV/Boston

Bite the Bullet *See* The ABC Sunday Night Movie

198 Black Beauty
The Big Event NBC Family Choice Presents
NBC
Program Type Limited Series
5 hours. 1/31/78–2/4/78. Fifteen-year saga of a horse. Adaptation of book by Anna Sewell. Music composed by John Addison.
Executive Producer Peter S. Fischer
Producer Ben Bishop
Company Universal Television Production
Director Daniel Haller
Writer Peter S. Fishcher
Narrator David Wayne
CAST
Tom Gray ....Martin Milner
Luke Gray (young) .... Ike Eisenmann
Henry Gordon ....Cameron Mitchell
Mistress Gordon ....Diane Ladd
Joe Green ....Dennis Dimster
John Manly .... William Devane
Enos Sutton .... Farley Granger
Anne ....Simone Griffith

Black Beauty *Continued*

Reuben Smith	Clu Gulager
Luke Gray (older)	Kristoffer Tabori
Lewis Barry	Edward Albert
Jonas McBride	Jack Elam
Phyllis Carpenter	Glynnis O'Connor
Jerry Barker	Warren Oates
Martin Tremaine	Don DeFore
Nicholas Skinner	Mel Ferrer
Horace Tompkins	Van Johnson

199   Black Filmmakers Hall of Fame
PBS
Program Type Parades/Pageants/Awards Special
90 minutes. Premiere date: 4/22/78. The fifth Oscar Micheaux Awards ceremony honoring blacks in motion pictures. Taped in February at the Paramount Theatre in Oakland, Calif. Program made possible by a grant from the Corporation for Public Broadcasting.
Executive Producer Christopher Lukas
Producer Carol Munday Lawrence
Company KQED-TV/San Francisco
Director Robert N. Zagone
Hosts Lou Gossett, Nancy Wilson, Don Cornelius, Vonetta Mcghee
Guests Linda Hopkins, Michael Schultz, Ted Lange, Brock Peters, The Nicholas Brothers, Ronald V. Dellums, Shirley Temple Black.

200   Black Market Baby   ABC
The ABC Friday Night Movie
Program Type TV Movie
2 hours. Premiere date: 10/7/77. A young college girl becomes pregnant and she and the father-to-be are caught in the middle of a struggle with a black market adoption ring. Based on the novel by Elizabeth Christman.
Executive Producer James Green
Producer Milton Sperling
Company Brut Productions
Director Robert Day
Writer Andrew Peter Marin
CAST

Anne Marcarino	Linda Purl
Steve Aletti	Desi Arnaz, Jr.
Mrs. Carmino	Jessica Walter
Mr. Carmino	David Doyle
Dr. Brantford	Tom Bosley
Mr. Freemont	Bill Bixby
Mrs. Krieg	Lucille Benson
Linda	Annie Potts
Babs	Tracy Brooks Swope
Mr. Marcarino	Allen Joseph
Mario	Mark Thomas

Black Orpheus *See* PBS Movie Theater

201   Black Perspective On the News   PBS
Program Type Public Affairs Series
30 minutes. Fridays. Fifth season premiere: 9/2/77. Taped around the country with black media journalists interviewing newsmakers. Series funded by the Ford Foundation, the Corporation for Public Broadcasting and Public Television Stations.
Producers Reginald Bryant, Acel Moore
Company WHYY-TV/Wilmington/Philadelphia
Director J. M. Van-Citters
Research Associate Shirley Jones
Host/Moderator Reginald Bryant

202   Black Sheep Squadron   NBC
Program Type Drama Series
60 minutes. Wednesdays/Thursdays as of 3/23/78. Formerly called "Baa Baa Black Sheep." Premiere date: 9/21/76. Second season premiere: 12/14/77. Based on the exploits of World War II ace Gregory "Pappy" Boyington as told in "Baa Baa Black Sheep." Boyington appeared in two episodes 1/18/77 and 3/8/77 in the role of Gen. Kenley. Music by Mike Post and Peter Carpenter
Executive Producer Stephen J. Cannell
Supervising Producer Don Bellisario
Producer Alex Beaton
Company Universal Television in association with NBC-TV
Directors Various
Writers Various
Technical Consultant Gregory "Pappy" Boyington
CAST

Maj. Gregory "Pappy" Boyington	Robert Conrad
Gen. Moore	Simon Oakland
Col. Lard	Dana Elcar
Lt. J. Bragg	Dirk Blocker
Lt. T. J. Wiley	Robert Ginty
Lt. Bob Anderson	John Larroquette
Lt. L. Casey	W. K. Stratton
French	Jeff MacKay
Boyle	Larry Manetti
Sgt. Andy Micklin	Red West

203   Blind Sunday
ABC Holiday Weekend Specials   ABC
Program Type Children's Special
30 minutes. Premiere date: 4/21/76. Season premiere: 12/24/77. Young people's drama of a friendship between a blind girl and a sighted boy. Music by Michel Legrand.
Producer Daniel Wilson
Company Daniel Wilson Productions, Inc.
Director Larry Elikann
Writers Arthur Barron Fred Pressburger
CAST

Mrs. Hays	Betty Beaird
Eileen	Jewel Blanch

Jeff .... Leigh J. McCloskey
Jeff's Father .... Robert Ridgely
Lifeguard .... Corbin Bernsen
Ticket Taker .... Ivan Bonar
Marge .... Cindy Eilbacher
Cab Driver .... Bill Elliot
Pam .... Debi Storm
Erik .... Steve Tanner
Math Teacher .... Carol Worthington

204 A Blind Teacher in a Public School
Americana   PBS
Program Type Documentary/Informational
Special
30 minutes. Premiere date: 4/22/77. Repeat
date: 11/29/77. A look at David Ticchi, a blind
7th grade English teacher in Newton, Massachu-
setts. Program made possible by grants from
Braille Services Club, Inc., Frederick E. Weber
Charities Corporation, Maurice Falk Medical
Foundation, Reader's Digest Foundation and
Polaroid Foundation.
Producer Pauline McCance
Company WGBH-TV/Boston

Blue Angle *See* PBS Movie Theater

205 Blue Collar Capitalism   PBS
Program Type Documentary/Informational
Special
60 minutes. Premiere date: 5/9/78. Film docu-
ments what happened when mine workers de-
cided to buy their company to save their jobs.
Program made possible by a grant from Corpora-
tion for Public Broadcasting.
Producer Joelle Shefts
Company Vermont Educational Television

206 The Blue Hotel
The American Short Story   PBS
Program Type Dramatic Special
60 minutes. Premiere date: 4/19/77. Repeat
date: 10/17/77. Adaptation of a short story by
Stephen Crane set in a rustic inn at the edge of
a Nebraska town in the 1880s. Program pre-
sented by South Carolina Educational Television
and made possible by a grant from the National
Endowment for the Humanities.
Executive Producer Robert Geller
Producer Ozzie Brown
Company Learning in Focus, Inc.
Director Jan Kadar
Writer Harry M. Petrakis
Costume Designer Juul Haalmeyer
Scenic Designer Charles Rosen
Host Colleen Dewhurst
CAST
Swede ....David Warner
Journalist .... Geddeth Smith
Cowboy .... John Bottoms

Scully .... Rex Everhart
Johnnie ....James Keach
The Stranger ....Tom Aldredge
Additional Cast Red Sutton, Lisa Pelikan, Cynthia
Wright

207 Bob Hope Desert Classic   NBC
Program Type Sports Special
Coverage of golf tournament from Bermuda
Dunes Country Club, Eldorado Country Club,
Indian Wells Country Club and LaQuinta Coun-
try Club—All in Palm Springs, Calif. 2/11/78
and 2/12/78.
Executive Producer Don Ohlmeyer
Producer Larry Cirillo
Company NBC Sports
Director Harry Coyle
Host Bob Hope
Commentators Jim Simpson, Jay Randolph,
John Brodie, Bob Goalby, Bruce Delvin

208 The Bob Newhart Show   CBS
Program Type Comedy Series
30 minutes. Saturdays. Premiere date: 9/16/72.
Sixth season premiere 9/24/77. Last show:
9/2/78. Series created by David Davis and
Lorenzo Music. Story centers around Chicago
psychologist. Music by Pat Williams.
Executive Producer Michael Zinberg
Producers Les Charles, Glen Charles
Company MTM Enterprises, Inc.
Directors Various
Writers Various
CAST
Bob Hartley .... Bob Newhart
Emily Hartley ....Suzanne Pleshette
Jerry Robinson .... Peter Bonerz
Howard Bordon .... Bill Daily
Carol Kester Bondurant ....Marcia Wallace

209 The Body Human: The Miracle
Months   CBS
Program Type Documentary/Informational
Special
60 minutes. Premiere date: 3/16/77. Repeat
date: 8/27/78. Informational special on human
birth with the emphasis on problem pregnancies.
Music by Teo Macero.
Executive Producer Thomas W. Moore
Producer Alfred R. Kelman
Co-Producer Vivian R. Moss
Company Tomorrow Entertainment/Medcom
Company
Director Alfred R. Kelman
Writer Robert E. Fuisz, M.D.
Choreographer Robert Elfstrom
Film Editor Peter Eliscu
Narrator Alexander Scourby

210   The Body Human: The Red River
CBS
Program Type Documentary/Informational
Special
60 minutes. Premiere date: 3/6/78. Informational special about the human heart and circulatory system. Music by Teo Macero. Animation by Dolphin Productions. Photography by Robert Elfstrom. Special fetal photography by John L. Marlow.
Executive Producer Thomas W. Moore
Producers Alfred R. Kelman, Vivian R. Moss
Company Tomorrow Entertainment/Medcom Company
Director Robert Elfstrom
Writer Robert E. Fuisz
Film Editor Peter Eliscu
Narrator Alexander Scourby

211   The Body Human: The Vital Connection
CBS
Program Type Documentary/Informational
Special
60 minutes. Premiere date: 5/11/78. Informational special about the human brain and the nervous system. Music by Teo Macero. Animation by Robert Glansky.
Executive Producer Thomas W. Moore
Producers Alfred R. Kelman, Vivian Moss, John Savage
Company Tomorrow Entertainment/Medcom Company
Directors Alfred R. Kelman; Robert Elfstrom
Writer Robert E. Fuisz
Film Editor Robert Brady
Narrator Alexander Scourby
Fetal Photography John L. Marlow
Brain Photography Arnold Schiebel

212   Boley, Oklahoma—Alive and Well
Americana
PBS
Program Type Documentary/Informational
Special
30 minutes. Premiere date: 6/3/77. Repeat date: 3/9/78. A look at one of the oldest all-Black towns in the United States now famous for its annual rodeo.
Producer Ed Clay
Company Nebraska Educational Television Network
Director Ed Clay
Cinematographer Drew Suss
Host Mal Adams

213   Bonnie Raitt and Mose Allison
In Performance at Wolf Trap
PBS
Program Type Music/Dance Special
60 minutes. Premiere date: 10/20/75. Repeat date: 7/8/78. Two separate concerts of blues and jazz performed by Bonnie Raitt and Mose Allison at the Wolf Trap Farm Park in Arlington, Va. Program made possible by a grant from the Atlantic Richfield Company.
Executive Producer David Prowitt
Producer Ruth Leon
Company WETA-TV/Washington, D.C.
Hosts Beverly Sills, David Prowitt
Executive-in-Charge Jim Karayn

214   Book Beat
PBS
Program Type Educational/Cultural Series
30 minutes. Wednesday. Premiered in 1965. Continuous. Weekly interview show with authors. Series funded by grants from the corporation for Public Broadcasting, the Ford Foundation and Public Television Stations.
Producer Chuck Tyler
Company WTTW-TV/Chicago
Director Chuck Tyler
Host Robert Crombie

215   The Boston Pops in Hollywood   PBS
Program Type Music/Dance Special
90 minutes. Premiere date: 3/8/76. Repeat date: 11/29/77. The first performance of the Boston Pops Orchestra on the West Coast. Filmed at the Century Plaza Hotel in Los Angeles 9/13/75. Special lyrics to "California Here I Come" by Sammy Cahn performed by the Johnny Mann Singers. Program made possible by a grant from Gulf Oil Coporation.
Executive Producer Loring d'Usseau
Producer William Cosel
Company KCET-TV/Los Angeles
Director William Cosel
Writer Marc London
Conductor Arthur Fiedler
Host Charlton Heston
Guest Stars Edgar Bergen; Anthony Paratore, Joseph Paratore

216   The Bowl Games: College Football's Second Season
ABC
Program Type Sports Special
30 minutes. Premiere date: 12/18/77. Previews of college teams competing in 1977-78 football games, including the Rose, Orange and Cotton Bowls.
Executive Producer Roone Arledge
Producer Terry O'Neill
Company ABC Sports
Director Ric LaCivita
Host Keith Jackson

217   Boxing Doubleheader
CBS
Program Type Sports Special
Boxing special promoted by Madison Square

Garden from the Indiana Convention and Exposition Center in Indianapolis between lightweights Howard Davis and Norman Goins. Additional bout by lightweights Larry Stanton and Johnny Copeland.
Company CBS Sports
Announcers Tim Ryan, Angelo Dundee, Gil Clancy

218 Boxing Special   CBS
Program Type Sports Special
Coverage of bout between heavyweights Leon Spinks and Alfio Righetti from Las Vegas, Nevada.
Producer Frank Chirkinian
Company CBS Sports
Director Frank Chirkinian
Announcers Brent Musburger, Ken Norton

219 Boxing Tripleheader   ABC
Program Type Sports Special
Live coverage from Caesars Palace in Las Vegas of World Boxing Council World Heavyweight Championship fight between Ken Norton and Larry Holmes; Bantamweight fight between Emilio Hernandez and Carlos Zarate; and Featherweight fight between Danny Lopez and Juan Malvarez, 6/9/78.
Executive Producer Roone Arledge
Producer Chet Forte
Company ABC Sports
Director Joe Aceti
Commentators Howard Cosell, Chris Schenkel

220 The Boy in the Plastic Bubble
The ABC Friday Night Movie   ABC
Program Type TV Movie
2 hours. Premiere date: 11/12/76. Repeat date: 3/10/78. Story by Joseph Morgenstern and Douglas Day Stewart. Concerns a boy born without immunities and forced to live in an incubator-like environment. Music by Mark Snow. "What Would They Say?" composed and sung by Paul Williams.
Executive Producers Aaron Spelling, Leonard Goldberg
Producers Joel Thurm, Cindy Dunne
Company Spelling/Goldberg Productions
Director Randal Kleiser
Writer Douglas Day Stewart
Art Director Paul Sylos
CAST
Tod Lubitch .... John Travolta
Gina Biggs .... Glynnis O'Connor
Johnny Lubitch .... Robert Reed
Mickey Lubitch .... Diana Hyland
Martha Biggs .... Karen Morrow
Pete Biggs .... Howard Platt
Dr. Gunther .... Ralph Bellamy

Roy Slater .... John Friedrich
Himself .... Col. Edwin E. "Buzz" Aldrin, Jr.

Boy Named Charlie Brown *See* CBS Special Movie Presentations

Brannigan *See* CBS Special Movie Presentations

Breakhart Pass *See* The CBS Wednesday Night Movies CBS Special Movie Presentations

Breaking the Sound Barrier *See* PBS Movie Theater

221 Breaking Up
ABC Theatre, ABC Special Monday   ABC
Program Type Dramatic Special
2 hours. Premiere date: 1/2/78. Drama of a woman fighting to rediscover her personal identity when her marriage ends. Music composed and conducted by Walter Levinsky. Filmed in Toronto and New York.
Executive Producer David Susskind
Producer Frederick Brogger
Company A Time-Life Television Production
Director Delbert Mann
Editor Gene Milford
Writer Loring Mandel
Art Director Ben Edwards
Director of Photography Gil Taylor, B.S.C.
CAST
JoAnn Hammil .... Lee Remick
Tom Hammil .... Granville Van-Dusen
Amy Hammil .... Vicki Dawson
T. C. Hammil .... David Stambaugh
Tony .... Fred Scollay
Gabe .... Stephen Joyce
Edie .... Cynthia Harris
Ira .... Michael Lombard
Louise Crawford .... Meg Mundy
George .... Ed Crowley
Mickey .... Linda Sorensen
Vancrier .... Kenneth McMillan
Haberle .... James Noble
Vic .... Bruce Gray
Toby .... Lois Markle
Alice .... Jill Andre
Robert Crawford .... Frank Latimore

Breakout *See* NBC Saturday Night at the Movies

Breezy *See* NBC Monday Night at the Movies

Brief Encounter *See* PBS Movie Theater

222   Brink's: The Great Robbery
The CBS Wednesday Night Movies   CBS
Program Type TV Movie
2 hours. Premiere date: 6/21/78. Dramatization
of an actual F.B.I. case.
Executive Producer Quinn Martin
Producer Philip Saltzman
Company Quinn Martin Production
Director Marvin Chomsky
Writer Robert W. Lenski
CAST
Paul Jackson .... Carl Betz
Donald Nash .... Stephen Collins
Ernie Heideman .... Burr DeBenning
Mario Russo .... Michael Gazzo
Danny Conforti .... Cliff Gorman
James McNally .... Darren McGavin
Julius Mareno .... Art Metrano
Norman Houston .... Leslie Nielsen
Maggie Hefner .... Jenny O'Hara
Ted Flynn .... Bert Remsen
Dennis Fisher .... Jerry Douglas
Russ Shannon .... Laurence Huddon
Less Hayes .... Philip Kenneally
Jerry Carter .... Byron Mabe
Thomas Preston .... Barney Phillips
Bill Shaddix .... Frank Borone
Robert Block .... David Bradon
Lt. Lorin Pope .... Hank Brandt
Stoughton cop .... Dort Clark
Doctor .... Nick Ferris

223   British Grand Prix   CBS
Program Type Sports Special
2 hours. 7/16/78. Coverage of auto race from
Brands Hatch, England.
Company CBS Sports
Announcer Ken Squier
Analysts Brock Yates, David Hobbs

224   British Open   ABC
2 hours. Taped coverage of final round of the
107th annual golf tournament from St. Andrews
Old Course in Scotland.
Company ABC Sports
Announcers Jim McKay, Dave Marr, Bob Rosburg

225   The Brontes   PBS
Program Type Dramatic Special
60 minutes. Premiere date: 2/19/78. One-woman
drama about the Bronte sisters.
Company WHA-TV and UWEX-Telecommuni-
cations Center, Madison
Producer Phil Samuels
Director Phil Samuels
Star Sybil Robinson

The Browning Version *See* PBS Movie
Theater

**226   Brunswick World Open Bowling
Tournament**   NBC
Program Type Sports Special
90 minutes. Premiere date: 11/19/77. Top men
professional bowlers compete in 6-day tourna-
ment at the Brunswick Northern Bowl, Glendale
Heights, Ill.
Company NBC Sports

Buffalo Bill and the Indians *See* The
CBS Wednesday Night Movies

The Bug *See* The CBS Friday Night
Movies

227   Bugs Bunny in Space   CBS
Program Type Animated Film Special
30 minutes. Premiere date: 9/6/77. Repeat date:
4/18/78. Animated adventures of Bugs Bunny in
space drawn from previously released produc-
tions.
Executive Producer Hal Geer
Company Warner Bros., Inc.
Animation Directors Chuck Jones, Friz Freleng
Voices Mel Blanc

228   Bugs Bunny's Howl-oween Special
CBS
Program Type Animated Film Special
30 minutes. Premiere date: 10/26/77. Halloween
adventures of animated character Bugs Bunny
and his pals.
Executive Producer Hal Geer
Company Warner Bros., Inc.
Writers Cliff Roberts, Tedd Pierce, Warren Fos-
ter, Michael Maltese, John Dunn
Sequence Directors Robert McKimson; Chuck
Jones; Friz Freleng; Abe Levitow, Maurice
Noble, Dave Detiege
Musicians Carl Stalling, Milt Franklin, Bill Lava
Voices Mel Blanc, June Foray

Burn! *See* The CBS Saturday Night
Movie

229   The Business of Newspapers   CBS
Program Type News Special
60 minutes. Premiere date: 7/14/78. The Ameri-
can daily newspaper and how newspaper journal-
ism is affected by newspaper economics.
Executive Producer Perry Wolff
Producer Irina Posner
Director Irina Posner

Writer Irina Posner
Film Editor Dena Levitt
Cinematographer Greg Cooke
Researcher Madeline Nelson
Special Consultant Ben H. Bagdikian
Reporter Hughes Rudd

Buster and Billie *See* The ABC Friday Night Movie

230 The Busters   CBS
Program Type Dramatic Special
60 minutes. Premiere date: 5/28/78. Pilot action drama. Music by Jerrold Immel.
Executive Producer Stu Erwin
Producer Jim Byrnes
Company MTM Enterprises, Inc.
Director Vincent McEveety
Writer Jim Byrnes
CAST
Chad Kimbrough .... Bo Hopkins
Albie McCrea .... Brian Kerwin
Wister Kane .... Slim Pickens
Marti Hamilton .... Devon Ericson
Billy Burnet .... Buck Taylor
Nick Carroll .... Chris Robinson
Mel Drew ....Lance Le-Gault
Joanna Bailey .... Susan Howard

231 Byron Nelson Golf Classic   ABC
Program Type Sports Special
Live coverage of the final two rounds of the 1978 Byron Nelson Golf Classic 5/6/78 and 5/7/78 from Dallas, Texas.
Executive Producer Roone Arledge
Producer Bob Goodrich
Company ABC Sports
Directors Jim Jennett, Terry Jastrow
Commentators Chris Schenkel, Bill Flemming
Expert Commentators Byron Nelson, Dave Marr, Bob Rosburg, Vern Lundquist

232 C. B. Bears/Go, Go Globetrotters   NBC
Program Type Animated Film Series
60 minutes. Saturdays. Premiere: 9/10/77. Became segment of "Go, Go Globetrotters," as of 2/4/78. Three bears get themselves into various capers.
Executive Producers William Hanna, Joseph Barbera
Writers Various
Story Editor Ray Parker
Associate Producer Alex Lovy
Musical Director Hoyt Curtin
Musical Supervisor Paul DeKorte
Company Hanna-Barbera
Additional Voices Scatman Crothers, Meadowlark Lemon

233 Calypso's Search for Atlantis   PBS
Program Type Science/Nature Special
Two part special, each part 60 minutes. Premiere dates: 5/1-2/78. Existence of lost civilization of Atlantis probed by Jacques Cousteau. Music is composed and conducted by Manos Hadjidakis. Program made possible by a grant from Atlantic Richfield Company.
Executive Producers Jacques Cousteau; Philippe Cousteau
Producer Andrew W. Solt
Company Cousteau Society in association with KCET-TV/Los Angeles
Writer Theodore Strauss
Narrator Theodore Strauss

234 Calypso's Search for the Britannic   PBS
Program Type Science/Nature Special
60 minutes. Premiere date: 11/22/77. Story of the mysterious World War I sinking of His Majesty's Hospital Ship Britannic. Music composed and conducted by Elmer Bernstein and performed by the Royal Philharmonic Orchestra. Program made possible by a grant from Atlantic Richfield Company.
Executive Producers Jacques Cousteau; Philippe Cousteau
Producer Andrew W. Solt
Company KCET-TV/Los Angeles
Writer Theodore Strauss
Narrator Theodore Strauss

235 Camera Three   CBS
Program Type Educational/Cultural Series
30 minutes. Sundays. Local premiere on WCBS-TV/New York: 5/16/53. National premiere date: 1/22/56. 22nd season network premiere: 9/18/77. Experimental series dealing with arts and sciences.
Executive Producer John Musilli
Producers John Musilli, Roger Englander and others
Company WCBS-TV/New York
Directors John Musilli, Roger Englander and others

236 Canadian Open   CBS
Program Type Sports Special
Live and taped coverage of the final two rounds of the Canadian Open golf championship at Glen Abbey Golf Club in Toronto, Canada 7/24/78 and 7/25/78.
Executive Producer Frank Chirkinian
Associate Producer Bob Dailey
Company CBS Television Network Sports
Commentators Vin Scully, Pat Summerall, Ben Wright, Frank Glieber, Jack Whitaker, Ken Venturi

237 Canal Zone   PBS
Program Type Documentary/Informational
Special
3 hours. Premier date: 10/9/77. Documentary
on the daily life of American residents in the
Panama Canal Zone.
Producer Frederick Wiseman
Company WNET-TV/New York

238 Canine Hall of Fame   NBC
Program Type Music/Comedy/Variety Special
60 minutes. Premiere date: 9/12/78. Entertain-
ment special devoted to dogs both real and imagi-
nary. Created by Lawrence Needleman.
Executive Producer George A. Heinemann
Producer Charles Andrews
Company NBC Television Network
Director Lloyd Gross
Writers Charles Andrews, Tony Geiss
Host Joe Garagiola
Special Guests Jerry Stiller, Anne Meara
Composer/Arranger Dick Hyman

Capone *See* The CBS Tuesday Night
Movies

239 The Captain & Tennille in Hawaii
                                      ABC
Program Type Music/Comedy/Variety Special
60 minutes. Premiere date: 5/5/78.
Producer Bill Lee
Company Moonlight and Magnolias, Inc. in as-
sociation with dick clark teleshows, inc.
Director John Moffitt
Stars Daryl Dragon, Toni Tennille
Guest Stars Kenny Rogers, David Soul, Melissa
Tennille, Louisa Tennille, Don Knotts,
Makaha Sons of Ni'ihua

**240 The Captain & Tennille in New
Orleans**   ABC
Program Type Music/Comedy/Variety Special
60 minutes. Premiere date: 4/3/78.
Producer Bill Lee
Director John Moffitt
Stars Daryl Dragon, Toni Tennille
Guest Stars Hal Linden, Fats Domino, John
Byner, Louisa Tennille, Melissa Tennille

241 Captain Kangaroo   CBS
Program Type Children's Series
60 minutes. Monday–Friday mornings. Premiere
date: 10/3/55. 23rd season premiere: 9/12/77.
Created by Bob Keeshan. Set in "The Captain's
Place." Cosmo Allegretti is the voice of many
characters: Dancing Bear, Mr. Moose, Bunny
Rabbit, Miss Frog, etc. Hugh "Lumpy" Bran-

num plays various characters: Percy, Mr.
Bainter, the Painter, The Professor, etc. Joel Ko-
sofsky and Frank Alesia producers as of
4/18/78.
Producer Jim Hirschfeld
Company Robert Keeshan Associates, Inc.
Director Peter Birch
Head Writer Bob Colleary
Costume Designer Hugh Holt
Puppeteer Cosmo Allegretti
CAST
Captain Kangaroo ....Bob Keeshan
Mr. Green Jeans .... Hugh "Lumpy" Brannum
Dennis, the Apprentice .... Cosmo Allegretti
Mr. Baxter .... Jimmy Wall
Debbie .... Debbie Weems

242 Captains Courageous
Bell System Special   ABC
Program Type Dramatic Special
2 hours. Premiere date: 12/4/77. Based on story
by Rudyard Kipling. Music by Allyn Ferguson.
Filmed off the coast of Maine.
Producer Norman Rosemont
Company Norman Rosemonnt Productions, Inc.
Director Harvey Hart
Writer John Gay
Cinematographer Philip Lathrop
Film Editor John McSweeney
CAST
Disko Troop .... Karl Malden
Harvey Cheyne .... Jonathan Kahn
Dan ....Johnny Doran
Little Penn .... Neville Brand
Long Jack .... Fred Gwynne
Tom Platt .... Charles Dierkop
Salters .... Jeff Corey
Harvey Cheyne, Sr. ....Fritz Weaver
Manuel .... Ricardo Montalban
Cook .... Stan Haze
Phillips .... Redmond Gleeson
Chief Steward ....Shay Duffin
Mr. Atkins .... Milton Frome
Mrs. Cheyne .... Stanja Lowe

243 Captioned ABC Evening News PBS
Program Type News Series
30 minutes. Mondays–Fridays. ABC (7 p.m.)
news captioned for the hearing-impaired at
WGBH-TV/Boston. Program funded by the
U.S. Department of Health, Education and Welfare—Bureau of Education for the Handicapped.
(*See* "ABC Evening News With Harry Reasoner
and Barbara Walters" for credits.)

Car Wash *See* NBC Monday Night at
the Movies

244 Card Sharks
Program Type Game/Audience Participation Series
30 minutes. Monday–Friday. Premiere date: 4/24/78. Two contestants try to complete a consecutive block of five playing cards.
Executive Producer Chester Feldman
Producer Jonathan M. Goodson
Company Goodson-Todman Productions
Director Marc Breslow
Host Jim Perry

245 Caribou: The Incredible Journey
NBC
Program Type Documentary/Informational Special
60 minutes. Premiere date: 4/12/78. Film follows a 2,000-mile trip by a herd of approximately 125,000 caribou from the Yukon Territory to an area in Alaska north of the Arctic Circle and back.
Executive Producer Aubrey Buxton
Producer David deVries
Company Survival Anglia Ltd. in association with the World Wildlife Fund
Writer Colin Wollock
Cinematographer David deVries
Narrator Michael Landon

246 Carnivore
Documentary Showcase   PBS
Program Type Documentary/Informational Special
60 minutes. Premiere date: 12/3/76. Season premiere: 12/6/77. (Closed captions for the hearing-impaired.) An objective look at America's meat eating habits.
Producer John Beyer
Company Iowa Public Broadcasting Network
Director John Beyer
Writer John Beyer
Cinematographer Ron Burnell
Film Editor Ron Burnell
Narrator Matthew James Faison

247 The Carol Burnett Show   CBS
Program Type Music/Comedy/Variety Series
60 minutes. Saturdays/Sundays (as of 12/11/77.) Premiere date: 9/11/67. Eleventh season premiere: 9/24/77. Last show: 3/29/78, 2-hour special. Regular features include "Mrs. Wiggins and Mr. Tudball," "As the Stomach Turns" and "The Family." Musical theme, "It's Time to Say So Long," words and music by Joe Hamilton.
Executive Producer Joe Hamilton
Producer Ed Simmons
Company Whacko, Inc.
Director Dave Powers

Head Writer Ed Simmons
Writers Ed Simmons, Roger Beatty, Rick Hawkins, Liz Sage, Robert Illes, James Stein, Franelle Silver, Larry Siegel, Tim Conway
Musical Director Peter Matz
Costume Designer Bob Mackie
Art Directors Paul Barnes, Bob Sanson
Stars Carol Burnett, Dick Van Dyke, Tim Conway, Vicki Lawrence, Ernest Flatt Dancers

248 The Carpenters at Christmas   ABC
Program Type Music/Comedy/Variety Special
60 minutes. Premiere date: 12/9/77. The Carpenters host guest stars in a warm musical presentation of old favorites interspersed with humorous sketches.
Executive Producer Jerry Weintraub
Producer Bob Henry
Company A Downey-Bronx Production
Director Bob Henry
Writers Bill Larkin; Stephen Spears
Musical Director Billy May
Choreographer Bob Thompson
Costume Designer Bill Belew
Art Director Romain Johnston
Stars Karen Carpenter, Richard Carpenter
Guest Stars Harvey Korman, Kristy McNichol, Burr Tillstrom and puppets Kukla and Ollie
Featuring The Bob Thompson Dancers and Cal State Long Beach Choir

249 The Carpenters ... Space Encounters   ABC
Program Type Music/Comedy/Variety Special
60 minutes. Premiere date: 5/17/78. Laser effects by Laser Media, Inc. Animated sequences by Image West.
Executive Producer Jerry Weintraub
Producer Bob Henry
Company A Downey-Bronx Production
Director Bob Henry
Writers Bill Larkin, Stephen Spears, Tom Sawyer, Joe Neustein
Musical Director Peter Knight
Choreographer Bob Thompson
Art Director Romain Johnston
Stars Richard Carpenter, Karen Carpenter
Guest Stars Suzanne Somers, Charlie Callas, John Davidson

250 Carter Abroad: An Assessment   NBC
Program Type News Special
30 minutes. Correspondent Garrick Utley chaired a round-table discussion 1/6/78 on President Carter's trip abroad.
Executive Producer Gordon Manning
Producer Kenneth Donoghue
Company NBC News
Anchor John Chancellor

251   Carter and the Dollar: Back from the Summit   NBC
Program Type News Special
20 minutes. 7/17/78. John Chancellor summarizes the results of President Carter's participation in the international economic summit meeting in Bonn, West Germany.
Executive Producer Paul Greenberg
Producer Ray Lockhart
Company NBC News

252   Carter Country   ABC
Program Type Comedy Series
30 minutes. Thursdays/Tuesdays (as of 5/2/78.) Premiere date: 9/15/77. Comedy about the relationship between a police chief in a small southern town and his new sergeant, a young black policeman from New York City. Taped before a studio audience in Hollywood, Calif. Created by Phil Doran and Douglas Arango. Developed by Bud Yorkin, Bernie Orenstein and Saul Turteltaub. Music by Pete Rugolo. Bud Yorkin directed the premiere episode. Douglas Arango and Phil Doran Executive Producers as of December 19, 1977.
Executive Producers Bud Yorkin; Bernie Orenstein; Saul Turtletaub
Producers Phil Doran, Douglas Arango
Company A TOY Production
Director Peter Baldwin
Head Writers Al Gardan, Jack Mendelsohn
Writers Various
Art Director Edward Stephenson
CAST
Chief Roy Mobey .... Victor French
Deputy Curtis Baker .... Kene Holliday
Mayor Teddy Burnside ....Richard Paul
Lucille Banks .... Vernee Watson
Cloris Phebus .... Barbara Cason
Harley Puckett .... Guich Koock
Deputy Jasper DeWitt Jr. .... Harvey Vernon

253   Carter's 365th Day   PBS
Program Type Public Affairs Special
30 minutes. 1/19/78. Special on the limitations on the power and authority of the U.S. Presidency.
Company WGBH-TV/Boston with the Institute of Politics, Kennedy School of Government, Harvard University
Host Doris Kearns

Casque d'Or *See* PBS Movie Theater

254   Catastrophe: Airships   Syndicated
Program Type Documentary/Informational Special
30 minutes. Premiere data: 3/28/78. Documentary about dirigible disasters.

Executive Producer Charles Denton
Producer Brian Lewis
Company ITC Entertainment
Directors Brian Lewis, Franc Roddam
Writer Warren Trabent
Narrator Glenn Ford

255   Cavalleria Rusticana
Great Performances   PBS
Program Type Music/Dance Special
90 minutes. Premiere date: 10/26/77. One-act opera by Pietro Mascagni performed by the La Scala Orchestra and Chorus. Program made possible by a grant from Exxon Corporation.
Company Unitel
Director Ake Falck
Conductor Herbert von Karajan
Staged by Georgia Strehler
CAST
Turiddu ....Gianfranco Cecchele
Lola ....Adriana Martino
Alfio .... Giangiacomo Guelfi
Santuzza ....Fiorenza Cossotto

256   Cavalleria Rusticana/Pagliacci
Live from the Metropolitan Opera   PBS
Program Type Music/Dance Special
3 Hours. Premiere date: 4/5/78. Two operas aired live from the Metropolitan Opera, New York: "Cavalleria Rusticana" by Pietro Mascagni and "Pagliacci" by Ruggiero Leoncavallo. Program made possible by grants from Texaco, Inc. and The National Endowment for the Arts.
Executive Producer Michael Bronson
Producer Christopher Sarson
Company Metropolitan Opera Association and WNET-TV/New York
Director Kirk Browning
Conductor James Levine
Stage Direction Fabrizio Melano
Lighting Designer Gil Wechsler
Production, Set and Costume Design Franco Zeffirelli
Host Tony Randall
Cast for Cavalleria Rusticana
CAST
Santuzza .... Tatiana Troyanos
Lola .... Isola Jones
Lucia ....Jean Kraft
Turiddu .... Placido Domingo
Alfio .... Vern Shinall
Cast for Pagliacci
Nedda .... Teresa Stratas
Canio .... Placido Domingo
Tonio .... Sherrill Milnes
Silvio .... Allan Monk
Beppe ....James Atherton
Villagers ....Arthur Apy, Domenico Simeone

257 **CBS: On the Air**   CBS
Program Type Music/Comedy/Variety Special
Premiere date: 3/26/78. 9-1/2 hour special be-
ginning Sunday for 2 hours, Monday through
Friday for 1 hour, and concluding on Saturday,
April 1, for 2-1/2 hours. Show commemorating
the first 50 years of CBS broadcasting. Conceived
and written by Hildy Parks. Special material by
Norman Corwin. Special musical material by
Jerry Herman; Hank Beebe; Bill Heyer; Cy Cole-
men; Betty Comden and Adolph Green; Jules
Styne; Sammy Cahn; Stan Freeman; Artie Mal-
vin; Leonard Bernstein
Executive Producer Alexander H. Cohen
Producer Lee Miller
Company CBS Entertainment
Directors Clark Jones; Sid Smith
Musical Director Elliot Lawrence
Choreographer Alan Johnson
Costume Designer Alvin Colt
Hosts Mary Tyler Moore; Walter Cronkite
Co-Hosts and Guest Stars Sunday: Mary Tyler
Moore and Walter Cronkite and co-hosts Telly
Savalas, Jean Stapleton and guest stars Alfred
Hitchcock and Bob Keeshan. Monday: Mary
Tyler Moore and co-hosts Beatrice Arthur,
Lucille Ball, George Burns and Arthur God-
frey. Tuesday: Mary Tyler Moore and Walter
Cronkite and co-host Alan Alda and guest
stars Garry Moore and Phil Silvers. Wednes-
day: Co-hosts Buddy Ebsen, Danny Kaye,
Cicely Tyson, Dick Van Dyke, and the
animated "Peanuts" characters. Thursday:
Mary Tyler Moore, co-host, Richard Thomas
and the cast of "The Waltons": Ellen Corby,
Kami Cotler, Will Geer, Michael Learned,
Mary McDonough and Ralph Waite. Friday:
Mary Tyler Moore and co-hosts Eve Arden,
Bert Convy, Richard Crenna, Bonnie Frank-
lin, Linda Lavin, Jim Nabors and guest star
Lauren Bacall. Saturday: Mary Tyler Moore
and Walter Cronkite and co-hosts Carol Bur-
nett, Art Carney, Sherman Hemsley, Art
Linkletter, Tony Randall, Carroll O'Connor,
Isabel Sanford, and guest star Danny Thomas;
and cameo appearances by Beatrice Arthur,
Edward Asner, Ken Berry, Andy Griffith,
Valerie Harper, Jim Nabors and Ester Rolle.

258 **CBS All-American Thanksgiving
Day Parade**   CBS
Program Type Parades/Pageants/Awards
Special
3 hours. Premiere date: 11/24/77. Highlights of
the Macy's Parade in New York, the Gimbel's
Parade in Philadelphia, the J. L. Hudson Parade
in Detroit, Hawaii's Aloha Floral Parade and
Eaton's Santa Calus Parade in Toronto.
Executive Producer Mike Gargiulo
Producers Wilf Fielding (Toronto), Vern Dia-
mond (New York, Toronto), Clarence Schim-
mel (Detroit), Jim Hirschfeld (Philadelphia),
Malachy Wienges (Hawaii)
Writers Beverly Schanzer, Carolyn Miller, Betty
Cornfield, Chuck Horner
Parade Hosts Pat Harrington and Loretta Swit
(New York), Bess Armstrong and Lynnie
Greene (Toronto), Ja'net DuBois and Kevin
Dobson (Philadelphia), Jack Lord (Hawaii)
and Linda Lavin and Ned Beatty (Detroit)
Special Host William Conrad

259 **CBS Evening News (Saturday
Edition)**   CBS
Program Type News Series
30 minutes. Saturday evenings. Continuous.
Executive Producer Joan Richman
Producer Elizabeth Midgley
Company CBS News
Anchor Bob Schieffer

260 **CBS Evening News (Sunday
Edition)**   CBS
Program Type News Series
30 minutes. Sunday evenings. Continuous.
Executive Producer Joan Richmann
Producer Elizabeth Midgley
Company CBS News
Anchor Morton Dean

261 **CBS Evening News with Walter
Cronkite**   CBS
Program Type News Series
30 minutes. Premiere date: 9/2/63. Mondays–
Fridays. Continuous. First 30-minute evening
news program on television. Regular feature "On
the Road" with Charles Kuralt. "What Else Is
New?" feature began 4/19/78. Eric Sevareid
retired 11/30/77.
Producer David Horwitz, Christie Basham
Company CBS News
Anchor Walter Cronkite

262 **The CBS Family Film Classics** CBS
Program Type Feature Film Series
2 hours (generally). Premiere date: 5/23/78. A
series of popular theatrically released films with
family appeal. The films are "Charlotte's Web"
(1973) shown 8/8/78 and 8/15/78, "National
Velvet" (1945) shown 6/6/78 and 6/13/78,
"Tom Sawyer" (1973) shown 7/18/78 and
7/25/78, "Where the Lilies Bloom" (1974)
shown 6/27/78 and 7/4/78, and "The Yearling"
(1947) shown 5/23/78 and 5/30/78.

263 The CBS Festival of Lively Arts for Young People CBS
Program Type Children's Series
60 minutes. Monthly. Sundays. Season premiere: 12/18/77. Music, dance, poetry and dramatic specials. Shows seen during the 1977–78 season are: "Dance of the Athletes," "Henry Winkler Meets William Shakespeare," "Music and Your Emotions," "The Secret of Charles Dickens," "What's a Museum for, Anyway," and "You're a Poet and Don't Know It! ... The Poetry Power Hour." (*See* individual titles for credits.)

264 The CBS Friday Night Movies CBS
Program Type Feature Film Series – TV Movie Series
2 hours. Fridays. Season premiere: 12/2/77. A combination of made-for-TV movies and theatrically released feature films. The made-for-TV movies are: "Big Mo," "Deadman's Curve," "Forever," "The Gypsy Warriors," "The President's Mistress," "Ski Lift to Death," and "Thaddeus Rose and Eddie." (*See* individual titles for credits.) The feature films are: "The Bible" (1966) shown 12/23/77, "The Bug" (1975) shown 1/20/78, "The Four Musketeers" (1975) shown 12/2/77 "Smile" (1975) shown 10/14/77, "White Lightning" (1973) shown 12/9/77, and "Zorro" (1975) shown 12/30/77.

265 CBS Late Movie CBS
Program Type Feature Film Series – TV Movie Series
A combination of made-for-television films and theatrically released features. Monday-Friday nights. Included are repeats of television series: "Kojak," "Hawaii Five-O," "M*A*S*H," "Columbo," "McCloud," and "McMillan and Wife."

266 CBS Mid-Day News with Douglas Edwards CBS
Program Type News Series
5 minutes. Mondays-Fridays. Premiere date: 10/2/61. Continuous. Edwards has anchored the news since February 1968.
Company CBS News
Anchor Douglas Edwards

267 CBS Morning News CBS
Program Type News Series
60 minutes. Monday–Fridays. Premiere date: 9/2/63. Continuous. Hughes Rudd anchors from New York, Leslie Stahl from Washington, DC. Richard Threlkeld replaced Rudd as co-anchor in October 1977.
Senior Producer Peter Larkin

Producer David Miller
Anchors Hughes Rudd, Leslie Stahl

268 CBS News Specials CBS
Program Type News Series
Special news and documentary broadcasts presented throughout the year. Programs shown during the 1977–78 season are: "Anatomy of a Scandal," "The Business of Newspapers," "A Conversation with Eric Sevareid," "The Hidden Heritage," "Is Anyone Out There Learning?: A CBS Report Card on American Public Education," "1968," "The Politics of Abortion," "President Carter at West Berlin Town Meeting," "President Carter's Travels," "Reply to Carter's Energy Message," "State of the Union Address," "Times of Exquisite Felicity," "What's Happened to Cambodia," "The World of Charlie Company," and "Your Turn: Letters to CBS News." (*See* individual titles for credits.)

269 CBS Reports CBS
Program Type Documentary/Informational Series
60 minutes. Special documentary broadcasts presented throughout the year. Multi-story editions began 1/24/78. Programs shown during the 1977–78 season are: "The Aliens," "The Battle for South Africa," "The Battle Over Panama," "The CIA's Secret Army," "Farm Strike," "The Fire Next Door," "The Fire Next Door-Updated," "Going, Going ... Gone," "Goodbye, Congress," "Into the Mouths of Babes ... ," "New Orleans," "The Politics of Abortion," "Promise Now, Pay Later," "Since Gary Gilmore," "Soul of Freedom," "The Taiwan Dilemma," "Who's Minding the Bank?" and "You Can Beat City Hall." (*See* individual titles for credits.)

270 The CBS Saturday Film Festival CBS
Program Type Feature Film Series
30 minutes. Saturdays. 11th season premiere date: 9/17/77. Formerly titled "CBS Children's Film Festival." Films for children from around the world.
Company CBS Television

271 The CBS Saturday Night Movie CBS
Program Type Feature Film Series – TV Movie Series
2 hours (generally). Saturdays. Season premiere: A combination of made-for-TV movies and theatrically released feature films. The made-for-TV movies are: "The Girl Called Hatter Fox," "Mary Jane Harper Cried Last Night," and "The

Islander." (*See* individual titles for credits.) The feature films are: "Burn!" (1970) shown 8/5/78, "Come Back Charleston Blue" (1972) shown 8/19/78, "Conrack" (1974) shown 7/1/78, "Fear Is the Key" (1973) shown 7/15/78, "For Better, For Worse" (1974, originally titled "Zandy's Bride") shown 6/17/78, "The French Connection" (1971) shown 7/8/78, "From Noon Till Three" (1976) shown 5/27/78, "Juggernaut" (1974) shown 7/29/78, "The Life and Times of Judge Roy Bean" (1972) shown 9/2/78, and "Magnum Force" (1973) shown 9/9/78.

272   CBS Special Movie Presentations
CBS

Program Type TV Movie Series

2 hours (generally). A selection of theatrically released feature films shown on different days of the week. Films shown are: "Bank Shot" (1974) shown 7/7/78, "A Boy Named Charlie Brown" (1969) shown 5/29/78, "Brannigan" (1975) shown 5/14/78, "Breakheart Pass" (1976) shown 5/13/78, "The Cheyenne Social Club" (1970) shown 5/6/78, "Gator" (1976) shown 2/12/78, "Grand Theft Auto," (1977) shown 9/15/78, "Hannie Caulder" (1971) shown 5/20/78, "Mitchell" (1975) shown 10/18/77, "Mr. Majestyk" (1974) shown 5/21/78, "Night Moves" (1975) shown 11/11/77, "Papillon" (1973) shown 10/6/77, "The Private Life of Sherlock Holmes" (1970) shown 7/28/78, "Scalawag" (1973) shown 7/14/78, "The Secret of Santa Vittoria" (1969) shown 6/24/78, "That's Entertainment, Part 2" (1976) shown 9/25/77, "Three Days of the Condor" (1975) shown 11/27/77, "The Three Musketeers" (1974) shown 11/18/77, "Vanishing Point" (1971) shown 6/10/78, "A Warm December" (1973) shown 8/4/78, and "The Wizard of Oz" (1939) shown 3/26/78.

273   CBS Sports Spectacular   CBS
Program Type Sports Series

90 minutes. Saturdays. Coverage of sports events from around the world, including the 110th Belmont Stakes, the 37th Daytona "200" Motorcycle Race and international Chunichi Cup from Japan.

Coordinating Producer Perry Smith
Producers Various
Company CBS Television Network Sports
Directors Various
Commentators Gary Bender, Tom Brookshier, Don Criqui, Phyllis George, Brent Musburger, Ken Squier, Jack Whitaker, Frank Wright, Charlie Cantey, Chic Anderson, Tim Ryan, Pat Summerall, Tony Trabert, Christine Craft, Sam Renick

274   The CBS Tuesday Night Movies
CBS

Program Type Feature Film Series – TV Movie Series

2 hours (generally). Tuesdays. Premiere date: 1/31/78. A combination of made-for-TV movies and theatrically released films. The made-for-TV movies are: "The Amazing Howard Hughes," "Escape from Bogen County," "Last of the Good Guys," "Perfect Gentlemen," and "A Question of Guilt." (*See* individual titles for credits.) The feature films are: "The Alamo" (1960) shown 5/9/78, "Capone" (1975) shown 8/22/78, "Chinatown" (1974) shown 1/31/78, "The Happy Ending" (1969) shown 4/11/78, "Hell Boats" (1970) shown 8/8/78, "Hondo" (1953) shown 9/12/78, "Hustle" (1975) shown 2/7/78, "In the Heat of the Night" (1967) shown 6/27/78, "It's a Mad, Mad, Mad, Mad World" (1963) shown 5/16/78, "The Magnificent Seven Ride" (1972) shown 7/18/78, "Magnum Force" (1973) shown 2/28/78, "Man on a Swing" (1974) shown 7/25/78, "A Man Called Horse" (1970) shown 4/18/78, "Moonshine County Express" (1977) shown 4/4/78, "Play It Again Sam" (1972) shown 6/13/78, "Pocket Money" (1972) shown 7/4/78, "The Russians Are Coming, the Russians Are Coming" (1966) shown 8/1/78, "The Spikes Gang" (1974) shown 6/6/78, "Submarine X-1" (1969) shown 8/15/78, "Twilight's Last Gleaming" (1977) shown 2/14/78, "Support Your Local Gunfighter" (1971) shown 3/21/78, and "West Side Story" (1961) shown 7/11/78.

275   The CBS Wednesday Night Movies
CBS

Program Type Feature Film Series – TV Movie Series

2 hours (generally). Wednesdays. Season premiere: 9/21/77. A combination of made-for-TV movies and theatrically released feature films. The made-for-TV movies are: "Brink's: The Great Robbery," "Daddy I Don't Like It Like This," "A Death in Canaan," "Death Moon," "Getting Married," "The Greatest Thing that Almost Happened," "Mary Jane Harper Cried Last Night," "A Killing Affair," "Mad Bull," "Maneaters Are Loose!" "Murder at the Mardi Gras," "Siege," "Special Olympics," and "Tarantulas: The Deadly Cargo." (*See* individual titles for credits.) The feature films are: "The Big Bus" (1976) shown 3/22/78, "Breakhart Pass" (1976) shown 11/2/77, "Buffalo Bill and the Indians" (1976) shown 9/13/78, "Challenge To Be Free" (1975) shown 5/31/78, "The Conversation" (1974) shown 8/2/78, "The Deadly Trap" (1972) shown 8/16/78, "Framed" (1974) shown 4/12/78, "From Noon Till Three" (1976) shown 11/16/77, "The Great Scout and

The CBS Wednesday Night Movies
Continued
Cathouse Thursday" (1976) shown 1/4/78, "The Hawaiians" (1970) shown 8/9/78, "Jackson County Jail" (1976) shown 9/28/77, "Jacqueline Susann's Once Is Not Enough" (1975) shown 11/9/77, "The Killer Elite" (1975) shown 10/19/77, "Mahogany" (1975) shown 3/8/78, "The Next Man" (1976) shown 12/14/77, "The Parallax View" (1974) shown 8/23/78, "Posse" (1975) shown 4/19/78, "Race With The Devil" (1975) shown 4/5/78, "Rancho Deluxe" (1975) shown 6/28/78, "T. R. Baskin" (1971) shown 7/19/78, "The Train Robbers" (1973) shown 1/25/78, "Up The Sandbox" (1972) shown 6/14/78, "Uptown Saturday Night" (1974) shown 12/7/77, and "Vigilante Force" (1976) shown 1/11/78.

276   CBS Youth Invitational ... Frisbee
CBS
Program Type Children's Special
30 minutes. Premiere date: 8/27/77. Repeat date: 3/25/78. Eight of the top junior and senior frisbee champions in competition. Taped 7/12/77 and 7/13/77 at Six Flags Over Georgia in Atlanta, Ga.
Executive Producer Jack Dolph
Producer Jim Cross
Company Jack Dolph Associates, Inc.
Director Jim Cross
Host Tom Brookshier
Expert Commentator Peter Bloeme

277   CBS Youth Invitational ... Skateboarding
CBS
Program Type Children's Special
30 minutes. Premiere date: 2/12/77. Season premiere: 12/31/77. Six teenage skateboarders in three events. Taped at The Dark Continent, Busch Gardens, Tampa, Florida.
Executive Producers Jack Dolph, Bill Riordan
Producer Jim Cross
Company Jack Dolph Associates, Inc.
Director Jim Cross
Host Tom Brookshier
Expert Analyst Denis Shufeldt

278   A Celebration at Ford's Theatre
NBC
Program Type Music/Comedy/Variety Special
60 minutes. Premiere date: 2/2/78. Actors, singers and dancers appear at historic Ford's Theatre, Washington, DC, saluting a decade of performances on its stage.
Executive Producer Joseph Cates
Producer Peter Dohanos
Company Cates Brothers Production
Director Gilbert Cates

Writer Frank Slocum
Host Lorne Greene
Stars Alexis Smith, Henry Fonda, James Whitmore, Billy Dee Williams, Vincent Price, Linda Hopkins, John Houseman, Delores Hall, Roderick Cook, Bill Schustidk, The Acting Company

279   Celebration of Women
PBS
Program Type Public Affairs Special
60 minutes. 11/21/77. Special on 1977 National Women's Conference from Dallas, Texas. Program made possible by a grant from the Corporation for Public Broadcasting.
Executive Producer Nazaret Cherkezian
Producer Susan Caudill
Company KERA-TV/Dallas-Fort Worth
Narrator Susan Caudill

280   Celebrity Bowling
Syndicated
Program Type Sports Series
30 minutes. Daily and weekly. Preceded by "The Celebrity Bowling Classic" in 1969. In syndication since 1/71. Four guest celebrities in team bowling.
Producers Joe Siegman, Don Gregory
Company 7–10 Productions
Distributor Syndicast Services, Inc.
Director Don Buccola
Host Jed Allan

281   Celebrity Challenge of the Sexes
CBS
Program Type Sports Series
30 minutes. Tuesdays. Premiere date: 1/31/78. Last show: 2/28/78. Half-hour form of the two-hour special of the same name.
Executive Producer Howard Katz
Producer Mel Ferber
Company CBS Sports and Trans World International
Director Bernie Hoffman
Writers Howard Albrecht, Sol Weinstein
Celebrity Coaches MacLean Stevenson, Barbara Rhoades
Competitors Various

282   Celebrity Tennis
Syndicated
Program Type Sports Series
30 minutes. Weekly. Four guest celebrities in doubles matches.
Producers Joe Siegman, Don Gregory
Company 7–10 Productions
Distributor Syndicast Services, Inc.
Director Don Buccola
Host Bobby Riggs

283 **Challenge of the Sexes** CBS
Program Type Limited Sports Series
45 minutes. Sundays. Premiere date: 1/10/76.
Third season premiere: 1/8/78. Last show of se-
ries. 4/9/78 ("Best of Challenge of the Sexes").
Top male and female athletes competing against
each other in a variety of sports. Taped at Mis-
sion Viejo, Calif. and Mt. Tremblant, Quebec,
Canada. (*See also* "Celebrity Challenge of the
Sexes.")
Producers Jay Michaels, Rudy Tellez
Company Trans World International
Director Tony Verna
Host Vin Scully, Phyllis George

Challenge to Be Free *See* The CBS
Wednesday Night Movies

284 **A Charlie Brown Christmas** CBS
Program Type Animated Film Special
30 minutes. Premiere date: 12/9/65. Repeat
date: 12/12/77. Created by Charles M. Schulz.
Music by Vince Guaraldi. 12/12/77. Repeat
date:
Executive Producer Lee Mendelson
Producers Lee Mendelson, Bill Melendez
Company Lee Mendelson-Bill Melendez Produc-
tion in cooperation with United Features Syn-
dicate, Inc.
Director Bill Melendez
Writer Charles M. Schulz
Musical Director Vince Guaraldi
Music Supervisor John Scott Trotter
VOICES
Charlie Brown .... Peter Robbins
Lucy .... Tracy Stratford
Linus .... Christopher Shea

285 **A Charlie Brown Thanksgiving** CBS
Program Type Animated Film Special
30 minutes. Created by Charles M. Schulz. Mu-
sic composed by Vince Guaraldi. Premiere date:
11/20/73. Season premiere: 11/21/77.
Producers Lee Mendelson, Bill Melendez
Company A Lee Mendelson-Bill Melendez Pro-
duction
Directors Bill Melendez, Phil Roman
Writer Charles M. Schulz
Musical Director Vince Guaraldi
Music Supervisor John Scott Trotter
VOICES
Charlie Brown .... Todd Barbee
Linus .... Stephen Shea
Peppermint Patty .... Christopher Defaria
Lucy .... Robin Kohn
Sally .... Hilary Momberger
Marcie .... Jimmy Ahrens
Franklin .... Robin Reed

286 **Charlie's Angels** ABC
Program Type Crime Drama Series
60 minutes. Wednesdays. Premiere date:
9/22/76. Second season premiere: 9/14/77 (2-
hour special). Action-adventure about three private investigators working for a never-seen boss
who communicates with them by phone. Created
by Ivan Goff and Ben Roberts. Pilot aired
3/21/76 and 9/14/76. Music by Jack Elliott and
Allyn Ferguson. Filmed at 20th Century Fox
Studios and various Southern California loca-
tions.
Executive Producers Aaron Spelling, Leonard
Goldberg
Producers Ronald Austin, James Buchanan, Ed-
ward J. Lasko
Company A Spelling/Goldberg Production
Directors Various
Story Editors Jack V. Fogarty, Edward J. Lakso
Writers Various
Art Director Les Green
Cinematographer Richard L. Rawlings
Film Editors Leon Carrere, Jack Harnish, John
Woodcock
CAST
Sabrina Duncan .... Kate Jackson
Kelly Garrett .... Jaclyn Smith
Bosley .... David Doyle
Kris Munroe .... Cheryl Ladd
Charlie Townsend .... John Forsythe

287 **A Chat with Country Music Artist**
Doc Williams PBS
Program Type Documentary/Informational
Special
30 minutes. Premiere date: 7/23/77. Season
premiere: 4/10/78. An interview with Doc Wil-
liams.
Producer David R. Hopfer
Company WWVU-TV/Morgantown, W.Va.
Director David R. Hopfer
Interviewer Carl Fleischhauer

288 **Cher ... Special** ABC
Program Type Music/Comedy/Variety Special
60 minutes. Premiere date: 4/3/78.
Executive Producers Raymond Katz; Sandy Gal-
lin
Producer Art Fisher
Company Isis Production
Director Art Fisher
Writers Buz Kohan, Patricia Resnick, Rod War-
ren
Creative Consultant Joe Layton
Art Director Brian C. Bartholomew
Star Cher
Guest Stars Dolly Parton, Rod Stewart

The Cheyenne Social Club *See* CBS Special Movie Presentations

289   Chico and the Man   NBC
Program Type Comedy Series
30 minutes. Fridays. Premiere date: 9/13/74. Fourth season premiere: 9/16/77. Last Show: 7/21/78. Comedy series about a garage owner in the barrio of east Los Angeles and his young Chicano partner. Music by Jose Feliciano. Created by James Komack.
Executive Producer James Komack
Producers Jerry Ross, Charles Stewart
Company The Komack Company, Inc. in association with the Wolper Organization and NBC-TV
Director Jack Donohue
Executive Story Editor Gary Belkin
Writers Various
Art Director Roy Christopher
CAST
Ed Brown .... Jack Albertson
Della Rogers .... Della Reese
Louie Wilson .... Scatman Crothers
Raul .... Gabriel Melgar
Woody Rogers .... Franklin Ajaye

290   Chico and the Man (Daytime)   NBC
Program Type Comedy Series
30 minutes. Mondays–Fridays. Premiere date: 5/9/77. Morning reruns of the evening series. For credit information, *see* "Chico and the Man."

Chinatown *See* The CBS Tuesday Night Movies

291   CHiPs   NBC
Program Type Crime Drama Series
60 minutes. Thursdays. Premiere date: 9/15/77. Action series about work and play of two young motorcycle officers of the California Highway Patrol (CHP). Created by Rick Rosner.
Producer Rick Rosner
Company Rosner Television in association with MGM-TV and NBC-TV
Directors Various
Writers Various
Art Director Joseph M. Altadonna
CAST
Jon Baker .... Larry Wilcox
"Ponch" Poncherello .... Erik Estrada
Sgt. Joe Getraer ....Robert Pine

292   Choreography by Balanchine
Dance in America/Great Performances   PBS
Program Type Music/Dance Special
Work of renowed choreographer George Balanchine shown in two parts.

Choreography by Balanchine, Part I
60 minutes. Premiere date: 12/14/77. Performed by members of the New York City Ballet with introductions by Edward Villella. Program consists of three pieces: "Tzigane," with music by Ravel, featuring Suzanne Farrell and Peter Martins; the "Andante Movement from Divertimento No. 15," music by Mozart, with dancers Merrill Ashley and Robert Weiss; and "The Four Temperaments," music by Hindemuth, with dancers Merrill Ashley; Bart Cook; Daniel Duell; Colleen Neary; and Adam Luders.

Choreography by Balanchine, Part II
90 minutes. Premiere date: 12/21/77. Performed by members of the New York City Ballet with introductions by Edward Villella. Three selections from "Jewels" are featured, including excerpts from "Emeralds," music by Faure, with dancers Karin von Aroldingen and Sean Lavery; pas de deux from "Rubies," music by Stravinsky, danced by Patricia McBride and Robert Weiss; and pas de deux from "Diamonds," music by Tchaikovsky, danced by Suzanne Farrell and Peter Martins; "Stravinsky Violin Concerto," danced by Kay Mazzo, Peter Martins, Bart Cook and Karin von Aroldingen. Programs made possible by the National Endowment for the Arts, the Corporation for Public Broadcasting and the Exxon Corporation.
Executive Producer Jac Venza
Producers Emile Ardolino, Merrill Brockway
Company WNET-TV/New York
Director Merrill Brockway
Writer Arlene Croce

293   Christina's World   PBS
Program Type Documentary/Informational Special
60 minutes. Premiere date: 8/1/78. Film profile of Christina Olson, the woman who modeled for Andrew Wyeth
Producer Linda Salwasser
Company Hard Times Movie Company
Director Sonja Gilligan
Writer Sonja Gilligan

294   Christmas Around the World   PBS
Program Type Music/Dance Special
60 minutes. 12/24/77. A musical production originating simultaneously in seven countries coordinated by Britain's BBC. Program made possible by a grant from The Sun Company, Inc.
Company South Carolina Educational TV (U.S. segment)
Narrator Raymond Burr

295 **Christmas at Pops**   PBS
Program Type Music/Dance Special
60 minutes. Premiere date: 12/23/74. Repeat
date: 12/21/77. Arthur Fiedler conducts the
Boston Pops Orchestra and the Tanglewood Festival Chorus. Program funded by the Martin Marietta Corporation.
Producer Bill Cosel
Company WGBH-TV/Boston

296 **Christmas at Washington Cathedral**
                                            NBC
Program Type Religious/Cultural Special
60 minutes. Premiere date: 12/25/77. Live cov-
erage of the Christmas Day Service from the
Washington (D.C.) National Cathedral cele-
brated by the Rt. Rev. William F. Creighton.
Christmas message by the Very Rev. Francis B.
Sayre, Jr.
Producer Doris Ann
Company NBC Television Religious Programs
  Unit in association with the National Council
  of Churches
Director Richard Cox
Musical Director Dr. Paul Callaway
Organist William Stokes

297 **A Christmas Carol**
Famous Classic Tales   CBS
Program Type Animated Film Special
60 minutes. Premiere date: 12/13/70. Season
premiere: 12/10/77. Adaptation of the Christ-
mas story by Charles Dickens. Music composed
by Richard Bowden.
Producer Walter J. Hucker
Company Air Programs International
Writer Michael Robinson
Animation Director Zoran Janjic

298 **A Christmas Celebration**   PBS
Program Type Music/Dance Special
30 minutes. Premiere date: 12/20/76. Repeat
date: 12/22/77. The traditions and customs of
the Christmas season traced through music and
historical narrative. Music performed by the
Hofstra University Collegium Musicum and the
Renaissance Street Trio. Taped at the Cloisters in
New York City. Program made possible by a
grant from the Corporation for Public Broad-
casting.
Producers Gail Macandrew, Gail Jansen
Company WNET-TV/New York
Director Jon Merdin
Host Richard Kiley

299 **Christmas Miracle in Caulfield
U.S.A.**
NBC Monday Night at the Movies/NBC

World Premiere movie   NBC
Program Type Dramatic Special
2 hours. Premiere date: 12/26/77. Coal miners
try to reach safety after being trapped under-
ground by an explosion.
Company 20th Century-Fox
Director Jud Taylor
Writer Dalene Young
                    CAST
Mathew ....Mitchell Ryan
Johnny .... Kurt Russell
Arthur .... Andrew Prine
Rachael .... Barbara Babcock
Grampa .... John Carradine
Matilda .... Karen Lamm
Caufield .... Don Porter
Kelly .... Melissa Gilbert
Willie .... Bill McKinney

300 **Christmas, Rome 1977**   NBC
Program Type Religious/Cultural Special
75 minutes. Premiere date: 12/25/77 (12 mid-
night to 1:15 a.m.). The Christmas Eve Midnight
Mass from St. Peter's Basilica in Vatican City
celebrated by Pope Paul VI. English language
commentary by the Rev. Agnellus Andrew,
O.F.M.
Executive Producer Doris Ann
Producer Martin Hoade
Company NBC Television Religious Programs
  Unit in association with the Office for Film
  and Broadcasting of the United States Catho-
  lic Conference
Director Martin Hoade

301 **Christmastime with Mister Rogers**
                                            PBS
Program Type Children's Special
60 minutes. Premiere date: 12/20/77. Music,
dance and fantasy special with regulars from
"Mister Rogers' Neighborhood" Series. Program
made possible by a grant from The Sears-
Roebuck Foundation. (Closed captions for the
hearing impaired.)
Company Family Communications, Inc.
Star Fred Rogers
Regulars Francois Clemmons, Betty Aberlin,
  Joe Negri, Elsie Neal, Audrey Roth, David
  Newell, Betsy Nadas

302 **Christopher Closeup**   Syndicated
Program Type Religious/Cultural Series
30 minutes. Weekly. Premiere date: 10/52. Inter-
view-talk show originally produced by Father
James Keller, M.M., founder of the Christo-
phers. Interpreter for the hearing impaired:
Carol Tipton.
Executive Producer Jeanne Glynn
Producer Ceil Harriendorf
Company Christopher, Inc.

Christopher Closeup Continued
Director Father John Catoir
Hosts Jeanne Glynn, Father John Catoir

303   Chuck Barris Rah Rah Show   NBC
Program Type Music/Comedy/Variety Series
60 minutes. Tuesdays. Premiere date: 12/20/77
(as special). Series premiere: 2/28/78. Last show:
4/11/78. Taped at the Los Angeles Forum.
Executive Producer Chuck Barris
Producer Gene Banks
Company Chuck Barris Productions
Musical Director Milton Delugg
Stars The Bay City Rollers, Michelle Phillips,
Stephen Bishop, Chet Atkins, Jaye P. Morgan,
The Temptations, The Mills Brothers, Jamie
Farr, Linda Hopkins, Redd Foxx
Host Chuck Barris

304   Chulas Fronteras   PBS
Program Type Educational/Cultural Special
60 minutes. 8/1/78. Film depicting the lifestyle
and music of the people who live along the Tex-
as-Mexico border. Originally aired in 1977 as
part of "The Real World" series of anthropologi-
cal films.
Producer Chris Strachwitz
Company WNET/TV/New York
Director Les Blank
Choreographer Les Blank
Film Editor Les Blank

305   The CIA's Secret Army—Updated
CBS Reports   CBS
Program Type Documentary/Informational
Special
Premiere date: 1/24/78. Update on what hap-
pened to "The CIA's Secret Army" after the
6/10/77 broadcast investigating U.S. policies to-
ward Cuba.
Executive Producer Howard Stringer
Producer Jonnet Steinbaum
Company CBS News

306   Cinderella   PBS
Program Type Music/Dance Special
60 minutes. Premiere date: 12/25/76. Repeat
date: 12/18/77. The ballet by Sergei Prokofiev
performed by the Columbia City Ballet of South
Carolina with recorded music by the Moscow
Symphony.
Company South Carolina Educational Televi-
sion Network
Director Sidney Palmer
Production Designer Ann Brodie
CAST
Cinderella ....Mimi Wortham
Prince Charming .... Henry Everett
Fairy Godmother .... Lou Martin

307   Cindy
The ABC Friday Night Movie   ABC
Program Type TV Movie
2 hours. Premiere date: 3/24/78. An all-black
cast in a musical "Cinderella" story. Songs writ-
ten by Stan Daniels. Other music composed, ar-
ranged, and orchestrated by Howard Roberts.
Producers James L. Brooks; Stan Daniels; David
Davis; Ed. Weinberger
Company Charles Walters Productions
Director William H. Graham
Choreographer Donald McKayle
Costume Designer Sandra Stewart
Art Director Jim Vance
CAST
Cindy .... Charlaine Woodward
Father .... Scoey Mitchell
Stepmother .... Mae Mercer
Olive .... Nell-Ruth Carter
Venus .... Alaina Reed
Joe Prince ....Clifton Davis
Michael ....Cleavant Derricks
Niles Archer .... W. Benson Terry
Wilcox ....John Hancock

308   Clapper's   NBC
Program Type Comedy Series
30 minutes. Premiere date: 6/28/78. Pilot about
two secretaries in Clapper's Department Store in
Philadelphia.
Producer Patricia Nardo
Company Pheebo Productions and Columbia
Pictures TV
Director Hal Cooper
Writer Patricia Nardo
CAST
Secretaries ....Jennifer Perito, Leah Ayres
Boss .... Morgan Farley
New boss .... Larry Breeding

Class of '65 See Whatever Happened to
the Class of '65

Claudine See The ABC Summer Movie

309   Cleo Laine and John Dankworth
In Performance at Wolf Trap   PBS
Program Type Music/Dance Special
60 minutes. Premiere date: 11/15/76. Repeat
date: 9/14/78. Jazz concert by Cleo Laine, John
Dankworth and the Dankworth Ensemble (Ken
Clare, Brian Torff and Paul Hart) performed at
the Wolf Trap Farm Park for the Performing
Arts in Arlington, Va. Program made possible by
a grant from the Atlantic Richfield Company.
Executive Producer David Prowitt
Producer Ruth Leon
Company WETA-TV/Washington, D.C.
Director Stan Lathan
Conductor John Dankworth

Cleopatra Jones *See* ABC Tuesday Movie of the Week

310 The Clone Master
NBC World Premiere Movie/NBC Wednesday Movie of the Week   NBC
Program Type TV Movie
Two hours. Premiere date: 9/14/78. Biochemist clones 13 replicas of himself.
Director Don Medford
Writer John D. F. Black
CAST
Simon .... Art Hindle
Gussie .... Robyn Douglas
Ezra .... Ralph Bellamy
Salt ....John Van Dreelen
Harry .... Mario Roccuzzo
Bender .... Ed Lauter

311 Colgate-Dinah Shore Winners Circle Golf Championship   NBC
Program Type Sports Special
Live coverage of final round from the Mission Hills Country Club in Rancho Mirage, Calif. 4/1/78 and 4/2/78
Executive Producer Don Olhmeyer
Company NBC Sports
Producer Larry Cirillo
Host Dinah Shore
Commentators Jim Simpson, Carol Mann, Susan O'Connor, Marlene Floyd, Cathy Duggan, Debbie Meisterlin, Arnold Palmer

312 Colgate European Open   PBS
Program Type Sports Special
2 hours. 8/5/78 and 8/6/78. Top professional women golfers compete at Sunningdale Golf Club in Berks, England.
Company KERA-TV/Dallas-Fort Worth
Anchor Carol Mann

313 Colgate Hall of Fame Golf Classic
ABC
Program Type Sports Special
90 minutes, 8/26/78. Two hours, 8/27/78. Live coverage of the final two rounds of the 1978 Colgate Hall of Fame Golf Classic from the Pinehurst Country Club, North Carolina.
Executive Producer Roone Arledge
Producer Chuck Howard
Company ABC Sports
Director Jim Jennett, Andy Sidaris
Commentators Jim McKay, Peter Alliss
Expert Commentator Dave Marr
Reporters Bob Rosburg, Vern Lundquist

314 Colgate Triple Crown LPGA Match Play Championship   PBS
Program Type Sports Special
4 hours. 1/28/78 and 1/29/78. Live coverage of semi-finals and finals women's golf tournament from Mission Hills Country Club, Rancho Mirage, California. Program made possible by a grant from Sarah Coventry.
Company KERA-TV/Dallas-Fort Worth

315 College Basketball '78 (NCAA Basketball)   NBC
Program Type Limited Sports Series
Live coverage of 90 regular-season national and regional college basketball games. Saturdays and Sundays. Season premiere: 1/8/78. Last regular season game: 3/5/78. Dick Enberg; Billy Packer and Al McGuire cover national games.
Executive Producer Scotty Connal
Producers Various
Company NBC Sports in association with TVS
Directors Various
Announcers Merle Harmon, John Ferguson, Dick Enberg, Jim Karavelas, Jay Randolph, Al Meltzer, Monte Moore, Ross Porter, Connie Alexander, Phil Samp, Tom Hedrick, Frank Glieber, Bill O'Donnell, Marv Albert, Curt Gowdy, Les Keiter
Color Analysts John Andariese, Billy Packer, Ron Pinkney, Omar Williams, Fred Taylor, Joe Dean, Gary Thompson, Tom Hawkins, Bill Strannigan, Rudy Davalos, Larry Conley, Bucky Walters, Dick Stockton, Steve Grad, Gary Griffith
Special Commentator Al McGuire

316 College Can Be Killing   PBS
Program Type Documentary/Informational Special
60 minutes. Premiere date: 6/27/78. An investigative report on the way universities deal with student stress, anxiety and potential suicide. Program made possible in part by a grant from the Van Amerigen Foundation, Inc.
Producer Michael Hirsh
Company WTTW-TV/Chicago

317 College Football '78: It's Anybody's Ballgame   ABC
Program Type Sports Special
60 minutes. Premiere date: 9/1/77. Season premiere: 9/2/78. Special focusing on the top college football teams in the six NCAA geographical regions.
Executive Producer Roone Arledge
Producers Terry O'Neil; Keith Jackson
Company ABC Sports
Director Robert Riger
Host Keith Jackson

318   College Football '77   ABC
Program Type Limited Sports Series
60 minutes. Sundays. Season premiere: 9/11/77.
Last show of season: 11/27/77 13-week series.
Highlights of the important collegiate games and
players of the week.
Executive Producer Dennis Cryder
Producer Kemper Peacock
Company NCAA Films
Director Kemper Peacock
Host Bill Flemming

319   Colonial National Invitation   CBS
Program Type Sports Special
Final two rounds of the $200,000 Colonial Na-
tional Invitation from the Colonial Country Club
in Fort Worth, Tex. 5/13/78 and 5/14/78.
Producer Frank Chirkinian
Company CBS Television Network Sports
Directors Bob Dailey, Frank Chirkinian
Commentators Vin Scully, Jack Whitaker, Pat
Summerall, Frank Glieber, Ben Wright, Ken
Venturi

320   Colorado C.I.   CBS
Program Type Dramatic Special
60 minutes. Premiere date: 5/26/78. Detective
drama pilot. Music by Dave Grusin.
Executive Producer Philip Saltzman
Producer Christopher Morgan
Company Woodruff Production in association
with Quinn Martin Productions
Director Virgil Vogel
Writer Robert W. Lenski
CAST
Mark Gunnison .... John Elerick
Pete Gunnison .... Marshall Colt
Hoyt Gunnison .... L. Q. Jones
Chris Morrison .... Laurette Spang
Carla Winters .... Christine Belford
David Royce .... David Hedison
Niles .... Bill Lucking
Piper Collins .... Chris De Lisle
Capt. Cochran .... Van Williams
Stan Cusek .... Randy Powell
Frank Bannock .... Lou Frizzell
Kessler .... John Karlen
George Hopkins .... George Wallace
Phone Operator ....Joan Roberts
Hazel Bicker .... Anne H. Bradley
Murphy .... Michael Palmer
Cop .... Bill McLaughlin
First County Deputy ....Richard Jamison
Second Deputy .... Dick Newton

321   Columbo
The Big Event/NBC Movie of the Week/NBC
Saturday Night at the Movies   NBC
Program Type Crime Drama Series
Broadcast irregularly as part of the "NBC Movie
of the Week" and "NBC Saturday Night at the

Movies." Premiere date: 9/15/71. Seventh season premiere: 11/21/77. Original pilots: "The
Conspirators" shown 5/13/78, repeated 9/1/78;
"How to Dial a Murder" shown 4/15/78, repeated 8/7/78; "Make Me a Perfect Murder"
shown 2/25/78, repeated 7/9/78; "Murder Under Glass" shown 1/30/78, repeated 7/31/78;
and "Try and Catch Me" shown 11/21/77, repeated 6/23/78. Created by Richard Levinson
and William Link. Series revolves around a slow-
moving detective in a rumpled raincoat.
Producer Richard Alan Simmons
Company Universal Television in association
with NBC-TV
Directors Various
Writers Various
CAST
Lt. Columbo .... Peter Falk

Come Back Charleston Blue See the CBS Saturday Night Movie

322   Come Back Little Sheba
NBC Saturday Night at the Movies   NBC
Program Type TV Movie
2 hours. Premiere date: 12/31/77. New adapta-
tion of play by William Inge about the sad and
troubled lives of a middle-age couple.
Executive Producer Derek Granger
Producer Sir Laurence Olivier
Company Granada Television, Ltd. in associa-
tion with NBC-TV
Director Silvio Narizzano
CAST
Lola .... Joanne Woodward
Doc ....Sir Laurence Olivier
Marie ....Carrie Fisher
Turk .... Nicholas Campbell
Mrs. Coffman ....Patience Collier
Bruce .... Jay Benedict
Postman .... Bill Hootkins

323   The Comedy Company   CBS
Program Type TV Movie
2 hours. Premiere date: 7/21/78. An ex-
comedian fights to keep a failing nightclub work-
shop for aspiring young comics.
Executive Producer Jerry Adler
Producer Merrit Malloy
Company MGM Television
Director Lee Philips
Writer Lee Kalcheim
CAST
Barney Bailey .... Jack Albertson
Jake .... Abe Vigoda
Russell Dodd ....Lawrence-Hilton Jacobs
Paul Lester .... Michael Brandon
Linda Gray ....Susan Sullivan
Roger Gray .... Howard Hesseman
Lester Dietz ....Herb Edelman
Ellen Dietz .... Joyce Van Patten

Comedy Team Ernst Emling, Jeff Doucette
Regulars Don Calfa, Christopher Roberts
Guest Star George Burns

324 Comedy Time   NBC
Program Type Comedy Series
30 minutes. Premiere date: 4/21/78. Series of comedy pilots. Shows aired are: "The Last Chance," "Space Force," and "Wild About Harry." (*See* titles for credits.)

325 The Concord String Quartet Plays Bartok and Haydn   PBS
Program Type Music/Dance Special
60 minutes. Premiere date: 12/4/77. Program made possible by a grant from the National Endowment for the Arts.
Producer Barry G. Baker
Company New Hampshire Public Television
Director Barry G. Baker
Violins Mark Sokol, Andrew Jennings
Viola John Kochanowski
Cello Norman Fischer

326 A Connecticut Rabbit in King Arthur's Court   CBS
Program Type Animated Film Special
30 minutes. Premiere date: 2/23/78. Music composed and conducted by Dean Elliott. Animated story of Bugs Bunny in King Arthur's Court.
Producer Chuck Jones
Company Chuck Jones Enterprises
Director Chuck Jones
Voice Characters Mel Blanc

327 A Connecticut Yankee in King Arthur's Court
Once Upon a Classic   PBS
Program Type Dramatic Special
60 minutes. Premiere date: 5/23/78. Classic tale by Mark Twain. Presented by WQED-TV/Pittsburgh and McDonald's Local Restaurants Assn.
Executive Producer Jay Rayvid
Producers Jay Rayvid, Chiz Schultz, Shep Greene.
Company Time-Life Television/BBC-TV
Writer Stephen Dick
Host Bill Bixby
CAST
King Arthur .... Richard Basehart
Hank Morgan ....Paul Rudd
Merlin .... Roscoe Lee Browne
Lady Alisandre .... Tovah Feldshuh

Conrack *See* the CBS Saturday Night Movie

328 The Consul
Great Performances   PBS
Program Type Music/Dance Special
2 hours. Premiere date: 3/29/78. Pulitzer-prize winning opera by Gian Carlo Menotti taped at the Spoleto Festival U.S.A. in Charleston, South Carolina. Made possible by a grant from Exxon Corporation and support from PBS stations.
Executive Producers Jac Venza, Charles S. Morris
Company South Carolina ETV Network, WNET-TV/New York and Unitel
Musical Director Christopher Keene
Conductor Christopher Keene
CAST
Magda Sorel .... Marvalee Cariaga
Husband ....David Clatworthy
Additional Cast Sandra Walker, Fredda Rakusin, Vern Shinall, Jerold Sizna

329 Consumer Survival Kit   PBS
Program Type Educational/Cultural Series
30 minutes. Wednesdays. Premiere date: 1/9/75. Fourth season premiere: 1/16/78. Consumer series with a variety format. Regular features include: consumer update, con of the week, and survivor of the week. Program funded by the Corporation for Public Broadcasting, the Ford Foundation and Public Television Stations.
Executive Producer Donna Faw
Producer Anne Jarrell
Company Maryland Center for Public Broadcasting
Director Tom Barnett
Host Lary Lewman
Regulars Rhea Feikin, Fran Johanson, Bob Smith

330 Continuing Creation   NBC
Program Type Religious/Cultural Special
60 minutes. Premiere date: 2/19/78. Documentary examining the effects of scientific discoveries on religion filmed in Italy, England and the United States. of Churches
Executive Producer Doris Ann
Company NBC Television Religious Programs Unit in association with the National Council of Churches
Director Joseph Vadala
Writer Philip Scharper
Cinematographer Joseph Vadala
Film Editor Ed Williams
Narrator Douglass Watson
NCC Representative Rev. D. W. McClurken

331 Contract on Cherry Street
The Big Event   NBC
Program Type Dramatic Special
2 hours. Premiere date: 11/19/77. Repeat date: 8/1/78. A police inspector operates outside of

Contract on Cherry Street *Continued*
established procedures to break an organized
crime ring. Based on a novel by Philip Rosen-
berg.
Executive Producer Renee Valente
Producer Hugh Benson
Company Columbia Pictures Television produc-
tion in association with NBC-TV
Director W. E. Graham
CAST
Frank Hovannes .... Frank Sinatra
Emily Hovannes ....Verna Bloom
Ron Polito .... Harry Guardino
Roberto Obregon ....Henry Silva
Ernie Weinberg .... Martin Balsam
Lou Savage .... Michael Nouri
Tommy Sinardos ....Jay Black
Jack Kittens ....Richard Ward
Paul Gold .... Sol Weiner
Al Palmini .... James Luisi
Otis Washington .... Johnny Barnes
Flo Weinberg .... Estelle Omens
Cecelia .... Ruth Rivera
Harry Diamond .... Nicky Blair

332   The Conversation *See* The CBS
Wednesday Night Movies

**333   A Conversation with Archbishop
John R. Quinn**   NBC
Program Type Religious/Cultural Special
60 minutes. Premiere date: 1/22/78. Philip
Scharper interviews John R. Quinn.
Executive Producer Doris Ann
Producer Martin Hoade
Company NBC Television Religious Programs
   Unit in association with the Office for Film
   and Broadcasting of the U.S. Catholic Confer-
   ence
Director Martin Hoade

**334   A Conversation with Dr. Chaim
Potok**
Eternal Light   NBC
Program Type Religious/Cultural Special
60 minutes. Premiere date: 11/6/77. Dr. Chaim
Potok interviewed by Edwin Newman.
Producer Martin Hoade
Producer for Seminary Milton E. Krents
Company NBC Television Religious Programs
   Unit in association with Jewish Theological
   Seminary of America
Director Martin Hoade

**335   A Conversation with Dr. Willard
Gaylin**   NBC
Program Type Religious/Cultural Special
60 minutes. Premiere date: 7/9/78. Interview
with Dr. Willard Gaylin.
Company NBC Religious Programs Unit in co-

operation with the National Council of
Churches
Correspondent Betty Rollin

336   A Conversation with Eric Sevareid
                    CBS
Program Type News Special
60 minutes. Premiere date: 12/13/77. Charles
Kuralt interviews Eric Sevareid about his four
decades of journalism.
Executive Producer Perry Wolff
Company CBS News
Film Editor Nobuko Organesoff
Photographers Robert Clemens, Isadore Bleck-
   man, Robert Peterson
Researcher Emily Lodge

**337   A Conversation with Howard
Thurman**   PBS
Program Type Religious/Cultural Special
60 minutes. 2/26/78. Howard Thurman interviewed by Landrum Bolling. Program made possible in part by a grant from the Lilly Endowment.
Company WGBH-TV/Boston

**338   A Conversation With Rabbi Louis
Finkelstein**
Eternal Light   NBC
Program Type Religious/Cultural Special
30 minutes. Premiere date: 10/3/76. Repeat
date: 10/3/77. A discussion with Rabbi Louis
Finkelstein in honor of Yom Kippur.
Producer Doris Ann
Company NBC Television Religious Programs
   Unit in association with the Jewish Theologi-
   cal Seminary of America
Director Robert Priaulx
Moderator Sol M. Linowitz

**339   A Conversation with Rabbi Stanley
J. Schachter**
Eternal Light   NBC
Program Type Religious/Cultural Special
30 minutes. Premiere date: 12/4/77. Rabbi Stan-
ley J. Schachter interviewed by Martin Book-
span.
Producer Martin Hoade
Producer for Seminary Milton E. Krents
Company NBC Television Religious Programs
   Unit in association with Jewish Theological
   Seminary of America
Director Martin Hoade

340 A Conversation with Robert N. Bellah NBC
Program Type Religious/Cultural Special
60 minutes. Premiere date: 9/17/78. University of California (Berkeley) sociologist Robert N. Bellah interviewed by Edwin Newman.
Executive Producer Doris Ann
Producer Martin Hoade
Director Martin Hoade
Company NBC Television Religious Programs Unit with the Communication Commission of the National Council of Churches
NCC Representative Rev. Dave Pomeroy

341 Copland Conducts Copland
Music in America/Great Performances PBS
Program Type Music/Dance Special
60 minutes. Premiere date: 3/17/76. Repeat date: 7/8/78. First "Music in America" concert. Aaron Copland conducts the Los Angeles Philharmonic Orchestra in a selection of his own works. Roger Wagner directs the Los Angeles Master Chorale. Taped at the Dorothy Chandler Pavilion in the Music Center in Los Angeles, Calif. January 1976. Program funded by a grant from the Exxon Corporation.
Executive Producers Jac Venza, Klaus Hallig
Producer David Griffiths
Company WNET-TV/New York and International Television Trading Corporation
Conductor Aaron Copland
Guest Soloist Benny Goodman

342 Coppelia
Live from Lincoln Center/Great Performances PBS
Program Type Music/Dance Special
3 hours. Premiere date: 1/31/78. Ballet by New York City Ballet danced by Patricia McBride and Helgi Tomasson. Program made possible by grants from Exxon Corporation, the National Endowment for the Arts, and the Corporation for Public Broadcasting.
Producer John Goberman
Company Lincoln Center with WNET-TV/New York
Choreographers George Balanchine, Alexandra Danilova
Host Robert MacNeil

343 The Cops and Robin
The Big Event NBC
Program Type Dramatic Special
2 hours. Premiere date: 3/28/78. Drama about a robot programmed to be the perfect cop.
Executive Producers Tony Wilson, Gary Damsker
Producer William Kayden
Company Paramount Television

Director Allen Reisner
Writers John T. Dugan, Brad Radnitz, Dawning Forsyth
CAST
Joe Cleaver .... Ernest Borgnine
John Haven .... Michael Shannon
Sgt. Bundy .... John Amos
Robin .... Natasha Ryan
Dr. Alice Alcott .... Carol Lynley
Marge Loren .... Elizabeth Farley
Dutton .... Terry Kiser
Richard .... James York
Tyler .... Gene Rutherford

344 'Copter Kids PBS
Program Type Children's Special
60 minutes. Premiere date: 8/17/78. A man and his children use a helicopter to chase cattle rustlers. Presented by WQED-TV/Pittsburgh.
Executive Producer John B. Rabourne
Producer Ronald Spencer
Company Pacesetter Productions for the Children's Film Foundation
Director Ronald Spencer
Writer Patricia Latham
CAST
Capt. Peters ....Eric Fowlds
Liz ....Sophie Neville
Jill .... Sophie Ward
Bill .... Jonathan Scott-Taylor

345 Cosmic Christmas Syndicated
Program Type Religious/Cultural Special – Animated Film Special
30 minutes. Premiere date: 12/7/77. Christmas story about a small boy, his pet goose and a space ship. Music written and performed by Sylvia Tyson.
Executive Producer Jeffrey Kirsch
Producers Michael Hirsh, Patrick Loubert
Company Nelvana Productions, Viacom
Director Clive Smith
Writers Ida Nelson Fruet, Martin Lavut, Laura Paull, Ken Sobol

346 Cotton Bowl CBS
Program Type Sports Special
3 hours. Live coverage of the Cotton Bowl football game between The University of Texas and The University of Notre Dame, in Dallas, Tex. 1/2/78.
Producer Bob Stenner
Company CBS Television Network Sports
Director Bob Dailey
Announcer Lindsey Nelson
Analyst Paul Hornung

347   **Cotton Bowl Festival Parade**   CBS
Program Type Parades/Pageants/Awards
Special
90 minutes. 1/2/78. Live coverage of the 22nd
annual parade from Dallas, Texas.
Executive Producer Mike Gargiulo
Producer Mike Gargiulo
Director Mike Gargiulo
Parade Hosts William Conrad, Ja'Net DuBois,
and Shields and Yarnell

348   **Count Dracula**
Festival '78   PBS
Program Type Dramatic Special
3 hours. Wednesdays. shown: 3/1/78, 3/8/78
and 3/15/78. Entire show on 3/18/78 as part of
Marathon Viewing of Festival '78. Classic horror
story by English author Bram Stoker. Program
made possible by a grant from Exxon Corpora-
tion and member PBS stations.
Executive Producer Jac Venza
Producers Ann Blumenthal, Morris Barry
Company WNET-TV/New York and BBC-TV
Writer Gerald Savory
CAST
Count Dracula ....Louis Jourdan
Jonathan Harker ....Bosco Hogan
Mina Westenra .... Judi Bowker
Lucy .... Susan Penhaligon
Dr. Seward .... Mark Burns
Quincey ....Richard Barnes
Prof. Van Helsing ....Frank Finlay

349   **Country Corner**   PBS
Program Type Music/Dance Special
30 minutes. Premiere date: 9/14/77. Repeat
date: 12/27/77. Documentary on the centuries-
old tradition of contra-dance, originally brought
to America from the British Isles and now flour-
ishing in New England. Features Dudley Lauf-
man and the Canterbury Orchestra and the Ed
Larken Dancers. Program made possible by
grants from the National Endowment for the
Arts and the Corporation for Public Broadcasting.
Company WITF-TV/Hershey
Cinematographer Bob Fiore
Choreographers Bob Fiore, Dick Nevell

350   **Country Moods**   PBS
Program Type Music/Dance Special
30 minutes. Premiere date: 7/23/77. Season
premiere: 4/8/78. A concert by Doc Williams
and The Border Riders of Wheeling, W.Va.:
Chickie Williams, vocalist; Karen McKenzie, vocalist; Roy Scott, vocalist, fiddler and guitarist;
Randy Bethune, banjoist; Marion Mar tin, cor-
dovoxist; Billy Miedel, drummer.
Producer David R. Hopfer

Company WWVU-TV/Morgantown, W.Va.
Director David R. Hopfer

351   **Country Music Association Awards**
CBS
Program Type Parades/Pageants/Awards
Special
90 minutes. Eleventh annual awards presentation
10/10/78 from the Grand Ole Opry House in
Nashville, Tenn.
Producer Robert Precht
Director Walter C. Miller
Writers Donald K. Epstein, Martin Ragaway
Musical Director Bill Walker
Art Director Bill Bohnert
Performers/Presenters Bill Anderson, Chet At-
kins, June Carter Cash, Roy Clark, Jerry
Clower, Dave and Sugar, Danny Davis and the
Nashville Brass, Mac Davis, Crystal Gayle,
Merle Haggard, Loretta Lynn, Barbara Man-
drell, Ronnie Milsap, Dolly Parton, Minnie
Pearl, Charley Pride, Jerry Reed, Kenny Rog-
ers, The Statler Brothers, Mel Tillis, Conway
Twitty, Don Williams and Tammy Wynette.

352   **Country Night of the Stars**   NBC
Program Type Music/Comedy/Variety Special
2 hours. Premiere date: 5/23/78. Country music
extravaganza.
Executive Producers Joseph Cates, Gilbert Cates
Producer Chet Hagan
Company Cates Brothers Company Production
Director Ivan Cury
Writers Chet Hagan, Frank Slocum
Musical Director Bill Walker
Hosts Charley Pride, Tennessee Ernie Ford
Guest Stars Johnny Paycheck, Barbara Man-
drell, Bill Anderson, Jimmy Dean, Gary Stew-
art, La Costa, Dave and Sugar Trio, Tom T.
Hall, Ronnie Milsap, Jeannie C. Riley, John
McEwen, Freddy Fender, Bobby Bare, George
Jones, Anne Murray, Conway Twitty

353   **Country Night of the Stars II** NBC
Program Type Music/Comedy/Variety Special
2 hours. Premiere date: 5/30/78.
Producer Chet Hagan
Company Cates Brothers Company Production
Director Ivan Cury
Writers Chet Hagan, Frank Slocum
Musical Director Bill Walker
Hosts Crystal Gayle, Eddy Arnold
Guest Stars Roger Miller, Asleep at the Wheel,
Jim Ed Brown, Helen Cornelius, Charlie Dan-
iels Band, Jimmie Davis, Lester Flatt, Nash-
ville Brass, Janie Fricke, Don Gibson, the
Kendalls, Pee Wee King, Ronnie McDowell,
Patti Page, Ray Price, Eddie Rabbitt, Dottie
West

354 Country Tales: The Miracle of Brother Humphrey
Festival '78   PBS
Program Type Comedy Special
30 minutes. Premiere date: 3/6/78. Comic film about the trials and tribulations of a monastery misfit.
Company BBC
Director Brian Miller
Narrator Hedley Goodall
CAST
Brother Humphrey .... Tony Robinson

355 The Courage and the Passion
NBC Saturday Night at the Movies   NBC
Program Type TV Movie
2 hours. Premiere date: 5/27/78. Drama concerning an Air Force colonel involved in a crisis on an isolated desert base. Created by Vince Edwards.
Producer Jay Daniel
Company David Gerber production in association with Columbia Pictures Television
Director John L. Lewellyn Moxey
Writer Richard Fielder
CAST
Col. Joe Agajanian .... Vince Edwards
Col. Jim Gardener .... Don Meredith
Capt. Kathy Wood .... Linda Foster
Brett Gardener .... Laraine Stephens
Lt. Lisa Rydell .... Trisha Noble
Sgt. Tom Wade .... Desi Arnaz, Jr.
Tracy .... Donna Wilkes
Gen. Sam Brewster .... Monty Hall
Tuyet Berkle .... Irene Yah-Ling Sun
Airman Donald Berkle .... Robert Ginty

356 The Court-Martial of George Armstrong Custer
Hallmark Hall of Fame   NBC
Program Type Dramatic Special
2 hours. Premiere date: 12/1/77. Adaptation of novel by Douglas C. Jones tells what might have happened if the military leader had survived the massacre at Little Bighorn.
Producer Norman Rosemont
Company Norman Rosemont Production in association with Warner Bros. Television
Director Glenn Jordon
Writer John Gay
CAST
Allan Jacobson .... Brian Keith
Maj. Asa B. Gardiner .... Ken Howard
Maj. Gen. Schofield .... Stephen Elliott
George Armstrong Custer .... James Olson
Elizabeth Custer .... Blythe Danner
Gen. William Sherman .... J. D. Cannon
Gen. Philip Sheridan .... Nicolas Coster
Maj. Reno .... William Daniels
President Grant .... Richard Dysart
Gen. Terry .... Biff McGuire
Mrs. Slaughter .... Susan Sullivan
Jefferson Quinton .... Anthony Zerbe

Chief Goes Ahead .... Dehl Berti
Wadkins .... James Blendick
Col. Miles .... John Cunningham
Lt. Bradley .... Duncan Gamble
Col. Williams .... Rick Goldman
Chambers .... John Horn
Col. Gibbon .... Laurence Hugo
Aide to Custer .... Christopher Pennock
Capt. Smith .... Lane Smith

357 Cousteau/Oasis in Space   PBS
Program Type Science/Nature Series
30 minutes. Saturdays. Premiere date: 11/13/76. Season premiere: 1/2/78. Six programs about the global environment. Series made possible by grants from the Corporation for Public Broadcasting, the Ford Foundation and Public Television Stations.
Executive Producer Philippe Cousteau
Producer Andrew W. Solt
Company The Cousteau Society in association with Andrew Solt Productions and in cooperation with KAMU-TV/College Station, Texas
Directors Philippe Cousteau, Andrew W. Solt
Writer Andrew W. Solt
Host Philippe Cousteau

358 The Cousteau Odyssey   PBS
Program Type Science/Nature Series
60 minutes. Premiere date: 11/22/77. Underwater explorations by Jacques Cousteau and his crew in the ship "Calypso." Programs shown in the 1977-78 season are: "Calypso's Search for Atlantis", "Calypso's Search for the Britannic," (*See* individual titles for credits.)

359 CPO Sharkey   NBC
Program Type Comedy Series
30 minutes. Fridays. Premiere date: 12/1/76. Season premiere: 10/21/77. Last show: 7/28/78. Comedy about a chief petty officer in command of a training unit at the San Diego Naval Training Center. Created by Aaron Ruben.
Executive Producer Aaron Ruben
Producer Gene Marcione
Company R & R Production
Directors Various
Writers Various
CAST
CPO Sharkey .... Don Rickles
Chief Robinson .... Harrison Page
Seaman Pruitt .... Peter Isacksen
Daniels .... Jeff Hollis
Kowalski .... Tom Ruben
Skolnick .... David Landsberg
Lt. Whipple .... Jonathan Daly
Rodriguez .... Richard Beauchamp
Capt. "Buck" Buckner .... Richard X. Slattery
Apocada .... Philip Sims

Crescendo *See* ABC Tuesday Movie of the Week

360   Crisis at Sun Valley
NBC Movie of the Week   NBC
Program Type TV Movie
2 hours. Premiere date: 3/29/78. Double feature about a sheriff and his deputy in a contemporary ski resort. "Outward Bound" and "The Vanishing Kind" were filmed in Sun Valley, Idaho, and Sawtooth National Forest.
Director Paul Stanley
Writers Carl Gottlieb , Alvin Boretz
CAST
Sheriff Stedman .... Dale Robinette
Deputy Archie .... Taylor Lacher
Buchanan ....Bo Hopkins
Sheila .... Tracy Brooks Swope
Poole .... Paul Brinegar
Derry ....Jason Johnson
Hubbard .... John McIntyre
Thorndike .... Ken Swofford
Eva .... Susan Adams
Jenny ....Julie Parsons

361   The Critical List
The Big Event/NBC Monday Night at the
Movies   NBC
Program Type Dramatic Special
2 hours each. Premiere dates: 9/11/78 and 9/12/78. Based on the novel by Marshall Goldberg. Drama about a hospital director who fights a local battle for his staff and a national battle against government officials involved in a federal health funds fraud.
Director Lou Antonio
Writer Jerry McNeely
CAST
Dan Lassiter .... Lloyd Bridges
Nick Sloan .... Robert Wagner
Charles Sprague ....Buddy Ebsen
Lem Harper .... Louis Gossett Jr.
Angela Adams .... Barbara Parkins
Matt Kinsella .... Richard Basehart
Jimmy Regosi .... Pat Harrington
Kris Lassiter .... Melinda Dillon
Nels Freiborg .... Ken Howard

362   Crockett's Victory Garden   PBS
Program Type Educational/Cultural Series
30 minutes. Saturdays/Sundays. Premiere date: 4/11/76. Third season premiere: 6/10/78. Weekly series on gardening of plants and vegetables. Series made possible by a grant from Public Television Stations.
Producer Russ Morash
Company WGBH-TV/Boston
Director Russ Morash
Writer James Underwood Crockett
Host James Underwood Crockett
Gardener Gary Mottau

363   The Cross-Wits   Syndicated
Program Type Game/Audience Participation Series
30 minutes. Mondays–Fridays. Premiere date: 12/75. Third season premiere: 11/77. Two teams of three players each try to guess words in a crossword puzzle. Four guest celebrities weekly.
Executive Producer Ralph Edwards
Producers Ray Horl, Ed Bailey
Company Gemini Productions
Distributor Metromedia Producers Corporation
Director Richard Gottlieb
Host Jack Clark
Announcer John Harlan

364   The Crowded Life   PBS
Program Type Documentary/Informational Special
90 minutes. Premiere date: 1/17/78. Repeat date: 9/7/78. Eric Hoffer is profiled. Program made possible by a grant from Inez Andreas.
Company WPBT-TV/Miami
Executive Producer Shep Morgan
Producer Jeanne Wolf
Director Shep Morgan
Writer Jeanne Wolf
Narrator Richard Basehart

365   Cruise into Terror
The ABC Friday Night Movie   ABC
Program Type TV Movie
2 hours. Premiere date: 2/3/78. Discovery of an ancient sarcophagus on a Caribbean cruise ship.
Producers Aaron Spelling, Douglas S. Cramer
Company Aaron Spelling Productions
Director Bruce Kessler
Writer Michael Braverman
CAST
Simon .... Dirk Benedict
Matt .... Frank Converse
Rev. Mather ....John Forsythe
Neal Barry .... Christopher George
Sandra Barry ....Lynda Day George
Judy .... JoAnn Harris
Lil Mather .... Lee Meriwether
Dr. Bakkun .... Ray Milland
Andy ....Hugh O'Brian
Marilyn .... Stella Stevens
Debbie .... Hilary Thompson
Bennett .... Marshall Thompson

366   The Cruise of the Courageous
The Winners   CBS
Program Type Children's Special
30 minutes. Premiere date: 2/9/78. Three teenagers attempt a rescue at sea. Special effects by J. B. Jones. Music by Michael Sahl.
Executive Producer Richard Slote
Producer Victor Kanefsky
Company Signet Productions

Director Richard Slote
Writer Richard Slote
Film Editor Victor Kanefsky
CAST
Mark .... Alan Amick
Steve .... Dennis McKiernan
Amy .... Kristen Vigard
Fisherman .... Mal Jones

Cry the Beloved Country *See* PBS Movie Theater

367 Cuba-Marquette Basketball Game
NBC
Program Type Sports Special
Coverage of basketball game between National Team of Cuba and champion Marquette Warriors 11/12/77 from the Milwaukee Arena.
Company NBC Sports and TVS
Play-by-play Announcer Dick Enberg
Analyst Billy Packer
Half-time Reporter Al McGuire

368 Curse of the Black Widow
The ABC Friday Night Movie   ABC
Program Type TV Movie
2 hours. Premiere date: 9/16/77. Drama about the search for a killer whose victims are wrapped in a spider-like web. Music by Robert Cobert.
Producer Steven North
Company A Dan Curtis Production for ABC Circle Films
Director Dan Curtis
Writers Robert Blees, Earl W. Wallace
Art Director Phil Barber
Film Editor Leon Carrere
Special Effects Roy Downey
CAST
Mark Higbie .... Anthony Franciosa
Leigh Lockwood .... Donna Mills
Laura Lockwood .... Patty Duke Astin
Mrs. Lockwood .... June Lockhart
Olga .... June Allyson
Ragsdale .... Max Gail
Aspa .... Jeff Corey
Flaps .... Roz Kelly
Lazlo Cozart .... Sid Caesar
Lt. Conti .... Vic Morrow
Carlo Lenzi .... Michael DeLano
Jeff Wallace .... Robert Burton
Watchman .... Bryan O'Byrne
Jennifer .... Rosanna Locke
Morgue Attendant .... Robert Nadder
Gymnast .... Tracy Curtis

Custer of the West *See* The ABC Sunday Night Movie

369 Daddy I Don't Like It Like This
The CBS Wednesday Night Movies   CBS
Program Type TV Movie
2 hours. Premiere date: 7/12/78. Concerns mental child abuse in a family in New York City. Music by David Shire. Filmed in the New York City borough of Queens.
Executive Producer Merrit Malloy
Producer Jay Daniel
Director Adell Aldrich
Writer Burt Young
CAST
Carol Agnelli .... Talia Shire
Rocco Agnelli .... Burt Young
Peter .... Doug McKeon
Margaret .... Erica Yohn
Sister St. Theresa .... Tresa Hughes
Michael .... Bobby Cassidy
Girl in hotel room .... Melanie Griffith
Tommy .... Jamie Aff
Marge .... Constance McCashion
Mother Superior .... Beverly May
Bob .... Lee Weaver
Store owner .... Frank Robles
Morty .... Morton Lewin
Mill worker .... Jessica James
Florist .... John Wylie
Tony .... Raymond Barry
Jennifer .... Vicky Perry
Alice .... Diane Stilwell
Milkman .... Clinton Allmon
Helen .... Jennifer Cooke
Joey .... Bob Mora
Johnny .... Wayne Harding
Giovanni .... Adam Monti
Juanita .... Susie Cebulski
First boy .... Matthew Anton
First girl .... Chris Langner
First gang boy .... Shawn Firtell
Second gang boy .... G. Adam Gifford
Third gang boy .... Eric Ohanien
Giovanni .... Larry Silvestri
Class child .... Brenden Ward

370 The Dain Curse
CBS
Program Type Limited Series
6 hours, 5/22/78–5/24/78. Based on the novel by Dashiell Hammett. Developed for television by Robert W. Lenski. Music by Charles Gross. Filmed in Sheltery Island, NY; Easton, Pa; and New York City
Executive Producer Bob Markell
Producers Martin Poll, Wm. C. Gerrity
Company Martin Poll Production
Director E.W. Swackhamer
Costume Designer Stanley Simmons
CAST
Hamilton Nash .... James Coburn
Ben Feeney .... Hector Elizondo
Owen Fitzstephan .... Jason Miller
Aaronia Haldorn .... Jean Simmons
The Old Man .... Paul Stewart
Alice Dain Leggett .... Beatrice Straight
Gabrielle .... Nancy Addison
Sgt. O'Gar .... Tom Bower

The Dain Curse *Continued*

Jack Santos	David Canary
Marshall Cotton	Beeson Carroll
Eric Collinson	Martin Cassidy
Tom Vernon	Brian Davies
Daisy Cotton	Roni Dengel
Foley	Clarence Felder
Mr. Leggett	Paul Harding
Maria Grosso	Karen Ludwig
Mickey	Malachy McCourt
Tom Fink	Brent Spiner
Judge Cochran	Ronald Weyand
Minnie Hershey	Hattie Winston
Hubert Collinson	Roland Winters
Joseph Haldorn	Ellis Rabb

371   Dallas   CBS
Program Type Limited Series
5 hours. Sundays. Premiere date 4/2/78. Drama about two Texas families involved in long-standing feud. Music by Jerrold Immel. Created by David Jacobs.
Executive Producers Lee Rich, Philip Capice
Producer Leonard Katsman
Company Lorimar Productions, Inc.
Directors Robert Day, Irving J. Moore
Writer David Jacobs
Art Director Ed Graves
CAST

Eleanor Southworth Ewing	Barbara Bel Geddes
John "Jock" Ewing	Jim Davis
Bobby Ewing	Patrick Duffy
J.R. Ewing	Larry Hagman
Pamela Barnes Ewing	Victoria Principal
Lucy Ewing	Charlene Tilton
Sue Ellen Ewing	Linda Grey
Ray Krebbs	Steve Kanaly
Cliff Barnes	Ken Kercheval
Digger Barnes	David Wayne
Julie	Tina Louise

372   Damien   PBS
Program Type Religious/Cultural Special
90 minutes. 1/24/78. Repeat dates: 1/29/78, 8/31/78. One-character play about Father Damien de Veuster, the leper priest of Molokai (Hawaii). Program made possible by grants from the Hawaii Committee for the Humanities, the Bank of Hawaii, Foodland Super Market, Ltd., Meadow Gold Dairies.
Producer Nino J. Martin
Company Hawaii Public Television
Director Nino J. Martin
Writer Aldyth Morris
CAST

Father Damien	Terence Knapp

373   Dan Haggerty Goes to the Circus
NBC
Program Type Music/Comedy/Variety Special
60 minutes. Premiere date: 5/30/78. Dan Haggerty hosts performances by world-famous acts featuring excerpts from the motion picture, "Circus in the Circus."
Director Milt Altman
Writer Daniel A. Segal
Host Dan Haggerty

374   Dance at Dawn   PBS
Program Type Music/Dance Special
30 minutes. Premiere date: 5/6/78. Special uses the symbolism of dance to show that man and his technology have affected Florida's beaches, and that this in turn has affected man. Music composed and performed by Wes McKenzie. Filmed on location at Canaveral National Seashore, Daytona and New Smyrna beaches.
Producer Heinz Bachfisch
Company WFSU-TV/Tallahassee, Florida
Director Heinz Bachfisch
Choreographer Kip Watson

375   Dance for Camera   PBS
Program Type Music/Dance Series
30 minutes. Tuesdays. Premiere date: 6/15/76. Season premiere: 1/16/78. Dances choreographed for television: "District One/Pale Cool Pale Warm," "George's House." (*See* individual titles for credits.)

376   Dance in America
Great Performances   PBS
Program Type Music/Dance Special
60 minutes. Special dance performances by leading American companies. Programs presented during the 1977–78 season are: "American Ballet Theatre," "Choreography by Balanchine," "Merce Cunningham and Dance Company," "Paul Taylor Dance Company," "The Pennsylvania Ballet," "Pilobolus Dance Theatre," "Trailblazers of Modern Dance," (*See* individual titles for credits.)

377   Dance of the Athletes
The CBS Festival of Lively Arts for Young People   CBS
Program Type Children's Special
60 minutes. Premiere date: 9/26/76. Repeat date: 5/28/78. A young people's special focusing on the similarities shared by sports figures and dancers. Music by Gordon Lowry Harrel.
Producer Edward Villella
Company Prodigal Productions
Director David Saperstein
Writer Douglas Howard Gray
Choreographer Edward Villella
Costume Designer John Rager
Art Director Michael Dennison
Star Edward Villella
Athletes Tom Seaver, Jerry Grote, Bob Griese,

Virginia Wade, George McGinnis, Muriel Grossfeld
Principal Dancers Edward Villella, Anna Aragno
Dancers Stephen Caras, Bart Cook, Elise Flagg, Laura Flagg, Susan Hendl, Jay Jolley, Laurence Matthews, Susan Pilarre, Bryan Pitts, Marjorie Spohn

378 The Dancing Bear
Visions   PBS
Program Type Dramatic Special
90 minutes. Premiere date: 10/23/77. Tragicomedy written by Conrad Bromberg about a character actor whose debts are piling up.
Executive Producer Barbara Schultz
Producer Barbara Schultz
Company KCET-TV/Los Angeles
Director Burt Brinckerhoff
CAST
Cubby Doucette .... Charles Durning
Ann .... Tyne Daly
Mrs. Doucette .... Verna Bloom
Daughter Bitsy .... Quinn Cummings
Director Alan Stone .... Burt Brinckerhoff
Additional Cast Joshua Bryant, Lou Wills, Jessica Rains, Robert Gibbons, Lesley Woods

379 Daniel Foster, M.D.   PBS
Program Type Educational/Cultural Series
30 minutes. Premiere date: 4/8/77. Second season premiere: 10/8/77, (formerly titled "M.D.") Series of conversations on various medical subjects between Daniel Foster and guest medical experts. Third 13-week series began 1/7/78 and fourth series began 7/8/78. Program made possible by a grant from Cecil and Ida Green.
Producer Pat Alexander
Company KERA-TV/Dallas Fort Worth in cooperation with The University of Texas Health Science Center at Dallas
Director David Dowe
Host Dr. Daniel W. Foster

380 Danny and the Mermaid   CBS
Program Type Comedy Special
30 minutes. Premiere date: 5/17/78. Pilot about an oceanographer who meets a mermaid. Music by Al Allen. Story by Ivan Tors. Filmed in Hollywood, Miami and Silver Springs, Florida.
Producer Ivan Tors
Company Ivan Tors Corporation
Director Norman Abbott
Underwater Director Ricou Browning
Writer Budd Crossman
CAST
Danny Stevens .... Patrick Collins
Aqua .... Harlee McBride
The Professor .... Ray Walston
Turtle .... Rick Fazel

The Psychiatrist .... Conrad Janis
Pilot .... Ancel Cook

381 Danny Thomas Memphis Classic
CBS
Program Type Sports Special
Final two rounds of golf classic 6/10/78 and 6/11/78 from Colonial Country Club in Cordova, Tenn.
Executive Producer Frank Chirkinian
Company CBS Sports
Directors Bob Dailey, Frank Chirkinian

382 Dark Secret of Harvest Home
The Big Event/NBC Monday Night at the Movies/NBC Novel for television   NBC
Program Type Dramatic Special
5 hours. Premiere dates: 1/23/78 and 1/24/78. Based on novel by Tom Tryon. Chronicles the events that beset a New York commerical artist when he and his wife and daughter move to a rustic New England village they visited during their travels.
Producer Jack Laird
Company Universal TV in association with NBC-TV
Director Leo Penn
Writers Jack Guss, Charles E. Israel
Costume Designer Bill Jobe
CAST
Nick Constantine .... David Ackroyd
Beth Constantine .... Joanna Miles
Kate Constantine .... Rosanna Arquette
Widow Fortune .... Bette Davis
Justin Hooke .... John Calvin
Sophie Hooke .... Laurie Prange
Tamar Penrose .... Lena Raymond
Missy Penrose .... Tracy Gold
Jack Stump .... Rene Auberjonois
Amys Penrose .... Norman Lloyd
Worthy Pettinger .... Michael O'Keefe
Robert Dodd .... Stephen Joyce
Maggie Dodd .... Linda Marsh
Jimmy Minerva .... Stephen Gustafson
Mrs. Buckley .... Phoebe Alexander
Asia Minerva .... Kathleen Howland
Roy Soakes .... Dick Durock
Old Man Soakes .... John Daheim
Elsie Pounder .... Lori Street

Darker Than Amber *See* The Big Event

Darling Lili *See* The ABC Sunday Night Movie

David and Lisa XR *See* PBS Movie Theater

383   **David Frost Presents the 7th Guinness Book of World Records**   ABC
Program Type Documentary/Informational Special
90 minutes. Premiere date: 4/25/78.
Hosts Richard Dawson, Michele Lee

384   **David Horowitz: Consumer Buyline**
Syndicated
Program Type Public Affairs Series
30 minutes. Premiere date: 1/14/78. Dissatisfied consumers bring problems to Horowitz.
Producer Lloyd Thaxton
Company Burt Rosen Co.
Host David Horowitz

385   **Davy Crockett on the Mississippi**
CBS
Famous Classic Tales
Program Type Animated Film Special
60 minutes. Premiere date: 11/20/76. Repeat date: 10/22/77. Adventures of the American folklore hero during his days as a frontiersman. "Davy Crockett" theme by Gairden Cooke and Hoyt Curtin. Graphics by Iraj Paran.
Executive Producers William Hanna, Joseph Barbera
Producer Iwao Takamoto
Company Hanna-Barbera Productions, Inc.
Director Charles A. Nichols
Writer Sid Morse
Musical Director Hoyt Curtin
Animators Carlos Alfonso, Oliver E. Callahan, Ken Muse, Juan Pina, Carlo Vinci
Voices Mike Bell, Ron Feinberg, Randy Gray, Kip Niven, Pat Parris, John Stephenson, Ned Wilson

Day of the Dolphin *See* NBC Movie of the Week

386   **A Day to Remember: August 28, 1963**   PBS
Program Type Documentary/Informational Special
30 minutes. Premiere date: 8/27/78. Commemoration of the day that over 250,000 people gathered at the Lincoln Memorial in Washington, DC, for the largest peaceful civil rights demonstration of the 1960s. Dr. Martin Luther King delivered his famous "I Have a Dream" speech at this meeting. Features a new cantata composed by C. Edward Thomas performed by Joy Simpson, the gospel singers of the Zion Baptist Church of Philadelphia and the Bethlehem Lutheran Choir of Minneapolis, the University of Minnesota Concert Bank Ensemble and a jazz trio. Program made possible by a grant from the Corporation for Public Broadcasting, the Jerome Foundation and the Minnesota Humanities Commission.
Producer Cyrus Bharucha
Company KTCA-TV/St. Paul-Minneapolis

387   **Days of Our Lives**   NBC
Program Type Daytime Drama Series
60 minutes. Mondays–Fridays. Premiere date; 11/8/65. Continuous. Second regularly scheduled 60-minute daytime drama (as of 4/21/75). Created by Ted Corday, Irna Phillips and Allan Chase. Series revolves around the Horton Family of Salem, U.S.A. Macdonald Carey, Frances Reid and John Clarke are original cast members. Cast list is alphabetical.
Executive Producers Betty Corday, H. Wesley Kenney
Producer Jack Herzberg
Company Corday Productions, Inc. and Columbia Pictures Television in association with NBC-TV
Directors Joseph Behar, Alvin Rabin, Frank Pacelli
Head Writer Ann Marcus
Writers Rocci Chatfield, Michael Robert David, Raymond Goldstone, Joyce Perry, Elizabeth Harrower, Laura Olsher

CAST

Don Craig	Jed Allan
Donna Temple	Tracy Bregman
Dr. Cunningham	Peter Brandon
Theresa Harper	Elisabeth Brooks
Dr. Greg Peters	Peter Brown
Dr. Tom Horton	Macdonald Carey
Mickey Horton	John Clarke
Robert LeClare	Robert Clary
Mrs. Evans	Dianna Douglas
Michael Horton, Jr.	Wesley Eure
Toni Johnson	Chip Fields
Dr. Laura Horton	Rosemary Forsyth
Amanda Peters	Mary Frann
Dr. Neil Curtis	Joseph Gallison
David Banning	Richard Guthrie
Dr. Marlena Evans	Deidre Hall
Doug Williams	Bill Hayes
Julie Williams	Susan Seaforth Hayes
Samantha Evans	Andrea Hall Lovell
Dr. Tommy Horton, Jr.	John Lupton
Melissa Phillips	Debbie Lytton
Dr. Paul Whitman	Peter MacLean
Phyllis Curtis	Elizabeth MacRae
Dr. Bill Horton	Edward Mallory
Linda Phillips	Margaret Mason
JoAnn Barnes	Corinne Michaels
Alice Horton	Frances Reid
Maggie Horton	Suzanne Rogers
Rosie Carlson	Fran Ryan
Hope Williams	Natasha Ryan
Mary Anderson	Barbara Stanger
Jeri Clayton	Kaye Stevens
Bob Anderson	Mark Tapscott
Chris Kositchek	Josh Taylor
Sister Marie Horton	Kate Woodville
Margot Anderman	Suzanne Zenor

388 **The Daytime Emmy Awards** ABC
Program Type Parades/Pageants/Awards
Special
90 minutes. Premiere date: 5/12/77. Live tele-
cast of the fifth annual Daytime Emmy awards
from the Grand Ballroom of the New York
(City) Hilton Hotel 6/7/78.
Producers Bill Carruthers, Joel Stein
Director Bill Carruthers
Host Richard Dawson

389 **The Deadly Game**
The Big Event/NBC World Premiere movie
NBC
Program Type Dramatic Special
2 hours. Premiere date: 12/3/77. Repeat date:
8/8/78. Police chief suspects terrorists are re-
sponsible when a truckload of chemicals is in-
volved in a highway accident.
Director Lane Slate
Writer Lane Slate
CAST
Abel .... Andy Griffith
Doc .... Sharon Spelman
John .... Hunter Von Leer
Fred ....Claude Earl Jones
Gloria .... Mitzi Hoag
Malcolm .... James Cromwell
Corporal .... O. W. Tuthill
Vernon Brea .... Steffen Zacharias
Col. Stryker .... Dan O'Herlihy
Barkeep .... Ellen Blake
Emma .... Ysabel MacCloskey
Polly .... Miriam Byrd Nethery
Whit .... Bill McLean
Mrs. Beezly ....Fran Ryan
Sgt. Redman ....Med Flory
Tiny ....Chuck Gradi
Goldstone ....Ted Noose
Amy Franklin .... Rebecca Balding
Jake .... John Perak
Jeff .... Christopher Tenney

390 **Deadman's Curve**
The CBS Friday Night Movies CBS
Program Type TV Movie
2 hours. Premiere date: 2/3/78. Biographical
film dealing with the Jan & Dean singing duo of
the late 1950s and 1960s. Music by Fred Karlin.
Executive Producer Roger Gimbel
Producer Pat Rooney
Company EMI Television Programs, Inc.
Director Richard Compton
Writer Dalene Young
CAST
Jan Berry .... Richard Hatch
Dean Torrence .... Bruce Davison
Annie .... Pamela Bellwood
Dr. Vivian Sheehan ....Floy Dean
Susan .... Denise Dubarry
Linda .... Priscilla Cory
Billy ....Kelly Ward
Nancy .... Eddie Benton

Mr. Berry .... George Wallace
Mrs. Berry .... June Dayton
The Jackal ....Wolfman Jack
Mr. Torrence ....Hank Brandt
Rainbow ....Susan Sullivan
Surgeon .... David Byrd
Army Sergeant ....Art Bradford
Herb Alpert ....Leonard Stone
Engineer .... James Oliver
Jim Arlett .... Noah Keen
Dick Clark .... Dick Clark
Mike Love ....Mike Love
Bruce Johnston ....Bruce Johnston

391 **Dean Martin Celebrity Roast: Betty
White** NBC
Program Type Comedy Special
60 minutes. Premiere date: 5/31/78. Special hon-
oring Betty White.
Producer Greg Garrison
Company A Sasha Production in association
with Greg Garrison Productions
Director Greg Garrison
Host Dean Martin
Guest of Honor Betty White
Celebrities Allen Ludden, Georgia Engel, John
Hillerman, Phyllis Diller, Milton Berle, Peter
Marshall, Bonnie Franklin, Dan Haggerty,
Orson Welles, Jimmie Walker, LaWanda
Page, Abe Vigoda

392 **Dean Martin Celebrity Roast: Dan
Haggerty** NBC
Program Type Comedy Special
60 minutes. Premiere date: 11/2/77. First
"roast" of the season. Taped at the MGM Grand
Hotel, Las Vegas.
Producer Greg Garrison
Company A Sasha Production in association
with Greg Garrison Productions
Director Greg Garrison
Host Dean Martin
Guest of Honor Dan Haggerty
Celebrities Rich Little, Jimmie Walker, Red But-
tons, Foster Brooks, LaWanda Page, Denver
Pyle, William Conrad, Marilyn Michaels, Abe
Vigoda, Tom Dreesen, Jackie Gayle, Harry
Morgan, Roger Miller, Pat Harrington, Orson
Welles

393 **Dean Martin Celebrity Roast:
Frank Sinatra** NBC
Program Type Comedy Special
2 hours. premiere date: 2/7/78. Special honoring
Frank Sinatra. Taped at the MGM Grand Hotel,
Las Vegas.
Producer Greg Garrison
Company A Sasha Production in association
with Greg Garrison Productions
Director Greg Garrison

Dean Martin Celebrity Roast: Frank Sinatra *Continued*
Writer Harry Crane
Guest of Honor Frank Sinatra
Celebrities Milton Berle, Ernest Borgnine, George Burns, Red Buttons, Ruth Buzz., Charlie Callas, Dom DeLuise, Peter Falk, Redd Foxx, Gene Kelly, Jack Klugman, Rich Little, LaWanda Page, Ronald Reagan, Don Rickles, Telly Savalas, James Stewart, Orson Welles, Flip Wilson, Jonathan Winters

394   Dean Martin Celebrity Roast: George Burns   NBC
Program Type Comedy Special
90 minutes. Premiere date: 5/17/78. Special honoring George Burns. Taped at MGM Grand Hotel, Las Vegas.
Producer Greg Garrison
Company A Sasha Production in association with Greg Garrison Productions
Director Greg Garrison
Writer Harry Crane
Host Dean Martin
Guest of Honor George Burns
Celebrities Milton Berle, Abe Vigoda, Gene Kelly, Ruth Buzzi, James Stewart, Dom DeLuise, LaWanda Page, Tom Dreesen, Phyllis Diller, Red Buttons, Orson Welles, Frank Welker, Jack Carter, Ronald Reagan, Charlie Callas, Connie Stevens, Don Rickles

395   Dean Martin Celebrity Roast: Jack Klugman   NBC
Program Type Comedy Special
60 minutes. Premiere date: 3/17/78. Special honoring Jack Klugman. Taped at the MGM Grand Hotel, Las Vegas.
Producer Greg Garrison
Company A Sasha Production in association with Greg Garrison Productions
Director Greg Garrison
Writers Harry Crane, Larry Markes, John Shea, Ed Hider, Paul Pumpian, Martin Ragaway, Arthur Phillips, Mel Chase, Robert L. Mills, Jay Burton, Stan Burns, David Axelrod
Host Dean Martin
Guest of Honor Jack Klugman
Celebrities Tony Randall, Milton Berle, Red Buttons, Joey Bishop, Dick Martin, LaWanda Page, Abbe Lane, Phyllis Diller, Ruth Buzzi, Robert Guillaume, Dr. Joyce Brothers, Foster Brooks, Connie Stevens, Katherine Helmond, Kay Medford, Sandi Herdt

396   Dean Martin Celebrity Roast: Jimmy Stewart   NBC
Program Type Comedy Special
60 minutes. Premiere date: 5/10/78. Special honoring Jimmy Stewart. Taped at the MGM Grand Hotel, Las Vegas.
Producer Greg Garrison
Company A Sasha Production in association with Greg Garrison Productions
Director Greg Garrison
Writers Harry Crane, Larry Markes, John Shea, Howard Albrecht, Sol Weinstein, Martin Ragaway, Arthur Phillips, Mel Chase, Robert L. Mills, Jay Burton, Stan Burns, David Axelrod
Host Dean Martin
Guest of Honor Jimmy Stewart
Celebrities Milton Berle, Lucille Ball, Sen. Barry Goldwater, Ruth Buzzi, June Allyson, Mickey Rooney, LaWanda Page, Janet Leigh, Henry Fonda, George Burns, Greer Garson, Foster Brooks, Eddie Albert, Red Buttons, Tony Randall, Rich Little, Jesse White, Don Rickles, Orson Welles

397   Dean Martin's Christmas in California   NBC
Program Type Music/Comedy/Variety Special
60 minutes. Premiere date: 12/18/77. Dean Martin gets on a horse to herald the holiday season in a music-and-comedy special. Music by Van Alexander.
Executive Producer Greg Garrison
Producer Lee Hale
Company A Sasha Production in association with Greg Garrison Productions
Directors Greg Garrison, Hugh Lambert
Host Dean Martin
Guests Jonathan Winters, Gabriel Melgar, Crystal Gayle, Linda Lavin, Mireille Mathieu, the Golddiggers

398   Dear Lovey Hart (I Am Desperate!)
ABC Out-of-School Specials/ABC Weekend Specials   ABC
Program Type Children's Special
60 minutes. Premiere date: 5/19/76. Repeat date: 3/25/78. Young people's comedy-drama about a high school newspaper editor and his secret lonely hearts columnist. Based on the novel by Ellen Conford.
Executive Producer Martin Tahse
Producer Fred Bennett
Company Martin Tahse Productions, Inc.
Director Larry Elikann
Writer Bob Rodgers
Art Director Ray Markham
CAST
Carrie Wasserman .... Susan Lawrence
Skip Custer .... Meegan King

Susan	Barbara Timko
Linda	Elyssa Davalos
Mar	Del Hinkley
Bernice	Bebe Kelly
Jeff Wasserman	Al Eisenmann
Marty	Stephen Liss
Bob	Benny Medina
Barker	Craig Hundley
Sam	John Starr
2nd Tennis Player	Helene T. Nelson
1st Tennis Player	Sheri Jason
Freddie	Bruce Caton

399 A Death in Canaan

The CBS Wednesday Night Movies   CBS
Program Type TV Movie
2-1/2 hours. Premiere date: 3/1/78. Fight of a handful of Canaan, Conn., citizens to insure justice for an 18-year-old accused of murdering his mother. Based on the book by Joan Barthel. Music arranged by John Addison.
Producers Robert W. Christiansen, Rick Rosenberg
Company Chris-Rose Productions in association with Warner Bros. Television
Director Tony Richardson
Writers Thomas Thompson, Spencer Eastman
CAST

Joan Barthel	Stefanie Powers
Lt. Bragdon	Tom Atkins
Mildred Carston	Jacqueline Brookes
Peter Reilly	Paul Clemens
Barny Parsons	Brian Dennehy
Sgt. Case	Charles Haid
Thomas Lanza (Prosecutor)	Floyd Levine
Sgt. Scully	Kenneth McMillan
Father Mark	Gavan O'Herlihy
Dr. Samura	Yuki Shimoda
Jim Barthel	James Sutorius
Teresa Noble	Bonnie Bartlett
Judge Revere (1st Judge)	William Bronder
Judge Vincent (2nd Judge)	Pat Corley
Sweeney	Trent Dolan
Cpt. Sebastian	Charles Hallahan
Sarah Biggens	Mary Jackson
Barbara Gibbons	Sally Kemp
Nurse Pynne	Doreen Lang
Bob Hartman	Lane Smith
Trooper Miles	Michael Talbot
Cliff Parsons	Marc Vahanian
Anne Barthel	Paige Mellon
Robert Keeper (2nd Prosecutor)	Dan Miller
CBS Interviewer	Brad Willis
Philip Pitts	Brian McGibbon
Carla Pitts	Olan Shepard

400 Death Moon

The CBS Wednesday Night Movies   CBS
Program Type TV Movie
2 hours. Premiere date: 5/31/78. Executive thinks his Hawaiian romance has overcome his tensions until the supernatural powers of a native curse begin to effect him. Filmed in Kauai, Hawaiian Islands.

Executive Producer Roger Gimbel
Producer Jay Benson
Company A Roger Gimbel Production for EMI Television Programs, Inc.
Director Bruce Kessler
Writer George Schenck
CAST

Jason Palmer	Robert Foxworth
Rick Bladen	Joe Penny
Diane May	Barbara Trentham
Tapulua	France Nuyen
Lt. Russ Cort	Dolph Sweet
Sherry Weston	Debralee Scott
Earl Wheelie	Charles Haid
Mrs. Jennings	Joan Freeman
Mr. Jennings	Mitch Mitchell
Vince Tatupu	Branscombe Richmond
Dr. Restin	Albert Harris
Tami Waimea	Carole Kai
Julie Chin	Lydia Lei Kayahara
Dr. Erlich	Don Pomes
Judy	Terry Takada
Dora	Donna White
Harry	Bob Witthans
Wolf Man	Jose Bulatao
Marsh	Robert I. Preston
Kay	Carole Avery
Jenner	Alan Vicencio
Walt	Chris Bailey

Death of Her Innocence *See* NBC Monday Night at the Movies

401 The Death of Pope Paul VI   NBC

Program Type News Special
45 minutes. Report on the death of Pope Paul VI 8/6/78 and 8/7/78.
Company NBC News
Anchor Edwin Newman
Correspondents Bob Kur; Brian Ross; Jim Bitterman

402 The Death of Richie

NBC Big Event Movie   NBC
Program Type Dramatic Special
2 hours. Premiere date: 1/10/77. Repeat date: 7/11/78. Fact-based drama based on "Richie" by Thomas Thompson about the effect of a teenager's drug addiction on his family. Music by Fred Karlin.
Executive Producer Charles B. FitzSimons
Producer Michael Jaffe
Company Henry Jaffe Enterprises, Inc. in association with NBC-TV
Director Paul Wendkos
Writer John McGreevey
Art Director James Hulsey
CAST

George Werner	Ben Gazzara
Richie Werner	Robby Benson
Carol Werner	Eileen Brennan
Russell Werner	Lance Kerwin

The Death of Richie Continued

Brick .... Charles Fleischer
Peanuts .... Clint Howard
Mark .... Harry Gold
Sheila .... Susan Neher
Mrs. Norlon .... Shirley O'Hara
Elaine .... Jennifer Rhodes

403   The Defection of Simas Kudirka
CBS

Program Type Dramatic Special
2 hours. Premiere date: 1/23/78. Special about a Lithuanian seaman who jumped from a Russian freighter to a Coast Guard cutter in 1970. Music by David Shire.
Executive Producers Gerald I. Eisenberg, Gerald W. Abrams
Producer Richard Briggs
Company The Jozak Company in association with Paramount Television
Director David Lowell Rich
Writer Bruce Feldman
Film Editor John A. Martinelli
CAST
Simas Kudirka .... Alan Arkin
Comdr. Devon .... Richard Jordan
Capt. Popov .... Donald Pleasence
Gruzauskas ....George Dzundza
Phillip Chadway ....John McMartin
Genna Kudirka .... Shirley Knight
Comdr. Burkalis .... Marvin Silbersher
Mott .... Peter Evans
Blain .... Ted Shackelford
Dr. Paegle .... Barton Heyman
Kabek ....Jack Blessing
Baltrunar .... Nicholas Guest
Petras .... Matthew Arkin
Ass't. Supervisor .... Salem Ludwig

Deliverance *See* The ABC Sunday Night Movie

404   Derbyweek: An American Tradition
ABC

Program Type Sports Special
60 minutes. 5/5/78. Sports special preceding the running of the Kentucky Derby horse race.
Executive Producer Roone Arledge
Producer Ric LaCivita
Company ABC Sports
Director Roger Goodman
Hosts Cheryl Tiegs, Frank Gifford
Reporters Howard Cosell, Jim McKay

405   The Devil's Work
Ourstory   **PBS**

Program Type Dramatic Special
30 minutes. Premiere date: 1/20/76. Repeat date: 10/24/77. Dramatization of the life and work of an itinerant theater company in the mid-1800s. Music by Dave Conner. Filmed in part at

Old Bethpage Village Restoration, Nassau County, N.Y. Program funded by a grant from the National Endowment for the Humanities.
Executive Producer Don Fouser
Producer Ron Finley
Company WNET-TV/New York
Director Ron Finley
Writer Stephen Jennings
Costume Designer John Boxer
Art Director Stephen Hendrickson
Host Bill Moyers
CAST
Joseph Jefferson .... Jerry Mayer
Cornelia Jefferson .... Betty Buckley
Joe Jr. .... John Dunn
Will McBride .... Frederick Coffin
Ella McBride .... Elizabeth Farley
Tom .... Bobby Grober
Abe Lincoln .... Stephen Keep
Rev. Scanlon ....Gil Rogers
Mayor Peebles ....John C. Becher
Mr. Fitch .... Tom Spratley
Mrs. Powell .... Elaine Eldridge
Ned .... Sam McMurray
Eustace .... Christopher Curry
Wagon Driver .... Richard Hamilton

406   Diamond Rivers
PBS

Program Type Documentary/Informational Special
30 minutes. Premiere date: 6/1/77. Repeat dates: 10/17/77 and 1/31/78. A look at an 80-year-old diamond prospector in the Brazilian state of Bahia. Program made possible by a grant from Sandgren & Murtha, Inc.
Producer Bill Benenson
Company WNET-TV/New York

Diamonds Are Forever *See* The ABC Sunday Night Movie

407   The Dick Cavett Show
PBS

Program Type Talk/Service/Variety Series
30 minutes. Premiere date: 10/10/77. Monday through Friday. Weeknightly interview show. Series made possible by grants from Public Broadcasting's Station Program Cooperative, The Chubb Group of Insurance Companies, Gulf and Western Industries, Inc.
Executive Producer Joan Konner
Producer Christopher Porterfield
Company WNET-TV/New York and Daphne Productions, Inc.
Director Gordon Rigsby
Host Dick Cavett

408   Dick Clark's Good Ol' Days: From Bobby Sox to Bikinis
The Big Event   NBC
Program Type Music/Comedy/Variety Special
2 hours. Premiere date: 10/11/77. Nostalgia for the late 1950s and early 1960s is spotlighted.
Executive Producer Dick Clark
Producers Bill Lee, Al Schwartz
Company dick clark teleshows, inc.
Director Jeff Margolis
Writers Robert Illes, James Stein
Stars Edd "Kookie" Byrnes, Freddie Cannon, Joey Dee, Bo Diddley, Dion, Fabian, Connie Francis, Lesley Gore, The Kingston Trio, Robert Klein, Anne Meara, Martha Reeves and the Vandellas, Mort Sahl, The Shirelles, Jerry Stiller
Hosts Frankie Avalon, Annette Funicello
Special Appearances The Beach Boys, Dr. Joyce Brothers, The Captain and Tennille, Angela Cartwright, Dick Clark, Noreen Corcoran, Johnny Crawford, Elinor Donahue, Evel Knievel, Snooky Lanson, Mickey Mantle, Jerry Mathers, Larry Mathews, Cubby O'-Brien, Ken Osmond, O.J. Simpson, Connie Stevens, Brian Wilson

409   The Dick Hanna Story   PBS
Program Type Public Affairs Special
30 minutes. Premiere date: 6/4/78. Former Orange County (Calif.) Congressman Richard T. Hann discusses the Korean influence-buying scandal.
Company KOCE-TV/Huntington Beach in association with the Arkansas Educational Television Network
Host Jim Cooper

410   Die Fledermaus   Syndicated
Program Type Music/Dance Special
2 hours. Premiere date: 12/31/77. Opera by Johann Strauss performed by The Royal Opera in London's Covent Garden.
Company Metromedia
Conductor Zubin Mehta
Hosts Tony Randall, Humphrey Burton
Lead Roles Kiri Te Kanawa, Hermann Prey

411   Died Young   PBS
Program Type Documentary/Informational Special
30 minutes. Premiere date: 4/14/75. Repeat date: 2/11/78. The rise and decline of the Union Terminal Railroad Station in Cincinnati.
Executive Producer Charles Vaughan
Producer Gene Walz
Company WCET-TV/Cincinnati
Director Gene Walz

Writer Jack Gwyn
Narrator Cecil Hale

412   Dinah!   Syndicated
Program Type Talk/Service/Variety Series
90 minutes. Mondays–Fridays. Premiere date: 10/21/74. Continuous. Successor to "Dinah's Place."
Executive Producer Henry Jaffe
Producer Fred Tatashore
Company Winchester Productions
Distributor 20th Century-Fox Television
Director Glen Swanson
Musical Director John Rodby
Host Dinah Shore
Announcer Johnny Gilbert

413   Dionne Warwick
In Performance at Wolf Trap   PBS
Program Type Music/Dance Special
60 minutes. Premiere date: 12/1/75. Season premiere: 8/5/78. A concert by Dionne Warwick performed at the Wolf Trap Farm Park in Arlington, Va. Program made possible by a grant from the Atlantic Richfield Company.
Executive Producer David Prowitt
Producer Ruth Leon
Company WETA-TV/Washington, D.C.
Director Clark Santee
Hosts Beverly Sills, David Prowitt

414   Direction '78: Morality of Television   PBS
Program Type Public Affairs Special
60 minutes. 9/10/78. Highlights symposium at Tulane University, New Orleans, held in early 1978. Made possible by grants from Mushroom Charitable Trust, Popeye's Fried Chicken, Charthouse Inc., Lucy Products, AMOCO, Tulane University
Company WYES-TV/New Orleans and Tulane University
Producer David Frentz
Director David Frentz
Host Martin Agronsky
Panelists Virginia Carter, Harlan Ellison, Robert Mulholland, Daniel Schorr

415   Directions   ABC
Program Type Religious/Cultural Series
30 minutes. Sundays. Premiere date: 11/13/60. Became 52-week show during 1976–77 season. Continuing theme: "Conscience of America" begun during the 1975–76 season.
Executive Producer Sid Darion
Producers Various
Company ABC News Public Affairs

Directions *Continued*
Directors Various
Writers Various

Dirty Harry *See* NBC Monday Night at
the Movies

Dirty Mary Crazy Larry *See* The ABC
Friday Night Movie

416   The Displaced Person
The American Short Story   PBS
Program Type Dramatic Special
60 minutes. Premiere date: 4/12/77. Repeat
date: 10/10/77. Adaptation of a short story by
Flannery O'Connor set in the late 1940s on a
Georgia farm. Music by Bill Conti. Program pre-
sented by South Carolina Educational Television
and funded by a grant from the National Endow-
ment for the Humanities.
Executive Producer Robert Geller
Producer Matthew N. Herman
Company Learning in Focus, Inc.
Director Glenn Jordan
Writer Horton Foote
Costume Designer Joseph Aulisi
Scenic Designer Charles Bennett
Host Colleen Dewhurst
CAST
Mrs. McIntyre .... Irene Worth
Father Flynn .... John Houseman
Mr. Guizac .... Noam Yerushalmi
Mrs. Shortley .... Shirley Stoler
Mr. Shortley .... Lane Smith
Field Hand ....Robert Earl Jones

417   District One/Pale Cool Pale Warm
Dance for Camera   PBS
Program Type Music/Dance Special
30 minutes. Premiere date: 6/15/76. Repeat
date: 1/16/78. Two original dances choreo-
graphed for television: "District One" by Rudy
Perez and "Pale Cool Pale Warm" by Elizabeth
Keen. Program made possible by a grant from
the Rockefeller Foundation, the National En-
dowment for the Arts and the Corporation for
Public Broadcasting.
Producer Nancy Mason
Company WGBH New Television Workshop/
Boston
Directors Fred Barzyk; John Budde
Host Carmen de-Lavallade

418   Diving for Roman Plunder
Festival '78   PBS
Program Type Science/Nature Special
60 minutes. Premiere date: 3/14/78. Chronicles
an underwater archaeological search by Captain

Jacques Cousteau and divers from his research
ship Calypso to recover Greek treasures from an
ancient Roman ship. Music composed and con-
ducted by Elmer Bernstein and performed by the
Royal Philharmonic Orchestra. Program made
possible by a grant from the Atlantic Richfield
Company.
Executive Producers Jacques Cousteau, Philippe
Cousteau
Production Executive Charles Allen
Producer Andrew W. Solt
Company KCET-TV/Los Angeles and The
Cousteau Society
Narrator Theodore Strauss
Narrator Melina Mercouri

Doctor *See* Dr.

419   The Doctors   NBC
Program Type Daytime Drama Series
30 minutes. Mondays–Fridays. Premiere date:
4/1/63. Continuous. Series revolves around the
Powers, Aldrich and Dancy families. Set primar-
ily in Hope Memorial Hospital in Madison,
U.S.A. Cast list is alphabetical.
Producer Chuck Weiss
Company Channelex, Inc.
Directors Gary Bowen, Ivan Cury
Writer Linda Grover
CAST
Stephanie Aldrich .... Bridget Breen
Dr. Maggie Powers .... Lydia Bruce
Bill Aldrich ....Shawn Campbell
Sweeney .... Peggy Cass
Jason Aldrich ....Glenn Corbett
Michael Paul Powers .... John Downes
Dr. Colin Wakefield .... Philip English
Sara Dancy .... Dorothy Fielding
Erich Aldrich .... Thor Fields
Greta Powers ....Jennifer Houlton
Doreen Aldrich ....Pamela Lincoln
Mona Croft .... Meg Mundy
Dr. Steve Aldrich ....David O'Brien
Dr. Matt Powers ....James Pritchett
Carolee Aldrich ....Jada Rowland
Dr. Speer ....Martin Shakar
Dr. Mike Powers ....John Shearin
Luke Dancy .... Frank Telfer
Nola Aldrich ....Kathleen Turner
Barney Dancy .... Larry Webber
M. J. Carroll .... Lauren White

420   Doctors' Private Lives
The ABC Monday Night Movie   ABC
Program Type TV Movie
2 hours. Premiere date: 3/20/78. Two heart sur-
geons in a story about medical ethics. Story by
Peggy Elliott and James Henerson. Music by
Richard Markowitz.
Executive Producer David Gerber
Producer Robert Stambler

Company David Gerber Productions in association with Columbia Pictures Television
Director Steven Stern
Writers Peggy Elliott, James Henerson
Art Directors Ross Bellah, John Beckman
Film Editors David Wages, Ronald LaVine
CAST
Dr. Jeffrey Latimer .... John Gavin
Dr. Beth Demery .... Donna Mills
Dr. Mike Wise .... Ed Nelson
Frances Latimer .... Barbara Anderson
Sylvia .... Bettye Ackerman
Irv ....John Randolph
Dr. Rick Calder .... Randy Powell
Phyllis .... Fawne Harriman
Kenny .... Leigh J. McCloskey
Kitty .... Kim Hamilton
Mona Wise .... Elinor Donahue
Howard Weese .... John Lupton
Harriet Wise .... Viola Harris
Lou Wise ....Ross Elliott
Sheila .... Robin Mattson
Tania .... Pamm Kenneally

421 Documentary Showcase   PBS
Program Type Documentary/Informational Series
60 minutes. Fridays. Premiere date: 11/5/76. Season premiere: 9/16/77. A collection of documentaries produced by different PBS stations and independent producers. Programs captioned for the hearing-impaired in repeat showings. Programs shown during the 1977-78 season are: "The Amish: People of Preservation," "Carnivore," "Song at Twilight," "TVTV Looks at the Oscars." (*See* individual titles for credits.)

422 Don Giovanni
Festival '78 live from the Metropolitan Opera
PBS
Program Type Music/Dance Special
3 hours. Premiere date: 3/16/78. Opera by Wolfgang Amadeus Mozart live from the stage of the Metropolitan Opera. Made possible by a grant from Texaco, Inc. and additional funding from the National Endowment for the Arts.
Executive Producer Michael Bronson
Producer Christopher Sarson
Company Metropolitan Opera Association
Director Kirk Browning
Conductor Richard Bonynge
Choreographer Zachary Solov
Costume Designer Eugene Berman
Host Tony Randall
CAST
Donna Anna .... Joan Sutherland
Donna Elvira .... Julia Varady
Zerlina ....Huguette Tourangeau
Don Giovanni .... James Morris
Don Ottavio .... John Brecknock
Leporello ....Gabriel Bacquier
Masetto .... Allan Monk
The Commendatore ....John Macurdy

423 Don Kirshner's New Rock Concert
Syndicated
Program Type Music/Dance Series
90 minutes. Weekly. Premiere date: 9/73. Fifth season premiere: 9/10/77. Late night show with different rock stars weekly. First show to use radio simulcasts.
Executive Producer Don Kirshner
Producer David Yarnell
Company Don Kirshner Productions
Distributor Viacom International, Inc.
Host Don Kirshner

424 Donahue   Syndicated
Program Type Talk/Service/Variety Series
60 minutes. Mondays–Fridays. Premiere date: 11/6/67 (as "The Phil Donahue Show.") Continuous. Hour-long discussion show with questions from the studio audience.
Executive Producer Richard Mincer
Producer Patricia McMillen
Company Avco Broadcasting
Distributor Multimedia Program Sales
Director Ron Weiner
Host Phil Donahue

425 Donny & Marie   ABC
Program Type Music/Comedy/Variety Series
60 minutes. Fridays. Premiere date: 1/23/76. Third season premiere: 9/23/77. Music and variety. Regular features: skating act, country/rock concerts taped at studios in Hollywood, Calif. until 11/77; then Orem, Utah.
Executive Producers Raymond Katz; The Osmond Brothers
Producers Art Fisher, Arnie Kogen
Company An Osmond Production
Producer/Director Art Fisher
Producer/Head Writer Arnie Kogen
Writers Bill Dana, Ed Hider, Mort Scharfman, Rod Warren, Paul Pumpian, Harvey Weitzman, Bruce Vilanch
Dance Choreographer Carl Jablonski
Ice Choreographer Bob Paul
Costume Designers Ret Turner, Bob Mackie
Animation Director Bill Bohnert
Stars Donny Osmond Marie Osmond
Regulars The Ice Angels

426 A Doonesbury Special   NBC
Program Type Animated Film Special
30 minutes. Premiere date: 11/27/77. Characters created by Garry Trudeau for his comic strip, "Doonesbury," assembled for first animated special. Harmonica solos by John B. Sebastian. Original songs by Jimmy Thudpucker.
Producers John Hubley, Faith Hubley, Garry Trudeau

A Doonesbury Special *Continued*
Company John and Faith Hubley Films, Ltd. in association with Universal Press Syndicate
Directors John Hubley, Faith Hubley, Garry Trudeau

VOICES

Joanie Caucus	Barbara Harris
Referee	Jack Guilford
Sportscaster	Will Jordan
Rev. Scot Sloan	Rev. William Sloane Coffin
Zonker Harris	Richard Cox
Mark Slackmeyer/Ralphie	Charles Levin

427   Doral Eastern Open   CBS
Program Type Sports Special
Final two rounds of the 17th Open from the Doral Country Club in Miami, Fla. 3/11/78 and 3/12/78.
Producer Frank Chirkinian
Company CBS Television Network Sports
Directors Frank Chirkinian, Bob Dailey
Commentators Vin Scully, Pat Summerall, Jack Whitaker, Ben Wright, Frank Glieber, Ken Venturi

428   Dorothy Hamill Presents Winners
ABC
Program Type Sports Special
60 minutes. Premiere date: 4/28/78. Special starring 1976 Olympic figure skating gold medalist Dorothy Hamill in a salute to other award winners.
Executive Producer Jerry Weintraub
Producer Nick Vanoff
Company Dor-Jer Productions, Inc.
Director Stan Harris
Writers Frank Peppiatt, John Aylesworth, Barry Adelman, Barry Silver
Musical Director Eddie Karam
Costume Designers Bill Belew, David Doucette
Choreographer Rob Iscove
Art Director Charles Lisanby
Star Dorothy Hamill
Guest Stars Hal Linden, Bruce Jenner

429   Doug Henning's World of Magic
NBC
Program Type Music/Comedy/Variety Special
60 minutes. Premiere date: 12/15/77. Live magic show with ten original illusions.
Executive Producer Jerry Goldstein
Producer Walter C. Miller
Company Doug Henning Magic, Inc.
Director Walter C. Miller
Writer Buz Kohan
Musical Director Peter Matz
Choreographer Anita Mann
Costume Designer Bill Hargate
Art Director Charles Lisanby
Star Doug Henning

Host Glen Campbell
Guest Star Sandy Duncan

430   Down Home   CBS
Program Type Dramatic Special
60 minutes. Premiere date: 8/16/78. Pilot about a couple who uproot their family and move from Detroit to a small town in the South.
Producer Philip Barry
Company MTM Enterprises, Inc.
Director Fielder Cook
Writer Melvin Van Peebles

CAST

Nate Simmons	Robert Hooks
Priscilla Simmons	Madge Sinclair
Aunt Velvet	Beah Richards
Joe Mayfield	Lincoln Kilpatrick
Junior Simmons	Kevin Hooks
Highpockets Simmons	Eric Hooks
Helen Mayfield	Beverly Hope Atkinson
Trunk	Sonny Jim Gaines
Sarah Claypool	Anne Seymour
Mrs. Winston	Norma Connolly
Darlene Simmons	Tia Rance
Julie Mayfield	Dena Crowder
Abner Claypool	Edward Binns
Burt Pritchard	William Watson
Benjamin Pritchard	Paul Koslo
Bobby Pritchard	Tim Scott
Mr. Winston	Woodrow Parfrey
Frank Simmons	Boyd Bodwell
Billy Joe Pritchard	Mickey Jones
Jeeter Simmons	John Gilgreen
Dr. Johnson	George McDaniel
Doc	Edward Beagle
Customer	Mark Taylor
Sheriff	Andrew Duggan

431   Dr. Scorpion
The ABC Friday Night Movie   ABC
Program Type TV Movie
2 hours. Premiere date: 2/24/78. A genius threatens world peace with a scheme involving the theft of atomic missiles from the United States. Music by Peter Carpenter and Mike Post.
Executive Producer Stephen J. Cannell
Producer Alex Beaton
Company A Stephen J. Cannell Production in association with Universal Television
Director Richard Lang
Writer Stephen J. Cannell
Film Editors Diane Adler, George R. Rohrs

CAST

John Shackelford	Nick Mancuso
Tania Reston	Christine Lahti
Bill Worthington	Richard T. Herd
Sandra Shackelford	Sandra Kerns
Dr. Cresus	Roscoe Lee Browne
The Dane	Denny Miller
Terry Batliner	Granville Van Dusen
Admiral Gunwilder	Philip Sterling
Eddie	Lincoln Kilpatrick
Lt. Reed	Joseph Ruskin
Whitey Ullman	Bill Lucking

432 Dr. Seuss' The Hoober-Bloob Highway CBS
Program Type Animated Film Special
30 minutes. Premiere date: 2/19/75. Repeat date: 11/15/77. First "Dr. Seuss" story created for television. Music by Dean Elliott; lyrics by Theodor Geisel.
Executive Producer David H. DePatie
Producer Friz Freleng, Theodor Geisel
Company DePatie-Freleng Production
Director Alan Zaslov
Writer Theodor Geisel
Voices Bob Holt

433 Dr. Seuss' Horton Hears a Who CBS
Program Type Animated Film Special
30 minutes. Repeat date: 3/19/70. Season premiere: 8/4/78. Created by Theodor Geisel. Music by Eugene Poddany; lyrics by Theodor Geisel.
Producers Theodor Geisel; Chuck Jones
Director Chuck Jones
Writer Theodor Geisel
Narrator Hans Conried

434 Dr. Seuss' How the Grinch Stole Christmas CBS
Program Type Animated Film Special
30 minutes. Based on the book by Theodor Geisel. Premiere date: 12/18/66. Repeat date: 12/10/77. Music composed by Albert Hague; lyrics by Theodor Geisel.
Producers Chuck Jones; Theodor Geisel
Company MGM Television
Director Chuck Jones
Writer Theodor Geisel
Narrator Boris Karloff
VOICES
Christmas Spoiler ....Boris Karloff

435 Dr. Seuss' The Lorax CBS
Program Type Animated Film Special
30 minutes. Premiere date: 2/14/72. Season premiere: 8/4/78. Based on the book by Theodor Geisel. Music by Dean Elliott; lyrics by Theodor Geisel.
Executive Producer David H. DePatie
Producers Friz Freleng, Theodor Geisel
Company DePatie-Freleng Production
Director Hawley Pratt
Writer Theodor Geisel
Narrator Eddie Albert
Voices Bob Holt, Helen Carraher

436 Dr. Strange CBS
Program Type Dramatic Special
2 hours. Premiere date: 9/6/78. Occult-adven-ture drama based on Marvel Comics characters created by Stan Lee.
Executive Producer Philip DeGuere
Producer Alex Beaton
Company Universal Television
Director Philip DeGuere
Writer Philip DeGuere
Art Director William H. Tuntke
CAST
Dr. Stephen Strange ....Peter Hooten
Morgan Le Fay ....Jessica Walter
Clea .... Eddie Benton
Wong .... Clyde Kusatsu
Lindmer ....John Mills
The Nameless One .... David Hook
Sarah .... June Barrett
Head Nurse .... Diana Webster
Dr. Frank Taylor .... Philip Sterling
Dept. Chief .... Blake Marion
Intern .... Bob Delegall
Nurse .... Sarah Rush
Orderly ....Frank Catalano
Magician .... Larry Anderson
Announcer ....Inez Pedroza
Driver #2 ....Richard Washington
Taxi Driver ....Michael Clark
Mrs. Sullivan ....Lady Rowlands

437 Drought PBS
Program Type Documentary/Informational Special
60 minutes. Premiere date: 10/6/77. Documentary special filmed in Arizona, California, Colorado, Idaho and Washington examines how individuals cope with the lack of water. Program made possible in part by a grant from the Rocky Mountain Public Broadcasting Network.
Executive Producer Joyce Campbell
Producer Mike Kirk
Company KUID-TV-Moscow, Ida. and KCTS-TV/Seattle
Choreographer Tom Coggins

438 Drum Corps International Championships—1978 PBS
Program Type Music/Dance Special
4 hours. Live coverage of the seventh annual Drum Corps International Championship from the Mile High Stadium in Denver, Colorado 8/8/78. Program made possible in part by a grant from public television stations.
Producer Syrl Silberman
Company WGBH-TV/Boston
Hosts Gene Rayburn, Helen Rayburn, Peter Emmons

439 The Dupont-Columbia Awards PBS
Program Type Parades/Pageants/Awards Special
2 hours. Premiere date: 2/14/78. Awards to news and public affairs programs.

The Dupont-Columbia Awards *Continued*
Producer Gail Macandrew
Company WNET-TV/New York
Director Jon Merdin

440   Dynamic Duos   NBC
Program Type Limited Sports Series
30 minutes. Premiere date: 1/22/78. 7-part series
featuring teams of famous athletes competing
against each other in a single elimination bowling
format.
Producer Don Ohlmeyer
Company TWI
Director Don Ohlmeyer
Dynamic Duos Mickey Mantle and Willie Mays,
Arnold Palmer and Ray Floyd, Cale Yar-
borough and Johnny Rutherford, Dick Butkus
and Ray Nitschke, Oscar Robertson and Wilt
Chamberlain, Eddie Arcaro and Willie Shoe-
maker, Jim Brown and Jim Taylor, Tom
Seaver and Johnny Bench.

**441   The Easter Bunny Is Comin' to
Town**   ABC
Program Type Animated Film Special
60 minutes. Premiere date: 4/6/77. Repeat date:
3/20/78. Animated musical special about Easter
customs using dimensional stop-motion photog-
raphy. Music by Maury Laws; lyrics by Jules
Bass.
Producers Arthur Rankin, Jr., Jules Bass
Company A Rankin/Bass Production
Directors Arthur Rankin, Jr., Jules Bass
Writer Romeo Muller
Musical Director Bernard Hoffer
Narrator Fred Astaire
                        VOICES
Sunny the Easter Bunny ....Skip Hinnant
Chugs .... Robert McFadden
Hallelujah Jones .... Ron Marshall
King Bruce .... James Spies
Lilly Longtooth .... Meg Sargent
Additional Voices Allen Swift, Jill Choder, Ray Owens,
Karen Dahle, Michael McGovern, Laura Dean,
George Brennan, Gia Anderson, Stacey Carey

**442   Easter Services from Covenant
House**   CBS
Program Type Religious/Cultural Special
60 minutes. Premiere date: 3/26/78. Live cover-
age of Easter Sunday services from the Chapel of
Covenant House in New York City's Times
Square area.
Executive Producer Pamela Ilott
Producer Alan Harper
Company CBS News

443   Easter Sunday Mass   NBC
Program Type Religious/Cultural Special
60 minutes. Premiere date: 3/26/78. Live cover-
age of Easter Sunday mass from the National
Shrine of the Immaculate Conception in Wash-
ington, DC. Principal celebrant is His Eminence,
William Cardinal Baum, Archbishop of Wash-
ington.
Executive Producer Doris Ann
Company NBC Television Religious Programs
Unit
Director Richard Cox

444   Economically Speaking   PBS
Program Type Public Affairs Series
30 minutes. Premiere date: 7/28/78. Weekly series about government action, business and judicial decisions, and national and world events, on
the economic well-being of the nation and its
citizens. Program made possible by a grant from
L. E. Phillips Charities, Melvin S. Cohen Foundation, National Presto Foundation.
Executive Producer Robert Chitester
Producer Craig Perry
Company WQLN-TV/Erie Public Communications
Host Marina v. N. Whitman

445   The Edelin Conviction   PBS
Program Type Documentary/Informational
Special
2 hours. Premiere date: 5/3/78. Repeat date:
8/1/78. Dramatic re-enactment of the trial of
Dr. Kenneth Edelin, charged with the death of a
viable infant in the course of a legal abortion.
Producers Susan Mayer, Peter Cook
Director Bruce Shah
Company WGBH-TV/Boston
Host Bill Moyers

446   The Edge of Night   ABC
Program Type Daytime Drama Series
30 minutes. Mondays–Fridays. Premiere date:
4/2/56. Continuous. "The Edge of Night" and
"As the World Turns" were the first two 30-
minute daytime dramas. Moved from CBS to
ABC 12/1/75. Crime detection and intrigue set
in the fictional midwest city of Monticello.
Created by Irving Vendig. Theme music by Paul
Taubman. Cast listed alphabetically.
Producer Erwin Nicholson
Company Procter & Gamble Productions, Inc.
Directors John Sedwick, Andy Weyman
Head Writer Henry Slesar
                        CAST
Carol Barclay .... Polly Adams
Steve Guthrie .... Denny Albee
Nicole Drake ....Jayne Bentzen
Winter Austen .... Lori Cardille
Mike Karr .... Forrest Compton

Ben Everett .... Mel Cobb
Draper Scott .... Tony Craig
Miles Cavanaugh ....Joel Crothers
April Scott ....Terry Davis
Kevin Jamison ....John Driver
Deborah Saxon .... Frances Fisher
Nancy Karr .... Ann Flood
Raven Jamison .... Sharon Gabet
John (the Whitney Butler) .... George Hall
Trudy (the Whitney Maid) .... Mary Hayden
Geraldine Whitney ....Lois Kibbee
Chief Bill Marceau .... Mandel Kramer
Logan Swift .... Joseph Lambie
Calvin Stoner ....Irving Lee
Raney Cooper ....Kiel Martin
Tree ....Marilyn Randall
Denise Cavanaugh .... Holland Taylor
Tony Saxon .... Louis Turenne
Dr. Norwood .... Wyman Pendleton

447 Egyptian President Anwar Sadat's Visit to Israel ABC
Program Type News Special
60 minutes. Premiere date: 11/20/77. Barbara Walters jointly interviewing Israeli Prime Minister Menachem Begin and Egyptian President Anwar Sadat after the two leaders addressed the Knesset.
Executive Producer Jeff Gralnick
Supervising Producers Tom Capra, Robert Siegenthaler
Guest Commentator Abba Eban
Correspondents John Scali, Peter Jennings, Ted Koppel, Lou Croffi, Frank Reynolds, Sam Donaldson, Barrie Dunsmore, Jack Smith, Bill Seamans, Barbara Walters

448 Eight Is Enough ABC
Program Type Drama Series
60 minutes. Wednesdays. Premiere date: 3/22/77. Second season premiere: 9/14/77. Comedy-drama about a couple with eight children. Based on the book "Eight Is Enough" by Thomas Braden. Created by William Blinn. Music by Earle Hagen. Main theme by Fred Werner.
Executive Producers Lee Rich, Philip Capice
Producer Robert L. Jacks
Company Lorimar Productions, Inc.
Directors Various
Exec. Story Editor Greg Strangis
Story Editor Peter Lefcourt
Writers Various
Art Director Jim Bachman
Executive Consultant William Blinn
CAST
Tom Bradford ....Dick Van Patten
Sandra Sue Abbott (Abbey) .... Betty Buckley
David Bradford .... Grant Goodeve
Mary Bradford .... Lani O'Grady
Joannie Bradford .... Lauri Walters
Susan Bradford ....Susan Richardson
Nancy Bradford .... Dianne Kay
Elizabeth Bradford ....Connie Newton

Tommy Bradford .... Willie Aames
Nicholas Bradford .... Adam Rich
Dr. Maxwell .... Michael Thoma
Daisy Maxwell .... Virginia Vincent
Donna .... Jennifer Darling

449 Eleanor and Franklin
The ABC Friday Night Movie ABC
Program Type Dramatic Special
ABC Theatre
4 hours. Premiere dates: 1/11/76 and 1/12/76. Repeat dates: 6/2/78 and 6/3/78. Dramatization of the private lives of Franklin and Eleanor Roosevelt, based on the biography by Joseph P. Lash. Music by John Barry. Filmed in part in Tacoma and Seattle, Wash., Burkeville and Keysville, Va., Georgetown, Washington, D.C., Warm Springs, Ga. and Hyde Park, N.Y.
Executive Producer David Susskind
Producers Harry Sherman, Audrey Maas
Company A Talent Associates Ltd. Production
Director Daniel Petrie
Writer James Costigan
Conductor John Barry
Costume Designer Joe Tompkins
Story Consultants Franklin Delano Roosevelt, Jr., Joseph P. Lash
CAST
Franklin Delano Roosevelt .... Edward Herrmann
Eleanor Roosevelt ....Jane Alexander
Sara Delano Roosevelt .... Rosemary Murphy
Anna Hall ....Pamela Franklin
Elliott Roosevelt, Sr. ....David Huffman
Eleanor (age 14) ....Mackenzie Phillips
Mlle. Souvestre ....Lilia Skala
Louis Howe .... Ed Flanders
Daisy .... Helen Kleeb
Grace Tully .... Peggy McCay
Laura Delano .... Anna Lee
Mary Hall .... Irene Tedrow
Corinne Robinson .... Devon Ericson
Theodore Roosevelt .... William Phipps
Franklin (age 16) ....Ted Eccles
Lucy Mercer ....Linda Kelsey
Joe McCall .... Edward Winter
Mistress of Ceremonies .... Sari Price
Presidential Aide .... Timothy Jecko
Steve Early ....Harry Holcombe
Adm. McIntyre .... Len Wayland
Franklin (age 5) ....Brett Salomon
Eleanor (age 2) .... Hilary Stolla
Eleanor (age 6) .... Tiffani Boli
Groom ....Elie Liardet
Nun .... Irene Robinson
Eleanor (age 10) .... Shannon Terhune
Marjorie Bennett ....Lindsay Crouse
Bunny Pierpoint .... Evan Morgan
Fraulein Schreiber .... Lidia Kristen
Elsbeth McEachern .... Cynthia Latham
Hall Roosevelt ....John Earle Burnett
Maid .... Ellen Blake
Conductor .... Derrick Lynn-Thomas
Rev. Endicott Peabody ....Ned Wilson
Chief Petty Officer ....Carl Blackwell Lester
Western Union Boy ....Steve Tanner

Eleanor and Franklin *Continued*

Cora	Nora Heflin
Gladys	Cherry Davis
Porter	Alvin Childress
Anna Roosevelt (age 7)	Teresa Steenhoek
James Roosevelt (age 6)	Chris Le Fontone
Elliott Roosevelt (age 3)	Zachery Tiegen
Franklin Roosevelt (age 4–6)	Paul Thornton
Governess	June Whitley Taylor
John Roosevelt (age 2)	Warren Johnson
Anna Roosevelt (age 12)	Robin Fenton
James Roosevelt (age 11–13)	Jeff Roberts
Elliott Roosevelt (age 8–11)	Curt Beau
John Roosevelt (age 5)	Mike Adler
Anna Roosevelt (age 15)	Cindy Henderson
Dr. Lovett	Peter Brandon
Lead Folk Singer	Herbert Kenny
Farmer	Vaughn Taylor
Arthur Prettyman	Arthur Adams
Paul Leonard	Jack Stauffer

450   Eleanor and Franklin: The White House Years

ABC Theatre   ABC
Program Type Dramatic Special
3 hours. Premiere date: 3/13/77. Repeat date: 6/4/78. Dramatization of the lives of Eleanor and Franklin Delano Roosevelt from 1932–1945. Based on the biography "Eleanor and Franklin" by Joseph P. Lash. Music by John Barry. Filmed in part in Washington, D.C., Hyde Park, N.Y. and Pasadena, Calif.
Executive Producer David Susskind
Producer Harry R. Sherman
Company A Talent Associates Ltd. Production
Director Daniel Petrie
Writer James Costigan
Conductor John Barry
Costume Designer Joe I. Tompkins
Production Designer Jan Scott
Story Consultants Franklin Delano Roosevelt, Jr., Joseph P. Lash
CAST

Eleanor Roosevelt	Jane Alexander
Franklin Delano Roosevelt	Edward Herrmann
Missy Lehand	Priscilla Pointer
Louis Howe	Walter McGinn
Sara Delano Roosevelt	Rosemary Murphy
Anna Roosevelt	Blair Brown
Theodore Roosevelt	David Healy
Grace Tully	Peggy McCay
Harry Hopkins	Donald Moffat
Malvina Thompson	Toni Darnay
Dr. Carr	John Beal
Marian Anderson	Barbara Conrad
Plog	Morgan Farley
Robert Dunlap	Mark Harmon
Laura Delano	Anna Lee
Lucy Mercer	Linda Kelsey
Ike Hoover	Colin Hamilton
James Roosevelt	Ray Baker
John Roosevelt	Brian Patrick Clarke
Elliott Roosevelt	Don Howard
Franklin D. Roosevelt, Jr.	Joseph Hacker
Irvin McDuffie	Charles Lampkin

Electra Glide in Blue *See* ABC Tuesday Movie of the Week

451   The Electric Company

PBS
Program Type Children's Series
30 minutes. Mondays–Fridays (usually twice daily). Premiere date: 10/25/71. Seventh season premiere: 10/17/77. Informational series teaching basic reading skills to second through fourth graders. Skits, music, audience involvement in a magazine format. Teen rock group Short Circus members: June Angela, Todd Graff, Rejane Magloire, Janina Mathews, Rodney Lewis. Series funded by grants from the U.S. Office of Education—Dept. of Health, Education and Welfare, Public Television Stations, the Ford Foundation, the Corporation for Public Broadcasting, and the Carnegie Corporation of New York.
Executive Producer Samuel Y. Gibbon, Jr.
Producer Andrew B. Ferguson, Jr.
Company Children's Television Workshop
Director John Tracy
Head Writer Tom Whedon
Writers John Boni, Sara Compton, Tom Dunsmuir, Thad Mumford, Jeremy Stevens, Jim Thurman
Musical Director Dave Conner
Choreographers Patricia Birch, Liz Thompson
Costume Designer Mostoller
Production Designer Ronald Baldwin
Set Decorator Nat Mongioi
CAST

Dr. Doolots/Pedro	Luis Avalos
Paul the Gorilla/Blue Beetle/ J. Arthur Crank	Jim Boyd
Easy Reader	Morgan Freeman
Jennifer of the Jungle/ Julia Grownup	Judy Graubart
Fargo North, Decoder	Skip Hinnant
Pandora the Brat/Movie Director/ Millie-the-Helper	Rita Moreno
Spider-Man	Danny Seagren
The Fox/Valerie the Librarian	Hattie Winston
Milkman/Ken Kane	Bill Cosby
Vi	Lee Chamberlin

452   The Eleventh Year

Americana   PBS
Program Type Documentary/Informational Special
30 minutes. Premiere date: 1/21/77. Repeat date: 10/10/77. An interview with Robert La Pierre, paroled from the Bordentown Reformatory after eleven years in jail for murder.
Executive Producer Betty Adams
Company New Jersey Public Television/Trenton
Director Louis Presti
Interviewer Betty Adams

Elie Wiesel *See* The Itinerary of Elie Wiesel: From Sighet to Jerusalem

453 Eliza
Ourstory   PBS
Program Type Dramatic Special
30 minutes. Premiere date: 10/6/75. Repeat date: 10/3/77. Dramatization of the life of Eliza Lucas Pinckney who cultivated the first American indigo on her 18th century South Carolina plantation. Music composed by Luther Henderson. Filmed at the Middleburg Plantation and the Heyward-Washington House, Charleston, S.C. Program funded by a grant from the National Endowment for the Humanities.
Executive Producer Don Fouser
Producer Marcia Speinson
Company WNET-TV/New York
Director Don Fouser
Writer Don Fouser
Musical Director Luther Henderson
Costume Designer John Boxer
Art Director William Ritman
Set Decorator Charles Bennett
Host Bill Moyers
CAST
Eliza .... Tovah Feldshuh
Mrs. Lucas ....Polly Holliday
Col. Charles Pinckney ....Tom Klunis
Quash .... Howard E. Rollins, Jr.
Nicholas Cromwell .... Stephan Weyte
Young Officer .... Cyrus Newitt
Newspaper Publisher .... Mariett Wicks
Musicians Lucien De Groote, Suzanne G. Rollins, Larry Long
Messenger .... Quentin McGown IV
Polly .... Lee Gibbs
Little Girls .... Carletta Ball, Cleo Lyles
Slaves ....Charles Seabrook, Leroy Singleton, Myra Bennett
Field Hands ...... Pamela Robinson, Louise J. Waring
Additional Cast Fay King, Wendy Wofford, Jan Jenkins, Lenore Bender, Peggy Roehsler, Bill Bender, Norman Weber

Elizabeth of Lady Mead *See* PBS Movie Theater

454 An Elizabethan Christmas Celebration   PBS
Program Type Music/Dance Special
30 minutes. Premiere date: 12/18/77. Authentic songs and dances of the Elizabethan period staged in a simulated Elizabethan banquet hall with music performed on instruments used during the era. Features Indiana State University of Evansville Mid-America Singers under the direction of Dr. Jon Carlson.
Producer David Wilson
Company WNIN-TV/Evansville, Indiana
Director David Wilson

455 Elvis in Concert   CBS
Program Type Music/Dance Special
60 minutes. Premiere date: 10/3/77. Repeat date: 5/7/78. Taped at concerts in Omaha, Nebraska, and Rapid City, South Dakota.
Producers Gary Smith; Dwight Hemion
Director Dwight Hemion
Musical Director Joe Guercio
Star Elvis Presley

Elvis Presley *See* Memories of Elvis/Nashville Remembers Elvis on His Birthday

456 Emergency!
The Big Event/NBC Saturday Night at the Movies   NBC
Program Type Limited Series
2 hours (generally.) Saturdays. Premiere date: 1/22/72. The operations of the paramedics of Engine Company 51 of the Los Angeles County Fire Department and their liaison with Ramparts General Hospital. Shows broadcast irregularly during the 1977–78 season are: "The Steel Inferno" shown 1/7/78, "Survival on Charter #220" shown 3/25/78, "Most Deadly Passage" shown 4/4/78. Created by Harold Jack Bloom and Robert A. Cinader. Music by Billy May. Filmed in cooperation with the Los Angeles Fire Department.
Executive Producer Robert A. Cinader
Company Mark VII Ltd. Productions, in association with Universal Television and NBC-TV
Directors Various
Writers Various
CAST
John Gage .... Randolph Mantooth
Roy DeSoto .... Kevin Tighe
Dr. Kelly Brackett .... Robert Fuller
Dr. Joe Early ....Bobby Troup
Nurse Dixie McCall ....Julie London

457 The Emmy Awards   CBS
Program Type Parades/Pageants/Awards Special
2-1/2 hours. Live coverage of the 30th annual Emmy Awards from the Pasadena (Calif.) Civic Auditorium 9/17/78. Special music by Hank Beebe, Bill Hyer.
Producer Alexander H. Cohen
Company CBS Television
Director Clark Jones
Writer Hildy Parks
Musical Director Elliot Lawrence
Choreographer Ernest Flatt
Art Director Paul Barnes
Master of Ceremonies Alan Alda

Emmy Awards (Daytime) *See* The Daytime Emmy Awards

458   The Entertainer of the Year Awards
CBS
Program Type Parades/Pageants/Awards Special
90 minutes. Premiere date: 1/18/78. Eighth annual AGVA (American Guild of Variety Artists) Awards to its top performers. Taped at Caesar's palace in Las Vegas.
Executive Producer Robert Precht
Producer Saul Ilson
Company Sullivan Productions
Director Jeff Margolis
Writers Saul Ilson, Martin Ragaway
Musical Director Bob Rosario
Choreographer Jaime Rogers
Art Director Bill Bohnert
Presenters Rich Little, Phyllis Diller, Bernadette Peters, Steve Lawrence, Eydie Gorme, Mike Douglas, Roy Clark, Steve Landesberg, Bert Convy
Performers Totie Fields, Steve Martin, Barbra Streisand, Engelbert Humperdinck, Shirley MacLaine, Donny and Marie Osmond, Shields and Yarnell, Chicago, Dolly Parton, Fred the Bird, Milton Berle, Rita Moreno, Rich Little, Jim Bailey, Jack Haley, Sr., The Sylvers, The Third Generation Steps Dancers

459   Equal Justice Under the Law   PBS
Program Type Limited Series
30 minutes. Monday–Friday 9/12/77–9/19/77. 90 minutes, Saturdays, 9/24/77 and 10/1/77. Series repeated: 11/21/77. Dramatizations of several of the landmark judicial decisions made by Chief Justice John Marshall. Series made possible by a grant from the Judicial Conference of the United States.
Producers Mat von Brauchitsh; Bill Donovan
Company WQED-TV/Pittsburgh
Director Mat von Brauchitsch
Writer Mat von Brauchitsch
Host E. G. Marshall
CAST
Chief Justice Marshall .... Ed Holmes
Aaron Burr .... Nicholas Kepros

460   Equality   PBS
Program Type Documentary/Informational Special
60 minutes. Premiere date: 10/11/77. Repeat date: 1/17/78, Public affairs documentary on the views of such national figures as Gloria Steinem, Jesse Jackson, former U.S. Senator Fred Harris, as well as Americans from many walks of life. Created by Kenneth Stein. Program made possi-

ble by a grant from the New Jersey Committee for the Humanities.
Company New Jersey Public Television
Cinematographers Art Ciocco, Paul Buck

461   Erica   PBS
Program Type Miscellaneous Series
30 minutes. Premiere date: 1/4/76. Repeat dates: 9/5/77, 6/9/78 and 9/8/78. 13-week series of instruction in needlecraft.
Producer Margaret MacLeod
Director Russ Fortier
Writers Erica Wilson, Margaret MacLeod
Host Erica Wilson
Company WGBH-TV/Boston

462   The Erie War
Ourstory
Program Type Dramatic Special   PBS
30 minutes. Premiere date: 3/22/76. Repeat date: 10/31/77. A dramatization of Cornelius Vanderbilt's attempt to buy control of the Erie Railroad in 1868. Program funded by grants from the National Endowment for the Humanities, the Arthur Vining Davis Foundations and the George Gund Foundation.
Executive Producer Don Fouser
Producer Ron Finley
Company WNET-TV/New York
Director Ron Finley
Writer John Crowley
Costume Designer John Boxer
Art Director Stephen Hendrickson
Host Bill Moyers
Cartoonist Frank Springer
CAST
Cornelius Vanderbilt ....Gil Rogers
Jim Fisk ....Ron Faber
Jay Gould .... Lewis J. Stadlen
Daniel Drew .... Fred Stuthman
Thomas Nast .... Marshall Efron
Josie Mansfield .... Patricia Elliott
Erie Secretary ....Roy K. Stevens
Broker .... Gary Allen
Vanderbilt's Secretary .... William Duell
Office Boy .... Miles Chapin
Reporters .... Robert B. Silver, Page Johnson

463   Escapade   CBS
Program Type Dramatic Special
60 minutes. Premiere date: 5/19/78. Drama about U.S. secret agents. Music by Pat Williams.
Executive Producer Philip Saltzman
Producer Brian Clemens
Company Woodruff Production in association with Quinn Martin Productions
Director Jerry London
Writer Brian Clemens
CAST
Joshua .... Granville Van Dusen
Suzy .... Morgan Fairchild

Arnold Tulliver ....Len Birman
Paula ....Janice Lynde
Wences .... Alex Henteloff
Seaman ....Gregory Walcott
Charlie Webster .... Dennis Rucker

464 Escape from Bogen County
The CBS Tuesday Night Movies   CBS
Program Type TV Movie
2 hours. Premiere date: 10/7/77. Repeat date:
6/20/78. Drama of the wife of a political czar.
From a story by Christopher Knopf.
Executive Producer Howard W. Koch
Producers Frank Von Zerneck, Robert Greenwald
Company Moonlight Productions, Inc. in association with Paramount Television
Director Steven Stern
Writers Christopher Knopf, Judith Parker.
CAST
Maggie Bowman .... Jaclyn Smith
Ambler Bowman ....Mitchell Ryan
Jack Kern ....Michael Parks
Abe Rand .... Henry Gibson
Judge Henry Martin ....Pat Hingle
Harry Webb .... Philip Abbott
Emily Martin ....Julie Mannix
Sheriff Mason ....John Quade

465 Escape from Madness
NBC Reports   NBC
Program Type News Special
60 minutes. Premiere date: 6/28/78. Treatment
of several forms of mental illness by drugs and
psycho-social rehabilitation techniques examined.
Company NBC News
Reporter Tom Snyder

466 The Escape of a One-Ton Pet
ABC Weekend Specials/ABC Children's
Novel for Television   ABC
Program Type Children's Special
90 minutes. Premiere date: 1/7/78. Shown in
three parts, 30 minutes each on 1/7/78, 1/14/78
and 1/21/78. Repeat dates: 5/13, 5/20 and
5/27/78. A young girl raises a bull into a Blue
Ribbon winner.
Executive Producer Thomas W. Moore
Producer Jean Moore
Company A Tomorrow Entertainment Production
Director Richard Bennett
Writers Arthur Heinemann, George Lefferts
Photography Mario DiLeo
CAST
Pru Miller .... Stacy Swor
Dusty Miller ....James Callahan
Jaimie Lester .... Michael Morgan
Angela Montez .... Roxanna Bonilla Giannini
Stino Montez ....Richard Yniguez

467 Eternal Light   NBC
Program Type Religious/Cultural Series
30 minutes/60 minutes. Sundays. Religious-cultural programs presented by the Jewish Theological Seminar of America. Programs seen during
the 1977–78 season are: "A Conversation with
Dr. Chaim Potok," "A Conversation with Rabbi
Louis Finkelstein," "A Conversation with Rabbit Stanley J. Schachter," "The Itinerary of Elie
Wiesel: From Sighet to Jerusalem," "Sunlight
and Shadow—The Golden Age of Spanish
Jewry," and "The Tender Grass." (*See* individual titles for credits.)

468 Eugene Ormandy Conducts the Philadelphia Orchestra
Great Performances   PBS
Program Type Music/Dance Special
60 minutes. Premiere date: 2/1/78. Eugene Ormandy conducts the Philadelphia Orchestra in
"The Planets" by Gustav Holst at the Academy
of Music in Philadelphia with choral segments
performed by the Mendelssohn Club of Philadelphia. Program made possible by a grant from
Exxon and PBS stations.
Company Unitel and International Television
Trading Corporation for WNET-TV/New
York

469 The Eve of Christmas Eve   ABC
Program Type News Special
60 minutes. Premiere date: 12/23/77. Visits to
world news capitals for a look at Christmas,
1977, and what are likely to be major news stories
of 1978.
Executive Producer Jeff Gralnick
Company ABC News
Host Howard K. Smith
Correspondents Barbara Walters, Peter Jennings,
Frank Reynolds, Sylvia Chase, Jack Smith,
John Martin, Sam Donaldson, Ted Koppel,
Don Farmer, Stephen Geer

470 Even the Desert Will Bloom   PBS
Program Type Documentary/Informational
Special
60 minutes. Premiere date: 12/15/77. Documentary examines how we use and misuse our water.
Program made possible by a grant from the Corporation for Public Broadcasting.
Producer William M. Berg
Company WXXI-TV/Rochester
Director William M. Berg
Host Tom McCall
Narrator Tom McCall

471 **Evening at Pops**   PBS
Program Type Music/Dance Series
60 minutes. Sundays. Eighth season premiere
7/9/78. 13-week series featuring the Boston Pops
Orchestra in concert with guest singers, dancers
and musicians. Funding is provided by public
television stations.
Producer William Cosel
Company WGBH-TV/Boston
Director David Atwood
Conductor Arthur Fiedler

472 **An Evening at Pops Special: The
Esplanade**
Festival '78
Program Type Music/Dance Special   PBS
90 minutes. Premiere date: 3/7/78. Repeat date:
7/4/78. Arthur Fiedler and the Boston Pops Or-
chestra perform a Fourth of July concert on the
banks of Boston's Charles River. Program made
possible by a grant from Martin Marietta Corp.
Producer Bill Cosel
Company WGBH-TV/Boston
Conductor Arthur Fiedler

473 **Evening at Symphony**   PBS
Program Type Music/Dance Series
60 minutes/90 minutes. Sundays. Premiere date:
10/6/74. Fourth season premiere: 10/2/77. 13-
part series featuring the Boston Symphony Or-
chestra and guest conductors and soloists. Pro-
grams made possible by grants from Raytheon
Corporation, Public Television Stations, the
Ford Foundation and the Corporation for Public
Broadcasting.
Producer Jordan Whitelaw
Company WGBH-TV/Boston
Directors David Atwood; William Cosel
Musical Director Seiji Ozawa
Guest Conductors Colin Davis, Klaus Tennstedt

474 **Evening in Byzantium**   Syndicated
Program Type Dramatic Special
4 hours. Premiere date: 8/14/78 (Part II shown
8/21/78.) Adaptation of novel by Irwin Shaw.
Executive Producer Glen A. Larson
Supervising Producer Michael Sloan
Producer Robert F. O'Neill
Company GLP Productions and Universal TV
(MCA-TV)
Director Jerry London
Writers Glen A. Larson, Michael Sloan
CAST
Jesse Craig .... Glenn Ford
Bret Easton .... Vince Edwards
Constance Dobson .... Shirley Jones
Gail McKinnon .... Erin Gray
Brian Murphy .... Eddie Albert
Ian Wadleigh .... Patrick Macnee
Inspector Le Dioux .... Marcel Hillaire

Fabricio .... Gregory Sierra
Inspector DuBois .... Christian Marquand
Klein .... Simon Oakland
Sonia Murphy .... Gloria De Haven
Danny ....Michael Cole

475 **An Evening of Big-Band Swing**
Live from Wolf Trap   PBS
Program Type Music/Dance Special
2-1/2 hours. Premiere date: 8/21/78. An evening
of big band swing with Tex Beneke and his Orchestra with vocalists Helen O'Connell and Bob
Eberly. Program made possible by grants from
the Corporation of Public Broadcasting, PBS
member stations, and Allied Chemical Corporation.
Executive Producer David Griffiths
Producer Hal Hutkoff
Company WETA-TV/Washington

476 **An Evening of Blue Grass**
In Performance at Wolf Trap   PBS
Program Type Music/Dance Special
60 minutes. Premiere date: 11/8/77. Performance taped at Wolf Trap Park Farm featuring
the Dillards; Doc and Merle Watson; John Hartford and Bryan Bowers. Made possible by a grant
from Atlantic Richfield Company.
Executive Producer Ruth Leon
Company WETA-TV/Washington
Director Clark Santee

477 **An Evening of Championship
Skating (1977)**   PBS
Program Type Sports Special
60 minutes. Premiere date: 12/26/77. The fifth
annual exhibition of championship ice skating
taped at Watson Rink, Harvard University in
November 1977. Program made possible by a
grant from the Champion Spark Plug Company.
Producer Syrl Silberman
Company WGBH-TV/Boston
Director Russ Fortier
Host John Powers
Performers Charles Tickner, Robin Cousins, Su-
san Driano, Kristina Regoczy and Andras Sal-
lay, Lorna Wighton and John Dowding, Gail
Hamula and Frank Swieding.

478 **An Evening with Chuck Mangione**
Live from Wolftrap   PBS
Program Type Music/Dance Special
2 hours. Premiere date: 8/24/78. Composer/-
musician Chuck Mangione in a live concert from
Wolf Trap Farm Park. Program made possible
by grants from the Corporation for Public
Broadcasting, PBS member stations and Allied
Chemical Corporation.
Executive Producer David Griffiths

Producer Hal Hutkoff
Company WETA-TV/Washington
Director Robert Wynn

479 The Extremists: American Nazis Party and the Ku Klux Klan PBS
Program Type Documentary/Informational Special
60 minutes. Premiere date: 1/15/78. Examination of two extremist groups: American Nazis and the Ku Klux Klan. Nazi film by Ryan Wilson.
Producers Anthony L. Mahn, Gail Macandrew
Company KERA-TV/Dallas
Moderator Roger Wilkins
Panelists Seymour Martin Lipset, Irwin Suall, Bruce Ennis

480 Eyewitness PBS
Program Type Documentary/Informational Series
60 minutes. Premiere date: 8/25/77. Repeats began 11/15/77. Four shows realistically dramatizing the events and issues behind some of the most significant news stories of this era. Program made possible by a grant from the Corporation for Public Broadcasting.
Producer Thomas McCann
Company KERA-TV/Dallas-Fort Worth and Thomas McCann and Associates, Boston
Director Webster Lithgow
Writers Webster Lithgow, Lenny Glynn
Moderator Andrew Macmillan
Narrator Andrew Macmillan

481 Face the Nation CBS
Program Type Public Affairs Series
30 minutes. Sundays. Original premiere: 11/7/54. Ran through 4/20/61. Current series premiere: 9/15/63. Continuous. Interviews with people in the news. Generally originates live from Washington.
Producer Mary O. Yates
Company CBS News
Director Robert Vitarelli
Moderator George Herman

482 Faces of Communism PBS
Program Type Documentary/Informational Series
60 minutes. Premiere date: 7/9/78. Four-part series examining different forms of modern communism.
Producer John Fanshawe
Company WNET-TV/New York
Director Colin Nutley
Host Robert MacNeil
Reporter-Narrator Robert Kee

483 Falstaff
Opera Theater PBS
Program Type Music/Dance Special
2 hours. Premiere date: 7/10/78. Comic opera by Giuseppe Verdi performed in English with the English Chamber Orchestra. Libretto by Eric Crozier and Joan Cross. Program made possible by grants from PBS stations and the Nate B. and Frances Spingold Foundation.
Producer Cedric Messina
Company WNET-TV/New York
Director Basil Coleman
Conductor James Lockhart
CAST
Falstaff	Geraint Evans
Dame Quickly	Regina Resnik
Alice Ford	April Cantelo
Ford	Norman Bailey
Nanetta	Norma Burrowes
Genton	Neil Jenkins

Fame Is the Spur *See* PBS Movie Theater

484 Family ABC
Program Type Drama Series
60 minutes. Tuesdays. Premiere date: 3/9/76 (as six-week series.) Premiere date: 9/28/76 (as regular series). Second season premiere: 9/13/77. Story of a closely knit family in Pasadena, California. Created by Jay Presson Allen. Music by Pete Rugolo; theme by John Rubinstein.
Executive Producers Mike Nichols; Aaron Spelling; Leonard Goldberg
Producer Nigel McKeand
Company An Icarus Production in association with Spelling-Goldberg Productions
Directors Various
Executive Story Consultant Carol Evan McKeand
Writers Various
Story Consultant Jay Presson Allen
Art Director Paul Sylos
Cinematographer Emil Oster
Film Editor Jack Wheeler, James Faris, J. Frank O'Neill
CAST
Kate Lawrence	Sada Thompson
Doug Lawrence	James Broderick
Nancy Lawrence Maitland	Meredith Baxter Birney
Willie Lawrence	Gary Frank
Letitia "Buddy" Lawrence	Kristy McNichol

485 Family Circle Magazine Cup NBC
Program Type Sports Special
90 minutes each day. Live coverage of semi-final and final matches of the $125,000 women's tennis tournament from Sea Pines Plantation on Hilton Head Island, S.C. 4/15/78 and 4/16/78.
Executive Producer Don Ohlmeyer

Family Circle Magazine Cup *Continued*
Producer Ted Nathanson
Company NBC Sports
Director Ted Nathanson

486   Family Feud   ABC
Program Type Game/Audience Participation
Series
30 minutes. Mondays–Fridays. Premiere date:
7/12/76. Continuous. Question-and-answer
game in which two families compete trying to
match answers given by respondents in a nation-
wide survey.
Producer Howard Felsher
Company Goodson-Todman Productions
Director Paul Alter
Host Richard Dawson

Family Plot *See* NBC Monday/Saturday
Night at the Movies

487   A Family Upside Down
NBC World Premiere movie
Program Type TV Movie
2 hours. Premiere date: 4/9/78. A contemporary
love story which transcends the barriers of age.
Music by Henry Mancini.
Company Ross Hunter-Jacques Mapes
Director David Lowell Rich
Writer Gerald Di Pego
Cinematographer Joseph Biroc
CAST
Emma Long .... Helen Hayes
Ted Long .... Fred Astaire
Mike .... Efrem Zimbalist, Jr.
Carol .... Pat Crowley
Grandson .... Brad Rearden
Wendy .... Patty Duke Astin
Case .... Ford Rainey
Nurse Lovell .... Lanna Saunders
Al .... Karl Held
Mrs. Taka .... Miiko Taka
Paula .... Kim Hamilton

488   Famous Classic Tales   CBS
Program Type Animated Film Series
60 minutes. A series of animated specials for children based on classic tales. Programs shown during the 1977–78 season are: "A Christmas
Carol," "Davy Crockett on the Mississippi,"
"Five Weeks in a Balloon," and "Journey to the
Center of the Earth." (*See* individual titles for
credits.)

489   Fantasy Island   ABC
Program Type Drama Series
60 minutes. Premiere date: 1/28/78. Multiple
adventure-suspense, comedy and dramatic sto-

ries dealing with people's fantasies. Created by
Gene Levitt. Music by Laurence Rosenthal.
Executive Producers Aaron Spelling; Leonard
Goldberg
Producer Michael Fisher
Company A Spelling-Goldberg Production in as-
sociation with Columbia Pictures Television
Directors Various
Writers Various
Art Director Alfeo Bocchicchio
Cinematographer Don H. Birnkrant
Film Editor Dick Van Enger, Jr., A.C.E.
CAST
Roarke .... Ricardo Montalban
Tattoo .... Herve Villechaize

Farewell My Lovely *See* NBC Saturday
Night at the Movies

490   Fast Lane Blues
The ABC Saturday Comedy Special   ABC
Program Type Music/Comedy/Variety Special
60 minutes. Premiere date: 8/12/78. A crew of
"average Americans" participate in a cross-
country auto race
Producers William Blinn, Jerry Thorpe
Company Blinn/Thorpe Production
Director Jerry Thorpe
Writers Michael Leeson, William Blinn

491   The Fat Albert Christmas Special
CBS
Program Type Animated Film Special
30 minutes. Premiere date: 12/18/77. Music by
Yvette Blais and Jeff Michael.
Company A Filmation Production
Star Bill Cosby
Producers Lou Scheimer, Norm Prescott
Writers Bill Danch, Jim Ryan
Director Hal Sutherland
Art Director Alberto De-Mello
Director of Color Ervin L. Kaplan
Film Editor Jim Blodgett
Executive Producer William H. Cosby, Jr.
Educational Advisor Dr. Gordon L. Berry
Voices Bill Cosby, Jan Crawford, Gerald Ed-
wards, Eric Suter, Erika Carroll, Eric Greene,
Kim Hamilton, Julius Harris, Ty Henderson

492   The Fat Albert Halloween Special
CBS
Program Type Animated Film Special
30 minutes. Premiere date: 10/24/77. First
prime time venture of the award-winning series,
"Fat Albert and the Cosby Kids." Fat Albert and
his friends learn things are not always what they
seem as they go out on Halloween. Background
music by Yvette Blais and Jeff Michael.
Company Filmation Production

Producers Lou Scheimer, Norm Prescott
Director Hal Sutherland
Writers Bill Dancy, Jim Ryan
Art Director Alberto De Mello
Executive Producer William H. Cosby, Jr.
Educational Advisor Dr. Gordon L. Berry
Voices Bill Cosby, Jan Crawford, Gerald Edwards, Eric Suter, Erika Carroll

Fat City See The ABC Friday Night Movie

493 Fat Tuesday and All that Jazz!
In Performance at Wolf Trap   PBS
Program Type Music/Dance Special
90 minutes. Premiere date: 2/7/78. New Orleans Mardi Gras dance and music celebration featuring Arthur Hall Afro-American Dance Ensemble and the Dejan Olympia Brass Band from New Orleans' famed Preservation Hall. Program made possible by a grant from Atlantic Richfield Company.
Executive Producer Ruth Leon
Producer Wesley O. Brustad
Company WETA-TV Washington
Director Clark Santee
Musical Director Allan Jaffe

The Father See PBS Movie Theater

494 Father Knows Best Christmas Reunion
The Big Event   NBC
Program Type Dramatic Special
90 minutes. Premiere date: 12/18/77. The original cast of the "Father Knows Best" series are re-united for the Christmas holiday celebration.
Producer Hugh Benson
Exec. Consultant Eugene B. Rodney
Company Columbia Pictures Television Production
Writer Paul West
Director Norman Abbott
CAST
Jim Anderson .... Robert Young
Margaret Anderson .... Jane Wyatt
Betty Anderson .... Elinor Donahue
Bud Anderson .... Bill Gray
Kathy Anderson .... Lauren Chapin
Frank .... Jim McMullan
Jeanne .... Susan Adams
Jason Harper .... Hal England
Jennifer .... Cari Anne Warder
Robbie .... Christopher Gardner
Ellen .... Kyle Richard

Fear Is the Key See The CBS Saturday Night Movie

495 Feeling Free   PBS
Program Type Children's Series
30 minutes. Premiere date: 4/4/78. Six half-hour shows on kids and disabilities. Program made possible by grants from the Bureau of Education for the Handicapped and the Office of Career Education, U.S. Department of Health, Education and Welfare.
Executive Producer Christopher Sarson
Producer Mary Benjamin
Company Workshop on Children's Awareness, a division of the American Institutes for Research

496 Festival of the Stars: Mexico   CBS
Program Type Music/Comedy/Variety Special
2 hours. Premiere date: 5/18/78. Repeat date: 8/15/78. Musical-variety special taped in Acapulco, Guadalajara, Mexico City and other locations in Mexico.
Executive Producer Bob Stivers
Producers Bernard Rothman, Jack Wohl, Bob Synes
Company Bob Stivers Productions
Director Perry Rosemond
Writers Herbert Baker, Bunny Stivers
Musical Director George Wyle
Choreographer Ernest Flatt
Stars Steve Allen, Roy Clark, Gary Collins, Bert Convy, Jamie Lee Curtis, Barbara Eden, Freddie Fender, Mary Ann Mobley, Rita Moreno, Mummenschanz, Samantha Sang, Jerry Stiller, Anne Meara, Rip Taylor, Ballet Folklorico of Mexico, Boys Choir of Padre Barba, Charros of Guadalajara, Folklorico Ballet of Guadalajara, Mariachis of Guadalajara, Mexico State Symphony Orchestra conducted by Enrique Batiz, Rondalla Feminina
Hosts Suzanne Somers, John Ritter
Special Guest Host Ricardo Montalban

497 Festival '78   PBS
Program Type Miscellaneous Series
Annual drive for funds for Public Television Stations 3/1–18/78 during with a combination of music dance specials, dramatic specials, parts of limited series, educational/cultural series, science/nature specials and theatrically released films are shown. The music/dance specials are: "Austin City Limits," "Big Band Bash," Birthday Party for Josef Strauss," "Don Giovanni," "Evening at Pops Special: On the Esplanade," "The Johnny Mathis Special," "Live from the Grand Ole Opry," "Song by Song by Ira Gershwin," and "Soundstage." The dramatic specials are: "Count Dracula," "Country Tales: The Miracle of Brother Humphrey," and "The Strange Case of the End of Civilization as We Know It." Part of limited seried is: "Anna Karenina." Educational/cultural specials are: "Great American

Festival '78 *Continued*
Dream Machine Revisited," and the second season premiere of "Meeting of Minds." Science/-nature specials are: "The Case of the Ancient Astronauts" (Nova), "Diving for Roman Plunder," "The Living Sands of Namib," and "White Bear." Theatrically released films are "Great Expectations," (1947) shown 3/18/78 and "Hester Street" (1975) shown 3/14/78. (*See* individual titles for credits.)

498   Fiesta Bowl   CBS
Program Type Sports Special
3 hours. Live coverage of the Fiesta Bowl football game between the Arizona State University Sun Devils and the Pennsylvania State University Nittany Lions 12/25/77
Producer Tom O'Neil
Company CBS Television Network Sports
Director Tony Verna
Announcer Lindsey Nelson
Analyst Tom Matte

499   50 Years of Country Music
The Big Event   NBC
Program Type Music/Dance Special
3 hours. Premiere date: 1/22/78. Show taped January 4–11, 1978 at the Grand Ol' Opry House in Nashville.
Executive Producer Joseph Cates
Producer Chet Hagan
Director Walter C. Miller
Writers Chet Hagan, Frank Slocum
Musical Director Bill Walker
Art Director Don Shirley
Hosts Glen Campbell, Roy Clark, Dolly Parton

500   The Fighting Nightingales   CBS
Program Type Comedy Special
30 minutes. Premiere date: 1/16/78. Pilot about combat-weary nurses in the Korean War. Music by Steve Kagen.
Producers Barry Sand, Alan Uger
Company 20th Century-Fox Film Corporation
Producers Barry Sand, Alan Uger
Director George Tyne
Writers Alan Uger, Barry Sand
CAST
Maj. Kate Steele ....Adrienne Barbeau
Col. Jonas Boyette ....Kenneth Mars
Lt. Angie Finelli .... Livia Genise
Capt. "Irish" McCall .... Erica Yohn
Lt. Hope Phillips .... Stephanie Faracy
Pvt. Tyrone Vallone ....Randy Stumpf
Sgt. Barker .... George Whiteman
Patient No. 1 .... Jonathan Banks
Driver .... Frank Whiteman
Capt. Jules Meyers .... Jerry Hauser
Chaplain Billy Joe Lee ....Rod McCary
North Korean soldier ....Kim Iahana

501   The Final Tribute
NBC News Special   NBC
Program Type News Special
30 minutes. Premiere date: 1/16/78. A special program on the life of Senator Hubert Humphrey and a recap of the funeral and burial services.
Anchor Edwin Newman
Company NBC News

502   Findings–A Film about Reinhold Marxhausen   PBS
Program Type Documentary/Informational Special
60 minutes. Premiere date: 9/29/77. Documentary on Nebraska artist Reinhold Marxhausen. Program made possible in part by a grant from Bankers Life Nebraska.
Company Nebraska Educational Television Network

503   Fine Music Specials
Great Performances   PBS
Program Type Music/Dance Series
Times vary. Wednesdays. Classical music specials of concerts and operas. Programs presented during the 1977–78 season are: "Bernstein Conducts Mahler," "Madama Butterfly," "Rubinstein: Works of Chopin," and "Salome." (*See* individual titles for credits.)

504   Fire!
The Big Event   NBC
Program Type Dramatic Special
90 minutes. Premiere date: 5/8/77. Repeat date: 6/11/78. Drama about a forest fire threatening a mountain community. Based on a story by Norman Katkov. Music by Richard La Salle. Filmed on location in Oregon. Special effects by Cliff Wenger. Presented in conjunction with "Flood!" during the 1977–78 season.
Executive Producer Irwin Allen
Company An Irwin Allen Production in association with Warner Bros. Television and NBC-TV
Director Earl Bellamy
Writers Norman Katkov, Arthur Weiss
Art Director Ward Preston
CAST
Sam Brisbane .... Ernest Borgnine
Martha Wagner ....Vera Miles
Peggy Wilson .... Patty Duke Astin
Alex Wilson .... Alex Cord
Harriet Malone .... Donna Mills
Doc Bennett .... Lloyd Nolan
Larry Durant .... Neville Brand
Fleming ....Ty Hardin
Dan Harter ....Gene Evans
Judy .... Michelle Stacy
Frank .... Erik Estrada

505 The Fire Next Door
CBS Reports · CBS
Program Type Documentary/Informational Special
60 minutes. Premiere date: 3/22/77. Repeat date: 7/26/78. A look at the New York City neighborhood of the South Bronx.
Executive Producer Howard Stringer
Producer Tom Spain
Co-Producer Anne Chambers
Company CBS News
Director Tom Spain
Writers Bill Moyers, Tom Spain
Cinematographer Dan Lerner
Film Editor Peter C. Frank
Researcher Oliver Mobley
Reporter/Editor Bill Moyers

506 The Fire Next Door–Updated
CBS Reports · CBS
Program Type Documentary/Informational Special
Premiere date: 5/2/78. Update on view of life in New York City's South Bronx, shown 3/22/77.
Producer Jonnet Steinbaum
Cinematographers Dan Lerner, William J. Wagner
Film Editor Chris Dalrymple
Reporter Bill Moyers

Fires on the Plain *See* PBS Movie Theater

507 Firing Line
PBS
Program Type Public Affairs Series
60 minutes. Fridays. Show premiered in 1966. Continuous. Weekly interview show with people in the news. Series funded by grants from the Corporation for Public Broadcasting, the Ford Foundation, and Public Television Stations.
Producer Warren Steibel
Company Southern Educational Communications Association
Director Warren Steibel
Host William F. Buckley, Jr.

508 The First Easter Rabbit
CBS
Program Type Animated Film Special
30 minutes. Premiere date: 3/19/78. Animated Easter special. Original music by Maury Laws. Lyrics by Jules Bass. Animation by Toru Hara, Tsuguyuki Kubo.
Company Rankin/Bass
Producers Arthur Rankin, Jr., Jules Bass
Directors Arthur Rankin, Jr., Jules Bass
Conductor Maury Laws
VOICES
Stuffy .... Robert Morse
Flops .... Stan Freberg

Zero .... Paul Frees
Spats .... Paul Frees
Mother .... Joan Gardner
Whiskers ....Don Messick
Glinda .... Dina Lynn
Great Easter Bunny .... Burl Ives

509 First Mass of Pope John Paul I
ABC
Program Type News Special
Live coverage from Vatican City.
Executive Producer Jeff Grolnick
Company ABC News Special Events
Correspondents Frank Reynolds, Peter Jennings, Robert Trout
Guest Commentator Father Vincent O'Keefe

510 Fish
ABC
Program Type Comedy Series
30 minutes. Saturdays: Thursdays as of 1/12/78. Premiere date: 2/5/77. Second season premiere: 9/17/77. Last show: 6/1/78. Spin-off from "Barney Miller" about a detective and his wife who run a group home in New York City. Developed by Tony Sheehan; Danny Arnold and Chris Hayward. Music by Jack Elliott and Allyn Ferguson.
Executive Producer Danny Arnold
Producers Norman Barasch, Roy Kammerman
Company The Mimus Corporation
Directors Various
Story Editor Michael Loman
Writers Various
Art Director Thomas E. Azzari
CAST
Phil Fish .... Abe Vigoda
Bernice Fish .... Florence Stanley
Charlie Harrison .... Barry Gordon
Mike .... Lenny Bari
Loomis .... Todd Bridges
Victor .... John Cassisi
Jilly .... Denise Miller
Diane .... Sarah Natoli

511 The Fitzpatricks
CBS
Program Type Drama Series
60 minutes. Tuesdays. Premiere date: 9/20/77. Last show: 1/10/78. Special preview: 9/5/77. Contemporary drama about blue-collar, Irish-Catholic family in Flint, Michigan, created by John Sacret Young.
Executive Producer Philip Mandelker
Producer John Cutts
Company Warner Bros. Television
Directors Various
Writers Various
CAST
Mike Fitzpatrick .... Bert Kramer
Maggie Fitzpatrick .... Mariclare Costello
Maureen ....Michele Tobin
Sean .... Clark Brandon
Jack ....James Vincent McNichol
Max .... Sean Marshall

The Fitzpatricks *Continued*

R. J. .... Derek Wells
Kerry .... Helen Hunt

512   Five-Finger Discount

Special Treat   NBC
Program Type Children's Special
60 minutes. Premiere date: 11/1/77. Drama
about a 13-year-old girl who starts shoplifting to
impress other youngsters and become one of
their group. Music by Charles Albertine.
Producer Nancy Malone
Company Nancy Malone Productions in associa-
tion with 20th Century-Fox Television
Director Richard Bennett
Writer Jerry McNeely
Cinematographer Brianne Murphy
Film Editor Michael Goldman
                     CAST
Corny .... Dawn Lyn
Angela .... Dana Laurita
David .... Peter Donat
Jenna .... Nancy Malone
Sgt. Juden .... Elizabeth Allen
Mrs. Summerland .... Harriet Nelson

513   Five-Hundred-Mile Sculpture Garden

                                              PBS
Program Type Documentary/Informational
Special
60 minutes. Premiere date: 2/28/78. Story of Nebraska's Interstate-80 sculptures erected in
honor of the Bicentennial year. Program made
possible by grants from the Nebraska Arts Council and Nebraskans for Public Television, Inc.
Producer Byron Knight
Company Nebraska ETV Network

514   Five Weeks in a Balloon

Famous Classic Tales   CBS
Program Type Animated Film Special
60 minutes. Premiere date: 11/24/77. Adventure
about a trio traveling across the wilds of 19th
century Africa. Based on the novel by Jules
Verne.
Executive Producer Neil Balnaves
Company Hanna-Barbera Pty Ltd
Writer Kimmer Ringwald
Animation Director Chris Cuddington
Animators Cynthia Leach, Jean Tych, Susan
Beak, Peter Gardner, Ray Nowland, Gairden
Cooke, Greg Ingram, Di Rudder, Don Ezard,
Richard Dunn, Eden Anthony, John Martin,
Geoff Collins, Rodney D'Silva, Sebastian
Herpia, Paul Maron
Character Design Marija Miletic Dail, Jerry Ei-
senberg
Voices Brooker Bradshaw; Laren Lester, Gene
Whittington, Cathleen Cordell, Laurie Main,

Johnny Hayner, John Stephenson
Recording Director Alan Dinehart

515   A Flintstone Christmas

                                              NBC
Program Type Animated Film Special
60 minutes. Premiere date: 12/7/77. Animated
special with Fred and Wilma Flintstone, Barney
and Betty Rubble, their youngsters, Pebbles and
Bam Bam, and the Stone Age inhabitants of Be-
drock. Creative producer is Iwao Takamoto.
Story by Duane Poole and Dick Robbins.
Executive Producers William Hanna, Joseph
Barbera
Company Hanna-Barbera
Director Charles A Nichols
                    VOICES
Fred .... Henry Corden
Betty .... Gay Hartwig
Barney .... Mel Blanc

516   The Flintstone's Little Big League

                                              NBC
Program Type Animated Film Special
60 minutes. Premiere date: 4/6/78. Stone age
characters Fred Flintstone and his pal Barney
Rubble strain their friendship when they become
managers of competing baseball teams.
Executive Producers Joseph Barbera, William
Hanna
Assoc. Producer Neil Balnaves
Company Hanna-Barbera
Director Chris Cuddington
Writer Jameson Brewer

517   Flood!

The Big Event
Program Type Dramatic Special
90 minutes. Premiere date: 11/24/76. Repeat
date: 6/11/78. Drama of a small town hit by a
flood when a dam collapses. Filmed in part on
location in Eugene, Ore. Music by Richard La
Salle. Special effects by Cliff Wenger and Cliff
Wenger, Jr. Presented in conjunction with
"Fire!" during the 1977–78 season.
Executive Producer Irwin Allen
Company Irwin Allen Productions in association
with NBC-TV
Director Earl Bellamy
Writer Don Ingalls
Costume Designer Paul Zastupnevich
                    CAST
Steve Banning .... Robert Culp
Paul Blake .... Martin Milner
Abbie Adams .... Carol Lynley
Mary Cutler .... Barbara Hershey
Andy Cutler .... Eric Olson
John Cutler .... Richard Basehart
Alice Cutler .... Teresa Wright
Sam Adams .... Cameron Mitchell
Fisherman .... Roddy McDowall

Dr. Horne ....Whit Bissell
Daisy .... Francine York

518   Florida Citrus Open   NBC
Program Type Sports Special
Live coverage of the final rounds of the 13th annual Florida Citrus Open from the Rio Pinar Country Club in Orlando, Fla. 3/4/78 and 3/5/78.
Producer Larry Cirillo
Company NBC Sports
Director Harry Coyle
Commentators John Brodie, Jay Randolph, Bruce Devlin, Jim Simpson, Bob Goalby

519   The Flying Dutchman   PBS
Opera Theater
Program Type Music/Dance Special
3 hours. Premiere date: 5/11/76. Repeat dates: 9/6/77 and 7/24/78. First full-length television production of the opera by Richard Wagner. English translation by Peter Butler and Brian Large; production design by David Meyerscough Jones. Features the Ambrosian Opera Chorus and the Royal Philharmonic Orchestra. Program made possible by grants from the Ford Foundation, the Corporation for Public Broadcasting and Public Television Stations. Presented by WNET-TV/New York.
Coordinating Producers Linda Krisel, David Griffiths
Producer Brian Large
Company British Broadcasting Corporation and WNET-TV/New York
Conductor David Lloyd Jones
Chorus Master John McCarthy
CAST
Vanderdecken .... Norman Bailey
Senta .... Gwyneth Jones
Daland .... Stafford Dean
Eric .... Keith Erwen
Marie ....Joan Davies
The Steersman ....Robert Ferguson

520   Flying High   CBS
Program Type Dramatic Special
2 hours. Premiere date: 8/28/78. Pilot about airline stewardesses. Musical theme by David Shire. Musical score by Jonathan Tunick.
Producer Mark Carliner
Company Mark Carliner Productions, Inc.
Director Peter H. Hunt
Writers Marty Cohan, Dawn Aldredge
CAST
Pam Bellagio .... Kathryn Witt
Marcy Bower .... Pat Klous
Lisa Benton ....Connie Sellecca
Connie Martin ....Marcia Wallace
Captain March .... Howard Platt
Paul Mitchell .... Jim Hutton
Burt Stahl .... David Hayward

Bagranditello Jr. ....Martin Speer
Sally ....Lynn Marie Johnston
Desk Clerk .... Richard Hack
Dale ....Casey Biggs
First Stewardess Trainee .... Catherine Campbell
Miss Simmons ....Lilyan Chauvin
Mrs. Bellagio .... Carmen Zapata
Second Stewardess Trainee .... Cyndy James-Reese
Computer Expert .... Victoria Shaw

521   Football's Red Dogs, Fumbles, Flankers and Flickers: A Sports Magazine for Children   NBC
Program Type Sports Special
60 minutes. Premiere date: 12/3/77. First network sports special for youngsters.
Producer Don Ohlmeyer
Star Franco Harris
Hosts Allyson Johnson, John Brodie

For Better, For Worse *See* The CBS Saturday Night Movie

For Pete's Sake *See* The ABC Summer Movie

522   For Richer For Poorer   NBC
Program Type Daytime Drama Series
30 minutes. Monday–Friday. Premiere date: 12/6/77. Situations arising out of conflict of the young and their elders, and within the young in search of their own values. Created by Harding Lemay. Cast listed alphabetically.
Executive Producer Paul Fauch
Head Writer Tom King
Directors Jack Hofsiss, Barnet Kellman
Costume Designer Julie Weiss
Set designer James Leonard Joy
Company Proctor and Gamble Productions, Inc.
Announcer William Wolf
Writers Dorothy Purser, Joe LeSeuer, Tom Megdall
CAST
Bentley Saxton .... David Abbott
Austin Cushing .... Rod Arrants
Jason Saxton .... Richard Backus
Edith Cushing ....Laurinda Barrett
Violet Brewster .... Pat Barry
Roger Hamilton ....Charles Bateman
Connie Saxton .... Cynthia Bostick
Lee Ferguson .... Robert Skip Burton
Josie Saxton ....Patricia Englund
Stan Hillmer ....Michael Goodwin
Tessa Saxton .... Breon Gorman
Bill Saxton .... Tom Happer
Amy Cushing .... Christine Jones
George Kimball .... Stephen Joyce
Desmond Hamilton .... David Knapp
Wendy Prescott .... Connie LoCurto
Laurie Hamilton ....Julia MacKenzie
Barbara Manners .... Lynne MacLaren

For Richer For Poorer *Continued*

Paco .... Chu Chu Mulave
Megan Cushing .... Darlene Parks
Eleanor Kimball .... Flora Plumb
Ira Ferguson .... Roy Poole
Mildred Quinn .... Sloane Shelton
Lester Saxton .... Albert Stratton

Forbidden Games *See* PBS Movie Theater

523   Forest Hills Invitational Men's Tennis Championships   ABC

Program Type Sports Special
2 hours. 7/15/78. Finals shown on 7/16/78.
Tennis tournament live from West Side Tennis Club's historic Forest Hills Stadium in New York City.
Executive Producer Roone Arledge
Producer Ric LaCivita
Company ABC Sports
Director Chet Forte
Commentators Howard Cosell, Jim Lampley
Expert Commentator Pancho Gonzalez

524   Forever

The CBS Friday Night Movies   CBS
Program Type TV Movie
2 hours. Premiere date: 1/6/78. Story of a teenager's first love. Music by Fred Karlin. From the novel by Judy Blume.
Executive Producer Roger Gimbel
Producers Marc Trabulus, Merrit Malloy
Company EMI Television Programs, Inc.
Director John Korty
Writers A. J. Carothers, Joanna Crawford
CAST
Kath Danziger .... Stephanie Zimbalist
Michael .... Dean Butler
Artie .... John Friedrich
Erica .... Beth Raines
Sibyl .... Diana Scarwid
Theo Maxton .... Jordan Clark
Mr. Danziger .... Tom Dahlgren
Mrs. Danziger .... Judy Brock
Grandpa .... Woodrow Chambliss
Grandma .... Erica Chambliss

525   Forever Fernwood   Syndicated

Program Type Comedy Series
30 minutes. Monday–Friday. Premiere date: 10/3/77. Continuation of series titled "Mary Hartman, Mary Hartman" during the 1976–77 season. Created by Gail Parent, Ann Marcus, Jerry Adelman and Daniel Gregory Browne; developed by Norman Lear.
Producers Eugenie Ross Leming, Brad Buckner
Company TAT Communications
Director Jim Drake

Writers Jerry Adelman, Peggy Goldman, Karen Jones, Mara Lideks, Mitch Markowitz
CAST
Tom Hartman .... Greg Mullavey
Cathy .... Debralee Scott
Heather .... Claudia Lamb
Martha Shumway .... Dody Goodman
Loretta Haggers .... Mary Kay Place
Dr. Elliot .... William Bogert
Merle Jeeter .... Dabney Coleman
Wanda .... Marian Mercer
Eleanor Major .... Shelley Fabares
Dr. Winston .... Norman Parker
Penny .... Judy Kahan
Bartender .... Robert Stoneman

Forty Carats *See* The ABC Friday Night Movie

526   Four Feathers

Bell System Family Theatre/The Big Event   NBC
Program Type Limited Series
2 hours. Premiere date: 1/1/78. Based on book by A. E. W. Mason about an English officer accused of cowardice in the 1800s. Filmed in England and Spain. Recommended by the National Education Association. Music by Allyn Ferguson.
Producer Norman Rosemont
Company Trident Films in association with Norman Rosemont Productions
Director Don Sharp
Writer Gerald DiPego
Costume Designer Olga Lehmann
CAST
Harry Faversham .... Beau Bridges
Ethne Eustace .... Jane Seymour
Capt. Jack Durrance .... Robert Powell
William Trench .... Simon Ward
David Faversham .... Harry Andrews
Abou Fatma .... Richard Johnson
Willoughby .... David Robb
Wembol .... Richard Beale

The Four Musketeers *See* The CBS Friday Night Movies

527   The Fourth Annual International Circus Festival of Monte Carlo   CBS

Program Type Music/Comedy/Variety Special
60 minutes. Premiere date: 1/18/78. Taped at Monte Carlo, Monaco. Great acts in the world of circus, selected by a jury of circus critics and aficionados.
Executive Producers Irvin Feld, Kenneth Feld for Ringling Bros., and Barnum & Bailey Combined, Inc.
Producer John Moffitt
Director John Moffitt
Writer Robert Arthur

Hosts John Davidson, Brenda Vaccaro
Judges John Ringling North, Cary Grant, Horst Buchholz, Jacqueline Cartier

528 The Fourth King NBC

Program Type Animated Film Special
30 minutes. Premiere date: 12/23/77. Animated musical special for the Christmas season telling how the animal kingdom discovers and celebrates the Birth of Christ. Book by Alvin Cooperman and Seymour Reit. Lyrics written by Cooperman; music by Ralph Affoumado. Arrangements by Eddie Sauter.
Executive Producer Renato M. Pachetti
Producers Alvin Cooperman, Bruno Caliandro
Company RAI Television Production for NBC
Musical Director Elliot Lawrence
CAST VOICES
Lion .... Ted Ross
Sparrow .... Laurie Beechman
Turtle .... Arnold Stang
Beaver .... Bob McFadden
Rabbit .... Ed Clein

529 Fox and Leonard Go to the Movies
Syndicated
Program Type Talk/Service/Variety Series
30 minutes. Premiere date: 1/6/78. Series featuring clips from past and present films.
Executive Producer Don Davidson
Producer Sonny Fox
Director Bob Fitzpatrick
Writers Sonny Fox, Bob Leonard
Hosts Sonny Fox, Bob Leonard

Framed *See* The CBS Wednesday Night Movies

530 Francesca, Baby
ABC Afterschool Specials ABC
Program Type Children's Special
60 minutes. Premiere date: 10/6/76. Repeat date: 1/25/78. Drama of a 15-year-old girl trying to cope with the problems created by her mother's alcoholism. Adapted from the book by Joan Oppenheimer. Music composed by Hod David.
Producer Martin Tahse
Company Martin Tahse Productions, Inc.
Director Larry Elikann
Writer Bob Rodgers
CAST
Francesca .... Carol Jones
Lillian .... Melendy Britt
Bix .... Dennis Bowen
Kate .... Tara Talboy
Connie .... Alice Nunn
Gordon .... Peter Brandon
Jo Lynn .... Elizabeth Herbert
Mike .... Benny Medina
Patty .... Doney Oatman

Greg .... Scot Marc Sovie
Marion .... Mona Tera
Mrs. Handley .... Lee Kessler
Salesgirl .... Barbara England
Louise .... Jody Britt

531 Francis of Assisi: A Search for the Man and His Meaning NBC

Program Type Religious/Cultural Special
60 minutes. Premiere date: 12/11/77. Repeat date: 5/7/78. Documentary on Saint Francis of Assisi.
Producer Martin Hoade
Company NBC Television Religious Programs Unit with the U.S. Catholic Conference
Director Martin Hoade
Writer Philip Scharper
Narrators Rev. Agnellus Andrew, O.F.M., Lee Richardson

532 Fred Rogers: Won't You Be My Neighbor PBS

Program Type Documentary/Informational Special
30 minutes. Premiere date: 1/1/78. Documentary on Fred Rogers, creator/host of public television's longest running children's program, "Mister Rogers' Neighborhood."
Executive Producer Doris Ann
Company WLVT-TV/Allentown for the Pennsylvania Public Television Network
Musical Director John Costa
Interviewer Shelley Brown

533 Free Country ABC

Program Type Comedy Series
30 minutes. Saturdays. Premiere date: 6/24/78. Last show: 7/22/78. Traces the lines of an immigrant family from its arrival in America at the turn of the century to the present day.
Executive Producers Rob Reiner, Phil Mishkin
Producer Gareth Davies
Company Reiner/Mishkin Productions in association with Columbia Pictures Television
Directors Various
CAST
Joseph Bresner .... Rob Reiner
Anna Bresner .... Judy Kahan
Sidney Gewertzman .... Fred McCarren
Ida Gewertzman .... Renee Tippin
Cousin Willy .... Larry Hankin
Leo Gold .... Larry Gelman
Louie Peschi .... Joe Pantoliano

Freebie and the Bean *See* The ABC Friday Night Movie

534 Freeman

Visions   PBS
Program Type Dramatic Special
90 minutes. Premiere date: 10/9/77. Drama
about a young black man who cannot find a place
in a society of compromised values. Music by
Phil Moore.
Producer Barbara Schultz
Company KCET-TV/Los Angeles
Director Lloyd Richards
Writer Phillip Hayes Dean
Costume Designer Terence Tam Soon
Art Director Michael Baugh
CAST
Freeman .... Dick Anthony Williams
Osa Lee .... Chip Fields
Rex .... Lou Gossett
Ned .... Richard Ward
Teresa .... Paulene Myers

535 The French Chef   PBS

Program Type Educational/Cultural Series
30 minutes. Premiere date: 10/14/70. Repeat
date: 10/9/77. 39-week series featuring the fa-
mous chef Julia Child. Series made possible by
Public Television Stations and the Polaroid
Corp.
Producer Ruth Lockwood
Company WGBH-TV/Boston

The French Connection *See* The CBS Saturday Night Movie

536 Friends   CBS

Program Type Comedy Special
30 minutes. Premiere date: 8/19/78. Pilot about
a once-popular team of rock singers who decide
to become staff songwriters for a Hollywood
record company. Created and written by
Lorenzo Music and Steve Pritzker.
Producers Lorenzo Music, Steve Pritzker
Company Music/Pritzker Production in associa-
tion with Universal Television
Director Hy Averback
CAST
Teddy Serrano .... Michael Tucci
Scott Rollins .... Darrell Fetty
Leslie Frankel .... Doris Brenner
Susan Rollins .... Susan Buctner
J.B. Henderson .... Brian Cutler
Gordon Bass .... Larry Cedar
Andrea .... Diane Lander
Diane Miller .... Rae Dawn Chong

The Friends of Eddie Coyle *See* The ABC Sunday Night Movie

537 From Monticello   CBS

Program Type Educational/Cultural Special
60 minutes. Premiere date: 11/27/77. The con-
tributions of Thomas Jefferson to America's art
and architecture discussed at Monticello by J.
Carter Brown, Director of the National Gallery,
and Rep. John Bardemas, Marjority Whip of the
House of Representatives.
Executive Producer Pamela Ilott
Producer Ted Holmes
Host Ted Holmes

From Noon till Three *See* The CBS Saturday/Wednesday Night Movies

538 From Paris with Love: An Evening of French Television   PBS

Program Type Documentary/Informational
Special
3 hours. Premiere date: 7/14/78. Highlights of
French television including commercials.
Created by Fred Flaxman.
Company WETA-TV/Washington and Video
Centre International, Paris.
Host Evelyn Leclercq

539 Frosty the Snowman   CBS

Program Type Animated Film Special
30 minutes. Premiere date: 12/7/69. Repeat
date: 12/10/77. Based on the song by Jack Rol-
lins. Music and lyrics by Jules Bass, Maury
Laws.
Producers Arthur Rankin, Jr., Jules Bass
Director Arthur Rankin, Jr., Jules Bass
Writer Romeo Muller
Narrator Jimmy Durante
VOICES
Frosty .... Jackie Vernon
Prof. Hindle .... Billy DeWolfe

540 Frosty's Winter Wonderland   ABC

Program Type Animated Film Special
30 minutes. Premiere date: 12/2/76. Repeat
date: 12/3/77. Animated musical sequel to
"Frosty the Snowman" using dimensional stop-
motion photography.
Producers Arthur Rankin, Jr., Jules Bass
Company Rankin-Bass Productions
Directors Arthur Rankin, Jr., Jules Bass
Writer Romeo Muller
Musical Director Maury Laws
Narrator Andy Griffith
Animators Toru Hara, Tsuguyuki Kubo
VOICES
Mrs. Frosty .... Shelley Winters
Parson Brown .... Dennis Day
Frosty .... Jackie Vernon
Jack Frost .... Paul Frees

Additional Voices Shelley Hines, Erik Stern, Manfred Olea, Barbara Jo Ewing, The Wee Winter Singers

541   Funeral of Pope Paul VI   NBC
Program Type News Special
2 hours. Live coverage of the funeral of Pope Paul VI on 8/12/78.
Company NBC News
Anchor Edwin Newman
Correspondents Garrick Utley, John Palmer

542   Funny Business   CBS
Program Type Comedy Special
2 hours. Premiere date: 7/26/78. Special devoted to the great comedians of the 30s and 40s.
Executive Producer Leonard B. Stern
Producer Richard Schickel
Company Heyday Prods. & Universal TV
Director Richard Schickel
Writer Richard Schickel
Host Walter Matthau

Funny Girl *See* ABC Tuesday Movie of the Week

543   The Funny World of Fred and Bunni   CBS
Program Type Music/Comedy/Variety Special
60 minutes. Premiere date: 8/30/78. Musical variety combining live performances and animation. Special musical material by Dick Williams.
Executive Producer Joseph Barbera
Producers John Aylesworth, Frank Peppiatt
Company Hanna-Barbera Productions
Director Bill Davis
Writers John Aylesworth, Frank Peppiatt, Barry Adelman, Barry Silver, Pat Harrington, James Burr Johnson
Musical Directors Jack Elliott, Allyn Ferguson
Choreographer Rob Iscove
Costume Designer Ret Turner
Star Fred Travalena
Guest Stars Sandy Duncan, Pat Harrington, Vicki Lawrence

Futureworld *See* The ABC Friday Night Movie

Gable and Lombard *See* NBC Monday/Saturday Night at the Movies

544   Gabriel Kaplan Presents the Small Event   ABC
Program Type Music/Comedy/Variety Special
60 minutes. Premiere date: 10/23/77. Star of

"Welcome Back, Kotter," hosts a spoof of popular television specials.
Executive Producer Gabriel Kaplan
Producer Eric Cohen
Company Rotunda Productions, Inc.
Director Bill Davis
Writers Eric Cohen, David Panich, Peter Gallay, Ray Taylor, Gabriel Kaplan
Musical Director George Wyle
Costume Designer Frank Novak
Art Director Gene McAvoy
Film Sequences Group One
Host Gabriel Kaplan
Guest Stars Sid Caesar, Cindy Williams, Fred Willard
Cameo Appearances Henny Youngman, Pat Morita, Robert Hegyes, Ron Palillo, Lawrence-Hilton Jacobs, John Travolta, John Sylvester White

545   Gala Performance: Minnesota Orchestra's 75th Anniversary Concert   PBS
Program Type Music/Dance Special
2 hours. Premiere date: 6/13/78. 7th Anniversary concert of the Minnesota Orchestra from Orchestra Hall in Minneapolis. "In Praise of Music" composed by Dominick Argento. The Bach Society and the Minnesota Chorale combine forces for Beethoven's Ninth Symphony. Soloists include soprano Carole Farley; mezzosoprano Gabrielle Levigne; tenor Peter Lindroos and bass John Cheek. Program made possible in part by a grant from Northwestern Bell.
Producers Jordan Whitelaw, William Cosel
Company KTCA-TV/St. Paul
Musical Director Stanislaw Skrowaczewski

546   The Gardener's Son
Visions   PBS
Program Type Dramatic Special
2 hours. Premiere date: 1/6/77. Repeat date: 1/15/78. Drama based on fact about the murder of a South Carolina mill owner by a boy in the 1870s. Concept by Richard Pearce. Music by Charles Gross. Program made possible by grants from the Ford Foundation, the National Endowment for the Arts and the Corporation for Public Broadcasting.
Executive Producer Barbara Schultz
Producers Michael Hausman, Richard Pearce
Company KCET-TV/Los Angeles
Director Richard Pearce
Writer Cormac McCarthy
Costume Designer Ruth Morley
Art Director Patrizia Von Brandenstein
Scenic Designer Carl Copeland
CAST
Robert McEvoy .... Brad Dourif
James Gregg .... Kevin Conway

The Gardener's Son *Continued*

Mrs. Gregg ....Nan Martin
Patrick McEvoy .... Jerry Hardin
Martha McEvoy .... Anne O'Sullivan
Mrs. McEvoy .... Penelope Allen
Pinky .... Ned Beatty
W. J. Whipper .... Paul Benjamin
Dr. Perceval .... Earl Wynn
Daphne .... Esther W. Tate
Maryellen McEvoy .... Helen Harmon

547   Gardening from the Ground Up PBS
Program Type Educational/Cultural Series
30 minutes. Premiere date: 6/17/78. Series
aimed specifically at the interests and concerns of
the Western gardener. Program made possible by
a grant from Home Savings and Loan Associa-
tion.
Executive Producer Don Roman
Producer Walter Louie
Company KQED-TV/San Francisco
Director Walter Louie
Host John Bryan

548   The Gathering
ABC Theatre   ABC
Program Type Dramatic Special
2 hours. Premiere date: 12/4/77. Drama of an
estranged husband and father facing his last
Christmas and his attempt to arrange one more
traditional holiday celebration with his family.
Music composed and conducted by John Barry.
Filmed entirely on location in Chagrin Falls and
Hudson, Ohio.
Executive Producer Joseph Barbera
Producer Harry R. Sherman
Company Hanna-Barbera Productions, Inc.
Director Randal Kleiser
Writer James Poe
Costume Designer Joe I. Thompkins
Film Editor Allan Jacobs
Art Director Jan Scott
Set Decorator Anne D. McCully
                            CAST
Adam Thornton ....Edward Asner
Kate Thornton .... Maureen Stapleton
Julie Pelham .... Rebecca Balding
Clara ....Sarah Cunningham
George Pelham .... Bruce Davison
Helen Thornton .... Veronica Hamel
Bud Thornton .... Gregory Harrison
Bob Block ....James Karen
Tom Thornton .... Lawrence Pressman
Dr. Hodges .... John Randolph
Peggy Thornton .... Gail Strickland
Roger .... Edward Winter
Toni Thornton .... Stephanie Zimbalist

Gator *See* CBS Special Movie
    Presentations

549   Gator Bowl   ABC
Program Type Sports Special
Live coverage of the Gator Bowl football game
between the Pittsburgh Panthers and the Clem-
son Tigers from the Gator Bowl in Jacksonville,
Florida 12/30/77.
Executive Producer Roone Arledge
Producer Bob Goodrich
Company ABC Sports
Director Andy Sidaris
Play-by-Play Announcer Keith Jackson
Expert Color Commentator Frank Broyles

550   GE Theater   CBS
Originally premiered as 30-minute series 2/1/53.
Returned after a decade 12/18/73 as a series of
specials. Two dramas broadcast during the
1977–78 season: "See How She Runs," and "Tell
Me My Name." (*See* individual titles for credits.)

**551   Gene Kelly ... An American in
Pasadena**   CBS
Program Type Music/Dance Special
60 minutes. Premiere date: 3/13/78. Salute to
Gene Kelly taped at Ambassador Auditorium,
Pasadena, Calif. Special music by Ray Charles.
Executive Producers Marty Pasetta; Frank Ko-
nigsberg
Producer Buz Kohan
Company Konigsberg/Pasetta Productions
Director Marty Pasetta
Writer Buz Kohan
Musical Director Jack Elliott
Choreographer Danny Daniels
Costume Designer Bill Hargate
Art Directors Gene McAvoy, Tom Meleck
Film Sequences Stu Bernstein, Eytan Keller
Title Animation Hanna-Barbera
Star Gene Kelly
Special Guests Lucille Ball, Cyd Charisse, Danny
Daniels, Gloria de Haven, Betty Garrett, Ka-
thryn Grayson, Bridget Kelly, Janet Leigh,
Liza Minnelli, Alex Romero, Frank Sinatra,
Cindy Williams
Featured Ray Charles Singers, Irish Pipers Band
of San Francisco

552   General Hospital   ABC
Program Type Daytime Drama Series
45 minutes. Mondays–Fridays. Premiere date:
4/1/63. Continuous. Became 60-minute show
1/16/78. Series set in the Port Chester hospital.
Created by Frank Hursley and Doris Hursley.
John Beradino and Emily McLaughlin are original cast members. Peter Hansen joined the show
the first year. Cast listed alphabetically. Cast as
of 3/79.
Producer Gloria Monty

Directors Alan Pultz, Phil Sogard, Marlena Laird, Sam Sherman
Head Writer Douglas Marland
Musical Director Charles Paul

CAST

Dr. Leslie Webber	Denise Alexander
Audrey Hobart Hardy	Rachel Ames
Dr. Jeff Webber	Richard Dean Anderson
Dr. Gina Lansing	Donna Bacalla
Dr. Steve Hardy	John Beradino
P.J./Steven Lars	Robert Betzel
Cal Jamison	Larry Block
Roy DiSicco	Asher Brauner
Dr. Gail Adamson	Susan Brown
Diana Taylor	Brooke Bundy
Gary Lansing	Steve Carlson
Dr. Monica Webber Quartermaine	Leslie Charleson
Dorrie Fleming	Angela Cheyne
Alan Quartermaine	Stuart Damon
Bryan Phillips	Tod Davis
Mrs. Grant	Lieux Dressler
Tracy Quartermaine	Jane Elliot
Maggie Taylor	Nancy Fox
Laura Vining	Genie Ann Francis
Luke Spencer	Anthony Geary
Tommy Baldwin	Bradley Green
Lee Baldwin	Peter Hansen
Dr. Peter Taylor	Craig Huebing
Coleen Middleton	Joyce Jameson
Dan Rooney	Frank Maxwell
Jessie Brewer	Emily McLaughlin
Heather Grant Webber	Mary O'Brien
Anne Logan	Susan O'Hanlon
Mitch Williams	Chris Pennock
Susan Moore	Gail Ramsey
Dr. Rick Webber	Chris Robinson
Howard Lansing	Richard Sarradet
Scotty Baldwin	Kin Shriner
Jeremy Hewitt	Philip Tanzini
Spence Andrews	Dan Travanti
Larry Joe Baker	Hunter Von Leer
Bobbie Spencer	Jackie Zeman–Kaufman

553 Gentle Giants of the Pacific NBC
Program Type Documentary/Informational Special
60 minutes. Premiere date: 12/10/77. Special revealing the living habits of the endangered humpback whales. Based on research projects by the World Wildlife Fund, the New York Zoological Society, the National Geographic Society and the California Academy of Sciences. Music by Nelson Riddle.
Producer Aubrey Buxton
Company Survival Anglia Ltd.
Writer Colin Willock
Cinematographer Al Giddings
Narrator Richard Widmark
Experts Dr. Sylvia Earle, Dr. Roger Payne, Katy Payne

554 The George Burns One-Man Show
CBS
Program Type Music/Comedy/Variety Special
60 minutes. Premiere date: 11/23/77. Music arranged and conducted by Jack Elliott and Allyn Ferguson.
Executive Producer Irving Fein
Producer Stan Harris
Company GBF Productions
Director Stan Harris
Writers Elon Packard, Fred S. Fox, Seaman Jacobs
Choreographer Walter Painter
Art Director Rene Lagler
Star George Burns
Guest Stars Ann–Margret, The Captain and Tennille, Gladys Knight and the Pips, Bob Hope

555 George Crumb: Voice of the Whale
PBS
Program Type Music/Dance Special
60 minutes. Premiere date: 6/6/78. George Crumb plays some of his favorite compositions and talks with fellow artist Richard Wernick. Program made possible in part by a grant from the Corporation for Public Broadcasting.
Company Maryland Center for Public Broadcasting

556 George's House
Dance for Camera PBS
Program Type Music/Dance Special
30 minutes. Premiere date: 6/29/76. Repeat date: 1/23/78. Dances filmed on location in a 200-year-old farmhouse in New Hampshire. Bluegrass music composed by Don Stover and Paul Chrisman. Program made possible by grants from the Rockefeller Foundation, the National Endowment for the Arts and the Corporation for Public Broadcasting.
Producer Nancy Mason
Company WGBH New Television Workshop/ Boston
Director David Atwood
Choreographer Dan Wagoner
Host Carmen de Lavallade

557 Gerald R. Ford: Presidential Decisions
NBC News Special NBC
Program Type News Special
60 minutes. Premiere date: 4/26/78. John Chancellor interviews former President Gerald R. Ford.
Executive Producer Gordon Manning
Producer Kenneth Donaghue
Company NBC News
Director Marvin D. Einhorn

558   Getting Married

The CBS Wednesday Night Movies   CBS
Program Type TV Movie
2 hours. Premiere date: 5/17/78. Romantic
comedy about a persistent suitor. Music by Craig
Safan. Song, "Now That I've Found You," music
and lyrics by John Hudock.
Producers Frank Von Zerneck, Robert Green-
wald
Company Moonlight Productions, Inc., in asso-
ciation with Paramount Television
Director Steven Hilliard Stern
Writer John Hudock
CAST
Michael Carboni .... Richard Thomas
Kristy Lawrence .... Bess Armstrong
Sylvia Carboni .... Dena Dietrich
Wayne Spanka .... Fabian
Howie Lasser .... Mark Harmon
Vera Lasser .... Katherine Helmond
Phil Lawrence .... Van Johnson
Jenny .... Mimi Kennedy
Catherine Lawrence .... Audra Lindley
Burt Carboni .... Vic Tayback
Wedding Director .... Richard Deacon
Telegram Girl .... Ann Ryerson

559   The Ghost of Flight 401

NBC World Premiere Movie   NBC
Program Type TV Movie
2 hours. Premiere date: 2/18/78. Based on novel
by John Fuller. Re-creates airplane crash and
subsequent events dealing with psychic phenom-
ena.
Producer Emmet Lavery
Company Paramount Production in association
with NBC-TV
Director Steven Stern
Writer Robert Malcolm Young
Cinematographer Howard Schwartz
CAST
Dom Cimoli .... Ernest Borgnine
Jordan .... Gary Lockwood
Prissy .... Kim Basinger
Garrick .... Allan Miller
Maria Cimoli .... Carol Rossen
Val .... Tina Chen
Bowdish .... Robert F. Lyons
Dana .... Beverly Todd
Andrews .... Eugene Roche
Barton .... Alan Oppenheimer
Bailey .... Byron Morrow
Stockwell .... Howard Hesseman
Mrs. Collura .... Angela Clarke
Dutch .... Tom Clancy
Marshall .... John Quade

Gilbert and Sullivan See PBS Movie
Theater

560   The Girl Called Hatter Fox

The CBS Saturday Night Movies   CBS
Program Type TV Movie
2 hours. Premiere date: 8/12/78. Drama based
on the book by Marilyn Harris. Music by Fred
Karlin.
Executive Producer Roger Gimbel
Producer George Schaefer
Company EMI-TV
Director George Schaefer
Writer Darryl Ponicsan
CAST
Dr. Teague Summer .... Ronny Cox
Hatter Fox .... Joanelle Romero
Nurse Rhinehart .... Conchata Ferrell
Claude .... John Durren
Dr. Levering .... Donald Hotten
Mr. Winton .... S. John Launer
Mango .... Mira Santera
Belle .... Jeannie Stein
Reverend .... Jack Maguire
Policeman .... Danny Villaneueva
Nurse .... Denise Montoya
Indian Nurse .... Mona Lawrence
Matron .... Sabra Wilson
Waitress .... Caroline Rackley
Cabbie .... Biff Yeager

The Girl from Petrovka See NBC
Monday Night at the Movies

561   The Girl in the Empty Grave

NBC Monday Night at the Movies
Program Type Dramatic Special
2 hours. Premiere date: 9/20/77. Repeat date:
7/10/78. Crime drama about a small-town police
chief investigating several suspicious deaths.
Filmed on location in Big Bear, Calif.
Executive Producer Richard O. Linke
Producers Lane Slate, Gordon Webb
Company MGM-TV Production in association
with NBC-TV
Director Lou Antonio
Writer Lane Slate
CAST
Abel .... Andy Griffith
Doc .... Sharon Spelman
John .... Hunter von Leer
Fred .... Claude Jones
Gloria .... Mitzi Hoag
Dr. Peter Cabe .... Edward Winter
Courtland Gates .... Jonathan Banks
David Alden .... George Gaynes
Harry .... Leonard Stone
Gilda .... Mary Robin Redd
Jedidiah Partridge .... Robert F. Simon
MacAlwee .... Byron Morrow

562   Glen Campbell Los Angeles Open
Golf Championship   ABC

Program Type Sports Special
Live coverage of the Glen Campbell Golf Cham-

pionship from The Riviera Country Club in Pacific Palisades, Calif. 2/18/78 and 2/19/78.
Executive Producer Roone Arledge
Producer Chuck Howard
Company ABC Sports
Directors Terry Jastrow, Jim Jennett
Host Glen Campbell
Anchor Keith Jackson
Expert Commentators Dave Marr, Peter Alliss, Bill Flemming, Bob Rosburg

563 The Glittering Prizes   PBS
Program Type Limited Series
90 minutes. Mondays. Premiere date: 1/6/78. Six-part semi-autobiographical series by Frederic Raphael about a group of Cambridge students. Program made possible by a grant from Thomas Cadillac, Inc. of Los Angeles.
Producer Mark Shivas
Company Time-Life Television/BBC-TV
Directors Waris Hussein, Robert Knights
CAST
Adam Morris .... Tom Conti
Ba .... Barbara Kellerman
Alan Parks .... John Gregg
Anna Cunningham .... Emily Richard
Stephen Taylor .... Eric Porter

564 Go Go Globetrotters   NBC
Program Type Children's Series
2 hours. Saturdays. Premiere date: 2/4/78. Umbrella title for children's series including "C.B. Bears," adventures of Harlem Globetrotters basketball team, "The Herculoids," and "Space Ghost."
Company Hanna-Barbera
Voices Scatman Crothers, Meadowlark Lemon

565 Go West, Young Girl   ABC
Program Type Dramatic Special
90 minutes. Premiere date: 4/27/78. Two young women set out on a series of misadventures in search of Billy the Kid. Filmed in Tucson, Arizona.
Executive Producers Harve Bennett, Harris Katleman
Producer George Yanok
Company Bennet/Katleman Productions in association with Columbia Pictures Television
Director Alan Levi
Writer George Yanok
CAST
Netty Booth .... Karen Valentine
Gilda Corin .... Sandra Will
Deputy Shreeve .... Stuart Whitman
Billy .... Richard Jaeckel
Chato .... Cal Bellini
Nestor .... Michael Bell
Librado .... Pepe Callahan
Rev. Crane .... David Dukes
Capt. Anson .... Charles Frank

Griff .... Richard Kelton
Fanchon .... William Larsen
Payne .... Griff Palmer
Ingalls .... John Payne

The Godfather *See* The Big Event/NBC Monday Night at the Movies

566 Goin' Home   Syndicated
Program Type Miscellaneous Series
30 minutes. Premiere date: 1/5/78. Celebrity guests are taken back to their hometowns for a look at their roots.
Executive Producer Alan Lubell
Producers Paul Block, Anthony Eaton
Company Marathon Entertainment
Director Phil Olsmen
Host Ed McMahon

567 Going, Going ... Gone   CBS
CBS Reports
Program Type Documentary/Informational Special
Premiere date: 7/5/78. Report on the increasing number of blacks who are losing their land.
Executive Producer Howard Stringer
Producer Phillip Burton, Jr.
Company CBS News
Writer Phillip Burton, Jr.
Cinematographer Vic Losick
Editor Jonathan Pontell
Reporter Marlene Sanders

Gold *See* The ABC Sunday Night Movie

568 Golden Gloves Championship   ABC
Program Type Sports Special
Coverage of amateur boxing championship, New York vs. Chicago, from Chicago's Amphitheatre 4/16/78.
Executive Producer Roone Arledge
Producer Ned Steckel
Company ABC Sports
Director Craig Janoff

The Golden Voyage of Sinbad *See* The ABC Friday Night Movie

569 The Goldie Hawn Special   CBS
Program Type Music/Comedy/Variety Special
60 minutes. Premiere date: 3/1/78. Special music by Earl Brown.
Producer George Schlatter
Company George Schlatter Productions in association with Rutledge Productions
Director Don Mischer
Head Writer Digby Wolfe

The Goldie Hawn Special *Continued*
Musical Director Jack Elliott
Choreographer Patricia Birch
Costume Designer Bob Mackie
Art Director Robert Kelly
Star Goldie Hawn
Guest Stars George Burns, John Ritter, The Harlem Globetrotters (Meadowlark Lemon, Nat Branch, Curly Neal, Robert Paige, Jerry Venable)
Special Guest Shaun Cassidy

570   **The Gondoliers**   PBS
Opera Theater
Program Type Music/Dance Special
2 hours. Premiere date: 7/12/77. Repeat date: 7/31/78. A performance of the operetta by W. S. Gilbert and Arthur Sullivan updated to the early 1900s, with sets patterned after the paintings of Raoul Dufy. Music performed by the Royal Philharmonic Orchestra. Program presented by WNET-TV/New York and made possible by grants from Public Television Stations with additional funding from the Ford Foundation and the Corporation for Public Broadcasting.
Executive Producer Jac Venza
Coordinating Producers David Griffiths, Sam Paul
Producer Cedric Messina
Company British Broadcasting Corporation
Director Bill Hays
Conductor David Lloyd Jones
Scenic Designer Roger Andrews
CAST
The Grand Inquisitor .... Michael Langdon
Luiz .... Joseph Ward
Casilda .... Beverly Bergen
Duke of Plaza Toro .... Denis Dowling
Duchess of Plaza Toro .... Heather Begg
Inez .... Edith Coates
Marco .... John Brecknock
Tessa .... Delia Wallis
Giuseppe .... Thomas Allen
Gianetta .... Laureen Livingstone
Additional Cast Alan Charles, Sara De Javelin, Cynthia Buchan

571   **The Gong Show**   NBC
Program Type Game/Audience Participation Series
30 minutes. Mondays–Fridays. Premiere date: 6/14/76. Continuous. Season premiere: 9/12/77. Talent contest judged by a panel of celebrities and the studio audience. Created by Chuck Barris and Chris Bearde.
Executive Producer Chuck Barris
Producer Gene Banks
Company Chuck Barris/Chris Bearde Production
Director John Dorsey

Musical Director Milton Delugg
Host Chuck Barris

572   **The Gong Show (Evening)** Syndicated
Program Type Game/Audience Participation Series
30 minutes. Weekly. Premiere date: 9/76. Season premiere: 9/77. Evening version of daytime show with a celebrity panel judging offbeat acts. Created by Chuck Barris and Chris Bearde.
Producer Chuck Barris
Company Chuck Barris/Christ Bearde Productions
Distributor Firestone Syndication
Director John Dorsey
Musical Director Milton Delugg
Host Chuck Barris
Regulars Arte Johnson, Jaye P. Morgan, Jamie Farr

573   **Goober and the Truckers' Paradise**
                                                   CBS
Program Type Comedy Special
30 minutes. Premiere date: 5/17/78. Pilot about a truck-stop cafe. Theme written and performed by Ray Stevens.
Producer Rich Eustis
Company Akorpios/Lindsey & Lovello Productions
Directors Bill Wyse, Rich Eustis
Writers Rich Eustis, April Kelly, George Lindsey
CAST
Goober Pyle ....George Lindsey
Pearl .... Leigh French
Charlene .... Sandie Newton
Becky .... Audrey Landers
Toni .... Lindsay Bloom
Deputy Eagle Keyes ....John Chappell
Bible Bill .... Bill Medley
T-Bone .... Brion James
Catfish .... Bruce Fisher
Elwood Gunnite .... Robert Towers
Troll .... Mickey Jones
Bud ....Ken Johnson

574   **A Good Dissonance Like a Man**
                                                   PBS
Program Type Documentary/Informational Special
60 minutes. Premiere date: 10/11/77. Repeat dates: 10/14/77 and 9/9/78. Award-winning film biography of maverick American composer Charles Ives. Program made possible by grants from the National Endowment for the Arts, The New York State Council on the Arts, The Andrew W. Mellon Foundation and Mutual of New York.
Producer Theodor William Timreck
Company WNET-TV/New York
Director Theodor William Timreck

Cinematographer Peter M. Stein
CAST
Ives .... John Bottoms

575 Good Mornin' Blues PBS
Program Type Music/Dance Special
60 minutes. Premiere date: 6/20/78. Special about blues music from its earliest origins at the turn of the century through World War II.
Company Mississippi Center for Educational Television
Executive Producer Walt Lowe
Producers Walt Lowe, Rob Cooper
Writer Edward Cohen
Narrator B. B. King

576 Good Morning America ABC
Program Type News Magazine Series
2 hours. Monday–Friday mornings. Premiere date: 11/3/75. Continuous. Regular features include "Face Off" debates, "Men-Women" segments, "Inside Washington," "People in the News" and the "Good Morning America" baby Paula Kadanoff (on monthly visits).
Executive Producer Woody Fraser
Senior Producer George Merlis
Producers George Merlis, Merrill Mazuer, Bob Blum
Company The ABC Television Network
Director Jan Rifkinson
Hosts David Hartman, Sandy Hill
Anchor Steve Bell
Contributors Jack Anderson, F. Lee Bailey, Rona Barrett, Erma Bombeck, Helen Gurley Brown, John Coleman, Pat Collins, Howard Cosell, Bruce Jenner, Dr. Timothy Johnson, John Lindsay, Joan Lunden, Sylvia Porter, Geraldo Rivera, Dr. Lendon Smith, Al Ubell, Jeanne Wolf

577 Good News from Bethlehem: A Candlelight Celebration ABC
Program Type News Special
60 minutes. Premiere date: 12/25/77. Service at the historic First Methodist Church of Evanston, Illinois, where a ballet company, an orchestra and a choir take part in the celebration of the Christmas liturgy. Rev. Arthur Landwehr officiates.
Producer Sid Darion
Company ABC News Public Affairs in Cooperation with Communications Commission of the National Council of Churches

578 The Good Old Days of Radio PBS
Program Type Music/Comedy/Variety Special
60 minutes. Premiere date: 3/10/76. Repeat date: 11/29/77. Nostalgic tribute to the first 50 years of broadcasting. Music by Les Brown and his Band of Renown. Program taped 2/9/76 at the Century Plaza Hotel in Los Angeles and made possible in part by a grant from the Gulf Oil Corporation and Public Television Stations (with special assistance from Trans-American Video, Inc.)
Producer Loring d'Usseau
Company KCET-TV/Los Angeles
Director Marty Pasetta
Writers Don Bresnahan, Hal Kanter
Host Steve Allen
Announcer Bill Baldwin

579 Good Times CBS
Program Type Comedy Series
30 minutes. Wednesdays. Premiere date: 2/8/74. Fifth season premiere: 9/21/77. Series created by Eric Monte and Mike Evans developed by Norman Lear. Theme music by Marilyn Bergman; Alan Bergman and Dave Grusin. Concerns a black family in a Chicago ghetto. Paintings created by Ernie Barnes.
Executive Producers Irma Kalish, Austin Kalish
Producers Gordon Mitchell, Lloyd Turner
Company Tandem Productions, Inc.
Director Gerren Keith
Writers Various
CAST
Willona Woods .... Ja'net DuBois
J.J. .... Jimmie Walker
Michael ....Ralph Carter
Thelma .... Bernnadette Stanis
Nathan Bookman .... Johnny Brown
Penny Gordon .... Janet Jackson

580 Goodbye, Congress
CBS Reports CBS
Program Type Documentary/Informational Special
Premiere date: 5/2/78. Report on why Rep. Otis Pike is quitting Congress.
Executive Producer Howard Stringer
Producer Howard Stringer
Company CBS News
Cinematographer Dan Lerner
Film Editor Walter Katz
Reporter Bill Moyers

581 Gould World Cup Polo Championship
Festival '78 PBS
Program Type Sports Special
60 minutes. Premiere date: 3/5/78. International world champion polo players competing for top honors. Program made possible by a grant from the Polo Training Foundation.
Company WTTW-TV/Chicago
Announcer Joe Magee
Commentators Ami Shintzky, Marty Robinson

582   Grammy Awards Show   CBS
Program Type Parades/Pageants/Awards
Special
2 hours. 20th annual presentation honoring artistic and technical achievement in the recording industry. Live from the Shrine Auditorium, Los Angeles, Calif. Special music by Alan Copeland.
Executive Producer Pierre Cossette
Producer Marty Pasetta
Company Pierre Cossette Productions
Director Marty Pasetta
Writer Bob Arnott
Musical Director Jack Elliott
Art Director Charles Lisanby
Host John Denver
Performers/Presenters Count Basie, Stephen Bishop, Debby Boone, Cab Calloway, Shaun Cassidy, Chicago, James Cleveland and the Southern California Community Choir, Jerry Clower, Natalie Cole, Crosby, Stills & Nash, Roberta Flack, Crystal Gayle, Andy Gibb, Igor Kipnis, Erich Leinsdorf, Henry Mancini, Steve Martin, the Mills Brothers, Ronnie Milsap, Olivia Newton-John, Minnie Pearl, Lou Rawls, Joe Tex, Dionne Warwick, Andy Williams, Paul Williams

583   Grand Prix Masters Tennis Tournament   CBS
Program Type Sports Special
Live coverage of semi-finals and finals of $400,-000 tennis tournament from New York's Madison Square Garden 1/7/78 and 1/8/78.
Producer Perry Smith
Company CBS Sports
Director Bob Dailey
Announcer Pat Summerall

584   Grand Prix Tennis: Island Holidays Pro Tennis Classic   PBS
Program Type Sports Special
2 hours. 10/15/77 and 10/16/77. Presented by Holsum Hawaii Bakery Division of Ward Foods and Oroweat Foods, Inc., Aloha Airlines, and Western Airlines.
Company WGBH-TV/Boston

585   Grand Slam of Tennis   CBS
Program Type Sports Special
Live and taped coverage of the $200,000 Grand Slam of Tennis from Boca West, Fla. 1/21/78 and 1/22/78.
Producer Perry Smith
Company CBS Television Network Sports
Director Bob Dailey
Commentators Pat Summerall Tony Trabert

Grand Theft Auto *See* CBS Special Movie Presentations

586   Grandstand   NBC
Program Type Sports Series
15 minutes. Saturdays. Premiere date: 9/21/75 (special preview 9/20/75). Third season premiere: 9/3/77. Based on British Broadcasting Corporation series of the same name. Live program featuring sports news and features.
Executive Producer Don Ellis
Producer Bill Fitts
Company NBC Sports
Hosts Lee Leonard, Bryant Gumbel

587   Great American Dream Machine Revisited
Festival '78   PBS
Program Type Educational/Cultural Special
2 hours. Premiere date: 3/19/78. Retrospective of the first 25 years of public television in America.
Executive Producer Jack Sameth
Coordinating Producer Jacqueline Donnet
Company WNET-TV/New York
Director Jack Sameth

588   The Great American Laugh-Off
NBC
Program Type Music/Comedy/Variety Special
90 minutes. Premiere date: 10/22/77. Original comedy acts.
Producer George Schlatter
Director Don Mischer
Writers Donna Schuman, Judy Roche, Digby Wolfe
Star Nancy Bleiweiss
Guest Stars Lenny Schultz, Ben Powers, Jim Giovanni, Robin Williams, Toad the Mime, Ed Bluestone, Bill Rafferty, Duck's Breath, Michael Sklar, Wayland Flowers (Madame), The Graduates

The Great Dan Patch *See* PBS Movie Theater

Great Expectations *See* Festival '78

589   The Great Houdini
The ABC Friday Night Movie   ABC
Program Type TV Movie
2 hours. Premiere date: 10/8/76. Repeat date: 4/7/78. Drama based on the life of Harry Houdini. Music by Peter Matz.
Company An ABC Circle Film
Director Melville Shavelson
Writer Melville Shavelson

Technical Advisor Harry Blackstone, Jr.
CAST
Harry Houdini (Erich Weiss) ....Paul Michael Glaser
Bess Houdini .... Sally Struthers
Mrs. Weiss .... Ruth Gordon
Minnie ....Vivian Vance
Daisy White ....Adrienne Barbeau
Rev. Arthur Ford .... Bill Bixby
Theo Weiss .... Jack Carter
Conan Doyle .... Peter Cushing
Rev. LeVeyne ....Nina Foch
Supt. Melville .... Wilfrid Hyde-White
Dr. Crandon .... Geoffrey Lewis
Lady Doyle .... Maureen O'Sullivan
Dundas Slater .... Clive Revill
Margery .... Barbara Rhoades

590 Great Performances   PBS
Program Type Miscellaneous Series
Times vary. Wednesdays and/or Sundays. Premiere date: 10/17/74. Fourth season premiere: 10/5/78. A collection of various series in the arts including "Dance in America," "Five Music Specials," "Live from Lincoln Center," "Music in America," and "Theater in America" as well as individual programs: "Abide with Me," "All Over," "The Arcata Promise," "Cavalleria Rusticana," "The Consul," "Eugene Ormandy Conducts the Philadelphia Orchestra," "Herbert von Karajan and the Berlin Philharmonic," "The Julliard String Quartet Plays Beethoven," "Madama Butterfly," "The Marriage of Figaro," "The Norman Conquests," "Out of Our Father's House," "Pagliacci," "Professional Foul," "Requiem," "The Royal Family," "The San Francisco Ballet," "Sarah," "Shooting the Chandelier," "Sir Georg Solti Conducts the Chicago Symphony," "Tartuffe," "The Time of Your Life," "The Trial of the Moke," "Uncommon Women and Others," "Verna: U.S.O. Girl," and "Zubin Mehta and the Los Angeles Philharmonic." (*See* individual titles for credits.)

The Great Scout and Cathouse Thursday
See The CBS Wednesday Night Movies

591 The Great Wallendas
NBC Movie of the Week/NBC World
Premiere Movie   NBC
Program Type Dramatic Special
2 hours. Premiere date: 2/12/78. Fact-based drama about one of America's most famous circus families, known for performing a seven-member pyramid on a high wire without benefit of a safety net.
Executive Producer Daniel Wilson
Producer Linda Marmelstein
Company Daniel Wilson productions in association with NBC-TV
Director Larry Elikann

Writer Jan Hartman
CAST
Karl Wallenda .... Lloyd Bridges
Jenny Wallenda .... Britt Ekland
Helen Wallenda .... Taina Elg
Herman Wallenda ....John Van Dreelen
Jana Schmidt .... Cathy Rigby
Gunther Wallenda .... Ben Fuhrman
Lottie Schmidt .... Travis Hudson
Mario Wallenda .... Bruce Ornstein
Deiter Schmidt .... Bill Sadler
Dick Faughnan .... Stephen Parr
Edith Wallenda .... Isa Thomas
Arnold Fielding .... Michael McGuire
Gene Hallow .... Casey Biggs

592 The Great Whales
National Geographic Special   PBS
Program Type Documentary/Informational Special
60 minutes. Premiere date: 2/16/78. Repeat dates: 2/18/78, 8/23/78. Examinations of dangers to the world's whales and a look at the characteristics of whale species. Program made possible by a grant from Gulf Oil Corporation.
Executive Producers Thomas Skinner, Dennis B. Kane
Producer Nicolas Noxon
Company WQED-TV/Pittsburgh
Director Nicolas Noxon
Writer Nicolas Noxon
Host E.G. Marshall
Narrator Alexander Scourby

593 Greater Greensboro Open   NBC
Program Type Sports Special
Live coverage of the final rounds of the Greater Greensboro (N.C.) Open 4/1/78 and 4/2/78.
Executive Producer Don Ohlmeyer
Producer Roy Hammerman
Company NBC Sports
Director Harry Coyle
Commentators John Brodie, Bruce Devlin, Jay Randolph, Bob Goalby

594 Greatest Sports Legends   Syndicated
Program Type Sports Series
30 minutes.
Host Reggie Jackson

595 The Greatest Thing that Almost Happened
The CBS Wednesday Night Movies   CBS
Program Type TV Movie
2 hours. Premiere date: 10/26/77. Drama about a teenage athlete stricken by leukemia. Based on the novel by Don Robertson.
Executive Producers Charles Fries, Malcolm Stuart
Producer Herbert Hirschman

The Greatest Thing that Almost Happened *Continued*
Company Crestview Productions in association with Charles Fries Productions, Inc.
Writer Peter Beagle

CAST

Morris Bird III	Jimmie Walker
Morris Bird Jr.	James Earl Jones
Julie Sutton	Deborah Allen
Sandra Bird	Tamu
Aunt Edythe	Sandra Sharp
Miss Goldfarb	Valerie Curtin
Hoover	Kevin Hooks
Horton	Sam Laws
Bonner	Harry Caesar
Coach	Bill Traylor

596 Greenpeace Adventures: Voyages to Save the Whales   PBS
Program Type Documentary/Informational Special
60 minutes. Premiere date: 12/20/77. Story of the members of the Greenpeace Foundation tracking down whaling fleets at sea and putting themselves between the whales and Russian harpoons in an effort to focus world attention on the extermination of species of whales by international commercial interests.
Producer Michael Chechik
Company WGBH-TV/Boston
Director Michael Chechik
Cinematographers Ronald Precious, Fred Easton

597 A Ground of Faith   CBS
Program Type Religious/Cultural Special
60 minutes. Premiere date: 9/3/78. Profile of Andrew Young.
Executive Producer Pamela Ilott
Producer Bernard Seabrooks
Company CBS News
Writer Al Cox
Narrator Ted Holmes

598 Group Portrait   PBS
Program Type Documentary/Informational Special
60 minutes. Premiere date: 6/23/76. Repeat date: 9/22/77. A profile of four New York artists: Norman Bluhm; Mary Frank; Kenneth Snelson; John White. Program made possible by a grant from the New York State Council for the Arts and the Corporation for Public Broadcasting; presented by WNET-TV/New York.
Producer Russell Connor
Company Cable Arts Production
Director Russell Connor
Host Russell Connor

599 Grow U.S. Doubles Championships   PBS
Program Type Sports Special
Live coverage of semi-finals and finals on 9/17/77 and 9/18/77. Program made possible by grants from Aetna Life & Casualty, Fieldcrest Mills, E. & J. Gallo Winery and American Airlines.
Company WGBH-TV/Boston

600 Guale   PBS
Program Type Educational/Cultural Special
60 minutes. Premiere date: 7/18/78. Film about the Georgia coast islands and their natural and human history. Program made possible in part by a grant from the Corporation for Public Broadcasting.
Producers Albert Scardino, Marjorie Morris Scardino
Company WETV-TV/Atlanta

601 The Guardian   NBC
Program Type Religious/Cultural Special
60 minutes. Premiere date: 6/18/78. Drama about performers who are "born again" as they enact The Passion Play through mime.
Executive Producer Doris Ann
Producer William Cosmas
Company NBC Television Religious Programs Unit in association with the Office for Film and Broadcasting of the U.S. Catholic Conference
Director Marvin Einhorn
Writer Brother Augustine Towey
Host Helen Hayes

CAST

Custodian	Carl Don
Diane	Irene D'Auria
Bill	Joe Ferris
Jim	Kevin Ford
Eddie	Tom Hostomsky
Ann	Joanne Manley
Elizabeth	Mary Ellen Murray
Pat	Russ Papia
Joanne	Phyllis Scarpelli
John	Bill Whitaker
Arthur	Tom Zindle

602 The Guiding Light   CBS
Program Type Daytime Drama Series
60 minutes as of 11/7/77. Mondays–Fridays. Premiere date (on television): 6/30/52 after 15 years on radio. Continuous. Created by Irna Phillips. "La Lumiere" theme by Charles Paul. Drama about the Bauer and Thorpe families set in Springfield, U.S.A. Credits as of 1/5/77. Cast listed alphabetically. Charita Bauer is an original cast member.
Executive Producer Allen M. Potter
Producer Leslie Kwartin

Company Procter & Gamble Productions
Directors Harry Eggart, Michael Gliona, John Pasquin
Head Writers Jerome Dobson, Bridget Dobson
Writers Jean Rouverol, Virginia McDonnell, Nancy Ford, Bob White, Phyllis White

CAST

Dr. Sara McIntyre Werner	Millette Alexander
Bertha (Bert) Bauer	Charita Bauer
Barbara Norris Thorpe	Barbara Berjer
Alan Spaulding	Christopher Bernau
Elizabeth Spaulding	Lezlie Dalton
Dr. Peter Chapman	Curt Dawson
Holly Norris Bauer	Maureen Garrett
Eve Stapleton McFarren	Janet Grey
Dr. Ed Bauer	Mart Hulswit
Rita Stapleton	Lenore Kasdorf
Diane Ballard	Sofia Landon
Dr. Emmet Scott	Frank Latimore
Hillary Kincaid	Linda McCullough
Adam Thorpe	Robert Milli
Ann Jeffers	Maureen Mooney
Peggy Thorpe	Fran Myers
Dr. Justin Marler	Thomas O'Rourke
Katie Parker	Denise Pence
Jacqueline Marler	Cindy Pickett
Dean Blackford	Gordon Rigsby
Phillys Spaulding	Jarrod Ross
Dr. Stephen Jackson	Stefan Schnabel
Michael Bauer	Don Stewart
Viola Stapleton	Kate Wilkinson
Brandy Shellooe	Jo-beth Williams
Ben McFarren	Stephen Yates
Roger Thorpe	Michael Zaslow

603 Gunther Gebel-Williams: The Lord of the Ring   CBS

Program Type Music/Comedy/Variety Special
60 minutes. Premiere date: 11/25/77. Circus animal trainer is featured in circus special taped at the Forum, Inglewood, Calif., the MGM Grand Hotel, Las Vegas, and the San Diego Wild Animal Park.
Executive Producers Irvin Feld and Kenneth Feld
Producers John Moffitt, Robert Arthur
Company Ringling Brothers and Barnum & Bailey
Director John Moffitt
Writer Robert Arthur
Stars Gunther Gebel–Williams, Tony Curtis, Ray Berwick, Siegfried & Roy, Sigrid Gebel–Williams, Rina Gebel–Williams, Oliver Gebel–Williams

604 Gypsy in My Soul   CBS

Program Type Music/Comedy/Variety Special
60 minutes. Premiere date: 1/10/76. Repeat date: 6/18/78. Show celebrating the theatrical chorus; conceived by Cy Coleman and Fred Ebb. Original music by Cy Coleman; lyrics by Fred Ebb.
Executive Producer William O. Harbach

Producers Cy Coleman; Fred Ebb
Director Tony Charmoli
Writer Fred Ebb
Musical Director Donn Trenner
Choreographer Tony Charmoli
Costume Designer Stanley Simmons
Art Director Charles Lisanby
Star Shirley MacLaine
Guest Star Lucille Ball

605 The Gypsy Warriors

The CBS Friday Night Movies   CBS
Program Type TV Movie
60 minutes. Premiere date: 5/12/78. World War II drama about an assignment to prevent the enemy use of a deadly toxin.
Executive Producer Stephen J. Cannell
Producer Alex Beaton
Director Lou Antonio
Writers Stephen J. Cannell, Philip DeGuere

CAST

Capt Shelley Alhern	James Whitmore, Jr.
Capt Ted Brinkerhoff	Tom Selleck
Ganault	Joseph Ruskin
Lela	Lina Raymond
Androck	Michael Lane
Bruno Schlagel	Albert Paulsen
Schulman	Kenneth L. Tigar
Ramon Pierre Cammus	William Wheatley
Henry Desearu	Hubert Noel
Lady Britt Austin-Forbes	Kathryn Leigh Scott
Communications Officer	Chris Anders

Hail Hero! See NBC Saturday Night at the Movies

606 Hallmark Hall of Fame   NBC

Program Type Dramatic Special
2 hours (generally). 27th season premiere: 11/16/77. Dramatic specials aired during the 1977–78 season are: "The Court Martial of George Armstrong Custer," "Have I Got a Christmas for You," "The Last Hurrah," "Peter Pan," and "Taxi." (See individual titles for credits.)

607 Halloween Is Grinch Night   ABC

Program Type Animated Film Special
30 minutes. Premiere date: 10/29/77. A small boy is blown away from Whoville in a howling night wind and finds himself face to face with the dreaded Grinch atop Mt. Crumpit. Featuring the voice of Hans Conried. Music by Joe Raposo. Teleplay and lyrics by Theodor Geisel.
Executive Producers David H. DePatie, Friz Freleng
Producer Theodor Geisel
Company Dr. Seuss and A. S. Geisel in association with DePatie-Freleng Enterprises, Inc.
Director Gerad Baldwin

Halloween Is Grinch Night *Continued*
Conductor Eric Rogers
Film Editors Bob Gillis, Joe Siracusa, Rick Steward
Animation Lee Mishkin, Don Williams, Rudy Zamora, Chrystal Russell, Willy Pyle, John Gibbs, Fred Helmick; Bob Matz
Graphic Design Roy Morita; Bob Dranko
Backgrounds Richard H. Thomas
Voices Hal Smith; Gary Shapiro; Irene Tedrow; Jack DeLeon; Henry Gibson

608   Halloween with the New Addams Family
The Big Event   NBC
Program Type Dramatic Special
90 minutes. Premiere date: 10/30/77. Unusual residents of a mansion play host to a reunion of fun-loving spooks on Halloween night. Based on cartoons by Charles Addams.
Executive Producer Charles Fries
Producer David Levy
Company Charles Fries Productions, Inc.
Director Dennis Steinmetz
Writer George Tibbles
CAST
Little Bo Peep .... Patrick Campbell
Mikey .... Vito Scotti
Boss Crook .... Parley Baer
Gomez Addams .... John Astin
Morticia/Ophelia .... Carolyn Jones
Uncle Fester ....Jackie Coogan
Lurch .... Ted Cassidy
Pancho Addams .... Henry Darrow
Cousin Itt .... Felix Silla
Fake Gomez .... Dean Sothern
Wednesday Sr. .... Lisa Loring
Pugsley Sr. .... Ken Weatherwax
Countess Dracula .... Suzanne Krazna
Wednesday Jr. .... Jennifer Surprenant
Pugsley Jr. .... Kenneth Marquis
Mother Frump ....Elvia Allman
Grandmama .... Jane Rose
Hercules .... David Johns
Atlas ....Clinton Beyerle
Fake Morticia .... Terry Miller

609   Hambletonian   CBS
Program Type Sports Special
Live coverage of trotting's most prestigious race 9/2/78 from DuQuoin, Illinois
Producer Bud "E. S." Lamoreaux
Company CBS Sports
Director Arthur Struck
Announcer Frank Glieber
Racing Expert Stan Bergstein

Hamlet *See* PBS Movie Theater

610   Hanna-Barbera Happy Hour   NBC
Program Type Limited Series
60 minutes. Thursdays. Premiere date: 4/13/78. Five shows scheduled this session. Variety show hosted by two humanized puppets.
Executive Producer Joseph Barbera
Producers Joe Layton, Mitzi Welch, Joe Welch
Company Hanna-Barbera Production
Animation Director Iwao Takamoto
Puppetry and Special Effects Charles DeMuth

611   Hanna-Barbera's All Star Comedy Ice Revue   CBS
Program Type Animated Film Special
60 minutes. Premiere date: 1/13/78. Taped at the Bakersfield Civic Auditorium. Animation done at Hanna-Barbera, Hollywood.
Executive Producers Joseph Barbera, William Hanna
Producer Walt deFaria
Company Hanna-Barbera Productions, Inc., in association with deFaria Productions, Inc.
Director Walter C. Miller
Writers Marc London, Jay Burton
Animation Writers Duane Poole, Dick Robbins
Musical Director Don James
Stars Roy Clark, Bonnie Franklin, The Sylvers and The Ice Capades Skaters

Hannie Caulder *See* CBS Special Movie Presentations

612   Happily Ever After   CBS
Program Type Dramatic Special
2 hours. Premiere date: 9/5/78. Drama about an aspiring singer. Music by Peter Matz. Special musical material by Peter Matz and Mitzi Welch. Song, "You Made a Believer Out of Me" by Bobby Gosh.
Executive Producer Philip Barry
Producer Robert Lovenheim
Company Whitaker Production by Tri-Media III, Inc. in association with Hamel-Somers Entertainment
Director Robert Scheerer
Writer Garry Michael White
CAST
Mattie .... Suzanne Somers
Jack ....Bruce Boxleitner
Ross Ford .... Eric Braeden
Richy .... John Rubinstein
Lewis Gordon .... Bill Lucking
Construction Boss .... Ron Hayes
Del Gregory .... Arch Johnson
Rev. Hale ....Al Checco
Mrs. Hale .... Patsy Garrett
Tennis Court Mgr. ....William Lanteau
Jenny Welson .... Gloria Manners
Dealer .... Reno Nichols
Al .... Billy Snyder

Hotel Clerk	Ed King Cross
1st Workman	Steve Eastin
2nd Workman	Bill Cross
Policeman	Charles Bracy
Young Man	Scott Sachs

613 Happy Birthday, Bob NBC
Program Type Music/Comedy/Variety Special
3 hours. Premiere date: 5/29/78. 75th birthday
salute to Bob Hope. Taped at Kennedy Center,
Washington, DC.
Executive Producers James Lipton, Gerald M.
Rafshoon
Producers John Hamlin, Bob Wynn
Company James Lipton Productions Inc. and
Rafshoon Communications
Director Bob Wynn
Writers Bob Arnott, James Lipton
Stars Lynn Anderson, Ann-Margret, Pearl Bailey, Lucille Ball, George Burns, Charo, Bert
Convy, Kathryn Crosby, Mac Davis, Sammy
Davis, Jr., Redd Foxx, Elliott Gould, Dolores
Hope, Peter Isacksen, KC and the Sunshine
Band, Alan King, Dorothy Lamour, Carol
Lawrence, Fred MacMurray, the Muppets,
Tony Orlando, Donny Osmond, Marie Osmond, Charles Nelson Reilly, Don Rickles,
George C. Scott, Shields and Yarnell, Red
Skelton, David Soul, Elizabeth Taylor, Danny
Thomas, Fred Travalena

614 Happy Birthday, Las Vegas ABC
Program Type Music/Comedy/Variety Special
2 hours. Premiere date: 10/23/78. Behind-the-scenes look at the 24-hour life style of those who
live and work in Las Vegas. Special musical material by Billy Barnes.
Executive Producer Pierre Cossette
Producer Marty Pasetta
Company Pierre Cossette Productions, Inc.
Director Marty Pasetta
Writers Buz Kohan, Bob Arnott, Aubrey Tadman, Garry Ferrier
Musical Director Bill Byers
Choreographer Alan Johnson
Choreographer Bill Hargate
Art Director Ed Flesh
Stars Eddy Arnold, David Brenner, Foster
Brooks, Charo, Mike Curb Congregation,
Norm Crosby, Rodney Dangerfield, John Davidson, Sammy Davis, Jr., Lola Falana, Totie
Fields, Redd Foxx, Jack Jones, The Keane
Brothers, Lenny Kent, The Lennon Sisters,
Liberace, Anthony Newley, Wayne Newton,
Juliet Prowse, Don Rickles, Joan Rivers, Doc
Severinsen, Rip Taylor, Dionne Warwick,
Slappy White, Andy Williams
Hosts Don Meredith, Cindy Williams

615 Happy Days ABC
Program Type Comedy Series
30 minutes. Tuesdays. Premiere date: 1/15/74.
Fifth season premiere: 9/13/77. (60 minute special.) Jefferson High School student growing up
in Milwaukee in the 1950s enrolls at the University during the 1977–78 season. Created by Garry
K. Marshall. "Happy Days" music by Charles
Fox; lyrics by Norman Gimbel.
Executive Producers Thomas L. Miller, Edward
K. Milkis, Garry K. Marshall
Producers Tony Marshall, Jerry Paris, Bob
Brunner
Company Miller-Milkis Productions, Inc. and
Henderson Production Company in association with Paramount Pictures Corp.
Director Jerry Paris
Writers Various
Art Director Monty Elliott
Cinematographer Robert G. Hager
Film Editor Ed Cotter
CAST

Richie Cunningham	Ron Howard
Arthur "Fonzie" Fonzarelli	Henry Winkler
Howard Cunningham	Tom Bosley
Marion Cunningham	Marion Ross
Potsie Weber	Anson Williams
Ralph Malph	Donny Most
Joanie Cunningham	Erin Moran
Alfred	Al Molinaro
Chachi	Scott Baio

616 Happy Days (Daytime) ABC
30 minutes. Premiere date: 9/1/75. Monday–
Friday. Morning reruns of evening show. Continuous. (*See* "Happy Days" for credits.)

The Happy Ending *See* The CBS
Tuesday Night Movies

617 Hard Times
Great Performances PBS
Program Type Limited Series
60 minutes. Wednesday. Premiere date: 5/11/77.
Repeat date: 2/6/78. Four-part dramatization of
the novel by Charles Dickens about England during the Industrial Revolution. Program made
possible by grants from Exxon Corporation, the
National Endowment for the Humanities, the
Corporation for Public Broadcasting, the Ford
Foundation and Public Television Stations.
Executive Producer Jac Venza
Producer Peter Eckersley
Company Granada Television/London and
WNET-TV/New York
Director John Irvin
Writer Arthur Hopcraft
Scenic Designer Roy Stonehouse
CAST

Louisa Gradgrind	Jacqueline Tong

Hard Times *Continued*

Thomas Gradgrind .... Patrick Allen
Tom Gradgrind .... Richard Wren
Josiah Bounderby .... Timothy West
Sissy Juppe .... Michelle Dibnah
Stephen Blackpool .... Alan Dobie
Capt. Harthouse .... Edward Fox
Mrs. Sparsit .... Rosalie Crutchley
Mrs. Gradgrind .... Ursula Howells
Mr. Sleary .... Harry Markham
Rachel .... Barbara Ewing

Hard Times *See* NBC Saturday Night at the Movies

Hardy Boys Mysteries *See* Hardy Boys/Nancy Drew Mysteries

618   Hardy Boys/Nancy Drew Mysteries
                                                            ABC
Program Type Children's Series
60 minutes. Sundays. Premiere dates: 1/30/77 (Hardy Boys) and 2/6/77 (Nancy Drew). Combined series premiere date: 9/11/77. Based on the "Hardy Boys" books by Franklin W. Dixon. Music score, theme by Glen A. Larson. As of 2/12/78 Janet Louise Johnson plays Nancy Drew. Became "Hardy Boys Mysteries" in 1978–79 season.
Executive Producer Glen A. Larson
Supervising Producer Michael Sloan
Producers Joe Boston, Arlene Sidaris, Joyce Brotman
Company A Glen A. Larson Production in association with Universal Television
Directors Various
Story Editor Christopher Crowe
Writers Various
Costume Designer George R. Whittaker
Art Director Roy Steffenson
Cinematographers Don H. Birnkrant, Jack Woolf
Film Editors Buford F. Hayes, John Dumas
CAST
Joe Hardy .... Shaun Cassidy
Frank Hardy .... Parker Stevenson
Nancy Drew .... Pamela Sue Martin
Fenton Hardy .... Edmund Gilbert
Bess .... Ruth Cox

619   The Harpsichord Maker   PBS
Program Type Documentary/Informational Special
30 minutes. Premiere date: 1/29/78. Repeat date: 3/14/78. Peter Redstone, builder of harpsichords and other authentic 18th century keyboard instruments, seen at work in his daily life. Program made possible by a grant from the National Endowment for the Humanities and the

Virginia Commission of the Arts and Humanities.
Company WCVE-TV/Richmond
Cinematographer Gene Harris

620   Harry S. Truman: Plain Speaking
                                                            PBS
Program Type Dramatic Special
60 minutes. Premiere date: 10/5/76. Repeat date: 9/2/78. One-man show about Harry S. Truman based on the book by Merle Miller. Program made possible by grants from Nathan Cummings, Harmon International Industries, Inc., Richard and Edna Solomon, and the Corporation for Public Broadcasting.
Producer David Susskind
Company Talent Associates, Inc. in association with WQED-TV/Pittsburgh
Director Daniel Petrie
Writer Carol Sobieski
Scenic Designers Cletus Anderson, William Matthews
CAST
Harry S. Truman .... Ed Flanders

621   The Harvey Korman Show
Program Type Comedy Series   ABC
30 minutes. Tuesday/Saturday. Preview presentation: 1/31/78. Premiere date: 4/4/78. Last show: 7/22/78. Comedy about an actor who runs an acting academy in the home he shares with his daughter.
Executive Producer Hal Dresner
Producer Don Van Atta
Directors Various
Writers Various
CAST
Harvey Kavanaugh .... Harvey Korman
Maggie .... Christine Lahti
Stuart .... Barry Van Dyke
Jake .... Milton Selzer

622   The Haunted Trailer   ABC
Program Type Children's Special
ABC Holiday Weekend Specials
30 minutes. Premiere date: 3/26/77. Repeat date: 12/24/77. Comedy about a college girl trying to live in a trailer inhabited by a group of musical poltergeists. Based on a short story by Robert Arthur.
Executive Producer Allen Ducovny
Producer William Beaudine, Jr.
Company ABC Circle Films
Director Ezra Stone
Writer Robert Specht
Art Director Joe Aubel
CAST
Clifford .... Murray Matheson
Mr. Simpson .... Eddie Bracken
Sharon .... Lauren Tewes
Mickey .... Monie Ellis

The Sheriff	Stu Gilliam
Woman in Car	Sara Seegar
Gas Station Owner	Jim Boles

623 Have I Got a Christmas for You

Hallmark Hall of Fame   NBC
Program Type Dramatic Special
60 minutes. Premiere date: 12/16/77. Leader of a Jewish temple opposes other leaders who want to become on-the-job substitutes for Christians desiring to spend Christmas with their loved ones.
Executive Producers Gilbert Cates, Joseph Cates
Producer Patricia Rickey
Company Cates Brothers
Director Marc Daniels
Writer Jerome Coopersmith
CAST

Morris Glickstein	Milton Berle
Dan Levine	Alex Cord
Marcia Levine	Adrienne Barbeau
Leo Silver	Harold Gould
Adele Serkin	Sheree North
Kevin Grady	Jim Backus
Sidney Wineberg	Jack Carter
Rabbi	Herb Edelman
Barry Silver	Barry Pearl
Rita	Jayne Meadows
Martin Kaplan	Steve Allen
Chips Domino	Wolfman Jack
Rev. Powers	Don Chastaine
Horgan	Biff McGuire

624 Having Babies   ABC

Program Type Drama Series
60 minutes. Premiere date: 3/7/78. Based on TV movie which premiered 10/17/76. As of 3/28/78 name changed to "Julie Farr, M.D." Last show 4/18/78. Drama of couples experiencing childbirth.
Executive Producers Gerald I. Isenberg, Gerald W. Abrams
Supervising Producer B. W. Sandefur
Producer James Heinz
Company Jozak Company in association with Paramount television
Directors Various
Writers Various
CAST

Julie Farr, M.D.	Susan Sullivan
Dr. Ron Danvers	Dennis Howard
Kelly	Beverly Todd
Dr. Simmons	Mitchell Ryan

625 Having Babies II

The ABC Friday Night Movie
Program Type TV Movie   ABC
2 hours. Premiere date: 10/28/77. Emotional crises involving birth, adoption and first love affect the lives of several couples. Music by Fred Karlin. Story by Ann Marcus. Director of Photography Michael P. Joyce.

Executive Producer Gerald W. Abrams
Producer Richard Briggs
Company The Jozak Company
Director Richard Michaels
Writer Elizabeth Clark
Art Director William M. Hiney
Film Editor John A. Martinelli
CAST

Aaron Canfield	Tony Bill
Arthur Magee	Cliff Gorman
Sally Magee	Carol Lynley
Trish Canfield	Paula Prentiss
Jeff Kramer	Nicholas Pryor
Lou Plotkin	Wayne Rogers
Dr. Julie Farr	Susan Sullivan
Paula Plotkin	Cassie Yates
Danny Magee	Robbie Rist
Martha Cooper	Lee Meriwether
Jenny Cooper	Tracy Marshak
Chris Williams	Michael St. Clair

626 Having Babies III

The ABC Friday Night Movie   ABC
Program Type TV Movie
2 hours. Premiere date: 3/3/78. Doctors help three families face medical and emotional crises. Created by Peggy Elliott and Ann Marcus. Song, "There Will Be Love,"—lyrics by Alan and Marilyn Bergman; music by Lee Holdridge. Director of Photography William K. Jurgenson
Executive Producers Gerald I. Isenberg, Gerald W. Abrams
Producers B.W. Sandefur, James Heinz
Company Jozak Company in association with Paramount Television
Director Jackie Cooper
Writer Pamela Chais
CAST

Dr. Julie Farr	Susan Sullivan
Kelly Williams	Beverly Todd
Dr. Ron Daniels	Dennis Howard
Dr. Blake Simmons	Mitchell Ryan
Leslie Wexler	Patty Duke Astin
Dawn	Kathleen Beller
Chuck	Phil Foster
Marnie Bridges	Jamie Smith Jackson
Russ Bridges	Michael Lembeck
Gloria Miles	Rue McClanahan
Jim Wexler	Richard Mulligan

627 Hawaii Five-O   CBS

Program Type Crime Drama Series
60 minutes. Thursdays. Premiere date: 9/26/68. Tenth season premiere: 9/15/77. Created by Leonard Freeman. Crime drama set and filmed in Hawaii about the adventures of the Hawaiian police. Fred Brown supervising producer as of 10/7/78.
Supervising Producer B. W. Sandefur
Producers James Heinz, Douglas Green
Company The CBS Television Network
Directors Various
Exec. Story Consultant Curtis Kenyon

Hawaii Five-O *Continued*
Writers Various
Musical Director Morton Stevens
CAST
Steve McGarrett .... Jack Lord
Danny Williams ....James MacArthur
Chin Ho ....Kam Fong
Che Fong ....Harry Endo
Duke ....Herman Wedemeyer
Doc Bergman ....Al Eben

628 · **Hawaii Revisited**
James Michener's World   PBS
Program Type Documentary/Informational
Special
60 minutes. Premiere date: 12/13/77. Repeat
date: 9/12/78. Second special in a series of visual
essays. Presented by KCET, Los Angeles and
made possible by a grant from Mrs. Paul's Kitchens, Inc.
Producer Julian Krainin
Company Reader's Digest Association, Inc.
Director Julian Krainin
Writer Julian Krainin
Host James Michener

629 **Hawaiian Open Golf Championship**
ABC
Program Type Sports Special
Live coverage of the final two rounds from
Honolulu's Waialae Country Club 2/4/78 and
2/5/78.
Executive Producer Roone Arledge
Producer Bob Goodrich
Company ABC Sports
Directors Jim Jennett, Terry Jastrow
Anchor Chris Schenkel
Expert Commentators Dave Marr, Peter Alliss,
Bill Flemming, Bob Rosburg

630 **The Hawaiians** *See* The CBS
Wednesday Night Movies

631 **Headliners with David Frost**   NBC
Program Type Limited Series
60 minutes. Wednesdays. Premiere date:
5/31/78. Limited series on six consecutive weeks
includes live and taped interviews. Interviews
with John Travolta, The Bee Gees, and former
CIA Director Richard Helms (5/31/78); Paul
Newman, and Elton John (6/7/78); Jane Fonda,
Tom Hayden, Bob Hope (6/14/78); Kris Kristofferson, Rita Coolidge, Donna Summer, Christiaan Barnard, Joe Carson (6/21/78); Ryan O'-
Neal, Tatum O'Neal, Gerry Rafferty (6/28/78);
Muhammad Ali, John Ritter, Bonnie Tyler, Mel
Brooks (7/5/78). Features "Wrap-up of the
Week" by Liz Smith, an all-star "Headliners

Forum" and other late-breaking segments of
topical interest.
Executive Producer David Frost
Producer John Gilroy
Company David Paradine Television, Inc. in association with NBC-TV
Director Bruce Gowers
Host David Frost

632 **Health Care: Your Money or Your
Life**   PBS
Program Type Documentary/Informational
Special
2 hours. Premiere date: 11/22/77. Documentary
on Health care in America. Program made possible in part by a grant from the New York Council
for the Humanities.
Executive Producer David Loxton
Producers Jon Alpert, Keiko Tsuno
Company Downtown Community TV Center
and WNET-TV/New York
Directors Jon Alpert, Keiko Tsuno
Writers Jon Alpert, Keiko Tsuno

The Heart of the Matter *See* PBS Movie
Theater

633 **Hee Haw**   Syndicated
Program Type Music/Comedy/Variety Series
60 minutes. Weekly. Originally premiered on
CBS in 1969. In syndication since 1971. Season
premiere: 9/77. Produced on location in Nashville, TN. Regular features: Barber Shop, Truck
Stop, Cooking, Cornfield, Country Dictionary,
Grandpa's Almanac.
Executive Producers Frank Peppiatt, John
Aylesworth
Producer Sam Lovullo
Company Yongestreet Productions
Director Bob Boatman
Head Writers Frank Peppiatt, John Aylesworth
Hosts Roy Clark, Buck Owens
Featured Performers Archie Campbell, George
Lindsey, Minnie Pearl, The Hager Twins, Junior Samples, Louis M. Jones, Gordie Tapp,
Don Harron, Misty Rowe, Gunilla Hutton,
Lisa Todd, Cathy Baker, Marianne Gordon,
Gailard Sartain, Kenny Price, John Henry
Faulk, Roni Stoneman, Buck Trent

634 **The Hee Haw Honeys**   Syndicated
Program Type Comedy Series
30 minutes. Premiere date: 12/28/77. Comedy
series about three women who live in a Winnebago bus.
Executive Producers Frank Peppiatt; John
Aylesworth
Producer Sam Lovullo

Company Yongestreet Productions
Writers Frank Peppiatt, John Aylesworth, Barry Adelman, Barry Silver
Stars Kathie Epstein, Catherine Hickland, Muffi Durham, Kenny Price, John Tuell, Joe Higgins, Jackie Kahane, Bob McClurg, Roy Clark, Billy Carter

635 The Heisman Trophy Awards
Special   CBS
Program Type Parades/Pageants/Awards Special
60 minutes. Premiere date: 1/8/77. Presented since 1935, this is the first time that the college football award ceremony has been televised. Live from the New York Hilton Hotel.
Executive Producer Howard Katz
Company Trans World International
Director Don Mischer
Writer Marty Farrell
Hosts Elliott Gould, O.J. Simpson
Guest Stars Paul Hornung, Reggie Jackson, Robert Klein, Leslie Uggams, Connie Stevens

Hell Boats *See* The CBS Tuesday Night Movies

636 Henry Ford's America   PBS
Program Type Documentary/Informational Special
60 minutes. Premiere date: 1/9/78. Ambiguous results of America's love affair with cars is examined. Features and interview with Henry Ford, II.
Producer Donald Brittain
Company Canadian Broadcasting Corp.
Director Donald Brittain
Writer Donald Brittain
Narrator Donald Brittain

637 Henry Kissinger: On the Record
NBC News Special   NBC
Program Type News Special
90 minutes. Premiere date: 1/13/78. Former Secretary of State Kissinger with former President Ford and David Brinkley in a program on Eurocommunism. Interviews with European leaders by Brinkley and Garrick Utley also included.
Executive Producer Stuart Schulberg
Producers Thomas Tomizawa, William Cosmas
Company NBC News
Chief Correspondent David Brinkley

638 Henry Winkler Meets William Shakespeare
The CBS Festival of Lively Arts for Young People   CBS
Program Type Children's Special
60 minutes. Premiere date: 3/20/77. Repeat date: 12/18/77. Excerpts from the works of William Shakespeare taped at the American Shakespeare Theatre, Stratford, Conn.
Producer Daniel Wilson
Company Daniel Wilson Productions
Director Jeff Bleckner
Writer Lee Kalcheim
Costume Designer Fred Voelpel
Art Director Fred Voelpel
Star Henry Winkler
CAST
William Shakespeare ....Tom Aldredge
Romeo .... Henry Winkler
Falstaff .... George Ede
Petruchio .... Kevin Kline
Tybalt .... Robert Phelps
Mercutio .... Jordan Clarke
Kate .... Bruce Bouchard
Fencer ....Erik Fredrickson
Additional Cast Stephan Brennan, William Sadler, Bruce Weitz, Bill McIntyre, David Blessing, Franklin Seales

639 Herbert Von Karajan and the Berlin Philharmonic
Great Performances   PBS
Program Type Music/Dance Special
Premiere date: 12/3/75 (60 minutes). Repeat date: 7/15/78. Concert performed by the Berlin Philharmonic Orchestra: Brahm's Symphony No. 4 in E Minor and Wagner's Overture to Tannhauser. Presented by WNET-TV/New York. Program made possible by grants from Exxon Corporation.
Company Unitel Productions
Conductor Herbert Von Karajan

640 Here Comes Peter Cottontail   CBS
Program Type Animated Film Special
60 minutes. Premiere date: 4/18/76. Repeat date: 3/24/78. Based on the book "The Easter Bunny that Overslept" by Priscilla Friedrich and Otto Friedrich. Music and lyrics by Maury Laws and Jules Bass.
Producers Arthur Rankin, Jr., Jules Bass
Directors Arthur Rankin, Jr., Jules Bass
Writer Romeo Muller
Musical Director Maury Laws
Animation Director Kizo Nagashima
VOICES
Mr. Sassafrass .... Danny Kaye
Irontail .... Vincent Price
Peter .... Casey Kasem
Donna ....Iris Rainer
Additional Voices Paul Frees, Joan Gardner, Greg Thomas, Jeff Thomas

641 Here's Lucy   CBS
Program Type Comedy Series
30 minutes. Mondays–Fridays. Originally seen
between 1968–1974. Daytime rerun premiere;
5/2/77. Last show: 11/4/77. Comedy about a
widow with two children working at the Unique
Employment Agency.
Executive Producer Gary Morton
Producers Tommy Thompson, Cleo Smith
Company A Lucille Ball Production in associa-
tion with Paramount Television
Directors Various
Writers Various
CAST
Lucy Carter .... Lucille Ball
Uncle Harry .... Gale Gordon
Kim Carter .... Lucie Arnaz
Craig Carter .... Desi Arnaz, Jr.

642 Heritage Classic   CBS
Program Type Sports Special
Closing rounds covered in professional golf's
Heritage Classic 3/25/78 and 3/26/78 from
Harbour Town Golf Links, Hilton Head Island,
South Carolina.
Producer Frank Chirkinian
Company CBS Sports
Directors Bob Dailey, Frank Chirkinian
Commentators Vin Scully, Pat Summerall, Ben
Wright, Frank Glieber, Ken Venturi, Jack
Whitaker

Hester Street *See* Festival '78

643 Hewitt's Just Different
ABC Afterschool Specials   ABC
Program Type Children's Special
60 minutes. Premiere date: 10/12/77. A sensitive
story in which children cope with the problem of
mental retardation. Filmed on location in Los
Angeles.
Executive Producer Daniel Wilson
Producer Fran Sears
Associate Producer Joanne Curley
Company Daniel Wilson Productions, Inc.
Director Larry Elikann
Writer Jan Hartman
Film Editors Ken Wagner, Eddie Fricke
Original Music Sodden-Weber
Director of Photography Otto Nemenz
Production Manager David Donley
CAST
Hewitt Calder .... Perry Lang
Willie Arthur .... Moosie Drier
Mr. Arthur .... Peter Brandon
Mrs. Arthur .... Gloria Stroock
Mrs. Calder .... Peggy McCay
Mr. Calder .... Russell Johnson
Palumbo .... Christopher Maleki
Tally" .... Doney Oatman
Goose .... Jarrod Johnson

Nubby .... Tom Gulager
Coach Andrus .... Stack Pierce
Frank .... Mike Luther

644 The Hidden Heritage   CBS
Program Type News Special
60 minutes. Premiere date: 7/31/77. Repeat
date: 5/14/78. Special on the major art exhibit
"Two Centuries of Black American Art," filmed
at the High Museum, Atlanta, Ga.
Executive Producer Pamela Ilott
Producer Bernard Seabrooks
Company CBS News
Narrator David C. Driskell

645 High Hopes   Syndicated
Program Type Daytime Drama Series
30 minutes. Monday–Friday. Premiere date:
4/3/79. Last show: 5/12/78. Filmed in Toronto,
the story is about a divorced family counselor,
his teenage daughter, his sister-in-law and his
mother.
Executive Producer Dick Cox
Producers Robert M. Driscoll, Karen Hazzard
Company Y&R Productions and DCA Produc-
tions
Director Bruce M. Minniex
Writers Winnifred Wolfe, Mort Forer
CAST
Family Counselor .... Bruce Gray
Daughter .... Marianne McIsaac
Sister-in-law .... Nuala FitzGerald
Mother .... Doris Petrie
Additional Cast Barbara Kyle, Colin Fox, Jan Muszin-
ski, Gordon Thomson, Jayne Eastwood, Gina Dick,
Norma Reis, Michael Tait, Debra Turnbull

High Plains Drifter *See* The ABC
Sunday Night Movie

**646 Highlights of Ringling Bros. and
Barnum & Bailey Circus**   NBC
Program Type Music/Comedy/Variety Special
60 minutes. Premiere date: 3/8/78. International
array of circus acts from the 108th edition of The
Greatest Show on Earth. Taped in St. Peters-
burg, Florida.
Executive Producers Irvin Feld, Kenneth Feld
Producer John Moffitt
Director John Moffitt
Writer Ken Shapiro
Host Dick Van Dyke

The Hindenburg *See* NBC Saturday
Night at the Movies

647 The Hobbitt   NBC
Program Type Animated Film Special
90 minutes. Premiere date: 11/27/77. Animated
film based on book by J.R.R. Tolkien. Recom-
mended by the National Education Association.
Entire score composed, arranged and conducted
by Maury Laws. Lyrics were written and adapted
by Jules Bass. Theme, "The Greatest Adven-
ture," sung by Glen Yarbrough.
Producers Arthur Rankin, Jr., Jules Bass
Company Rankin/Bass Production in associa-
tion with Xerox Corporation
Directors Arthur Rankin, Jr., Jules Bass
Writer Romeo Muller
                    VOICES
Bilbo Baggins .... Orson Bean
Gandalf .... John Huston
Smaug .... Richard Boone
Elvenking .... Otto Preminger
Elrond .... Cyril Ritchard
Thorin Oakenshield .... Hans Conried
Gollum .... Theodore
Additional Voices Paul Frees, John Stephenson, Don
   Messick, Jack DeLeon

Hobson's Choice *See* PBS Movie Theater

**648 Hollywood Foreign Press
Association's 35th Annual Golden Globe
Awards**
The Big Event   NBC
Program Type Parades/Pageants/Awards
Special
2 hours. Premiere date: 1/29/78. Honoring the
best in motion pictures and television in the In-
ternational Ballroom of the Beverly Hilton Ho-
tel, Beverly Hills, Calif. Red Skelton received the
DeMille Award.
Producer Kjell F. Rasten
Director Bob Wynn
Writer Marty Farrell
Musical Director Nelson Riddle
Hosts Charles Bronson, Jill Ireland
Presenters Jenny Agutter, Marissa Berenson, Su-
   san Blakely, LeVar Burton, Cantinflas, Charo,
   Chevy Chase, Michael Douglas, Glenn Ford,
   Lee Grant, Mark Hamill, Richard Harris,
   Cheryl Ladd, Farrah Fawcett-Majors, Lee
   Majors, Lee Marvin, Peter O'Toole, Roy
   Scheider, Ann Turkel, Robert Wagner, Henry
   Winkler, Natalie Wood, Franco Zeffirelli
Performers Mary MacGregor, The Fifth Dimen-
   sion, Marvin Hamlisch, Lisa Hartman, Hal
   Linden

649 Hollywood on Trial   PBS
Program Type Documentary/Informational
Special
90 minutes. Premiere date: 12/2/77. Documen-
tary examines the Red Scare of the 1950s and its
influence on the lives and careers of several mem-
bers of the movie industry.
Producer James C. Gutman
Company Stephen R. Friedman, Irwin Meyer,
   Peter Crane
Director David Helpern, Jr.
Writer Arnie Reisman
Narrator John Huston

Hollywood Out-Takes *See* Marilyn
   Beck's Second Annual Hollywood
   Out-Takes

650 The Hollywood Squares   NBC
Program Type Game/Audience Participation
Series
30 minutes. Mondays–Fridays. Premiere date:
10/17/66. Continuous. Nine celebrity panelists
in a tic-tac-toe board answer questions for con-
testants.
Executive Producers Merrill Heatter, Bob Quig-
   ley
Producer Jay Redack
Company Heatter-Quigley Productions in asso-
   ciation with NBC-TV
Director Jerome Shaw
Host Peter Marshall
Regulars Rose Marie, George Gobel, Paul
   Lynde

651 Hollywood Squares (Evening)
                                        Syndicated
Program Type Game/Audience Participation
Series
30 minutes. Twice weekly. Season premiere:
9/77. Evening version of daytime game with nine
celebrities in tic-tac-toe box.
Executive Producers Merrill Heatter, Bob Quig-
   ley
Producer Jay Redack
Company Heatter-Quigley Productions
Distributor Rhodes Productions
Director Jerome Shaw
Host Peter Marshall
Announcer Ken Williams
Regulars Rose Marie, George Gobel, Paul
   Lynde

652 Hollywood Television Theatre   PBS
Program Type Drama Series
Times vary. Tuesdays. Premiere date: 5/17/70.
Season premiere: 1/10/78. Contemporary plays
by American and European dramatists. Plays
shown during the 1977–78 season are: "Actor,"
"And the Soul Shall Dance," and "The Ascent
of Mt. Fuji." (*See* individual titles for credits.)

653 Holocaust

The Big Event   NBC
Program Type Limited Series
9-1/2 hours. Premiere date: 4/16-19/78. Shown
on four consecutive nights. Original dramatiza-
tion of the systematic destruction by the Nazis of
millions of people. Original story and screenplay
by Gerald Green. Music composed by Morton
Gould.
Executive Producer Herbert Brodkin
Producers Herbert Brodkin, Robert "Buzz"
 Berger
Company Titus Productions, Inc.
Director Marvin Chomsky
Conductor Morton Gould
Production Designer Wilfred J. Shingleton
Art Directors Theo Harisch, Jurgen Kieback
Set Decorator Maxi Harieter
CAST
Eichmann .... Tom Bell
Rudi Weiss ....Joseph Bottoms
Helena Slomova .... Tovah Feldshuh
Herr Palitz .... Marius Goring
Berta Weiss .... Rosemary Harris
Muller .... Anthony Haygarth
Himmler .... Ian Holm
Uncle Sasha .... Lee Montague
Erik Dorf .... Michael Moriarty
Marta Dorf .... Deborah Norton
Lowy .... George Rose
Uncle Kurt Dorf .... Robert Stephens
Inga Helms Weiss .... Meryl Streep
Moses Weiss ....Sam Wanamaker
Heydrich ....David Warner
Josef Weiss ....Fritz Weaver
Karl Weiss .... James Woods
Hoefle .... Sean Arnold
Hans Frank .... John Bailey
Ana Weiss ....Blanche Baker
Hans Helms .... Michael Beck
Rahm .... John Collin
Hoess .... David Daker
Karp .... Vernon Dobtscheff
Biberstein ....Edward Hardwicke
Ohlendorf .... Nigel Hawthorne
Frau Lowy .... Kate Jaenicke
Dr. Kohn .... Charles Korvin
Herr Helms .... Werner Kreindl
Zalman .... Stanley Lebor
Aaron .... Jeremy Levy
Blobel ....T. P. McKenna
Kaltenbrunner .... Hans Meyer
Frau Palitz ....Nora Minor
Maria Kalova .... Irene Prador
Felscher .... George Pravda
Tesch ....Oscar Quitak
Levin .... Osman Ragheb
Nebe .... John Rees
Fr. Lichtenberg .... Llewellyn Rees
Kovel .... Toby Salaman
Analevitz .... Murray Salem
Frau Helms .... Nina Sandt
Weinberg .... Cyril Shaps
Cassidy .... Robert Sherman
Rabbi Samuel ....Gabor Vernon
Frey .... Peter Vogel

Peter Dorf, age 9 ....Jim Anbach
Eva .... Isolde Barth
Dr. Heintzen ....Hubert Berger
Nadya .... Vera Borek
Immigration Man .... Gottfried Blahovsky
Rabbi Karsh ....Martin Brandt
Seder Man .... Peter Capell
Vanya .... Ulli Chivall
Buchenwald Sgt. .... Otto Clemens
Yuri .... Peter Garell
Peter Dorf, age 15 .... Edward Gilkrist
Barski ....Klaus Guth
SS Guard .... Bernd Hall
Soviet Captain .... Nikolai Hantoff
Auschwitz Sergeant ....Ernst Hausknost
Laura Dorf .... Courtney Hill
Gestapo Policeman .... Harry Horisch
Buchenwald Prisoner .... Karl Hoss
Pfannenstiel ....Helmut Janatsch
Sarah the Nurse .... Kathina Kaiser
Berlin Doctor .... Gotz von Langheim
Engleman ....Wolfgang Lesowsky
Sofia Alatri .... Hanna Lessing
Woman with Infant .... Mirian Mahler
Anton .... Rudolf Melichar
Border Guard .... Peter Neusser
Auschwitz Kapo .... Elvira Neustadtl
Aaron's Classmate .... Ian Odle
Sgt. Foltz ....Stefan Paryla
Prague Policeman .... Walter Scheuer
Polish Policeman ....Karl Schulz
Ghetto Policeman ....Ortwin Speer
Buchenwald Typist ....Ervon Steinhauser
Kapo Melnick .... Bruno Thost
Czech Jew .... Joe Trummer
Sacristan ....Peter Weihs

654 Home to Stay   CBS

Program Type Dramatic Special
90 minutes. Premiere date: 5/2/78. Filmed in
Toronto and Greenbank, Ontario, Canada.
Drama about a farm owner and his granddaugh-
ter. Script by Suzanne Clauser. Adapted from the
book by Janet Majerus. Music by Hagood Hardy.
Director Delbert Mann
Company Time-Life Television
Art Director Ben Edwards
Executive Producer David Susskind
Producer Frederick Brogger
CAST
Grandpa .... Henry Fonda
Frank .... Michael McGuire
Sarah .... Kristen Vigard
Aunt Martha .... Frances Hyland
Joey ....David Stambaugh
Clara .... Pixie Bigelow
Richard ....Louis Del Grande
Hildy .... Trudy Young
Mrs. Strickmeyer ....Doris Petrie
Petrie .... David Thomas
Bill Brewster .... Judy Sinclair
Farmer .... Len Doncheff
Frances ....Eleanor Beacroft
Policeman ....James D. Morris
Neighbor .... Sandra Scott

655 Homer and the Wacky Doughnut Machine ABC
ABC Short Story Specials
Program Type Children's Special
30 minutes. Premiere date: 4/30/77. Repeat dates: 10/15/77 and 3/18/78. Comedy about a boy who saves his uncle's business. Adapted from the short story by Robert McCloskey.
Executive Producer Allen Ducovny
Producer Robert Chenault
Company ABC Circle Films
Director Larry Elikann
Writer Mark Fink
CAST
Uncle Ulysses .... David Doyle
Mr. Gabby .... Jesse White
Homer .... Michael LeClair
Kelly .... Tara Talboy
Additional Cast Natalie Schafer, Cliff Norton, Bob Hastings, Dodo Denney, Roy Stuart

656 Hometown Almanac PBS
Program Type Music/Dance Special
60 minutes. Premiere date: 5/13/78. Special featuring the Jack Daniel's Original Silver Cornet Band. Program made possible by a grant from the National Resources Group of Gulf & Western Industries, Inc.
Producer Bob Sabel
Company WDCN-TV/Nashville and Spring Branch Productions
Band Leader Dave Fulmer

657 Hometown Saturday Night PBS
Program Type Music/Dance Special
60 minutes. Premiere date: 12/10/75. Repeat date: 12/30/77. A nostalgic recreation of a turn-of-the-century small-town band concert with the new Jack Daniel's Original Silver Cornet Band. Concert staged in the Nashville Opryhouse in February 1975. Program made possible by a grant from Marquette Corporation.
Producer Bob Sabel
Company WDCN-TV/Nashville, Tenn.
Director Bob Boatman
Conductor Dave Fulmer
Narrator Dave Fulmer

Hondo *See* The CBS Tuesday Night Movies

658 The Honeymooners' Christmas Special ABC
Program Type Comedy Special
60 minutes. 11/28/77. Jackie Gleason and the Honeymooners present a version of "A Christmas Carol." Music arranged by George Williams. Music composed by Jackie Gleason. Originated from Guzman Hall, Miami, Florida.
Executive Producer Jack Philbin
Producer Ed Waglin
Company Peekskill Enterprises, Inc. Productions
Director Jackie Gleason
Writers Walter Stone, Robert Hilliard
CAST
Ralph Kramden .... Jackie Gleason
Alice Kramden .... Audrey Meadows
Ed Norton .... Art Carney
Trixie Norton .... Jane Kean

659 The Honeymooners' Valentine Special ABC
Program Type Comedy Special
60 minutes. Premiere date: 2/13/78. Ralph Kramden disguises himself as a woman to trap the gigolo he believes is tempting his wife to kill him. Music composed by Jackie Gleason. Music arranged by George Williams.
Executive Producer Jack Philbin
Producer Ed Waglin
Company Peekskill Enterprises, Inc. Productions
Writers Walter Stone, Robert Hilliard
CAST
Ralph Kramden .... Jackie Gleason
Alice Kramden .... Audrey Meadows
Ed Norton .... Art Carney
Trixie Norton .... Jane Kean

660 Hong Kong Phooey
Program Type Children's Series NBC
30 minutes. Premiere date: 2/4/78. Animated series about a dog who practices the martial arts.
VOICES
All characters .... Scatman Crothers

661 Horowitz at the White House PBS
Program Type Music/Dance Special
60 minutes. Premiere date: 2/26/78. Special White House performance by pianist Vladimir Horowitz. Program made possible under a special grant from the Corporation for Public Broadcasting.
Company WETA-TV/Washington, DC

662 The Horrible Honchos ABC
ABC Afterschool Specials
Program Type Children's Special
60 minutes. Premiere date: 3/9/77. Repeat date: 5/31/78. Story of a group of kids who ostracize a new boy in the neighborhood. Based on "The Seventeenth Street Gang" by Emily Cheney Neville. Original music by Joe Weber.
Executive Producer Daniel Wilson
Producer Fran Sears
Company Daniel Wilson Productions, Inc.
Director Larry Elikann
Writer Thomas Baum

The Horrible Honchos *Continued*
CAST

Minnow	Kim Richards
Hollis	Christian Juttner
Louise	Tara Talboy
Ivan	Billy Jacoby
C. C.	Christopher Maleki
Hollis' Dad	Laurence Haddon
Hollis' Mom	Davey Davison
Louise's Mom	Pat Delany
Louise's Dad	Jack Knight

663 The House Without a Christmas Tree
CBS

Program Type Dramatic Special
90 minutes. Premiere date: 12/3/72. Season premiere: 12/16/77. Drama focusing on the conflict within a Nebraska family during a Christmas season in the 1940s. Adapted from a story by Gail Rock.
Producer Alan Shayne
Company CBS Television Network
Director Paul Bogart
Writer Eleanor Perry
CAST

James Mills	Jason Robards
Grandmother	Mildred Natwick
Addie Mills	Lisa Lucas
Carla Mae	Alexa Kenin
Miss Thompson	Kathryn Walker
Billy Wild	Brady MacNamara
Mrs. Cott	Maya Kenin Ryan
Gloria Cott	Gail Dusome
Mr. Brady	Murray Westgate

664 Houston Open Golf
NBC

Program Type Sports Special
Live coverage of the final rounds of the Houston Open from the Woodlands Country Club 4/22/78 and 4/23/78.
Producer Larry Cirillo
Company NBC Sports
Director Harry Coyle
Commentators John Brodie; Jay Randolph; Jim Simpson; Bob Goalby; Bruce Devlin

665 How the Beatles Changed the World

Special Treat
NBC

Program Type Children's Special
60 minutes. Premiere date: 11/22/77. Program showing how the British rock group affected the world's music and life styles.
Executive Producers Charles Andrews; Ken Greengrass
Producer Charles Andrews
Company Greengrass Enterprises
Director Jean-Christophe Averty
Writer Charles Andrews
Stars Richie Havens, Melissa Manchester, Melanie, David Clayton-Thomas with Blood, Sweat & Tears, Frankie Valli
Narrator David Frost

666 How the West Was Won
ABC

Program Type Limited Series
60 minutes. Sundays. Season premiere: 2/12/78. First two shows were each three hours. A continuation of the saga of "The Macahans" (shown 1/19/76) and based on the motion picture "How the West Was Won." Developed for television by Albert S. Ruddy and Jim Byrnes. Filmed at Utah, Colorado, Arizona, California locations and at MGM studios, Culver City, Calif. Music by Jerrold Immel
Executive Producer John Mantley
Producer John G. Stephens
Company A John Mantley Production in association with MGM-TV
Directors Vincent McEveety, Bernard McEveety
Writers Colley Cibber, Calvin Clements, William Kelley, John Mantley, Katharyn Michaelian Powers, Earl W. Wallace
Executive Story Consultant Calvin Clements
Cinematographer Edward R. Plante
Art Director Arch Bacon
Music Supervisor Harry V. Lojewski
Men's Wardrobe Ed Sunley
Women's Wardrobe Gilda Craig
CAST

Zeb Macahan	James Arness
Luke Macahan	Bruce Boxleitner
Josh Macahan	William Kirby Cullen
Laura Macahan	Kathryn Holcomb
Jessie Macahan	Vicki Schreck
Mina	Lynn Benesch
Captain Poynton	Don Collier
Booster	Bruce Fischer
Shewelah	Silvana Gallardo
Woodley	Burton Gilliam
Major Drake	Peter Hansen
Tommy Gant	Kristopher Marquis
Maggie Taylor	Peggy McCay
Hubbard	Henry Olek
Captain MacAllister	Van Williams
Tobe Harker	Mark Withers
Molly Culhane	Fionnuala Flanagan

667 How to Survive the 70s and Maybe Even Bump into Happiness
CBS

Program Type Music/Comedy/Variety Special
60 minutes. Premiere date: 2/22/78. Dance music arranged by Wally Harper. Musical conductor and arranger is Jack Elliott. "Zodiac Dancers" and "Listen Here" written by David Frishberg.
Producer Bill Persky
Company MTM Enterprises, Inc.
Director Bill Persky
Writers Bill Persky, Phil Hahn, April Kelly, Wayne Kline, Tom Sawyer, Sam Bobrick
Choreographer Tony Stevens

Costume Designer Pete Menefee
Set Decorator Don Remacle
Art Director Roy Christopher
Star Mary Tyler Moore
Special Guest Harvey Korman
Guest Star John Ritter
Cast Catlin Adams, Candice Azzara, Ed Barth, Allen Case, Gene Conforti, Sam Denoff, Michael Durrell, Arny Freeman, Christopher Guest, Steve Landesberg, Alan Oppenheimer, Henry Polic, II, Beverly Sanders

668 How We Got Here   PBS
Program Type Documentary/Informational Special
30 minutes. Premiere date: 6/21/76. Repeat date: 1/5/78. History of the Chinese in the United States focusing mainly on the experiences of people living in America's Chinatowns. Program funded by grants from the Corporation for Public Broadcasting, the Ford Foundation and Public Television Stations.
Executive Producer Don Roman
Producer Loni Ding
Company KQED-TV/San Francisco
Director Loni Ding
Writer Loni Ding

669 The Hunted Lady
NBC Monday Night at the Movies/NBC World Premiere Movie   NBC
Program Type Dramatic Special
2 hours. Premiere date: 11/28/77. Drama about an undercover police woman.
Director Richard Lang
Writer William Robert Yates
CAST
Susan Reilly .... Donna Mills
Sgt. Stanley Arizzio .... Alan Feinstein
Dr. Arthur Sills .... Robert Reed
Capt. John Shannon .... Andrew Duggan
Robert Armstrong .... Lawrence Casey
James Radford .... David Darlow
Angie .... Mario Roccuzzo
Johnny Ute .... Panchito Gomez
Uncle George .... Will Sampson
Senator Clements .... Mark Miller
Lt. Henry Jacks .... Michael McGuire
Cathy Clements .... Patti Kohoon
Lewis Clements .... Robert Nathan
Mr. Eckert .... Geoffrey Lewis

670 Hunters of the Reef
NBC World Premiere Movie/NBC Saturday Night at the Movies   NBC
Program Type TV Movie
2 hours. Premiere date: 5/20/78. The owner of a salvage boat races to stake a claim on a submerged wreck. Filmed in Key West, Fla., and the Bahamas.
Executive Producer Stanley Kallis

Producer Ben Chapman
Company Writers Company production in association with Paramount Pictures Television and NBC-TV
Director Alex Singer
Writer Eric Bercovici
CAST
Jim Spanner .... Michael Parks
Dr. Tracey Russell .... Mary Louise Weller
Panama Cassidy .... William Windom
Winston L.T. St. Andrew .... Felton Perry
Mike Spanner .... Moosie Drier
La Salle .... Stephen Macht
Kris La Salle .... Katy Kurtzman

671 Hurry Tomorrow   PBS
Program Type Documentary/Informational Special
60 minutes. Premiere date: 10/20/77. Cinemaverite documentary shot inside a locked men's ward at Metropolitan State Hospital, Norwalk, Calif. Program made possible in part by a grant from the Corporation for Public Broadcasting
Company Halfway House
Cinematographers Richard Cohen, Kevin Rafferty

672 Husbands, Wives and Lovers   CBS
Program Type Comedy Series
60 minutes. Fridays. Pilot: 7/18/77. Premiere: 3/10/78. Last show: 6/30/78. Married people in an American suburb. Created by Hal Dresner and Joan Rivers. Music by Jack Elliott and Allyn Ferguson.
Executive Producer Hal Dresner
Producer Don Van Atta
Company 20th Century-Fox Television in association with the CBS Television Network
Director Bill Persky
Writers Various
CAST
Murray Zuckerman .... Alex Rocco
Paula Zuckerman .... Cynthia Harris
Harry Bellini .... Ed Barth
Joy Bellini .... Lynne Marie Stewart
Lennie Bellini .... Mark Lonow
Rita Delatorre .... Randee Heller
Ron Willis .... Ron Rifkin
Helene Willis .... Jesse Wells
Dixon Carter Fielding .... Charles Siebert
Courtney Fielding .... Claudette Nevins

Hustle *See* The CBS Tuesday Night Movies

673 Hyde Park   PBS
Program Type Documentary/Informational Special
60 minutes. Premiere date: 4/25/78. A close look at one of the most naturally beautiful areas in the Hudson River Valley. Program made possible by

Hyde Park *Continued*
grants from the New York State Council on the
Arts and the Corporation for Public Broadcast-
ing.
Producer Ralph Arlyck
Company WNET-TV/New York

**674   I Am the Greatest: The Adventures
of Muhammad Ali**   NBC
Program Type Animated Film Series
30 minutes. Saturdays. Premiere: 9/10/77. Ani-
mated series about Muhammad Ali's adventures.
Executive Producer Fred Calvert
Producer Janis Marissa Diamond
Company Farmhouse Films, Inc.
Director Fred Calvert
Writers Fred Calvert, Janis Marissa Diamond
Art Director Kimmie Calvert
Voice Muhammad Ali

675   I Can!
The Winners   CBS
Program Type Children's Special
30 minutes. Premiere date: 10/13/77. Repeat
date: 4/13/78. Debbie Phillips stars in her own
life story of how she overcame the handicap of a
serious birth defect to become a champion eques-
trienne. Horse handler: Stevie Myers.
Executive Producer Robert Guenette
Producers Paul Asselin, Diane Asselin
Company Guenette/Asselin Productions
Director Paul Asselin
Writer Hindi Brooks
Art Director John Told
Star Debbie Phillips
CAST
Jeff ....Jim Kester
Dr. Lindman .... George Cooper
Flip .... Bob Purvey
Phillip .... Dick Gjonola
Betsy .... Connie Hunter
Lisa .... Mary Matthews
Mrs. Lacy .... Gwen Van Dam

676   I, Claudius
Masterpiece Theatre   PBS
Program Type Limited Series
60 minutes. Premiere date: 11/6/77. 13-part se-
ries based on two novels by Robert Graves about
the Roman Emperor Claudius. Presented by
WGBH-TV/Boston; produced by Joan Sullivan.
Series made possible by a grant from Mobil Oil
Corporation. Title music by Wilfred Josephs; in-
cidental music by David Wulstan; performed by
David Wulstan and The Clerkes of Oxonford.
Producer Martin Lisemore
Company London Films-BBC Production
Director Herbert Wise
Story Editor Betty Willingale
Writer Jack Pulman

Host Alistair Cooke
CAST
Claudius ....Derek Jacobi
Livia .... Sian Phillips
Augustus .... Brian Blessed
Antonia .... Margaret Tyzack
Caligula .... John Hurt
Tiberius .... George Baker
Sejanus .... Patrick Stewart
Piso .... Stratford Johns
Messalina .... Sheila White
Drusus ....Ian Ogilvy
Julia ....Frances White
Germanicus .... David Robb
Livilla .... Patricia Quinn
Postumus .... John Castle
Herod ....James Faulkner

677   I Love You   NBC
Program Type Music/Comedy/Variety Special
60 minutes. Premiere date: 2/14/78. Nearly 30
celebrities offer different perspectives of love.
Executive Producer Ken Weinstock
Guest Stars Tony Orlando, Elaine Orlando, Paul
Anka, Anne Anka, Marilyn McCoo, Bill Da-
vis, Telly Savalas, Melissa Gilbert, Phyllis
Diller, Edgar Bergen, Big Bird, Oscar, Kristy
McNichol, Jimmy McNichol, Ed McMahon,
Doc Severinsen, Audra Lindley, Norman Fell,
Paul Lynde, Angie Dickinson, Will Geer, Jack
Albertson, Gabriel Melgar, Don Rickles, Bill
Hayes, Susan Seaforth, Steve Garvey, Cindy
Garvey, Ernest Borgnine, Roberta Linn,
Johnny Mathis

678   I Sought My Brother   PBS
Program Type Documentary/Informational
Special
90 minutes. Premiere date: 4/18/78. Two black
Americans, Dr. S. Allen Counter and David
Evans, visit descendants of rebel slaves in Suri-
nam. Program made possible by a grant from the
Corporation for Public Broadcasting.
Company WQED-TV/Pittsburgh
Host Alex Haley
Narrator James Earl Jones

679   I Want It All Now
NBC News Special   NBC
Program Type Documentary/Informational
Special
60 minutes. Premiere date: 7/20/78. Documen-
tary on the life styles and values of people who
live in Marin County.
Reporter Edwin Newman
Company NBC News
Producer Joe De Cola

680 The Image Makers: The Environment of Arnold Newman   PBS
Program Type Documentary/Informational Special
30 minutes. Premiere date: 8/31/77. Repeat dates: 11/24/77 and 1/5/78. A look at the work of portrait photographer Arnold Newman. Program made possible by a grant from the Nebraska Educational Television Network.
Producer Gene Bunge
Company Nebraska Educational Television Network
Director Linda Elliott

681 Images of Aging   PBS
Program Type Documentary/Informational Series
60 minutes. Premiere date: 1/21/76. Series repeated: 10/8/77. Eight-part series investigating American attitudes towards the elderly. Series made possible by a grant from the Corporation for Public Broadcasting.
Producer Robert Larson
Company WITF-TV/Hershey
Writer Robert Larson
Host Robert Larson

682 The Impossible Dream: Ballooning Across the Atlantic   CBS
Program Type Sports Special
60 minutes. 2/5/78. Coverage of successful Trans-Atlantic balloon crossing.
Producer Ed Goren
Company CBS Sports
Narrator Jack Whitaker

683 In Performance at Wolf Trap   PBS
Program Type Music/Dance Series
Times vary. Premiere date: 10/14/74. Fourth season premiere: 9/20/77. Music/dance series from the Wolf Trap Park Farm for the Performing Arts in Virginia. Programs shown during the 1977–78 season are: "Bonnie Raitt and Mose Allison," "Cleo Laine and John Dankworth," "Dionne Warwick," "An Evening of Blue Grass," "Fat Tuesday and All that Jazz!" "King of Swing," "Kostelanetz and Menuhin," "La Traviata," "Martha Graham Dance Company," "Mikhail Baryshnikov," "New England Conservatory Ragtime Ensemble and the Katharine Dunham Dancers," "The Nutcracker," "Roberto Devereaux," "Valerie and Galina Panov," "The Verde Requiem," and "The World Series of Jazz." (*See* individual titles for credits.) Series made possible by a grant from the Atlantic Richfield Company.

684 In Pursuit of Liberty   PBS
Program Type Public Affairs Series
60 minutes. Premiere date: 9/5/77. Series repeated: 1/9/78. Examines various civil and personal liberties fundamental to American society. Series made possible by a grant from the National Endowment for the Humanities, with additional support provided by the Edward W. Hazen Foundation.
Executive Producer Don Dixon
Company WNET-TV/New York
Director Jack Sameth
Host Charles Frankel
Writer Charles Frankel

685 In Search of the Real America   PBS
Program Type Educational/Cultural Series
30 minutes. Monthly. Premiere date: 2/15/77. Second season premiere: 5/18/78. Repeat of first series: 7/13/78. Six-part series examining America's institutions, attitudes and future. Regular feature: rebuttal arguments by guest critics. Series made possible by grants from the Corporation for Public Broadcasting, the Mobil Corporation, the John M. Olin Foundation, Inc., the Pfizer Foundation, Scaife Family Charitable Trusts, and the J. M. Foundation.
Executive Producer Gerald Lange
Producer Werner Bundschuh
Company WGBH-TV/Boston
Director Bruce Shah
Host Ben Wattenberg

686 In the Glitter Palace
NBC Monday Night at the Movies
Program Type Dramatic Special
2 hours. Premiere date: 2/23/77. Repeat date: 7/10/78. Drama of a lesbian accused of murder. Filmed in part on locations in Los Angeles. Music by John Parker.
Executive Producer Stanley Kallis
Producers Jerry Ludwig, Jay Daniel
Company Columbia Pictures Television in association with NBC-TV
Director Robert Butler
Writer Jerry Ludwig
CAST
Vince Halloran	Chad Everett
Ellen Lange	Barbara Hershey
Casey Walker	Diana Scarwid
Roy Danko	Anthony Zerbe
Raymond Travers	Howard Duff
Nathan Redstone	David Wayne
Grace Mayo	Tisha Sterling
Roger	Ron Rifkin
Judge Kendis	Salome Jens
Fred Ruggiero	Ron Masak
Daisy Dolon	Carole Cook

In the Heat of the Night *See* The CBS Tuesday Night Movies

687   In the Matter of Karen Ann Quinlan
NBC Saturday Night at the Movies/NBC World Premiere movie   NBC
Program Type TV Movie
2 hours. Premiere date: 9/16/77. Repeat date: 7/15/78. Fact-based-drama about a woman kept alive by a life support system.
Executive Producer Warren V. Bush
Producer Hal Sitowitz
Company Warren V. Bush Production in association with NBC-TV
Director Hal Jordan
Writer Hal Sitowitz
CAST
Joe Quinlan .... Brian Keith
Julie Quinlan .... Piper Laurie
Paul Armstrong ....David Huffman
Dr. Mason .... David Spielberg
Father Tom .... Biff McGuire
Mary Ellen .... Stephanie Zimbalist
Attorney General .... Byron Morrow
Sister Mary .... Louise Latham
Dr. Korein ....Bert Freed
Dr. Hanif ....Habib Ageli

688   In the News   CBS
Program Type News Special
Capsulized current-events broadcasts for young viewers.
Company CBS News
Narrator Gary Shepard

689   Including Me   PBS
Program Type Documentary/Informational Special
60 minutes. Premiere date: 9/15/77. A look at public education for handicapped children as a result of the passage of the Education for All Handicapped Children Act. Program captioned for the hearing-impaired and made possible by a grant from the 3M Company.
Producer Linda Janower
Company WQED-TV/Pittsburgh
Director Linda Janower
Writer Linda Janower

690   The Incredible Hulk   CBS
Program Type Dramatic Special
2 hours. Premiere date: 11/4/77. Science-adventure drama based on Marvel Comic hero which first appeared in 1962. Music by Joseph Harnell.
Producer Kenneth Johnson
Company Universal Television
Director Kenneth Johnson
Writer Kenneth Johnson

Film Editors Jack Shoengarth, Alan Marks
Director of Photography Howard Schwartz
CAST
David Bruce Banner .... Bill Bixby
The Hulk .... Lou Ferrigno
Elaina Marks ....Susan Sullivan
Mr. McGee ....Jack Colvin
Mrs. Maier ....Susan Batson
Ben .... Charles Siebert
Mr. Bram .... Mario Gallo
Policeman .... Eric Server
B. J. .... Eric Deon
Jerry .... Jake Mitchell
Laura Banner ....Lara Parker
Minister .... William Larsen
girl at lake .... Olivia Barash
man at lake .... George Brenlin
woman ....June Whitley
young man ....Terrence Locke

691   The Incredible Hulk   CBS
Program Type Drama Series
60 minutes. Premiere: 3/10/78. Fridays. Two movie specials, "The Incredible Hulk" and "The Return of the Incredible Hulk," telecast Fall, 1977. Series based on Marvel Comic Book character of research scientist whose radiation experiments transform him into raging beast with superhuman strength whenever he is angered. Music by Joseph Harnell.
Executive Producer Kenneth Johnson
Producers James D. Parriott, Charles Bowman
Company Universal Television
Directors Various
Writers Various
CAST
David Bruce Banner .... Bill Bixby
The Hulk .... Lou Ferrigno
Mr. McGee ....Jack Colvin

692   The Incredible Machine
National Geographic Special   PBS
Program Type Science/Nature Special
60 minutes. Premiere date: 10/28/75. Repeat date: 3/28/78. A look at the inner workings of the human body. Music by Billy Goldenberg. Program funded by a grant from Gulf Oil Corporation and presented by WQED-TV/Pittsburgh
Executive Producer Dennis B. Kane
Production Executive Nicholas Clapp
Producer Irwin Rosten
Company National Geographic Society in association with Wolper Productions
Director Irwin Rosten
Writer Irwin Rosten
Cinematographers Erik Daarstad, John Morrill, Lennart Nilsson, Rokuru Havashi
Film Editor Hyman Kaufman
Host E. G. Marshall
Narrator E. G. Marshall

693 The Incredible Rocky Mountain Race
NBC World Premiere Movie/NBC Saturday
Night at the Movies NBC
Program Type TV Movie
2 hours. Premiere date: 12/17/77. Mark Twain
races riverman Mike Fink from Missouri to the
Pacific Ocean via horse, canoe, and balloon.
Director James L. Conway
Writers Tom Chapman, Dave O'Malley
CAST
Mark Twain .... Christopher Connelly
Mike Fink .... Forrest Tucker
Jim Bridger .... Jack Kruschen
Chief Crazy Horse .... Mike Mazurki
Eagle Feather .... Larry Storch
Mayor ....Bill Zuckert
Simon Hollaway ....Whit Bissell
Sheriff Benedict ....Don Haggerty
Farley Osmond .... Parley Baer
Milford Petrie .... Sam Edwards

694 Indian Summer PBS
Program Type Documentary/Informational
Special
30 minutes. Premiere date: 10/14/75. Repeat
date: 9/25/77. Life on the Santa Ana Pueblo
Reservation as seen through the eyes of a 12-year
old Indian boy.
Company WGBH-TV/Boston

695 Indianapolis "500" ABC
Program Type Sports Special
2 hours. 5/28/78. Same-day coverage of 62nd
annual auto race from The Indanapolis Motor
Speedway.
Executive Producer Roone Arledge
Producers Chuck Howard, Bob Goodrich
Directors Chet Forte, Larry Kamm
Anchor Jim McKay
Reporters Jackie Stewart, Chris Schenkel, Chris
Economaki, Bill Flemming

696 Indanapolis "500" Festival Parade
ABC
Program Type Parades/Pageants/Awards
Special
2 hours. Taped coverage of the parade which
includes the Indanapolis 500's 33 starting drivers, 5/27/78.
Executive Producer Roone Arledge
Producers Chuck Howard, Bob Goodrich
Company ABC Sports
Directors Chet Forte, Larry Kamm
Hosts Bob Barker, Josephine Hauck

697 Infinity Factory PBS
Program Type Children's Series
30 minutes. Sundays, Tuesdays, Thursdays. Premiere date: 9/20/76. Season premiere: 10/2/77.
Series repeats: 1/3/78 and 4/18/78. Twice-
weekly magazine-format show designed to help
children 8–11 years old learn mathematics. Series made possible by a grant from the U.S. Office
of Education under the Emergency School Aid
Act plus additional funding from the Carnegie
Corporation of New York, John and Mary R.
Markle Foundation, JDR 3rd Fund, National
Science Foundation and Alfred P. Sloan Foundation.
Executive Producer Madeline Anderson
Producers Terri Payne Francis, D.B. Roderick
Company Education Development Center, Inc.,
Newton, Mass.
Director Allan Muir
Senior Advisor Jerrold Zacharias

698 The Initiation of Sarah
The ABC Monday Night Movie ABC
Program Type TV Movie
2 hours. Premiere date: 2/6/78. A freshman coed is drawn into the rites of a sorority. Story by
Tom Holland and Carol Saraceno. Music by
Johnny Harris. Special effects by Cliff Wenger.
Executive Producers Charles Fries, Dick Berg
Producer Jay Benson
Company A Stonehenge/Charles Fries Production
Director Robert Day
Writers Don Ingalls, Carol Saraceno, Kenette
Gfeller
Art Director Herman Zimmerman
CAST
Sarah .... Kay Lenz
Miss Erica ....Shelley Winters
Patti ....Morgan Brittany
Mrs. Goodwin .... Kathryn Crosby
Jennifer .... Morgan Fairchild
Paul Yates ....Tony Bill
Laura .... Elizabeth Stack
Bobbi .... Deborah Ryan
Barbara ....Nora Heflin
Mouse .... Tisa Farrow
Scott .... Robert Hays
Allison .... Talia Balsam
Tommy ....Doug Davidson
Kathy .... Jennifer Gay
Regina ....Susan Duvall
Pledge .... Karen Purcil
Freddie .... Michael Talbot
Clerk .... Madeline Kelly

699 Inner Tennis PBS
Program Type Limited Sports Series
30 minutes. Mondays. Premiere date: 5/16/76.
Series repeated: 8/8/77. Six-part series of tennis
lessons based on "The Inner Game of Tennis"
written by Tim Gallwey. Funded by a grant from
GAF Corporation.
Producer Mark Waxman
Company KCET-TV/Los Angeles

Inner Tennis *Continued*
Director Jerry Hughes
Host/Instructor Tim Galwey

700   Inner Visions—Beah Richards   PBS
Program Type Documentary/Informational
Special
30 minutes. Premiere date: 1/23/78. Beah Richards, poet, playwright and actress performs works from her book.
Producer Joe Phillips
Company KCET-TV/Los Angeles
Director Ed Scott
Host David Crippens

701   Inside CBS News
CBS News Special   CBS
Program Type Public Affairs Special
Series of broadcasts which allows the public access to decision makers and on-air reporters at CBS News.

Part V
60 minutes Premiere date: 11/6/77 (on national television). Originally produced and broadcast by WHP-TV/Harrisburg. Fifth program in the series.
Company CBS News
Moderator John Sebastian

Part VI
60 minutes. Premiere date: 4/15/78 (on national television). Originally produced and broadcast by WHAS-TV/Louisville. Sixth program in the series.
Company CBS News
Moderator Milton Metz

702   Inside the World of Jesse Allen   PBS
Program Type Documentary/Informational
Special
30 minutes. Premiere date: 8/10/78. Life and work of self-taught artist Jesse Allen.
Producers Steve and Elizabeth Grumette

703   Insight   Syndicated
Program Type Religious/Cultural Series
30 minutes. Weekly. Seventeenth year of weekly dramatic shows.
Executive Producer Rev. Ellwood E. Kieser
Producer Michael Rhodes
Company Paulist Productions
Directors Various
Writers Various

704   International Chess Coverage   PBS
Program Type Sports Special
2 hours each broadcast. Premiere date: 8/26/78.

Coverage of on-going world championship chess match between defending champion Anatoly Karpov and challenger Victor Korchnoi played in Baguio City, the Philippines. Continuous Saturday coverage of the tournment from 8/26/78 to completion. Program underwritten by The American Chess Foundation.
Company WGBY-TV/Springfield, Massachusetts

**705   International Grand Prix Tennis
Tournament**   CBS
Program Type Sports Special
Same-day coverage of final round from North Conway, New Hampshire 8/6/78.
Producer Perry Smith
Company CBS Sports
Director Bob Dailey
Announcers Tony Trabert, Rick Barry

**706   Interview with Prime Minister
Begin**
NBC News Special   NBC
Program Type News Special
30 minutes. Premiere date: 3/23/78. John Chancellor interviews Prime Minister Menachem Begin at Blair House in Washington, DC. NBC News correspondent Hilary Brown also participated.
Producer Gordon Manning
Company NBC News

707   Intimate Strangers
The ABC Friday Night Movie   ABC
Program Type TV Movie
2 hours. 11/11/77. Couple find their love for each other cannot overcome the emotions which threaten to destroy their marriage. Music by Fred Karlin.
Executive Producer Charles Fries
Producers Richard Shapiro, Esther Shapiro
Company Charles Fries Productions
Director John Llewellyn Moxey
Writers Richard Shapiro, Esther Shapiro
Art Director Bill Ross

CAST

Donald Halston	Dennis Weaver
Janis Halston	Sally Struthers
Karen	Tyne Daly
Mort	Larry Hagman
Father	Melvyn Douglas
Chris Halston	Brian Andrews
Peggy Halston	Quinn Cummings
Dr. Morgan	Julian Burton
Marilyn	Ellen Travolta
Bridget	Ellen Blake
Rest Home Director	Regis Cordic
Young Cop	James Keane
Older Officer	Ed Walsh
Charlotte Ames	Barbara Iley

708 Into the Mouths of Babes
CBS Reports   CBS
Program Type Documentary/Informational
Special
Premiere date: 7/5/78. Report on the controversy over the danger of the sale and use of infant formula in underdeveloped countries.
Executive Producer Howard Stringer
Producer Janet Roach
Company CBS News
Director Janet Roach
Writers Bill Moyers, Janet Roach
Cinematographer Robert Peterson
Film Editor Joanne Burke
Researcher Susan D. Werbe
Translator Maruta Friedler
Reporter Bill Moyers

709 Iowa
Visions   PBS
Program Type Dramatic Special
90 minutes. Premiere date: 10/2/77. Original drama about a reunion of family members who have not seen each other for some time.
Producer Barbara Schultz
Company KCET-TV/Los Angeles
Director Rick Bennewitz
Art Director Barbara Schultz
CAST
Neal .... Warren Stevens
Mary .... Bethel Leslie
Eileen .... Carol Fox
Margaret .... Nora Heflin
Grandmother .... Peggy Furey
Claudia .... Alma Beltran
Young Man .... John-Anthony Bailey
Nurse .... Ellen Travolta

710 Is Anyone Out There Learning?: A CBS News Report Card On American Public Education   CBS
Program Type News Special
3 hours. One hour three consecutive nights: 8/22-24/78. An examination of the problems in American public schools, their causes and possible solutions.
Executive Producer Leslie Midgley
Senior Producers Russ Bensley, Ernest Leiser
Producers Jane Bartels, Bernard Birnbaum, Hal Haley
Company CBS News
Director Ken Sable
Writers Russ Bensley, Ernest Leiser, Charles West
Anchor Walter Cronkite
Reporter Susan Spencer
Correspondents David Culhane, David Dow, Barry Serafin
Field Correspondent Charles Collingwood

711 The Islander
The CBS Saturday Night Movies   CBS
Program Type TV Movie
2 hours. Premiere date: 9/16/78. Retired mainland lawyer buys a small hotel in Honolulu. Filmed in Honolulu. Music by Stu Phillips.
Producer Glen A. Larson
Company Universal Television in association with Glen Larson Productions
Director Paul Krasny
Writer Glen A. Larson
CAST
Gable McQueen .... Dennis Weaver
Shauna Cooke .... Sharon Gless
Lt. Larkin .... Peter Mark Richman
Trudy Engles .... Bernadette Peters
Senator Stratton .... Robert Vaughn
Bishop Hatch .... John S. Ragin
Al Kahala .... Dick Jensen
Kimo .... Ed Kaahea
Lazarro .... Sheldon Leonard
Simms .... George Wyner
Paco .... Zitto Kazaan
Mac's Wife .... Leann Hunley
Wallace .... Glenn Cannon
Sgt. Chow .... Jimmy Borges
Sgt. Rojo .... Daniel Kamekona
Reporter .... Burt Marshall
Henchman .... Moe Keale
Charlie Soon .... John Fitzgibbon
Taxi Driver .... Galen W. Y. Kam
Tiny .... Kwan Hi Lim
Commentator .... Bob Sevey

712 The Islander   PBS
Program Type Documentary/Informational
Special
30 minutes. Premiere date: 2/8/78. Film portrait of the life of artist Walter Anderson. Program made possible in part by a grant from The Corporation for Public Broadcasting.
Producer Ron Harris
Company Mississippi Authority for Education Television
Director Ron Harris
Narrator Mary Anderson Stebly
CAST
Walter Anderson .... James Best
Mrs. Anderson .... Mary Anderson Stebly

713 Israel: A Search for Faith
James Michener's World   PBS
Program Type Documentary/Informational
Special
60 minutes. Premiere date: 6/21/77. Repeat date: 9/7/77. First in a series of four specials about different places Michener has written about. Program presented by KCET-TV/Los Angeles and made possible by a grant from Mrs. Paul's Kitchens, Inc.
Producer Albert Waller
Co-Producer Ken Golden
Company Reader's Digest Association, Inc.

Israel: A Search for Faith *Continued*
Director Albert Waller
Writer Albert Waller
Host James Michener

714   Issues and Answers   ABC
Program Type Public Affairs Series
30 minutes. Sundays. Premiere date: 10/60. 18th season premiere: 9/77. Live interview show with newsmakers; generally from Washington. Several shows devoted to inflation and the economy.
Producer Peggy Whedon
Company ABC News Public Affairs
Chief Correspondent Bob Clark

715   It Happened at Lakewood Manor
The ABC Friday Night Movie   ABC
Program Type TV Movie
2 hours. Premiere date: 12/2/77. Suspense drama about a group of people at a summer resort. Music by Kim Richmond. Special effects by Roy Downey. Filmed at Qualicam College Inn, Vancouver Island, B.C.
Executive Producer Alan Landsburg
Producer Peter Nelson
Company Alan Landsburg Productions, Inc.
Director Robert Scheerer
Writers Guerdon Trueblood, Peter Nelson
Art Director Ray Beal
Stunt Coordinator Roger Creed
Ant Coordinator Warren Estes
CAST
Gloria .... Suzanne Somers
Mike .... Robert Foxworth
Ethel Adams .... Myrna Loy
Valerie Adams ....Lynda Day George
Tony .... Gerald Gordon
Vince .... Bernie Casey
Richard .... Barry Van Dyke
Linda .... Karen Lamm
Peggy .... Anita Gillette
Tommy ....Moosie Drier
White ....Steve Franken
Fire Chief .... Brian Dennehy
Tom .... Bruce French
Marjorie .... Barbara Brownell
Doc .... Stacy Keach, Sr.
Luis .... Rene Enriquez
Peter .... Vincent Cobb

716   It Happened One Christmas
The ABC Sunday Night Movie   ABC
Program Type TV Movie
2-1/2 hours. Premiere date: 12/11/77. Story of a young woman and an apprentice angel. Based on 1946 film, "It's a Wonderful Life."
Producers Marlo Thomas, Carole Hart
Company Daisy Productions
Director Donald Wrye
Writer Lionel Chetwynd
Art Director John J. Lloyd

Set Decorator Hal Gausman
CAST
Mary Bailey .... Marlo Thomas
Angel ....Cloris Leachman
George Hatch .... Wayne Rogers
Potter ....Orson Welles
Uncle Willy .... Barney Martin
Bailey ....Richard Dysart
Mrs. Bailey .... Doris Roberts
Cousin Tillie .... Ceil Cabot
Harry Bailey .... Christopher Guest
Ernie .... Archie Hahn
Bert .... Morgan Upton
Violet .... Karen Carlson
Gower .... Dick O'Neill
Sam Wainwright .... Jim Lovelett

717   It Isn't Easy Being a Teenage Millionaire
ABC Afterschool Specials   ABC
Program Type Children's Special
60 minutes. Premiere date: 3/8/78. A teenage girl loses sight of the important things in life when she wins one million dollars. Based on the novel by Joan Oppenheimer. Filmed in and around San Francisco Bay area.
Executive Producer Joseph Barbera
Producer Terry Morse, Jr.
Company Hanna-Barbera Productions, Inc.
Director Richard Bennett
Writer Jim Inman
Music Hoyt Curtin
Sound Mike Eliot
Director of Photography Al Niggemeyer
CAST
Melissa Harrington ....Victoria Meyerink
Jeff Gardner .... Chris Dekker
Mrs. Catherine Harrington .... Karen Hurley
Mr. Harry Harrington ....Bob Hastings
Teague Harrington .... Lauri Hendler
Aunt Liz ....Susan O'Connell
Gail .... Danette Pachtner
Mrs. Scanlon .... Olwen Morgan
Mark Henderson .... Clark Brandon
Wendy Rogers .... Alice Cadogan
Mrs. Waverly ....Julie MacAskill
Jim McKrell .... Jim McKrell
Miss Plamer ....Judith Weston
Phil Davidson ....Chris Pray
Announcer .... Morgan Upton

718   It Must Be Love, ('Cause I Feel So Dumb!)
ABC Out-of-School Specials/ABC Weekend Specials   ABC
Program Type Children's Special
60 minutes. Premiere date: 10/8/75. Repeat date: 10/1/77. Young people's drama about love, filmed on location on Manhattan's upper West Side
Producers Arthur Barron, Evelyn Barron
Company Verite Productions
Director Arthur Barron

Writer Arthur Barron
Costume Designer Judith W. Pressburger
CAST
Erik .... Alfred Lutter
Cathy .... Denby Olcott
Lisa .... Vicki Dawson
Father .... Michael Miller
Mother .... Kay Frye
LeRoy .... P. R. Paul

719 The Itinerary of Elie Wiesel: From Sighet to Jerusalem
Eternal Light   NBC
Program Type Religious/Cultural Special
60 minutes. Premiere date: 5/21/72. Repeat date: 5/21/78. Filmed chronicle of the distinguished novelist's return to Sighet, Romania, for the first time since his deportation to the concentration camps of Nazi Germany in 1944.
Executive Producer Doris Ann
Producer Martin Hoade
Producer for the Seminary Milton E. Krents
Company NBC News with Jewish Theological Seminary of America
Director Martin Hoade

720 It's a Brand New World
Special Treat   NBC
Program Type Animated Film Special
60 minutes. Premiere date: 3/8/77. Repeat date: 12/5/77. Animated musical based on the Biblical stories of Noah and Samson. Original music and lyrics by Al Elias; Andy Badale and Murray Semos. "Noah's Ark" written by Romeo Muller and Max Wilk; "Young Samson" by Romeo Muller.
Executive Producer Eddie Elias
Producer Al Elias
Company An Elias Production
Writers Romeo Muller, Max Wilk
Animation Directors Ronald Fritz, Dan Hunn
Animators Martin Taras, Lucifer B. Guarnier, Paul Sparagano, Charles Harriton
Dialogue Director Jon Surgal
VOICES
Teacher/Noah .... Joe Silver
Elijah/Samson .... Malcolm Dodd
Aaron .... Dennis Cooley
Jezebel .... Boni Enten
Barnabas .... George Hirsch
Samson's Mother .... Charmaine Harma
Additional Voices Sylvester Fields, Hilda Harris, Maeretha Stewart

It's a Mad, Mad, Mad, Mad World *See* The CBS Tuesday Night Movies

721 It's a Mile from Here to Glory
ABC Afterschool Specials   ABC
Program Type Children's Special
60 minutes. Premiere date: 5/3/78. A teenaged athlete must win at all costs. Music by Glenn Paxton. Director of Photography: Bob Collins. Based on the book by Richard C. Lee.
Producer Martin Tahse
Associate Producer Fred Bennett
Company Martin Tahse Productions, Inc.
Director Richard Bennett
Writer Durrell Royce Crays
Art Director Ray Markham
Film Editor Vince Humphrey
Sound Bruce Bizenz
CAST
Early McLaren .... Steve Shaw
Billy Patnell .... Justin Lord
Coach Canepa .... David Haskell
Dave McLaren .... James G. Richardson
Mary Bruce .... Anne Gee Byrd
John Moody .... Woodrow Parfrey
Dizzy Cartwright .... Art Kimbro
Jimmy Plummer .... Cole Dammett
Dorothy Kidder .... Suzy Callahan
Tim Mahaney .... David Cole
Doctor .... Steve Eastin
Bus Driver .... Allan Lurie
Radio Announcer .... Dave Morick

722 It's Anybody's Guess   NBC
Program Type Game/Audience Participation Series
30 minutes. Mondays–Fridays. Premiere date: 6/13/77. Last show: 9/30/77. Contestants trying to guess whether a studio panel will come up with a predetermined reply to questions.
Executive Producer Stu Billett
Producer Steve Feke
Company Stefan Hatos-Monty Hall Production
Director Joseph Behar
Art Director Scott Ritenour
Host Monty Hall
Announcer Jay Stewart

723 It's Arbor Day, Charlie Brown   CBS
Program Type Animated Film Special
30 minutes. Premiere date: 3/8/76. Repeat date: 4/10/78. Created by Charles M. Schulz. Music by Vince Guaraldi.
Executive Producer Lee Mendelson
Producer Bill Melendez
Company A Lee Mendelson-Bill Melendez Production in cooperation with United Feature Syndicate, Inc., and Charles M. Schulz Creative Associates
Director Phil Roman
Musical Director Vince Guaraldi
VOICES
Charlie Brown .... Dylan Beach
Lucy .... Sarah Beach
Sally .... Gail M. Davis

It's Arbor Day, Charlie Brown *Continued*

Peppermint Patty ....Stuart Brotman
Schroeder .... Greg Felton
Linus .... Liam Martin
Re-Run ....Vinnie Dow
Frieda .... Michelle Muller

724 It's the Easter Beagle, Charlie Brown CBS

Program Type Animated Film Special
30 minutes. Premiere date: 4/9/74. Repeat date: 3/19/78. Created by Charles M. Schulz. Music composed by Vince Guaraldi.
Executive Producer Lee Mendelson
Producer Bill Melendez
Company A Lee Mendelson-Bill Melendez Production in cooperation with United Feature Synidcate, Inc. and Charles M. Schulz Creative Associates
Director Phil Roman
Writer Charles M. Schulz
Musical Director Vince Guaraldi
Music Supervisor John Scott Trotter
VOICES
Charlie Brown .... Todd Barbee
Lucy ....Melanie Kohn
Linus ....Stephen Shea
Peppermint Patty .... Linda Ercoli
Sally .... Lynn Mortensen
Marcie .... Jimmy Ahrens

725 It's Your First Kiss, Charlie Brown CBS

Program Type Animated Film Special
30 minutes. Premiere date: 10/24/77. Written and created by Charles M. Schulz. Music by Ed Bogas.
Executive Producer Lee Mendelson
Producer Bill Melendez
Company A Lee Mendelson-Bill Melendez Production in cooperation with United Feature Syndicate and Charles M. Schulz Creative Associates
Director Phil Roman
Film Editor Chuck McCann, Roger Donley
VOICES
Charlie Brown ....Arrin Skelley
Peppermint Patty .... Laura Planting
Linus ....Daniel Anderson
Lucy .... Michelle Muller
Franklin .... Ronald Hendrix

726 Jabberjaws ABC

Program Type Animated Film Series
30 minutes. Saturday mornings. Premiere date: 9/11/76. Season premiere: 9/11/77. Last show: 9/3/78. Commedy-adventure series set in an underwater civilization in 2021 A.D. about a lovable shark who is the mascot of four teenagers. Created by Joe Ruby and Ken Spears.

Executive Producers Joseph Barbera, William Hanna
Producer Iwao Takamoto
Company Hanna-Barbera Productions, Inc.
Story Editor Ray Parker
Writers George Atkins, Haskell Barkin, John Bates, Lars Bourne, Tom Dagenais, Robert Fisher
Animation Director Charles A. Nichols
Voices Tommy Cock, Regis J. Cordic, Ron Reinberg, Barry Gordon, Gay Hartwig, Hettie Lynn Hurtes, Casey Kasem, Keye Luke, Julie McWhirter, Don Messick, Pat Parris, Vic Perin, Barney Phillips, Hal Smith, John Stephenson, Janet Waldo, Lennie Weinrib, Frank Welker

727 Jack: A Flash Fantasy

Opera Theater PBS
Program Type Music/Dance Special
60 minutes. Premiere date: 7/26/77. Repeat date: 9/18/78. First rock opera musical-variety show commissioned for television. Music by Peter Mann. Program presented by WNET-TV/New York and made possible by grants from the Corporation for Public Television, the Ford Foundation and Public Television Stations.
Executive Producer Neil Sutherland
Coordinating Producers David Griffiths, Sam Paul
Producers Rob Iscove, Peter Mann
Company Canadian Broadcasting Corporation
Director Rob Iscove
Writers Rob Iscove, Peter Mann
Musical Director Rick Wilkins
Choreographer Rob Iscove
Costume Designer Csilla Marki
Scenic Designer Arthur Herriot
CAST
Jack (Spirit) .... Jeff Hyslop
Jill (Spirit) .... Laurie Hood
Jack of Hearts .... Victor Garber
Jill of Hearts .... Gilda Radner
Jack of Spades .... William Daniel Grey
Jill of Spades ....Vera Biloshisky
Jack of Diamonds .... Alan Thicke
Jill of Diamonds .... Patricia Gaul
Jack of Clubs .... Jerry Sroka
Jill of Clubs ....Valri Bromfield

728 Jackie & Darlene

The ABC Saturday Comedy Special ABC
Program Type Comedy Special
30 minutes. Premiere date: 7/8/78. Comedy pilot about a rookie policewoman.
Executive Producer Aaron Ruben
Producer Gene Marcione
Company An Andomar Production
Director Russ Petranto
CAST
Jackie .... Sarina Grant

Darlene .... Anna L. Pagan
Sgt. Guthrie .... Lou Frizzell

729 Jackie Gleason Inverrary Classic
CBS

Program Type Sports Special
Coverage of the Jackie Gleason Inverrary Classic
from the Inverrary Golf & Country Club in Lau-
derhill, Fla. 2/25/78 and 2/26/78.
Producer Frank Chirkinian
Company CBS Television Network Sports
Directors Bob Dailey, Frank Chirkinian
Commentators Vin Scully, Pat Summerall, Jack
  Whitaker, Ben Wright, Ken Venturi

Jackson County Jail *See* The CBS
Wednesday Night Movies

Jacqueline Susann's Once Is Not Enough
See The CBS Wednesday Night
Movies

730 Jacques Lipchitz   PBS
Program Type Documentary/Informational
  Special
60 minutes. Premiere date: 1/3/78. Repeat date:
6/6/78. Portrait of master-sculptor Jacques Lip-
chitz.
Producer Bruce W. Bassett
Company WNET-TV/New York
Director Bruce W. Bassett

731 Jade Snow
Ourstory   PBS
Program Type Dramatic Special
30 minutes. Premiere date: 5/10/76. Repeat
date: 11/14/77. Dramatization of the early years
of ceramicist/author Jade Snow Wong in San
Francisco's Chinatown in the 1920s. Based on
her book "Fifth Chinese Daughter." Program
funded by a grant from the National Endowment
for the Humanities.
Executive Producer Don Fouser
Producer Nola Safro
Company WNET-TV/New York
Director Ron Finley
Costume Designer John Boxer
Host Bill Moyers
Narrator Stephen Jennings
CAST
Jade Snow Wong .... Freda Foh Shen
Father .... James Hong
Mother ....Mary Mon Toy
Jade Snow (age 5) ....Jodi Wu
Jade Snow (age 11) .... Amy Mah
Joe ....Calvin Jung
Peg Milligan .... Claudette Sutherland
Al Milligan .... Joe Ponazecki
Nancy Milligan .... Denby Olcott

Richie Milligan ...." Douglas Grober
Uncle Jan .... Conrad Yama
Blessing (age 14) .... Don Wang
Admiral Kelly .... Vincent O'Brien

732 James at 15   NBC
Program Type Drama Series
60 minutes. Thursdays. Premiere date:
10/27/77. 2-hour pilot: 9/5/77. Last show:
7/27/78. Story of James Hunter, a teenager, and
his problems with growing up. Title changed to
"James at 16" 2/9/78.
Producer Ron Rubin
Company 20th Century Fox TV
Directors Various
Writers Various
CAST
James Hunter .... Lance Kerwin
Father .... Linden Chiles
Mother .... Lynn Carlin
Sandy Hunter .... Kim Erica Richards
Kathy Hunter .... Deirdre Berthrong
Marlene Mahoney .... Susan Myers
Sly Hazeltine ....David Hubbard

733 James Michener's World   PBS
Program Type Documentary/Informational
  Series
60 minutes. Premiere date: 9/7/77. Four specials
in which the celebrated author explores the ex-
otic lands of special interest to him. The shows
are "Hawaii Revisited," "Israel: A Search for
Faith," "The South Pacific: End of Eden?" and
"Spain: the Land and the Legend." (*See* individ-
ual titles for credits.) Series made possible by a
grant from Mrs. Paul's Kitchens, Inc. Closed
captions for the hearing impaired.
Producer Albert Waller
Company Reader's Digest Association, Inc.
Director Albert Waller
Writer Albert Waller

734 The Jeffersons   CBS
Program Type Comedy Series
30 minutes. Saturdays. Premiere date: 1/18/75.
Fourth season premiere: 9/24/77 (as one hour
special). 90 minute special: 2/25/78. Spin-off
from "All in the Family." Created by Don Ni-
choll; Michael Ross and Bernie West; developed
by Norman Lear. Theme song "Movin' On Up"
by Jeff Barry and Ja'net Dubois. Self-made suc-
cess (owner of dry cleaning stores) and family on
Manhattan's fashionable East Side.
Producers Don Nicholl; Michael Ross; Bernie
  West
Company T.A.T. Communications Company in
  association with NRW Productions
Director Jack Shea
Story Editors Mike Milligan; Jay Moriarty
Writers Various

The Jeffersons *Continued*
CAST
Louise Jefferson .... Isabel Sanford
George Jefferson ....Sherman Hemsley
Lionel Jefferson .... Damon Evans
Helen Willis .... Roxie Roker
Tom Willis .... Franklin Cover
Mother Jefferson ....Zara Cully
Jenny Willis .... Berlinda Tolbert
Harry Bentley .... Paul Benedict
Florence Johnson .... Marla Gibbs
Ralph (Doorman) ....Ned Wertimer
Marcus Henderson .... Ernest Harden, Jr.

735   **Jerusalem Peace**   PBS
Program Type Documentary/Informational
Special
60 minutes. Premiere date: 2/28/78. Repeat dates: 3/5/78, 7/11/78. Independently produced documentary film presenting a uniquely impressionistic view of the city of Jerusalem and the conflict which divides it. Program made possible by a grant from the Corporation for Public Broadcasting.
Company WPBT-TV/Miami
Directors Mark Benjamin, Elisabeth Fink Benjamin
Cinematographers Mark Benjamin, Elisabeth Fink Benjamin
Film Editor Sara Fishko

736   **Jerusalem Symphony**   CBS
Program Type Documentary/Informational
Special
60 minutes. Premiere date: 4/3/77. Repeat date: 4/16/78. Premiere performance of the "Jerusalem Symphony" composed by Ezra Laderman and performed by the Jerusalem Symphony Orchestra in Jerusalem.
Executive Producer Pamela Ilott
Producer Pamela Ilott
Company CBS News Religious Broadcast
Conductor Alfredo Antonini
Host Abraham Kaplan

737   **The Jim Nabors Show**   Syndicated
Program Type Talk/Service/Variety Series
60 minutes. Premiere date: 1/9/78. Last show: 7/9/78. Talk-variety show with audience participation.
Executive Producers Carolyn Raskin, Larry Thompson
Producers Ken Harris, Charles Colarusso
Company NTR Productions
Director Barry Glazer
Writers Ken Harris, Charles Colarusso, Cort Casady, Brian Pollack, Milt Larsen
Host Jim Nabors

738   **Joe and Valerie**   NBC
Program Type Limited Series
30 minutes. Mondays, Wednesdays. Premiere date: 4/24/78. Four episodes: 4/24/78, 5/1/78, 5/3/78, 5/10/78. Two teenagers from blue-collar families meet at disco and fall in love.
Executive Producer Linda Hope
Producer Bernie Kahn
Company Hope Enterprises
Director Bill Persky
Writers Various
CAST
Joe Pizo .... Paul Regina
Valerie Sweetzer .... Char Fontane
Frank Berganski ....Bill Beyers
Paulie Barone ....David Elliott
Vincent Pizo .... Robert Costanza
Stella Sweetzer .... Pat Benson
Thelma Medina ....Donna Ponterotto

739   **Joe Garagiola Tucson Open**   NBC
Program Type Sports Special
Live coverage of the final rounds of the Tucson Open from the Tucson National Golf Club 1/7/78 and 1/8/78.
Producer Larry Cirillo
Company NBC Sports
Director Harry Coyle
Host Joe Garagiola
Commentators John Brodie, Jay Randolph, Bruce Devlin, Jim Simpson, Bob Goalby

Joe Kidd *See* The ABC Sunday Night Movie

740   **The Joffrey Ballet Live from Artpark**   PBS
Program Type Music/Dance Special
2 hours. Premiere date: 8/23/78. The Joffrey Ballet performs live from Artpark in Lewistown, New York. Program made possible by grants from the Corporation for Public Broadcasting and the PBS stations of New York State.
Executive Producer David Griffiths
Producer Hal Hutkoff
Company WNED-TV/Buffalo with assistance from WNET-TV/New York

741   **John Cage**   PBS
Program Type Documentary/Informational
Special
30 minutes. Premiere date: 8/16/78. Interview with musician-composer John Cage.
Producer Gregg Burton
Company WSKG-TV/Binghamton

John Cappelletti *See* Something for Joey

742 The John Davidson Christmas Special ABC
Program Type Music/Comedy/Variety Special
60 minutes. Premiere date: 12/9/77. John Davidson and his family take a trip back in time to the England of the early 19th century in a Christmas special.
Producer Bob Finkel
Company Management III
Director Tony Charmoli
Writer Herbert Baker
Art Director Ray Klausen
Star John Davidson
Guest Star Tim Conway
Special Guest Star Betty White
Featured Singers David Wilson, Mike Redman, Bill Brown, Sue Allen, Julia Rinker, Edie Lehman

743 John Denver Celebrity Pro-Am ABC
Program Type Sports Special
60 minutes. Premiere date: 3/12/78. Winter festival and pro-am skiing competition at Aspen, Colorado.
Executive Producer Roone Arledge
Producer Doug Wilson
Director Andy Sidaris
Guests Josef Odermatt, Hank Kashiwa, Tyler Palmer, Jim Hunter, Werner Mattle, Werner Bleiner, Ed Reich, Andre Arnold, Jill St. John, David Soul, Clint Eastwood, Carol Wayne, Bruce Jenner

744 John Denver in Australia ABC
Program Type Documentary/Informational Special
90 minutes. Premiere date: 2/16/78. John Denver takes his music and his guest stars on a tour of Australia. Music arranged by Glen D. Hardin, Lee Holdridge, and Doug Gilmore. Filmed entirely in Australia and New Zealand.
Producers Al Rogers, Bill Davis
Company A John-Jer Production in association with ATN Channel 7, Sidney
Director Bill Davis
Writers Phil Hahn, George Geiger, Al Rogers
Additional Material April Kelly, Larry Murray
Musical Director Doug Gilmore
Conductor Glen D. Hardin
Costume Designer Warden Neil
Art Director Darrell Lass
Star John Denver
Special Guest Star Lee Marvin
Guest Stars Robby Benson, Debby Boone, John Newcombe, Susan Saint James

745 John Denver Rocky Mountain Christmas ABC
Program Type Music/Comedy/Variety Special
60 minutes. Premiere date: 12/10/75. Repeat dates: 12/14/76 and 12/23/77. Holiday special filmed in Aspen, Colorado.
Executive Producer Jerry Weintraub
Producers Al Rogers, Rich Eustis
Company A Jon-Jer Production
Director Bill Davis
Writers Jim Mulligan, April Kelly, Tom Chapman, Dave O'Malley, Steve Martin, Rich Eustis, Al Rogers
Art Director Ken Johnson
Star John Denver
Guest Stars Valerie Harper, Olivia Newton-John, Steve Martin

746 Johnny Cash Christmas Special CBS
Program Type Music/Comedy/Variety Special
60 minutes. Premiere date: 11/30/77. Taped at The Grand Ole Opry House in Nashville, Tenn., and Galilee and Bethlehem in Israel.
Executive Producers Joseph Cates, Marty Klein
Producer Chet Hagan
Company Joseph Cates Company
Director Walter C. Miller
Writers Chet Hagan, Frank Slocum
Musical Director Bill Walker
Art Director Don Shirley
Star Johnny Cash
Special Guest Roy Clark
Guest Stars June Carter Cash, the Carter Family, Jerry Lee Lewis, Roy Orbison, Carl Perkins, the Statler Brothers

747 Johnny Cash: Spring Fever CBS
Program Type Music/Dance Special
60 minutes. Premiere date: 5/7/78. Special taped at The Grand Ole Opry, Nashville, Tennessee.
Executive Producers Joseph Cates, Marty Klein
Producer Chet Hagan
Company Cates Brothers
Director Walter C. Miller
Writer Frank Slocum
Musical Director Bill Walker
Star Johnny Cash
Guest Stars June Carter Cash, Jessi Colter, the Carter Family, Roseanne Cash, Ray Charles, Waylon Jennings

748 The Johnny Mathis Special
Festival '78 PBS
Program Type Music/Dance Special
45 minutes. Premiere date: 3/5/78. Taped during tour of England by Johnny Mathis.
Producer Yvonne Littlewood
Company BBC-TV

Jolly Bad Fellow *See* PBS Movie Theater

749 Journey to the Center of the Earth
Famous Classic Tales   CBS
Program Type Animated Film Special
60 minutes. Premiere date: 11/13/77. Journey underneath the earth's surface to a prehistoric world based on book by Jules Verne. Special effects by Yamuna Adamson and Marika Sochacki.
Producer Walter J. Hucker
Company Air Programs International
Director Richard Slapczynski
Writer John Palmer
Animators Irena Slapczynski, Ray Nowland, Peter Luschwitz, Susan Beak, Don Ezard, Gairden Cook, Wal Logue, Geoff Collins, William Toh, Jean Tych

750 Journey to the Outer Limits
National Geographic Special   PBS
Program Type Documentary/Informational Special
60 minutes. Premiere date: 4/11/78. 19 city kids go through the training of the Colorado Outward Bound School. Presented by WQED, Pittsburg and made possible by a grant from Gulf Oil Corporation.
Company National Geographic and Wolper Productions
Host E.G. Marshall
Narrator Leslie Nielsen

751 Journey Together
The Winners   CBS
Program Type Children's Special
30 minutes. Premiere date: 3/9/78. Drama about woman who refuses to accept charity. Music by Don Heckman.
Executive Producer Robert Guenette
Producers Paul Asselin, Diane Asselin
Company Guenette/Asselin Productions
Director Paul Asselin
Writer Hindi Brooks
Film Editor Peter Wood
CAST
Shenandoah Griffin .... Ester Rolle
Shawn Leach ....Tina Andrews
Carolyn Leach .... Janet MacLachlan
Ted Young ....Ernie Hudson
Angie .... Candace Bowen
Diane .... Eugenia Wright
Freddy .... Raphael Douglas
Mr. Crowley .... Ed Call

Juggernaut *See* The CBS Saturday Night Movie

Jules and Jim *See* PBS Movie Theater

752 Julie Andrews: One Step Into Spring   CBS
Program Type Music/Comedy/Variety Special
60 minutes. Premiere date: 3/9/78. Musical-variety special.
Executive Producer Bob Banner
Producer Steve Pouliot
Company Bob Banner Associates
Director Jeff Margolis
Writer Kenny Solms
Musical Director Ian Fraser
Choreographer Paddy Stone
Orchestrated by Ralph Burns, Bill Byers, Peter Knight, David Lindup
Star Julie Andrews
Special Guest Alan King
The Muppet Performers Frank Oz with Jerry Nelson, Richard Hunt, David Goelz, Louise Gold, Jim Henson

Julie Farr, M.D. *See* Having Babies

753 The Julliard String Quartet Plays Beethoven
Great Performances   PBS
Program Type Music/Dance Special
90 minutes. Premiere date: 7/5/78. Program of chamber music by an American ensemble. Program made possible by a grant from Exxon and support from PBS stations.
Executive Producers Jac Venza, Fritz Buttenstedt
Producers David Griffiths, Helmut Bauer
Company WNET-TV/New York
Director Dr. Hugo Kach
Host Martin Bookspan
Performers Robert Mann (violin), Earl Carlyss (violin), Samuel Rhodes (viola), Joe Krosnick (cello).

754 Junior Almost Anything Goes   ABC
30 minutes. Premiere date: 9/4/77. "Almost Anything Goes" for youngsters.
Host Soupy Sales

755 Junior Davis Cup   PBS
Program Type Sports Special
2 1/2 hours. Live coverage of the tennis matches on 12/25/77.
Company WPBT-TV/Miami

Junior Olympic National Multi-Sport Championship *See* AAU Junior

Olympic National Multi-Sport
Championships

756 Just a Little Inconvenience
The Big Event/NBC World Premiere Movie
NBC
Program Type Dramatic Special
2 hours. Premiere date: 10/2/77. A Vietnam veteran attempts to rehabilitate his best friend. Filmed in Alberta, Canada, and Southern California.
Executive Producer Lee Majors
Producer Theodore J. Flicker
Company Fawcett-Majors Productions in association with Universal TV
Director Theodore J. Flicker
Writers Theodore J. Flicker, Allan Balter
Film Editor Bernard J. Small
CAST
Frank Logan .... Lee Majors
Kenny Briggs ....James Stacy
Nikki Klausing ....Barbara Hershey
Major Bloom .... Charles Cioffi
Dave Erickson .... Jim Davis

757 Just for Laughs NBC
Program Type Comedy Special
60 minutes. Premiere date: 2/7/78. Six comedy specials starring seasoned performers and newcomers.
Executive Producer George Schlatter
Producer Hal Kanter
Company George Schlatter Productions
Directors Dick McDonough, Dennis Steinmetz
Writers Hal Kanter, Milt Rosen, Bob O'Brien, Lorne Frohman, Ben Gordon

758 Just Me and You
NBC Monday Night at the Movies/NBC
World Premiere Movie NBC
Program Type TV Movie
2 hours. Premiere date: 5/22/78. Comedy about two mismatched people driving to Los Angeles over a period of four days.
Producer Roger Gimbel
Company E.M.I. Production
Director John Erman
Writer Louise Lasser
CAST
Jane .... Louise Lasser
Michael ....Charles Grodin

Kameradschaft *See* PBS Movie Theater

Kanal *See* PBS Movie Theater

759 Kate Bliss and the Ticker Tape Kid
The ABC Friday Night Movie ABC
Program Type TV Movie
2 hours. Premiere date: 5/26/78. Comedy western about a woman investigator. Music by Jeff Alexander. Story by John Zodorow. Filmed in Sonora, Calif., and Los Angeles.
Executive Producers Aaron Spelling, Douglas S. Cramer
Producer Richard E. Lyons
Company Aaron Spelling Productions
Director Burt Kennedy
Writers William Bowers, John Zodorow
Art Director Alfeo Bocchicchio
CAST
Kate Bliss .... Suzanne Pleshette
Clint Allison .... Don Meredith
Lord Devery .... Tony Randall
Hugo Peavey .... Harry Morgan
William Blackstone .... Burgess Meredith
Sheriff .... David Huddleston
Joe .... Buck Taylor
Tim ....Don Collier
Betty .... Alice Hirson
Fred ....Gene Evans
Bud ....Jerry Hardin
Luke ....Harry Carey, Jr.

760 Keefer ABC
Program Type Dramatic Special
90 minutes. Premiere date: 3/16/78. Drama of top Allied secret agents during World War II.
Executive Producers David Gerber, William Driskill
Producer James H. Brown
Company David Gerber Production in association with Columbia Pictures Television
Director Barry Shear
Writers William Driskill, Simon Muntner
CAST
Keefer .... William Conrad
Benny .... Michael O'Hare
Angel ....Cathy Lee Crosby
Amy ....Kate Woodville
Beaujolais .... Brioni Farrell
Kleist .... Jeremy Kemp
Maureau .... Marcel Hillaire
Hegel .... Bill Fletcher
Rudy ....Ian Abercrombie
Benson ....Jack L. Ging
Bemmel .... Richard Sanders
Vorst .... Norbert Weisser
Sergeant .... William H. Bassett
Duval .... Steffan Zaharaias
Madame Cerral .... Natalie Core
Jacques .... Alain Patrick
Folger .... Andre Landzaat

761 Keeper of the Wild Syndicated
Program Type Miscellaneous Series
30 minutes. Premiere date: 1/19/78. Pilot for jungle series.
Producer Leonard B. Kaufman

Keeper of the Wild *Continued*
Company Elbekay Productions, 20th Century-
Fox and Colgate-Palmolive
Director Dick Moder
Writer Leonard B. Kaufman

762   Keith Jarrett: Vermont Solo   PBS
Program Type Music/Dance Special
90 minutes. Premiere date: 8/29/78. Pianist-
composer Keith Jarrett gives a performance at a
country estate on the banks of Lake Champlain,
Shelburne, Vermont. Taped 8/26/77.
Producer George Lair
Company Vermont Educational Television

763   Kemper Open   CBS
Program Type Sports Special
Coverage of the final two rounds of the $250,000
Kemper Open golf tournament from the Quail
Hollow Country Club, Charlotte, N.C. 6/3/78
and 6/4/78.
Executive Producer Frank Chirkinian
Company CBS Television Network Sports
Directors Bob Dailey, Frank Chirkinian
Commentators Vin Scully, Jack Whitaker, Pat
Summerall, Frank Glieber, Ben Wright, Ken
Venturi

764   Ken Norton vs. Jimmy Young   ABC
Program Type Sports Special
Live coverage of bout between Ken Norton and
Jimmy Young, the two top contenders for
Muhammad Ali's heavyweight title from Caesars
Palace, Las Vegas on 11/5/77. Two other fights
between Sugar Ray Leonard and Augustin Es-
trada and Jerry Quarry and Lorenzo Zanon.
Executive Producer Roone Arledge
Producer Dennis Lewin
Company ABC Sports
Director Chet Forte

765   The Kentucky Derby   ABC
Program Type Sports Special
60 minutes. 5/6/78. Live coverage of the thor-
oughbred horse race from Churchill Downs in
Louisville, Kentucky.
Executive Producer Roone Arledge
Producer Chuck Howard
Director Chet Forte
Hosts Howard Cosell, Jim McKay
Commentator Eddie Arcaro
Caller Dave Johnson

766   Kentucky Pacing Derby   CBS
Program Type Sports Special
Live coverage of harness racing's top event for
two-year-olds from Louisville Downs 9/17/78.
Producer Bud Lamoreaux

Company CBS Sports
Director Arthur Struck
Announcer Frank Glieber
Racing Expert Stan Bergstein

767   The Key To the Universe   PBS
Program Type Science/Nature Special
2 hours. Premiere date: 5/24/77. Repeat date:
9/4/77. A look at recent scientific breakthroughs
shedding new light on the origins and laws of the
universe. Program made possible by a grant from
Hoffman-La Roche, Inc.
Producer Alec Nisbett
Company British Broadcasting Corporation and
WTTW-TV/Chicago
Writer Nigel Calder
Narrators Nigel Calder, James Ruddle

768   Kill Me If You Can
The Big Event   NBC
Program Type Dramatic Special
2 hours. Premiere date: 9/25/77. Drama about
Caryl Chessman.
Producer Peter Katz
Director Buzz Kulik
Writer John Gay
Company Columbia Pictures TV in association
with NBC-TV
CAST
Caryl Chessman .... Alan Alda
Rosalie Asher ....Talia Shire
Davis ....John Hillerman
Leavy .... Walter McGinn
Judge Fricke .... Barnard Hughes
Edmunds .... Ben Piazza
Judge Goodman .... John Randolph

The Killer Elite *See* The CBS
Wednesday Night Movies

769   Killer on Board
NBC Monday Night at the Movies/NBC
World Premiere Movie   NBC
Program Type Dramatic Special
2 hours. Premiere date: 10/10/77. Passengers on
a cruise ship are infected by a deadly virus.
Executive Producers Lee Rich, Peter Dunne
Producer Sandor Stern
Company Lorimar Productions
Director Philip Leacock
Writer Sandor Stern
CAST
Jan .... Jane Seymour
Julie .... Susan Howard
Norma Walsh .... Patty Duke Astin
Snowden .... William Daniels
Dr. Berglund .... Michael Lerner
Dr. Folger .... Murray Hamilton
Oscar Billingham .... Claude Akins
Beatrice Richmond .... Beatrice Straight

Glenn Lyle	George Hamilton
Dr. Paul Jeffries	Frank Converse
Mitch	Jeff Lynas

770 A Killing Affair

The CBS Wednesday Night Movies   CBS
Program Type TV Movie
2 hours. Premiere date: 9/21/77. Drama about white detective and her black partner who become involved in a love affair. Music by Richard Shores.
Executive Producer David Gerber
Producer James H. Brown
Company Columbia Pictures Television
Director Richard C. Sarafian
Writer E. Arthur Kean
Film Editor Ken Zemke

CAST

Viki Eaton	Elizabeth Montgomery
Woodrow York	O. J. Simpson
Beverly York	Rosalind Cash
Shoup	John Mahon
Judge Cudahy	Priscilla Pointer
Capt. Bullis	Allan Rich
Buck Fryman	Charlie Robinson
Flagler	John P. Ryan
Kenneth Switzer	Dean Stockwell
Scotty Neilson	Dolph Sweet
Todd York	Todd Bridges
Lukens Switzer	Fred Stuthman
Cooks	John Steadman
Cabrillo	Michael Durrell
Sgt. Boyle	Stephen Parr
Kagel	Ed Knight
Sgt. Gould	Michael J. London
Mr. Macy	Morgan Farley
Mrs. Macy	Georgia Schmidt
Mrs. Harrow	Natalie Core
Miss Slauson	Eleanor Zee
Sgt. Bandini	Karmin Murcelo
Jose Temple	Tony Perez
Dyer	Jay Ingram
Virginia Colorado	Joanna Lehmann
Mrs. May	Sari Price
Sgt. Holt	Robert Phalen
Vincent	Gil Stuart
Olive Laveta	Valentina Quinn
Feeney	Cheryl Carter
Carmenita	Mary Maldonado
Bluesuit	Danil Torppe
Mrs. Nogales	Yolanda Marquez
Tetley	Tim Wead
Saticoy	Jim Veres
M.D.	Fil Formicola
Black Dude	Billy Jackson
Driver	Frank Doubleday
Man	Bill J. Stevens

771 Killing Stone

NBC World Premiere Movie/The Big Event   NBC
Program Type Dramatic Special
2 hours. Premiere date: 5/2/78. Man attempts to pick up the pieces of his life after serving time in prison. Filmed in Southern California and Tucson, Arizona.
Producer Michael Landon
Company NBC-TV
Director Michael Landon
Writer Michael Landon

CAST

Gil Stone	Gil Gerard
Sheriff Harky	J.D. Cannon
Senator Tyler	Jim Davis
Earl Stone	Nehemiah Persoff
Christopher	Matthew Laborteaux
Ellen Rizzi	Corinne Michaels
Harold Rizzi	Joshua Bryant
Daniel Tyler	Dick De Coit
Cindy	Valentina Quinn
Barney Dawes	Ken Johnson

772 King

The Big Event/NBC Monday Night at the Movies   NBC
Program Type Limited Series
6 hours. Premiere date: 2/12–14/78. Drama about the career of Dr. Martin Luther King, Jr.
Executive Producer Edward S. Feldman
Supervising Producer William Finnegan
Producer Paul Maslansky
Company Abby Mann Productions in association with Filmways
Director Abby Mann
Writer Abby Mann
Film Editor Byron "Buzz" Brandt, Richard Meyer, David Berlatsky

CAST

Martin Luther King Jr	Paul Winfield
Coretta Scott King	Cicely Tyson
Martin Luther King Sr	Ossie Davis
A.D. King	Art Evans
Ralph Abernathy	Ernie Banks
Andrew Young	Howard Rollins
John F. Kennedy	William Jordan
Robert F. Kennedy	Cliff DeYoung
Philip Harrison	Roscoe Lee Browne
Mrs. Rosa Parks	Yolanda King
Mayor Richard Daley	Patrick Hines
Bull Connor	Kenneth McMillan
Malcolm X	Dick Anthony Williams
J. Edgar Hoover	Dolph Sweet
Mrs. Alberta King	Frances Foster
Dorothy Cotton	Sheila Frazier
Martin Luther King III	Tony Holmes
Reverend Parker	Martin Luther King III
Julian Bond	Julian Bond
Ramsey Clark	Ramsey Clark
Tony Bennett	Tony Bennett
E.D. Nixon	Ernie Hudson
Bernard Lee	Terry Alexander
Sullivan	Clu Gulager
Viola Liuzzo	Harriet Karr
Stanley Levison	Steven Hill
Rev. Shuttlesworth	Roger Robinson
Damon Lockwood	Al Freeman, Jr.

King Kong See NBC Saturday Night at the Movies

773   King of Swing
In Performance at Wolf Trap   PBS
Program Type Music/Dance Special
60 minutes. Premiere date: 12/6/77. Benny Goodman performing live from Wolf Trap Park Farm with his orchestra conducted by Morton Gould; pianist Patricia Prattis-Jennings. Program made possible by a grant from Atlantic Richfield Company.
Executive Producer Ruth Leon
Company WETA-TV/Washington

774   King of the Beasts   NBC
Program Type Animated Film Special
30 minutes. Premiere date: 4/9/77. Repeat date: 4/19/78. Animated musical in which a bumbling lion becomes king of the beasts after leaving Noah's Ark. Music by Michael Colicchio; lyrics by Wiley Gregor.
Executive Producer Charles G. Mortimer, Jr.
Company Westfall Productions, Inc.
Director Shamus Culhane
Writers John Culhane, Charles G. Mortimer, Jr., Shamus Culhane

VOICES
The Croc	Paul Soles
Female Baby Croc	Judy Sinclair
Female Elephant	Bonnie Brooks
Male Giraffe/Camel	Jay Nelson
Polar Bear	Don Mason
Noah	Henry Ramer
The Lion	Carl Banas
Ostrich/Female Penguin	Ruth Springford
Walrus	Jack Mather
Male Elephant	Murray Westgate
Mouse/Male Baby Croc	Cardie Mortimer

775   King of the Road   CBS
Program Type Comedy Special
60 minutes. Premiere date: 5/10/78. Pilot about a semi-retired, country-and-western singer who runs a motel in Muscle Shaoles, Ala. Created and written by Rod Parker.
Executive Producers Norman Lear, Jerry Weintraub
Producers Rod Parker, Hal Cooper
Company Management III/T.A.T. Communications Co. Production
Director Hal Cooper
Musical Directors Larry Cansler, Don Piestrup

CAST
Cotton Grimes	Roger Miller
Sam Braffman	Larry Haines
Mildred Braffman	Marian Mercer
Maureen Kenney	Lee Crawford
Billy Lee Huff	R.G. Brown
Rick	Ric Carrot
Himself	John Davidson

776   King Orange Jamboree Parade
Program Type Parades/Pageants/Awards Special   NBC
60 minutes. Live coverage of the 44th annual King Orange Jamboree Parade from Miami, FL 12/31/77.
Producer Elmer Gorry
Company NBC Television
Director Peter Fatovich
Writer Frank Slocum
Musical Director Milton Delugg
Hosts Joe Garagiola, Rita Moreno
Guest Stars Joey Heatherton, Gabriel Melgar, Gilda Radner

Knife in the Water See PBS Movie Theater

777   Knockout   NBC
Program Type Game/Audience Participation Series
30 minutes. Mondays–Fridays. Premiere date: 10/3/77. Last show: 4/21/78. Features three audience contestants who match wits to earn eight letters and be the first to score KNOCKOUT.
Producer Bruce Belland
Company Ralph Edwards Production
Director Arthur Forrest
Host Arte Johnson

778   Kojak   CBS
Program Type Crime Drama Series
60 minutes. Sundays/Saturdays as of 12/10/77. Premiere date: 10/24/73. Fifth season premiere: 10/2/77. Last show: 4/15/78. Police series about a New York City homicide squad. Created by Abby Mann. Music by John Cacavas; George Savalas previously acted in the series under the name Demosthenes. Filmed in part on location in New York City.
Executive Producer Matthew Rapf
Supervising Producer James McAdams
Producers Gene Kearney, Chester Krumholz
Company Universal Television
Directors Various
Writers Various

CAST
Lt. Theo Kojak	Telly Savalas
Capt. Frank McNeil	Dan Frazer
Det. Crocker	Kevin Dobson
Det. Stavros	George Savalas

779   Komedy Tonite   NBC
Program Type Comedy Special
60 minutes. Premiere date: 5/9/78. Special starring an ensemble comedy company of acclaimed black performers.
Executive Producers Raymond Katz, Sandy Gallin

Producers Lawrence Kasha; Mark Warren
Company Katz-Gallin Productions
Director Mark Warren
Writers Matt Robinson, Tony Peyser, J. Sanford
    Parker, Bob Hackett
Stars Cleavon Little, Paula Kelly, Marilyn Cole-
    man, Marion Ramsey, Shon Vaughn, Charles
    Valentino, Paul Lynde, Lawrence-Hilton
    Jacobs, Danielle Spencer, Todd Bridges

780   Koscuiszko: An American Portrait
PBS
Program Type Dramatic Special
60 minutes. Premiere date: 4/5/76. A dramatiza-
tion of the contributions to the American Conti-
nental Army of Thaddeus Koscuiszko. Filmed
on location at Fort Ticonderoga in New York
State. Program made possible by a grant from
Mrs. Paul's Kitchens, Inc.; presented by KCET-
TV/Los Angeles.
Producer Paul Asselin
Company Reader's Digest Films by Guenette-
    Asselin Productions
Director Paul Asselin
Writers Ray Sipherd, Robert Guenette
CAST
Kosciuszko ....William Lyman
Soldier .... Craig Wasson
Col. James Wilkinson .... Gregory Abels

781   Kostelanetz and Menuhin
In Performance at Wolf Trap   PBS
Program Type Music/Dance Special
60 minutes. Premiere date: 10/4/76. Repeat
date: 7/22/78. Originally shown as part of the
90-minute special "Happy Birthday to U.S."
which aired live at the Wolf Trap Farm Park for
the Performing Arts in Arlington, Va. 7/4/76.
Concert performed by the National Symphony
Orchestra. Program made possible by a grant
from the Atlantic Richfield Company.
Executive Producer David Prowitt
Producer Ruth Leon
Company WETA-TV/Washington, D.C.
Director Jack Sameth
Conductor Andre Kostelanetz
Guest Soloist Yehudi Menuhin

782   The Kraft 75th Anniversary Special
CBS
Program Type Music/Comedy/Variety Special
90 minutes. Premiere date: 1/24/78. A nostalgic
look at some memorable moments in broadcast-
ing history. Special music by Earl Brown.
Producers Gary Smith, Dwight Hemion
Company Smith-Hemion Productions
Director Dwight Hemion
Writers Buz Kohan, Marty Farrell, Jerry Perzi-
    gian, Don Seigel
Musical Director Ian Fraser

Choreographer Ron Field
Costume Designer Bill Hargate
Art Director Romain Johnston
Stars Bob Hope, Leslie Uggams, Bob Crosby,
    Hal Peary, Edgar Bergen, Milton Berle, Alan
    King, Donna McKechnie, Roy Clark

783   The Krofft Comedy Hour
The ABC Saturday Comedy Special   ABC
Program Type Comedy Special
60 minutes. Premiere date: 7/29/78. Two com-
plete comedy stories and other featured variety
acts.
Executive Producers Sid Krofft, Marty Krofft
Supervising Producer Bonny Dore
Company Sid and Marty Krofft Production
Directors Jack Regas, Howard Storm, Alan My-
    erson
Writers Michael Kagan, Dick Robins, Duane
    Poole, William Bickley, Michael Warren
Stars Sheryl Lee Ralph, Deborah Maone, Bart
    Braverman, Gene Conforti, Redd Foxx, Patty
    Harrison, Robin Tyler

784   The Krofft Supershow '77   ABC
Program Type Children's Series
60 minutes. Saturday mornings. Premiere date:
9/11/76. Season premiere: 9/10/77. Live-action
comedy adventures.
Executive Producers Sid Krofft, Marty Krofft
Supervising Producer Donald R. Boyle
Company Sid and Marty Krofft Productions

Wonderbug
Three teenagers and their magical car. Created
by Joe Ruby and Ken Spears.
Directors Jack Regas, Rick Locke
Cast David Levy, Carol Ann Seflinger, John An-
    thony Bailey

Magic Mongo
About a male geni whose magic often backfires.
Created by Joe Ruby and Ken Spears.
Director Jack Regas
Story Editors Doug Tibbles, Barbara Tibbles
Writers Various
Cast Lennie Weinrib, Helaine Lembeck, Paul
    Hinckley, Robin Dearden

Bigfoot and Wildboy
About a teenager reared by Bigfoot. Created by
Joe Ruby and Ken Spears.
Directors Irving J. Moore; Gordon Wiles
Cast Ray Young, Joe Butcher, Monika Ramirez

Kaptain Kool and the Kongs
Director Jack Regas
Writer Jim Parker
CAST
Kaptain Kool .... Michael Lembeck

The Krofft Supershow '77 *Continued*
Turkey .... Mickey McMeel
Superchick .... Deborah Clinger
Nashville ....Louise Duart

785　La Traviata (Italian)
In Performance at Wolf Trap　　　　PBS
Program Type Music/Dance Special
2-1/2 hours. Premiere date: 9/20/76. Repeat
date: 9/27/77. A new production by the San
Diego Opera Company and the Filene Center
Orchestra and Filene Center Chorus of the tragic
opera by Giuseppe Verdi with libretto by Fran-
cesco Maria Peave. Conceived and staged by Tito
Capobianco at the Wolf Trap Farm Park in Ar-
lington, Va. Program made possible by a grant
from the Atlantic Richfield Company.
Executive Producer David Prowitt
Producer Ruth Leon
Company WETA-TV/Washington, D.C.
Director Kirk Browning
Conductor Julius Rudel
Costume Designer Carl Toms
Scenic Designer Carl Toms
Host Beverly Sills
CAST
Violetta .... Beverly Sills
Flora Bervoix .... Fredda Rakusin
Dr. Grenvil ....John Cheek
Marquis d'Obigny .... Keith Kibler
Baron Douphol .... Robert Orth
Gastone .... Neil Rosenshein
Alfredo ....Henry Price
Annina .... Evelyn Petros
Giuseppe .... Roger Lucas
Georgio Germont ....Richard Fredricks
Gardener .... Christopher Deane

786　Lacy and the Mississippi Queen
The Big Event/NBC Movie of the Week　NBC
Program Type Dramatic Special
90 minutes. Premiere date: 5/17/78. Two sisters
track down a pair of train robbers for shooting
their father.
Executive Producer Lawrence Gordon
Producer Lew Gallo
Company Lawrence Gordon Productions and
Paramount TV
Director Robert Butler
Writers Kathy Donnell, Madeline DiMaggio
Wagner
CAST
Kate Lacy ....Kathleen Lloyd
Queenie .... Debra Feuer
Willie .... Jack Elam
Isaac Harrison .... Edward Andrews
Parker ....James Keach
Jennings .... Christopher Lloyd
Webber .... Les Lannom
Reynolds .... Matt Clark
Sam Lacy .... Anthony Palmer
Bixby .... David Byrd

Reverend ....Alvy Moore
Mitchell Beacon .... Sandy Ward

The Lady and the Outlaw *See* The ABC
Sunday Night Movie

787　Lamp Unto My Feet　　　　CBS
Program Type Religious/Cultural Series
30 minutes. Sunday mornings. Premiere date:
11/21/48. Continuous. Programs of a religious
nature. 30th anniversary year retrospective
shows began 3/5/78 on " . . . Behold Wondrous
Things."
Executive Producer Pamela Ilott
Producers Ted Holmes, Chalmers Dale, Bernard
Seabrooks, Joseph Clement, Marlene
Didonato and others
Company CBS News Religious Broadcast
Directors Various

788　Land of Hype and Glory　　　NBC
Program Type News Special
60 minutes. Premiere date: 1/10/78. Special ex-
amines the multi-billion-dollar business of pro-
moting the sale of movies, books, and rock
groups.
Producer Karen Lerner
Company NBC News
Director Tom Priestley
Writer Edwin Newman
Reporter Edwin Newman

789　Land of the Lost　　　　NBC
Program Type Children's Series
30 minutes. Saturdays. Premiere date: 9/7/74.
Fourth season premiere: 2/4/78. Last show:
4/1/78. Live-action and animation fantasy of a
family in an alternate universe. Music by Larry
Neiman and Jack Tillar.
Executive Producers Sid Krofft, Marty Krofft
Producer Jon Kubichan
Company Sid and Marty Krofft Productions
Directors Joseph L. Scanlan, Rick Bennewitz
Story Editor Sam Roeca
Writers Various
Animation Director Gene Warren
CAST
Will Marshall .... Wesley Eure
Holly Marshall .... Kathy Coleman
Uncle Jack ....Ron Harper

The Land That Time Forgot *See* NBC
Saturday Night at the Movies

790 Las Vegas Entertainment Awards

The Big Event   NBC
Program Type Parades/Pageants/Awards
  Special
2 hours. Premiere date: 12/4/77. Seventh annual
awards given by the Academy of Variety and
Cabaret Artists honoring performing artists in
the Las Vegas variety and cabaret fields. Origi-
nates from the Theatre of the Performing Arts,
Aladdin Hotel, Las Vegas.
Executive Producer George Le Fave
Producer Paul W. Keyes
Company Sedbar Productions, Inc.
Director Bill Carruthers
Writers Paul W. Keyes, Marc London, Bob
  Howard
Musical Director Nelson Riddle
Presenters/Performers Ann-Margret, David
Brenner, Charo, The Emotions, Donna Fargo,
Totie Fields, Shecky Greene, Merle Haggard,
Chuck Mangione, Jackie Mason, Don Rickles,
Seals and Crofts, Rip Taylor, Tina Turner

791 The Last Ballot

Ourstory   PBS
Program Type Dramatic Special
30 minutes. Premiere date: 12/16/75. Repeat
date: 10/17/77. Dramatization of the election of
Thomas Jefferson. Program funded by a grant
from the National Endowment for the Humani-
ties.
Executive Producer Don Fouser
Company WNET-TV/New York
Director Don Fouser
Costume Designer John Boxer
Art Director Warren Clymer
Set Director Hubert J. Oakes, Jr.
Host Bill Moyers
CAST

Bayard	Lee Richardson
Sedgwick	Gil Rogers
Lyon	Roy Poole
Livingston	Joseph Lambie
Smith	Thomas Toner
Jefferson	Jack Ryland
Burr	Edward Zag
Randolph	Noel Craig
Nicholson	Alan Langer
Clerk	Paul Nevins
Inebriate	George Hall

792 Last Chance

Comedy Time   NBC
Program Type Comedy Special
30 minutes. Premiere date: 4/21/78. Pilot about
wily juvenile delinquents who work at outwitting
their supervisors at a dude ranch that has been
converted into a rehabilitation center.
Executive Producers Lee Rich, Philip Capice
Producer Lew Gallo
Company Lorimar Production

Director Robert Moore
Writer Hal Dresner
CAST

Pat Gilhooley	Sorrell Booke
Counselor Crosby	Will MacKenzie
Cromwell	Jaison Walker
Ludlum	Steven Guttenberg
Angie	Albert Insinnia
Tim Honeywood	J. Andrew Kenney
Meredith Gilhooley	Debi Richter
Farkas	Alvin Kupperman
Feinberg	Lauren Frost
Drummond	Burton Gilliam

The Last Days of Dolwyn *See* PBS
  Movie Theater

793 The Last Dinosaur

The ABC Friday Night Movie   ABC
Program Type TV Movie
2 hours. Premiere date: 2/11/77. Repeat date:
7/14/78. Drama of a contemporary tycoon hunt-
ing a dinosaur in a prehistoric world. Music by
Maury Laws with lyrics by Jules Bass sung by
Nancy Wilson. Special effects by Tsuburaya Pro-
ductions Co., Ltd.
Producers Arthur Rankin, Jr., Jules Bass
Company A Rankin/Bass Production
Directors Alex Grasshoff, Tom Kotani
Writer William Overgard
CAST

Masten Thrust	Richard Boone
Frankie Banks	Joan Van Ark
Bunta	Luther Rackley
Chuck Wade	Steven Keats
Dr. Kawamoto	Tatsu Nakamura
Barney	Carl Hansen
Prehistoric Girl	Mamiya Sekia

The Last Holiday *See* PBS Movie
  Theater

794 The Last Hurrah

Hallmark Hall of Fame   NBC
Program Type Dramatic Special
2 hours. Premiere date: 11/16/77. Head of a po-
litical machine tries to stay in power and win a
fourth term. Based on the novel by Edwin O'-
Connor. Music composed and arranged by Peter
Matz.
Executive Producer Terry Becker
Producers Mike Wise, Franklin R. Levy
Company O'Connor-Becker Productions in asso-
  ciation with Columbia Pictures Television
Director Vincent Sherman
Writer Carroll O'Connor
CAST

Prudy Cass	Leslie Ackerman
Amos Force	John Anderson
Roger Shanley	Dana Andrews
Nat Gardiner	Robert Brown

The Last Hurrah *Continued*

Sam Weinberg .... Jack Carter
Ditto Boland .... Tom Clancy
Gorman .... Brendan Dillon
Hack Wiles .... Arthur Franz
George Sherrard .... Alan Hamel
Clare Gardiner .... Mariette Hartley
Cardinal Burke .... Burgess Meredith
Winslow .... Stewart Moss
Frank Skeffington .... Carroll O'Connor
Norman Cass .... Patrick O'Neal
Dr. Santangelo .... Paul Picerni
Robert Skeffington .... Patrick Wayne
Maeve Skeffington .... Kitty Winn

The Last Laugh *See* PBS Movie Theater

795 Last of the Good Guys

The CBS Tuesday Night Movies   CBS
Program Type TV Movie
2 hours. Premiere date: 3/7/78. Police drama.
Music by Dana Kaproff
Producer Jay Daniel
Company Columbia Pictures Television
Director Theodore J. Flicker
Writers John D. Hess, Theodore J. Flicker,
   Clark Howard
Art Director Robert Peterson
CAST
Sgt. Nichols .... Robert Culp
Officer Lucas .... Dennis Dugan
Officer Namaguchi .... Richard Narita
Officer Pulaski ....Ji Tu Cumbuka
Officer Talltree .... Hampton Fancher
Officer O'Malley .... Larry Hagman
Marnie .... Elta Blake
Dr. Cropotkin .... Jonathan Harris
Mr. Stit .... Roger Bowen
Lill O'Malley .... Marlyn Mason
El Caliph .... Ernie Hudson
Zapata .... Chu Chu Malave

796 The Last of the Mohicans

NBC Movie of the Week   NBC
Program Type Dramatic Special
2 hours. Premiere date: 11/23/77. Classic adventure based on book by James Fenimore Cooper.
Director James L. Conway
Writer Stephen Lord
CAST
Hawkeye ....Steve Forrest
Chingachgook .... Ned Romero
Heyward .... Andrew Prine
Uncas .... Don Shanks
Alice ....Jane Actman
Cora .... Michele Marsh
David Gamut ....Robert Easton
Magua ....Robert Tessier
Gen. Webb .... Whit Bissell

The Last Picture Show *See* ABC
Tuesday Movie of the Week

797 The Last Tenant

ABC Theatre   ABC
Program Type Dramatic Special
2 hours. Premiere date: 6/25/78. An aging man in failing health, resists the efforts of his family to place him in a nursing home. Teleplay won ABC Television's first "ABC Theatre Award." Filmed entirely on location in New York and Staten Island. Music by Dick Hyman.
Executive Producer Herbert Brodkin
Producer Robert Berger
Company Titus Productions, Inc.
Director Jud Taylor
Writer George Rubino
Costume Designer Joseph G. Aulisi
Art Director Patrizia von Brandenstein
Cinematographer Sol Negrin
Film Editor Robert Reitano
CAST
Joey .... Tony Lo Bianco
Carol .... Christine Lahti
Father .... Lee Strasberg
Marie ....Julie Bovasso
Carl .... Danny Aiello
Connie ....Anne DeSalvo
Vinnie .... Jeffrey DeMunn
Carmine .... Victor Arnold
Mrs. Farelli ....Joanna Merlin
Mrs. Korowski ....Ruth Jaraslow
Lucy .... Antonia Rey
Frankie .... Evan Michael Turz

798 Laugh-In   NBC

Program Type Limited Series
60 minutes. Six specials: 9/12/77, 10/10/77, 11/2/77, 12/20/77, 2/1/78, 2/8/78. Original special: 9/9/67. Original premiere: 1/22/68. Comedy-variety show featuring famous personalities as well as a regular cast. Created by George Schlatter.
Producer George Schlatter
Company George Schlatter Productions in association with NBC-TV
Head Writer Digby Wolfe
Director Don Mischer
Musical Director Tommy Oliver
Art Director Robert Kelly
Regulars Nancy Bleiweiss, Ed Bluestone, Kim Braden, Claire Faulkonbridge, Wayland Flowers, June Gable, Jim Giovanni, Ben Powers, Bill Rafferty, Michael Sklar, Lenny Schultz, Toad the Mime, Robin Williams

799 Laverne and Shirley   ABC

Program Type Comedy Series
30 minutes. Tuesdays. Premiere date: 1/27/76. Third season premiere: 9/20/77. Characters introduced on "Happy Days." Created by Garry K. Marshall; Mark Rothman and Lowell Ganz. Concerns two young women working in the bottle cap division of the Shotz Brewery in Milwau-

kee during the late 1950s. "Making Our Dreams Come True" music by Charles Fox; lyrics by Norman Gimbel.
Executive Producers Garry K. Marshall, Thomas L. Miller, Edward K. Milkis
Producers Arthur Silver, Nick Abdo
Company Miller-Milkis Productions, Inc. and Henderson Production Company, Inc. in association with Paramount Television
Directors Various
Writers Various

CAST

Laverne De Fazio	Penny Marshall
Shirley Feeney	Cindy Williams
Frank De Fazio	Phil Foster
Carmine Ragusa	Eddie Mekka
Andrew "Squiggy" Squiggman	David L. Lander
Lenny Kolowski	Michael McKean
Edna Babish	Betty Garrett

Law and Disorder *See* The ABC Sunday Night Movie/PBS Movie Theater

800 **The Lawrence Welk Show**
Syndicated
Program Type Music/Dance Series
60 minutes. Weekly. Premiere date: 7/2/55 as "The Dodge Dancing Party." In syndication since 9/71.
Executive Producer Sam J. Lutz
Producer James Hobson
Company Teleklew Productions, Inc.
Distributor Don Fedderson Productions, Inc.
Director James Hobson
Musical Director George Cates
Host Lawrence Welk
Regulars The Aldridge Sisters, Anaconi, Ava Barber, Bobby Burgess, Henry Cuesta, Dick Dale, Ken Delo, Arthur Duncan, Gail Farrell, Jo Feeney, Myron Floren, Sandi Griffiths, Larry Hooper, Guy Hovis, Ralna Hovis, Jack Imel, Bob Lido, Mary Lou Metzger, Tom Netherton, The Otwell Twins, Bob Ralston, Jim Roberts, Norma Zimmer

801 **Le Disco**
NBC
Program Type Music/Comedy/Variety Special
90 minutes. Premiere date: 8/19/78. 80 couples compete in a disco dance contest judged by Edie Adams; Trini Lopez; and Damita Jo Freeman.
Executive Producer Dick Clark
Producer Bob Arthur
Company Dick Clark Production
Director Barry Glazer
Musical Guests The Village People and The Spinners

802 **A Leaf from a Town Record**
PBS
Program Type Documentary/Informational Special
30 minutes. Premiere date: 9/7/77. Patriotic parade in a small town provides the focal point for an examination of loyalty. Program made possible by the N.Y. Council for the Humanities and the Corporation for Public Broadcasting.
Producer Jack Ofield
Company WMHT-TV/Schenectady
Director Jack Ofield

803 **Leapin' Lizards It's Liberace**
CBS
Program Type Music/Comedy/Variety Special
60 minutes. Premiere date: 2/1/78. Taped at the Las Vegas Hilton.
Executive Producer Bob Banner
Producer Steve Pouliot
Company Bob Banner Associates
Director Tony Charmoli
Musical Director Bo Ayars
Star Liberace
Guest Stars Debbie Reynolds, Barkley Shaw, Vince Cardell, The Chinese Acrobats of Taiwan
Cameo Guest Appearance Phyllis Diller

804 **Leave Yesterday Behind**
The ABC Sunday Night Movie
ABC
Program Type TV Movie
2 hours. Premiere date: 5/14/78. An injured college athlete, with the help of a young woman, learns to live again. Music by Fred Karlin. Song, "Leave Yesterday Behind," lyrics and music by Fred Karlin; sung by Shandi Sinnamon.
Producer Paul Harrison
Company ABC Circle Films
Director Richard Michaels
Writer Paul Harrison

CAST

Paul Stallings	John Ritter
Marny Clarkson	Carrie Fisher
Doc	Buddy Ebsen
Mr. Clarkson	Ed Nelson
Connie	Carmen Zapata
David	Robert Urich
Betty Stallings	Barbara Stuart
Howard Stallings	Walter Maslow
Kim	Lucia Stralser
Laura	Carol Ann Williams

805 **The Legacy of L.S.B. Leakey**
National Geographic Special
PBS
Program Type Documentary/Informational Special
60 minutes. Premiere date: 1/14/78. Story of anthropologist L. S. B. Leakey. Program made possible by a grant from Gulf Oil Corporation.
Executive Producers Dennis B. Kane, Thomas Skinner

The Legacy of L.S.B. Leakey *Continued*
Producer Irwin Rosten
Company WQED-TV/Pittsburgh
Writer Irwin Rosten
Host E. G. Marshall
Narrator E. G. Marshall

806   The Legend of Robin Hood   PBS
Once Upon a Classic
Program Type Drama Series
30 minutes. Thursdays/Saturdays. Premiere date: 10/6/77. 12-part series about the legendary crime-fighter. Presented by WQED-TV/Pittsburgh and McDonald's Local Restaurants Assn.
Executive Producer George Gallicco
Producer Jay Rayvid
Company Time-Life Television/BBC-TV
Director Eric Davidson
Writers Alistair Bell, Robert Banks Stewart, David Butler, Alexander Barron
Cinematographer Elmer Cossey
Host Bill Bixby
CAST
Robin Hood .... Martin Potter
Lady Marion .... Diane Keen
Sheriff of Nottingham .... Paul Darrow
Friar Tuck .... Tony Caunter
Little John .... Conrad Asquith

807   Legends of Golf   NBC
Program Type Sports Special
Live coverage of all-star tournament live from the Onion Creek Golf Course in Austin, Texas 4/29/78 and 4/30/78.
Executive Producer Don Ohlmeyer
Producer Larry Cirillo
Company NBC Sports
Director Harry Coyle
Commentators Jim Simpson, John Brodie, Jay Randolph, Bruce Devlin, Bob Goalby

808   Legs   NBC
Program Type Comedy Special
60 minutes. Premiere date: 5/19/78. Pilot about a Las Vegas showgirl and a comedienne raising two youngsters. Created by Garry K. Marshall; Bob Brunner and Arthur Silver.
Executive Producers Garry Marshall, Tony Marshall
Company Henderson Production
Director Alan Rafkin
Writers Walter Kempley, Marty Nadler
CAST
Stacy Turner .... Caren Kaye
Norma Kay Bates .... Marcia Lewis
Major Putnam .... David Ketchum
Franklin Bates .... Scott Baio
Melissa Turner .... Tammy Lauren
Angie .... Lynda Goodfriend
Rimshot .... Dawson Mays
Memphis .... Laurie Mahaffey

Dixie .... Sayra Hummel
Billy Joe .... Marv Dennis
Bubba Stump .... Ed Cree
Freddie .... Fred Fox, Jr.
Cochise .... Shirley Kirkes
Bridget .... Elaine Bolton

809   The Leningrad Ice Show   CBS
Program Type Music/Dance Special
60 minutes. Premiere date: 8/29/78. Ice skating special taped at Leningrad's Sports Palace.
Executive Producer Mike Gargiulo
Producer Lothaar Bock
Company LBA Associates
Directors Frank Marischka, Mike Gargiulo, Vern Diamond
Writer Chuck Horner
Hosts Sally Struthers, Harry Morgan

Let's Scare Jessica to Death *See* ABC Tuesday Movie of the Week

810   The Liars Club   Syndicated
Program Type Game/Audience Participation Series
30 minutes. Mondays–Fridays. Premiere date: 9/7/74 (KTLA-TV/Los Angeles). In syndication since 1975–76 season. Four celebrity guests make up stories about strange objects.
Executive Producer Ralph Andrews
Producer Larry Hovis
Company Ralph Andrews Productions in association with 20th Century-Fox Television and Golden West Television.
Distributor Sandy Frank Television Distributors, Inc.
Directors Bill Rainbolt, Chris Darley, Bill Foster, Charlie Stark
Host Allen Ludden
Regulars Larry Hovis, Dody Goodman
Semi-Regulars Betty White, Alan Sues, Dick Gautier, Buddy Hackett

811   Liberty Bowl   ABC
Program Type Sports Special
Live coverage of the Liberty Bowl football game between the North Carolina Tarheels and the Nebraska Cornhuskers from Memorial Stadium in Memphis, TN 12/19/77.
Executive Producer Roone Arledge
Producer Chuck Howard
Company ABC Sports
Director Andy Sidaris
Play-by-Play Announcer Keith Jackson
Expert Color Commentator Frank Broyles

812 Life Among the Lowly
Visions   PBS
Program Type Dramatic Special
90 minutes. Premiere date: 12/2/76. Repeat
date: 1/8/78. Drama of a 19th century slave
trader haunted by his past. Performed by the
Trinity Square Repertory Company of Provi-
dence. Music composed by Richard Cumming.
Program made possible by grants from the Ford
Foundation, the National Endowment for the
Arts and the Corporation for Public Broadcast-
ing.
Executive Producer Barbara Schultz
Producers Adrian Hall, Robin Miller
Company KCET-TV/Los Angeles
Directors Adrian Hall, Robin Miller
Writers Adrian Hall, Richard Cumming
Costume Designer Betsey Potter
Production Designer Eugene Lee
Set Decorator Sandra Nathanson
CAST
Abram .... Richard Kneeland
Young Abram .... Robert Black
Mother .... Marguerite Lenert
Abigail .... Rose Weaver
Helen .... Margo Skinner
Martha Sue .... Nancy Nichols
Dorothea Dix .... Mina Manente
Mr. Whitney .... William Cain
Slave Buyer .... Timothy Crowe
Capt. Wells .... William Damkoehler
Guard .... Ed Hall
Officer .... Richard K. Jenkins
Official .... David C. Jones
Crippled Man .... Richard Kavanaugh
Slave Buyer .... Howard London
Masterson .... George N. Martin
Guards .... Barbara Meek, Barbara Orson, Daniel Von
Bargen

813 The Life and Times of Grizzly Adams
NBC
Program Type Drama Series
60 minutes. Wednesdays. Premiere date: 2/9/77.
Season premiere: 9/28/77. Last show: 7/26/78.
Fictionalized portrait of an 1880s fugitive wild-
life adventurer whose constant companion is a
grizzly bear named Ben. Created by Charles E.
Sellier, Jr. in the 1974 film of the same name.
(Film shown 5/25/77 as two-hour special.)
Theme music written and performed by Thom
Pace. Other music by Don Perry. Filmed on lo-
cation in the Uinta Mountains, Utah and in
Arizona.
Executive Producer Charles E. Sellier, Jr.
Producer Jim Simmons
Company Schick Sunn Classic Productions in
association with NBC Television Network
Directors Various
Story Editor Paul Hunter
Writers Various
Wildlife Advisers Lloyd Beebe, Terry Rowlands

CAST
James "Grizzly" Adams .... Dan Haggerty
Mad Jack .... Denver Pyle
Nakuma .... Don Shanks

The Life and Times of Judge Roy Bean
See The CBS Saturday Night Movie

814 Life Goes to War: Hollywood and the Homefront
The Big Event   NBC
Program Type Documentary/Informational
Special
2 hours. Premiere date: 9/18/77. A look at
Americans during World War II. Suggested by
"Life Goes to War," a Time-Life Television
Book. Original music by Fred Karlin.
Producer Jack Haley, Jr.
Co-Producer Malcolm Leo
Company Time-Life Television and 20th Cen-
tury-Fox Television produced in association
with Jack Haley, Jr. Productions, Inc.
Director Jack Haley, Jr.
Writer Jack Haley, Jr.
Host/Narrator Johnny Carson

815 Lilias, Yoga and You   PBS
Program Type Educational/Cultural Series
30 minutes. Mondays-Fridays. Season premiere:
9/19/77. Physical fitness and mental well-being
through hatha yoga exercises demonstrated by
Lilias Folan. Programs funded by the Corpora-
tion for Public Broadcasting, the Ford Founda-
tion and Public Television Stations.
Executive Producer Charles Vaughan
Producer Len Goorian
Company WCET-TV/Cincinnati
Director Bill Gustin
Writer Lilias Folan

816 Lindsay Wagner—Another Side of Me
ABC
Program Type Music/Comedy/Variety Special
60 minutes. Premiere date: 11/7/77. Lindsay
Wagner explores favorite fantasies. Music ar-
ranged and conducted by Everett Gordon.
Executive Producers Ron Samuels; Dick Foster
Producer Dick Foster
Company Dick Foster Productions, Inc. and
Ron Samuels Productions, Inc.
Director Art Fisher
Writers Tom Egan, Mike Marmer
Choreographer Bob Banas
Costume Designer Gordon Brockway
Art Director Archie Sharp
Editor Keith Olson
Star Lindsay Wagner

Lindsay Wagner—Another Side of Me
Continued
Guest Stars Michael Brandon, Vincent Price, Avery Schreiber, Vito Scotti, Teddy Wilson
Featuring The Locke High School Band and Meraquas Synchronized Swim Team
Special Guest Star Paul Anka

Little Big Man *See* NBC Saturday Night at the Movies

817 The Little Drummer Boy Book II
NBC
Program Type Animated Film Special
30 minutes. Premiere date: 12/14/75. Repeat date: 12/23/77. Sequel to "The Little Drummer Boy." A new Christmas story using dimensional stop-motion photography. Title song by Katherine Davis, Henry Onorati and Harry Simeone. Original music and lyrics by Maury Laws and Jules Bass. "Do You Hear What I Hear?" by Noel Regney and Gloria Shayne.
Producers Arthur Rankin, Jr., Jules Bass
Company Rankin/Bass Productions, Inc.
Directors Arthur Rankin, Jr., Jules Bass
Writer Julian P. Gardner
Narrator Greer Garson
VOICES
Brutus .... Zero Mostel
Little Drummer Boy .... David Jay
Melchior .... Allen Swift
Simeon .... Ray Owens
Plato .... Robert McFadden

818 Little House on the Prairie NBC
Program Type Drama Series
60 minutes. Mondays. Premiere date: 9/11/74. Fourth season premiere: 9/12/77. Based on the "Little House" books by Laura Ingalls Wilder about her life in the West 100 years ago. Set in and around Walnut Grove, Minn., in the 1870s. Music by David Rose.
Executive Producer Michael Landon
Producers John Hawkins, William F. Claxton
Company An NBC Production in association with Ed Friendly
Directors Michael Landon, William F. Claxton
Writers Various
Art Director Walter M. Jeffries
CAST
Charles Ingalls .... Michael Landon
Caroline Ingalls .... Karen Grassle
Mary Ingalls .... Melissa Sue Anderson
Laura Ingalls .... Melissa Gilbert
Carrie Ingalls .... Lindsay Greenbush, Sidney Greenbush
Mr. Edwards .... Victor French
Grace Edwards .... Bonnie Bartlett
Nellie Oleson .... Alison Arngrim
Mrs. Oleson .... Katherine MacGregor
Mr. Oleson .... Richard Bull
Dr. Baker .... Kevin Hagen

819 Little Ladies of the Night
The ABC Monday Night Movie ABC
Program Type TV Movie
2 hours. Premiere date: 1/16/77. Repeat date: 3/27/78. Drama of teenage prostitution. Filmed in part in Los Angeles and Long Beach, Calif. Music by Jerry Fielding.
Executive Producers Aaron Spelling, Leonard Goldberg
Producer Hal Sitowitz
Company Spelling-Goldberg Productions
Director Marvin Chomsky
Writer Hal Sitowitz
Costume Designers Robert Harris, Maddie Sylos
Art Director Paul Sylos
CAST
Lyle York .... David Soul
Russ Garfield .... Lou Gossett
Hailey Atkins ....Linda Purl
Comfort ....Clifton Davis
Mrs. Atkins .... Carolyn Jones
Mr. Atkins .... Paul Burke
Maureen .... Lana Wood
Karen .... Kathleen Quinlan
Finch .... Vic Tayback
Mrs. Colby .... Katherine Helmond
Maggie .... Dorothy Malone
Matron .... Bibi Osterwald
Mrs. Brodwick .... Sandra Deel
Wally ....Claude Earl Jones
Brady .... David Hayward
First Senator ....James Ray
Second Senator .... Tom McDonald
Third Senator .... Byron Morrow
First John ....Matt Bennett
Female Guard .... Connie Sawyer

820 Little Mo
NBC World Premiere Movie/The Big Event
NBC
Program Type Dramatic Special
3 hours. Premiere date: 9/5/78. TV movie about Maureen Connelly, the first woman to win the Grand Slam of tennis (the American, English, French and Australian titles).
Executive Producer Jack Webb
Producer George Sherman
Company Mark VII Production in association with NBC-TV
Director Daniel Haller
Writer John McGreevey
Technical Advisor Nancy Chaffee Kiner
CAST
Maureen Connelly .... Glynnis O'Connor
"Teach" Tennant ....Michael Learned
Mother .... Anne Baxter
Folsom ....Martin Milner
Norman ....Mark Harmon
Gus .... Claude Akins
Fisher .... Leslie Nielsen

Sophie .... Anne Francis
Tony Trabert .... Tony Trabert
Aunt Gert .... Ann Doran

Live and Let Die *See* The ABC Sunday
Night Movie

821 Live from Lincoln Center
Great Performances   PBS
Program Type Music/Dance Series
Times vary. Live performances from Lincoln
Center for the Performing Arts in New York
City. Performances shown during the 1977–78
season: "Coppelia," "Luciano Pavarotti Re-
cital," "Manon," "Saint of Bleecker Street,"
"Theme and Variations," and "Zubin Mehta,
The New York Philharmonic and Shirley Ver-
rett." (*See* individual titles for credits.) Series
made possible by grants from Exxon Corpora-
tion, the National Endowment for the Arts, and
the Corporation for Public Broadcasting.

822 Live from the Grand Ole Opry PBS
Program Type Music/Dance Special
3 hours. Premiere date: 3/4/78. Repeat date:
8/19/78. An encore presentation of the first-ever
"live" television broadcast of Nashville's world-
famous Grand Ole Opry.
Stars Roy Acuff, Archie Campbell, Skeeter Davis, Don Gibson, Billy Grammer, George
Hamilton IV, Stonewall Jackson, Lonzo and
Oscar, Ronnie Millsap, Jimmy C. Newman,
Connie Smith, Hank Snow, The Stoney Mountain Cloggers, Porter Wagoner, The Wilburn
Brothers, Minnie Pearl, Del Reeves, The Osborne Brothers, Don Williams, Del Wood,
The Willis Brothers.

823 Live from the Metropolitan Opera
                                                              PBS
Program Type Music/Dance Series
2 1/2 hours. Premiere date: 11/7/77. Four operas televised live from the Metropolitan Opera.
The operas are "Cavalleria Rusticana/Pa-
gliacci," "Don Giovanni," and "Rigoletto."
(*See* individual titles for credits.) Made possible
by a major grant from Texaco, Inc. and an additional grant from the National Endowment for
the Arts.

824 Live from Wolftrap   PBS
Program Type Music/Dance Series
2 1/2 hours. Premiere date: 8/19/78. A series of
live music performances from Wolf Trap Park
Farm for the Performing Arts in Arlington, VA.
Programs during the 1977–78 season are "Bern-
stein 60/An Appreciation," "An Evening of Big-
Band Swing," "An Evening with Chuck Mang-

ione," "Pete Seeger and Arlo Guthrie," "Sarah
Vaughn," and "Tex Beneke." (*See* individual titles for credits.)

825 The Living Sands of Namib
Festival '78
National Geographic Special   PBS
Program Type Documentary/Informational
Special
60 minutes. Premiere date: 3/6/78. Portrait of
the extraordinary animal life which struggles to
survive in southwestern Africa's Namib Desert.
Made possible by a grant from Gulf Oil Corpora-
tion. (Closed captions for the hearing impaired.)
Producers David Saxon, David Hughes
Company WQED-TV/Pittsburgh
Directors David Saxon, David Hughes
Cinematographer David Hughes
Host E. G. Marshall
Narrator Burgess Meredith

826 Liza's Pioneer Diary
Visions   PBS
Program Type Dramatic Special
90 minutes. Premiere date: 11/18/76. Repeat
date: 12/25/77. Historical drama about a young
woman crossing the plains with a wagon train on
its way to the Oregon Territory. Filmed entirely
on location in the Southwest. Program made pos-
sible by grants from the Ford Foundation, the
National Endowment for the Arts and the Cor-
poration for Public Broadcasting.
Executive Producer Barbara Schultz
Producer Nell Cox
Company KCET-TV/Los Angeles
Director Nell Cox
Writer Nell Cox
                         CAST
Liza Stedman .... Ayn Ruymen
Eben Stedman .... Dennis Redfield
Hiram Stedman .... Patrick Burke
Martha Stedman ....Fran Ryan
Aunt Sara .... Katherine Helmond
Tyler Stedman .... Steven Wick
Buzzy Stedman .... Michael Harvey
Harrod .... Tim Scott
Kate Scofield ....Andra Akers
Jake Scofield .... David Ross
Jennie Scofield .... Kim Buss
Mrs. Zink .... Lucille Benson
Mr. Zink .... Luke Jones
Cousin Emma Zink .... Margaret Roberts
Mrs. Meece .... Cory Cudia
Mr. Meece ....Duke Sundt
Mr. Dunster .... Nobel Willingham
Mrs. Dunster ....Maralyn Millar
Dunster Children .... Glenna Picket, Patty Picket,
                                  Lisa Williams, Sean Williams
Zeke Trueblood ....Dixon Newberry
Trueblood Brother ....Jay Quintana
Mr. Johnson .... Rex King
Mrs. Johnson .... Helen Picket

Liza's Pioneer Diary *Continued*
Johnson Children .... Chris Williams, David Williams
Indian Girl .... Angie Espinoza

827 Logan's Run   CBS
Program Type Science Fiction Series
60 minutes. Fridays/Mondays (as of 10/10/77.)
Premiere date: 9/16/77 (as 90 minute special).
Last show: 1/16/78. Science fiction adventure
set 200 years in the future after nuclear holocaust
has destroyed most of earth's civilization.
Executive Producers Ivan Goff, Ben Roberts
Producer Leonard Katzman
Company Goff-Roberts-Steiner Productions
with MGM Television
Directors Various
Writers Various
CAST
Logan .... Gregory Harrison
Jessica .... Heather Menzies
Rem .... Donald Moffat
Francis .... Randy Powell

The Longest Yard *See* The ABC Sunday
Night Movie

828 Look Up and Live   CBS
Program Type Religious/Cultural Series
30 minutes. Sunday mornings. Premiere date:
1/3/54. Continuous. Cultural programs of a reli-
gious nature.
Executive Producer Pamela Ilott
Producers Chalmers Dale, Ted Holmes, Joseph
Clement, Alan Harper, Bernard Seabrooks
and others
Company CBS News
Directors Various

829 Loose Change
NBC Novel for Television/The Big
Event/NBC Monday Night at the Movies
Program Type Limited Series   NBC
6 hours. Premiere date: 2/26, 27/78. Dramatiza-
tion of book by Sara Davidson about the impact
of the turbulent 1960s on three young women.
Executive Producer Jules Irving
Producer Michael Rhodes
Company Universal Studios production in asso-
ciation with NBC-TV
Director Jules Irving
Writers Corinne Jacker, Charles E. Israel, Jen-
nifer Miller
CAST
Kate Evans .... Cristina Raines
Tanya Berenson .... Season Hubley
Jenny Reston .... Laurie Heineman
Joe Norman .... Ben Masters
Hank Okun .... Gregg Henry
Rob Kagan .... Guy Boyd
John Campbell .... John Getz

Irene Evans .... June Lockhart
Sol Berenson .... Joshua Shelley
Ed Thomas .... Carl Franklin
Roxanne .... Paula Wagner
Peter Lane .... Stephen Macht
Mark Stewart .... Michael Tolan
Dr. Moe Sinden .... David Wayne
George .... Gary Swanson
Rosemary .... Alice Hirson

The Lords of Flatbush *See* The ABC
Summer Movie

830 Lorna Doone   PBS
Once Upon a Classic
Program Type Drama Series
30 minutes. Premiere date: 2/23/78. 10-part se-
ries based on tale of adventure, intrigue, and a
Romeo-and-Juliet romance by R.D. Blackmore.
Presented by WQED-TV/Pittsburgh and Mc-
Donald's Local Restaurants Assn.
Producer Shep Greene
Company Time-Life Television/BBC-TV
Director Joan Crafts
Writer Stephen Dick
Host Bill Bixby
CAST
Young Lorna .... Jennifer Thanisch
Young John .... Richard Beaumont
Mature Lorna .... Emily Richard
John Somerville .... John Ridd
Carver Doone .... John Turner

**831 The Los Angeles Philharmonic at
the Hollywood Bowl**   PBS
Program Type Music/Dance Special
60 minutes. Premiere date: 9/12/78. Zubin
Mehta conducts the Los Angeles Philharmonic
Orchestra with violinist Itzhak Perlman. Meh-
ta's last televised appearance as conductor before
assuming his new role as director of the New
York Philharmonic. Program made possible by a
grant from Atlantic Richfield Company.
Executive Producer David Prowitt
Producer Jim Solt
Company Arts Program Group, Washington,
DC in cooperation with KCET-TV/Los An-
geles
Director Jack Sameth

832 Lou Grant   CBS
Program Type Drama Series
60 minutes. Tuesdays. Premiere date: 9/20/77.
Dramatic series with comedic overtones about a
city desk editor and his staff.
Executive Producers James L. Brooks; Allan
Burns; Gene Reynolds
Producer Gene Reynolds
Company MTM
Directors Various

Writers Various

CAST

Lou Grant	Edward Asner
Billie Newman	Linnda Kelsey
Charlie Hume	Mason Adams
Joe Rossi	Robert Walden
Carla Mardigian	Rebecca Balding
Margaret Pynchon	Nancy Marchand
Donovan	Jack Bannon
Animal	Daryl Anderson

---

833   A Love Affair: The Eleanor and Lou Gehrig Story

The Big Event   NBC
Program Type Dramatic Special
2 hours. Premiere date: 1/15/78. Fact-based story about the romance and marriage of the New York Yankees first baseman and the woman whose love and devotion sustained him in his battle against an incurable disease. Based on the book by Eleanor Gehrig and Joseph Durso. Music by Eddy Lawrence Manson. Filmed aboard the Queen Mary, at Yankee Stadium in New York City and at Los Angeles locations.
Executive Producers Charles Fries, Dick Berg
Producer David Manson
Company Stonehenge Productions in association with Charles Fries Productions, Inc. and NBC-TV
Director Fielder Cook
Writer Blanche Hanalis

CAST

Eleanor Gehrig	Blythe Danner
Lou Gehrig	Edward Hermann
Mrs. Gehrig	Patricia Neal
Babe Ruth	Ramon Bieri
Dr. Canlan	Michael Lerner
Claire Ruth	Georgia Engel
Joe McCarthy	Gerald S. O'Loughlin
Eleanor's mother	Jane Wyatt

---

834   The Love Boat   ABC

Program Type Drama Series
60 minutes. Premiere date: 9/24/77. (Originally aired 9/17/76 and 1/21/77 as two hour ABC Friday Night Movies, "The Love Boat," and "The Love Boat II.") Each episode is comprised of three vignettes, sometimes interwoven but usually separate in this comedy-adventure series set on a Pacific cruise ship. Developed by W. L. Baumes and suggested by Jeraldine Saunders' "The Love Boats." "The Love Boat Theme," by Charles Fox; lyrics by Paul Williams and sung by Jack Jones. Filmed at 20th Century-Fox Studios and at sea aboard the SS Pacific Princess.
Executive Producers Aaron Spelling, Douglas S. Cramer
Producers Gordon Farr, Lynne Farr, and Henry Coleman
Company Aaron Spelling Productions, Inc.
Directors Various

Writer Various
Cinematographer Arch Dalzell
Film Editors Michael McLean, Norman Wallerstein

CAST

Capt. Merril Stubing	Gavin MacLeod
Dr. Adam Bricker	Bernie Kopell
"Gopher" Smith	Fred Grandy
Isaac Washington	Ted Lange
Julie McCoy	Lauren Tewes

---

835   Love Is Not Enough

NBC Monday Night at the Movies   NBC
Program Type Dramatic Special
2 hours. Premiere date: 6/12/78. A black family moves from Detroit to Los Angeles in search of a better life. Created by Arthur Ross and Stanley G. Robertson.
Executive Producer Stanley G. Robertson
Director Ivan Dixon
Writer Arthur Ross

CAST

Mike Harris	Bernie Casey
Liz	Renee Brown
David	Stuart K. Robinson
J. P.	Lia Jackson
Tommy	Eddie Singleton
Richard Allen	Dain C. Turner
Charley Adams	Stu Gilliam
Angie Adams	Carol Tillery Banks

---

836   Love of Life   CBS

Program Type Daytime Drama Series
25 minutes. Mondays–Fridays. Premiere date: 9/24/51 (as 15-minute show). Expanded to 25 minutes 4/14/58. Continuous. The second longest-running daytime drama on television. Story of the Sterling and Aleata-Hart families set in Rosehill, U.S.A. Theme "The Life You Love" by Carey Gold. Cast listed alphabetically, as of 7/78.
Producer Jean Arley
Company CBS Television
Directors Larry Auerbach, Robert Myhrum
Writer Gabrielle Upton
Announcer Kenneth Roberts

CAST

Edouard Aleata	John Aniston
Ray Slater	Lloyd Battista
Dr. Joe Cusack	Peter Brouwer
Lynn Henderson	Amy Gibson
Mia Lowry Marriott	Veleka Gray
Ben Harper	Chandler Hill Harben
Andrew Marriott	Ron Harper
Elliot Hampton Lang	Ted Leplat
Andy Marriott, Jr.	Christian Marlowe
Charles Lamont	Jonathan Moore
Carrie Johnson Lovett	Peg Murray
Mary Jane Owens	Corinne Neuchateau
Vanessa Dale Sterling	Audrey Peters
Johnny Prentiss	Trip Randall
Dory Patten	Sherry Rooney
Sarah Caldwell	Joanna Roos
Cherie Manning	Elizabeth Stack

Love of Life Continued

Arlene Lovett Slater ....Birgitta Tolksdorf
Bruce Sterling ....Ron Tomme
Zachary Blye ....Jake Turner
Faith Manning ....Gretchen Walther
Tom Crawford .... Richard K. Weber
Meg Dale Hart .... Tudi Wiggins
T. J. Brogger ....Martin Zurla

837 Love's Dark Ride

The Big Event   NBC
Program Type Dramatic Special
2 hours. Premiere date: 4/2/78. True story of a
man who is accidentally blinded, then strength-
ened by a woman's love. "I Need You," com-
posed and sung by Tom Sullivan.
Producer Joseph M. Teritero
Director Delbert Mann
Writers Ann Beckett, Kane O'Connor, Dennis
Nemec

CAST

Stephen P. Ehlers .... Cliff Potts
Nancy Warren ....Carrie Snodgress
Diana .... Jane Seymour
Karl Sears ....Shelly Novack
Tom Scott .... Granville Van Dusen
Dr. Brad Smith .... Tom Sullivan
Dr. Kanlan ....Basil Hoffman
Dave Ramsey ....Fred Beir
Dr. Rush .... Bill Deiz
John Ehlers ....John Waldron
David Ehlers .... Jimmy Mair
Debbie ....Judy Jordan West

838 Lowell Thomas Remembers   PBS

Program Type Documentary/Informational
Series
30 minutes. Saturdays. Premiere date: 10/5/75.
Series repeated: 1/7/78. 39-part series of reminis-
cences by Lowell Thomas covering 1963–1975,
aviation between 1929–1939, and various world-
famous personalities. Put together with newsreel
films from the Movietone News Library. Series
funded by the Corporation for Public Broadcast-
ing, the Ford Foundation and Public Television
Stations.
Executive Producer James W. Jackson, Jr.
Producer James McQuinn
Company South Carolina ETV Network/ Columbia, S.C.
Director Marc Mangus
Writer Mackie Quavie
Film Editor Bryan Heath

839 The Loyal Opposition

NBC News Special   NBC
Program Type News Special
60 minutes. Premiere date: 1/29/78. Prominent
Republicans offer their observations and com-
ments on the condition of their party.
Producer Robert Asman

Company NBC News
Anchor Douglas Kiker

840 LPGA Championship   NBC

Program Type Sports Special
Live coverage of the final rounds of the 1978
LPGA Championship from the Jack Nicklaus
Golf Center at King's Island Entertainment Cen-
ter in Mason, Ohio 6/10/78 and 6/11/78.
Producer Larry Cirillo
Company NBC Sports
Director Don Ohlmeyer
Commentators Jim Simpson, Carol Mann, Susan
O'Connor, Mary Bea Porter, Cathy Duggan

841 LPGA Coca-Cola Gold Classic   PBS

Program Type Sports Special
2 hours. Coverage of the golf tournament at the
Forsgate Country Club in Jamesbury, New Jer-
sey 5/20/78. Made Possible by a Grant from the
New York, New Jersey and Fairfield County
Chrysler/Plymouth Dealers Association.
Company New Jersey Public Television
Tournament Director Peter V. Busatti

842 LPGA Lady Keystone Open   NBC

Program Type Sports Special
Coverage of golf tournament from Hershey
Country Club, Penna. 6/24/78 and 6/25/78.
Executive Producer Don Ohlmeyer
Company NBC Sports

843 Lucan   ABC

Program Type Drama Series
60 minutes. Mondays. Premiere date: 9/12/77.
Began limited run as of 12/26/77. A 20-year-old
youth who spent the first ten years of his life
running wild in the forest, where he was raised
by predatory animals, now strikes out on his own
in search of his identity. Created by Michael Za-
gor. Music by Fred Karlin.
Executive Producer Barry Lowen
Producer Harold Gas
Company A Barry Lowen Production in associa-
tion with MGM Television
Directors Various
Writers Various
Art Director Robert C. MacKichan
Cinematographer Harry May
Film Editor Herbert H. Dow

CAST

Lucan .... Kevin Brophy
Dr. Hoagland .... John Randolph
Prentiss .... Don Gordon

844 Luciano Pavarotti Recital
Live from Lincoln Center/Great Performances
PBS
Program Type Music/Dance Special
2 hours. Premiere date: 2/12/78. Recital by Metropolitan Opera star Luciano Pavarotti regarded as the reigning lyric tenor of the Italian repertory. First vocal artist ever to concertize from the Met. Made possible by grants from Exxon Corporation, the National Endowment for the Arts and the Corporation for Public Broadcasting.
Executive Producer John Goberman
Company Lincoln Center in collaboration with WNET-TV/New York

845 The Lucille Ball Special CBS
Program Type Comedy Special
60 minutes. Premiere date: 11/21/77.
Executive Producer Lucille Ball
Executive Producer Gary Morton
Company Lucille Ball Productions, Inc.
Director Marc Daniels
Writers Madelyn Davis, Bob Carroll, Jr.
Musical Director Morton Stevens
Star Lucille Ball
Co-Stars Vivian Vance, Gale Gordon, Mary Wickes
Guest Stars Ed McMahon, Steve Allen
Special Appearance Lillian Carter

846 Luke Was There
Special Treat NBC
Program Type Children's Special
60 minutes. Premiere date: 10/5/76. Repeat date: 4/4/78. Dramatization of the novel by Eleanor Clymer about a young boy in a children's shelter. Music by Joseph Horowitz.
Executive Producer Linda Gottlieb
Producer Richard Marquand
Company Learning Corporation of America
Director Richard Marquand
Writer Richard Marquand
CAST
Julius .... Scott Baio
Luke .... David Pendleton
Max .... Matthew Anton
Ricardo .... Kip Ford
Mrs. Cronkite .... Polly Holliday
Lady with a Quarter .... Estelle Omens
Lady with a Handbag .... Alice Yourman
Lady Traveller .... Harriet Sappington
Mother .... Tanya Berezin

M *See* PBS Movie Theater

847 Mac Davis ... I Believe in Christmas NBC
Program Type Music/Comedy/Variety Special
60 minutes. Premiere date: 12/7/77. Musical tour of Christmas, recalling various customs and childhood memories.
Executive Producers Raymond Katz, Sandy Gallin
Producers Joe Layton, Ken Welch, Mitzi Welch
Company Cauchemar Production in association with Welch/Layton/Welch Productions
Director Steve Binder
Writers Bill Dyer, Robert Shields
Host Mac Davis
Guests David Soul, Shields and Yarnell, Engelbert Humperdinck

848 Mac Davis Special NBC
Program Type Music/Comedy/Variety Special
60 minutes. Premiere date: 5/11/78. Singer Mac Davis and guests in music and comedy special, which takes you behind the scenes of a college concert.
Executive Producers Charles Koppelman, Gary Klein
Company The Entertainment Company
Producer Nick DeCaro
Guest Stars KC and the Sunshine Band, Donna Summer, Art Carney

849 MacNamara's Band ABC
Program Type Comedy Series
60 minutes. Premiere date: 5/14/77. Two new episodes shown during 1977–78 season: 12/5/77 and 6/10/78. Spoof of World War II adventure movies.
Executive Producers Jeff Harris, Bernie Kukoff
Producers Darrell Hallenbeck, Harry Colomby
Company Boiney Stoones, Inc.
Directors Bill Bixby, Roger Duchowny
Writers Jeff Harris, Bernie Kukoff
CAST
Johnny MacNamara .... John Byner
Frankie Milano .... Joe Pantoliano
Gaffney .... Bruce Kirby, Sr.
Zoltan .... Sid Haig
Aggie .... Steve Doubet

850 The MacNeil-Lehrer Report PBS
Program Type Public Affairs Series
30 minutes. Mondays–Fridays. Continuous. Premiere date: 1/5/76. (Began locally in New York City in November 1975.) An in-depth look at one major news story per day. Series made possible by grants from Public Television Stations, the Corporation for Public Broadcasting and Exxon Corporation.
Executive Producer Ray Weiss
Producers Howard Weinberg, Shirley Wershba, Linda Winslow
Company WNET-TV/New York and WETA-TV/Washington, D.C.
Director Duke Struck

The MacNeil-Lehrer Report *Continued*
Host Robert MacNeil
Co-Host Jim Lehrer

851 Macy's Thanksgiving Day Parade
Program Type Parades/Pageants/Awards
  Special   NBC
3 hours. Live coverage of the 51st annual parade
from New York City 11/24/77.
Producer Dick Schneider
Director Dick Schneider
Writer Herbert Hartig
Musical Director Milton Delugg
Host Ed McMahon
Co-Host Bryant Gumbel
Associate Hosts Orson Bean, Big Bird, Arte
  Johnson, Carol Lawrence, Andrea McArdle,
  Lou Rawls, Mel Tillis

852 'Mad as Hell'—The Taxpayers' Revolt
NBC News Special   NBC
Program Type News Special
Special report examining the rising tax revolt
across the country in the wake of the approval in
California of Proposition 13 limiting property
taxes 6/16/78.
Executive Producer Stuart Schulberg
Producers Kenneth Donoghue, Gene Farinet,
  Ray Lockhart
Company NBC News
Anchor David Brinkley

853 Mad Bull
The CBS Wednesday Night Movies   CBS
Program Type TV Movie
2 hours. Premiere date: 12/21/77. Love story
about a wrestler whose life in the ring has little
meaning. Music by Al De Lory.
Executive Producer Len Steckler
Producer Richard Rosenbloom
Company Steckler Production in association
  with Filmways Motion Pictures, Inc.
Directors Walter Doniger, Len Steckler
Writer Vernon Zimmerman
CAST
Iago (Mad Bull) Karkus .... Alex Karras
Christina .... Susan Anspach
Anthoney Karkus .... Chris DeRose
Jack (The White Knight) Braden .... Steve Sandor
Coley Turner ....Tracy Walter
Duke Sallow .... Nick Colasanto
Eddie Creech .... Danny Dayton
Sweeper .... Elisha Cook, Jr.
Black Bart .... Ernie Hudson
Yapopotsky .... Richard Karron
Queenie .... Eddra Gale
Maria .... Barbara Boles
Theo Karkus .... Titos Vandis
Alex Karkus .... K. C. Martel
Delia .... Laurie Heineman

Earl Lewis .... Dennis Burkley
Rafferty .... Eddie Quillan
TV Inverviewer .... Walker Edmiston
Referee Murphy .... Billy Varga
Ring Announcer .... Jimmy Lennon
Black Man .... Rozella Gayle
Mr. Clean .... Hard Boiled Haggerty
Tidy ....Mike Mazurki
Raymond Towne ....Regis Philbin
Dr. Brunton .... Harry Landers
Panhandler .... Charlie Waggenheim
Cabbie .... Russell Shannon
Mrs. Breedlove ....Ila Britton
Female teenager ....Bonnie Wiseman
Kewpie Doll .... Virginia Peters
Demented fan .... Douglas Deane
Captain ....Al Dunlap
Freckle face .... Bradley Lieberman
Grandmother ....Marie Earle
Nurse Ellen ....Dolores Sandoz
Slattern .... Kathleen Hiethala
Fan ....Simmy Bow
Body Shop Worker .... Patrick Campbell
Smitty ....Dale Ishimoto
Customer .... Hal Smith

854 Madama Butterfly
Fine Music Special/Great Performances   PBS
Program Type Music/Dance Special
3 hours. Premiere date: 10/20/76. Repeat date:
11/2/77. 1903 opera by Giacomo Puccini. Music
performed by the Vienna Philharmonic Orchestra. Program presented by WNET-TV/New
York and made possible by grants from Public
Television Stations, the Corporation for Public
Broadcasting, the Ford Foundation and Exxon
Corporation.
Executive Producer Fritz Buttenstedt
Producer David Griffiths
Company Unitel Productions
Director Jean-Pierre Ponnelle
Conductor Herbert von Karajan
CAST
Butterfly ....Mirella Freni
Benjamin Franklin Pinketton .... Placido Domingo
Suzuki ....Christa Ludwig
Consul Sharpless .... Robert Kerns

855 Made in America: Rome, New York
PBS
Program Type Documentary/Informational
  Special
60 minutes. Premiere date: 9/25/77. Documentary about a town that saved itself by creating a
national park and reconstructing historic sites.
Presented by WSKG-TV/Binghamton and
Rome Strip Steel Company, Inc.
Company WSKG-TV/Binghamton
Cinematographers Dennis Remick, Patricia
  Stanley

856 Magazine   CBS
Program Type News Magazine Series
60 minutes. Monthly. Premiered May 1974. Informational daytime series on subjects of particular interest to women.
Executive Producer Joseph Heller
Producers Various
Company CBS News
Director Vern Diamond
Editor Sharron Lovejoy

The Maggie *See* PBS Movie Theater

857 The Magical Mystery Trip Through Little Red's Head
ABC Out-of-School Specials/ABC Weekend Specials   ABC
Program Type Children's Special
60 minutes. Premiere date: 5/15/74. Season premiere: 4/29/78. Musical cartoon based on "Little Red Riding Hood." Music by Dean Elliott; lyrics by John Bradford.
Producers David H. DePatie, Friz Freleng
Company Depatie-Freleng Enterprises
Director Herbert Klein
Writer Larry Spiegel
VOICES
Timer .... Lennie Weinrib
Carol .... Diane Murphy
Larry .... Ike Eisenmann
Little Red .... Sarah Kennedy
Mother/Adeline/Diane .... Joan Gerber

The Magician *See* PBS Movie Theater

858 Magnificat—Mary's Song of Liberation   NBC
Program Type Religious/Cultural Special
60 minutes. Premiere date: 11/16/75. Repeat date: 8/13/78. Mary, as reflected in the art and cultures of 2,000 years. Filmed in England, France, Italy and the U.S.
Executive Producer Doris Ann
Producer Martin Hoade
Company NBC Television Religious Programs Unit in association with the U.S. Catholic Conference Division for Film and Broadcasting
Director Martin Hoade
Writer Philip Scharper
Narrator Marian Seldes

The Magnificent Seven Ride *See* The CBS Tuesday Night Movies

Magnum Force *See* The CBS Tuesday/Saturday Night Movies

Mahogany *See* The CBS Wednesday Night Movies

Major League Baseball Game-of-the-Week *See* Baseball Game-of-the-Week

Major League Baseball Championships *See* American League Championship/National League Championship

859 The Making of "Star Wars" as Told by C3PO and R2D2   ABC
Program Type Documentary/Informational Special
60 minutes. Premiere date: 9/16/77. A behind-the-scenes look at the making of the feature film "Star Wars." "Star Wars" music by John Williams.
Executive Producer Gary Kurtz
Producer Robert Guenette
Company A 20th Century-Fox Television Production in association with the Star Wars Company
Director Robert Guenette
Writer Richard Schickel
Hosts C3PO (Anthony Daniels), R2D2 (Kenny Baker)
Narrator William Conrad

860 Making Television Dance   PBS
Program Type Music/Dance Special
60 minutes. Premiere date: 10/4/77. Choreographer-dancer Twyla Tharp and the TV Lab at WNET, New York, explore the creative relationship between highly sophisticated television technology and the art of dance. Program made possible by grants from Andrew W. Mellon Foundation, Television Laboratory at WNET, Rockefeller Foundation, New York State Council on the Arts, National Endowment for the Arts, and Corporation for Public Broadcasting.
Executive Producer David Loxton
Company Twyla Tharp Dance Foundation and WNET Television Laboratory/New York
Director Don Mischer
Cinematographer Joel Gold
Film Editors Aviva Slesin, Girish Bhargava
Performers Twyla Tharp, Mikhail Baryshnikov, Snuffy Jenkins, Pappy Sherill and the Hired Hands.

A Man Called Horse *See* The CBS Tuesday Night Movies

861   The Man From Atlantis   NBC
Program Type Drama Series
60 minutes. Thursdays/Tuesdays (as of
10/18/77). Premiere date: 3/4/77. Season
premiere: 9/22/77. 2-hour special repeat of Pilot:
1/10/78. Show off air until 4/18/78. Last show:
8/8/78. Science-fiction drama about the last sur-
viving citizen of Atlantis who works with the
Foundation for Oceanic Research. Music by
Fred Karlin. Special effects created by Tom
Fisher. Filmed in part off the coast of Catalina in
Southern California.
Executive Producer Herbert F. Solow
Producer Herman Miller
Company Solow Production Company in associ-
ation with NBC-TV
Directors Various
Writers Various
Stunt Coordinator Paul Stader
CAST
Mark Harris .... Patrick Duffy
Dr. Elizabeth Merrill .... Belinda J. Montgomery
C. W. Crawford .... Alan Fudge

Man on a Swing *See* The CBS Tuesday
Night Movies

The Man with the Golden Gun *See* The
ABC Sunday Night Movie

862   Maneaters Are Loose!
The CBS Wednesday Night Movies   CBS
Program Type TV Movie
2 hours. Premiere date: 5/3/78. Drama about a
small American national forest community men-
aced by two huge tigers. Music by Gerald Fried.
Based on book, "Man-Eater," by Ted Willis.
Executive Producer Robert D. Wood
Producer William Finnegan
Company A Monda Production with Finnegan
Associates
Director Timothy Galfas
Writer Robert W. Lenski
CAST
John Gosford .... Tom Skerritt
David Birk .... Steve Forrest
Gordon Hale .... G. D. Spradlin
Toby Waites .... Harry Morgan
Taggart .... Frank Marth
Tom Purcell .... Joshua Bryant
Edith Waites .... Priscilla Morrill
Penny Halpern .... Jenifer Shaw
Deputy Parker .... Tony Swartz
Jill Gosford .... Susan Adams
Maud Pennington .... Carol Jones
Mira Crane .... Anita Dangler
Kevin Pennington .... Phil Brown
John Pennington .... Harry Northup
George Leppard .... John Welsh
Lucy .... Kit McDonough
Claude Davin .... Tom Mahoney

Peter Street .... Richard Caine
Deputy Miller .... Kurt Andon
Clarissa Pennington .... Pat van Patten
May Purcell .... Diana Muldaur
McCallum .... Dabney Coleman
Sheriff Rondel .... Arthur Roberts

863   Manon
Live from Lincoln Center/Great Performances
PBS
Program Type Music/Dance Special
3-1/2 hours. Premiere date: 10/18/77. Beverly
Sills sings title role in production by New York
City Opera. Simulcast in stereo. Program made
possible by grants from Exxon Corporation, Na-
tional Endowment for the Arts and the Corpora-
tion for Public Broadcasting.
Producer Tito Capobianco
Company Lincoln Center with WNET-TV/New
York
Writer Jules Massenet
Conductor Julius Rudel
CAST
Manon .... Beverly Sills
Lescaut .... Richard Fredricks
Des Grieux .... Samuel Ramey

864   The Many Loves of Arthur   NBC
Program Type Comedy Special
60 minutes. Premiere date: 5/23/78. Pilot about
a zoo veterinarian who relates to animals better
than people.
Producer Phil Berry
Company MTM Enterprises, Inc.
Director Bill Bixby
Writer Gerald DiPego
CAST
Dr. Arthur Murdock .... Richard Masur
Gail Corbett .... Caroline McWilliams
Karen .... Constance McCashin
Dr. Chase .... David Dukes
Mendoza .... Silvana Gallardo
Peg .... Paddy Edwards
Michelle .... Linda Lukens
Assistant .... Harv Selsby
Nancy .... Lee Bryant
Jake .... Robert Ridgely

865   Marilyn Beck's Second Annual
Hollywood Out-Takes   NBC
Program Type Documentary/Informational
Special
60 minutes. Premiere date: 3/27/77. Second sea-
son premiere: 3/26/78. Out-takes from 12 films
with 1978 Oscar nominations plus interviews
with people connected with the films. Show
created by Marilyn Beck.
Executive Producer Herman S. Saunders
Producers John Frederick, Bob Williams
Company Hollywood & Vine Productions
Director Dick Martin

Head Writer Elon Packard
Hosts Marilyn Beck, George Burns

866 The Mark Russell Comedy Special
PBS
Program Type Comedy Series
30 minutes. Tuesdays. Premiere date: 11/75. Third season premiere: 10/4/77. Comedy specials of political/topical humor aired live at the State University of New York at Buffalo. Programs made possible by grants from the Corporation for Public Broadcasting, the Ford Foundation and Public Television Stations.
Executive Producer John L. Hutchinson, Jr.
Producer Wiley Hance
Company WNED-TV/Buffalo
Director Will George
Scenic Designer Bryon Young
Star Mark Russell

867 The Marriage of Figaro
Great Performances PBS
Program Type Music/Dance Special
3 1/2 hours. Premiere date: 10/5/77. Opera by Wolfgang Amadeus Mozart sung in Italian. Staged by Jean-Pierre Ponnelle. Karl Boehm conducts the Vienna Philharmonic Orchestra. Made possible by a grant from EXXON.
CAST
Figaro .... Hermann Prey
Susanna ....Mirella Freni
Count .... Dietrich Fischer-Dieskau
Countess .... Kiri Te Kanawa
Cherubino .... Maria Ewing
Bartolo .... Paolo Montarsolo
Marcellina .... Heather Begg
Don Basilo .... John van Kesteren
Antonio .... Hans Kraemmer

868 Marshall Efron's Illustrated, Simplified and Painless Sunday School
CBS
Program Type Children's Series
30 minutes. Sunday mornings. Fifth season premiere: 7/23/78. Last show: 9/10/78. Religious program for children.
Executive Producer Pamela Ilott
Producer Ted Holmes
Company CBS News
Director Alvin Thaler
Writers Marshall Efron, Alfa-Betty Olsen
Host Marshall Efron

869 Martha Graham Dance Company
In Performance at Wolftrap PBS
Program Type Music/Dance Special
90 minutes. Premiere date: 4/4/78. Three works choreographed and introduced by Martha Graham performed by the Martha Graham Dance

Company: "Seraphic Dialogue," "O thou desire who are about to sing," and "Phaedra." Program funded by a grant from Atlantic Richfield Company.
Company WNET-TV/New York

870 Marty Robbins' Spotlight Syndicated
Program Type Music/Comedy/Variety Series
30 minutes. Premiere date: 9/77. Salutes a different artist each week.
Company Show Biz, Inc.
Executive Producer Bill Graham
Producer J. Reginald Dunlap
Director Bayron Binkley
Writers Bill Graham, Paul Elliott
Musical Director Timmy Tappan
Host Marty Robbins

871 Mary Jane Harper Cried Last Night
The CBS Wednesday/Saturday Night Movies
CBS
Program Type TV Movie
2 hours. Premiere date: 10/5/77. Drama about a deeply troubled young mother whose serious psychiatric problems lead her to take them out on her daughter. Music by Billy Goldenberg.
Producer Joanna Lee
Company Christiana Productions in association with Paramount Pictures
Director Allen Reisner
Writer Joanna Lee
Film Editor Kenneth R. Koch
CAST
Rowena Harper .... Susan Dey
Dave Williams .... Bernie Casey
Dr. Angela Buccieri .... Tricia O'Neil
Dr. Orrin Helgerson .... John Vernon
Mr. Atherton .... Kevin McCarthy
Mrs. Atherton .... Priscilla Pointer
Mr. Bernard .... Phillip R. Allen
Mary Jane Harper .... Natasha Ryan
Dr. Farnum .... James Karen
Mark Handelman .... Ray Buktenica
Bill Harper .... Chip Lucia
Mrs. Ramish .... Sandra Deel
Judge .... Ivan Bonar
Jeanne Williams .... Elizabeth Robinson
Joy .... Linda Gillian
Nancy West .... Fritzi Burr
Judy .... Rhea Perlman
Radiologist .... Pierrino Mascarino
Rowena at 7 .... Brandi Tucker
Billie Rae .... Pat Ast
Margo .... Susan Hickey
Tommy .... Christopher Ciampa
Miss Ramos .... Connie Izay
Officer Duncan .... Read Morgan

872 Mary Lou Williams CBS
Program Type Music/Dance Special
30 minutes. Premiere date: 12/24/77. Perfor-

Mary Lou Williams Continued
mance by Mary Lou Williams, an American jazz musician.
Producer Bernard Seabrooks
Company CBS News
Director Alvin Thaler
Star Mary Lou Williams

873   **Mary White**
ABC Theatre   ABC
Program Type Dramatic Special
2 hours. Premiere date: 11/18/77. Story based on the writings of Pulitzer Prize-winning newsman William Allen White after the death of his daughter in 1921. Filmed entirely on location in Emporia, Kansas and vicinity. Music by Leonard Roseman.
Producer Robert B. Radnitz
Company Radnitz/Mattel Productions, Inc.
Director Jud Taylor
Writer Caryl Ledner
Editor Fred Chulack
Costume Designer Joe Tompkins
Cinematographer Bill Butler, A.S.C.
CAST
William Allen White .... Ed Flanders
Sallie White .... Fionnuala Flanagan
Mary White ....Kathleen Beller
Bill White .... Tim Matheson
Sir James Barrie .... Donald Moffat
Jane Addams .... Diana Douglas
Selina .... Kaki Hunter
Richard Sloan III .... Howard McGillin

874   **M*A*S*H**   CBS
Program Type Comedy Series
30 minutes. Tuesdays/Mondays (as of 1/24/78). Premiere date: 9/17/72. Sixth season premiere: 9/20/77 (one-hour special). Based on the 1970 motion picture "M*A*S*H." Adventures of the 4077th Mobile Army Surgical Hospital during the Korean War. Theme music by Johnny Mandel.
Producer Burt Metcalfe
Company 20th Century-Fox Television
Directors Various
Executive Story Consultant Jay Folb
Writers Various
Art Director Rodger Maus
Music Supervisor Lionel Newman
CAST
Hawkeye .... Alan Alda
Capt. B. J. Hunnicut .... Mike Farrell
Col. Sherman Potter .... Harry Morgan
Maj. "Hot Lips" Houlihan .... Loretta Swit
Maj. Charles Winchester .... David Ogden Stiers
Radar O'Reilly .... Gary Burghoff
Corp. Klinger ....Jamie Farr
Father Mulcahy .... William Christopher

875   **Masterpiece Theatre**   PBS
Program Type Drama Series
60 minutes. Sundays. Umbrella title for a variety of limited dramas differing each season. Series premiered 9/69. Ninth season premiere: 11/6/77. Musical theme "Fanfare" by J. J. Mouret. Programs presented during the 1977–78 season: "Anna Karenina," "I, Claudius," "The Mayor of Casterbridge," "Our Mutual Friend," and "Poldark, II." (See individual titles for credits.) Funded by a grant from the Mobil Oil Corporation.
Producer Joan Sullivan
Company WGBH-TV/Boston
Host Alistair Cooke

876   **The Masters Tournament**   CBS
Program Type Sports Special
Highlights of early round action and live coverage of the final two rounds of the Masters from the Augusta (GA) National Golf Club 4/1/78 and 4/9/78.
Producer Frank Chirkinian
Company CBS Television Network Sports
Directors Bob Dailey, Frank Chirkinian
Commentators Vin Scully, Jack Whitaker, Pat Summerall, Ben Wright, Henry Longhurst, Frank Glieber, Jim Thacker

877   **Match Game '77–78**   CBS
Program Type Game/Audience Participation Special
30 minutes. Mondays–Fridays. Premiere date: 7/2/73. Continuous. Title changes yearly. Six celebrities seen each week; three are regulars.
Producer Ira Skutch
Company Goodman-Todman Productions
Director Marc Breslow
Host Gene Rayburn
Regulars Richard Dawson, Brett Somers, Charles Nelson Reilly

878   **A Matter of Size**
Americana   PBS
Program Type Documentary/Informational Special
30 minutes. Premiere date: 10/29/76. Repeat date: 3/7/78. A report on people in an era of increasing bigness. Program made possible by grants from the New York Council for the Humanities and the Corporation for Public Broadcasting.
Producer Joan Lapp
Company WMHT-TV/Schenectady, N.Y.
Director Michael Marton
Film Editor Ted Zborowski

879 Maude CBS
Program Type Comedy Series
30 minutes. Mondays/Saturdays as of 1/28/78.
Premiere date: 9/12/72. Sixth season premiere:
9/12/77. Last show: 4/29/78. Series created by
Norman Lear. An offshoot of "All in the Family" about a much-married liberal, Maude Findlay. Set in Tuckahoe, New York. Theme "And
Then There's Maude" by Marilyn Bergman;
Alan Bergman; Dave Grusin. Sung by Donny
Hathaway.
Executive Producers Rod Parker, Hal Cooper
Producer Charlie Hauck
Company Tandem Productions
Director Hal Cooper
Story Editors Thad Mumford, Michael Ender
Writers Various
CAST
Maude Findlay .... Beatrice Arthur
Walter Findlay .... Bill Macy
Carol ....Adrienne Barbeau
Dr. Arthur Harmon .... Conrad Bain
Vivian Harmon .... Rue McClanahan
Mrs. Naugatuck .... Hermione Baddeley
Phillip .... Kraig Metzinger
Victoria .... Marlene Warfield

Maureen Connelly *See* Little Mo

Maurice Stokes *See* Big Mo

880 The Mayor of Casterbridge
Masterpiece Theatre PBS
Program Type Limited Series
60 minutes. Premiere date: 9/3/78. Seven-part
adaptation of the novel by Thomas Hardy.
Theme music is untitled signature tune by Carl
Davis. Presented by WGBH-TV/Boston; produced by Joan Sullivan. Series made possible by
a grant from Mobil Oil Corporation.
Producer Jonathan Powell
Company BBC/Time-Life Television Production
Director David Giles
Writer Dennis Potter
CAST
Michael Henchard .... Alan Bates
Susan Henchard ....Anne Stallybrass
Elizabeth-Jane .... Janet Maw
Luceta Templeman .... Anna Massey
Donald Farfrae .... Jack Galloway
Mr. Fall .... Freddie Jones
Mrs. Goodenough .... Avis Brunnage
Mr. Jopp .... Ronald Lacey

881 The Maze—The Story of William Kurelek PBS
Program Type Documentary/Informational
Special
30 minutes. Premiere date: 9/17/76. Repeat

date: 1/16/78. The story of painter William
Kurelek. Presented by WNET-TV/New York.
Producer Dr. James B. Mass
Company Houghton-Mifflin Co.
Narrator William Kurelek

MD *See* Daniel Foster, M.D.

882 Me and Stella PBS
Program Type Documentary/Informational
Special
30 minutes. Premiere date: 11/16/77. A television portrait of Elizabeth Cotten$_{25}$and her guitar
"Stella." Program made possible by grants from
Commission for the Arts and Humanities, Washington, DC and the Corporation for Public
Broadcasting.
Producer Geri Ashur, Gerry Robert Byrne
Company WUNC-TV/Chapel Hill, NC
Director Geri Ashur, Gerry Robert Byrne
Filmmaker Geri Ashur

883 Meat PBS
Program Type Documentary/Informational
Special
2 hours. Premiere date: 11/13/76. Repeat date:
6/12/78. A look at the process by which Americans get their beef and lamb. Filmed in black and
white at Monfort of Colorado, Inc., a company
which owns feed lots and meat packing facilities.
Program made possible by a grant from the Ford
Foundation.
Producer Frederick Wiseman
Company WNET-TV/New York
Director Frederick Wiseman
Film Editor Frederick Wiseman

884 Medicine in America: Life, Death and Dollars
NBC News Special NBC
Program Type News Special
3 hours. Premiere date: 1/3/78. Program examining the quality and economics of medical care
in the United States.
Company NBC News
Executive Producer Daniel P. O'Connor
Supervising Producer Earl Ubell
Producers Adrienne Cowles, Darold Murray,
Bill Turque
Directors Joel Banow, Darold Murray
Writers Adrienne Cowles, Darold Murray, Janet
Pearce, Betty Rowlin, Karen Rutledge, Michael B. Silver, Tom Snyder, Carl Stern, Bill
Turque, Jean Sprain Wilson
Anchor Tom Snyder
Correspondents Edwin Newman, Jane Pauley,
Betty Rollin, Carl Stern

885   **Meet the Press**   NBC
Program Type Public Affairs Series
30 minutes. Sundays. Premiere date: 11/6/47 (in
New York). Network premiere: 11/20/47. Con-
tinuous. The longest-running show on television.
Live program, generally from Washington, D.C.,
with outstanding guests in the news questioned
by a panel of newspepole. Created by Lawrence
Spivak in October 1945 as a radio promotion for
American Mercury magazine.
Executive Producer Bill Monroe
Producer Betty Cole Dukert
Company NBC News
Moderator/Panelist Bill Monroe

886   **Meeting of Minds**   PBS
Program Type Educational/Cultural Series
60 minutes. Mondays. Premiere date: 1/10/77.
Second season premiere: 3/6/78. Repeats of
shows shown last season began: 4/17/78. Series
created by Steve Allen in which important per-
sonalities from various periods throughout his-
tory discuss major issues. Music composed by
Steve Allen. Series made possible by a grant from
E. F. Hutton & Company, Inc.
Executive Producer Loring d'Usseau
Producers Perry Rosemond, Loring d'Usseau
Company KCET-TV/Los Angeles
Directors Peter Levin, Bruce Franchini
Writer Steve Allen
Art Director John Retsek
Historical Consultant Dr. Robert L. Phillips
Host/Moderator Steve Allen
                    CAST
Theodore Roosevelt/Ulysses S. Grant ...... Joe Earley
St. Thomas Aquinas .... Peter Bromilow
Thomas Paine .... Joseph Sirola
Sir Thomas More .... Bernard Behrens
Attila the Hun .... Khigh Dhiegh
Emily Dickinson .... Katherine Helmond
Charles Darwin .... Murray Matheson
Frederick Douglas .... Roscoe Lee Browne
Voltaire .... John Hoyt
Plato .... David Hooks
Cesare Beccaria .... Robert Carricart
Tz'u-hsi .... Beulah Quo
Marquis de Sade .... Stefan Gierasch
Sir Francis Bacon .... James Booth
Cleopatra/Susan B. Anthony/Marie
   Antoinette/Florence Nightingale ..Jayne Meadows
Emiliano Zapata .... Juli Medina
Socrates/Galileo Galilei .... Alexander Scourby
Martin Luther/Dr Karl Marx .... Leon Askin

887   **Mel & Susan Together**   ABC
Program Type Music/Comedy/Variety Series
30 minutes. Saturdays. Premiere date: 4/22/78.
Last show: 5/13/78. Comedy sketches and mu-
sic.
Executive Producers The Osmond Brothers
Co-Producers Jerry McPhie, Toby Martin
Company An Osmond Television Production

Director Jack Regas
Writers Michael Kagan, Sonny Gordon, Carmen
   Finestra, Arthur Sellars
Comedy Consultant Ronny Graham
Stars Mel Tillis, Susan Anton

888   **Memorial Tournament**   CBS
Program Type Sports Special
Live and taped coverage of the final rounds of the
third Memorial Golf Tournament from Muir-
field Village Golf Club, Dublin, Ohio 5/20/78
and 5/21/78.
Executive Producer Frank Chirkinian
Company CBS Television Network Sports
Directors Bob Dailey, Frank Chirkinian
Commentators Vin Scully, Jack Whitaker, Pat
   Summerall, Frank Glieber, Ben Wright, Bob
   Halloran, Ken Venturi

889   **Memories of Elvis**
The Big Event   NBC
Program Type Music/Dance Special
3 hours. Premiere date: 11/20/77. Repeat date:
8/29/78. Tribute to the singer, Elvis Presley.
Production is combination of programs previ-
ously telecast 12/3/68 and 4/4/73.
Host Ann-Margret

890   **Men of Bronze**   PBS
Program Type Documentary/Informational
   Special
60 minutes. Premiere date: 11/8/77. Repeat
date: 5/30/78. Documentary about a regiment of
black American soldiers who served under the
Fourth French Army during World War I. Program made possible by grants from the Corporation for Public Broadcasting and the National
Endowment for the Arts.

891   **Merce Cunningham and Dance
Company**
Dance in America/Great Performances   PBS
Program Type Music/Dance Special
60 minutes. Premiere date: 1/5/77. Repeat date:
1/18/78. Selections from nine works performed
by Merce Cunningham and Dance Company.
Music composed by John Cage and David Tu-
dor; scenery and costume design by Robert
Rauschenberg, Andy Warhol, Jasper Johns,
Frank Stella, Remy Charlip, Mark Lancaster.
Program made possible by grants from Exxon
Corporation, the National Endowment for the
Arts and the Corporation for Public Broadcast-
ing.
Executive Producer Jac Venza
Producer Emile Ardolino
Company WNET-TV/New York

892 The Merry Widow   PBS
Program Type Music/Dance Special
2 hours. Premiere date: 11/28/77. English-language presentation of the light romantic operetta by the San Diego Opera Company taped at San Diego's Civic Theater. Music by Franz Lehar. Libretto by Ursula Eggers and Joseph De Rugeriis. Carl Toms designed the sets and costumes. Tito Capobianco is Director of the San Diego Opera Company. Program made possible by a grant from the Atlantic Richfield Company. Program recorded in stereophonic sound for stereo simulcasts in selected cities.
Producer David Prowitt
Company KCET-TV/Los Angeles and the Arts Program Group, Washington, DC
Director Kirk Browning
Conductor Theo Alcantara
CAST
Anna Glawari .... Beverly Sills
Baron Zeta .... Andrew Foldi
Count Danilo .... Alan Titus

893 The Merv Griffin Show   Syndicated
Program Type Talk/Service/Variety Series
90 minutes. Mondays–Fridays. Show first produced in 1964. Current syndication started in 1972. Continuous. Daytime talk/variety series.
Producer Bob Murphy
Company Merv Griffin Productions in association with Metromedia Producers Corporation
Director Dick Carson
Writers Merv Griffin, Bob Murphy, Tony Garofalo
Musical Director Mort Lindsay
Host Merv Griffin

894 Michel's Mixed-Up Musical Bird
ABC Afterschool Specials   ABC
Program Type Children's Special
60 minutes. Premiere date: 2/15/78. Based on a story by Michel Legrand and George Mendoza. Music by Michel Legrand; lyrics, John Bradford.
Executive Producer Nat Shapiro
Producers David H. DePatie, Friz Freleng
Company DePatie-Freleng Enterprises, Inc. in association with Ennes Productions, Ltd
Director Michel Legrand
Writers Dick Robbins, Duane Poole
Director of Photography Otto Nemenz
Animation Camera Ray Lee, Bob Mills, Steve Wilzbach, Gary Gunther
Animation Directors Tom Yakutis, Brad Case, Gerry Chiniquy
Film Editor Bill Moore
Star Michel Legrand
CAST
Eugenie .... Olivia Barash
VOICES
Young Michel .... Michael Barbera

Madame Footy .... Rita Lynn
Professor Latouche .... Hal Smith

895 Microbes and Men   PBS
Program Type Drama Series
60 minutes. Fridays. Premiere date: 2/21/77. Series repeated: 11/18/77. Six-part series dramatizing the lives and accomplishments of 19th-century medical pioneers based on the book by Robert Reid. Regular feature: "Epilogue," produced at the Salk Institute by KCET-TV/Los Angeles, in which research scientists at the institute discuss new frontiers in medical research. Series presented by KCET-TV/Los Angeles and made possible by grants from Hoffman-La Roche, Inc. and the Arthur Vining Davis Foundations.
Producer Peter Goodchild
Company British Broadcasting Corporation and Time-Life Films
Host Dr. Jonas Salk

The Invisible Enemy
Director John Glenister
Writer Martin Worth
CAST
Ignaz Semmelweis .... Robert Lang
Hebra .... David Garfield
Skoda .... Wolfe Morris
Klein ....John Gill
Marcusovsky .... Nigel Lambert
Beck ....Tim Meats
Marie .... Sandra Payne
Hildenbrand .... Donald Bisset
Rokitansky .... Leonard Maguire

A Germ is Life
Director Peter Jones
Writer Martin Worth
CAST
Louis Pasteur ....Arthur Lowe
Robert Koch .... James Grout
Marie Pasteur .... Antonia Pemberton
Biot ....Donald Eccles
Raulin .... Richard Kane
Emmy Koch .... Patricia Heneghan

Men of Little Faith
Director Peter Jones
Writer John Wiles
CAST
Louis Pasteur ....Arthur Lowe
Robert Koch .... James Grout
Emile Roux .... Charles Kay
Chamberland .... Michael Griffiths
Marie Pasteur .... Antonia Pemberton
Emmy Koch .... Patricia Heneghan
Thuillier ....Ioan Meredith
Loir .... Keith Drinkel

Certain Death
Director Peter Jones
Writer Bruce Norman
CAST
Louis Pasteur ....Arthur Lowe

Microbes and Men *Continued*

Emile Roux .... Charles Kay
Metchnikoff ....Jacob Witkin
Prof. Peter .... Aubrey Richards
Loir .... Keith Drinkel
Grancher .... John Normington
Vulpian .... Geoffrey Lumsden

A Tuberculin Affair
Writer Martin Worth
CAST

Robert Koch .... James Grout
Paul Ehrlich .... Milo O'Shea
Emil Behring ....David Swift
Von Gossler ....Geoffrey Toone
Emmy Koch .... Patricia Heneghan
Bergmann .... Charles Morgan

The Search for the Magic Bullet
Director Denis Postle
Writer Martin Worth
CAST

Paul Ehrlich .... Milo O'Shea
Sir Almroth Wright ....Michael Gough
Hedwig Ehrlich ....Stephanie Bidmead
Herxheimer .... Clifford Rose
Bertheim ....Vernon Dobtcheff
Wasserman ...., Jack Woolgar

896   The Midnight Special   NBC
Program Type Music/Comedy/Variety Series
90 minutes. Friday (1 a.m.). Premiere date:
2/3/73. Sixth season premiere: 9/16/77. First
"Midnight Special" broadcast 8/19/72. Musical
show featuring top acts in rock, pop, soul, coun-
try, and comedy.
Executive Producer Burt Sugarman
Producer Ken Ehrlich
Company Burt Sugarman, Inc. Productions
Director Kip Walton
Announcer Wolfman Jack

Midway *See* The Big Event

897   Mighty Moose and the Quarterback Kid
ABC Afterschool Specials   ABC
Program Type Children's Special
60 minutes. Premiere date: 12/1/76. Repeat
date: 12/7/77. Comedy-drama based on a story
by Jeff Miller about a 12-year old who prefers
photography to football. Music by Glen Ballard.
Executive Producer Alex Karras
Producer Harry Bernsen
Co-Producer Nick Frangakis
Company Harry Bernsen Productions, Inc. in
association with Karavan Productions, Inc.
Director Tony Frangakis
Writers Gerald Gardner, Kay Cousins Johnson
CAST

Benny Singleton .... Brandon Cruz
Coach Puckett .... Dave Madden

Mr. Singleton ....Joseph Mascolo
Alex "Mighty Moose" Novak .... Alex Karras
Suzy .... Nancy Puthuff
L.J. .... Charles Everett
Morris .... Peter Halton
Robbie .... Matthew Robert
Luncheonette Owner .... Larry Gelman
Additional Cast The Northridge Knights Junior Midget
Team

898   The Mike Douglas Show   Syndicated
Program Type Talk/Service/Variety Series
90 minutes. Mondays–Fridays. Premiered in
1961. Continuous. Show has new guest co-host
each week. Moved to Los Angeles 1977.
Executive Producer Frank Miller
Producers Vince Calandra, Erni Di Massa, Brad
Lachman
Company Group W/Westinghouse Broadcast-
ing Company, Inc. in association with Mike
Douglas Entertainments, Inc.
Distributor Group W/Westinghouse Broadcast-
ing Company, Inc.
Director Martin Morris
Host Mike Douglas

899   Mikhail Baryshnikov
In Performance at Wolf Trap   PBS
Program Type Music/Dance Special
60 minutes. Premiere date: 12/6/76. Repeat
date: 8/26/78. Selections from five ballets in a
concert at the Wolf Trap Center for the Performing Arts in Arlington, Va.: "Pas de Deux" from
"Coppelia" with music by Leo Delibes; "Le
Spectre de la Rose" with music by Carl Maria
von Weber and staged by Andre Eglevsky; "Ves-
tris" with music by G. Banshchikov; "Prelude
and First Movement" from "Push Comes to
Shove" with music by Franz Joseph Haydn and
Joseph Lamb arranged by David E. Bourne; "Pas
de Deux" from "Don Quixote" with music by
Leon Minkus. Music performed by the Filene
Center Orchestra. Program made possible by a
grant from the Atlantic Richfield Company.
Executive Producer David Prowitt
Producer Ruth Leon
Company WETA-TV/Washington, D.C.
Director Stan Lathan
Conductor Akiro Endo

Pas de Deux—Coppelia
Choreographer Arthur Saint-Leon
Dancers Mikhail Baryshnikov, Gelsey Kirkland

Le Spectre de la Rose
Choreographer Michel Fokine
Costume Designers Leon Bakst, Stanley Sim-
mons
Dancers Mikhail Baryshnikov, Marianna Tcher-
kassky

Vestris
Choreographer Leonid Jacobson
Dancer Mikhail Baryshnikov

Prelude and First Movement—Push Comes to Shove
Choreographer Twyla Tharp
Costume Designer Santo Loquasto
Dancers Mikhail Baryshnikov, Marianna Tcherkassky, Martine Van Hamel

Pas de Deux—Don Quixote
Choreographer Marius Petipa
Dancers Mikhail Baryshnikov, Gelsey Kirkland

900 Milwaukee 150 USAC Race CBS
Program Type Sports Special
2 hours. Coverage of auto race from West Allis, Wisconsin 6/18/78.
Company CBS Sports
Director Bernie Hoffman
Announcers Ken Squier, Brock Yates, Dan Gurney

901 Milwaukee 200 Race CBS
Program Type Sports Special
2 hours. Live coverage of auto race at the Wisconsin State Fair Park at West Allis, Wisconsin 8/20/78.
Producer Bernie Hoffman
Director Bob Dunphy
Announcers Ken Squier, Brock Yates, David Hobbs

902 Mime Dreaming of a White Christmas PBS
Program Type Music/Comedy/Variety Special
30 minutes. Premiere date: 12/11/77. Interpretation of Christmas scenes by the Great American Mime Experiment of Cleveland. Original music by Tim Staron. Created and written by Randy Martin and Sandra Hughes. Presented by Women's Council of WVIZ and the Corporation for Public Broadcasting.
Company WVIZ-TV/Cleveland

A Minute to Pray, A Second to Die *See* The ABC Summer Movie

Miss Julie *See* PBS Movie Theater

903 Miss Universe Beauty Pageant CBS
Program Type Parades/Pageants/Awards Special
2 hours. Live coverage via satellite from Acapulco, Mexico, 7/24/78.
Executive Producer Harold L. Glasser

Producer Sid Smith
Director Clark Jones
Writer Donald K. Epstein
Musical Director Elliot Lawrence
Choreographer Judy Houghton
Art Director Don Shirley, Jr.
Hosts Bob Barker, Helen O'Connell

904 Miss USA Beauty Pageant CBS
Program Type Parades/Pageants/Awards Special
2 hours. Live coverage of the finals of the 27th annual Miss USA Beauty Pageant from Gaillard Municipal Auditorium, Charleston, S.C. 4/29/78.
Executive Producer Harold L. Glasser
Producer Sid Smith
Company Miss Universe, Inc.
Director Clark Jones
Musical Director Elliot Lawrence
Choreographer Gene Bayliss
Art Director Don Shirley, Jr.
Hosts Bob Barker, Helen O'Connell
Guest Star Jack Jones
Featured Guest Kimberly Louise Tomes

Mr. Majestyk *See* CBS Special Movie Presentations

905 Mister Rogers' Neighborhood PBS
Program Type Children's Series
30 minutes. Monday mornings–Friday mornings. Premiere date: 5/22/67. Continuous. Title changed from "Misterogers' Neighborhood" in Sept. 1970. The longest-running children's show on PBS. Created by Fred Rogers. Regular feature: visits to the puppet-populated Neighborhood of Make-Believe. Series funded by grants from Sears Roebuck Foundation, the Corporation for Public Broadcasting, the Ford Foundation, Public Television Stations and Johnson and Johnson Baby Products.
Executive Producer Fred Rogers
Producer Bill Moates
Company Family Communications, Inc. in association with WQED-TV/Pittsburgh
Director Bill Moates
Writer Fred Rogers
Musical Director John Costa
Art Director Jack Guest
Host Fred Rogers
Puppeteers Fred Rogers, William P. Barker, Robert Trow
CAST
Lady Aberlin .... Betty Aberlin
Chef Brockett .... Don Brockett
Francois Clemmons .... Francois Clemmons
Pilot Ito .... Yoshi Ito
Mrs. McFeely .... Betsy Nadas
Elsie Neal .... Elsie Neal

Mister Rogers' Neighborhood *Continued*

Handyman Negri ....Joe Negri
Mr. McFeely .... David Newell
Audrey Cleans Everything (A.C.E.)/
Audrey Pauliffcate ....Audrey Roth
Robert Troll/Bob Dog/Bob Trow .... Robert Trow
VOICES
X the Owl/King Friday XIII/Queen Sara Saturday/
Cornflake S. Pecially/Lady Elaine Fairchilde/
Henrietta Pussycat/Grandpere/Edgar Cooke/
Daniel Striped Tiger/Donkey Hodie
.... Fred Rogers
Dr. Duckbill Platypus/Mrs. Elsie Jean Platypus
William P. Barker
Harriett Elizabeth Cow ....Robert Trow

906   Mr. Speaker: A Portrait of Tip O'Neil   PBS

Program Type Documentary/Informational
Special
60 minutes. Premiere date: 7/18/78. An hour
long look at the job of the Speaker of the U.S.
House of Representatives and the Congressman
from Cambridge who fills it—Tip O'Neil.
Producer Nancy Porter
Company WGBH-T/Boston

907   Miss America Pageant

Program Type Parades/Pageants/Awards
Special   NBC
2 hours. Finale of the 1978 Miss America Pag-
eant live from Convention Hall, Atlantic City,
NJ 9/9/77. Production numbers produced and
directed by George Cavalier. Original music and
lyrics by Edna Osser and Glenn Osser.
Executive Producer Albert A. Marks, Jr.
Producer John L. Koushouris
Company NBC Television
Director Dave Wilson
Writer Stuart Hersch
Musical Director Glenn Osser
Choreographer Ron Poindexter
Art Director Herb Andrews
Hosts Bert Parks, Phyllis George, Lee
Meriwether
Special Guest Star John McCook
Entertainers Dorothy Benham, Scott Heyden

908   Miss Teenage America Pageant

Program Type Parades/Pageants/Awards
Special   NBC
90 minutes. Live coverage of the 17th annual
pageant from Dallas, TX, 11/25/77.
Producer Joseph Cates
Company Joseph Cates Production
Director Sidney Smith
Writer Frank Slocum
Musical Director James Gaertner
Host Richard Thomas
Guests Garry Moore Singers

909   Miss World 1977

Program Type Parades/Pageants/Awards
Special   NBC
90 minutes. Live via satellite of the 1977 Miss
World Beauty Contest from Royal Albert Hall,
London 11/17/77.
Executive Producers Ken Weinstock, Seymour
Sietz, Hal Blake
Producer Michael Begg
Company Trans World International/BBS Pro-
ductions
Director Michael Begg
Musical Director Phil Tate
Set Decorator John Hurst
Host Andy Williams
Entertainers Cindy Breakspeare

Misty *See* The Big Event

Mitchell *See* CBS Special Movie
Presentations

910   Mitzi ... What's Hot, What's Not   CBS

Program Type Music/Comedy/Variety Special
60 minutes. Premiere date: 4/6/78. Musical se-
quences by Bill Dyer and Dick DeBenedictis.
Executive Producer Jack Bean
Company Green Isle Enterprises
Director Tony Charmoli
Writer Jerry Mayer
Musical Director J. Hill
Choreographer Tony Charmoli
Costume Designer Bob Mackie
Star Mitzi Gaynor
Guest Stars Gavin MacLeod, John McCook,
Jimmy Murphy

911   Mixed Team Championship Golf   CBS

Program Type Sports Special
Final two rounds of golf action from Bardmoor
Country Club in Largo, Florida 12/3/77 and
12/4/77.
Producer Frank Chirkinian
Company CBS Sports
Director Bob Dailey
Anchor Vin Scully

912   Mobile Maidens

The Winners   CBS
Program Type Children's Special
30 minutes. Premiere date: 11/10/77. Drama of
three young girls who rescued "seconds" of fruits
and vegetable crops to sell them inexpensively to
migrant workers. Music by Tom Adair and Will
Schaefer.

Producer William Beaudine, Jr.
Director John Tracy
Writer Jerome Alden
CAST
Louisa .... Kenia Borell
Rose .... Nita Dee
Sally ....Julie Piekarski
Mrs. Hanson .... Laura Wallace
Roberto .... Eddie Martinez

913 **Model Railroading Unlimited** PBS
Program Type Documentary/Informational
Special
30 minutes. Premiere date: 10/1/77. Story of a
young model train enthusiast who saves a huge
train layout from disaster. Special effects advisor
is Robert E. Rogers.
Producer Mike O'Connell
Company Liberty Pictures, Inc.
Writer Robert E. Rogers
Post-Production Supervisor Larry Wright

914 **Mom and Dad Can't Hear Me**
ABC Afterschool Specials ABC
Program Type Children's Special
60 minutes. Premiere date: 4/5/78. A 15-year-
old girl is embarrassed by the prospect of bring-
ing new friends home to meet her deaf parents.
Original music by Sodden-Weber
Executive Producer Daniel Wilson
Producer Fran Sears
Company Daniel Wilson Productions, Inc.
Director Larry Elikann
Writers Irma Reichert, Daryl Warner
Cinematographers Dennis Dalzell, Eric Saarinen
Film Editor Vince Humphrey
CAST
Charlotte Meredith ....Rosanna Arquette
Mrs. Meredity .... Priscilla Pointer
Dan Meredith .... Stephen Elliott
David .... Eric Scott
Joyce .... Wendy Rastartter
Alice ....Noelle North
Hughie ....David Hollander
Bob Tomasino .... David Burns
Martha .... Susan Myers
Mrs. Egan .... Victoria Shaw
Mrs. Wagner ....Loretta Lottman

Monday Night Baseball *See* ABC's
Monday Night Baseball

Monday Night Football *See* ABC's
Monday Night Football

915 **The Moneychangers**
The Big Event/NBC Monday Night at the
Movies NBC
Program Type Limited Series
6 hours. Premiere date: 12/4–19/76. Repeat da-

tes: 4/23–25/78. Based on the novel by Arthur
Hailey about a power struggle in a banking em-
pire. Music composed by Henry Mancini. Filmed
in part on locations in Los Angeles.
Producers Ross Hunter, Jacque Mapes
Company Ross Hunter Productions, Inc. in asso-
ciation with Paramount Television and NBC-
TV
Director Boris Sagal
Writers Dean Riesner, Stanford Whitmore
Art Director Jack DeShields
CAST
Alex Vandervoort .... Kirk Douglas
Roscoe Heyward ....Christopher Plummer
Miles Eastin .... Timothy Bottoms
Margot Bracken .... Susan Flannery
Edwina Dorsey .... Anne Baxter
Nolan Wainwright .... Percy Rodrigues
Jerome Patterton .... Ralph Bellamy
Avril Devereaux .... Joan Collins
Tony Bear ....Robert Loggia
Beatrice Heyward .... Jean Peters
Harold Austin .... Patrick O'Neal
George Quartermain .... Lorne Greene
Dr. McCartney .... Helen Hayes
Juanita .... Amy Tivell
Lewis Dorsey .... Hayden Rorke

Monte Walsh *See* NBC Saturday Night
at the Movies

Moonshine County Express *See* The CBS
Tuesday Night Movies

916 **More Music from Aspen** PBS
Program Type Music/Dance Special
60 minutes. Premiere date: 1/11/76. Repeat
date: 1/5/78. A behind-the-scenes look at a cho-
ral concert of Wolfgang Amadeus Mozart's C
Minor Mass performed by a 135-voice chorus
and 66 piece orchestra. Taped during the sum-
mer of 1975 at the Aspen Music Festival. Pro-
gram made possible by grants from Atlantic
Richfield Company, the National Endowment
for the Arts and the Corporation for Public
Broadcasting.
Executive Producer Zev Putterman
Producer Christopher Lukas
Company KQED-TV/San Francisco
Director Christopher Lukas
Musical Director Fiora Contino
Soloists Susan Davenny Wyner, Jan De Gaetani,
John McCollum, Thomas Paul

917 **Mother, Juggs & Speed** ABC
Program Type Comedy Series
30 minutes. Premiere date: 8/17/78. Pilot about
three paramedics working for an ambulance
company. Based on the 1976 film, "Mother, Jugs
& Speed."

Mother, Juggs & Speed *Continued*
Director John Rich
Writer Tom Mankiewicz
CAST
Mother ....Ray Vitte
Juggs ....Joanne Nail
Speed .... Joe Penny
Murdock ....Rod McCary
Fishbine ....Harvey Lembeck
Mrs. Fishbine .... Barbara Minkus Barron

Mountain Man *See* NBC Movie of the Week

918 **Mowgli's Brothers**   CBS
Program Type Animated Film Special
30 minutes. Premiere date: 2/11/76. Repeat date: 4/4/78. Third in a series of adaptations from "The Jungle Books" by Rudyard Kipling Music by Dean Elliott.
Producers Chuck Jones, Oscar Dufau
Company Chuck Jones Enterprises
Directors Chuck Jones, Hal Ambro
Writer Chuck Jones
Narrator Roddy McDowall
VOICES
Mowgli/Shere Khan/Akela/Tabaqui/Bagheera/
Baloo .... Roddy McDowall
Mother Wolf .... June Foray

919 **Mulligan's Stew**   NBC
Program Type Comedy Series
90 minutes. Tuesdays. Premiere date: 6/20/77. Season premiere: 10/25/77. Last show: 12/13/77. Comedy about the family of the high school coach who inherit four orphans.
Producer Joanna Lee
Company Christiana Production in association with Paramount Television
Directors Various
Writers Various
CAST
Michael Mulligan .... Lawrence Pressman
Jane Mulligan .... Elinor Donahue
Mark ....Johnny Doran
Jimmy .... K. C. Martel
Melinda ....Julie Haddock
Stevie .... Suzanne Crough
Adam .... Christopher Ciampa
Polly .... Lory Kochheim
Kimmy ....Sunshine Lee

920 **The Muppet Show**   Syndicated
Program Type Music/Comedy/Variety Series
30 minutes. Weekly. Premiere date: 9/76. Season premiere: 9/12/77. The Muppets plus guests in a comedy-variety show emceed by Kermit the Frog and starring Miss Piggy. Developed in co-operation with the CBS-TV owned and operated stations.
Executive Producer Dave Lazer

Company ITC Entertainment and Henson Associates
Producer Jim Henson
The Muppets Frank Oz, Jerry Nelson, Richard Hunt, Dave Goelz, Jim Henson

921 **Murder at the Mardi Gras**
The CBS Wednesday Night Movies   CBS
Program Type TV Movie
2 hours. Premiere date: 5/10/78. A pair of tourists share romance and intrigue during the famed New Orleans Carnival. Filmed in New Orleans. Music by Peter Matz.
Executive Producer Gerald W. Abrams
Producers Richard Nader, Matthew N. Herman
Company A Richard Nader Production in association with The Jozak Company and Paramount Television
Director Ken Annakin
Writer Stanley Ralph Ross
CAST
Barbi Benton .... Barbi Benton
Julie Evans .... Didi Conn
Jack Murphy .... Bill Daily
Harry Benson ....David Groh
Randy Brian ....Gregg Henry
Jim Bob Jackson .... Harry Morgan
Larry Cook .... Ron Silver
Janet Murphy .... Joyce Van Patten
Mickey Mills .... David Wayne
Nancy ....LaVerne Hooker
Andrew .... Duncan McCord
Lisa .... Andrea Piwetz
Fenton .... Don Hood
Cedric .... Louis Dezseran
Sutton .... Don Lutenbacher
Desk clerk .... Joe Mullane
Wolfman Jack ....Wolfman Jack

922 **Murder at the World Series**
The ABC Sunday/Friday Night Movie   ABC
Program Type TV Movie
2 hours. Premiere date: 3/20/77. Repeat date: 8/27/78. Drama of a kidnapping during the World Series in Houston. Music by John Cacavas. Filmed on location in Houston and Los Angeles.
Producer Cy Chermak
Company ABC Circle Films
Director Andrew V. McLaglen
Writer Cy Chermak
Art Director Elayne Barbara Ceder
CAST
Margo Mannering ....Lynda Day George
Harvey Murkison .... Murray Hamilton
Lois Marshall .... Karen Valentine
Moe Gold ....Gerald S. O'Loughlin
Larry Marshall ....Michael Parks
Karen Weese .... Janet Leigh
Governor .... Hugh O'Brian
Alice Dakso .... Nancy Kelly
Severino .... Johnny Seven
Liza .... Tamara Dobson

Sam	Joseph Wiseman
Cisco	Bruce Boxleitner
Vawn	Larry Mahan
Frank Gresham	Cooper Huckabee
Kathy	Maggie Wellman
Jane Torres	Cynthia Avila
Barbara Gresham	Monica Gayle

923 Murder in Peyton Place
NBC Monday Night at the Movies/NBC
World Premiere Movie   NBC
Program Type Dramatic Special
2 hours. Premiere date: 10/3/77. Drama focuses on the events surrounding the slaying of a young couple.
Producer Peter Katz
Company 20th Century-Fox production in association with NBC-TV
Director Bruce Kessler
Writer Richard DeRoy
CAST

Allison MacKenzie	Mia Farrow
Norman Harrington	Christopher Connelly
Jill Harrington	Joyce Jillson
Steven Cord	David Hedison
Carla Cord	Linda Gray
Betty Anderson	Janet Margolin
Elliot Carson	Tim O'Connor
Constance MacKenzie	Dorothy Malone
Dr. Michael Rossi	Ed Nelson
Bonnie Buehler	Kimberly Beck
Billie Kaiserman	David Kyle
Denise Haley	Charlotte Stewart
Stan Haley	Jonathan Goldsmith
Jay Kamens	Normann Burton
Tommy Crimpton	James Booth
Andy Considine	Chris Nelson
Bo Buehler	Royal Dano
Mae	Priscilla Morrill
Tristan	Robert Deman
Stella Chernak	Stella Stevens
David Roerick	Ed Bell
Springer	Kaz Garas
Kaiserman	Charles Siebert
Ruth	Gale Sladstone
Chauffeur	Fred Lerner
Ellen	Marg Dusay
Dr. Jensen	Jerome Thor
Linda	Catherine Bach

Murder on the Orient Express *See* The ABC Sunday Night Movie

924 Music   PBS
Program Type Music/Dance Series
30 minutes. Saturdays/Sundays. Premiere date: 10/8/77. Series repeated: 1/3/78. 10-part series aimed at expanding the musical knowledge and understanding of upper elementary school children. Features the National Symphony Orchestra. Program made possible through a contract with HEW's Office of Education and a grant from Allied Chemical Corporation.

Executive Producer Ruth Leon
Coordinating Producer Hal Hutkoff
Company WETA-TV/Washington, DC
Director Clark Santee
Curriculum Director Toby Levine
Host Murry Sidlin

925 Music and Your Emotions
The CBS Festival of Lively Arts for Young People   CBS
Program Type Children's Special
60 minutes. Premiere date: 3/19/78. Erich Leinsdorf conducts the New York Philharmonic Orchestra and Beverly Sills sings to demonstrate how music evokes emotions. Taped live from Avery Fisher Hall at Lincoln Center in New York City.
Producer Hank Saroyan
Directors Joshua White, Andrew Wilk
Writers Sean Kelly, Robert Jacobson
Music Coordinators Patrick Holland, Richard Vitzhum
Conductor Erich Leinsdorf
Hostess-Commentator Beverly Sills

926 Music from Aspen   PBS
Program Type Music/Dance Special
60 minutes. Premiere date: 1/4/76. Repeat date: 12/29/77. First of two specials blending performances taped at the 1975 Aspen Music Festival with the beauty of the Colorado Rockies. (*See also* "More Music from Aspen.") Music performed by the Aspen Festival Philharmonia Orchestra. Program made possible by grants from Atlantic Richfield Company, the National Endowment for the Arts and the Corporation for Public Broadcasting.
Executive Producer Zev Putterman
Producer Christopher Lukas
Company KQED-TV/San Francisco
Director Christopher Lukas
Conductor Sergiu Comissiona
Performers Itzhak Perlman, Pinchas Zukerman, Ronald Leonard

927 Music in America
Great Performances   PBS
Program Type Music/Dance Special
Two classical music shows seen as part of the "Great Performances" series: "Copland Conducts Copland" and "The Music of Ernest Bloch." (*See* individual titles for credits.)

928 Music in Jerusalem   PBS
Program Type Music/Dance Special
60 minutes. Premiere date: 8/16/77. Repeat date: 7/11/78. A look at the Jerusalem Music Center. Filmed over four years. Program made

Music in Jerusalem *Continued*
possible by a grant from Automatic Data Processing, Inc.
Executive Producer Ruth Leon
Producer Paul Salinger
Company WETA-TV/Washington, D.C.
Director Paul Salinger
Host/Narrator Isaac Stern

929   The Music of Ernest Bloch
Music in America/Great Performances   PBS
Program Type Music/Dance Special
60 minutes. Premiere date: 5/19/76. Repeat date: 9/2/78. The Cleveland Symphony Orchestra performing the works of Ernest Bloch. Program funded by a grant from Exxon Corporation.
Executive Producer Jac Venza
Producers David Griffiths, Klaus Hallig
Company WNET-TV/New York and the International Television Trading Corporation
Conductor Lorin Maazel
Guest Soloist Leonard Rose

930   The Music School
The American Short Story   PBS
Program Type Dramatic Special
60 minutes. Premiere date: 5/10/77. Repeat date: 11/14/77. Adaptation of the short story by John Updike about a middle-aged writer in contemporary society. Music by Ed Bogas. Program presented by South Carolina Educational Television and made possible by a grant from the National Endowment for the Humanities.
Executive Producer Robert Geller
Producer Dan McCann
Company Learning in Focus, Inc.
Director John Korty
Writer John Korty
Host Colleen Dewhurst
CAST
Alfred Schweigen .... Ronald Weyand
Schweigen's Wife .... Dana Larsson
Scientist .... Tom Dahlgren
Scientist's Wife .... Vera Stough
Country Priest .... Frank Albertson
Maggie Johns .... Elizabeth Huddle Nyberg
Divorced Woman .... Anne Lawder

Mutual of Omaha's Wild Kingdom *See*
Wild Kingdom

931   My Dear Uncle Sherlock
ABC Short Story Specials   ABC
Program Type Children's Special
30 minutes. Premiere date: 4/16/77. Repeat date: 12/24/77. Story of a 12-year-old boy and his uncle who solve a mystery using deductive

reasoning. Based on the short story by Hugh Pentecost.
Executive Producer Allen Ducovny
Producer William Beaudine, Jr.
Company ABC Circle Films
Director Arthur H. Nadel
Writer Manya Starr
CAST
Joey Trimble .... Robbie Rist
Uncle "Sherlock" George ....Royal Dano
Bill Leggett .... John Karlen
Off. Gilligan .... Vaughn Armstrong
Dave Taylor .... John Milford
Mr. Trimble .... John Carter
Mrs. Trimble .... Inga Swenson

932   My Mom's Having a Baby
ABC Afterschool Specials   ABC
Program Type Children's Special
60 minutes. Premiere date: 2/16/77. Repeat date: 11/16/77. Story explaining the facts of human reproduction using drama, animation and a videotaped birth sequence showing Candace Farrell giving birth to her child. Music by Dean Elliott lyrics by John Bradford.
Executive Producers David H. DePatie, Friz Freleng
Producer Robert Chenault
Company DePatie-Freleng Enterprises
Director Larry Elikann
Writers Susan Fichter Kennedy, Elaine Evans Rushnell
Art Director Ray Markham
Animation Director Tom Yakutis
Animators Don Williams, Nelson Shin, Bob Richardson, John Gibbs
CAST
Dr. Lendon Smith .... Lendon Smith
Petey Evans .... Shane Sinutko
Oscar .... Jarrod Johnson
Kelly .... Rachel Longaker
Anne Evans .... Candace Farrell
Peter's Father .... Ed Rombola
Nurse .... Karen Glow Carr
Receptionist .... Dodo Denney

My Name Is Nobody *See* The Big Event/NBC Saturday Night at the Movies

933   Mysterious Castles of Clay   NBC
Program Type Documentary/Informational Special
60 minutes. Premiere date: 3/18/78. Photographic study of the busy world of the blind African termites. Photographed in the bushlands of East Africa by Alan Root. Music by Marc Wilkinson.
Executive Producer Aubrey Buxton
Producer Alan Root

Company Survival Anglia Ltd. in association with the World Wildlife Fund
Writer Alan Root
Narrator Orson Welles.

934 Mystery Murals of Baja California
PBS
Program Type Documentary/Informational Special
30 minutes. Premiere date: 11/17/75. Repeat date: 8/6/78. An exploration of ancient cave paintings found in Baja California, Mexico. Program made possible by grants from KPBS-TV/San Diego and the Corporation for Public Broadcasting.
Producer Wayne Smith
Company KPBS-TV/San Diego Office of Scientific Affairs
Narrator Harry Williams Crosby

Name that Tune See The $100,000 Name that Tune

Nancy Drew Mysteries See Hardy Boys/Nancy Drew Mysteries

935 Nanook Taxi
Visions   PBS
Program Type Dramatic Special
90 minutes. Premiere date: 11/27/77. Original drama about an Inuit Eskimo in the Canadian Northwest Territories. Music by Itulu and Susan Peta, Tomasie Quissak, Sugluc Band and Frobisher Bay Senior Citizens.
Executive Producer Barbara Schultz
Producer Jeffrey Hayes
Company KCET-TV/Los Angeles
Director Edward Folger
Writer Edward Folger
Cinematographer Paul Glickman
CAST
Ningiuksiak ....Joanasie Salomonie
Mukittuq .... Kanayuk Salomonie
Ashoona .... Mickey Turqtuq
Leona ....Elisapee Davidee

Nashville See The ABC Sunday Night Movie

936 Nashville International Invitational Swim Meet
PBS
Program Type Sports Special
2 hours. Premiere date: 5/7/78. Highlights of swim meet which brought together over 700 swimmers from the U.S. and six foreign countries and saw two Women's Breast Stroke records broken.

Producers Harmon McBride; Michael J. Kroger
Company WDCN-TV/Nashville
Associate Producer Virginia C. Wynne
Director Charles Lewis
Announcer Bud Collins
Expert Commentators Wendy Boglioli, Steve Tyrrell, and Bernie Boglioli

937 Nashville Remembers Elvis on His Birthday
The Big Event   NBC
Program Type Music/Dance Special
90 minutes. Premiere date: 1/8/78. Special honoring Elvis Presley's memory on the occasion of his 43rd birthday anniversary.
Executive Producers Joseph Cates, Gilbert Cates
Producers Bobby Brenner, Bill Siegler
Director Ivan Cury
Writer Frank Slocum
Musical Director Bill Walker
Host Jimmy Dean
Guest Stars Chubby Checker, Larry Gatlin, Jordanaires, Jerry Lee Lewis, Roy Orbison, Carl Perkins, Charlie Rich, Dottie West, Merle Haggard, Ronnie McDowell, Tanya Tucker
Special Appearances Jack Albertson, Bill Bixby, Edith Head, Gary Lockwood, Mary Ann Mobley, Sheree North, Arthur O'Connell, Nancy Sinatra, Stella Stevens

938 The Natalie Cole Special
CBS
Program Type Music/Comedy/Variety Special
60 minutes. Premiere date: 4/27/78.
Executive Producers Kevin Hunter, Dick Clark
Producer Robert Arthur
Company dick clark teleshows, inc. in association with R.A.Y. Productions
Director Tim Kiley
Writer Robert Arthur
Musical Director Nelson Riddle
Choreographer George Faison
Star Natalie Cole
Guest Stars Earth, Wind & Fire, Johnny Mathis, Stephen Bishop

939 The National Cheerleading Championships
CBS
Program Type Parades/Pageants/Awards Special
90 minutes. Premiere date: 4/24/78. Five cheerleading teams from around the country compete for the national title live from the Los Angeles Sports Arena.
Producers Brad Marks, Lee Mendelson
Company Interpublic Television
Director Walter C. Miller
Writers Brad Marks, Lee Mendelson, Fred S. Fox, Seaman Jacobs
Guest Stars George Burns, Phyllis George,

The National Cheerleading Championships *Continued*
Bruce Jenner, Gene Kelly, Lou Rawls, Cheryl Ladd

940 National Geographic Specials   PBS
Program Type Documentary/Informational Series
Times vary. Premiere date: 10/28/75. Third season premiere: 12/5/77. Monthly specials produced by the National Geographic Society. Programs shown during the 1977–78 season: "The Great Whales," "Journey to the Outer Limits," "The Legacy of L.S.B. Leakey," "The Living Sands of Namib," "Search for the Great Apes," "Strange Creatures of the Night," "Treasure," "The Volga," "Voyage of the Holule'a," and "Yukon Passage." (*See* individual titles for credits.)

941 National Kids' Quiz   NBC
Program Type Children's Special
60 minutes. Premiere date: 1/28/78. Focuses on opinions of youngsters, 8–13, about themselves and their relationships with family, friends and school. Created by Jane Norman.
Executive Producer Sonny Fox
Producers Jane Norman, Jack Kuney
Director Jack Kuney
Star Michael Landon

942 National League Championship (Baseball)   ABC
Program Type Sports Special
Live coverage of the National League Championship games between the Philadelphia Phillies and the Los Angeles Dodgers beginning 10/4/77. Producer and director in Los Angeles for Games 1 and 2 are George Finkel and Harry Coyle. Additional games produced by Mike Weisman and directed by Harry Cole.
Executive Producer Roone Arledge
Company ABC Sports

943 National Love, Sex and Marriage Test   NBC
Program Type Game/Audience Participation Special
90 minutes. Premiere date: 3/5/78. Home viewers rate themselves in the most common male-female relationships. Test created in collaboration with noted marriage counsellor Dr. Thomas Laswell and Professor Eleen Bauman.
Producer Norman Sedawie
Company Warren V. Bush Production in cooperation with the American Association of Marriage and Family Counselors
Director Joel Tator

Writers Ruben Carson, Michael Kagan, Karyl Miller, Norman Sedawie
Hosts Tom Snyder, Suzanne Somers
Guests Ann Landers, Bonnie Franklin, Abe Vigoda, Joan Rivers, Lynn Redgrave, Rich Little, Phyllis Diller, Don Knotts, Jo Anne Worley, Barbara Rhoades, Marty Allen, Misty Rowe, Greg Mullavey, Jim Backus, George Gobel, Debralee Scott, Audra Lindley, Della Reese, Vicki Lawrence

944 National Open Long Driving Championship   ABC
Program Type Sports Special
Coverage of the finals of the 4th annual National Open Long Driving Championship from the Oakmont Country Club, Pittsburgh, Pennsylvania 8/6/78.
Executive Producer Roone Arledge
Producer Terry Jastrow
Company ABC Sports
Director Jim Jennett
Hosts Dave Marr, Dan Jenkins

945 National Pro-Am Racquetball   PBS
Program Type Sports Special
60 minutes. Premiere date: 12/18/77. Racquetball matches held at King's Racquetball Court, Westminster, California. Underwritten by Robert Kendler, Sr.
Company KOCE-TV/Huntington Beach

946 National Women's Conference, 1977   PBS
Program Type Public Affairs Special
60 minutes. 11/21/77. Live coverage of the National Women's Conference from Houston, Texas. Program made possible by a grant from the Corporation for Public Broadcasting.
Company KERA-TV/Dallas-Fort Worth

947 NBA All-Star Game   CBS
Program Type Sports Special
2-1/2 hours. Live coverage of the 28th annual National Basketball Association East-West All-Star game from the Omni in Atlanta, GA. 2/5/78.
Producer Chuck Milton
Company CBS Sports
Director Sandy Grossman
Announcers Brent Musburger, Don Criqui
Expert Analyst Keith Erickson

948 NBA on CBS (National Basketball Association Games)   CBS
Program Type Limited Sports Series
Live coverage of regular-season, play-off and

championship games. Fifth season premiere: 10/28/77. Regular Sunday games began 1/2/78. Playoffs began 4/14/78. Championship games began 5/25/78 between the Seattle SuperSonics and the Washington Bullets. Half-time features include "H-O-R-S-E," the third season of "Red on Roundball" with Red Auerbach, and "The Greek's Grapevine on Basketball" with Jimmy "The Greek" Snyder.

Producers Chuck Milton, Bob Stenner
Company CBS Sports
Directors Sandy Grossman, Tony Verna
Announcers Brent Musburger, Don Criqui, Gary Bender, Jerry Gross, Bob Costas, Frank Glieber, Tim Ryan, Jim Karavelas, Bill Mazer
Expert Analysts Mendy Rudolph, Billy Cunningham, Steve Jones, Peter Maravich, John Havlicek, Rick Barry, Cazzie Russell, Jon McGlocklin, Keith Erickson, Gus Johnson, Stu Lantz

949 NBC: The First Fifty Years—A Closer Look
The Big Event   NBC
Program Type Music/Comedy/Variety Special
2-1/2 hours. Premiere date: 10/23/77. A salute to NBC-TV variety and special programming going back to TV's early days.
Executive Producer Greg Garrison
Producer Lee Hale
Company NBC in association with Greg Garrison Productions, Inc.
Director Greg Garrison
Writer Jess Oppenheimer
Conductor Van Alexander
Film Editor George Pitts
Animation Bill Melendez Productions, Inc.

NBC Family Choice *See* Black Beauty

950 NBC Junior Hall of Fame   NBC
Program Type Children's Series
90 seconds. Saturdays: 8:57, 9:27, 11:27 AM. Premiere: 9/10/77. Tribute to young people 15 year of age and under who have achieved excellence in the fields of arts, sciences, sports, public service, overcoming a physical handicap.
Company Alan Landsburg Productions

951 NBC Monday Night at the Movies
NBC
Program Type Feature Film Series – TV Movie Series
2 hours (generally). Mondays. Season premiere: 9/12/77. A combination of made-for-television movies and theatrically released feature films. Films which are longer than two hours are shown in part on NBC Saturday Night at the

Movies and The Big Event. The made-for-TV movies are: "The Awakening Land: The Saga of an American Woman," "Billy: Portrait of a Street Kid," "Christmas Miracle in Caulfield U.S.A.," "Columbo," "The Critical List," "Dark Secret of Harvest Home," "The Girl in the Empty Grave," "Holocaust," "The Hunted Lady," "In the Glitter Palace," "Just Me and You," "Killer on Board," "King," "Loose Change," "Love Is Not Enough," "The Moneychangers," "Murder in Peyton Place," "The Night They Took Miss Beautiful," "Nowhere to Run," "Once an Eagle," "Sergeant Matlovich vs. U.S. Air Force," "Seventh Avenue," "79 Park Avenue," "Sharon: Portrait of a Mistress," "The Storyteller," "Sunshine Christmas," "Sybil," "To Kill a Cop," "Wheels," and "Wilma." (*See* individual titles for credits.) The feature films are "Adam at 6 A.M." (1970) shown 7/24/78, "Breezy" (1973) shown 7/24/78, "Breakout" (1975) shown 8/14/78, "Car Wash" (1976) shown 1/9/78, "Death of Her Innocence" (1974—released theatrically as "Our Time") shown 3/13/78, "Dirty Harry" (1972) shown 8/28/78, "Family Plot" (1976) shown 7/24/78, "Gable and Lombard" (1976) shown 9/19/77, "The Girl from Petrovka" (1974) shown 6/26/78, "The Godfather" (1972) and "The Godfather, Part II" (1974) shown on TV as "Mario Puzo's The Godfather: The Complete Novel for Television" on four successive nights beginning 11/12/77, "Midway" (1976) shown 2/6/78, "The War Between the Men and Women" (1972) shown 3/20/78, "The Wind and the Lion" (1975) shown 4/3/78.

952 NBC Movie of the Week   NBC
Program Type Feature Film Series – TV Movie Series
2 hours (generally). Season premiere: 12/27/77. A combination of made-for-TV movies and theatrically released feature films. The made-for-TV movies are "The Beasts Are in the Streets," "The Great Wallendas," "Lacy and the Mississippi Queen," "The Last of the Mohicans," "Peter Lundy and the Medicine Hat Stallion," "Pine Canyon Is Burning," and "Terraces." (*See* individual titles for credits.) The feature films are "Adventures of Frontier Freemont" (1976) shown 8/2/78, "Against a Crooked Sky" (1975) shown 12/25/77, "Day of the Dolphin" (1973) shown 6/25/77 and repeated 8/30/78, "Mountain Man" (1976) shown 2/15/78, "Rooster Cogburn" (1975) shown 5/24/78, "Starship Invasions" (1978) shown 9/15/78, "Who Is Harry Kellerman, and Why Is He Saying Those Terrible Things About Me?" (1971) shown 4/12/78, "Willy Wonka and the Chocolate Factory" (1971) shown 1/15/78 and repeated 8/23/78.

953   **NBC News Update**   NBC
Program Type News Series
60 seconds. Daily. Premiere date: 8/6/75. Continuous. Lloyd Dobyns is anchor Monday–Friday. Originates from Washington, DC, on Saturday and Sunday with various newscasters. John Schubeck is anchor in the West.
Company NBC News
Anchors Lloyd Dobyns, John Schubeck

954   **NBC News Update (Daytime)**   NBC
Program Type News Series
60 seconds each. Mondays–Fridays. Premiere date: 1/3/77.
Company NBC News
Anchors Jane Pauley, Edwin Newman, Chuck Scarborough

955   **NBC Nightly News**   NBC
Program Type News Series
30 minutes. Mondays–Fridays. Premiere date: 8/1/70. Continuous.
Executive Producer Joseph Angotti, Herb Dudnick as of 2/21/78.
Producers Herb Dudnick, Harry Griggs, Alfred Robbins, William Wheatley, William Chesleigh as of 2/21/78.
Company NBC News
Director Norman Cook
Anchors John Chancellor, David Brinkley

956   **NBC Novel for Television**   NBC
Program Type TV Movie Series
Times vary. Premiere date: 10/16/77. TV movies based on novels: "Aspen," "Dark Secret of Harvest Home," "Loose Change," "79 Park Avenue," and "Wheels." (*See* individual titles for credits.)

957   **NBC Reports/NBC News Special**
NBC
Program Type Documentary/Informational Series
Live and taped coverage of special events and reports. Programs shown during the 1977–78 season are: "Bakke Case," "Escape from Madness," "The Final Tribute," "Gerald R. Ford: Presidential Decisions," "Henry Kissinger: On the Record," "I Want It All Now," "Interview with Prime Minister Begin," "Land of Hype and Glory," "The Loyal Opposition," " 'Mad as Hell' - The Taxpayers' Revolt," "Medicine in America: Life, Death and Dollars," "Pope John Paul I: The Ministry Begins," "Pope John Paul I and the Church," "President Carter's 9-day Trip to Europe and the Middle East," "President Carter's Vacation/Grand Teton Park," "The President in Berlin: A Town Meeting," "Resig-

nation of Bert Lance," "Sadat's Visit to Israel," "Special Report on the Fighting in the Middle East," "Spying for Uncle Sam," "State of the Union Address," "Trouble in Coal Country," and "Wherever We Lodge." (*See* individual titles for credits.)

958   **NBC Saturday Night at the Movies**
NBC
Program Type Feature Film Series – TV
  Movie Series
2 hours (generally). Saturdays. Season premiere: 9/17/77. A combination of made-for-TV movies and theatrically released feature films. The TV movies are "Aspen," "Columbo," "Come Back Little Sheba," "The Courage and the Passion," "Emergency!," "The Ghost of Flight 401," "Hunters of the Reef," "In the Matter of Karen Ann Quinlan," "The Incredible Rocky Mountain Race," "Lacy and the Mississippi Queen," "Police Story: Day of Terror, Night of Fear," "Police Story: River of Promises," "The Rhinemann Exchange," "Ring of Passion," "A Sensitive, Passionate Man," "Sex and the Married Woman," "Sharon: Portrait of a Mistress," "Standing Tall," and "The War between the Tates." (*See* individual titles for credits.) The feature films are "Airport '75" (1974) shown 4/22/78, "Alice Doesn't Live Here Anymore" (1975) shown 5/6/78, "Family Plot" (1976) shown 11/26/77, "Farewell My Lovely" (1975) shown 2/11/78, "Gable and Lombard" (1976) shown 9/2/78 "The Golden Heist" (1975) shown 8/12/78, "Hail Hero!" (1969) shown 4/29/78, "Hard Times" (1975) shown 9/24/77 "The Hindenburg" (1975) shown 7/8/78, " In Search of Noah's Ark" (1976) shown 12/24/77, "King Kong" (1976) shown 9/6/78 and 9/17/78, "The Land That Time Forgot" (1975) shown 8/5/78, "Little Big Man" (1970) shown 10/22/77, "McQ" (1974) shown 4/8/78, "Monte Walsh" (1970) shown 10/29/77, "My Name Is Nobody" (1974) shown 4/1/78, "Rafferty and the Highway Hustlers" (1975) shown 6/3/78, "The Reivers" (1969) shown 10/1/77, "Rio Lobo" (1970) shown 10/8/77 and repeated 3/18/78, "Russian Roulette" (1975) shown 3/11/78, "Something Big" (1971) shown 10/15/77 and repeated 8/19/78, "Stranger in the House" (1975) shown 1/28/78, and "W.C. Fields and Me" (1976) shown 12/10/77.

959   **NBC Saturday Night News**   NBC
Program Type News Series
30 minutes. Saturdays. Continuous.
Executive Producer Joseph Angotti
Producers Herb Dudnick, Harry Griggs, Alfred Robbins, William Wheatley
Company NBC News

Director Norman Cook
Anchor John Hart

960 NBC Special on Middle East Fighting NBC
Program Type News Special
30 minutes. Special report on the Israeli invasion of South Lebanon.
Executive Producer Gordon Manning
Company NBC News
Anchor Edwin Newman

961 NBC Sunday Night News NBC
Program Type News Series
30 minutes. Sundays. Continuous.
Executive Producer Joseph Angotti
Producers Herb Dudnick, Harry Griggs, Alfred Robbins, William Wheatley
Company NBC News
Director Norman Cook
Anchor Jessica Savitch as of 11/6/77.

962 NBC Tuesday Movie of the Week NBC
Program Type TV Movie Series
2 hours (generally). Tuesdays. Season premiere: 9/13/77. Made-for-TV movies: "The Girl in the Empty Grave," "79 Park Avenue," and "Sex and the Married Woman." (*See* individual titles for credits.)

963 NBC Wednesday Night at the Movies NBC
Program Type Feature Film Series – TV Movie Series
2 hours (generally). Wednesdays. Season premiere: 11/30/77. A combination of made-for-TV movies and theatrically released feature films. The TV movies are: "The Beasts Are in the Streets," "The Clone Master" and "Crisis in Sun Vally." (*See* individual titles for credits.) The feature films are "The Adventures of Frontier Freemont" (1976) shown 2/2/78; "Earthquake" (1974) shown 11/30/77; "Rooster Cogburn" (1975) shown 5/24/78; "Who Is Harry Kellerman and Why Is He Saying those Terrible Things about Me?" (1971) shown 4/12/78.

964 NBC World Premiere Movies NBC
Program Type TV Movie Series
2 hours. Premiere date: 9/12/77. Times vary. Made-for-TV movies shown during the 1977–78 season are "Amelia Earhart," "The Awakening Land: The Saga of an American Woman," "Billy: Portrait of a Street Kid," "Christmas Miracle in Caulfield U.S.A.,", "The Deadly Game," "A Family Upside Down," "The Ghost

of Flight 401," "The Great Wallendas," "In the Matter of Karen Ann Quinlan," "Just a Little Inconvenience," "Just Me and You," "Killer on Board," "Killing Stone," "Little Mo," "Loves's Dark Ride," "Murder in Peyton Place," "The Night They Took Miss Beautiful," "Nowhere to Run," "The Other Side of Hell," "Peter Benchley's Mysteries of the Deep," "Ring of Passion," "Scott Joplin: King of Ragtime," "Sergeant Matlovich Versus the U.S. Air Force," "Sharon: Portrait of a Mistress," "Standing Tall," "The Storyteller," "Terraces," "To Kill a Cop," "Top Secret," "Wilma," and "Ziegfeld: The Man and His Women." (*See* individual titles for credits.)

965 NBC's Best Sellers NBC
Program Type Feature Film Specials
2 hours. Premiere date: 9/30/76. Season premiere: 7/2/78. Repeats of novels made into TV movies shown during 1977–78 season are: "Once an Eagle," "The Rhineman Exchange," and "Seventh Avenue," (*See* individual titles for credits)

966 NBC's Saturday Night Live NBC
Program Type Comedy Series
90 minutes. Saturdays. Premiere date: 10/11/75. Season premiere: 9/24/77. Live show from NBC's Studio 8H in New York with comedy built around a resident repertory company—the Not Ready for Prime Time Players—and each week's guest host. Created by Lorne Michaels.
Producer Lorne Michaels
Company NBC
Director Dave Wilson
Writers Dan Aykroyd, Anne Beatts, John Belushi, James Downey, Al Franken, Tom Davis, Lorne Michaels, Marilyn Suzanne Miller, Bill Murray, Michael O'Donoghue, Herb Sargent; Tom Schiller, Rosie Shuster, Alan Zweibel
Musical Director Howard Shore
Costume Designers Eugene and Franne Lee
Announcer Don Pardo
Repertory Company Dan Aykroyd, John Belushi, Jane Curtin, Garrett Morris, Bill Murray, Laraine Newman, Gilda Radner

967 NBC's Star Salute to 1978 NBC
Program Type Parades/Pageants/Awards Special
90 minutes. Premiere date: 1/1/78. Preview of TV programs for 1978, interviews with stars and look at Pasadena Tournament of Roses Parade.
Hosts Kelly Lange, Michael Landon
Announcer Bryant Gumbel

NCAA Basketball *See also* College
Basketball '78

968   NCAA Basketball Championship
                                    NBC
Program Type Sports Special
Live coverage of the NCAA championship be-
tween the Duke Blue Devils and the Kentucky
Wildcats 3/27/78 from the Checkerdome in St.
Louis, MO.
Producer George Finkel
Company NBC Sports
Director Harry Coyle
Announcers Curt Gowdy, Dick Enberg, Billy
Parker, Al McGuire

969   NCAA Basketball Semi-Finals NBC
Program Type Sports Special
Live coverage of doubleheader semifinals from
the Checkerdome in St. Louis, Mo., 3/25/78 be-
tween the University of Kentucky Wildcats and
the University of Arkansas Razarbacks and the
Duke University Blue Devils and the University
of Notre Dame Fighting Irish.
Producer George Finkel
Company NBC Sports and TVS
Director Harry Coyle
Announcers Dick Enberg, Curt Gowdy, Al
McGuire, Billy Packer

970   NCAA Basketball Tournament NBC
Program Type Sports Special
Live coverage of regional play-offs, semi-finals
and finals 3/11/78, 3/12/78 and 3/27/78.
Producer George Finkel
Company NBC Sports in association with TVS
Director Harry Coyle
Announcers Dick Enberg, Billy Packer, Al
McGuire

971   NCAA Football   ABC
Program Type Sports Special
30 minutes. 12/11/77. Twenty-five collegiate
All-Americans selected by the Football Writers
Association of America are highlighted.
Executive Producer Dennis Cryder
Coordinating Producer Ric LaCivita
Producer Bill Flemming
Company ABC Sports
Host Bill Flemming

**972   NCAA Football (NCAA Game of
the Week)**
Coordinating Producer Ric LaCivita
Producer Bill Flemming
Company ABC Sports
Host Bill Flemming

**973   NCAA Football (NCAA Game of
the Week)**   ABC
Program Type Limited Sports Series
Live coverage of national, regional and double-
header college football games. Saturdays. 12th
season premiere: 9/10/77. Last show of season:
12/3/77. Keith Jackson is the principal play-by-
play announcer. "NCAA Football" includes
coverage of the Pioneer Bowl, Grantland Rice
Bowl, Knute Rockne Bowl and Amos Alonzo
Stagg Bowl.
Executive Producer Roone Arledge
Producers Chuck Howard and others
Company ABC Sports
Directors Andy Sidaris and others
Play-by-Play Announcers Keith Jackson, Chris
Schenkel, Verne Lundquist, Chris Lincoln, Al
Michaels, Jim Lampley, Bill Flemming, Ron
Pinkney
Expert Commentators Ara Parseghian, Lee
Grosscup, Steve Davis, Rick Forzano, Ron
Johnson, Frank Broyles
Sideline Reporter Jim Lampley
Special Features Reporter Jim Lampley
Pre-Game/Halftime Host Bill Flemming

**974   Neil Diamond Special: I'm Glad
You're Here with Me Tonight**   NBC
Program Type Music/Dance Special
60 minutes. Premiere date: 11/17/77. Neil Dia-
mond, in concert at Woburn Abbey, England; on
location in Paris, France; and in Hollywood. FM
Stereo broadcast transmitted via 17 radio sta-
tions from New York to California at the same
time the special is telecast.
Executive Producer Jerry Weintraub
Producer Art Fisher
Company Arch Angel Productions and Art
Fisher Productions
Director Art Fisher
Writer Rod Warren
Star Neil Diamond

**975   Nestor, the Long-Eared Christmas
Donkey**   ABC
Program Type Animated Film Special
30 minutes. Premiere date: 12/3/78. Animated
film of the donkey who carried Mary to Bethle-
hem. Narrated and sung by Roger Miller. Music
arranged and conducted by Maury Laws. Music
and lyrics by Maury Laws and Jules Bass, respec-
tively, for songs, "Nestor, the Long-Eared
Christmas Donkey," and "Don't Laugh and
Make Somebody Cry."
                    VOICES
Tillie .... Brenda Vaccaro
Nestor .... Erik Stern
Nestor's mother .... Linda Gary
Olaf .... Paul Frees
Girl Donkey No. 1 .... Iris Rainer

Girl Donkey No. 2 .... Shelley Hines
Roman soldier .... Don Messick
Producers Arthur Rankin, Jr., Jules Bass
Directors Arthur Rankin, Jr., Jules Bass
Writer Romeo Muller
Sound John Curcio
Design Paul Coker, Jr.

976 New Adventures of Robin Hood
Syndicated
Program Type Children's Series
30 minutes. Premiere date: 4/19/78. Adventures of the thief of Sherwood Forest who robs from the rich to give to the poor.
Producer Robert D. Cardona
Company Trident Films Ltd
Director Peter Duffell
Writer Terry Nation
CAST
Robin Hood .... Barry Andrews
Maid Marion .... Briony McRoberts
Prince John .... Michael Culver

977 New Adventures of Wonder Woman
CBS
Program Type Drama Series
60 minutes. Fridays. Premiere date: 10/13/76 on ABC. Premiere on CBS: 9/16/78 (90 minute special). Last show on ABC: 7/30/77. Adventures of Amazon princess from Paradise Island fighting the Nazis during World War II. Based on the comic book characters created by Charles Moulton and developed for television by Stanley Ralph Ross in three specials which aired during the 1975–76 season. "Wonder Woman" music by Charles Fox; lyrics by Norman Gimbel.
Executive Producers Douglas S. Cramer; W. L. Baumes
Producer Mark Rodgers
Company Douglas S. Cramer Company in association with Warner Bros. Television
Directors Various
Writers Various
CAST
Wonder Woman/Diana Prince .... Lynda Carter
Maj. Steve Trevor .... Lyle Waggoner
Joe Atkinson .... Normann Burton

978 The New Archies/Sabrina Hour/Superwitch/The Bang–Shang Lalapalooza Show
NBC
Program Type Animated Film Series
60 minutes. Premiere: 9/10/77. Became two half-hour shows, 12/10/77, called "Superwitch" and "The Bang–Shang Lalapalooza Show." Last show: 1/28/78. Contemporary teenage attitudes and aspects of teenage life. Based on comic characters created by John L. Goldwater and originally designed by Bob Montana. Sabrina is a teenage sorceress.

Executive Producers Lou Scheimer, Norm Prescott
Producer Don Christensen
Company Filmation Studios
Writers Various
Animation Directors Rudy Larriva, Marsh Lamore, Lou Zukor, Gwen Wetzler, Hal Sutherland
Voices Dallas McKennon, Howard Morris, John Irwin, Jane Webb, Jose Flores

979 The New England Conservatory Ragtime Ensemble and the Katherine Dunham Dancers
In Performance at Wolf Trap   PBS
Program Type Music/Dance Special
60 minutes. Premiere date: 11/3/75. Repeat date: 7/9/78. A performance of American ragtime music and dance performed at the Wolf Trap Farm Park in Arlington, Va. by the New England Conservatory Ragtime Ensemble and the Katherine Dunham Dancers. Program made possible by a grant from the Atlantic Richfield Company.
Executive Producer David Prowitt
Producer Ruth Leon
Company WETA-TV/Washington, DC
Director Clark Santee
Conductor Gunther Schuller
Choreographer Katherine Dunham
Hosts Beverly Sills, David Prowitt

980 The New High Rollers   NBC
Program Type Game/Audience Participation Series
30 minutes. Monday–Friday. Premiere date: 4/24/78. New Version of "High Rollers" shown 7/1/74–6/11/76.
Host Alex Trebek

981 The New Jokers Wild   Syndicated
Program Type Game/Audience Participation Series
30 minutes. Premiere date: 9/77.
Company Jack Barry & Dan Enright Production
Executive-in-Charge Jim Karayn

982 The New Maverick
The ABC Sunday Night Movie   ABC
Program Type TV Movie
2 hours. Premiere date: 9/3/78. Western crime-drama about the Maverick brothers. Music composed and conducted by John Rubinstein. Filmed at Old Tucson, Arizona.
Executive Producer Meta Rosenberg
Producer Bob Foster
Company Warner Bros. Television
Director Hy Averback

The New Maverick *Continued*
Writer Juanita Bartlett
Art Director John Jefferies
CAST
Bret Maverick .... James Garner
Ben Maverick .... Charles Frank
Bart Maverick .... Jack Kelly
Nell .... Susan Blanchard
Judge Crupper .... Eugene Roche
Poker Alice .... Susan Sullivan
Vinnie .... George Loros
Leveque .... Woodrow Parfrey
Dobie .... Gary Allen
Mrs. Crupper .... Helen Paige Camp
Homer .... Jack Garner
Lambert .... Graham Jarvis

983   New Orleans
CBS Reports   CBS
Program Type Documentary/Informational
Special
Premiere date: 1/24/78. The economics of the
"New South" in New Orleans in relationship to
old social problems.
Executive Producer Howard Stringer
Producer Janet Roach
Company CBS News
Reporter Bill Moyers

**984   New Orleans Concerto for Piano
and Orchestra**   PBS
Program Type Music/Dance Special
60 minutes. Premiere date: 2/28/78. Roger
Dickerson traces the development of the concerto from its inception to its premiere in New
Orleans in January 1977. Pianist Leon Bates
solos with the New Orleans Symphony Orchestra; conducted by Werner Torkanowsky; soprano soloist is Marilyn Thomas Bernard. Program made possible by grants from the National
Endowment for the Humanities and the Corporation for Public Broadcasting.
Company Institute for Services to Education,
Washington, DC and WETA-TV/Washing-
ton.

985   The New Tic Tac Dough   CBS
Program Type Game/Audience Participation
Series
30 minutes. Premiere date: 7/3/78. Regeneration
of "Tic Tac Dough" broadcast from 1956–1959.
Supervising Producer Ron Greenberg
Company Jack Barry/Dan Enright Production
Director Richard Kline
Editorial Supervisor Howard Kuperberg
Host Wink Martindale

986   The New Truth or Consequences
Syndicated
Program Type Game/Audience Participation
Series
30 minutes. Premiere date: 10/15/77.
Company A Ralph Edwards Production
Distributor Metromedia Productions
Host Bob Hilton

**987   New Year's Eve with Guy
Lombardo's Royal Canadians**   CBS
Program Type Music/Dance Special
90 minutes. Premiere date: 12/31/77. 49th con-
secutive broadcast with Victor Lombardo now
conducting live from the Waldrof Astoria Hotel
and Times Square in New York City.
Executive Producer Kevin O'Sullivan
Producer Albert Hartigan
Company Worldvision Enterprises Inc. in associ-
ation with CBS-TV
Director Robert Myhrum
Stars Guy Lombardo's Royal Canadians
Guest Stars Leslie Uggams, Paul Williams
Times Square Host Lee Jordan

988   New Year's Rockin' Eve 1978   ABC
Program Type Music/Dance Special
90 minutes. Premiere date: 12/31/77. Live New
Year's Eve celebration from Hollywood in Los
Angeles and Times Square in New York City.
Executive Producer Dick Clark
Producers Larry Klein, Barry Glaser
Company dick clark teleshows, inc.
Director Barry Glaser
Writer Robert Arthur
Hosts Dick Clark, Suzanne Somers, Robert
Hegyes
Guests Crystal Gayle, K.C. and The Sunshine
Band, Johnny Rivers, Andy Gibb, The Ohio
Players

Newman's Law *See* The ABC Sunday
Night Movie

989   Newsbreak   CBS
Program Type News Series
60 seconds. Nightly. Premiere date: 1/1/77.
Continuous. Nightly 60-second news headline
service.
Producer Ralph Paskman
Company CBS News
Anchors Morton Dean (Sundays–Fridays), Ste-
phani Shelton (Saturdays)

The Next Man *See* The CBS Wednesday
Night Movies

990 The Next Step Beyond Syndicated
Program Type Drama Series
30 minutes. Premiere date: 1/5/78. Series dramatizes occurrences which are beyond the grasp of present-day explanation.
Executive Producer Collier Young
Producer Alan Jay Factor
Company Factor-Newland Productions
Director John Newland
Writer Merwin Gerard
Host John Newland

991 NFC Championship CBS
Program Type Sports Special
3 hours. Live coverage of the National Football Conference Championship game between the Minnesota Vikings and the Dallas Cowboys from Texas Stadium, Irving, TX 1/1/78.
Producer Chuck Milton
Company CBS Sports
Director Sandy Grossman
Announcer Vin Scully
Analyst Alex Hawkins

992 NFC Play-Offs (Game I) CBS
Program Type Sports Special
3 hours. Live coverage of the National Football Conference play-off between the Chicago Bears and the Dallas Cowboys from Texas Stadium, Irving, TX 12/26/77.
Producer Chuck Milton
Company CBS Sports
Director Sandy Grossman
Announcer Pat Summerall
Analyst Tom Brookshier

993 NFC Play-Offs (Game II) CBS
Program Type Sports Special
3 hours. Live coverage of the National Football Conference play-off between the Minnesota Vikings and the Los Angeles Rams from Los Angeles Memorial Coliseum, Los Angeles, CA 12/26/77.
Producer Bob Stenner
Company CBS Sports
Director Tony Verna
Announcer Vin Scully
Analyst Alex Hawkins

994 NFL Game of the Week NBC
Program Type Sports Series
Live coverage of 93 regular-season National Football League games including eight doubleheaders. Season premiere: 9/18/77. Last regular season game: 12/18/77.
Executive Producer Don Ohlmeyer
Producers Ted Nathanson, George Finkel, Ken Edmundson, John Kerwin, Sam Kirshman, Roy Hammerman, David Stern, Larry Cirillo, Jim Marooney, Dick Auerbach, Mike Weisman
Company NBC Sports
Directors Ted Nathanson, John Gonzalez, Dick Cline, Jim Cross, Harry Coyle, Barry Stoddard, Ken Fouts, Dave Caldwell
Announcers Marv Albert, Jack Buck, Dick Enberg, Curt Gowdy, Charlie Jones, Stu Nahan, Jay Randolph, Jim Simpson, Dick Stockton, Sam Nover
Analysts Lionel Aldridge, John Brodie, Len Dawson, Mike Haffner, Jimmy Johnson, Floyd Little, Paul Maguire, Merlin Olsen, Andy Russell, Ed Podolak, Bob Trumphy, Paul Warfield

995 NFL on CBS CBS
Program Type Limited Sports Series
3 hours. Sundays (some Saturdays). 22nd season premiere: 9/18/77. Last regular show: 12/18/77. Live coverage of 88 regular-season national and regional games.
Producer Various
Company CBS Sports
Directors Various
Announcers Pat Summerall, Frank Glieber, Gary Bender, Lindsey Nelson, Don Criqui, Vin Scully, Jim Thacker, Bob Costas, Tim Ryan
Analysts Tom Brookshier, Alex Hawkins, Johnny Unitas, Sonny Jurgensen, Johnny Morris, Emerson Boozer, Paul Hornung, Tom Matte, Nick Buoniconti, Jim Brown, Roy Jefferson

996 NFL Pre-Season Games (ABC) ABC
Program Type Sports Special
Live coverage of three pre-season NFL football games on 7/29/78, 8/18/78, and 8/25/78.
Executive Producer Roone Arledge
Producer Dennis Lewin
Company ABC Sports
Director Chet Forte

997 NFL Pre-Season Games (NBC)
NBC
Program Type Sports Special
Live coverage of two pre-season football games 8/20/78 and 8/26/78.
Executive Producer Don Ohlmeyer
Producers George Finkel, Ted Nathanson, Mike Weisman
Company NBC Sports
Directors Ted Nathanson, Ken Fouts
Announcers Curt Gowdy, John Brodie

998   NFL '77   NBC
Program Type Sports Series
30 minutes. Premiere date: 9/18/77. Pre-game, half-time and post-game adjunct to NFL games featuring STATZ, the computerized robot who serves as the ace handicapper and forecaster on NBC Sports.
Executive Producer Don Ohlmeyer
Producer Larry Merchant, Bill Fitts
Company NBC Sports
Hosts Lee Leonard, Bryant Gumbel, Regina Haskins
Commentators Larry Merchant, Fran Tarkenton

999   The NFL Today   CBS
Program Type Limited Sports Series
Premiere: 9/18/77. Last show of season: 12/18/77. Live pre-game, half-time and post-game show presented during regular season games and National Football Conference play-offs and championship. Series covers the major NFL games played that day, other sports events during the weekend, and features such as "The Greek's Grapevine" with Jimmy "The Greek" Snyder.
Producers Mike Pearl
Company CBS Television Network Sports
Director Bob Fishman
Host Brent Musburger, Irv Cross, Phyllis George, Jack Whitaker
Analyst Jimmy "The Greek" Snyder

1000   Night Cries
The ABC Sunday Night Movie   ABC
Program Type TV Movie
2 hours. Premiere date: 1/29/78. Drama about a young mother. Music by Paul Chihara.
Executive Producers Dick Berg, Charles Fries
Producer David Manson
Company A Stonehenge Production in association with Charles Fries Productions
Director Richard Lang
Writer Brian Taggert
Art Director Bill Ross
CAST
Jeannie Haskins .... Susan Saint James
Dr. Whelan .... William Conrad
Mitch Haskin .... Michael Parks
Nurse Green .... Dolores Dorn
Mrs. Delesande .... Cathleen Nesbitt
Peggy Barton .... Jamie Smith Jackson
Mrs. Thueson .... Diana Douglas
Mrs. Whitney .... Ellen Geer

Night Moves *See* CBS Special Movie Presentations

1001   Night of the Champions   CBS
Program Type Sports Special
Boxing special featuring two world championship bouts and two reigning Olympic champions 9/13/77. WBC world welterweight championship fight between Carlos Palomino and Everaldo Costa Azevedo; WBC featherweight bout between Danny Lopez and Jose Torres; Michael Spinks and Ray Elson; Howard Davis, Jr. and Arturo Pineda. Live from Los Angeles Olympic Auditorium.
Company CBS Sports

1002   The Night of the Empty Chairs
                                                     PBS
Program Type Dramatic Special
60 minutes. Premiere date: 7/15/78. Works of political prisoners and dissidents performed by Joel Grey, Lauren Bacall, Art Buchwald, Richard Widmark, Leonard Bernstein, Arthur Miller, and Vincent Gardenia. Created by Art Buchwald. Produced for Amnesty International, USA, by Arts, Letters and Politics, Inc. with Jamie Bernstein.
Producer Anthony L. Mahn
Company WNET-TV/New York

1003   The Night They Took Miss Beautiful
NBC Monday Night at the Movies/NBC World Premiere Movie   NBC
Program Type Dramatic Special
2 hours. Premiere date: 10/24/77. A terrorist group hijacks an airliner with five beauty pageant finalists abroad.
Director Robert Michael Lewis
Writer George Lefferts
CAST
Marv .... Phil Silvers
Kate .... Stella Stevens
Layla ....Sheree North
Mike ....Chuck Connors
Rolly .... Henry Gibson
Paul .... Gary Collins
Damon .... Peter Haskell
Smitty .... William H. Bassett
Momma .... Marcia Lewis
Omar .... Gregory Sierra
Buck .... Jonathan Banks
Hector .... Santos Morales
Barney .... Burke Byrnes
Cindy .... Karen Lamm
April ....Rosanne Katon
Toni .... Suzette Carroll

Night Watch *See* ABC Tuesday Movie of the Week

1004 **A Night with the Heavyweights**
NBC
Program Type Sports Special
3 hours. Live coverage of four 10-round heavyweight bouts from Caesars Palace in Las Vegas 9/14/77: Ken Norton vs. Lorenzo Zanon, Jimmy Young vs. Jody Ballard, Ron Lyle vs. Stan Ward and Larry Holmes vs. Fred Houpe.
Producer Ted Nathanson
Co-Producer Jim Marooney
Company NBC Sports
Director Ted Nathanson
Host Joe Garagiola
Announcer Stu Nahan
Analyst Bryant Gumbel
Special Reporters Larry Merchant, Marv Albert
Commentators Muhammad Ali, Earnie Shavers

The 1978 Miss Universe Pageant *See* Miss Universe Beauty Pageant

1005 **1968**
CBS
Program Type News Special
2 hours. Premiere date: 8/25/78. An assessment of the events of the year of 1968.
Executive Producer Perry Wolff
Producer Shareen Blair Brysac
Writer Perry Wolff
Film Editors John Dullaghan, Sarah Stein, Nobuko Oganesoff
Anchor Harry Reasoner

1006 **1968: A Crack in Time**
ABC
Program Type News Special
60 minutes. Premiere date: 6/11/78. News special on the events of one decade ago.
Executive Producer Jeff Gralnick
Producer Bruce Cohn
Company ABC News
Director Joel Tator
Writers Bruce Cohn, Frank Reynolds
Art Directors Scott G. Ritenour, Jr., Ken Davis
Hosts Cliff Robertson, Frank Reynolds

1007 **No Way to Run a Government** PBS
Program Type Public Affairs Special
60 minutes. Premiere date: 6/30/78. Explores the question of civil service reform.
Executive Producer Linda Winslow
Producer Gregg Ramshaw
Company WETA-TV/Washington, DC

1008 **Noah's Animals**
NBC
Program Type Animated Film Special
30 minutes. Premiere date: 4/5/76. Repeat date: 12/25/77. Adventures aboard the Ark, adapted

from the Bible story. Music by Michael Colicchio; lyrics by Wiley Gregory.
Executive Producer Charles G. Mortimer, Jr.
Company Shamus Culhane Productions, Inc. for Westfall Productions
Director Shamus Culhane
Writers Shamus Culhane, John Culhane
Voices Paul Soles, Judy Sinclair, Bonnie Brooks, Jay Nelson, Ruth Springford, Don Mason, Henry Ramer, Wendy Thatcher, Carl Banas, Jack Mather, Murray Westgate, Cardie Mortimer

1009 **The Norman Conquests**
Great Performances
PBS
Program Type Dramatic Special
Premiere date: 6/14/78. Play by Alan Ayckbourn shown in three parts: First part, 2 hours; second, 90 minutes; third, 2 hours. Comic trilogy about middle-class marriage. Each part is totally independent, yet all concern the same weekend in the country. Although the time span remains the same, each part takes place in a different area of the family home. Programs made possible by a grant from Exxon Corporation and by support from PBS stations.
Company Thames International Television and WNET-TV/New York
Director Herbert Wise
CAST
Norman .... Tom Conti
Annie .... Penelope Wilton
Ruth .... Fiona Walker
Sarah .... Penelope Keith
Reg .... Richard Briers
Tom .... David Troughton

1010 **North American Youth Soccer Championships**
PBS
Program Type Sports Special
2 hours. Coverage of soccer matches held in August 1977 in Tacoma, Washington shown 3/21/78.
Company KCPQ-TV/Tacoma
Announcer Bob Robertson

1011 **North Star: Mark di Suvero** PBS
Program Type Documentary/Informational Special
60 minutes. Premiere date: 7/18/78. Portrait of sculptor Mark di Suvero.
Producers Francois de Menil, Barbara Rose
Company WETA-TV/Washington

1012 **Nova**
PBS
Program Type Science/Nature Series
60 minutes. Wednesdays. Premiere date: 3/3/74. Fifth season premiere: 1/4/78. Repeats began 7/5/78. Weekly series focusing on a variety of

Nova *Continued*
science-related topics produced with the advice and cooperation of the American Association for the Advancement of Science. Captioned for the hearing-impaired. Series made possible by grants from Exxon Corporation, the National Science Foundation, Public Television Stations, the Ford Foundation and the Corporation for Public Broadcasting.
Executive Producer John Angier
Producers Various
Company WGBH-TV/Boston

1013   Now You Are Light   CBS
Program Type Religious/Cultural Special
60 minutes. Premiere date: 4/30/78. Selections from the Holy Week services of the Greek Orthodox Church.
Executive Producer Pamela Ilott
Producer Joseph Clement
Director Joseph K. Chomyn
Writer Leon Contos
Narrator Leon Contos

1014   Nowhere to Run
NBC Monday Night at the Movies/NBC
World Premiere Movie   NBC
Program Type Dramatic Special
2 hours. Premiere date: 1/16/78. Drama of a man who devises a winning blackjack system. Based on the novel by Charles Einstein.
Producer Jim Brynes
Company MTM Enterprises in association with NBC-TV
Director Richard Lang
Writer Jim Byrnes
CAST
Harry Adams .... David Janssen
Marian Adams .... Stefanie Powers
Herbie Stoltz .... Allen Garfield
Amy Kessler .... Linda Evans
Joe Anasto .... Anthony Eisley
Mother .... Neva Patterson
Father .... John Randolph
McEnerney .... James Keach
Charleen .... Ahna Capri

1015   The Nunundaga
ABC Children's Novel for Television   ABC
Program Type Children's Special
60 minutes. Premiere date: 12/3/77. Shown in two parts on 12/3/77 and 12/10/77. An Indian youth faces a challenge when his tribe, on the verge of starvation, has its sacred bow stolen by an enemy. Music by Andrew Belling. Director of Photography: Duke Callaghan. Filmed entirely in the Coronado National Memorial Grounds in Cochise County, Arizona.
Producer Edgar J. Scherick

Company Palomar Pictures International in association with 20th Century Fox Television
Director John Llewellyn Moxey
Writer I. C. Rapoport
Art Director Stewart W. Campbell
Film Editor John Martinelli
CAST
Painted Bear .... Ned Romero
Snake Eyes .... Guillermo San Juan
One Feather .... John War Eagle
Wind Song .... Monika Ramirez
Low Wolf .... Joe Renteria
Star Fire .... Victoria Racimo
White Bull .... Emilio Delgado
Yellow of the Fire .... Madeline Taylor Holmes
Back Eagle .... Richard Romancita
Night Crier .... Oscar Valdez

1016   The Nutcracker   CBS
Program Type Music/Dance Special
90 minutes. Premiere date: 12/16/77. The National Philharmonic orchestra conducted by Kenneth Schermerhorn. Puppets by E. J. Taylor.
Executive Producer Herman Krawitz
Producer Yanna Kroyt Brandt
Company Jodav Productions, Inc.
Director Tony Charmoli
Writer Yanna Kroyt Brandt
Costume Designer Frank Thompson
Narrator Norman Rose
CAST
Drosselmeyer .... Alexander Minz
Mr. Stahlbaum .... Gayle Young
Mrs. Stahlbaum .... Sallie Wilson
Clara .... Gelsey Kirkland
Fritz .... Warren Conover
Harlequin .... Gregory Osborne
Doll .... Rebecca Wright
Moor .... George De La Pena
Nutcracker/Prince .... Mikhail Baryshnikov
King of Mice .... Marcos Paredes
Snowflake Waltz Soloists .... Cynthia Harvey,
Jolinda Menendez
Court Buffoons .... Rodney Gustafson, Eric Nesbitt,
Charles Maple, Gregory Osborne
Spanish Dance .... Jolinda Menendez, Clark Tippet
Chinese Dance .... Hilda Morales, Kirk Peterson
Shepherds .... Aurea Hammerli, Warren Conover
Russian Dance ... George De La Pena, Roman Jasinski
Waltz Soloists ...... Nanette Glushak, Marie Johansson,
Richard Schafer, Victor Barbee

1017   The Nutcracker
In Performance at Wolf Trap   PBS
Program Type Music/Dance Special
60 minutes. Premiere date: 12/23/74. Repeat date: 12/20/77. British actress Rohan McCullough joins Andre Kostelanetz and the National Symphony Orchestra in a Christmas concert with music by Peter Tchaikovsky including "Romeo and Juliet," "The Coronation March," and the "Nutcracker Suite" (with verses by Og-

den Nash). Program made possible by a grant from the Atlantic Richfield Company.
Company WETA-TV/Washington, DC

1018 The Nutcracker   NBC
Program Type Music/Dance Special
90 minutes. Premiere date: 12/18/77. Ballet taped 9/23/77 at Moscow's Bolshoi Theatre. First act performed by Yekaterina Maximova and her husband Vladimir Vasiliev who injured a leg muscle. Performance continued with Nadia Pavlova and Vyacheslav Gordeyevin the leading roles. Betty Ford hosted; Mrs. Ford's script by Catherine Faulconer.
Producer Patrick Trese
Company Lothar Bock Associates and Gosteleradio-Moscow
Director Elena Maceret
Conductor Alexander Kopylov
Choreographer Yuri Gregorovich

1019 The Ocean City International Tennis Tournament   PBS
Program Type Sports Special
4 hours. Live coverage of the Ocean City, Maryland tennis tournament 2/26/78.
Producer John H. Davis
Company Maryland Center for Public Broadcasting

1020 Of Race and Blood   PBS
Program Type Documentary/Informational Special
90 minutes. Premiere date: 2/14/78. Repeat date: 7/25/78. Story behind the creation of Nazi art. Program made possible by grants from the Council for Public Television and the Corporation for Public Broadcasting.
Producer Jim Connolly
Company KRMA-TV/Denver
Director Jim Connolly
Writer Jim Connolly
Consultant Capt. Gordon Gilkey

1021 Off-Hollywood   NBC
Program Type Comedy Special
90 minutes. Premiere date: 1/14/78. Satirical exploration of contemporary California society.
Executive Producer Kenneth B. Belsky
Producer Mario Beguiristain
Company Pierre Cossett Production
Director Sterling Johnson
Writers David Garber, Kevin Hartigan, Mario Beguiristain, David Curry, Vic Dunlop, Christopher Durang, Marty Farrell, Peter Krikes, Steve Meerson, Chase Newhart, Frank Prendergast
Performers Glenn Daniels, Susan Elliot, Cyndy

James-Reese, Dizzy Llowell, Chase Newhart, Lorna Patterson

1022 Old Friends ... New Friends   PBS
Program Type Documentary/Informational Series
30 minutes. Premiere date: 4/15/78. Series repeats began: 6/3/78. 7-part Series about how people of various ages live and grow with one another. Series made possible by a grant from The Richard King Mellon Foundation.
Producer Arthur Barron
Company Family Communications, Inc. for WQED-TV/Pittsburgh
Director Arthur Barron
Host Fred Rogers
Features Hoagy Carmichael, William Wasson, Helen Hayes, Millie Jewett, Milton Berle, Joe Restivo, Nick Failla, Lesley Frost Ballantine, William Sloan Coffin, Jr., John Jackson

1023 Olivia   ABC
Program Type Music/Dance Special
60 minutes. Premiere date: 5/17/78. Musical segments produced by Jimmy Webb.
Executive Producer Lee Kramer
Producer Steve Binder
Company ONJ Television Productions, Inc. in association with Steve Binder Productions
Director Steve Binder
Writers Alan Thicke, Steve Binder, Susan Elliot, William F. Williams
Musical Director Dennis McCarthy
Choreographer Lester Wilson
Costume Designer Fleur Thiemeyer
Art Director Jim Tompkins
Star Olivia Newton-John
Guest Stars ABBA, Andy Gibb, The James Cleveland Choir

1024 On Death and Dying   NBC
Program Type Documentary/Informational Special
60 minutes. Premiere date: 11/24/74. Repeat date: 10/2/77. Interview with Dr. Elisabeth Kubler-Ross.
Executive Producer Doris Ann
Producer Martin Hoade
Company NBC Television Religious Programs Unit
Director Martin Hoade

1025 On Our Own   CBS
Program Type Comedy Series
30 minutes. Sundays. Premiere date: 10/9/77. Last show: 8/20/78. Story about two young women who work in a New York advertising agency. Created by Bob Randall.

On Our Own *Continued*
Executive Producer David Susskind
Producer Sam Denoff
Company Time-Life Television
Directors Various
Writers Various
CAST
Julia Peters .... Bess Armstrong
Maria Teresa Bonino .... Lynnie Greene
Toni McBain .... Gretchen Wyler
April Baxter .... Dixie Carter
Craig Boatwright .... Dan Resin
Eddie Barnes .... John Christopher Jones

1026   On Trial   Syndicated
Program Type Drama Series
30 minutes. Premiere date: 1/30/78. Court-room
drama series.
Executive Producer Alan Sloan
Producer Robert Justman
Company Alan Sloan Inc.
Director Joseph L. Scanlan
Writer Anthony Lawrence

1027   Once an Eagle
The Big Event/NBC's Best Seller/NBC
Monday Night at the Movies   NBC
Program Type Limited Series
6 hours. Premiere date: 12/9 and 12/16/76. Se-
ries repeated: 7/2/78.
Dramatization of the novel by Anton Myrer
about two Regular Army officers in the years
between 1918–1945. Filmed in part on locations
in the Napa Valley and Los Angeles, Calif. and
in Hawaii.
Executive Producer William Sackheim
Producer Peter S. Fischer
Company Universal Television in association
with NBC-TV
Directors E. W. Swackhamer, Richard Michaels
Writer Peter Fischer
CAST
Sam Damon .... Sam Elliott
Courtney Massengale .... Cliff Potts
Tommy Damon ....Darleen Carr
Emily Massengale .... Amy Irving
George Caldwell .... Glenn Ford
Lt. Merrick .... Clu Gulager
Marge Krisler ....Lynda Day George
Ben Krisler .... Robert Hogan
Donny Damon (as a boy) ....John Waldron
Jinny Massengale .... Melanie Griffith
Joe Brand .... Kario Salem
Donny Damon (as an adult) .... Andrew Stevens
Ryetower .... Kip Niven

1028   Once Upon a Brothers Grimm CBS
Program Type Children's Special
2 hours. Premiere date: 11/23/77. Story of the
brothers who collected legends that became
world-famous fairy tales. Original musical score

by Mitch Leigh (music) and Sammy Cahn (lyr-
ics).
Producers Bernard Rothman; Jack Wohl
Director Norman Campbell
Company Rothman/Wohl Productions
Writer Jean Holloway
Choreographer Ron Field
Costume Designer Bill Hargate
Art Director Ken Johnson
Set Decorator Robert Checci
CAST
Jacob Grimm .... Dean Jones
Wilhelm Grimm .... Paul Sand
Wood Nymph ....Betsy Beard
King of Hesse .... Sorrell Booke
Selfish and Mean .... Arte Johnson
Queen Astrid .... Ruth Buzzi

The Bremen Town Musicians
CAST
The Ass .... Don Correia
The Rooster .... Joe Giamalva
The Hound .... Gary Morgan
The Cat .... Maria Pogge

Cinderella
CAST
Cinderella .... Stephanie Steele
Fairy Godmother ....Corinne Conley
Prince Charming .... John McCook
Carriage Driver .... Gordon Connell

Hansel and Gretel
CAST
Gretel .... Mia Bendixsen
Hansel .... Todd Lookingland
Esmerelda .... Edie McClurg
Gingerbread Lady .... Chita Rivera

The Frog Prince
CAST
The King .... Ken Olfson
Princess ....Terri Garr

Little Red Riding Hood
CAST
Little Red Riding Hood .... Susan Silo
Wolf ....Cleavon Little
Grandmother .... Dean Jones

The King with Eight Daughters
CAST
Prime Minister ....Dan Tobin
Rumpelstiltskin .... Clive Revil

Sleeping Beauty
CAST
Sleeping Beauty ....Johnna Kirkland
The Prince ....John Clifford

The Mazurka
CAST
Dancers ....Los Angeles Ballet Company

1029   Once Upon a Classic   PBS
Program Type Drama Series
30 minutes/60 minutes. Thursdays. Premiere

date: 10/6/76. Season premiere: 10/8/77. Adaptations of literary classics for children plus modern-day original dramas. Programs presented during the 1977–78 season are: "Avalanche," "A Connecticut Yankee in King Arthur's Court," "'Copter Kids," "Lorna Doone," "Robin Hood," "Robin Hood Jr.," "Sky Pirates," and "What Katy Did." (*See* individual titles for credits.)

1030 One Day at a Time   CBS
Program Type Comedy Series
30 minutes. Tuesdays/Mondays (as of 1/30/78). Premiere date: 12/16/75. Third season premiere: 9/27/77. Series created by Whitney Blake and Allan Mannings and developed by Norman Lear. Comedy about a newly divorced mother of two teen-age daughters.
Executive Producers Norman Paul, Jack Elinson
Producers Dick Bensfield, Perry Grant
Company A Norman Lear T.A.T. Communications Company and Allwhit, Inc. Productions
Director Herbert Kenwith
Writers Various
CAST
Ann Romano .... Bonnie Franklin
Julie Cooper .... Mackenzie Phillips
Barbara Cooper .... Valerie Bertinelli
Dwayne Schneider .... Pat Harrington

1031 $100,000 Name That Tune
Syndicated
Program Type Game/Audience Participation Series
30 minutes. Weekly. Premiere date: 9/74. Fourth season premiere: 11/77. Evening version of daytime show that went off the air 1/3/75. Show created by Harry Salter for radio in 1951. Two contestants compete to name the songs being played. Changed name in the 1976–77 season to indicate top prize.
Executive Producer Ralph Edwards
Producer Ray Horl
Company A Ralph Edwards Production
Distributor Sandy Frank Station Syndication, Inc.
Director Richard Gottlieb
Writer Richard Gottlieb
Conductor Tommy Oliver
Host Tom Kennedy
Announcer John Harlan
Musicologist Harvey Bacal
Music Coordinator Richard Gottlieb

1032 $128,000 Question   Syndicated
Program Type Game/Audience Participation Series
30 minutes. Weekly. Premiere date: 9/76. Revival of the 1950s quiz show "The $64,000 Ques-

tion" created by Steve Carlin with unlikely experts in specific fields.
Executive Producer Steve Carlin
Producer Willie Stein
Company Cinelar Associates
Distributor Viacom International
Director Dick Schneider
Host Alex Trebek

1033 One Life to Live
Program Type Daytime Drama Series   ABC
45 minutes. Mondays–Fridays. Premiere date: 7/15/68. Continuous. Became 1-hour show 1/16/78. Set in Llanview, U.S.A. Created by Agnes Nixon. Cast list is alphabetical.
Producer Joseph Stuart
Company An ABC Television Network Presentation
Directors David Pressman, Peter Miner, Norman Hall
Head Writer Gordon Russell
Writers Sam Hall, Don Wallace, Peggy O'Shea
CAST
Marco Dane .... Gerald Anthony
Melinda Cramer .... Jane Badler
Luke Jackson .... Marshall Ingram
Dr. Jack Scott .... Arthur Burghardt
Edwina Lewis .... Margaret Clenck
Patricia Kendall .... Jacqueline Courtney
Dr. Pamela Shepherd .... Kathleen Devine
Paul Kendall .... Tom Fuccello
Dr. Will Vernon .... Tony George
Jenny Wolek .... Katherine Glass
Ina Hopkins .... Sally Gracie
Cathy Lord .... Jennifer Harmon
Sadie Gray .... Lillian Hayman
Carla Hall .... Ellen Holly
Vinnie Wolek .... Michael Ingram
Wanda Wolek .... Lee Lawson
Karen Wolek .... Judith Light
Tony Lord .... Philip MacHale
Anna Craig .... Kathleen Maguire
Dr. Dorian Lord .... Claire Malis
Samantha Vernon .... Julie Montgomery
Danny Wolek .... Eddie Moran
Joe Riley .... Lee Patterson
Dr. James Craig .... Nat Polen
Dr. Peter Janssen .... Jeffrey Pomerantz
Richard Abbott .... David Reilly
Talbot Huddleston .... Byron Sanders
Victoria Riley .... Erika Slezak
Dr. Larry Wolek .... Michael Storm
Rebecca Lee Hunt .... Jill Voight

1034 Only the Best   NBC
Program Type Sports Special
30 minutes. Premiere date: 3/11/78. A look at college basketball's finest preceding coverage of the 40th annual National Collegiate Basketball championship.
Company NBC Sports
Hosts Dick Enberg, Billy Packer, Al McGuire

1035 The Only Thing I Can't Do Is Hear   PBS
Program Type Documentary/Informational Special
30 minutes. Premiere date: 8/12/78. Documentary about innovative programs that help prepare deaf students for college.
Company WETA-TV/Washington, DC

1036 Opera Theater   PBS
Program Type Music/Dance Series
Times vary. Mondays. Premiere date: 4/27/76. Series repeated: 7/3/78. Series of operas and operettas in English. Shows seen during the 1977–78 season: "Albert Herring," "Falstaff," "The Flying Dutchman," "Gondoliers," "Santa Fe Opera," "Transformations," "Trouble in Tahiti," and "Yeoman of the Guard." (*See* individual titles for credits.)

1037 Operation Petticoat
Program Type Comedy Series   ABC
30 minutes. Saturdays. Premiere date: 9/17/77. (2-hour pilot shown 9/4/77.) Based on the 1959 motion picture and a story by Paul King and Joe Stone.
Executive Producer Leonard B. Stern
Producers David J. O'Connell, Si Rose
Company Heyday Productions and Universal Television
Directors John Astin, William Asher, Hollingsworth Morse
Writers Various
Story Editor John Fenton Murray
Art Director Edward Ruder
Cinematographer Sy Hoffberg
CAST
Lt. Cmdr. Matthew Sherman .... John Astin
Lt. Nick Holden .... Richard Gilliland
Maj. Edna Howard .... Yvonne Wilder
Yeoman Hunkle .... Richard Brestoff
Ensign Stovall .... Christopher J. Brown
Seaman Dooley .... Kraig Cassity
Molumphrey .... Wayne Long
Williams .... Richard Marion
Seaman Gossett .... Michael Mazes
Tostin .... Jack Murdock
Seaman Horwich .... Peter Schuck
Lt. Watson .... Raymond Singer
Seaman Broom .... Jim Varney
Lt. Crandall .... Melinda Naud
Lt. Duran .... Jamie Lee Curtis
Lt. Colfax .... Dorrie Thomson
Lt. Reid .... Bond Gideon
Ramon Gallardo .... Jesse Dizon

1038 Operation Runaway   NBC
Program Type Limited Series
Premiere date: 4/27/78 (2 hours). Thursdays. Last show: 8/31/78. Specialist deals with teen-agers and young adults who become runaways and/or missing persons.
Executive Producer William Robert Yates
Producer Mark Rodgers
Company Quinn Martin
Directors Various
Writers Various
CAST
David McKay .... Robert Reed

1039 Orange Bowl   NBC
Program Type Sports Special
Live coverage of the 46th Orange Bowl game between the Oklahoma Sooners and the Arkansas Razorbacks from Miami, Fla. 1/2/78.
Executive Producer Scotty Connal
Producer Mike Weisman
Company NBC Sports
Director Ken Fouts
Announcers Jim Simpson, Merlin Olsen

1040 The Oregon Trail   NBC
Program Type Drama Series
60 minutes. Wednesdays. Premiere date: 9/21/77 (as 2-hour special). Last show: 11/30/77. Story of westward-bound pioneers and their adventures. Created by Michael Gleason.
Executive Producer Michael Gleason
Supervising Producer Richard Collins
Producer Carl Vitale
Company Universal Television in association with NBC-TV
Directors Various
Writers Various
Art Director Fred Tuch
CAST
Evan Thorpe .... Rod Taylor
Margaret Devlin .... Darleen Carr
Luther Sprague .... Charles Napier
Andrew Thorpe .... Andrew Stevens
William Thorpe .... Tony Becker
Rachel Thorpe .... Gina Marie Smika

1041 The Originals: Women in Art PBS
Program Type Educational/Cultural Series
30 minutes. Mondays. Premiere date: 2/6/78. Six 30-minute shows and one 60-minute show. Focuses on the richness and diversity of the art of American women artists. Series made possible by grants from the National Endowment for the Arts and the Corporation for Public Broadcasting. The artists featured are: Alice Neel, Georgia O'Keeffe, Helen Frankenthaler, Mary Cassatt, Louise Nevelson, Betye Saar and handcrafts of women of the 18th and 19th century.
Executive Producer Perry Miller Adato
Company WNET-TV/New York
Directors Nancy Baer, Susan Fanshel, Jill Godmilow

Filmmakers Nancy Baer, Mirra Bank, Perry Miller Adato, Suzanne Bauman

1042 The Originals: The Writer in America   PBS
Program Type Educational/Cultural Series
30 minutes. Mondays. Premiere date: 3/20/78. Ten shows documenting the lives of eight contemporary writers. The writers are: Janet Flanner, John Gardner, Toni Morrison, Wright Morris, Eudora Welty, Ross MacDonald, Muriel Rukeyser, and Robert Duncan. Series made possible by a grant from the National Endowment for the Arts, the Corporation for Public Broadcasting and the Robert Sterling Clark Foundation.
Producer Richard O. Moore
Company WNET-TV/New York
Director Richard O. Moore

1043 Oscar Presents John Wayne and the War Movies   ABC
Program Type Documentary/Informational Special
2 hours. Premiere date: 11/27/77. John Wayne hosts special that traces the story of World War II as depicted by the motion picture industry. Music by Nelson Riddle.
Producer Alan Landsburg
Associate Producer Harrison Engle
Director Mel Stuart
Writer Charles Champlin
Art Director Bill Morris
Guest Hosts John Wayne, Jeff Bridges, Louise Fletcher, Walter Matthau, Brenda Vaccaro

1044 Oscar's Best Actors   ABC
Program Type Documentary/Informational Special
60 minutes. Premiere date: 5/23/78. Special honoring the 50 men who have won the Academy Award for Best Actor.
Producer Howard W. Koch
Company The Academy of Motion Picture Arts and Sciences
Director Howard W. Koch
Writers William Ludwig, Leonard Spigelgass
Hosts William Holden, Gene Kelly, Marsha Mason, John Wayne

1045 The Osmond Brothers Special ABC
Program Type Music/Comedy/Variety Special
60 minutes. Premiere date: 5/26/78.
Executive Producers The Osmond Brothers
Producer Art Fisher
Director Art Fisher
Writers Jim Parker, Michael Kagan
Musical Director Bob Rozario

Costume Designer Marie Osmond
Art Director Bill Bohnert
Stars Alan Osmond, Wayne Osmond, Merrill Osmond, Jay Osmond
Guest Stars Bob Hope, Crystal Gayle, Andy Gibb, Jimmie Walker, The Dallas Cowboys Cheerleaders, Gunda Reid, Johnny Ryder, The Knudsen Brothers
Dancers Kim Sullivan, Ellen Mathias

1046 The Other Side of Hell
The Big Event/NBC World Premiere Movie
                                                    NBC
Program Type TV Movie
2 hours. Premiere date: 1/17/78. Man tries to win his release from a hospital for the criminally insane.
Producers James T. Aubrey, Ronald Lyon
Company Aubrey/Lyon, Inc. in association with NBC-TV
Director Jan Kadar
Writer Leon Tokatyan
CAST
Frank Dole .... Alan Arkin
Jim Baker .... Roger Mosley
Johnson .... Morgan Woodward
Donahue .... Seamon Glass
The Rev. Wyler .... Richard Hawkins
Pudgy Man .... Al Checco
Morelli ....Leonard Stone
Miller ....Shay Duffin
Carlo ....Tony Karloff

1047 Otto: Zoo Gorilla   PBS
Program Type Documentary/Informational Special
60 minutes. Premiere date: 8/30/78. Documentary of the Lincoln Park Zoo in Chicago and the move of the zoo's 27 great apes to a new primate house.
Company WTTW-TV/Chicago

Our Daily Bread *See* PBS Movie Theater

1048 Our Mutual Friend
Masterpiece Theatre   PBS
Program Type Limited Series
60 minutes. Premiere date: 4/16/78. Drama adapted from last completed work of Charles Dickens. Presented by WGBH-TV/Boston; produced by Joan Sullivan. Series made possible by a grant from Mobil Oil Corporation. Music composed and conducted by Carl Davis.
Producer Martin Lisemore
Company BBC/Time-Life Productions
Director Peter Hammond
Story Editor Betty Willingale
Writers Julia Jones, Donald Churchill

Our Mutual Friend *Continued*
Designer Chris Pemsel
Host Alistair Cooke
CAST

Bella Wilfer	Jane Seymour
John Rokesmith	John McEnery
Nicodemus Boffin	Leo McKern
Mrs. Boffin	Kathleen Harrison
Lizzie	Lesley Dunlop
Charley Hexam	Jack Wild
Jenny Wren	Polly James
Mortimer Lightwood	Andrew Ray
Silas Wegg	Alfie Bass

1049 Our Town
Bell System Special   NBC
Program Type Dramatic Special
2 hours. Premiere date: 5/30/77. Repeat date: 6/5/78. The Pulitzer Prize-winning play by Thornton Wilder in a production specially designed for TV, about people in a small New England town.
Executive Producer Saul Jaffe
Producer George Schaefer
Company Hartwest Productions, Inc.
Director George Schaefer
Writer Thornton Wilder
Costume Designer Noel Taylor
Production Designer Roy Christopher
Creative Consultant Robert Hartung
CAST

Stage Manager	Hal Holbrook
Dr. Gibbs	Ned Beatty
Mrs. Webb	Barbara Bel Geddes
George Gibbs	Robby Benson
Mr. Webb	Ronny Cox
Emily Webb	Glynnis O'Connor
Mrs. Gibbs	Sada Thompson
Mrs. Soames	Charlotte Rae
Howie Newsome	William Lanteau
Simon Stimson	David Cryer
Constable Warren	Don Beddoe
Joe Stoddard	Ford Rainey
Sam Craig	Charles Cyphers
Rebecca Gibbs	Elizabeth Cheshire
Joe Crowell, Jr.	Allen Price
Si Crowell	Michael Sharrett
Wally Webb	Scott Atlas

1050 Ourstory   PBS
Program Type Drama Series
30 minutes. Monday mornings. Premiere date: 9/30/75. Series repeated: 9/19/77. Historical dramatizations from Colonial times to the present originally designed to coincide with monthly American Issues Forum discussions. Programs shown during the 1977–78 season: "The Devil's Work," "Eliza," "The Erie War," "Jade Snow," "The Last Ballot," "The Peach Gang," "The Queen's Destiny," "The World Turned Upside Down." (*See* individual titles for credits.)

1051 Out of Our Fathers' House
Great Performances   PBS
Program Type Dramatic Special
60 minutes. Premiere date: 8/2/78. Drama based on book by Eve Merrian titled "Growing Up Female." Program made possible by a grant from Exxon Corporation and support from PBS stations.
Producer Judy Kinberg
Executive Producer Jac Venza
Company WNET-TV/New York
Director Jack Hofsiss
CAST

Eliza Southgate	Carol Kane
Elizabeth Cady Stanton	Kaiulani Lee
Maria Mitchell	Jackie Burroughs
"Mother" Mary Jones	Jan Miner
Dr. Anna Howard Shaw	Maureen Anderman
Elizabeth Gertrude Stern	Dianne Wiest

1052 Over Easy   PBS
Program Type News Magazine Series
30 minutes. Premiere dates: 9/13/76 and 9/14/76. Second season premiere: 11/14/77. Magazine-variety programs, featuring celebrity interviews, consumer advice, public service news and special features, all geared toward the mature viewer. Programs made possible by funding from the U.S. Department of Health, Education and Welfare—Administration on Aging and the Corporation for Public Broadcasting.
Executive Producer Richard R. Rector
Producers Jules Power, Christopher Lucas
Company KQED-TV/San Francisco
Directors Haig Mackey, Paul Blake, Vincent Casalaina
Writers Steve Yafka, Jennifer Alps
Host Hugh Downs

1053 Over-Under, Sideways-Down
Visions   PBS
Program Type Dramatic Special
90 minutes. Premiere date: 10/30/77. Dramatic film about a young blue-collar worker who dreams of being a professional baseball player. Music composed by Ozzie Ahlers.
Executive Producer Barbara Schultz
Producer Steve Wax
Company KCET-TV/Los Angeles
Directors Eugene Corr, Peter Gessner, Steve Wax
Writers Eugene Corr, Peter Gessner
Production Designer John Hanson
Art Director Judy Irola
Cinematographer Stephen Lighthill
CAST

Roy Stennis	Robert Viharo
Jan Stennis	Sharon Goldman
Roy's children	Vera Conrat, Jordan Weiner
Baseball Scout	Joe Bellan
Coach	Eugene Anselm Corr

Wilbur	Roy Andrews
Frank	Robert A. Behling
Rich	Michael Cavanaugh
Luke	Lonnie Ford
A.J.	Fran Furey
Johnson	Larry Patterson
Old Man	Charles Meyers
Tomas	Esteban Oropreza
Shop Steward	Max Segar

1054 P. J. & the President's Son

ABC Afterschool Specials   ABC
Program Type Children's Special
60 minutes. Premiere date: 11/10/76. Repeat date: 4/19/78. Update of Mark Twain's "The Prince and the Pauper" about the 15-year-old son of a President of the United States and his look-alike who exchange life styles for a few days. Music composed by Joe Weber. Filmed in part in Washington, D.C.
Executive Producer Daniel Wilson
Producer Fran Sears
Company Daniel Wilson Productions
Director Larry Elikann
Writer Thomas Baum
Costume Designer Ann Hannon
Special Consultant Jack Ford
CAST

P. J./Preston	Lance Kerwin
Grandma McNulty	Irene Tedrow
Mr. Nolan	Laurence Haddon
Piccard	Robert Miller Driscoll
Tina	Patti Cohoon
Bascomb	Milton Selzer
Reporter	Carol Worthington
Ambassador's Daughter	Rosalind Chao
The President	Peter Brandon
The First Lady	Jane Brandon
The Ambassador	Chao-Li Chi
The Chef	Fritz Feld

1055 P.O.W.: Atlanta Revisited   PBS

Program Type Documentary/Informational Series
30 minutes. Premiere date: 5/29/78. Former World War II German Prisoner of War William Oberdieck revisits camp near the small Nebraska town of Atlanta. Produced by the public affairs unit of University of Nebraska Television.
Company KETV-TV/Omaha

1056 Pagliacci

Great Performances   PBS
Program Type Music/Dance Special
90 minutes. Premiere date: 3/19/75. Repeat date: 10/19/77. 1968 film version of the opera by Ruggiero Leoncavallo performed at La Scala Opera House in Milan, Italy with the La Scala Opera Orchestra and Chorus. Program presented by WNET-TV/New York and funded by a grant from Exxon Corporation.
Coordinating Producer David Griffiths

Producer Paul Hager
Company Cosmotel S.A. Production
Conductor Herbert von Karajan
CAST

Canio/Pagliaccio	Jon Vickers
Nedda/Columbine	Raina Corsi-Kabaivanska
Tonio/Taddeo	Peter Glossop
Beppo/Harlequin	Sergio Lorenzi
Silvio	Rolando Panerai

1057 The Pallisers   PBS

Program Type Limited Series
60 minutes. Mondays. Premiere date: 1/24/77 (90 minutes). Repeat date: 9/3/78. 22-part dramatization of six Victorian novels by Anthony Trollope. Filmed in England. Series presented by WNET-TV/New York and made possible by a grant from Prudential Insurance Company of America.
Producer Martin Lisemore
Company British Broadcasting Corporation and Time-Life Television
Directors Hugh David, Ronald Wilson
Writer Simon Raven
Host Sir John Gielgud
CAST

Plantagenet Palliser	Philip Latham
Lady Glencora M'Cluskie Palliser	Susan Hampshire
Alice Vavasor	Caroline Mortimer
Duke of Omnium	Roland Culver
Phineas Finn	Donal McCann
Lady Dumbello	Rachel Herbert
Burgo Fitzgerald	Barry Justice
George Vavasor	Gary Watson
Countess Midlothian	Fabia Drake
Marchioness of Auld Reekie	Sonia Dresdel
Mme. Max Gosler (Marie Finn)	Barbara Murray
Lady Laura Standish	Anna Massey
Violet Effingham	Mel Martin
Kennedy	Derek Godfrey
Mary	Maire Ni Ghrainne
Lizzie Eustace	Sarah Badel
Frank	Martin Jarvis
Lord George	Terence Alexander
Mrs. Carbuncle	Helen Lindsay
Rev. Emilius	Anthony Ainley
Lord Fawn	Derek Jacobi
Mr. Bonteen	Peter Sallis
Silverbridge	Roderick Shaw
Adelaide	Jo Kendall
Gerard	Jeremy Clyde
Dolly Longstaffe	Donald Pickering
Lopez	Stuart Wilson
Emily	Sheila Ruskin
Wharton	Brewster Mason
Lady Mary	Kate Nicholls
Frank Tregear	Jeremy Irons
Gerald	Michael Cochrane
Duke of St. Bungay	Roger Livesey
Lord Silverbridge	Anthony Andrews
Isabel	Lynne Frederick
Lady Mabel Grex	Anna Carteret
John Grey	Bernard Brown

1058   Palm Sunday Worship Service
NBC
Program Type Religious/Cultural Special
60 minutes. Premiere date: 3/19/78. Palm Sunday Worship Service in the Broadway Baptist Church in Fort Worth, Texas. Dr. Welton Gaddy delivers the sermon. Southern Baptist Radio and Television Commission Representative is Dr. Paul M. Stevens.
Executive Producer Doris Ann
Company NBC Television Religious Programs Unit
Director Richard Cox

1059   Panama Canal Treaties   ABC
Program Type News Special
30 minutes. Formal signing of the Panama Canal Treaties by Pres. Carter and Pres. Torrijos live from Panama 6/16/78.
Executive Producer Jeff Gralnick
Company ABC News Special Events
Correspondents Frank Reynolds, Sam Donaldson; Bernard Shaw

Pandora's Box See PBS Movie Theater

1060   Papa and Me
Special Treat   NBC
Program Type Children's Special
60 minutes. Premiere date: 2/10/76. Repeat date: 1/10/78. Drama about the loving relationship between an elderly man who is dying and his grandson.
Executive Producer George A. Heinemann
Producer Michael McLean
Director William P. D'Angelo
Writers William P. D'Angelo, Harvey Bullock, Ray Allen

CAST

Papa D'Amico	Joseph Mascolo
Nana	Renata Vanni
Joseph	Matthew Laborteaux
Dominick	Paul Picerni
Lily	Dimitra Arliss
Aunt Olga	Rhoda Gemignani
Uncle Al	Lou Tiano
Uncle Guido	Len Scaletta
"Red Nose"	John Mitchum
Father McKenna	Robert Ginty
Aunt Rose	Paula Picerni
Richard	Bradley Green
Tom	Eugene Mazzolo
Dr. Rella	Ernest Sarracino
Nickie	Frank Alesia

1061   The Papal Selection   ABC
Program Type News Special
Live coverage of the procession of the College of Cardinals into Sistine chapel as the selection of new pope begins 8/25/78.

Executive Producer Jeff Gralnick
Company ABC News Special Events
Correspondents Peter Jennings, Robert Trout, Frank Reynolds
Guest Commentator Father Vincent O'Keefe

Papillon See CBS Special Movie Presentations

The Parallax View See The CBS Wednesday Night Movies

1062   Parent Effectiveness   PBS
Program Type Educational/Cultural Series
30 minutes. Saturdays. Premiere date: 10/8/77. Series for parents blending dramatization with role playing and location filming at parent effectiveness classes. Series made possible by grants from the Corporation for Public Broadcasting, Ford Foundation, and Public Television Stations.
Company KPBS-TV/San Diego

1063   Pasadena Tournament of Roses Parade
Program Type Parades/Pageants/Awards Special   NBC
2-1/2 hours. Live coverage of the 89th annual parade from Pasadena, CA 1/2/78.
Producer Dick Schneider
Company NBC Television
Director Dick Schneider
Writer Barry Downes
Hosts Michael Landon, Kelly Lange, Bryant Gumbel

1064   Pass the Buck   CBS
Program Type Game/Audience Participation Special
30 minutes. Monday–Fridays. Premiere date: 4/3/78. Last show: 6/29/78.
Executive Producer Bob Stewart
Producer Sande Stewart
Company Bob Stewart Production
Director Mike Gargiulo
Host Bill Cullen

1065   Pat Boone and Family   ABC
Program Type Music/Comedy/Variety Special
60 minutes. Premiere date: 4/8/78. Musical-variety special with singer Pat Boone, his family, and guests.
Executive Producer Jerry Weintraub
Producers Bernard Rothman, Jack Wohl
Company Management Three/Cooga Mooga Productions
Director Perry Rosemond

Writers Burt Styler, Adele Styler, Tom Sawyer, Joe Neustein, Bernard Rothman, Jack Wohl
Choreographer Walter Painter
Costume Designer Bill Hargate
Art Director Roy Christopher
Musical Supervisor George Wyle
Music Consultant Ray Charles
Stars Pat Boone, Shirley Boone, Cherry Boone, Lindy Boone, Laury Boone, Debby Boone
Guest Stars Fran Ryan, Perry Lang, Greg Lewis, Dick Van Patten

1066 Patrick Henry: Give Me Liberty or Give Me Death PBS
Program Type Educational/Cultural Special
30 minutes. Premiere date: 9/13/76. A reenactment of the historic speech filmed on location in the church where it was delivered—St. John's Church, Richmond, Virginia. Features a troupe of players from the Barksdale Theatre in Hanover, VA, under the direction of Muriel McCauley. Prologue written by Virginia Dabney. Program made possible by a grant from the Sons of the Revolution in Virginia and the American Revolution Bicentennial Administration. Script "The Proceedings of the Virginia Convention in the Town of Richmond on the 23rd of March, 1775" published in 1927 by Robert Lecky, Jr.
Company WCVE-TV/Richmond

1067 Paul Anka in Monte Carlo CBS
Program Type Music/Comedy/Variety Special
60 minutes. Premiere date: 8/27/78. Special musical material by Larry Grossman. Music arranged by Mike Barone.
Producer Marty Pasetta
Director Marty Pasetta
Writer Buz Kohan
Choreographer Alan Johnson
Costume Designer Bill Hargate
Star Paul Anka
Guest Stars Suzanne Somers, Donna Summer

1068 The Paul Lynde Comedy Hour ABC
Program Type Music/Comedy/Variety Special
60 minutes. Premiere date: 5/20/78. All the wishes of the host and his guest stars are granted, with surprising and humorous results.
Executive Producers Raymond Katz, Sandy Gallin
Producers Mitzi Welch, Joe Layton, Ken Welch
Company Hoysyl Productions
Directors Jim Washburn, Joe Welch
Writer Stan Hart
Musical Director Alf Clausen
Choreographer Joe Layton
Costume Designer Ret Turner
Art Director Charles Lisanby

Star/Host Paul Lynde
Guest Stars Harry Morgan, Juliet Prowse, Brenda Vaccaro

1069 The Paul Simon Special NBC
Program Type Music/Comedy/Variety Special
60 minutes. Premiere date: 12/8/77. The singer-composer performs a number of his popular compositions.
Producer Lorne Michaels
Company Above Average-Peregrine Productions
Director Dave Wilson
Writers Lorne Michaels, Paul Simon, Chevy Chase, Charles Grodin, Lily Tomlin, Al Franken, Tom Davis, Alan Zweibel
Star Paul Simon
Guest Stars Chevy Chase, Jesse Dixon Singers, Art Garfunkel, Charles Grodin, Lily Tomlin

1070 Paul VI: Minister and Witness CBS
Program Type Religious/Cultural Special
30 minutes. Premiere date: 8/13/78. Religious leaders of major faith groups discuss Pope Paul VI.
Executive Producer Pamela Ilott
Producer Marlene Didonato
Company CBS News
Moderator Ted Holmes
Discussants Bernard Law, Dr. Eugene Carson Blake, Marc Tannenbaum

1071 Paul Taylor Dance Company
Great Performances/Dance in America PBS
Program Type Music/Dance Special
60 minutes. Premiere date: 1/4/78. Performances of two dance compositions by Paul Taylor: "Esplanade," to the music of Bach's E major and D minor Violin Concertos; and the Druidic-inspired "Runes." Program made possible by the National Endowment for the Arts, Corporation for Public Broadcasting and Exxon Corporation.
Company WNET-TV/New York

1072 PBS Movie Theater PBS
Program Type TV Movie Series
Times vary. Saturdays. 9/10/77–12/31/77 and 7/22/78–9/23/78. Feature films from the Janus Film Collection purchased with the help of a grant from the Exxon Corporation. Films aired during the 1977–78 season are: "As You Like It" (1936) shown 7/29/78, "Barrier" (1966) shown 11/12/77, "Beauty and the Beast" (1946) shown 10/22/77, "Black Orpheus" (1959) shown 10/15/77, "The Blue Angel" (1930) shown 12/3/77, "Breaking the Sound Barrier" (1952) shown 2/4/78, "Brief Encounter" (1946) shown

PBS Movie Theater *Continued*

9/10/77, "The Browning Version" (1951) shown 9/24/77, "Casque d'Or" (1952) shown 11/5/77, "Cry the Beloved Country" (1952) shown 1/21/78, "David and Lisa" (1962) shown 12/3/77, "Elizabeth of Ladymead" (1948) shown 2/11/78, "Fame Is the Spur" (1949) shown 10/1/77 "The Father" (1966) shown 7/15/78, "Fires on the Plain" (1959) shown 9/2/78, "Forbidden Games" (1951) shown 12/10/77, "Gilbert and Sullivan" (1953), shown 1/28/78, "The Great Dan Patch" (1949) shown 7/22/78, "Hamlet" (1948) shown 8/5/78, "The Heart of the Matter" (1953) shown 7/29/78, "Hobson's Choice" (1954) shown 9/17/77, "Jolly Bad Fellow" (1964) shown 8/5/78, "Jules and Jim (1961) shown 10/22/77, "Kamerad-schaft" (1931) shown 11/26/77, "Kanal" (1957) shown 10/29/77, "Knife in the Water" (1962) shown 11/5/77, "The Last Days of Dolwyn" (1949) shown 2/18/78, "Last Holiday" (1950) shown 9/3/77, "Last Laugh" (1924) shown 12/31/77, "Law and Disorder" (1958) shown 8/12/78, "M" (1931) shown 12/17/77, "The Maggie" (1954) shown 10/15/77, "The Magician" (1958) shown 9/9/78, "Miss Julie" (1950) shown 11/19/77, "Our Daily Bread" (1934) shown 10/8/77, "Pandora's Box" (1928) shown 12/24/77, "The Plough and the Stars" (1936) shown 7/22/78, "Port of Call" (1948) shown 9/16/78, "Rashomon"(1951) shown 8/26/78, "Richard III" (1955) shown 8/12/78, "A Run for Your Money" (1949), "The Servent" (1963) shown 10/22/77, shown 6/3/78, "Shameless Old Lady" (1965) shown 7/8/78, "Shoot the Piano Player" (1962) shown 1/7/78, "Three Men in a Boat" (1956) shown 2/25/78, "Virgin Spring" (1959) shown 9/23/78.

1073   The Peach Gang

Ourstory   PBS
Program Type Drama Series
60 minutes. Premiere date: 9/22/75. Repeat dates: 9/19/77 and 9/26/77 (30 minutes each). Dramatizes the conflict between English and Indian concepts of justice in 17th century America. Filmed at Plimoth Plantation, Plymouth, Mass. Music by Wladimir Selinsky. Program funded by the National Endowment for the Humanities.
Executive Producer Don Fouser
Producer Don Fouser
Company WNET-TV/New York
Director William A. Graham
Writer Allan Sloane
Conductor Wladimir Selinsky
Host Bill Moyers
CAST
Arthur Peach .... Daniel Tamm
Canonicus .... Chief Dan George
Roger Williams .... James Tolkan
Thomas Prence .... Gil Rogers

William Bradford .... David Hooks
Miles Standish .... John Carpenter
Miantonomo .... William Wilcox
John Alden .... Patrick Gorman
Young Indian/Penowanyanquis .... Billy Drago
Richard Stinnings .... Michael Kimberly
Thomas Jackson .... Michael L. Barlow
Steven Hopkins .... Ron Faber
Dorothy Temple .... Annie O'Neill
Dr. James .... William Shust
Matthew Fletcher .... Gary Cookson
Strongheart Sekatau .... Eric Thomas
Mudjewis .... John Brown III
Firefly Song of Wind .... Ella Thomas
Princess Evening Star .... Gertrude Aiken

1074   Peanuts to the Presidency: The Jimmy Carter Campaign   Syndicated

Program Type Public Affairs Special
90 minutes. Premiere date: 3/18/78. Documentary of the 1976 Presidential campaign.
Producer Chuck Braverman
Company Baverman Picture Corp
Director Chuck Braverman
Writer Kandy Stroud
Narrator Joseph Campanella

1075   Peeping Times   NBC

Program Type Comedy Special
60 minutes. Premiere date: 1/25/78. Comedy special spoofing TV news magazine shows.
Executive Producers David Frost, Marvin Minoff
Producers Rudy DeLuca, Barry Levinson
Company Paradine-DeLuca-Levinson Production
Directors Rudy DeLuca, Barry Levinson
Head Writers Rudy DeLuca, Barry Levinson
Writers Bill Richmond, Gene Perret, Robert Illes, James Stein, Christopher Guest
CAST
Miles Rathbourne .... Alan Oppenheimer
Dan Cochran .... David Letterman
Ofc. Hansen .... Charles Murphy
Seedy Man .... Lee Delano
Mr. X .... Johnie Decker
Monk .... Ron Carey
Angelo Bertinelli .... J. J. Barry
Dr. Burnett .... Murphy Dunne
Eva Braun .... Sharon Spelman
Mayor of Ewell .... Michael Fairman
Prisoner #2 .... Bill Fiore

1076   The Pennsylvania Ballet

Dance in America/Great Performances   PBS
Program Type Music/Dance Special
60 minutes. Premiere date: 6/2/76. Repeat date: 9/4/77. Excerpts from "Madrigalesco" by Benjamin Harkarvy, "Grosse Fugue" and "Adagio Hammerklavier" by Hans van Manen, "Concerto Barocco" by George Balanchine, and "Concerto Grosso" by Charles Czarny. Taped in

Philadelphia and Nashville. Program made possible by grants from the National Endowment for the Arts, the Corporation for Public Broadcasting and Exxon Corporation.
Executive Producer Jac Venza
Producer Emile Ardolino
Series Producer Merrill Brockway
Company WNET-TV/New York
Director Merrill Brockway
Narrator Barbara Weisberger
Featured Dancers Dane LaFontsee, Edward Myers, Jerry Schwender, Janek Schergen, Alba Calzada, Marcia Darhower, Michelle Lucci, Lawrence Rhodes

1077 **Pennsylvania Lynch**
Visions   PBS
Program Type Dramatic Special
90 minutes. Premiere date: 12/9/76. Repeat date: 1/1/78. Drama about turn-of-the-century Hungarian immigrants in a small Pennsylvania town. Based on a historical incident. Program made possible by grants from the Ford Foundation, the National Endowment for the Arts and the Corporation for Public Broadcasting.
Producer Barbara Schultz
Company KCET-TV/Los Angeles
Directors Jeff Bleckner, Rick Bennewitz
Writer David Epstein
Costume Designer Sandra Stewart
Art Director Lynn Griffin
CAST
Robert Dayka .... Tom Atkins
Eva Dayka .... Lelia Goldoni
Paul Dayka .... Bill Whitaker
Sandor .... Bo Brundin
Gretta .... Lenka Peterson
Sheriff .... Richard Venture
Zachariah Walker .... Bob Delegall
Mr. James .... Jason Wingreen
Nmika .... Fritz Feld
Kosko .... Harry Frazier
Cronin .... Ken O'Brien
Thomson .... Lincoln Demyan
District Attorney .... Herb Armstrong
Stanley Huff .... Will Mackenzie
Grundy .... Ralph Lev Mailer
Village Idiot .... John Megna
Officer .... Herman Poppe
Phillips .... Marius Mazmanian
Reporters .... Robert Chapel, Louis Plant, Frank Coppola, Brett Dunham, Wally Berns
Black Men .... Ken Men'ard, Frenchia Guizon

1078 **The People vs. Inez Garcia**   PBS
Program Type Dramatic Special
90 minutes. Premiere date: 5/25/77. Repeat date: 8/8/78 Docudrama edited from the trial of Inez Garcia and adapted from the stage production of Rena Down. Program made possible by a grant from the Corporation for Public Broadcasting (unedited version).

Executive Producer Zev Putterman
Producers Rena Down, Christopher Lukas
Company KQED-TV/San Francisco
Directors Rena Down, Christopher Lukas
Writer Rena Down
Scenic Designer Henry May
Narrator Jessica Epstein
CAST
Inez Garcia .... Silvana Gallardo
Charles Garry .... Robert Loggia
Braudrick .... Marc Jacobs
Judge .... Robert Haswell
Luis Castillo .... Jearado Carmona
Dr. Oldden .... Barbara Oliver
Juan Garcia .... Carlos Baron
Raul Garcia .... Julio Rossetti
Worthington .... David Klein
Freddie Medrano .... Manuel Gonzales
Courtroom Interpreter .... Judith Weston
Additional Cast Louis Winfield Bailey, Loretta Sheridan, Patrick Taffe, Raymond L. Lopez

1079 **The People's Choice Awards**   CBS
Program Type Parades/Pageants/Awards Special
2 hours. 2/20/78. Fourth annual awards live from Hollywood.
Executive Producer Bob Stivers
Producer Bob Finkel
Director Tony Charmoli
Writer Herbert Baker
Hosts Dick Van Dyke, Army Archerd

1080 **People's Command Performance**
CBS
Program Type Music/Comedy/Variety Special
2 hours. Premiere date: 1/13/78. Repeat date: 6/22/78. Performances by entertainers selected in a public-opinion survey.
Company People's Command Performance Productions, Inc.
Executive Producer Bob Stivers
Producer Bob Finkel
Director Tony Charmoli
Writer Herbert Baker
Musical Directors Jack Elliott, Allyn Ferguson
Choreographer Tony Charmoli
Costume Designer Madeline Ann Graneto
Art Directors Anthony Sabatino, William Harris

1081 **Perfect Gentlemen**
The CBS Tuesday Night Movies   CBS
Program Type TV Movie
2 hours. Premiere date: 3/14/78. Comedy-drama of a million dollar heist. Music by Dominic Frontiere.
Executive Producer Bud Austin
Producer Jackie Cooper
Company A Bud Austin Production in association with Paramount Television

Perfect Gentlemen *Continued*
Director Jackie Cooper
Writer Nora Ephron
CAST

Lizzie Martin	Lauren Bacall
Mama Cavagnaro	Ruth Gordon
Sophie Rosenman	Sandy Dennis
Annie Cavagnaro	Lisa Pelikan
Ed Martin	Robert Alda
Murray Rosenman	Stephen Pearlman
Vinnie Cavagnaro	Steve Allie Collura
Mr. Auletta	Rick Garia
Desk Clerk	Ken Olfson
Nick Auletta	Rick Garia
Johnson	Robert Kya-Hill

1082   Perry Como's Easter by the Sea
ABC
Program Type Music/Comedy/Variety Special
60 minutes. Premiere date: 3/22/78. Holiday special from San Diego's Sea World Park. Featuring Shamu, the Killer Whale; Seamore the Sea Lion and Flo the Walrus.
Executive Producer Bob Banner
Producer Steve Pouliot
Company Bob Banner Associates, Inc., in association with Roncom Productions
Director David Acumba
Writer Jim Mulligan
Musical Director Nick Periot
Choreographer Bob Thompson
Art Director Keith Gonzales
Star Perry Como
Guest Star Debby Boone, Kenny Rogers, The Navy Sea Chanters, Hiromichi Bando Dancers, Minobu Miki and the Japan Karate Organization

1083   Perry Como's Olde English Christmas
ABC
Program Type Music/Comedy/Variety Special
60 minutes. Premiere date: 12/14/77. Perry Como and his guests celebrate a traditional Christmas in English locations including a 15th-century castle and St. Paul's Cathedral, London. Choirmaster, St. Paul's Cathedral is Barry Rose. Script and special material by Eric Merriman.
Producer Yvonne Littlewood
Director Yvonne Littlewood
Company A BBC Production in association with Como's Roncom Productions
Musical Director Nick Periot
Conductor Raymond Cohen
Choral Director Ray Charles
Art Director Tony Abbott
Costume Designer Joyce Mortlock
Star/Host Perry Como
Guest Stars Petula Clark, Leo Sayer, John Curry, Gemma Craven
Also appearing: The Gillian Lynne Dancers, The Tony Mansell Singers, The Boys Choir of St. Paul's Cathedral

1084   Person to Person: Selected Interviews 1953–1959
PBS
Program Type Documentary/Informational Series
30 minutes. Premiere date: 7/6/78. 13-week series with Edward R. Murrow interviewing newsmakers of the fifties. "Person to Person" originally aired on the CBS Television Network which granted permission to the Eastern Educational Television Network to repeat several of the episodes on a one-time basis.
Coordinating Producer Liz Oliver
Company WNET-TV/New York

Pete 'n Tillie *See* ABC Tuesday Movie of the Week

1085   Pete Seeger and Arlo Guthrie
Live from Wolf Trap
PBS
Program Type Music/Dance Special
90 minutes. Premiere date: 8/22/78. Pete Seeger and Arlo Guthrie serenade the Wolf Trap Farm Park audience with music drawn from folk, ragtime, country blues, and Revolutionary and Civil War ballads. Program made possible by grants from the Corporation for Public Broadcasting, PBS member stations, and Allied Chemical Corporation.
Company WETA-TV/Washington
Executive Producer David Griffiths
Producer Hal Hutkoff

1086   Peter Lundy and the Medicine Hat Stallion
NBC Movie of the Week
NBC
Program Type Dramatic Special
2 hours. Premiere date: 11/6/77. Repeat date: 8/9/78. Frontier teenager comes of age as a Pony Express rider in the late 1800s. Based on "San Domingo—the Medicine Hat Stallion," by Marguerite Henny. Teleplay by Jack Turley. Music by Morton Stevens. Filmed in New Mexico.
Producer Ed Friendly
Company Ed Friendly Productions in association with NBC-TV
Director Michael O'Herlihy
CAST

Peter Lundy	Leif Garrett
Jethro Lundy	Mitch Ryan
Emily Lundy	Bibi Besch
Grandma Lundy	Ann Doran
Brisly	Milo O'Shea
Adam	John Quade
Jim	Brad Rearden
Majors	John Anderson
Muggeridge	James Lydon

Slade .... Charles Tyner
Red Cloud .... Ned Romero
Horse ....Domengo

1087 Peter Pan
Hallmark Hall of Fame   NBC
Program Type Dramatic Special
2 hours. Premiere date: 12/12/76. Repeat date: 3/16/78. New musical adaptation of the 1904 play by Sir James M. Barrie about a boy who won't grow up. "Once Upon a Bedtime" sung by Julie Andrews. Musical and dramatic sequences supervised by Michael Kidd. Music and lyrics by Anthony Newley and Leslie Bricusse. Stereosimulcast on local FM radio stations.
Executive Producers Gary Smith, Dwight Hemion
Producer Gary Smith
Company An ATV/ITC Production in association with NBC
Director Dwight Hemion
Writers Jack Burns, Andrew Birkin
Musical Director Ian Fraser
Conductors Ian Fraser, Jack Parnell
Costume Designer Sue Le Cash
Art Director David Chandler
Narrator Sir John Gielgud
CAST
Peter Pan ....Mia Farrow
Capt. Hook/Mr. Darling .... Danny Kaye
Mrs. Darling .... Virginia McKenna
Tiger Lily .... Paula Kelly
Wendy .... Briony McRoberts
John .... Ian Sharrock
Michael .... Adam Stafford
Nana/Crocodile .... Peter O'Farrell
Slightly .... Jerome Watts
Tootles .... Nicky Lyndhurst
Nibs .... Adam Richens
Curly .... Michael Deeks
First Twin .... Simon Mooney
Second Twin ....Andrew Mooney
Smee .... Tony Sympson
Starkey ....Joe Melia
Pirates ....Oscar James, George Harris, Michael Crane, Max Latimer, Fred Evans, Peppi Borza
Wendy (older) .... Jill Gascoine
Jane .... Linsey Baxter

1088 PGA Golf Championship   ABC
Program Type Sports Special
90 minutes, 8/5/78. 2-1/2 hours, 8/6/78. 30 minutes, 8/4/78. 60th PGA Golf Championship from The Oakmont Country Club, Pittsburgh, Pennsylvania.
Executive Producer Roone Arledge
Producer Chuck Howard
Company ABC Sports
Directors Jim Jennett, Terry Jastrow
Commentators Jim McKay, Keith Jackson, Peter Alliss

Expert Commentators Dave Marr, Bill Flemming, Bob Rosburg

1089 The Phantom of the Open Hearth
Visions   PBS
Program Type Dramatic Special
90 minutes. Premiere date: 12/23/76. Repeat date: 12/18/77. Comedy about a 1940s Junior Prom. Adapted by the author from his book "Wanda Hickey's Night of Golden Memories, and Other Disasters." Presented by KCET-TV/Los Angeles. Program made possible by grants from the Ford Foundation, the National Endowment for the Arts and the Corporation for Public Broadcasting.
Executive Producer Barbara Schultz
Producers Fred Barzyk, David Loxton
Company WNET Television Laboratory/New York and WGBH New Television Workshop/Boston
Directors Fred Barzyk, David Loxton
Writer Jean Shepherd
Costume Designer Jennifer Von Mayrhauser
Art Director John Wright Stevens
CAST
Ralph (as man) ....Jean Shepherd
Ralph (as boy) .... David Elliott
Father .... James Broderick
Mother .... Barbara Bolton
Randy .... Adam Goodman
Daphne Bigelow .... Tobi Pilavin
Wanda Hickey ....Roberta Wallach
Uncle Carl .... Ed Huberman
Schwartz .... Bryan Utman
Flick .... William Lampley
John .... Carlton Power
Halfback .... Steve Nuding
Sherby .... David Pokat
Gertz .... Chris Clark
Awkie ....Joe Mayo
Zudock .... David Howard
Mr. Doppler .... Frank Dolan
Al .... Joey Faye
Morty .... John Peters
Clara Mae ....Andrea McCullough
Budge .... Peter Graham
Arlita .... Leigh Brown
Steelworker .... Michael Stein
Deliveryman ....James Bonnell
Waiter .... Sol Schwade

1090 Phase IV
The ABC Summer Movie
Program Type TV Movie   ABC
90 minutes. Premiere date: 6/22/78. Science fiction drama about a woman hunted by a colony of ants.
Producer Paul Radin
Company Paramount Pictures
Director Saul Bass
Photography Dick Bush
Special Ant Photography Ken Middleham

Phase IV *Continued*

CAST

Ernest Hubbs .... Nigel Davenport
James Lesko .... Michael Murphy
Kendra .... Lynne Frederick
Mr. Eldridge .... Alan Gifford
Mrs. Eldridge .... Helen Horton
Clete .... Robert Henderson

1091   The Phenomenon of Benji   ABC
Program Type Documentary/Informational
Special
30 minutes. Premiere date: 5/4/78. Documentary on canine star, Benji.
Executive Producer Joe Camp
Producer Richard Baker
Company Mulberry Square Productions
Director Stan Harris
Writers Joe Camp, Dan Witt, Richard Baker
Musical Director Evel Box
Star Benji
Guest Stars Charlie Rich, Meredith MacRae, Edgar Buchanan, Jesse Davis, Frank Inn

1092   Phil Ochs Memorial Concert   PBS
Program Type Music/Dance Special
90 minutes. Premiere date: 7/9/77. Repeat date: 7/4/78. Concert-tribute to Phil Ochs taped at Madison Square Garden in New York City 5/28/76. Program made possible in part by a grant from the Corporation for Public Broadcasting.
Producer Douglas Bailey
Company WHYY-TV/Philadelphia-Wilmington
Directors Douglas Bailey, Russell Kneeland
Performers Dan Van Ronk, Pete Seeger, Fred Hellerman, Eric Andersen, Tim Harden, Tom Rush, Melanie, Oscar Brand, Bob Gibson, Jim Glover, David Blue, Peter Yarrow

1093   Philadelphia Golf Classic   CBS
Program Type Sports Special
Live coverage of final two rounds 7/22/78 and 7/23/78 from Whitemarsh Valley Country Club in Lafayette Hills, Pennsylvania.
Executive Producer Frank Chirkinian
Company CBS Sports
Directors Bob Dailey, Frank Chirkinian
Commentators Vin Scully, Pat Summerall, Jack Whitaker, Ben Wright, Ken Venturi

1094   Phoenix Open   CBS
Program Type Sports Special
60 minutes each day. Live coverage of the final two rounds of the Phoenix Open from the Phoenix (Ariz.) Country Club 1/14/78 and 1/15/78.
Producer Frank Chirkinian
Company CBS Television Network Sports

Directors Frank Chirkinian, Bob Dailey
Commentators Pat Summerall, Jack Whitaker, Ben Wright, Ken Venturi, Frank Beard

1095   A Piece of Cake
A Special Treat   NBC
Program Type Children's Special
60 minutes. Premiere date: 10/11/77. A student reporter passes along some unsupported gossip on a school's closed circuit TV station and spurs a student strike.
Producers Marilyn Olin, Lee Polk
Director J. Philip Miller
Writer Paul Ritts

CAST

Star-Shimah .... Star-Shimah
Mr. Eglin .... Ossie Davis
Jerry Hudson .... Al Freeman, Jr.
Mr. Johnson .... David Faulkner
Ronnie Bennett .... Peter Wise
Mr. Bennett .... Arthur French
Ziggy .... Wendell Brown
Amity .... Alexa Brown
Jack .... Darren Edwards

1096   Pilobolus Dance Theatre
Dance in America/Great Performances   PBS
Program Type Music/Dance Special
60 minutes. Premiere date: 5/4/77. Repeat date: 12/28/77. Dance troupe combines dance, acrobatics, design, sculpture and humor in four selections from its repertoire: "Ocellus," "Monkshood's Farewell," "Ciona," and "Untitled." Program made possible by the National Endowment for the Arts, Corporation for Public Broadcasting and the Ford Foundation.
Executive Producer Jac Venza
Producers Emile Ardolino, Judy Kinberg
Company WNET-TV/New York
Director Merrill Brockway
Dancers Moses Pendelton, Jonathan Wolken, Alison Chase, Robby Barnett, Martha Clarke, Michael Tracy

1097   The Pinballs   ABC
ABC Afterschool Specials
Program Type Children's Special
60 minutes. Premiere date: 5/18/77. Repeat date: 10/26/77. Drama about three youngsters from different backgrounds placed in a foster home together. Based on the novel by Betsy Byars.
Producer Martin Tahse
Company Martin Tahse Productions, Inc.
Director Richard Bennett
Writer Jim Inman
Art Director Ray Markham

CAST

Carlie Higgins .... Kristy McNichol
Harvey .... Johnny Doran
Thomas J. .... Sparky Marcus

Mrs. Mason	Priscilla Morrill
Mr. Mason	Walter Brooke
Harvey's Father	Barry Coe
Ms. Harris	Jacque Lynn Colton
Policeman	James Chandler
Nurse	Beverly Hope Atkinson

1098 Pine Canyon Is Burning
NBC Movie of the Week   NBC
Program Type Dramatic Special
90 minutes. Premiere date: 5/18/77. Repeat date: 12/27/77. Dramatic pilot about a small-town firefighter raising his two children alone.
Executive Producer Robert A. Cinader
Producers Gino Grimaldi, Hannah Shearer
Company Universal Television in association with the NBC Television Network
Director Christian Nyby III
Writer Robert A. Cinader
Art Director George Renne
CAST

Capt. William Stone	Kent McCord
Margaret Stone	Megan McCord
Michael Stone	Shane Sinutko
Sandra	Diana Muldaur
Charlie Edison	Dick Bakalyan
Anne Walker	Brit Lind
Capt. Ed Wilson	Andrew Duggan
Edna Wilson	Doreen Lang
Whitey Olson	Curtis Credel

1099 Pioneer Bowl   ABC
Program Type Sports Special
Live coverage of the Pioneer Bowl game between the Lehigh Engineers and the Jacksonville State Gamecocks from Memorial Stadium, Wichita Falls, TX 12/10/77.
Executive Producer Roone Arledge
Producer Bob Goodrich
Company ABC Sports
Director Larry Kamm
Play-by-Play Announcer Bill Flemming
Expert Color Commentator Lee Grosscup

1100 The Plant Family   CBS
Program Type Comedy Special
30 minutes. Premiere date: 9/2/78. Pilot about an ex-taxi dancer married to one of her best ex-customers.
Executive Producers Bud Austin, Robert D. Wood
Producer Monica Johnson
Company Paramount Television Productions
Director James Burrows
Writers Monica Johnson, Jordan Tabat
CAST

Lyla Plant	Joyce Van Patten
Augie Plant	Norman Alden
Geneva	Jo Marie Payton
Leo Harrell	Jesse White
Homer Jay	DeWayne Jessie
Ava	Kay Heberle

Art	Larry Hankin
Aerilio	Peter Elbling
Eddie Guabo	Anthony Sirico
Patty	Willie Tjan

Play It Again, Sam *see* The CBS Tuesday Night Movies

Plaza Suite *see* ABC Tuesday Movie of the Week

1101 Pleasantville
Visions   PBS
Program Type Dramatic Special
90 minutes. Premiere date: 11/6/77. Drama about a young girl's visit to her eccentric and reclusive grandmother. Music composed and performed by Michael Reisman.
Executive Producer Barbara Schultz
Producers Vicki Polon, Kenneth Locker
Company KCET-TV/Los Angeles
Directors Vicki Polon, Kenneth Locker
Writers Vicki Polon, Kenneth Locker
Production Designer William Strom
Cinematographer Walter Lassally
Film Editor Jill Godmilow
CAST

Ora Drummond	Gale Sondergaard
Samantha	Suzanne Weber
Matthew	Michael Del Viscovo, Jr.
Desmond Slattery,	Robert Hitt
George Pocello	John Bottoms
Jo Pocello	Marcia Jean Kurtz
Pocello Children	Mickey Giordana, Michael Cornell, Sari Kershnar, Timothy Stewart, Spencer Holden

The Plough and the Stars *see* PBS Movie Theater

1102 The Poisoning of Michigan   PBS
Program Type Documentary/Informational Series
60 minutes. Premiere date: 10/4/77. True story of accidental poisoning of thousands of cattle.
Executive Producer Christie Basham
Producers John Fielding and Thames Television "This Week" team

1103 Poldark, II
Masterpiece Theatre   PBS
Program Type Limited Series
60 minutes. Sundays and Thursdays. Premiere date: 6/4/78. 13-part romantic adventure set in late 18th-century Cornwall adapted from the "Poldark" novels of Winston Graham. Music by Kenyon Emrys-Roberts. Presented by WGBH-TV/ Boston; produced by Joan Sullivan. Series

Poldark, II *Continued*

made possible by a grant from Mobil Oil Corporation.
Producers Tony Coburn, Richard Beynon
Company BBC Production
Directors Philip Dudley, Roger Jenkins
Writers Alexander Baron, John Wiles, Martin Worth
Costume Designer Penny Lowe
CAST

Ross Poldark	Robin Ellis
Isaac Ward	Jay Neill
Verity Blamey	Norma Streader
Agatha Poldark	Eileen Way
George Warleggan	Ralph Bates
Jud Paynter	Paul Curran
Demelza Poldark	Angharad Rees
Elizabeth Warleggan	Jill Townsend
Drake Carne	Kevin McNally
Sam Carne	David Delve
Zachy Martin	Forbes Collins
Tom Harry	Gertan Klauber
Geoffrey Charles	Stefan Gates
Joe Nanfan	Peter Diamond
Lucy Pipe	Ingrid Evans
Dr. Behenna	Hugh Dickson
Nicholas Warleggan	Alan Tilvern
Caroline Penvenen	Judy Geeson
Prudie	Mary Wimbush
Morwenna Chynoweth	Jane Wymark
Comte de Sombreuil	Michael Petrovitch
Vicomte de Maresi	Tim Morand
Trencrom	Leon Sinden
Hugh Armitage	Brian Stirner
Dwight Enys	Michael Cadman
Harris Pascoe	Preston Lockwood
John Trelawney	Shaun Curry
Rev. Ossie Whitworth	Christopher Biggins
Sid Rowse	Michael Graham Cox
Valentine Warleggan	Catharine Bowler; Wayne Brooks
Rowella	Julie Dawn Cole
Arthur Solways	Stephen Reynolds
Monk Adderley	Malcolm Tierney
Lord Falmouth	Hugh Manning

1104 Police Story

The Big Event   NBC
Program Type Crime Drama Series
2 hours. Premiere date: 10/2/73. Fifth season premiere: 9/27/77. Broadcast irregularly as part of "The Big Event." Original pilots: "Pressure Point" shown 9/27/77, "Stigma" shown 11/9/77 and repeated 8/6/78, "River of Promises" shown 1/14/78 and repeated 8/13/78, "Day of Terror, Night of Fear" shown 3/4/78 and repeated 8/20/78, "The Broken Badge" shown 3/19/78, "No Margin for Error" shown 4/30/78 and repeated 9/3/78, and "A Chance to Live" shown 5/28/78. Anthology series created by Joseph Wambaugh Developed for television by E. Jack Neuman. Theme music by Jerry Goldsmith.
Executive Producer David Gerber

Producers Mel Swope, Larry Brody
Company David Gerber Productions in association with Columbia Pictures Television and NBC-TV
Directors Various
Executive Story Consultant Larry Brody
Writers Various

1105 The Police Tapes   PBS

Program Type Documentary/Informational Series
90 minutes. Premiere date: 8/3/78. Documentary about the daily life of policemen in New York's 44th Precinct.
Cinematographers Susan and Alan Raymond

1106 Police Woman   NBC

Program Type Crime Drama Series
60 minutes. Tuesdays/Wednesdays as of 12/14/77. Thursdays as of 3/23/78. Premiere date: 9/13/74. Fourth season premiere: 10/25/77. Spin-off from "Police Story" episode entitled "The Gamble." Crime drama of an undercover police woman in a large city. Theme music by Morton Stevens. Special effects by Bill Clove.
Executive Producer David Gerber
Producer Douglas Benton
Company David Gerber Productions in association with Columbia Pictures Television and NBC-TV
Directors Various
Executive Story Editor Ed DeBlasio
Writers Various
Art Director Bob Purcell
CAST

Sgt. Pepper Anderson	Angie Dickinson
Sgt. Bill Crowley	Earl Holliman
Joe Styles	Ed Bernard
Pete Royster	Charles Dierkop

1107 The Politics of Abortion

CBS Reports   CBS
Program Type Documentary/Informational Special
60 minutes. Premiere date: 4/22/78. Report on the movement to reverse the 1973 Supreme Court decision legalizing abortion.
Executive Producer Howard Stringer
Producer Andrew Lack
Company CBS News
Director Andrew Lack
Writers Andrew Lack, Bill Moyers
Cinematographer Chuck Levey
Film Editor Joanne Burke
Correspondent Bill Moyers

1108 Pope John Paul I: A Ministry Begins CBS
Program Type Religious/Cultural Special
Live coverage from Rome of the solemn mass marking the beginning of the pontificate of Pope John Paul I; 9/3/78.
Producer Russ Bensley
Anchors Harry Reasoner, Winston Burdett

1109 Pope John Paul I: The Ministry Begins NBC
Program Type News Special
Live coverage by satellite of the solemn mass to be celebrated by Pope John Paul I for the beginning of his ministry.
Executive Producer Paul Greenberg
Producers Ray Lockhart, Kenneth Donoghue
Company NBC News
Anchor Edwin Newman
Reporter Garrick Utley (Rome)

1110 Pope John Paul I and the Church.
NBC News Special NBC
Program Type News Special
60 minutes. Premiere date: 8/26/78. Coverage of the election of Pope John Paul I.
Executive Producer Paul Greenberg
Producers Ray Lockhart, Kenneth Donoghue
Company NBC News
Anchor Edwin Newman
Correspondents Robert Hager, Ford Rowan, Fred Francis, Richard Hunt, Rick Davis, John Palmer, John Cochrane

1111 Pope Paul VI Burial CBS
Program Type Religious/Cultural Special
Live special report on the burial services of Pope Paul VI 8/12/78.
Company CBS News
Correspondents Harry Reasoner, Dan Rather, Winston Burdett, Jerry Bowen

1112 The Popeye Show CBS
Program Type Animated Film Special
30 minutes. Premiere date: 9/13/78. Animated adventures of the comic strip sailor.
Executive Producers William Hanna, Joseph Barbera
Producer Alex Lovy
Creative Producer Iwoa Takamoto
Company Hanna-Barbera Productions, Inc.
Directors Ray Patterson, Carl Urbano
Story Editor Larz Bourne
Writers Glenn Leopold, Dalton Sandifer, Jack Hanrahan, Tom Dajenai
VOICES
Popeye .... Jack Mercer
Additional Voices Allan Melvin, Marilyn Schreffler, Daws Butler

Port of Call *see* PBS Movie Theater

1113 The Porter Wagoner Show
Syndicated
Program Type Music/Comedy/Variety Series
30 minutes. Weekly. Premiered in 1960. 18th season premiere: 9/77. Country music/variety show.
Executive Producer Bill Graham
Producer J. Reginald Dunlap
Company Show Biz, Inc.
Distributor Show Biz, Inc.
Director Gene Birke
Musical Director Porter Wagoner
Star Porter Wagoner

1114 Portrait of Grandpa Doc
ABC Weekend Specials/ABC Short Story
Specials ABC
Program Type Children's Special
30 minutes. Premiere date: 11/5/77. Repeat date: 4/22/78. A gentle and loving grandfather sees, respects and encourages the wonder in a child's eyes. Portrait of Grandpa Doc painted by Robert Redding. Music by Charles Albertine. Filmed on location in Seaside Park, NJ, and Los Angeles.
Executive Producer Barbara Bryant
Producer Diane Baker
Company Phoenix Films
Director Randal Kleiser
Writer Randal Kleiser
CAST
Grandpa Doc .... Melvyn Douglas
Bruce (young man) .... Bruce Davison
Bruce (boy) .... Keith Blanchard
Mother .... Barbara Rush
Grandmother .... Anne Seymour

The Poseidon Adventure *See* The ABC Sunday Night Movie

Posse *See* The CBS Wednesday Night Movies

1115 Possum Trot PBS
Program Type Documentary/Informational Special
30 minutes. Premiere date: 4/4/78. Film documenting the art of the late Calvin Black. Program made possible in part by a grant from the Corporation for Public Broadcasting.
Producers Allie Light, Irving Saraf
Company SCTS-TV/Seattle

1116 **The Preakness**   ABC
Program Type Sports Special
60 minutes. 5/20/78. Live coverage of the 103rd running of the Preakness Stakes from Pimlico Race Course, Baltimore, Maryland.
Executive Producer Roone Arledge
Producer Chuck Howard
Director Chet Forte
Hosts Jim McKay, Howard Cosell
Commentator Eddie Arcaro
Caller Dick Woolley

1117 **Prep Championships: Indiana Boys' Basketball**   PBS
Program Type Sports Special
90 minutes. Premiere date: 4/23/78. National championship of high school basketball with semi-finals in the afternoon and finals the same evening. Program made possible by a grant from the Corporation for Public Broadcasting.
Company KAET-TV/Phoenix

1118 **Prep Championships: Iowa Girls' Basketball**   PBS
Program Type Sports Special
90 minutes. Premiere date: 4/16/78. 59th annual girl's high school tournament from Des Moine's Veterans Memorial Auditorium. Program made possible by a grant from the Corporation for Public Broadcasting.
Company KAET-TV/Phoenix

1119 **Prep Championships: Minnesota Boys' Hockey**   PBS
Program Type Sports Special
90 minutes. Premiere date: 4/30/78. Hockey tournament held in St. Paul, Minnesota. Made possible by a grant from the Corporation for Public Broadcasting.
Company KAET-TV/Phoenix

1120 **President Carter at West Berlin Town Meeting**   CBS
Program Type News Special
Coverage of President Carter's participation in a West Berlin Town Meeting at Congress Hall, 7/15/78.
Executive Producer Russ Bensley
Company CBS News
Anchor Bob Schieffer

1121 **President Carter's 9-Day Trip to Europe and The Middle East**
NBC News Special   NBC
Program Type News Special
Live and taped coverage via satellite of President Carter's nine-day trip to Europe and the Middle East. John Chancellor, co-anchor of "NBC Nightly News" traveled with the President. Also included were NBC News White House correspondents Bob Jamieson and Judy Woodruff and "Segment 3" correspondent John Dancy. Coverage began 12/30/77 with live coverage of the President's news conference in Warsaw, Poland, and continued with the President's New Year's message to Americans gathered at Teheran Airport 1/1/78; live coverage of a major address to the Indian Parliament in New Delhi on 1/2/78 and a major speech in Paris 1/4/78. Other correspondents were Tom Brokaw, Garrick Utley, John Palmer, Fred Briggs, and Steve Delaney.
Producer Ray Lockhart
Company NBC News
Director Thomas R. Wolzien

1122 **President Carter's Travels**   CBS
Program Type News Special
Special coverage highlighting Pres. Carter's visits to India, Egypt, France and Belgium, January 2–6, 1978.

The President in India
30 minutes. 1/2/78. Highlights of a major speech in New Delhi, and other activities of the day, including visit to Gandhi's tomb, meeting with Prime Minister Desai, and a reception and state dinner. Reporter: Peter Collins.

The President in Egypt
30 minutes. 1/4/78. Talks with Egyptian President Anwar El-Sadat. Reporter: John Sheahan.

The President in France
20 minutes. 1/5/78. Highlights of visit to Omaha Beach, reception at the Palace of Versailles, and interview with French President Valery Giscard D'estaing. Reporter: Tom Fenton.

The President Comes Home
20 minutes. 1/6/78. Highlights of activities in Brussels, including meeting with NATO and the European economic community, his return home to Andrews Air Force Base, evaluation of the impact of the President's trip. Reporter in Belgium: Mike Lee.
Executive Producer Russ Bensley
Company CBS News
Anchor Roger Mudd
Newspeople Accompanying the President and Mrs. Carter Bob Schieffer, Ed Bradley, Robert Pierpoint, Lee Thornton

1123 **President Carter's Trip to Six Nations**   ABC
Program Type News Special
Various times from 12/29/77–1/6/78. Barbara Walters covering President Carter's trips to Po-

land, Iran, India, Saudi Arabia, France and Belgium. Highlights of the trips shown on "ABC Evening News with Harry Reasoner and Barbara Walters," "Good Morning America," "ABC Saturday News" and "ABC Weekend News."
Company ABC News
Correspondents Barbara Walters, Sam Donaldson, Ann Compton, David Garcia, Ted Koppel, Steve Bell, Frank Reynolds, Bill Seamans, Irv Chapman, Jerry King, Jack Smith, Sylvia Chase

1124 President Carter's Vacation/Grand Teton Park
NBC News Special   NBC
Program Type News Special
Coverage of President Carter's 10-day Grand Teton Park vacation beginning 8/24/78.
Director Thomas R. Wolzien
Company NBC News

1125 The President in Berlin: A Town Meeting
NBC News Special   NBC
Program Type News Special
Live coverage on the President's appearance at a town hall meeting in Berlin, West Germany 7/15/78.
Executive Producer Paul Greenberg
Producer Ray Lockhart
Company NBC News

1126 The President in Germany   ABC
Program Type News Special
Live coverage of President Carter's "Town Meeting" in Berlin 7/15/78. Special report of Pres. Carter's trip to Germany for the economic summit meeting of world leaders presented on 7/16/78.
Company ABC News
Correspondents Peter Jennings, Sam Donaldson
Anchors Vic Ratner, Don Fisher

1127 The President's Mistress
The CBS Friday Night Movies   CBS
Program Type TV Movie
2 hours. Premiere date: 2/10/78. Drama of a man and his sister, who is mistress of a U.S. president. Music by Lalo Schifrin. Based on a novel by Patrick Anderson.
Executive Producer Stephen Friedman
Producer Herbert Hirschman
Company Stephen Friedman/Kings Road Production in association with Richard Bright
Director John Llewellyn Moxey
Writer Tom Lazarus
CAST
Ben Morton .... Beau Bridges
Donna Morton .... Karen Grassle

Mugsy .... Susan Blanchard
Gilkrist .... Joel Fabiani
Murphy .... Larry Hagman
Craig .... Don Porter
Gordon .... Thalmus Rasulala
Gwen .... Gail Strickland
Anatoly .... Titos Vandis
Bradley .... Michael Bell
Jan .... Janice Carroll
Claire Whitmore .... Patricia Wilson
Kinkaid .... Richard Blain
Josef .... Gregory Gay
Phil .... John S. Fox
Analyst .... Ellen Travolta
Alvina .... Virginia Wing
Boy at Zoo .... Steve Shaw
Minor Official .... Jason Wingreen
Peters .... Wes Dawn
Cabbie .... Biff Yeager
Mrs. Gilkrist .... Laurie Jefferson
Charlie .... Morton Lewis
Cleaning Lady .... Connie Sawyer
DMV Supervisor .... Anita Dangler
Nurse .... Juli Bridges
First Guard .... Tom Moses
Second Guard .... Dale Ware
Murphy's Secretary .... Abigail Shelton

1128 Previn and the Pittsburgh   PBS
Program Type Music/Dance Series
60 minutes. Sundays. Premiere date: 2/27/77. Second season premiere: 3/26/78. Eight-part series of musical discussion and performances with guest artists and the Pittsburgh Symphony. Series made possible by a grant from the Alcoa Foundation.
Executive Producer Jay Rayvid
Producers James A. DeVinney, Virginia K. Bartlett
Company WQED-TV/Pittsburgh
Director Ian Engelmann
Conductor Andre Previn
Host Andre Previn

1129 The Price is Right   CBS
Program Type Game/Audience Participation Special
60 Minutes. Mondays–Fridays. New series premiere: 9/4/72. Continuous. Show originally seen in 1956. Became television's first regularly scheduled 60-minute daytime game show 11/3/75.
Executive Producer Frank Wayne
Producer Jay Wolpert
Company Goodson-Todman Productions
Director Marc Breslow
Host Bob Barker
Announcer Johnny Olson

1130 The Priceless Treasures of Dresden
                                     PBS
Program Type Documentary/Informational

The Priceless Treasures of Dresden
Continued
Series
60 minutes. Premiere date: 6/27/78. Special inspired by "The Splendor of Dresden: Five Centuries of Art Collecting, An Exhibition from the German Democratic Republic." Taped in Dresden and at the National Gallery of Art in Washington, DC, where the exhibition opened 6/1/78. Program made possible by a grant from IBM.
Producer Al Perlmutter
Company WNET-TV/New York
Director Sid Smith
Writer Lou Solomon
Narrator Jose Ferrer

1131   The Prince of Homburg
Theater in America/Great Performances   PBS
Program Type Dramatic Special
2 hours. Premiere date: 4/27/77. Repeat date: 7/19/78. The Chelsea Theater Center of New York in a production of the 1811 psychological drama by Heinrich von Kleis translated by James Kirkup. Taped at the Biltmore House in Asheville, N.C. Program made possible by grants from Exxon Corporation, the Corporation for Public Broadcasting, the Ford Foundation and Public Television Stations.
Executive Producer Jac Venza
Producer Lindsay Law
Company WNET-TV/New York and WRKL-TV/Columbia, S.C.
Directors Robert Kalfin, Kirk Browning
Writer Heinrich von Kleist
Host Hal Holbrook
CAST
Prince	Frank Langella
Natalia	Randy Danson
Elector	K. Lype O'Dell
Col. Kottwitz	Roger DeKoven
Elector's Wife	M'El Dowd

Additional Cast George Morfogen, Robert Einekel, Frank Anderson, Jon Peter Benson, William Myers, Larry Swansen

1132   The Prison Game   PBS
Visions
90 minutes. Premiere date: 1/13/77. Repeat date: 12/11/78. Drama about a "To-Tell-the-Truth"-type game show in which three women claim to be a murderer. Program made possible by grants from the Ford Foundation, the National Endowment for the Arts and the Corporation for Public Broadcasting.
Producer Barbara Schultz
Company KCET-TV/Los Angeles
Director Robert Stevens
Writer Susan Yankowitz
Costume Designer Terence Tam Soon
Art Director John Retsek

CAST
Anna I	Edith Diaz
Anna II	Jessica Walter
Anna III	Cara Williams
Henry Stokes	Peter Bonerz
Marion Kostine	Neva Patterson
Marvin Simeon	Severn Darden
Moderator (Chuck Cooper)	Bo Kaprall
Husband I	Chu Chu Malave
Husband II	David Hayward
Husband III	Ryan MacDonald
Carrie	Migdia Varela
Psychiatrist	Tom Palmer

1133   The Prisoner   PBS
Program Type Drama Series
60 minutes. Season premiere: 1/16/78. Intellectual thriller first produced for British television over 11 years ago. Each episode followed by Dr. Roderic Gorney commenting on the series' psychological intricacies. Producer for the Gorney segments is Mark Waxman; Director, Jerry Hughes. Original series created by Patrick McGoohan who plays the title role.
Company Independent Television Corporation
Host Dr. Roderic Gorney
Star Patrick McGoohan

The Private Life of Sherlock Holmes *See* CBS Special Movie Presentations

1134   Pro Bowl   ABC
Program Type Sports Special
Live coverage of The Pro Bowl football game between the Dallas Cowboys and the Miami Dolphins from Tampa Stadium, Tampa Bay, FL 1/23/78.
Executive Producer Roone Arledge
Producer Dennis Lewin
Company ABC Sports
Director Chet Forte
Announcers Howard Cosell, Frank Gifford, Don Meredith

1135   Professional Bowlers Association National Championship Tournament   CBS
Program Type Limited Sports Series
2 hours. Live coverage of the finals of the championship tournament from Reno, Nevada 6/18/78. CBS Sports-Gary Bender
Producer Bob Stenner
Company CBS Television Network Sports
Director Tony Verna
Announcer Gary Bender
Commentator Carmen Salvino

1136   Professional Bowlers Tour   ABC
Program Type Limited Sports Series
90 minutes. Saturday afternoons. Premiere date:

1/6/62. 17th season premiere: 1/7/78. Last show of season: 4/22/78. 16-week series of live telecasts of bowling tournaments.
Executive Producer Roone Arledge
Producers Dick Buffinton, Ric LaCivita, Bob Goodrich
Company ABC Sports
Directors Roger Goodman, Lou Volpicelli, Jim Jennett
Announcers Chris Schenkel (regular announcer), Al Michaels, Dave Diles
Expert Commentator Nelson Burton, Jr.

1137 Professional Foul
Great Performances   PBS
Program Type Dramatic Special
90 minutes. Premiere date: 4/26/78. Play about a Cambridge professor who delivers a philosophy symposium paper in Prague. Program made possible by a grant from Exxon Corporation.
Producer Mark Shivas
Company WNET-TV/New York
Director Michael Lindsay-Hogg
Writer Tom Stoppard
CAST
Professor Anderson .... Peter Barkworth
Additional Cast John Shrapnel, Stephen Rea, Richard O'Callaghan, Shane Rimmer, Bernard Hill, Billy Hamon, David de Keyser

1138 Professional Racquetball   PBS
Program Type Sports Special
60 minutes. 6/11/78. Coverage of the men's and women's finals of the Phoenix stop on the Colgate Pro-Am Racquetball Tour taped at the Arizona Athletic Club. Expert tips on the game by Charlie Brumfield and Jean Sauser. Program made possible by a grant from Robert W. Kendler, Sr. and Twin City Concrete.
Company KAET-TV/Phoenix

1139 Project U.F.O.   NBC
Program Type Drama Series
60 minutes. Sundays. Premiere: 2/19/78. True-to-life dramatization of the U.S. Air Force's investigation of mysterious sightings. These investigations are based on the Air Force "Blue Book" files.
Executive Producer Jack Webb
Producers William Coleman, Don Widener
Company Mark VII Ltd.
Directors Various
Writers Various
CAST
Maj. Jake Gatlin .... William Jordan
S/Sgt. Harry Fitz .... Casey Swaim
Libby .... Aldine King

1140 Promise Now, Pay Later
CBS Reports   CBS
Program Type Documentary/Informational Special
Premiere date: 5/2/78. Report on the cost of Civil Service pensions to taxpayers.
Executive Producer Howard Stringer
Producer Esther Kartiganer
Cinematographer Greg Cooke
Film Editor Chris Dalrymple
Researcher Teresa Styles
Reporter Marlene Sanders

1141 Pssst! Hammerman's After You!
ABC Out-of-School Specials/ABC Weekend Specials   ABC
Program Type Children's Special
60 minutes. Premiere date: 1/16/74. Repeat date: 12/17/77. Based on "The 18th Emergency" by Betsy Byars.
Producer Martin Tahse
Company Entertainment Media Productions
Director Jack Regas
Writer Bob Rodgers
CAST
Mouse Fawley .... Christian Juttner
Marv Hammerman .... Jim Sage
Ezzie .... Lance Kerwin
Mr. Casino .... Titos Vandis
Mr. Stein .... Jack Manning
Mouse's Mother .... Jay MacIntosh
Mrs. Schwartz .... Lillian Adams
Viola .... Lark Geib
Margy .... Ann D'Andrea

1142 Psychic Phenomena: Exploring the Unknown
The Big Event   NBC
Program Type Documentary/Informational Special
90 minutes. Premiere date: 10/30/77. Special depicting several of the world's most remarkable psychic feats.
Producer Alan Neuman
Writer Alan Neuman
Director Alan Neuman
Host Burt Lancaster

1143 Psychic Surgeons: Miracle or Illusion?   PBS
Program Type Documentary/Informational Special
75 minutes. Premiere date: 2/27/78. Documentary probe of a new and lucrative international trade in "miracles." Acquired for PBS by Eastern Educational Network.
Company Granada Television International

1144   Quark   NBC
Program Type Comedy Series
30 minutes. Fridays. Premiere date: 5/7/77. Second season premiere: 2/24/78 (as one-hour special). Last show of series: 4/14/78. Science-fiction comedy pilot about the commander of the United Galaxy Sanitation Patrol in the year 2222 A.D.
Executive Producers David Gerber, Mace Neufeld
Producer Bruce Johnson
Company David Gerber Productions in association with Columbia Pictures Television
Directors Various
Writers Various
CAST
Adam Quark ....Richard Benjamin
Gene/Jean ....Timothy Thomerson
Betty I .... Tricia Barnstable
Betty II .... Cyb Barnstable
Otto Palindrome ....Conrad Janis
The Head .... Alan Caillou
Andy the Robot ....Bobby Porter
Ficus ....Richard Kelton
The Source .... Hans Conreid

1145   ¿ Que Pasa, U.S.A.?   PBS
Program Type Comedy Series
30 minutes. Premiere date: 1/14/78. 18-part bilingual situation-comedy about the Penas, a Cuban-American family. Taped before an audience at WPBT, Miami. Series made possible by a grant from the U.S. Department of Health, Education and Welfare Office of Education's Emergency Aid Act (ESAA–TV). Series created by Manuel Mendoza.
Project Director Jose Bahamonde
Supervising Executive Shep Morgan
Company WPBT-TV/Miami and Community Action and Research, Inc.
Director Bernard Lechowick
Story Editor Luis Santiero
CAST
Grandparents .... Velia Martinez, Louis Oquendo
Parents .... Ana Margarita Martinez-Casado;
                                             Manolo Villaverde
Teenagers .... Rocky Echevarria,
                                             Ana Margarita Menendez

1146   The Queen's Destiny
Ourstory   PBS
Program Type Dramatic Special
30 minutes. Premiere date: 4/12/76. Repeat date: 11/7/77. A dramatization of the overthrow of Queen Liliuokalani of Hawaii in 1893. Funded by grants from the National Endowment for the Humanities, the Arthur Vining Davis Foundations and the George Gund Foundation.
Executive Producer Don Fouser
Producer Don Fouser
Company WNET-TV/New York
Director Don Fouser

Writer Robert Pendlebury
Costume Designer John Boxer
Host Bill Moyers
CAST
Queen Liliuokalani .... Miriam Colon
Samuel Parker ....Manu Tupou
A. P. Peterson .... George Pentecost
W. H. Cornwell .... Bill Moor
John F. Colburn .... Wayne Maxwell
Wilson .... Tom Martin
Princess .... Nai Bonet

1147   A Question of Guilt
The CBS Tuesday Night Movies   CBS
Program Type TV Movie
2 hours. Premiere date: 2/21/78. Drama about woman accused of murdering her child. Music by Artie Kane.
Executive Producers Lee Rich, Philip Capice
Producer Peter Katz
Writers Jack and Mary Willis
Director Robert Butler
CAST
Doris Winters ....Tuesday Weld
Det. Louis Kazinsky .... Ron Liebman
Wharton .... Peter Masterson
Mel Duvall .... Alex Rocco
Dr. Rosen .... Viveca Lindfors
Elizabeth Garson ....Lana Wood
Herman Golob ....Stephen Pearlman
Assistant D.A. Verrell .... Ron Rifkin
Dick Tarcher .... David Wilson
Larry Winters .... Jim Antonio
McCartney ....M. Emmet Walsh
Mrs. Wharton .... Kelly Peters
Miriam Hamlish .... Mari Gorman
Mrs. Winters ....Katharine Bard
Mrs. Kazinsky .... Lisa Richards
Norman Picker ....Robert Costanza
Dan Mazzo ....James Ingersoll
Carmines .... Nicky Blair
Polygraph Technician ....Brian Farrell
Judge Williams .... Sid McCoy
Man on Stand .... Michael Fairman
Daly ....John Fitzpatrick
Rappaport ....Philip Halverson
D.A. Koch ....Bernard Behrens

1148   Quincy   NBC
Program Type Crime Drama Series
60 minutes. Fridays. Premiere date: 10/3/76. Second season premiere: 9/16/77. Mystery drama involving a medical examiner in the Los Angeles City Coronor's Office. Created by Glen A. Larson and Lou Shaw. Music by Stu Phillips.
Executive Producers Judy Kinberg, Glen A, Larson, Richard Irving
Supervising Producer B. W. Sandefur
Producers Christopher Morgan, Peter J. Thompson, Edward J. Montagne, Robert F. O'Neill
Company Glen A. Larson Productions in association with Universal Television and NBC-TV
Directors Various
Writers Various

CAST

Quincy	Jack Klugman
Lt. Frank Monahan	Garry Walberg
Dr. Robert Astin	John S. Ragin
Sam Fujiyama	Robert Ito
Danny Tovo	Val Bisoglio
Sgt. Brill	Joseph Roman

Race With the Devil *See* The CBS Wednesday Night Movies

1149 Rafferty   CBS
Program Type Drama Series
60 minutes. Mondays. Premiere date: 9/5/77.
Last show: 11/28/77. Drama about retired
Army doctor in civilian practice.
Executive Producer Jerry Thorpe
Producer James Lee
Company Warner Bros. Television
Directors Various
Writers Various

CAST

Dr. Sid Rafferty	Patrick McGoohan
Nurse Vera Welsh	Millie Slavin
Dr. Daniel Gentry	John Getz

Rafferty and the Highway Hustlers *See* NBC Saturday Night at the Movies

1150 The Rag Business
The ABC Saturday Comedy Special   ABC
30 minutes. Premiere date: 7/1/78. Comedy
about garment workers.
Executive Producer Aaron Ruben
Producer Gene Marcione
Company Andomar Production
Director Russ Petranto
Writers Ronald Wolfe, Ronald Chesney

CAST

Connie	Conchata Ferrell
Mr. Fisher	Dick O'Neil
Alma	Sudie Bond
Jackie	Sarina Grant
Susan	Susan Lawrence
Coco	Jeannie Linero
Dennis	Fred McCarren
Darlene	Anna L. Pagan
Rita	Peggy Pope

1151 The Rag Tag Champs
ABC Afterschool Specials   ABC
Program Type Children's Special
60 minutes. Based on the novel by Alfred Slote.
Premiere date: 3/22/78. Special about a team of
14-year-old baseball players. Filmed on location
in Los Angeles.
Producer Robert Chenault
Company ABC Circle Films
Director Virgil Vogel
Writer E. Jack Kaplan

Art Director Ray Markham
Film Editor Peter Parasheles, A.C.E.
Music Tommy Leonetti
Director of Photography Otto Nemenz

CAST

Jake Wrather	Larry Scott
Lenny Johnson	Glynn Turman
Mrs. Bradbury	Madge Sinclair
Jesus Sanchez	Claudio Martinez
Cindy Franks	Shannon Terhune
Tony DeVito	Guillermo San Juan
Pat McCleod	Chris Petersen
Mr. McCleod	John Durren
Mrs. Fulton	Jacque Lynn Colton
Policeman	Joseph Clark
Jerry	James Bridges

1152 Raid on Entebbe
The Big Event
Program Type Dramatic Special   NBC
3 hours. Premiere date: 1/9/77. Repeat date:
6/13/78. Dramatization of the 7/4/76 Israeli
raid on Entebbe airport. Music by David Shire.
Executive Producers Edgar J. Scherick; Daniel
H. Blatt
Company Edgar J. Scherick Associates in associ-
ation with 20th Century-Fox Television and
NBC-TV
Director Irvin Kershner
Writer Barry Beckerman
Production Designer W. Stewart Campbell
Art Director Kirk Axtell

CAST

Gen. Dan Shomron	Charles Bronson
Prime Minister Rabin	Peter Finch
Pres. Idi Amin	Yaphet Kotto
Gen. Mordechai Gur	Jack Warden
Dan Cooper	Martin Balsam
Wilfred Boese	Horst Bucholz
Capt. Bacos	Eddie Constantine
Cohen	Allan Arbus
Gen. Allon	Robert Loggia
Gen. Peled	John Saxon
Begin	David Opatoshu
Dora Block	Sylvia Sidney
Krieger	Mariclare Costello
Yonni Netanyahu	Stephen Macht

Additional Cast Tige Andrews, Warren Kemmerling,
James Woods, Lou Gilbert, Alex Colon, Harvey
Lembeck, Peter Brocco, Aharon Ipale

Rancho Deluxe *See* The CBS Wednesday Night Movies

1153 The Ransom of Red Chief
ABC Weekend Specials/ABC Short Story
Specials   ABC
Program Type Children's Special
30 minutes. Premiere date: 10/22/77. Repeat
date: 3/11/78. Two old drifters plan the kidnap-
ing of a young boy as a way of putting together
a stake which will get them to California. Based

The Ransom of Red Chief *Continued*
on story by O. Henry. Teleplay by Jim Carlson
and Terrence McDonnell. Music by Tommy
Leonetti.
Executive Producer Robert Chenault
Company An ABC Circle Film
Director Jeffrey Hayden
Cinematographer Otto Nemenz
CAST
Billy ....Strother Martin
Sam .... Jack Elam
Ebeneezer Dorset .... William Mims
Red Chief .... Patrick J. Petersen

Rashomon *See* PBS Movie Theater

1154 Razzmatazz   CBS
Program Type News Magazine Series
30 minutes. Saturday/Thursday (as of 4/13/78.)
Premiere date: 11/5/77. (60 minute pilot shown
4/16/77.) News magazine series for young peo-
ple.
Company CBS News in cooperation with Scho-
lastic Magazine
Producer Vern Diamond
Director Vern Diamond
Executive Producer Joel Heller
Film Editor Kenneth Baldwin
Host Barry Bostwick

1155 Rebop   PBS
Program Type Children's Series
30 minutes. Sundays. Premiere date: 10/9/76.
Season premiere: 10/2/77. 26-week multi-cul-
tural series for children ages 9–13. Two weekly
film portraits of young people from different cul-
tural backgrounds. Series made possible by
grants from the U.S. Department of Health, Edu-
cation and Welfare, Parker Brothers, Kenner
Products and Fundimension Division of General
Mills, Inc.
Executive Producer Topper Carew
Producers Lois H. Johnson, Jesus Henrique Mal-
donaldo, Dasal Banks, Tanya Hart, David K.
Liu, Hazel V. Bright, Peter Cook
Company WGBH-TV/Boston
Cinematographers Tim Hill, Werner Bund-
schuh, Henry Johnson, Elvida Abella

1156 The Red Hand Gang   NBC
Program Type Children's Series
30 minutes. Saturday. Premiere date: 9/10/77.
Last show: 1/21/78. Adventures of five city chil-
dren. Serialized stories of varying length.
Executive Producer William P. D'Angelo; Ray
Allen; Harvey Bullock
Company D'Angelo/Bullock/Allen Productions
Director William P. D'Angelo (first five weeks)
Writers Various

CAST
Frankie .... Matthew Laborteaux
J.R. .... J. R. Miller
Doc ....James Bond
Joanne ....Jolie Newman
Lil Bill .... Keith Mitchell

1157 Redd Foxx   ABC
Program Type Music/Comedy/Variety Series
60 minutes. Thursdays. Premiere date: 9/15/77.
Last show: 1/26/78. Veteran entertainer Redd
Foxx and his special brand of comedy. Among
the regular segments was "Redd's Corner," a
showcase for talented performers never before
seen on national television.
Executive Producer Redd Foxx
Producers Allan Blye, Bob Einstein
Company A Blye-Einstein Production in associa-
tion with Redd Foxx Productions
Director Donald Davis
Writing Supervisors Bob Einstein, Allan Blye
Writers Pat Proft, Lenny Ripps, Andrew John-
son, Levi Taylor, Stuart Birnbaum, Matt Neu-
man, Joe Shulkin, Henry Wallace
Musical Director Gerald Wilson
Choreographer Lester Wilson
Costume Designer Bill Whitten
Art Director Jack McAdam
Regulars Slappy White, Damita Jo, LaWanda
Page, Bill Saluga, Hal Smith, Joe Clayton, Tim
Thomerson

1158 The Redd Foxx Special   ABC
Program Type Music/Comedy/Variety Special
90 minutes. Premiere date: 4/4/78.
Producers Allan Blye; Bob Einstein
Company Blye-Einstein Production in associa-
tion with Redd Foxx Productions
Director Donald Davis
Star Redd Foxx
Guest Stars Lorne Greene, Red Buttons, Rip
Taylor, Slappy White, Bill Saluga, Susan An-
ton

The Reivers *See* NBC Saturday Night at
the Movies

**1159 Renascence: Where All Things
Belong**   PBS
Program Type Documentary/Informational
Special
30 minutes. Premiere date: 12/27/76. Repeat
date 2/1/78. A television essay celebrating the
process of rebirth in the natural world. Program
made possible by a grant from the Weyerhaeuser
Company Foundation.
Producer Richard Gilbert
Company KCTS-TV/Seattle

Director Richard Gilbert
Writer James Halpin

1160 Rene Levesque: A Portrait of Independence   PBS
Program Type Documentary/Informational Special
60 minutes. Premiere date: 4/21/78. Rene Levesque gives his first extended interview to American television.
Producer Peter N. Hartberg
Company Vermont Education Television
Director Peter N. Hartberg
Interviewer Jack Barry

1161 Reply to Carter's Energy Message   CBS
Program Type News Special
30 minutes. Premiere date: 11/15/77. Republican view of President Carter's Nov. 8 energy message presented by Congressman John B. Anderson of Illinois and Senator Bob Packwood of Oregon.
Company CBS News

1162 Requiem   CBS
Program Type Religious/Cultural Special
60 minutes. Premiere date: 9/18/77. Jewish community in Hungary commemorates the Jewish High Holy Days, Rosh Hashanah and Yom Kippur.
Executive Producer Pamela Ilott
Company CBS News
Cinematographer Imre Lazar

1163 Requiem
Great Performances   PBS
Program Type Music/Dance Special
90 minutes. Premiere date: 3/22/78. Classic work of inspirational music by Giuseppe Verdi with La Scala Orchestra and Chorus. Program made possible by a grant from Exxon Corporation and support from PBS.
Executive Producer Jac Venza
Producer David Griffiths
Company Unitel for WNET-TV/New York
Director Henri-Georges Clouzot
Conductor Herbert von Karajan
Soloists Leontyne Price, Fiorenza Cossotto, Luciano Pavarotti, Nicolai Ghiaurov

1164 The Resignation of Bert Lance   ABC
Program Type News Special
2 hours. Live coverage of Budget Director Bert Lance before the Senate Governmental Affairs Committee 9/15/77.
Executive Producer Robert Siegenthaler

Company ABC News Special Events
Producer Jeff Gralnick
Correspondents Frank Reynolds, Dan Cordtz, Sam Donaldson, Bill Wordham

1165 The Resignation of Bert Lance I
NBC News Special   NBC
Program Type News Special
30 minutes. 9/15/77. Special report on Budget Director Bert Lance appearing before the Senate Governmental Affairs Committee.
Producer Ray Lockhart
Company NBC News
Anchor John Hart
Commentators Tom Pettit, Irving R. Levine, Marilyn Berger, Jackson Bain

1166 The Resignation of Bert Lance II
NBC News Special   NBC
Program Type News Special
30 minutes. 9/17/77. Special report on Budget Director Bert Lance appearing before the Senate Governmental Affairs Commitee.
Producer Ray Lockhart
Company NBC News
Anchor Bob Jamieson
Commentator Irving R. Levine

1167 The Resignation of Bert Lance III
NBC News Special   NBC
Program Type News Special
30 minutes. 9/21/77. Special report on Budget Director Bert Lance appearing before the Senate Governmental Affairs Committee. Tom Pettit interviewed Elizabeth Drew and David Broder.
Producer Ray Lockhart
Company NBC News
Anchor David Brinkley
Commentators Bob Jamieson, Judy Woodruff, Jessica Savitch, Robert Jimenez

1168 The Return of Captain Nemo   CBS
Program Type Limited Series
60 minutes. Wednesdays. Premiere date: 3/8/78. Continued: 3/15/78, 3/22/78. Pilot series based on the Jules Verne novel, the underseas adventure is set in contemporary times. Created by Irwin Allen. Underwater sequences directed by Paul Stader. Special photo effects by L. B. Abbot. Special effects by Chuck Gaspar. Music by Richard LaSalle.
Executive Producer Arthur Weiss
Producer Irwin Allen
Company Warner Bros. Television and Irwin Allen Productions
Director Alex March
Writers Norman Katkov, Preston Wood, Robert

The Return of Captain Nemo *Continued*
Block, William Keys, Larry Alexander, Robert C. Dennis, Mann Rubin
Costume Designer Paul Zastupnevich
CAST
Capt. Nemo .... Jose Ferrer
Lt. Jim Porter .... Burr DeBenning
Cmdr. Tom Franklin .... Tom Hallick
Prof. Waldo Cunningham .... Burgess Meredith
Mr. Miller .... Warren Stevens
Tor .... Med Flory
Kate .... Lynda Day George
Cook .... Mel Ferrer
Tibor .... Horst Buchholz

1169   The Return of the Incredible Hulk
CBS
Program Type Dramatic Special
2 hours. Premiere date: 11/28/77. Repeat date: 5/5/78. Further adventures of a scientist whose radiation experiments turned him into a homeless wanderer-raging beast looking for a cure for the ray's monsterous effect.
Director Alan Levi
Writer Kenneth Johnson
Company Universal Television
CAST
David Bruce Banner .... Bill Bixby
The Hulk .... Lou Ferrigno;
McGee .... Jack Colvin
Julie Griffith .... Laurie Prange
Margaret Griffith .... Dorothy Tristan
Denny .... Gerald McRaney
Dr. Bonifant .... William Daniels

The Return of the Pink Panther *See* The ABC Friday Night Movie

1170   Return to Earth
Tuesday Movie of the Week   ABC
Program Type TV Movie
90 minutes. Premiere date: 5/14/76. Repeat date: 8/1/78. Fictionalized account of the Apollo 11 astronaut, based on the book, "Return to Earth" by Col. Edwin E. "Buzz" Aldrin, Jr. and Wayne Warga. Filmed in part at NASA in Houston, Tex. Music by Billy Goldenberg.
Executive Producers Alan King, Rupert Hitzig
Producer Jud Taylor
Company A King-Hitzig Production
Director Jud Taylor
Writer George Malko
CAST
Col. Edwin E. "Buzz" Aldrin, Jr. .... Cliff Robertson
Joan Aldrin .... Shirley Knight
Col. Edwin E. Aldrin, Sr. .... Ralph Bellamy
Marianne .... Stefanie Powers
Dr. Sam Mayhill .... Charles Cioffi
Andy Aldrin .... Kraig Metzinger
Jan Aldrin .... Alexandra Taylor
Mike Aldrin .... Tony Marks
Dr. Holtfield .... Stephen Pearlman

1171   Return to Fantasy Island
The ABC Friday/Sunday Night Movie   ABC
Program Type TV Movie
2 hours. Premiere date: 11/20/77. Repeat date: 1/20/78. Six people fly to a plush island resort where they are given the opportunity to live out their fantasies. This sequel to "Fantasy Island" is the forerunner of the series, "Fantasy Island" which premiered 1/28/78. Music by Laurence Rosenthal.
Executive Producers Aaron Spelling, Leonard Goldberg
Producer Michael Fisher
Company A Spelling-Goldberg Production
Director George McCowan
Writer Marc Brandell
Art Director Alfeo Bocchicchio
CAST
Roarke .... Ricardo Montalban
Margo Dean .... Adrienne Barbeau
Charles .... Horst Buchholz
Brian .... Joseph Campanella
Pierre .... George Chakiris
Mr. Grant .... Joseph Cotten
Lucy .... Pat Crowley
Mrs. Grant .... Laraine Day
Benson .... George Maharis
Raoul .... Cameron Mitchell
Kito .... France Nuyen
Janet .... Karen Valentine
Tattoo .... Herve Villechaize
Dr. Croyden .... John Zaremba
Pat .... Kevi Kendall
Carol .... Kristine Ritzke
Ann .... Nancy McKeon

1172   Rex Humbard World Outreach Ministry
Syndicated
Program Type Religious/Cultural Series
60 minutes. Weekly. Syndicated for over 25 years from the Cathedral of Tomorrow near Akron, Ohio. Sermons by Rex Humbard.
Executive Producer Rex Humbard, Jr.
Producer Bob Anderson
Company The Cathedral of Tomorrow-World Outreach Ministry
Director Bob Anderson
Musical Director Mary Adams
Regulars The Rex Humbard Family Singers, Cathedral Choir
Featured Soloists Maude Aimee Humbard, Elizabeth Humbard

1173   The Rhinemann Exchange
NBC's Best Seller/The Big Event
Program Type Limited Series   NBC
5 hours. Premiere date: 3/10/77. Repeat date: 7/29/78. Dramatization of the novel by Robert Ludlum about espionage during World War II. Filmed on location in Mexico City and Cuernavaca, Mexico.
Executive Producer George Eckstein

Producer Richard Collins
Company Universal Television in association with NBC-TV
Director Burt Kennedy
Writer Richard Collins
Costume Designer Yvonne Wood
Art Director William H. Tuntke
Set Decorator Richard Friedman
CAST

David Spaulding	Stephen Collins
Dr. Lyons	Rene Auberjonois
Bobby Ballard	Roddy McDowall
Dr. Azevedo	Ben Wright
Col. Pace	Larry Hagman
Leslie Jenner Hawkewood	Lauren Hutton
Kendall	Claude Akins
Irene	Trisha Noble
Altmuller	Werner Klemperer
Dietricht	John van Dreelen
Stoltz	Bo Brundin
Rhinemann	Jose Ferrer
Swanson	Vince Edwards
Asher Feld	Len Berman
Col. Meehan	Ramon Bieri
Lt. Funes	Pedro Armendariz, Jr.
Amb. Granville	John Huston
Mrs. Cameron	Kate Woodville
Alex Spaulding	William Prince
Indian Girl	Victoria Racimo
Geoffrey Moore	Jeremy Kemp

1174 **Rhoda** CBS
Program Type Comedy Series
30 minutes. Sundays. Premiere date: 9/9/74. Fourth season premiere: 10/2/77. Spin-off from "The Mary Tyler Moore Show" created by James L. Brooks and Allan Burns. Comedy about a window dresser in New York City. Music by Billy Goldenberg.
Executive Producer Charlotte Brown
Producers Don Reo; Allan Katz
Company MTM Enterprises, Inc.
Directors Various
Writers Various
CAST

Rhoda Morgenstern Gerard	Valerie Harper
Brenda Morgenstern	Julie Kavner
Gary Levy	Ron Silver
Benny Goodwin	Ray Buktenica
Johnny Venture	Michael DeLano
Jack Doyle	Kenneth McMillan
Ramon	Rafael Campos
Carlton the Doorman	Lorenzo Music

1175 **Rich Little's Washington Follies**
ABC
Program Type Comedy Special
60 minutes. Premiere date: 5/13/78. Impressionist Rich Little raises a comical eyebrow at government.
Executive Producer Jerry Goldstein
Producer Saul Ilson

Company Dudley Enterprises in association with Saul Ilson Productions, Inc.
Director Stan Harris
Writers Hal Goldman, Jeffrey Barron, Wayne Kline, Kevin Hartigan, David Garber, Saul Ilson
Musical Director Bob Hughes
Choreographer Kevin Carlisle
Costume Designer Bill Hargate
Art Director Bill Bohnert
Star Suzanne Somers
Host Rich Little
Guest Stars Dick Van Patten, Robert Guillaume, Tom Bosley

1176 **The Richard Pryor Show** NBC
Program Type Comedy Series
60 minutes. Tuesdays/Thursdays (as of 10/20/77.) Premiere: 9/13/77. Last show: 10/20/77. Comedy-variety show, starring Richard Pryor with guests.
Executive Producer Burt Sugarman
Producers Rocco Urbisci, John Moffitt
Company Burt Sugarman Productions in association with Richard Pryor Enterprises and NBC-TV
Director John Moffitt
Writers Various

Richard III *See* PBS Movie theater

1177 **The Richard Pryor Special?** NBC
Program Type Music/Comedy/Variety Special
60 minutes. Premiere date: 5/5/77. Repeat date: 10/11/77. Richard Pryor's first television special.
Executive Producer Burt Sugarman
Producer Bob Ellison
Company Burt Sugarman Production in association with Richard Pryor Enterprises and NBC
Director John Moffitt
Writers Richard Pryor, Bob Ellison, Rocco Urbisci, Paul Mooney, Alan Thicke
Star Richard Pryor
Guest Stars John Belushi, Mike Evans, LaWanda Page, Shirley Hemphill, Maya Angelou, Glynn Turman, Timothy Thomerson, the Pips

1178 **Richie Brockelman, Private Eye**
NBC
Program Type Limited Series
60 minutes. Thursdays/Fridays. Premiere date: 3/16/78. Last show: 4/14/78. Adventures of a 23-year-old, college-educated private eye who tries to avoid violence. "Richie Brockelman: Missing 24 Hours" was a 90-minutes film, telecast May 1977 as "NBC Movie of the Week."

Richie Brockelman, Private Eye
Continued
Also, 2/24/78, special two-hour, "The Rockford Files", featured "Brockelman."
Executive Producers Stephen J. Cannell; Steven Bochco
Supervising Producer Alex Beaton
Producer Peter S. Fischer
Company Universal Television Production in association with NBC-TV
Directors Various
Writers Various
CAST
Richie Brockelman .... Dennis Dugan
Sharon .... Barbara Bosson
Sgt. Coopersmith .... Robert Hogan

1179   Rigoletto
Live from the Metropolitan Opera   PBS
Program Type Music/Dance Special
3 hours. Premiere date: 11/7/77. Classic Giuseppe Verdi opera airs live from the Metropolitan Opera, New York. Program made possible by grants from Texaco and the National Endowment for the Arts.
Executive Producer Michael Bronson
Producer Christopher Sarson
Company Metropolitan Opera Association and WNET-TV/New York
Director Kirk Browning
Musical Director James Levine
Host Tony Randall
CAST
Rigoletto .... Cornell MacNeil
Gilda .... Ileana Cotrubas
Duke .... Placido Domingo
Maddalena .... Isola Jones
Sparafucile .... Justino Diaz
Monterone .... John Cheek

1180   Rikki-Tikki-Tavi   CBS
Program Type Animated Film Special
30 minutes. Premiere date: 1/9/75. Repeat date: 1/23/78. Adapted from "The Jungle Books" by Rudyard Kipling.
Producer Chuck Jones
Company Chuck Jones Enterprises, Inc.
Director Chuck Jones
Writer Chuck Jones
Narrator Orson Welles
VOICES
Rikki-Tikki-Tavi .... Orson Welles
Additional Voices June Foray, Les Tremayne, Michael LeClair, Lennie Weinrib, Shep Menken

1181   Ring of Passion
NBC Saturday Night at the Movies/NBC World Premiere Movie   NBC
Program Type Dramatic Special
2 hours. Premiere date: 2/4/78. Drama about Joe Louis's two historic heavyweight fights with Germany's Max Schmeling.
Director Robert Michael Lewis
Writer Larry Forrester
CAST
Joe Louis .... Bernie Casey
Max Schmeling .... Stephen Macht
Anny Ondra .... Britt Ekland
Marva Trotter Louis .... Denise Nicholas
Joe Jacobs .... Mordecai Lawner
Damon Runyon .... Allen Garfield
Paul Gallico .... Joseph Campanella
Lilly Brooks .... Beah Richards
Roxborough .... Percy Rodriques

1182   Ringo   NBC
Program Type Music/Comedy/Variety Special
60 minutes. Premiere date: 4/26/78. Ringo Starr plays himself and his look-alike in this rock-musical comedy. Based loosely on "The Prince and the Pauper" by Mark Twain.
Executive Producers Robert Meyrowitz, Peter Kauff, Alan Steinberg
Producer Ken Ehrlich
Company DIR Broadcasting Productions and Montico Corp
Director Jeff Margolis
Writers Neil Israel, Pat Proft
Musical Director Jimmy Webb
Star Ringo Starr
Guest Cast John Ritter, Angie Dickinson, George Harrison, Carrie Fisher, Art Carney, Mike Douglas, Vincent Price

Rio Lobo See NBC Saturday Night at the Movies

1183   The Rita Moreno Show   CBS
Program Type Comedy Special
30 minutes. Premiere date: 5/2/78. Pilot about the owner of a small resort in the Poconos.
Executive Producers Mark Rothman; Lowell Ganz
Company Hayoudo Productions, Inc.
Director Tony Mordente
Writers Mark Rothman, Lowell Ganz
CAST
Marie Constanza .... Rita Moreno
Leo .... Victor Buono
Mr. Gladstone .... Louis Nye
Carol Constanza .... Kathy Bendett
Esteban .... Bert Rosario
Miss Forbush .... Kit McDonough
Mr. Leopold .... Ron Vernan
Mrs. Murphy .... Virginia Peters
Mrs. Kleppner .... Lee Bryant
Doris .... Shirley Mitchell

1184 Robert F. Kennedy Pro-Celebrity Tennis Tournament ABC
Program Type Sports Special
90 minutes. 8/27/78. Tennis tournament from Forest Hills Tennis Stadium, New York, to benefit the Robert F. Kennedy Memorial.
Executive Producer Roone Arledge
Producer Ric LaCivita
Company ABC Sports
Director Roger Goodman
Hosts Howard Cosell; Arthur Ashe

1185 Roberto Devereux
In Performance at Wolf Trap PBS
Program Type Music/Dance Special
2 1/2 hours. Premiere date: 10/6/75. Repeat date: 9/20/77. The opera by Gaetano Donizetti performed by the Wolf Trap Company and the Filene Center Orchestra at the Wolf Trap Farm Park in Arlington, Va. Program made possible by a grant from the Atlantic Richfield Company.
Executive Producer David Prowitt
Producer Ruth Leon
Company WETA-TV/Washington, D.C.
Director Kirk Browning
Conductor Julius Rudel
Hosts Beverly Sills, David Prowitt
Executive-in-Charge Jim Karayn
CAST
Queen Elizabeth I .... Beverly Sills
Roberto Devereux ....John Alexander
Sara, Duchess of Nottingham .... Susanne Marsee
Nottingham ....Richard Fredricks
Raleigh .... David Rae Smith

Robin Hood *See* The Legend of Robin Hood

1186 Robin Hood Jr. PBS
Once Upon a Classic
Program Type Dramatic Special
60 minutes. Premiere date: 12/29/77. Special production of classic tale with all principal roles played by youngsters. Presented by WQED-TV/Pittsburg and McDonald's local Restaurants Association.
Company Time-Life Television/BBC-TV
Host Bill Bixby
CAST
Robin Hood .... Keith Chegwin
Marion ....Mandy Tulloch
Edmund ....Dean Lawrence
Lord Gilbert ....Alexander John
Baron .... Maurice Kaufmann

1187 The Rock 'N' Roll Sports Classic NBC
Program Type Sports Special
2 hours. Premiere date: 5/3/78. More than 50

TV and pop music stars compete in a 20-event Olympic-style contest.
Executive Producer Bob Finkel
Producer Tony Verna
Company Aucoin/Alvin Ross/Bob Finkel/-Teram Production
Director Tony Verna
Hosts Alex Karras, Ted Knight, Kristy McNichol, Ed McMahon

1188 The Rock Rainbow ABC
Program Type Dramatic Special
60 minutes. Premiere date: 7/15/78. Pilot about three women seeking superstardom in the music world.
Executive Producer Martin Starger
Producer Alan Sacks
Co-Producer Robert Scheerer
Company Marstar Productions in association with TTC Productions, Inc.
Musical Director Tony Berg
CAST
Jess .... Ellen Greene
Catherine ....Susan Bigelow
Lil ....Louisa Flaningam
Speed ....John V. Shea
Mack .... John Aprea
David ....Scott Porter
Jim .... Kenneth Tigar

1189 The Rockford Files NBC
Program Type Crime Drama Series
60 minutes. Fridays. Premiere date: 9/13/74. Fourth season premiere: 9/16/77. Action drama revolving around an ex-con/private investigator who takes on unsolved police cases. Created by Roy Huggins and Stephen J. Cannell. Theme music by Mike Post and Peter Carpenter.
Executive Producer Meta Rosenberg
Supervising Producer Stephen J. Cannell
Producers David Chase, Charles F. Johnson
Company A Roy Huggins/Public Arts Production in association with Cherokee Productions; Universal Television and NBC-TV
Directors Various
Writers Various
CAST
Jim Rockford .... James Garner
Joseph "Rocky" Rockford ....Noah Beery
Det. Dennis Becker ....Joe Santos
Angel Martin .... Stuart Margolin
Beth Davenport .... Gretchen Corbett

1190 Roll of Thunder, Hear My Cry ABC
Program Type Limited Series
3 hours. Premiere date: 6/2-4/78. A 13-year-old girl is inspired by her family's struggle to keep the land that has been its own for three generations. Based on the novel by Mildred Taylor. Developed for television by Dorothy Gilbert.

Roll of Thunder, Hear My Cry
Continued
Music by Fred Karlin. Song, "One Step at a Time" by Fred Karlin and Rob Reyer. Filmed near Jackson, Mississippi.
Executive Producer Thomas W. Moore
Producer Jean Anne Moore
Company Tomorrow Entertainment, Inc.
Director Jack Smight
Writer Arthur Heinemann
Cinematographer Robert Hauser
CAST
Mary .... Janet MacLachlan
David .... Robert Christian
Big Ma .... Claudia McNeil
Cassie .... Lark Ruffin
Stacey .... Tony Ross
Little Man .... Eric Dunaway
Christopher John .... Rodney Adams
Morrison .... Rockne Tarkington
Hammer .... Morgan Freeman
Avery .... Lou Walker
T.J. .... Larry Scott
Mrs. Berry .... Colia Lafayette
Granger .... Roy Poole
Lillian Jean .... Lisa Whittington
Jeremy .... Mark Keith
Miss Crocker .... Joan Lewis
Kaleb Wallace .... Charles Briggs
Jamison .... John Cullum

1191 Rollergirls   NBC
Program Type Comedy Series
30 minutes. Mondays/Wednesdays (as of 5/3/78.) Premiere: 4/24/78. Funny adventures of an all-girl roller derby team. Last show: 5/10/78. James Komack is creator.
Executive Producer James Komack
Producers Stan Cutler, Neil Rosen, George Tricker
Co-Producer Tom Cherones
Company Komack Co., Inc. in association with NBC-TV
Director Burt Brinckerhoff
Writers Stan Cutler, Neil Rosen, George Tricker
CAST
Don Mitchell .... Terry Kiser
Mongo Sue Lampert .... Rhonda Bates
J. B. Johnson .... Candy Ann Brown
Selma "Books" Cassidy .... Joanna Cassidy
Honey Bee Novak .... Marcy Hanson
Shana "Pipeline" Akira .... Marilyn Tokuda
Howie Devine .... James Murtagh

1192 Rolling Stone: The 10th Anniversary   CBS
Program Type Music/Dance Special
2 hours. Premiere date: 11/25/77. Title music theme by Jimmy Webb.
Executive Producer Janna Wenner
Producer Steve Binder
Company Steve Binder/Rolling Stone Television Production

Director Steve Binder
Head Writer Mike Marmer
Writers Ben Fong-Torres, David Felton, Steve Martin, Bill Angelos, Mason Williams, Don Clark, Susan Clark
Musical Director Jack Nitzsche
Choreographer Ron Field
Guest Stars Richard Baskin, The Coasters, Chief Ed Davis, Yvonne Elliman, Ben Fong-Torres, Art Garfunkel, Terri Garr, Richie Havens, Gladys Knight and the Pips, Patti LaBelle, Jerry Lee Lewis, Mike Love, Melissa Manchester, Steve Martin, Jim Messina, Bette Midler and the Harlettes, Keith Moon, Ted Neeley, Billy Preston, Rubinoos, Martin Sheen, Phoebe Snow, Sissy Spacek, Lesley Ann Warren, Jimmy Webb, Janna Wenner, The Lester Wilson Dancers

1193 Romagnolis' Table   PBS
Program Type Educational/Cultural Series
30 minutes. Mondays. Premiere date: 1/19/75. Second series repeated: 6/5/78 and 9/4/78. Authors of "The Romagnolis' Table"—Margaret and G. Franco Romagnoli demonstrate their recipes for traditional Italian cooking. Program made possible by grants from the Corporation for Public Broadcasting, the Ford Foundation and Public Television Stations.
Producer Margaret MacLeod
Company WGBH-TV/Boston
Directors Howie Lowe, David Atwood

1194 Rookie of the Year
ABC Weekend Specials/ABC Afterschool Special   ABC
Program Type Children's Special
60 minutes. Premiere date: 10/3/73. Repeat date: 10/8/77. Based on "Not Bad for a Girl" by Isabella Taves. Filmed in Stony Point, NY.
Producer Daniel Wilson
Company Daniel Wilson Productions
Director Larry Elikann
Writer Gloria Banta
CAST
Sharon Lee .... Jodie Foster
Mark .... Dennis McKiernan
Kenny .... Joey Marvel
Charlie .... David Perkins
Paul .... Mike Scheer
Greg .... Mitchell Spera

Rooster Cogburn *See* NBC Movie of the Week

1195 Roots
ABC Novel for Television   ABC
Program Type Limited Series
12 hours. Premiere date: 1/23/77. Last show:

1/30/77. Repeat date: 9/5/78. Shown on eight consecutive nights. Dramatization based on the book by Alex Haley tracing the lives of his family from Africa in 1750 to Tennessee after the Civil War. Developed for television by William Blinn. Filmed in part in and around Savannah, GA. and on the ship *Unicorn.* Music by Gerald Fried and Quincy Jones.
Executive Producer David L. Wolper
Producer Stan Margulies
Company A David L. Wolper Production
Directors Marvin Chomsky, John Erman, David Greene; Gilbert Moses
Writers William Blinn, M. Charles Cohen, Ernest Kinoy, James Lee
Costume Designer Jack Martell
Production Designer Jan Scott
Art Director Joseph R. Jennings
Script Supervisor William Blinn
Consultant Alex Haley

CAST

Kunta Kinte	LeVar Burton
Kunta Kinte (Toby)	John Amos
Binta	Cicely Tyson
Capt. Davies	Edward Asner
Kadi Touray	O. J. Simpson
Third Mate Slater	Ralph Waite
Nyo Boto	Maya Angelou
The Wrestler	Ji-Tu Cumbuka
The Kintango	Moses Gunn
Omoro	Thalmus Rasulala
Brima Cesay	Harry Rhodes
Gardner	William Watson
Fanta	Ren Woods
Fiddler	Lou Gossett
John Reynolds	Lorne Greene
Mrs. Reynolds	Lynda Day George
Ames	Vic Morrow
Carrington	Paul Shenar
William Reynolds	Robert Reed
Bell	Madge Sinclair
Grill	Gary Collins
Fanta (as an adult)	Beverly Todd
The Drummer	Raymond Saint Jacques
Tom Moore	Chuck Connors
Missy Anne	Sandy Duncan
Noah	Lawrence-Hilton Jacobs
Ordell	John Schuck
Kizzy	Leslie Uggams
Squire James	Macdonald Carey
Matilda	Olivia Cole
Mingo	Scatman Crothers
Stephen Bennett	George Hamilton
Mrs. Moore	Carolyn Jones
Sir Eric Russell	Ian McShane
Sister Sara	Lillian Randolph
Sam Bennett	Richard Roundtree
Chicken George	Ben Vereen
Evan Brent	Lloyd Bridges
Tom	Georg Stanford Brown
Ol' George	Brad Davis
Lewis	Hilly Hicks
Jemmy Brent	Doug McClure
Irene	Lynne Moody
Martha	Lane Binkley
Justin	Burl Ives

1196 Roots—One Year Later   ABC
Program Type Documentary/Informational Special
60 minutes. Premiere date: 1/23/78. Examines the far-reaching impact of David L. Wolper's epic 12-hour television production and Alex Haley's Pulitzer Prize-winning best-seller. Special appearance by LeVar Burton. Music by Gerald Fried. Filmed in The Gambia (Africa), Virginia, North Carolina and Los Angeles.
Executive Producer David L. Wolper
Producer Robert Guenette
Associate Producer Frances Guenette
Company A David L. Wolper Production in association with Warner Bros.
Director Robert Guenette
Writer Robert Guenette
Photographers Erik Daarstad, Thomas Ackerman, Andre Gunn
Editors N. H. Cominos; Peter Wood
Host/Narrator Lou Gossett.

1197 Rose Bowl   NBC
Program Type Sports Special
Live coverage of the 64th Rose Bowl game between the Michigan Wolverines and the Washington Huskies from Pasadena, Calif. 1/2/78.
Producer Dick Auerbach
Company NBC Sports
Director Harry Coyle
Announcers Curt Gowdy, John Brodie

1198 The Rosenberg-Sobell Case Revisited   PBS
Program Type Documentary/Informational Special
90 minutes. Premiere date: 7/1/78. Update of 1974 award-winning documentary, "The Unquiet Death of Julius and Ethel Rosenberg," by producer Alvin H. Goldstein.
Company WETA-TV/Washington in association with KTCA-TV/St. Paul-Minneapolis

1199 Rosetti and Ryan   NBC
Program Type Comedy Series
60 minutes. Thursdays. Premiere: 9/22/77. Last show: 11/10/77. 2-hour pilot telecast on "NBC Monday Night at the Movies" 5/23/77. Two lawyers from diverse backgrounds become involved in difficult cases in this comedy—mystery series.
Executive Producer Leonard B. Stern
Supervising Producers Gordon Cotler, Don M. Mankiewicz
Producer Jerry Davis
Company Heyday Productions in association with Universal Television and NBC-TV
Directors Various
Writers Various

Rosetti and Ryan Continued
CAST

Joseph Rosetti	Tony Roberts
Frank Ryan	Squire Fridell
Jessica Hornesby, Asst. D.A.	Jane Elliot

1200 The Royal Family
Great Performances   PBS
Program Type Dramatic Special
2 hours. Premiere date: 11/9/77. Play by Edna Ferber and George S. Kaufman about an American theatrical clan. Program made possible by a grant from Exxon Corporation.
Producer Ken Campbell
Company WNET-TV/New York
Directors Ellis Rabb; Kirk Browning
CAST

Fanny	Eva LeGallienne
Tony	Ellis Rabb
Herbert	Keene Curtis
Julie	Rosemary Harris

1201 Royal Heritage   PBS
Program Type Documentary/Informational Special
60 minutes. Premiere date: 1/29/78. Nine 1-hour shows chronicles Britain's royal treasures and art collection. Program made possible by a grant from International Flavors & Fragrances Inc. and the Rosalind P. Walter Foundation.
Producer Michael Gill
Company BBC

1202 Rubinstein: Works of Chopin
Fine Music Specials/Great Performances PBS
Program Type Music/Dance Special
60 minutes. Premiere date: 12/24/75. Repeat date: 7/29/78. The London Symphony Orchestra in a Christmas concert of works by F. Chopin, Johannes Brahms and Franz Schubert. Filmed at Fairfield Halls, Croyden, England. Program presented by WNET-TV/New York and made possible by grants from Exxon Corporation, the Corporation for Public Broadcasting, the Ford Foundatin and Public Television Stations.
Executive Producer Fritz Buttenstedt
Coordinating Producer David Griffiths
Producers Fritz Buttenstedt, David Griffiths
Company Unitel Productions
Conductor Andre Previn
Guest Artist Arthur Rubinstein

1203 Ruby and Oswald   CBS
Program Type Dramatic Special
3 hours. Premiere date: 2/8/78. Dramatization of an almost minute-by-minute account, over a four-day span preceding and following the assassination of President John F. Kennedy in Dallas. Filmed mostly in Dallas, Texas.

Executive Producer Alan Landsburg
Producer Paul Freeman
Company Alan Landsburg Productions, Inc.
Director Mel Stuart
Writers John McGreevey; Michael McGreevey
CAST

Jack Ruby	Michael Lerner
Lee Harvey Oswald	Frederic Forrest
Eva	Doris Roberts
Captain J. Will Fritz	Lou Frizzell
Robert Oswald	Bruce French
District Attorney Wade	Sandy McPeak
Marina Oswald	Lanna Saunders
Chief Curry	Sandy Ward
Judge Johnston	James E. Brohead
George Paulsen	Brian Dennehy
Little Lynn	Gwynne Gilford
Clyde Gaydosh	Gordon Jump
Andy Armstrong	Eric Kilpatrick
George	Walter Matthews
"Ike" Pappas	Michael Pataki
Nat Ryan	Al Ruscio
Phyllis Noonan	Jodean Russo
Agent Kelley	Richard Sanders
Wanda Killiem	Vickery Turner
Deputy Eugene Boone	Max Anderson
FBI Agent	Lewis Arquette
Smokey	Robert Bryan Berger
Policeman	Dean Brooks
Cecil McWatters	Ed Call
Jim Chaney	Raymond Colbert
Woman on Bus	Molly Dodd
Wesley Frazier	David Leroy Dorr
Older Woman	Jessie Lee Fulton
William Whaley	John William Galt
Ottney Gurley	Phyllis Glick
Marilyn Moon	Margie Gordon
Postal Clerk	James Hall
Doctor	Bill Joyce
Junior Jarman	Delbert Henry Knight, Sr.
Policeman	Jim Lough
John Brewer	Chip Lucia
Secretary	Lillah McCarthy
Reporter	Dick McGarvin
Policeman	John R. MacLean
Charles Batchelor	Jim Mendenhall
Bail Bondsman	Anthony Palmer
Lydia Witcher	Georgie Paul
H. D. Holmes	Richard Roat
Reporter	Michael Schwartz
Helen Markham	Adriana Shaw
June	Amanda Sherman
Rabbi Hillel Silverman	Rabbi Hillel Silverman
Drunk Businessman	Bill Sorrells
Detective	Jon Terry
Ruth	Lesley Woods

1204 Rudolf Serkin: Master Musician
PBS
Program Type Documentary/Informational Special
60 minutes. Premiere date: 3/8/78. Isaac Stern interviews famed pianist Rudolf Serkin in a 75th birthday tribute. Also present are conductor Eugene Ormandy, cellist Marta Casals Istomin and

Mstislav Rostropovich, violinist Alexander Schneider, and pianist Claude Frank.
Executive Producer Ruth Leon
Company WETA-TV/Washington

1205 Rudolph the Red-Nosed Reindeer
CBS
Program Type Animated Film Special
60 minutes. Premiere date: 12/64. Repeat date: 11/30/77. Based on the song by Johnny Marks. Additional music and lyrics by Johnny Marks; orchestration by Maury Laws. Adapted from a story by Robert L. May.
Producers Arthur Rankin, Jr., Jules Bass
Company Videocraft International Production
Director Larry Roemer
Writer Romeo Muller
Narrator Burl Ives
VOICES
Sam the Snowman .... Burl Ives
Rudolph .... Billie Richards
Yukon Cornelius .... Larry Mann
Santa Claus .... Stan Frances
Hermy the Elf .... Paul Soles
Clarice .... Janet Orenstein
Additional Voices Alfie Scopp, Paul Klugman, Corinne Connely, Peg Dixon

1206 Rudolph's Shiny New Year   ABC
Program Type Animated Film Special
60 minutes. Premiere date: 12/10/76. Repeat date: 12/1/77. A sequel to "Rudolph the Red-Nosed Reindeer" with music and lyrics by Johnny Marks. Filmed in Animagic—dimensional stop-motion photography.
Producer Arthur Rankin, Jr., Jules Bass
Company Rankin-Bass Productions
Writer Romeo Muller
Musical Director Maury Laws
Narrator Red Skelton
VOICES
Father Time .... Red Skelton
Sir Tentwothree .... Frank Gorshin
One Million B.C. .... Morey Amsterdam
Big Ben .... Hal Peary
Eon .... Paul Frees
Rudolph .... Billie Richards
Additional Voices Don Messick, Iris Rainer

A Run for Your Money *See* PBS Movie Theater

1207 The Runaways   CBS
Program Type Dramatic Special
90 minutes. Premiere date: 4/1/75. Season premiere: 4/25/78. Based on Victor Canning novel.
Executive Producer Lee Rich
Producer Philip Capice
Company Lorimar Productions, Inc.

Director Harry Harris
Writer John McGreevey
CAST
Angela Lakey .... Dorothy McGuire
Joe Ringer .... Van Williams
George Collingwood .... John Randolph
Alice Collingwood .... Neva Patterson
Johnny Miles .... Josh Albee
Mrs. Wilson .... Lenka Peterson
Lew Brown .... Steve Ferguson
Haines .... Don Matheson
Bob Davis .... Tierre Turner
Mrs. Pickerel .... Janice Carroll
Al Pritchard .... John Pickard
Rita Armijo .... Gina Alvarado
Capt. Baker .... Leonard Stone
Kelly .... George Reynolds
Mr. Morgan .... Norman Andrews
Capt. Cole .... Ray A. Stephens
Sgt. Coonan .... Wayne A. Jones
Soldier .... Tony Huston

Russian Roulette *See* NBC Saturday Night at the Movies

The Russians Are Coming, the Russians are Coming *See* The CBS Tuesday Night Movies

1208 Ryan's Hope   ABC
Program Type Daytime Drama Series
30 minutes. Mondays–Fridays. Premiere date: 7/7/75. Continuous. Created by Claire Labine and Paul Avila Mayer. Set in the Riverside section (upper west side) of Manhattan. Cast listed alphabetically.
Executive Producers Paul Avila Mayer; Claire Labine
Producer Robert Costello, Ellen Barret
Company A Labine-Mayer Production in association with the ABC Television Network
Directors Lela Swift, Jerry Evans
Writers Claire Labine, Paul Avila Mayer, Mary Munisteri, Judith Pinsker, Allan Leicht
CAST
Jillian Coleridge .... Nancy Addison
Johnny Ryan .... Bernard Barrow
Faith Coleridge .... Faith Catlin
Dr. Buckminster "Bucky" Carter .... Justin Deas
Nick Szabo .... Michael Fairman
Dr. Seneca Beaulac .... John Gabriel
Maeve Ryan .... Helen Gallagher
Dr. Pat Ryan .... Malcolm Groome
Ramona Gonzalez .... Rosalinda Guerra
Dr. Roger Coleridge .... Ron Hale
Det. Bob Reid .... Earl Hindman
Delia Reid Ryan .... Ilene Kristen
Ed Coleridge .... Frank Latimore
Jack Fenelli .... Michael Levin
Mary Ryan Fenelli .... Mary Car
Dr. Clem Moultrie .... Hannibal Penney, Jr.
Frank Ryan .... Andrew Robinson
Nell Beaulac .... Diana van der Vlis

1209   Sadat's Visit to Israel I
NBC News Special   NBC
Program Type News Special
90 minutes. 11/19/77. Live coverage of Egyptian President Anwar Sadat visiting Israel to seek a peaceful solution to the Middle East crisis.
Company NBC News
Anchors Edwin Newman, John Hart
Commentators Richard Hunt, Garrick Utley, Bob Jamieson, David Burrington

1210   Sadat's Visit to Israel II
NBC News Special   NBC
Program Type News Special
3 hours. 11/20/77. Live coverage of speeches of President Anwar Sadat and Prime Minister Menachem Begin before the Israeli Parliament.
Company NBC News
Anchors Edwin Newman, John Hart, Richard Valeriani
Commentator Henry Kissinger

1211   The Saint-Galy Tiles   PBS
Program Type Documentary/Informational Special
30 minutes. Premiere date: 4/11/78. Program focuses on artist Geza Saint-Galy who was commissioned to create an historical perspective of Williamsburg in tile. Program made possible by a grant from the W.H. Brady Foundation, Inc. of Milwaukee.
Producer Walter McGhee
Company WCVE-TV/Richmond
Director Ernest Skinner
Cinematographer Ernest Skinner

1212   Saint of Bleecker Street
Live from Lincoln Center/Great Performances
                                                        PBS
Program Type Music/Dance Special
2-1/2 hours. Premiere date: 4/19/78. Opera by Gian Carlo Menotti performed by New York City Opera. Simulcast in stereo. Story of Italian-American life in the "Little Italy" section of Greenwich Village in New York. Program made possible by grants from Exxon Corporation, the National Endowment for the Arts and the Corporation for Public Broadcasting.
Producer John Goberman
Company WNET-TV/New York
Conductor Cal Stewart Kellogg
Staged by Francis Rizzo
                        CAST
Annina .... Catherine Malfitano
Michele ....Enrico di Giuseppe
Desideria .... Sandra Walker
Additional Cast Diana Soviero, Irwin Densen

1213   Salome
Fine Music Specials/Great Performances   PBS
Program Type Music/Dance Special
2 hours. Premiere date: 2/2/77. Repeat date: 10/12/77. Filmed version of the 1905 one-act German opera by Richard Strauss based on the play by Oscar Wilde. Music performed by the Vienna Philharmonic Orchestra. Program stereo-simulcast on local FM radio stations. Presented by WNET-TV/New York and made possible by grants from Exxon Corporation, the Corporation for Public Broadcasting, the Ford Foundation and Public Television Stations.
Executive Producer Fritz Buttenstedt
Producer David Griffiths
Company Unitel Productions
Director Goetz Friedrich
Conductor Karl Bohm
                        CAST
Salome .... Teresa Stratas
Herod ....Hans Beirer
Herodias ....Astrid Varnay
Jokanaan (John the Baptist) .... Bernd Weikl
Narraboth .... Wieslaw Ochman
Page ....Hanna Schwarz

1214   Sam   CBS
Program Type Crime Drama Series
30 minutes. Tuesdays. Premiere date: 3/14/78. Last show: 4/18/78. Man and dog patrol of Los Angeles Police Department. Created by Jack Webb and Dan Noble. Music by Billy May.
Executive Producer Jack Webb
Producer Leonard B. Kaufman
Company Mark VII Ltd.
Directors Various
Writers Various
                        CAST
Sam .... Sam
Officer Mike Breen ....Mark Harmon
Captain Tom Clagett .... Len Wayland

1215   Sammy Davis Jr. Greater Hartford Open   CBS
Program Type Sports Special
Live coverage of final rounds of golf event 7/29/78 from Wethersfield Country Club in Wethersfield, Conn.
Executive Producer Frank Chirkinian
Company CBS Sports
Directors Bob Dailey, Frank Chirkinian
Commentators Vin Scully, Jack Whitaker, Ben Wright, Rick Barry, Ken Venturi

1216   San Francisco Ballet
Dance in America/Great Performances   PBS
Program Type Music/Dance Special
2 hours. Premiere date: 6/7/78. Repeat date: 6/11/78. Three-act version of "Romeo and Juliet" with music by Prokoviev. Made possible

by grants from Exxon Corporation, The National Endowment for the Arts, Corporation for Public Broadcasting and member stations of PBS.
Company WNET-TV/New York
Choreographer Michael Smuin
CAST
Romeo .... Jim Sohm
Juliet .... Diana Weber

1217 The San Pedro Beach Bums   ABC
Program Type Comedy Series
60 minutes. Mondays. Premiere date: 9/19/77. Based on TV movie, "The San Pedro Bums," shown 5/13/77, about five young men who live on an old boat. Last show 12/12/77. Created by E. Duke Vincent. Music and lyrics by Mark Snow and Carol Connors. Filmed at San Pedro, Calif., and at 20th Century-Fox Studios.
Executive Producers Aaron Spelling, Douglas S. Cramer
Supervising Producer E. Duke Vincent
Producer Earl Barret
Company An Aaron Spelling Production
Directors Various
Writers Various
Animation Director Al Smith
CAST
Buddy ....Christopher Murney
Boychick .... Chris DeRose
Dancer .... John Mark Robinson
Stuf .... Stuart Pankin
Moose .... Darryl McCullough
Louise .... Louise Hoven
Suzi .... Susan Mullen
Marge .... Lisa Reeves
Ralphie .... Christoff St. John
Julie .... Nancy Morgan
Lou .... Raymond O'Keefe
Cherry .... Jenny Sherman
Nate .... Lou Tiano
Nurse Gomez .... Lee Leonard

1218 Sanford and Son (Daytime)   NBC
Program Type Comedy Series
30 minutes. Mondays–Fridays. Premiere date: 6/14/76. Last show: 4/21/78. Continuous. Morning reruns of evening series.
Executive Producer Bud Yorkin
Producers Saul Turteltaub, Bernie Orenstein
Company A Bud Yorkin/Norman Lear/Tandem Production through Norbud Productions, Inc. in association with NBC-TV
Directors Various
Writers Various
Costume Designer Lee Smith
Art Director Edward Stephenson
CAST
Fred Sanford .... Redd Foxx
Lamont Sanford .... Demond Wilson
Aunt Esther .... LaWanda Page
Grady Wilson ....Whitman Mayo
Bubba .... Don Bexley

Rollo .... Nathaniel Taylor
Donna Harris ....Lynn Hamilton
Woody .... Raymond Allen
Hoppy .... Howard Platt
Smitty ....Hal Williams
Janet ....Marlene Clark
Roger ....Edward Crawford

1219 Sanford Arms   NBC
Program Type Comedy Series
30 minutes. Fridays. Premiere date: 9/16/77. Last show: 10/14/77. Spin-off from "Sanford and Son" shown on ABC. Based on British TV comedy series "Steptoe and Son" created by Ray Galton and Alan Simpson. Music by Quincy Jones
Executive Producers Bud Yorkin, Saul Turteltaub, Bernie Orenstein
Producer Woody Kling
Company TOY Productions
Directors Various
Writers Various
CAST
Phil Wheeler .... Theodore Wilson
Esther .... LaWanda Page
Jeannie .... Bebe Drake Hooks
Grady ....Whitman Mayo
Bubba .... Don Bexley
Woody .... Raymond Allen
Angela .... Tina Andrews
Nat .... John Earl

1220 Santa Claus Is Coming to Town
ABC
Program Type Animated Film Special
60 minutes. Premiere date: 12/13/70. Repeat date 12/1/77. Animated special using dimensional stop-motion photography. Music by Maury Laws, lyrics by Jules Bass. Title song composed by J. Fred Coots, lyrics by Haven Gillespie
Producers Arthur Rankin, Jr., Jules Bass
Company Rankin/Bass Productions
Directors Arthur Rankin, Jr., Jules Bass
Writer Romeo Muller
Narrator Fred Astaire

1221 Santa Fe Opera
Opera Theater   PBS
Program Type Music/Dance Special
90 minutes. Premiere date: 7/5/77. Repeat date: 7/3/78. Documentary-and-performance special celebrating the Santa Fe Opera's 20th year. Taped in the summer of 1976 with excerpts from "The Mother of Us All" with music by Virgil Thomson and text by Gertrude Stein, "The Marriage of Figaro" by Wolfgang Amadeus Mozart, "La Traviata" by Giuseppe Verdi, "L'Egisto" by Francesco Cavalli, and "Salome" by Richard Strauss. Program made possible by grants from Public Television Stations with additional fund-

Santa Fe Opera *Continued*
ing from the Ford Foundation and the Corporation for Public Broadcasting.
Executive Producer Jac Venza Barry Gavin
Producers Humphrey Burton, David Griffiths
Company WNET-TV/New York and the British Broadcasting Corporation
Director David Chesire
Host Donald Gramm
Narrator Donald Gramm

The Mother of Us All
Director Peter Wood
Conductor Raymond Leppard
Costume Designer Robert Indiana
Scenic Designer Robert Indiana
CAST
Susan B. Anthony .... Mignon Dunn
Anne .... Batyah Godfrey
Jo the Loiterer ....James Atherton
Angel More .... Ashley Putnam
John Adams ....William Lewis
Constance Fletcher .... Helen Vanni

The Marriage of Figaro
Conductor Robert Baustian
CAST
Figaro .... Donald Gramm
Cherubino .... Faith Esham
Susanna .... Sheri Greenawald

La Traviata
Conductor John Crosby
CAST
Violetta ....Ellen Shade
Alfredo ....William Lewis

L'Egisto
Conductor Raymond Leppard
CAST
Clori .... Linn Maxwell
Egisto .... Jerold Norman
Climene .... Ellen Shade
Four Seasons .... Susan Peterson, Ashley Putnam,
Cheryl Boatwright, Patricia McCaffrey

Salome
CAST
Joakanaan .... William Dooley

1222   Sarah
Great Performances   PBS
Program Type Dramatic Special
2 hours. Premiere date: 11/30/77. Play by Suzanne Grossman about the actress Sarah Bernhardt. Program made possible by a grant from Exxon Corporation.
Executive Producer Jac Venza
Producer Robert Sherrin
Company WNET-TV/New York
Director Waris Hussein
CAST
Sarah ....Zoe Caldwell
Edward Jarrett .... Donald Davies
Additional Cast Jean Leclerc, Dawn Greenhalgh

1223   Sarah Coventry Golf Tournament
                                                            PBS
Program Type Sports Special
Live coverage of the final two rounds in the Sarah Coventry competition, one of the last stops on the 1977 Ladies Professional Golf Association Tour 9/24/77 and 9/25/77. Special interviews with players by Greg Morris. Program made possible by a grant from Colgate-Palmolive Company.
Company KERA-TV/Dallas-Fort Worth
Anchor Bob Halloran
Commentators Carol Mann, Mary Bea Porter, Bob Goalby

1224   Sarah Vaughn Live from Wolf Trap
Live from Wolf Trap   PBS
Program Type Music/Dance Special
2-1/2 hours. Premiere date: 8/19/78. Singer Sarah Vaughan and the National Symphony Orchestra with all-Gershwin concert from Wolf Trap Farm Park. Program made possible by grants from the Corporation for Public Broadcasting, PBS member stations, and Allied Chemical Corporation.
Executive Producer David Griffiths
Producer Hal Hutkoff
Company WETA-TV/Washington

1225   Sara's Summer of the Swans
ABC Out-of-School Specials   ABC
Program Type Children's Special
60 minutes. Premiere date: 10/2/74. Repeat date: 4/15/78. Based on the book, "The Summer of the Swans" by Betsy Byars. Story about a tall and awkward teenage girl who discovers that people can appreciate the beauty within.
Producer Martin Tahse
Company An Entertainment Media Production
Director James B. Clark
Writer Bob Rodgers
Animation Director David Brain
CAST
Sara Godfrey .... Heather Totten
Joe Melby ....Chris Knight
Aunt Willie .... Priscilla Morrill
Gretchen Wyant .... Eve Plumb
Wanda .... Betty Ann Carr
Mary .... Doney Oatman
Frank ....Scott McCartor
Charlie .... Reed Diamond

1226   Savages
Tuesday Movie of the Week   ABC
Program Type TV Movie
90 minutes. Premiere date: 9/11/74. Repeat date: 4/18/78. Filmed partly on location in the Mojave Desert, California. Based on the novel "Death Watch" by Robb White.
Producer Aaron Spelling, Leonard Goldberg

Company Spelling/Goldberg Productions
Director Lee H. Katzin
Writer William Wood
CAST
Horton Maddock .... Andy Griffith
Ben Whiting ....Sam Bottoms
George Whiting ....Noah Beery
Sheriff Hamilton .... James Best
Dep. Haycroft .... Randy Boone
Les Hanford .... Jim Antonio
The Doctor .... Jim Chandler

1227 Say Brother Pays Tribute to Webster Lewis With an Evening on the Town   PBS
Program Type Music/Dance Special
60 minutes. Premiere date: 6/19/77. Repeat date: 7/1/78. A concert performed by the 50-member Webster Lewis Orchestra and the Post Pop Space Rock Be-Bop Gospel Tabernacle Chorus.
Producer Barbara Barrow
Company WGBH-TV/Boston
Director David Atwood
Conductor Webster Lewis

1228 Say Uncle   NBC
Program Type Comedy Special
30 minutes. Premiere date: 8/4/78. Pilot about a middle-aged man who meddles in his nephew's budding musical career.
Producers Ron Friedman, Gene Marcione
Company Don Kirshner Production
Director Burt Brinckerhoff
Writer Ron Friedman
CAST
Uncle Jack ....Richard B. Shull
Billy .... Dennis Cooley
Frizz .... Del Russell
Brother Fly .... Theodore Wilson
Cabbie .... Louis Guss
Harlin Floyd .... Renny Temple
Marlene .... Carol Ann Williams
Snake Eyes .... Deborah Harmon
Hairdresser .... Michael Byers

Scalawag See CBS Special Movie Presentation

1229 The School for Scandal
Theater in America/Great Performances   PBS
Program Type Dramatic Special
2 hours. Premiere date: 4/2/75. Repeat date: 2/19/78. Television adaptation of the 18th century English comedy by Richard Brinsley Sheridan performed by the Guthrie Theater Company of Minneapolis. Music by Stanley Silverman with additional lyrics by Christopher Langham. Program funded by grants from Exxon Corporation and the Corporation for Public Broadcasting.

Executive Producer Jac Venza
Producer David Griffiths
Company WNET-TV/New York in association with KTCA-TV/St. Paul
Directors Michael Langham, Nick Havinga
Writers Richard Brinsley Sheridan, Michael Bawtree
Musical Director Roland Gagnon
Costume Designer Sam Kirkpatrick
Scenic Designer Jack Barkla
Host Hal Holbrook
CAST
Sir Oliver Surface ....Larry Gates
Joseph Surface .... Nicholas Kepros
Charles Surface .... Kenneth Welsh
Lady Teazle .... Blair Brown
Mrs. Candour ....Barbara Bryne
Lady Sneerwell .... Patricia Conolly
Sir Peter Teazle ....Bernard Behrens
Sir Benjamin Backbite .... Mark Lamos
Maria .... Sheriden Thomas
Rowley .... Macon McCalman
Careless .... Lance Davis
Sir Harry Bumper/Crabtree .... Jeff Chandler
Snake .... Ivar Brogger
Alfred ....Frank Scott
Moses .... Oliver Cliff
Trip .... Henry J. Jordan
William ....John Newcome
Additional Cast Dennis Babcock, Valery Daemke, James Harris, Maryann Lippay, Gary Martinez, William Schoppert, Cleo Simonett, Kendrick Wilson

1230 Schoolhouse Rock   ABC
Program Type Animated Film Series
3 minute films shown during children's programming at intervals on a rotating basis on Saturday and Sunday mornings. Premiered in 1972-73 season with "Multiplication Rock." "Grammar Rock" introduced 9/8/73. "America Rock" "Bicentennial- oriented history and government" premiered 9/7/74. "Rufus Xavier Sarsaparilla" (one of seven "Grammar Rock" segments designed to explain graphically the parts of speech) and "Mother Necessity" (song and animation illustration of old adage, "Necessity is the mother of invention") premiered 9/10/77. "Science Rock" premiered 3/11/78. Series is based on an idea by David B. McCall. "America Rock" was developed in consultation with Prof. John A. Garraty.
Executive Producer Tom Yohe
Producers George Newall, Radford Stone
Company Newall & Yohe, Inc.
Musical Director Bob Dorough
Animators Kim & Gifford

1231 The Scooby-Doo/Dynomutt Hour   ABC
Program Type Animated Film Series
90 minutes (as of 12/4/76). Saturday mornings. Premiere date for "Scooby-Doo" cartoons: 9/71

The Scooby-Doo/Dynomutt Hour
Continued

(on CBS). Series about a dog and his young friends who solve mysteries. "Dynomutt, Dog Wonder" premiere: 9/11/76. Cartoon featuring a robot dog who fights crime with the Blue Falcon. Created by Joe Ruby and Ken Spears. Program re-titled "Scooby's All-Star Laff-A-Lympics" in 1978 and the Dynomutt episodes omitted.

Executive Producers William Hanna, Joseph Barbera
Producers Alex Lory, Don Jurwich
Creative Producer Iwao Takamoto
Head Writers Duane Poole, Dick Robbins

Captain Caveman and the Teen Angels
VOICES

Captain Caveman .... Mel Blanc
Dee Dee .... Vernee Watson
Brenda .... Marilyn Schraffler
Taffy .... Laurel Page

Dynomutt
VOICES

Dynomutt .... Frank Welker
Narrator & Focus I .... Ron Feinberg
Blue Falcon .... Gary Owens
Mayor .... Larry McCormick

Scooby-Do
VOICES

Freddy .... Frank Welker
Daphne Blake .... Healther North
Shaggy .... Casey Kasem
Velma .... Nicole Jaffe
Scooby-Doo .... Don Messick

Laff-A-Lympics

Announcers
VOICES

Snagglepuss .... Daws Butler
Mildew Wolf/Doggie Daddy .... John Stephenson

The Yogi Yahooeys
VOICES

Yakky Doodle .... Frank Welker
Huckleberry Hound/Hokie Wolf/Wally Gator/Yogi/
   Blabber/Snooper/Augie Doggie/Quick
   Draw/Dixie/Jinx .... Daws Butler
Boo Boo/Pixie .... Don Messick
Grape Ape .... Bob Holt
Cindy .... Julie Bennett

The Scooby Doobys
VOICES

Hong Kong Phooey .... Scatman Crothers
Jeannie .... Julie McWhirter
Babu .... Joe Besser
Tinker/Dynomutt .... Frank Welker
Speedy Bugg/Shaggy .... Casey Kasem
Scooby Doo .... Don Messick
Scooby Dum .... Daws Butler
Blue Falcon .... Gary Owens
Dee Dee Skyes .... Vemee Watson
Brenda Chance .... Marilyn Schreffler
Taffy Dare .... Laural Page
Captain Caveman .... Mel Blanc

The Really Rottens
VOICES

Daisy Mayhem .... Marilyn Schreffler
Sooey Pig/Magic Rabbit .... Frank Welker
Orful Octopus/Dinky .... Bob Holt
The Creepleys .... Laural Page, Don Messick
Dread Baron/Fondoo .... John Stephenson
Mumbly .... Don Messick
Dalton Brothers .... Don Messick, Daws Butler

1232   Scott Joplin: King of Ragtime
The Big Event/NBC World Premiere Movie

NBC

Program Type Dramatic Special
2 hours. Premiere date: 6/20/78. Drama about ragtime composer. Joplin's music arranged and performed by Richard Hyman. Song, "Hang Over Blues," written by Harold Johnson.
Executive Producers Rob Cohen, Berry Gordy
Producer Stan Hough
Director Jeremy Paul Kagan
Writer Christopher Knopf
CAST

Scott Joplin .... Billy Dee Williams
John Stark .... Art Carney
Chauvin .... Clifton Davis
Belle Joplin .... Margaret Avery
Tom Turpin .... Godfrey Cambridge
Poor Alfred .... Taj Mahal
Will Williams .... Eubie Blake
Dr. Jaelki .... Seymour Cassel
John the Baptist .... Dewayne Jessie
Left Hand of God .... Spo-De-Odee

1233   The Seagull
Theater in America/Great Performances   PBS
Program Type Dramatic Special
2 hours. Premiere date: 1/29/75. Repeat date: 11/23/77. Classic 1896 Russian comedy/drama adapted from a production of the Williamstown Festival Theatre, Williamstown, Mass. Filmed on location in the Berkshire hills. Program made possible by grants from Exxon Corporation and the Corporation for Public Broadcasting.
Executive Producer Jac Venza
Producer David Griffiths
Company WNET-TV/New York
Directors Nikos Psacharopoulos, John Desmond
Writer Anton Chekhov
Host Hal Holbrook
CAST

Treplev .... Frank Langella
Irina Arkadina .... Lee Grant
Nina .... Blythe Danner
Trigorin .... Kevin McCarthy
Masha .... Marian Mercer
Pauline Andreevna .... Olympia Dukakis
Sorin .... William Swetland
Medvedenko .... David Clennon

1234   Search and Rescue: The Alpha Team
30 minutes. Saturdays. Premiere date: 9/10/77. Last show: 1/28/78. Live-action adventure series about widower and his two teenage children, who train animals for search and rescue missions. Created by Seymour Berns
Executive Producer Seymour Berns
Producers Sam Strangis; Lew Lehman
Company An NTA Production in association with 10/4 Productions and CTV of Canada
Directors Various
Writers Various
CAST
Bob Donell .... Michael J. Reynolds
Kathy Donell .... Donann Calvin
Jim Donell .... Michael Tough
Dr. Liz Warren ....Helen Shaver

1235   Search for the Great Apes   PBS
National Geographic Special
Program Type Documentary/Informational Special
60 minutes. Premiere date: 1/13/76. Repeat date: 4/25/78. Filmed over seven years, program shows Birute M. F. Galdikas-Brindamour studying the orangutan in Borneo, and Dian Fossey working with mountain gorillas in Rwanda. Music composed by Walter Scharf. Program funded by a grant from Gulf Oil Corporation and presented by WQED-TV/Pittsburgh.
Executive Producer Dennis B. Kane
Producers Christine Z. Wiser, David Saxon
Company National Geographic Society in association with Wolper Productions
Directors Robert M. Young, Robert M. Campbell, Christine Z. Wiser
Narrator Richard Kiley

1236   Search for Tomorrow   CBS
Program Type Daytime Drama Series
30 minutes. Mondays–Fridays. Premiere date: 9/3/51 (in 15-minute format). Continuous. The longest-running daytime drama on television. Created by Agnes Nixon. Drama about the family of Joanne Vincente, the Phillips family and the Bergman family in Henderson, USA. "Search for Tomorrow" theme by Jon Silberman. Mary Stuart is an original cast member. Cast listed alphabetically.
Executive Producer Mary-Ellis Bunim
Associate Producers Robert Getz
Company Procter & Gamble Productions
Directors Ned Stark, Robert A. Schwarz
Writers Chuck Dizenzo, Patti Dizenzo, Sam Reese, Henry Slesar
Announcer Dwight Weist
CAST
David Sutton ....Lewis Arlt
Kylie Halliday .... Lisa Buck
Stephanie Pace Wyatt .... Marie Cheatham

John Wyatt .... Val Dufour
Stu Bergman ....Larry Haines
William Mendell .... Robert Heitman
Tom Bergman .... John James
Dr. Gary Walton .... Richard Lohman
Eric Phillips ....Christopher Lowe
Lisa Kaslo .... Sherry Mathis
Carolyn Hanley ....Marilyn McIntyre
Suzie Wyatt .... Stacey Moran
Steve Kaslo .... Michael Nouri
Wendy Wilkins .... Lisa Peluso
Scott Phillips .... Peter Ratray
Donna Davis ....Leslie Ann Ray
Chance Halliday .... George Shannon
Kathy Phillips .... Courtney Sherman
Ralph Heywood ....Drew Snyder
Joanne Vincent .... Mary Stuart
Janet Collins .... Millee Taggart
Ellie Bergman ....Billie Lou Watt

1237   A Season of Light and Peace   CBS
Program Type Religious/Cultural Special
90 minutes. Premiere date: 12/25/77. Special on the United Nations, Christmas and world peace.
Executive Producer Pamela Ilott
Producer Joe Clement
Company CBS News
Director Alvin Thaler

1238   The Second Annual Circus of the Stars   CBS
Program Type Music/Comedy/Variety Special
2 hours. Premiere date: 1/10/77. Repeat dates: 12/5/77 and 6/11/78. Television and movie stars performing circus acts.
Executive Producer Bob Stivers
Producers Dan Kibbe, Michael Viner
Director Buddy Bregman
Writer Herbert Baker
Musical Director John Caper
Art Directors Anthony Sabatino, Bill Harris
Stars Marty Allen, Lucie Arnaz, Lucille Ball, George Burns, Lynda Carter, Gary Collins, Robert Conrad, Jamie Lee Curtis, Anny Duperey, Lola Falana, Peter Fonda, Richard Hatch, Earl Holliman, Jack Klugman, Tony Lo Bianco, Jimmy and Kristy McNichol, Penny Marshall, Lee Merriwether, Mary Ann Mobley, David Nelson, Beth Nufer, Valerie Perrine, Mackenzie Phillips, Deborah Raffin, Richard Roundtree, Telly Savalas, Susan Saint James, Tom Sullivan, Ann Turkel, Abe Vigoda, Betty White, Cindy Williams, Paul Williams, Michael York
Ringmasters Lucille Ball, Telly Savalas, Cindy Williams, Michael York

1239   The Second Barry Manilow Special   ABC
Program Type Music/Comedy/Variety Special
60 minutes. Premiere date: 2/24/78. Composer/-

The Second Barry Manilow Special
Continued
performer Barry Manilow entertains with many of his songs.
Executive Producer Miles J. Lourie
Producers Ernest Chambers, Barry Manilow
Company Ernest Chambers Productions in association with Kamikazi Music Corporation
Director George Schaefer
Writers Ernest Chambers, Barry Manilow
Star Barry Manilow
Guest Star Ray Charles

1240   Second City TV   Syndicated
Program Type Dramatic Special
60 minutes. Premiere date: 8/27/78. Chicago improvisional theatre troupe in a pilot evolving around a fictitious TV station.
Producer Andrew Alexander, Jack E. Rhodes, Bernard Sahlins
Company Rhodes Productions
Directors George Bloomfield, Milad Bessada
Writers Brian Doyle-Murray, Sheldon Patinkin
Regulars John Candy, Joe Flaherty, Eugene Levy, Andrea Martin, Catherine O'Hara, Harold Ramis, David Thomas

1241   The Secret Life of John Chapman
GE Theater   CBS
Program Type Dramatic Special
90 minutes. Premiere date: 12/27/76. Repeat date: 4/25/78. Drama based on the real-life experiences of John R. Coleman taken from his book "Blue Collar Journal." Filmed in part in King County, WA, and Washington, DC. Music by Fred Myrow.
Executive Producer Gerald I. Isenberg
Producer Gerald W. Abrams
Company The Jozak Company
Director David Lowell Rich
Writer Albert Rubin
Art Director Trevor Williams
CAST
John Chapman .... Ralph Waite
Wilma .... Susan Anspach
Gus Reed ....Pat Hingle
Meredith Chapman .... Elayne Heilveil
Andy Chapman .... Brad Davis
College Chariman .... Maury Cooper
Charlie ....Charlie Watters
Phil .... Reuben Sierra
Victor .... Gardner Hayes
"Dammit" Stanley .... Bill Treadwell
Al .... Teotha Dennard
Grady .... John Aylward
Wally .... Curtis Jackson
Factory Clerk .... Peter Fisher
Manager .... John Roeder
Secretary .... Zoaunne Leroy
Trustee .... Richard Arnold
Dump Truck Driver .... Thomas Ross
Back Hoe Operator ....Earnest M. Simon

Waiter .... Norman Bernard
Hard Hat .... Richard Hawkins
Boss .... Joe Brazil

1242   The Secret Life of T.K. Dearing
ABC Out-of-School Specials/ABC Weekend Specials   ABC
Program Type Children's Special
60 minutes. Premiere date: 4/23/75. Repeat date: 12/31/77. Based on the book by Jean Robinson. A young girl develops a sensitive relationship with her grandfather. Filmed in Topanga Canyon and West Los Angeles, California.
Producer Daniel Wilson
Company Daniel Wilson Productions, Inc.
Director Harry Harris
Writer Bob Rodgers
CAST
T.K. Dearing .... Jodie Foster
Grandpa Kindermann .... Eduard Franz
Walter Dearing ....Leonard Stone
Ruth Dearing .... Zoe Karant
Potato Tom .... Brian Wood
Dugger .... Brian Part
Alvin .... Michael Link
Alice .... Robin Stone
Jerry .... Tierre Turner
Mrs. Whitfield ....Barbara Morrison
Mr. Crane .... Norman Andrews
Sheriff .... Ted Jordan

1243   The Secret of Charles Dickens
The CBS Festival of Lively Arts for Young People   CBS
Program Type Children's Special
60 minutes. Premiere date: 4/16/78. Drama about Charles Dickens taped in London. Special effects by John Burgess.
Executive Producer Daniel Wilson
Producer Linda Marmelstein
Director Sheldon Larry
Writer Lee Kalcheim
Art Director David Perry
Star Valerie Bertinelli
CAST
Charles Dickens .... Alan Badel
Kate .... Elizabeth Springgs
Georgina .... Linda Polan
Director ....Richard Wilson
Sidney ....Luke Batchelor
Henry .... Michael Mannion
Edward .... Benjie McKie

The Secret of Santa Vittoria *See* CBS
Special Movie Presentations

1244   Secret Service
Theater in America/Great Performances   PBS
Program Type Dramatic Special
2 hours. Premiere date: 1/12/77. Repeat date: 7/12/78. The Phoenix Repertory Company of

New York in a revival of the turn-of-the-century melodrama of Civil War espionage by William Gillette. Civil War songs arranged by Arthur Miller. Program made possible by grants from the Corporation for Public Broadcasting. Public Television Stations, the Ford Foundation and Exxon Corporation.
Executive Producer Jac Venza
Producer Ken Campbell
Company WNET-TV/New York
Directors Daniel Freudenberger, Peter Levin
Writer William Gillette
CAST
Thorne .... John Lithgow
Edith .... Meryl Streep
Arrelsford .... Charles Kimbrough
Caroline .... Marybeth Hurt
Wilfred .... Don Scardino
Mrs. Varney .... Alice Drummond
Henry Dumont .... Lenny Baker
Lt. Maxwell .... Frederick Coffin
Cpl. Matson ....Joe Grifasi
Jonas ....David Harris
Sgt. Wilson .... Jeffrey Jones
Tel. Mess. B .... Arthur Miller
Cavalry Orderly .... Moultrie Patton
Lt. Allison .... Jonathan Penzner
Gen. Randolph .... Roy Poole
Lt. Foray .... Rex Robbins
Tel. Mess. A ....Hansford Rowe
Martha .... Louise Stubbs
Pvt. Eddinger .... Stuart Warmflash

1245 A Secret Space
Visions   PBS
Program Type Dramatic Special
90 minutes. Premiere date: 12/4/77. Original comedy-drama about a 12-year-old boy who finds himself drawn to orthodox Judaism to the dismay of his liberal parents. Music by Arlon Ober and Harry Manfredini.
Executive Producer Barbara Schultz
Producer Roberta O. Hodes
Company KCET-TV/Los Angeles
Director Roberta O. Hodes
Writers Roberta O. Hodes, Rosalyn Regelson
Film Editor Jack Sholder
CAST
David .... Jon Matthews
Ann .... Phyllis Newman
Ted .... Sam Schacht
Grandma ....Virginia Graham
Kevin King .... Lester Rawlins
Rebbe ....Robert Klein
Eli .... Robert Fields
Shamos .... Leib Lensky
Ben .... Howard Berger
Hershel ....Michael Gorrin
Michelle ....Janet League
Fran .... Madeline Lee
Jonah .... John Seidman
Amy .... Lin Shaye
Rabbi Hillman ....Berkeley Harris
Psychiatrist .... Mel Howard

1246 Secrets
The ABC Friday Night Movie   ABC
2 hours. Premiere date: 2/20/77. Season premiere: 4/21/78. Drama of a compulsively promiscuous woman. Music by George Aliceson Tipton. "Dream Away" written by Susan Blakely. Puppets by Bob Baker Marionette Productions. Filmed on location in Southern California.
Executive Producer Gerald I. Isenberg
Producer Gerald W. Abrams
Company The Jozak Company
Director Paul Wendkos
Writer James Henerson
CAST
Andrea Fleming .... Susan Blakely
Herb Fleming .... Roy Thinnes
Helen Warner .... Joanne Linville
Ed Warner .... John Randolph
Laura Fleming .... Melody Thomas
Dr. Lee .... Frances Lee McCain
Phyllis Turner .... Charlotte Stewart
Chrissie .... Michelle Stacy
Taxi Driver .... Brian Cutler
Larry Bleier .... Anthony Eisley
Joanne Weese ....Rosanne Covy
Joel Corcoran .... Andrew Stevens
Phyllis Turner .... Charlotte Stewart
Piano Tuner .... Paul Itkin
Andrea (age 7) .... Elizabeth Cheshire

1247 See How She Runs
GE Theater   CBS
2 hours. Premiere date: 2/1/78. Dramatic special about a woman who attempts to complete the grueling 26-mile Boston Marathon. Music composed by Jimmy Haskell.
Producer George Englund
Company CLN Productions
Director Richard T. Heffron
Writer Marvin A. Gluck
Art Director Charles Bailey
Film Editor Gary Griffen
CAST
Betty Quinn .... Joanne Woodward
Larry Quinn ....John Considine
Janey Quinn .... Lissy Newman
Kathy Quinn ....Mary Beth Manning
John Matusak .... Barnard Hughes
Evelyn .... Barbara Meek
Handsome man ....James Houghton

1248 Seige
The CBS Wednesday Night Movies   CBS
Program Type TV Movie
2 hours. Premiere date: 4/26/78. Drama about an urban community and a neighborhood gang. Music by Charles Gross. Filmed in New York.
Executive Producer Herbert Brodkin
Producer Robert Berger
Company Titus Productions, Inc.
Director Richard Pearce

Seige *Continued*
Writer Conrad Bromberg
CAST

Henry Fancher	Martin Balsam
Lillian Gordon	Sylvia Sidney
Simon	Dorian Harewood
Lt. Don Riegel	James Sutorius
Mrs. Shapiro	Raschel Novikoff
Mrs. Terranova	Antonia Rey
Mr. Lubin	Albert M. Ottheimer
Mrs. Doyle	Lesslie Nicol
Mr. Johnson	Ted Butler
Mr. Hegen	Joe Sullivan
Mrs. Mikowski	Jety Herlick
Mrs. Comacho	Mila Conway
Sgt. Doan	Lloyd Hollar
Sgt. Bermudez	Alex Colon
Ronald	Larry Scott
Mikey	Peter Acevedo
Carlos	Dadi Pinero
Renee	Wanda Velez

1249 Self to Self   Syndicated
Program Type Talk/Service/Variety Series
30 minutes. Premiere date: 4/27/78. Talk show with people speaking about their own experiences.
Producer Alexandra Self
Company Self to Self Interviews
Director Arnie Nocks
Host Alexandra Self

1250 Senior Bowl   NBC
Program Type Sports Special
Live coverage of the 29th annual Senior Bowl from Ladd Memorial Stadium in Mobile, Ala. 1/7/78.
Producers Ted Nathanson, George Finkel
Company NBC Sports
Director Ted Nathanson
Commentators Charlie Jones, Len Dawson

1251 A Sensitive, Passionate Man
NBC Saturday Night at the Movies   NBC
2 hours. Premiere date: 6/6/77. Repeat date: 6/24/78. Drama about a marriage threatened by a husand's alcoholism. Based on the novel by Barbara Mahoney. "My Sensitive, Passionate Man" lyrics by David Janssen and Carol Connors; music by Carol Connors and Bill Conti; sung by Melba Moore.
Producer Alan Jay Factor
Company Factor-Newland Productions in association with NBC-TV
Director John Newland
Writer Rita Lakin
Art Director Elayne Barbara Ceder
CAST

Marjorie Delaney	Angie Dickinson
Michael Delaney	David Janssen
Dan Delaney	Todd Lookinland
Kerry Delaney	Justin Randi

Pat Morris	Mariclare Costello
Jack Morris	Richard Venture
John Chapin	Rhodes Reason
Dr. Lazerow	Richard Bull

The Sentry Collection Presents *See* Ben Vereen—His Roots.

1252 Sergeant Matlovich Versus the U.S. Air Force
NBC World Premiere Movie/NBC Monday Night at the Movies   NBC
Program Type Dramatic Special
2 hours. Premiere date: 8/21/78. Based on the real-life story of a sergeant discharged from the U.S. Air Force.
Executive Producer Thomas W. Moore
Producer Paul Lear
Company Tomorrow Entertainment in association with NBC-TV
Director Paul Leaf
Writer John McGreevey
CAST

Leonard Matlovich	Brad Dourif
Jason	Marc Singer
Addlestone	David Spielberg
Applegate	Mitch Ryan
Mat's Father	Stephen Elliott
Father Veller	William Daniels
Jaenicke	Frank Converse
Mat's Mother	Rue McClanahan
Susan	Barra Grant

Serpico *See* The ABC Sunday Night Movie

The Servant *See* PBS Movie Theater

1253 A Service of Lessons and Carols
CBS
Program Type Religious/Cultural Special
60 minutes. Premiere date: 12/24/77. Services from Pine United Methodist Church, San Francisco, Calif., the mother church of Japanese Methodism.
Executive Producer Pamela Ilott
Director Ben Hill
Pastor Rev. Nobuhiro Imaizumin

1254 Sesame Street   PBS
Program Type Children's Series
60 minutes. Monday–Friday mornings. Premiere date: 11/10/69. Ninth season premiere: 11/8/77. Magazine format for preschool children. Muppets created by Jim Henson. Series made possible by grants from the U.S. Department of Health, Education and Welfare—Office of Education, Public Television Stations, the Ford Foundation,

the Corporation for Public Broadcasting, and the Carnegie Corporation of New York. Wednesday programs include specially prepared segments for children with learning disabilities.
Executive Producer Jon Stone
Producer Al Hyslop
Company Children's Television Workshop
Directors Robert Myhrum, Jon Stone, Emily Squires, Jimmy Baylor, Bob Schwarz
Writers Ray Sipherd, Emily Perl Kingsley, Joseph Bailey, David Korr, Judy Freudberg, Tony Geiss, Sara Compton
Musical Director Sam Pottle
Costume Designer Domingo Rodriguez
Art Director Alan J. Compton
Set Decorator Nat Mongioi
CAST
David .... Northern J. Calloway
Luis .... Emilio Delgado
Mr. Hooper .... Will Lee
Susan .... Loretta Long
Maria .... Sonia Manzano
Bob .... Bob McGrath
Gordon .... Roscoe Orman
Big Bird/Oscar .... Carroll Spinney
Puppeteers Jim Henson, Frank Oz, Jerry Nelson, Richard Hunt, Peter Friedman, Caroly Wilcox

1255   Seventh Avenue
NBC's Best Seller/The Big Event/NBC Monday Night at the Movies
Program Type Limited Series
6 hours. Premiere date:2/24/77. Series repeated: 7/18/78. Dramatization of the novel by Norman Bogner about New York City's garment industry. Filmed on location in New York.
Executive Producer Franklin Barton
Producer Richard Irving
Company Universal Television in association with NBC-TV
Directors Richard Irving, Russ Mayberry
Writer Laurence Heath
Production Designer Philip Rosenberg
Art Director Lloyd Papez
CAST
Jay Blackman .... Steven Keats
Rhoda Gold Blackman .... Dori Brenner
Eva Meyers .... Jane Seymour
Myrna Gold .... Anne Archer
Al Blackman .... Kristoffer Tabori
Frank Topo .... Richard Dimitri
Douglas Fredericks .... Ray Milland
Harry Lee .... Alan King
Joe Vitelli .... Herschel Bernardi
Marty Cass .... John Pleshette
Mr. Finkelstein .... Jack Gilford
Gus Farber .... Eli Wallach
John Meyers .... William Windom
Celia Blackman .... Anna Berger
Morris Blackman .... Mike Kellin
Barney Green .... Josh Mostel
Dave Shaw .... Paul Sorvino
Neal Blackman .... Joshua Freund

1256   79 Park Avenue
The Big Event/NBC Monday Night at the Movies/ Tuesday Movie of the Week   NBC
Program Type Limited Series
6 hours. Premiere date: 10/16–18/78. Based on best-seller by Harold Robbins. Music by Nelson Riddle. Developed for television by Richard DeRoy.
Executive Producer George Eckstein
Producer Paul Wendkos
Company Universal Television in association with Harold Robbins International Co., Ltd.
Director Paul Wendkos
Writers Richard DeRoy, Jack Guss,Lionel E. Siegel
Costume Designer Yvonne Wood
Art Director Lloyd Papez
Director of Photography Enzo A. Martinelli
Film Editors Robert F. Shugrue (I and III); Rod Stephens (II)
CAST
Marja/Marianne .... Lesley Ann Warren
Mike Koshko .... David Dukes
Ross Savitch .... Marc Singer
Ben Savitch .... Michael Constantine
Armand Perfido .... Raymond Burr
Peter Markevich .... Albert Salmi
Joker Martin .... Jack Weston
Vera .... Polly Bergen
Harry Vito .... John Saxon
Stevens .... Lloyd Haynes
Whitfield .... Peter Marshall
Frannie .... Jane Marla Robbins
Kaati .... Barbara Barrie
Joey .... Sandy Helberg
Paulie .... Matthew Laborteaux
Myrna .... Margaret Fairchild

1257   Sex and the Married Woman
NBC Saturday/Tuesday Night at the Movies
Program Type TV Movie
2 hours. Premiere date: 9/13/77. Repeat date: 6/17/78. Comedy about a couple whose marriage flounders after the wife writes a book about the sexual experiences of married women.
Executive Producer George J. Santoro
Producer Jack Arnold
Company Universal Television in association with NBC-TV
Director Jack Arnold
Writer Michael Norell
CAST
Leslie Fitch .... Joanna Pettet
Alan Fitch .... Barry Newman
Uncle June .... Keenan Wynn
Duke Skaggs .... F. Murray Abraham
Louie Grosscup .... Dick Gautier
Peter Nebben .... Angus Duncan
Virginia Ladysmith .... Fannie Flagg
Irma Caddish .... Jayne Meadows
Arnie .... Larry Hovis
Carolyn .... Jeanne Lange
Hedi Lomax .... Nita Talbot
Jim Cutler .... Chuck McCann

1258 **Sha Na Na**   Syndicated
Program Type Music/Comedy/Variety Series
30 minutes. Premiere date: 9/27/77. 10-man
rock 'n' roll group host music-comedy-variety
show.
Executive Producer Pierre Cossette
Producers Bernard Rothman; Jack Wohl
Company Pierre Cossette Productions
Distributor Lexington Broadcast Services, Inc.
Director Tom Trbovich
Writers Bernard Rothman, Jack Wohl
Stars Sha Na Na

1259 **Shades of Greene**   PBS
Program Type Drama Series
60 minutes. Premiere date: 10/2/77. 12-part an-
thology based on the short stories of Graham
Greene.
Producer Alan Cooke
Company Thames Television
Director Alastair Redi

Shameless Old Lady *See* PBS Movie
   Theater
Writer John Mortimer

1260 **Sharks: The Death Machines** NBC
Program Type Educational/Cultural Special
60 minutes. Premiere date: 9/6/77. True stories
of 3 Americans' encounters with great white
sharks.
Executive Producer James W. Packer
Producers Ken Shapiro, Nicolas Webster
Company Tiburon Productions in association
   with the NBC Television Network
Director Nicolas Webster
Writer Peter A. Lake
Cinematographers Ron Taylor, Valerie Taylor

1261 **Sharon: Portrait of a Mistress**
NBC Monday Night at the Movies/NBC
World Premiere Movie   NBC
Program Type Dramatic Special
2 hours. Premiere date: 10/31/77. Drama of a
woman is a mistress to a series of married men.
Song, "The Days Have No Names," music by
Roger Kellaway; lyrics by Gene Lees; sung by
Sarah Vaughn.
Producer Frank von Zerneck
Company Moonlight Productions, Inc., in asso-
   ciation with Paramount-TV and NBC-TV
Director Robert Greenwald
Writer Nancy Greenwald
CAST
Sharon Blake .... Trish Van Devere
Ed Dowling .... Patrick O'Neal
Carol .... Janet Margolin
Timothy .... Sam Groom
Mrs. Blake .... Gloria De Haven

David .... Mel Ferrer
Anne Dowling .... Rose Gregorio
Terri .... Salome Jens
Dr. Greenberg .... Arthur Storch

1262 **Shields and Yarnell**   CBS
Program Type Music/Comedy/Variety Series
30 minutes, Tuesdays. Premiere date: 6/13/77.
Season Premiere: 1/31/78. Last show: 3/28/78.
Mime, singing, dancing and comedy.
Executive Producer Steve Binder
Producers Frank Peppiatt, John Aylesworth
Company A Steve Binder Production; Get the
   Hook Productions and Youngestreet Enter-
   tainment Corp.
Director Steve Binder
Writers Barry Adelman, Robert Shields, Barry
   Silver, Gailard Sartain, Jim Millaway
Musical Director Norman Mamey
Art Director Gene McAvoy
Stars Robert Shields, Lorene Yarnell

1263 **Shipshape**   CBS
Program Type Comedy Special
30 minutes. Premiere date: 8/1/78. Pilot about
an ambitious young ensign who must train a
group of "misfit" sailors if she wants to get ahead
in the Navy. Musical theme by Michael Lloyd.
Executive Producer James Komack
Producers Al Gordon, Jack Mendelsohn
Company James Komac Company, Inc.
Directors James Komack, Gary Shimokawa
Writers George Tricker, Neil Rosen, Gary Bel-
   kin, Stan Cutler
CAST
Ensign Leslie O'Hara .... Deborah Ryan
Capt. Lash .... Earl Boen
Lucky Lorenzo .... Lorenzo Lamas
Beltyman .... Andrew Block
Watkins .... Gary Veney
Demo .... Demetre Phillips
Sweetzer .... Shell Kepler

1264 **Shoot for the Stars**   NBC
Program Type Game/Audience Participation
   Series
30 minutes. Mondays–Fridays. Premiere date:
1/3/77. Last show: 9/30/77. Word-association
paraphrase game with teams of contestants and
celebrities.
Executive Producer Bob Stewart
Producer Bruce Burmester
Company A Bob Stewart Production
Director Mike Gargiulo
Host Geoff Edwards
Announcer Bob Clayton

Shoot Out *See* The ABC Sunday Night
   Movie

Shoot the Piano Player *See* PBS Movie Theater

1265 Shooting the Chandelier
Great Performances   PBS
Program Type Dramatic Special
90 minutes. Premiere date: 5/10/78. A historian serving in the Russian army as a junior catering officer joins with a member of Stalin's secret police to commandeer a dilapidated country house during the 1945 "liberation" of Czechoslovakia.
Company WNET-TV/New York
Writer David Mercer
Stars Edward Fox, Denholm Elliott

1266 Showdown at the Hoedown   PBS
Program Type Music/Dance Special
60 minutes. Premiere date: 12/27/77. Forty thousand fiddlers, square dancers, and pickers of all kinds assemble at Smithville, Tennessee for a hoedown. Presented on PBS by the Southern Educational Communications Association.
Producers Blaine Dunlap, Sol Korine
Company WETV-TV/Atlanta

1267 Showdown of the Dream Teams
                                            Syndicated
Program Type Game/Audience Participation Series
30 minutes. Premiere date: 2/8/78. Two teams of celebrities of four members each compete against each other in four tests of team ability.
Executive Producer Alan Sloan
Producer George Vosburgh
Company Alan Sloan Inc.
Director Arthur Forrest
Writer E. Jack Kaplan
Host Gary Owens

1268 Significant Religious Events 1977
                                                  CBS
Program Type Religious/Cultural Special
60 minutes. Premiere date: 1/1/78. Prominent American churchmen discuss the major religious news of the past year.
Executive Producer Pamela Ilott
Producer Ted Holmes

1269 The Silent Minority   PBS
Program Type Documentary/Informational Special
30 minutes. Premiere date: 5/20/78. Documentary exploring the active and varied lives of a number of deaf individuals.
Company WHA Televison, UWEX Television and UWEX Telecommunications Center in Madison, Wisconsin

1270 Sinatra and Friends
Program Type Music/Dance Special   ABC
60 minutes. Premiere date: 4/21/77. Repeat date: 8/9/78. All-music special. Production numbers by Hugh Lambert.
Producer Paul W. Keyes
Co-Producer Marc London
Company A Paul W. Keyes Production
Director Bill Davis
Writers Paul W. Keyes, Marc London
Musical Director Nelson Riddle
Art Director E. Jay Krause
Music Coordinator Irving Weiss
Star/Host Frank Sinatra
Guest Stars Tony Bennett, Natalie Cole, John Denver, Loretta Lynn, Dean Martin, Robert Merrill, Leslie Uggams

1271 Since Gary Gilmore
CBS Reports   CBS
Program Type Documentary/Informational Special
Premiere date: 3/7/78. Update of a story on capital punishment and the Gary Gilmore case.
Executive Producer Howard Stringer
Producer Jonnet Steinbaum
Company CBS News
Cinematographer William J. Wagner
Reporter Marlene Sanders

1272 Sing a Sign   PBS
Program Type Music/Dance Special
30 minutes. Premiere date: 5/20/78. Original musical revue in sign language. Program made possible by a grant from the American Telephone and Telegraph Company. Music composed and conducted by Steve Swab with lyrics by Susan Davidoff, Vince DiZebba, and Susan Smith.
Producer Susan Smith
Company Cara Smith Production presented by WETA-TV/Washington, DC
Director Sterling Smith
Writer Susan Smith
Choreographer Vince DiZebba
Performers Bernard Braff Rita Corey, Vince DiZebba, Donna Gadling, Rodney Johnson, Ogden Whitehead, Martie Stephens, Tracy Tuttle, David MacFarlane

1273 Sing America Sing   PBS
Program Type Music/Dance Special
60 minutes. Premiere date: 3/22/76. Repeat date: 7/4/78. Highlights of the stage production and opening night reception at the John F. Kennedy Center, Washington, D.C. of the Bicentennial musical "Sing America Sing." Program made possible by a grant from the Prudential Insurance Company of America.
Producers Robert L. Stevens, Sidney Palmer

Sing America Sing *Continued*
Company South Carolina Educational Television Network
Directors Oscar Brand, Philip Gay
Writer Oscar Brand
Musical Director Ron Frangipane
Choreographer Tony Stevens
CAST
Eyewitness .... John Raitt

1274   Sing We Noel   PBS
Program Type Music/Dance Special
30 minutes. Premiere date: 12/18/77. Mormon Youth Symphony and Chorus featured in Christmas music special.
Company KBYU-TV/Provo and Bonneville Productions

1275   Sir Georg Solti Conducts the Chicago Symphony Orchestra
Great Performances   PBS
Program Type Music/Dance Special
90 minutes. Premiere date: 2/22/78. Sir Georg Solti conducts the Chicago Symphony Orchestra in three works by Richard Strauss. Program made possible by a grant from Exxon and support from PBS stations.
Executive Producers Klaus Hallig, Jac Venza
Producer David Griffiths
Company International Television Trading Corporation for WNET-TV/New York
Director Humphrey Burton

1276   Sister Terri   ABC
Program Type Comedy Special
30 minutes. Premiere date: 5/27/78. Comedy pilot about a former gang leader.
Executive Producers Bob Brunner, Arthur Silver
Company Paramount Pictures Production
Director Jerry Paris
CAST
Sister Terri .... Pam Dawber
Mother Superior Helen .... Allyn Ann McLerie
Sister Agatha .... Amy Johnston
Sam .... Robbie Lee
Angel .... Scott Colomby
Jenny .... Kimberly La Page

Sisters *See* Tuesday Movie of the Week

1277   Six American Families   PBS
Program Type Documentary/Informational Series
60 minutes. Tuesdays. Premiere date: 4/4/77. Repeat date: 4/4/78. Six documentaries looking at contemporary family life in the United States. Series presented by KQED-TV/San Francisco and made possible by a grant from the Travelers Insurance Companies.

Executive Producer George Moynihan
Producers Bill Jersey, Albert Maysles, David Maysles, Arthur Barron, Mark Obenhaus
Company Group W (Westinghouse Broadcasting Company) in association with the United Church of Christ and the United Methodist Church
Directors Bill Jersey, Albert Maysles, David Maysles, Arthur Barron, Mark Obenhaus
Host Paul Wilkes

1278   The Six Million Dollar Man   ABC
Program Type Crime Drama Series
60 minutes. Sundays. Mondays as of 1/30/78. Premiere date: 1/14/74. Fifth season premiere: 9/11/77. Last show: 3/6/78. Based on the novel "Cyborg" by Martin Caidin and pilot "The Six Million Dollar Man" originally broadcast 3/7/73. Action-adventures of bionic man working for the U.S. Office of Scientific Information (O.S.I.).
Executive Producer Harve Bennett
Producer Lionel E. Siegel, Allan Balter
Company A Harve Bennett Production in association with Universal Television
Directors Various
Writers Various
Producers Fred Freiberger, Richard Landau
Special Effects Joe Goss
CAST
Steve Austin .... Lee Majors
Oscar Goldman .... Richard Anderson
Dr. Rudy Wells .... Martin E. Brooks

1279   Sixty Minutes   CBS
Program Type News Magazine Series
60 minutes. Sundays. Premiere date: 9/24/68. Tenth season Premiere: 9/11/77. Became 52-week primetime show 12/7/75. Three reports weekly. Regular features: "Mail" (viewer response) and "Point-Counter-Point" with Shana Alexander and James J. Kilpatrick.
Executive Producer Don Hewitt
Producers Various
Company CBS News
Co-Editors Mike Wallace, Morley Safer, Dan Rather

1280   The Skating Rink
ABC Out-of-School Specials/ABC Weekend Specials   ABC
Program Type Children's Special
60 minutes. Premiere date: 2/5/75. Repeat date: 10/29/77. Based on the book by Mildred Lee. Music by Glenn Paxton. Skating choreographer: Bill Blackburn. The discovery of self-respect and the faith of a friend help a teenage stutterer deal with his handicap.
Producer Martin Tahse
Company Martin Tahse Productions, Inc.

Director Larry Elikann
Writer Bob Rodgers
CAST

Pete Degley	Jerry Dexter
Lilly Degley	Devon Ericson
Ida Faraday	Betty Beaird
Myron Faraday	Rance Howard
Tuck Faraday	Stewart Petersen
Elva Grimes	Cindy Eilbacher
Tom Faraday	Billy Bowles
Clete Faraday	Robert Clotworthy
Karen Faraday	Tara Talboy
Mrs. Bayliss	Molly Dodd
Tuck's Real Mother	Patricia Stevens
Young Tuck	Sparky Marcus

1281 Ski Lift to Death
The CBS Friday Night Movies   CBS
Program Type TV Movie
2 hours. Premiere date: 3/3/78. Drama about several people trapped in two derailed ski lift gondolas. Music by Barry DeVorzon. Filmed in Banff and Lake Louise, Alberta, Canada.
Executive Producer Gerald W. Abrams
Producers Richard Briggs, Bruce J. Sallan
Company The Jozak Company in association with Paramount Television
Director William Wiard
Writer Laurence Heath
CAST

Lee Larson	Deborah Raffin
Dick Elston	Charles Frank
Ben Forbes	Howard Duff
Ron Corley	Don Galloway
Vicki Gordon	Gail Strickland
Mike Sloan	Don Johnson
Andrea Mason	Veronica Hamel
Marv Gillman	Clu Gulager
Wendy Brant	Lisa Reeves
Clevenger	Pierre Jalbert
Ski Patroller	Suzy Chaffee

Skullduggery *See* Tuesday Movie of the Week

1282 Sky Pirates   PBS
Program Type Children's Special
60 minutes. Premiere date: 5/11/78. Two brothers and an ex-pilot become involved with diamond smugglers. Presented by WQED-TV/Pittsburg.
Producer Frank Godwin
Company Ansus Production for Children's Film Foundation
Director Pennington Richards
Writer Pennington Richards
CAST

Mike	Adam Richens
Harry	Michael McVey
Maggie	Sylvia O'Donnell
Charlie	Bill Maynard

Sky Terror *See* The ABC Sunday Night Movie

Smash-Up on Interstate 5 *See* Tuesday Movie of the Week

Smile *See* The CBS Friday Night Movies

1283 Snavely   ABC
Program Type Comedy Special
30 minutes. Premiere date: 6/24/78. Comedy pilot about the inept owners of a resort hotel. Based on the BBC series, "Fawlty Towers." Created by John Cleese and Connie Booth.
Company Strathmore Production in association with Viacom Enterprises
Director Hal Cooper
Writers Roland Kibbee, Dean Hargrove
CAST

Henry Snavely	Harvey Korman
Gladys Snavely	Betty White
Petro	Frank LaLoggia
Chief	Ivor Francis
Connie	Deborah Zon
Mr. Bishop	Jack Dodson
Mr. Foley	George Pentecost

1284 Snoopy, Come Home   CBS
Program Type Animated Film Special
90 minutes. Premiere date: 11/5/76. Repeat date: 11/5/77. Snoopy returns to his first owner. Music and lyrics by Richard M. Sherman and Robert Sherman; arranged and conducted by Don Ralke.
Producers Lee Mendelson, Bill Melendez
Director Bill Melendez
Writer Charles M. Schulz
VOICES

Charlie Brown	Chad Webber
Lucy	Robin Kohn
Linus	Stephen Shea
Schroeder	David Carey
Lila	Johanna Baer
Sally	Hilary Momberger
Peppermint Patty	Christopher Defaria
Clara	Linda Ercoli
Frieda	Linda Mendelson
Snoopy	Bill Melendez

1285 Snoopy's Musical on Ice   CBS
Program Type Music/Comedy/Variety Special
60 minutes. Premiere date: 5/24/78. Variety ice show. Music arranged and directed by Ed Bogas and Judy Munsen.
Executive Producer Charles M. Schulz
Producers Lee Mendelson, Warren Lockhart
Director Walter C. Miller
Choreographers Helen and Bob Maxson
Costume Designer Bill Hargate

Snoopy's Musical on Ice Continued
Stars Peggy Fleming, Charles M. Schulz, Judy Sladky (Snoopy)
Guest Stars Skippy Baster, Lisa Carey, Mr. Frick, Chris Harrison, Dan Henry, Lisa Illsley, Karen Kresge, Amy Schulz, Atoy Wilson, Pat Baker, Robert Steiner, Suzanna Leduc, David Thomas, Mary Ellen Kinsey, Julie Lockhart, Vicki Lockhart, Robert Lockhart

1286 Snowbeast
The Big Event   NBC
Program Type TV Movie
2 hours: Premiere date: 4/28/77. Repeat date: 6/6/78. Drama about a ski resort terrorized by a killer beast. Music by Robert Prince. Special effects by Marlowe Newkirk. Filmed on location in Gunnison County, Colorado.
Executive Producer Douglas S. Cramer
Producer W. L. Baumes
Company Douglas Cramer Productions in association with NBC-TV
Director Herb Wallerstein
Writer Joseph Stefano
Art Director Steven Sardanis
CAST
Gar Seberg .... Bo Svenson
Ellen Seberg .... Yvette Mimieux
Tony Rill .... Robert Logan
Sheriff Paraday .... Clint Walker
Carrie Rill ....Sylvia Sidney
Snowbeast .... Michael J. London
Buster .... Thomas Babson
Jennifer .... Kathy Christopher
Heidi .... Anne McEncroe

1287 Snowbound
Special Treat   NBC
Program Type Children's Special
60 minutes. Premiere date: 2/7/78. A teen-age boy and girl learn to respect each other while stranded in a blizzard. Based on the book by Harry Mazer.
Company Learning Corporation of America
Director Andrew Young
Writers Edward Pomerantz, Kurt Villadsen
CAST
Tony .... Michael Mullins
Cindy ....Lisa Jane Persky
Jeanine .... Vicki Dawson
Roller rink cashier .... Shirley Stoler

1288 Soap   ABC
Program Type Comedy Series
30 minutes. Tuesdays. Premiere date: 9/13/77. Series repeated in late night viewing Mondays and Tuesdays 6/5/78. Created by Susan Harris. Continuing adult character comedy which follows the lives of two sisters. Jessica Tate and Mary Campbell. Music by George Aliceson Tip-

ton. Taped before a studio audience in Hollywood, Calif.
Executive Producers Paul Junger Witt, Tony Thomas
Supervising Producer Susan Harris
Producer Susan Harris
Company A Witt/Thomas/Harrison Production
Director Jay Sandrich
Writer Susan Harris
Announcer Rod Roddy
CAST
Billy Tate ....Jimmy Baio
Corinne Tate .... Diana Canova
Jodie Dallas .... Billy Crystal
Mary Campbell .... Cathryn Damon
Benson ....Robert Guillaume
Jessica Tate .... Katherine Helmond
The Godfather .... Richard Libertini
Chester Tate .... Robert Mandan
Burt Campbell .... Richard Mulligan
The Major .... Arthur Peterson
Claire .... Kathryn Reynolds
Eunice Tate .... Jennifer Salt
Peter (Tennis Player) ....Robert Urich
Danny Dallas .... Ted Wass

1289 The Soap Factory   Syndicated
Program Type Music/Dance Series
30 minutes. Saturdays. Premiere date: 7/18/78. Disco dance show.
Executive Producer David Bergman
Producer Andrew Baddish
Company DMB Productions
Director Joe Lo-re
Host Paul Harriss

1290 Soap Retrospective II   ABC
Program Type Comedy Special
90 minutes. 8/31/78. Highlights of the first year of new comedy series.
Executive Producers Paul Junger Witt, Tony Thomas
Producer Susan Harris
Company Witt-Thomas Production
Director Jay Sandrich
Writer Susan Harris
CAST
Jessica Tate .... Katherine Helmond
Chester Tate .... Robert Mandan
Corinne Tate .... Diana Canova
Eunice Tate .... Jennifer Salt
Billy Tate ....Jimmy Baio
Benson ....Robert Guillaume
Burt Campbell .... Richard Mulligan
Mary Campbell .... Cathryn Damon
Jodie Dallas .... Billy Crystal
Danny Dallas .... Ted Wass
Peter Campbell ....Robert Urich
Chuck Campbell .... Jay Johnson
Carol .... Rebecca Balding
Elaine .... Dinah Manoff
Congressman McCallum .... Edward Winter
Father Timothy Flotsky .... Sal Viscuso
Dennis Phillips .... Bob Seagren

Judge Petrillo ....Charles Lane
E. Ronald Mallu ....Eugene Roche

Dr. Klunick .... David Garfield
Mark ....Kevin McKenzie

1291 Soccer Made In Germany PBS
Program Type Sports Special
60 minutes. Premiere date: 10/14/77. Series repeated: 8/27/78. Eighteen 1-hour taped highlights of the top game played the preceding Saturday in the 18-team West German First Division (Bundesliga).
Coordinating Producer Jim Scalem
Company German Educational Television Network and KQED-TV/San Francisco

1292 Some of the Presidents' Men PBS
Program Type Documentary/Informational Special
60 minutes. Premiere date: 5/28/78. Former White House press secretaries Pierre Salinger, George Reedy, Ron Ziegler and Ron Nessen discuss their careers. Program made possible in part by a grant from the Corporation for Public Broadcasting.
Producer Mike Kirk
Company KCTS-TV/Seattle and KSPS-TV/Spokane
Director Bruce Franchini
Anchor Mike Kirk
Reporters Seymour Hersh, Liz Trotta

Something Big *See* NBC Saturday Night at the Movies

1293 Something for Joey CBS
Program Type Dramatic Special
2 hours. Premiere date: 4/6/77. Repeat date: 9/8/78. Dramatizaton of the true-life relationship between Heisman Trophy winner John Cappelletti and his brother Joey. Music by David Shire.
Producer Jerry McNeely
Company MTM Enterprises, Inc.
Director Lou Antonio
Writer Jerry McNeely
Art Director Sydney Z. Litwack
CAST
Anne Cappelletti .... Geraldine Page
John Cappelletti, Sr. ....Gerald S. O'Loughlin
John Cappelletti .... Marc Singer
Joey Cappelletti .... Jeff Lynas
Joyce Cappelletti ....Linda Kelsey
Marty Cappelletti .... Brian Farrell
Jean Cappelletti .... Kathy Beller
Mike Cappelletti .... Steven Guttenberg
Joe Paterno .... Paul Picerni
Eddie O'Neil .... Stephen Parr
Archbishop ....David Hooks
Mrs. Frone .... June Dayton
Dr. Wingreen .... James Karen

1294 Something Personal PBS
Program Type Documentary/Informational Series
30 minutes. Saturdays. Premiere date: 7/16/7. Series repeated: 9/10/77. Nine-part series of documentary films showing the variety and uniqueness of American women. Series made possible by grants from the National Endowment for the Arts and the Corporation for Public Broadcasting.
Executive Producer Nancy Porter
Producers Nancy Porter, Joyce Chopra, Ann Hershey, Miriam Weinstein, Mitchell Block, Mirra Bank, Lynne Littman
Company WGBH-TV/Boston

1295 Song at Twilight: An Essay on Aging
Documentary Showcase PBS
Program Type Documentary/Informational Special
60 minutes. Premiere date: 1/21/77. Repeat date: 10/21/77. A look at the aging process and society's attitude toward older people.
Producer Paul Cabbell
Company KOCE-TV/Huntington Beach, Calif.
Director Thom Eberhardt
Writer Paul Cabbell
Narrator Paul Cabbell

1296 Song by Song by Ira Gershwin
Festival '78 PBS
Program Type Music/Dance Special
60 minutes. Premiere date: 3/7/78. Musical tribute to the lyrics of Ira Gershwin.
Producer Ned Sherrin
Company BBC
Director Brian Whitehouse
Stars Ned Sherrin, Millicent Martin, Julia McKenzie, David Kernan

1297 Soul of Freedom
CBS Reports CBS
Program Type Documentary/Informational Special
Premiere date: 3/7/78. Profile of Soviet defector Simas Kudirka.
Producer Howard Stringer
Company CBS News
Cinematographer Tom Spain
Film Editor Maurice Murad
Researchers Peter Schweitzer, Susan D. Werbe
Reporter Bill Moyers

1298   The Sounds of Christmas Eve NBC
Program Type Religious/Cultural Special
30 minutes. Premiere date: 12/24/73. Repeat
date: 12/24/77. Original and traditional Yule-
tide music and readings.
Producer Dick Schneider
Director Dick Schneider
Writer Shelly Cohen
Host Doc Severinsen
Guests Henry Mancini, Victor Buono, Choir of
St. Charles Borromeo Church, Los Angeles

1299   Soundstage PBS
Program Type Music/Dance Series
60 minutes. Saturdays. Premiere date: 11/12/74.
Fourth season premiere: 1/21/78. Weekly con-
temporary music series featuring guest stars.
Funded by the Corporation for Public Broad-
casting, the Ford Foundation and Public Televi-
sion Stations.
Producers William Heitz, Charles Mitchell
Company WTTW-TV/Chicago
Director Richard Carter

1300   Soup and Me
ABC Weekend Specials   ABC
Program Type Children's Special
30 minutes. Premiere date: 2/4/78. A modern-
day Tom Sawyer and Huck Finn find all their
ideas turning into trouble. Music by Tommy
Leonetti. Based on stories by Robert Newton
Peck. Teleplay by Mark Fink.
Producer Robert Chenault
Company An ABC Circle Film
Director Dennis Donnelly
Art Director Ray Markham
CAST
Mr. Sutter ....Frank Cady
Rob ....Shane Sinutko
Soup ....Christian Berrigan
Janice ....Mary Margaret Patts
Delivery Man ....Owen Bush
Mrs. Stetson ....Kathleen Freeman

1301   The South Pacific: End of Eden?
James Michener's World   PBS
Program Type Documentary/Informational
Special
60 minutes. Premiere date: 6/20/78. Fourth in
series of specials about places of which author
has written. Presented by KCET, Los Angeles
and made possible by a grant from Mrs. Paul's
Kitchens, Inc.
Producer Julian Krainin
Company Reader's Digest Association, Inc.
Director Julian Krainin
Writer Julian Krainin
Host James Michener

1302   Southie! PBS
Program Type Documentary/Informational
Special
60 minutes. Premiere date: 8/17/78. Documentary about the Irish-American community of
South Boston, Mass., its traditions and its impact
on the city of Boston as a whole.
Company WGBH-TV/Boston and Irish television

1303   Space Force
Comedy time   NBC
Program Type Comedy Special
30 minutes. Premiere date: 4/28/78. Pilot for-
merly titled "Fort Leo," about the zany crew of
a starcraft spaceship coping with the threat of
inter-galactic war.
Producers John Boni, Norman Stiles
Company Columbia Pictures TV
Director Peter Baldwin
Writers John Boni, Norman Stiles
CAST
Cmdr. Irving Hinkley ....William Phipps
Capt. Thomas Edison Woods ....Fred Willard
Pvt. Arnold Fleck ....Larry Block
Capt. Leon Stoner ....Jim Boyd
D.O.R.K. ....Richard Paul
Capt. Robert Milford ....Hilly Hicks
Sgt. Eve Bailey .... Maureen Mooney
Lt. Kabar .... Joe Medalis

The Space Sentinels *See* The Young
Sentinels

1304   Spain: The Land and the Legend
James Michener's World   PBS
Program Type Documentary/Informational
Special
60 minutes. Premiere date: 3/21/78. Repeat
date: 9/19/78. Third special in a series of docu-
mentaries on places of which the author has writ-
ten. Presented by KCET, Los Angeles and made
possible by a grant from Mrs. Paul's Kitchens,
Inc.
Producers Albert Waller, Ken Golden, Nan Se-
german
Company Reader's Digest Association, Inc.
Director Albert Waller
Writer Albert Waller
Host James Michener

1305   The Spark PBS
Program Type Documentary/Informational
Special
30 minutes. Premiere date: 11/16/77. Documen-
tary on two Hasidic communities of New York.
Producer Melvin Epstein
Director Melvin Epstein
Narrator David Horowitz

1306 Sparrow CBS
Program Type Dramatic Special
60 minutes. Premiere date: 8/11/78. Slightly different remake of a pilot shown 1/12/77; this one about a self-educated crime-buff who joins a large detective agency. Created by Larry Cohen.
Executive Producer Herbert B. Leonard
Producer Walter Bernstein
Company L & B Productions
Director Jack Sold
Writer Walter Bernstein
CAST
Jerry Sparrow .... Randy Herman
Medwick .... Gerald S. O'Loughlin
Valerie .... Cathy Hicks
Mrs. Benet ....Lillian Gish
Dory .... Jonelle Allen
Rhino .... Kurt Knudsen
Landon .... Dolph Sweet

1307 Special Edition Syndicated
Program Type News Magazine Series
30 minutes. Premiere date: 9/17/77. Magazine format with Barbara Feldon as host.
Producer Alan Sloan
Company Columbia Pictures TV
Director Steve Katten
Writer Ron Raley
Host Barbara Feldon

1308 A Special Evening with Carol Burnett CBS
Program Type Music/Comedy/Variety Special
2 hours. Premiere date: 3/29/78. The last taping of "The Carol Burnett Show."
Executive Producer Joe Hamilton
Producer Ed Simmons
Director David Powers
Star Carol Burnett
Regulars Vicki Lawrence, Tim Conway, The Ernest Flatt Dancers
Guest Stars in sequences from past shows are Ray Charles, Perry Como, Bing Crosby, Buddy Ebsen, Ella Fitzgerald, Eydie Gorme, Rita Hayworth, Bob Hope, Rock Hudson, Steve Lawrence, Liza Minelli, Jim Nabors, Burt Reynolds, Wayne Rogers

1309 Special Olympics
The CBS Wednesday Night Movies CBS
Program Type TV Movie
2 hours. Premiere date: 2/22/78. Drama of a widower who comes to terms with his younger son's mental retardation. Filmed entirely in Albuquerque and Santa Fe, New Mexico. Music by Peter Matz.
Executive Producer Roger Gimbel
Producers Merrit Malloy, Marc Trabulus
Company EMI Television Programs, Inc.
Director Lee Philips

Writer John Sacret Young
CAST
Carl Gallitzin .... Charles Durning
Elmira Gallitzin .... Irene Tedrow
Janice Gallitzin .... Mare Winningham
Michael Gallitzin .... Phil Brown
Matthew Gallitzin .... George Parry
Doug Ransom .... Herb Edelman
Sherry Hensley .... Debra Winger
Trina Cunningham .... Constance McCashin
Dr. Brennerman .... James Calvin Nelson
Ron Burton .... Nat Simmons

1310 Special Report on the Fighting in the Middle East
NBC News Special NBC
Program Type News Special
30 minutes. Special report on fighting in the Middle East with electronic camera coverage transmitted via satellite 3/15/78.
Executive Producer Gordon Manning
Producer Gordon Manning
Company NBC News
Anchor Edwin Newman
Correspondents Hilary Brown, Garrick Utley, Richard Hunt, David Burrington, Tom Pettit, Richard Valeriani, Judy Woodruff

1311 Special Treat NBC
Program Type Children's Series
60 minutes. Tuesdays. Premiere date: 10/21/75. Third season premiere: 10/11/77. Specials shown during the 1977–78 season are: "Big Henry and the Polka Dot Kid," "Five-Finger Discount," "How the Beatles Changed the World," "It's a Brand New World," "Luke Was There," "Papa and Me," "A Piece of Cake," and "Snowbound." (*See* individual titles for credits.)

1312 A Special Valentine with the Family Circus NBC
Program Type Animated Film Special
30 minutes. Premiere date: 2/10/78. Bill Keane brings his comic panel, "The Family Circus," to TV for the first time. "If Every Day Were Valentine's Day," by Sammy Fain and E. Y. (Yip) Harburg is sung by Fain.
Producer Edward Cullen
Company Cullen-Kasdan Production
Director Al Kouzel
Writer Joseph C. Cavella

The Spikes Gang *See* The CBS Tuesday Night Movies

1313 The Spirit of '78: The Flight of Double Eagle II ABC
Program Type Sports Special
60 minutes. 8/27/78. On-the-scene story of the

The Spirit of '78: The Flight of Double Eagle II *Continued*
first successful crossing of the Atlantic in a balloon by Ben Abruzzo, Max Anderson and Larry Newman of Albuquerque, New Mexico.
Executive Producer Roone Arledge
Producer John Wilcox
Company ABC Sports
Director John Wilcox

1314   Spiritual Birth   NBC
Program Type Religious/Cultural Special
30 minutes. Premiere date: 6/25/78. Discussion of the experience of being born again with Dr. Donald McKnight, district superintendent of the Evangelical Methodist Church; Dr. Joseph Stowell, national representative of the General Association of Regular Baptist Churches; and the Rev. B. Robert Biscoe, executive secretary of the American Council of Christian Churches.
Producer Doris Ann
Company American Council of Christian Churches in association with NBC Television Religious Programs Unit
Director Robert Priaulx

1315   Spoleto: The Festival of Two Worlds   PBS
Program Type Documentary/Informational Special
30 minutes. Premiere date: 5/22/77. Repeat date: 3/28/78. A look at the Festival of Two Worlds in Spoleto, Italy and in Charleston, South Carolina. Program made possible by a grant from the Corporation for Public Broadcasting.
Producer Sidney Palmer
Company South Carolina Educational Television Network
Director Sidney Palmer
Writer Sidney Palmer

1316   SportsWorld   NBC
Program Type Sports Series
Times vary. Premiere date: 1/22/78. Sunday afternoon series highlighting Olympics-oriented sports, world championship events and a wide variety of other sports.
Executive Producer Don Ohlmeyer
Producer Don Ellis
Company NBC Sports
Cinematographer Bud Greenspan

1317   Springfield International Tennis Classic   PBS
Program Type Sports Special
2 hours 2/11/78 and 2/12/78. Live coverage of the singles semi-finals held at the Civic Center in Springfield, Massachusetts.
Company WGBY-TV/Springfield

1318   Spying for Uncle Sam
NBC News Special   NBC
Program Type News Special
60 minutes. Premiere date: 3/28/78. Special program examining life inside the Central Intelligence Agency as viewed by Caleb and Claudia Bach.
Producer Robert Rogers
Company NBC News
Reporter Edwin Newman

S*P*Y*S *See* The ABC Summer Movie

1319   SST Disaster in the Sky
The ABC Sunday Night Movie   ABC
Program Type TV Movie
2 hours. Premiere date: 2/25/77. Repeat date: 3/26/78. Drama about sabotage aboard the first flight of a U.S. supersonic transport. Based on a story by Guerdon Trueblood. Music by John Cacavas. Filmed in and around Los Angeles and Ventura County, Calif.
Producer Ron Roth
Company ABC Circle Films
Director David Lowell Rich
Writers Robert L. Joseph, Meyer Dolinsky
Art Director Peter Wooley
CAST
Carla Stanley .... Barbara Anderson
Tim Vernon .... Bert Convy
Paul Whitley .... Peter Graves
Marshall Cole .... Lorne Greene
Anne Redding .... Season Hubley
Mae ....Tina Louise
Les Phillips .... George Maharis
Willy Basset .... Burgess Meredith
Hank Fairbanks .... Doug McClure
Lyle Kingman ....Martin Milner
Dr. Ralph Therman .... Brock Peters
Capt. Walsh .... Robert Reed
Nancy Kingman ....Susan Strasberg
Angela Garland .... Misty Rowe
David .... Billy Crystal
Bob Connors .... John de Lancie
Kathy ....Chrystie Jenner

1320   The Stages of Preston Jones   PBS
Program Type Documentary/Informational Special
30 minutes. Premiere date: 6/28/77. Repeat date: 10/25/77. A look at the career of playwright Preston Jones. Filmed in New York, Dallas and West Texas. Program made possible by grants from the Texas Commission for the Arts and Humanities, the National Endowment for

the Arts and the Corporation for Public Broadcasting.
Executive Producer Bill Porterfield
Producers Patsy Swank, Kenneth Harrison
Company KERA-TV/Dallas-Fort Worth
Director Kenneth Harrison
Cinematographer Kenneth Harrison
Film Editor Kenneth Harrison

1321 Standing Tall
NBC Saturday Night at the Movies/NBC
World Premiere Movie   NBC
Program Type TV Movie Series
2 hours. Premiere date: 1/21/78. Small-time cattle rancher is harassed when he refuses to merge his property with that of another rancher.
Company Quinn Martin Production in association with NBC-TV
Director Harvey Hurt
Writer Franklin Thompson
CAST
Luke Shasta .... Robert Forster
Jill Shasta .... Linda Evans
Lonny Moon .... Will Sampson
Major Hartline ....Chuck Connors
Nate Rackley .... L. Q. Jones
George Fewster .... Buck Taylor
Anne Klinger .... Faith Quabius
Sheriff Brumfield .... Robert Donner
Ginny Tarver .... Dani Janssen

1322 Star of India: Iron Lady of the Seas   PBS
Program Type Documentary/Informational Special
30 minutes. Premiere date: 7/3/78. Documentary which chronicles the 114-year history of the oldest iron-hulled merchant ship afloat. Program made possible in part by a grant from Jane and Norman Neely.
Producer Wayne Smith
Company KPBS-TV/San Diego
Director Wayne Smith
Narrator Aaron Fletcher

1323 Star Soccer   PBS
Program Type Limited Sports Series
60 minutes. Weekly. Season premiere: 11/76. Second season premiere: 10/1/77. 28-week series of soccer matches from the top two divisions of the English Football League. 90-minute games are taped, edited and aired one week later on U.S. television.
Company Incorporated Television Company, Ltd. (I.T.C.)
Distributor Eastern Educational Network through KCET-TV/Los Angeles
Host/Announcer Mario Machado

1324 The Stars Salute Israel at 30 ABC
Program Type Music/Comedy/Variety Special
2 hours. Premiere date: 5/8/78. Entertainment gala celebrating the 30th anniversary of the State of Israel. Taped at the Dorothy Chandler Pavilion, Los Angeles Music Center.
Executive Producers James Lipton, Charles Fishman
Producer Marty Pasetta
Company James Lipton Productions
Director Marty Pasetta
Stars Anne Bancroft, Daniel Barenboim, Mikhail Baryshnikov, Debby Boone, Pat Boone, Sammy Davis, Jr., Kirk Douglas, Henry Fonda, Hermione Gingold, Barbara Heuman, Kate Jackson, Gape Kaplan, Gene Kelly, Larry Kert, Alan King, Billie Jean King, Gelsey Kirkland, Los Angeles Philharmonic Orchestra, Barry Manilow, Dean Martin, Millicent Martin, Zubin Mehta, Paul Newman, Valery and Galina Panov, Bernadette Peters, Jean Stapleton, Barbra Streisand, Sally Struthers, Cicely Tyson, Ben Vereen, John Williams, Flip Wilson, Henry Winkler, Joanne Woodward

Starship Invasions *See* NBC Movie of the Week

1325 Starsky and Hutch   ABC
Program Type Crime Drama Series
60 minutes. Saturdays. Wednesdays as of 1/25/78. Premiere date: 9/10/75. Third season premiere: 9/17/77 (2 hour special). Police drama about two plainclothes detectives. Series created by William Blinn. 90-minute pilot originally telecast 4/30/75. Music by Mark Snow. Theme by Tony Scott.
Executive Producers Aaron Spelling, Leonard Goldberg
Producer Joseph T. Naar
Company Spelling/Goldberg Productions
Directors Various
Writers Various
CAST
Ken "Hutch" Hutchinson .... David Soul
Dave Starsky ....Paul Michael Glaser
Capt. Harold Dobey .... Bernie Hamilton
Huggy Bear ....Antonio Fargas

1326 Starsky and Hutch (Late Night)   ABC
Program Type Crime Drama Series
60 minutes. Wednesdays. Premiere date: 9/21/77. Late-night repeat presentations of the primetime series. (For credit information, *see* "Starsky and Hutch.")

1327 State of the Nation—Republican View   CBS
Program Type News Special
60 minutes. Republican view of the State of the Union 1/27/78.
Company CBS News

1328 State of the Union Address (ABC)
ABC
Program Type News Special
60 minutes. Live coverage of the State of the Union Address to Congress by President Jimmy Carter 1/19/78.
Company ABC News Special Events Unit

1329 State of the Union Address (CBS)
CBS
Program Type News Special
Live coverage of President Carter's State of the Union Address before a joint session of Congress 1/19/78.
Producer Sanford Socolow
Company CBS News

1330 State of the Union Address (NBC)
NBC News Special   NBC
Program Type News Special
Live coverage of President Carter's State of the Union Address to a joint session of Congress in the House of Representatives Chamber.
Company NBC News

1331 The State of the Union: Alternate Views   ABC
Program Type News Special
30 minutes. 1/26/78: Senator Howard Baker, minority leader of the Senate, Representative John Rhodes, minority leader of the House of Representatives, and Bill Brock, chairman of the Republican National Committee respond to President Carter's State of the Union Address. Correspondent Frank Reynolds moderates.
Company ABC News

The Stepford Wives *See* The ABC Sunday Night Movie

1332 Steve & Eydie Celebrate Irving Berlin   NBC
Program Type Music/Dance Special
90 minutes. Premiere date: 8/22/78.
Executive Producers Steve Lawrence, Gary Smith
Producers Gary Smith; Dwight Hemion
Company Stage 2 Production in association with Smith-Hemion Productions

Director Dwight Hemion
Writer Harry Crane
Stars Steve Lawrence; Eydie Gorme
Guests Leslie Brown, Carol Burnett, Sammy Davis, Jr., Oscar Peterson

1333 Stickin' Together
The ABC Friday Night Movie   ABC
Program Type TV Movie
90 minutes. Premiere date: 4/14/78. Comedy-drama about five orphaned children living in Hawaii. Music by John Rubinstein. Filmed in Oahu, Hawaii.
Producers Jerry Thorpe, William Blinn
Company Blinn/Thorpe Productions in association with Viacom Enterprises
Director Jerry Thorpe
Writer William Blinn
Art Director Gibson Holley
Film Editor Byron Chudnow
CAST
Grace Geary .... Talia Balsam
Officer Stanbery .... Santos Morales
Lead Actor .... Richard Venture
Miss Farrell .... Deborah White
Miss Steigler .... Gwen Arner

1334 The Storyteller
NBC World Premiere Movie/NBC Monday Night at the Movies   NBC
Program Type Dramatic Special
2 hours. Premiere date: 12/5/77. Drama about television violence and its effects on children.
Producers Richard Levinson, William Link
Company Fairmount/Foxcroft Production in association with Universal Studios and NBC-TV
Director Bob Markowitz
Writers Richard Levinson, William Link
CAST
Ira Davidson .... Martin Balsam
Marion .... Doris Roberts
Sue .... Patty Duke Astin
Mrs. Eberhardt .... Rose Gregorio
Huston .... James Daly
Donaldson .... David Spielberg
Eberhardt .... Tom Aldredge
Lee Gardner .... Peter Masterson
Reporter .... James Staley
Curry .... Milt Kogan
Chrissie .... Shelby Balik
Whitman .... Ivan Bonar

1335 A Storyteller's Town
Americana   PBS
Program Type Documentary/Informational Special
30 minutes. Premiere date: 3/18/77. Repeat date: 10/4/77. A look at Clyde, Ohio, Sherwood Anderson's boyhood home and the setting for "Winesburg, Ohio." Program made possible by

grants from the Ohio College Bicentennial Program and the George Gund Foundation.
Producer Patrick Fitzgerald
Company WBGU-TV/Bowling Green, Ohio
Director Patrick Fitzgerald
Writer Gene Dent
Narrator Leonard Slominski
CAST
Sherwood Anderson .... Eric Vaughn

1336 The Strange Case of the End of Civilisation as We Know It
Festival '78   PBS
Program Type Comedy Special
60 minutes. Premiere date: 3/18/78. Spoof of adventure-mystery films.
Executive Producer Kenneth Harper
Producer Humphrey Barclay
Company Shearwater Films Production in association with London Weekend TV
Director Joseph McGrath
CAST
Arthur Sherlock Holmes .... John Cleese
Dr. Gropinger .... Arthur Lowe
Additional Cast Joss Ackland, Denholm Elliott, Stratford Johns, Connie Booth

1337 Strange Creatures of the Night
National Geographic Special   PBS
Program Type Documentary/Informational Special
60 minutes. Premiere date: 6/27/78. Explores the behavior and environments of mysterious, nocturnal creatures. Program presented by WQED, Pittsburgh and made possible by a grant from Gulf Oil Corporation.
Company National Geographic Society and Wolper Productions
Narrator Leslie Nielsen

1338 Studio See
                                      PBS
Program Type Children's Series
30 minutes. Sundays. Premiere date: 1/25/77. Series repeated: 12/18/77. 26-week magazine-format series for youngsters 10–15 years old created by Jayne Adair and produced at locations throughout the country. Three–four features weekly plus regular "poetry power" and animation segments contributed by children. Series made possible by grants from the Corporation for Public Broadcasting, the Ford Foundation and Public Television Stations.
Executive Producer Gene Upright
Producer Jayne Adair
Company South Carolina Educational Television Network
Supervision Director Hugh Martin

Submarine X-1 *See* The CBS Tuesday Night Movies

1339 Sugar Bowl   ABC
Program Type Sports Special
Live coverage of the Sugar Bowl football game between the Ohio State Buckeyes and the Alabama Crimson Tide from the Superdome in New Orleans, LA 1/2/78.
Executive Producer Roone Arledge
Producer Chuck Howard
Company ABC Sports
Director Andy Sidaris
Play-by-Play Announcer Keith Jackson
Expert Color Commentator Ara Parseghian

1340 Sugar Time!
Program Type Comedy Series   ABC
30 minutes. Mondays. Premiere date: 8/13/77. Second season premiere: 4/10/78. Comedy series about three aspiring rock singers in a group called "Sugar" who work at the Tryout Room. Series created by James Komack and developed for television by Hank Bradford.
Executive Producer James Komack
Producers Hank Bradford, Martin Cohan
Company James Komack Company, Inc.
Directors Bill Hobin, Stan Cutler
Story Editors Iris Rainer, Dawn Aldredge
Writers Various
CAST
Maxx ....Barbi Benton
Diane .... Didi Carr
Maggie .... Marianne Black
Al Marks .... Wynn Irwin
Paul Landson .... Mark Winkworth
Lightning Jack Rappaport .... Charles Fleischer

1341 Summer Semester   CBS
Program Type Educational/Cultural Series
30 minutes/three times a week. 15th season premiere: 5/15/78. Two courses 17 weeks in length three times a week. "Alternative Futures," shown Mondays/Wednesdays/Fridays. Produced under the auspices of St. John's University, New York City with Winston L. Kirby, coordinator. "Paradox of Power: U.S. Foreign Policy," shown Tuesdays/Thursdays/Saturdays. Produced under the auspices of Bergen Community College, Paramus, NJ. with Dr. Philip C. Dolce as coordinator.
Producer Roy Allen
Company WCBS-TV/New York
Director Roy Allen

1342 Sun Bowl   CBS
Program Type Sports Special
3 hours. Live coverage of the 43rd Sun Bowl football game between the Louisiana State Uni-

Sun Bowl *Continued*
versity Tigers and the Stanford University Cardinals from El Paso, Tex. 12/31/77
Producer Tom O'Neill
Company CBS Television Network Sports
Director Tony Verna
Announcer Pat Summerall
Analyst Tom Brookshier
Special Guest Burt Reynolds

CAST

Sam Hayden	Cliff DeYoung
Cody	Barbara Hershey
Joe	Pat Hingle
Bertha	Eileen Heckart
Jill	Elizabeth Cheshire
Nora	Meg Foster
Weaver	Bill Mumy
Givits	Corey Fischer

1343   Sunlight and Shadow—The Golden Age of Spanish Jewry
Eternal Light   NBC
Program Type Religious/Cultural Special
60 minutes. Premiere date: 4/2/78. Documentary/essay filmed in southern Spain. Music composed by John Duffy. Krents was producer for the Seminary.
Executive Producer Doris Ann
Producers Martin Hoade, Milton E. Krents
Company NBC Television Religious Programs Unit in association with the Jewish Theological Seminary of America
Director Martin Hoade
Writer Marc Siegel
Host Dr. Gerson D. Cohen

1344   Sunrise Semester   CBS
Program Type Educational/Cultural Series
30 minutes each day. Monday–Saturday mornings. Premiered locally (WCBS-TV/New York): 9/23/57. Network premiere: 9/22/63. Fall season premiere: 9/19/77. Two courses given each semester by professors at New York University. "Discipline in the classroom: Social and Emotional Problems" presented by Dr. Lawrence Balter shown Mondays/Wednesdays/Fridays. "Man's Place in Nature" presented by Prof. John Buettner-Janusch Tuesdays/Thursdays/Saturdays. Spring premiere: 1/23/78. "Teaching Critical Thinking to Children and Adolescents" presented by Dr. Bernice E. Cullinan Mondays/-Wednesdays/Fridays. "Physics and Society" presented by Prof. Benjamin Bederson Tuesdays/Thursdays/Saturdays.
Producer Roy Allen
Company WCBS-TV/New York
Director Roy Allen
Supervisors for New York University Myron Price; Hope Chasin

1345   Sunshine Christmas
NBC Monday Night at the Movies   NBC
Program Type Dramatic Special
2 hours. Premiere date: 12/12/77. Original cast of series, "Sunshine," star in a holiday love story.
Director Glenn Jordan
Writer Carol Sobieski

1346   Super Bowl XII   CBS
Program Type Sports Special
Live coverage of the 12th Super Bowl football game between the Denver Broncos and the Dallas Cowboys form the Louisiana Superdome, New Orleans, LA, 1/15/78.
Producer Bob Stenner
Company CBS Sports
Director Tony Verna
Announcer Pat Summerall
Analyst Tom Brookshier

1347   The Super Bowl Today   CBS
Program Type Sports Special
90 minutes. Live Pre-game look at various locations in New Orleans plus highlights of past Super Bowl games.
Producer Mike Pearl
Company CBS Sports
Director Bob Fishman
Commentators Brent Musburger, Phyllis George, Irv Cross, Jack Whitaker, Jimmy "The Greek" Snyder

1348   Super Friday   CBS
Program Type Children's Special
90 minutes. Premiere date: 11/25/77. Special Thanksgiving presentation of three popular children's series regularly seen in the Saturday morning line-up: "Fat Albert and the Cosby Kids," "Tarzan: Lord of the Jungle," and "Space Academy." (*See* individual titles for credits.)

1349   Super Night at the Super Bowl
                                                      CBS
Program Type Music/Comedy/Variety Special
90 minutes. Premiere date: 1/14/78. Third annual gala all-star special saluting football, Super Bowl XII and New Orleans. Special music material by Billy Barnes.
Executive Producer Pierre Cossette
Producer Marty Pasetta
Company Pierre Cossette Production
Director Marty Pasetta
Writers Buz Kohan, Bob Arnott, Pat McCormack
Musical Director Jack Elliott
Choreographer Walter Painter
Costume Designer Bill Hargate

Hosts Joe Namath, Andy Williams, Paul Williams
Guest Stars Jim Bailey, Bon Amis, Foster Brooks, Billy Carter, Natalie Cole, Norm Crosby, Irv Cross, Peter Falk, Pete Fountain, Phyllis George, Happy Whistlers, Doug Kershaw, Vicki Lawrence, Henry Mancini, Mills Brothers, Money Changers, Brent Musburger, Minnie Pearl, Scotts's football playing Boxer dog act, Southern University marching band, Jerry Stiller, Anne Meara, Mel Tillis, Uncle Heavy's Pork Chop Revue, Wild Magnolias

1350 Superdome ABC
Program Type Dramatic Special
2 hours. Premiere date: 1/9/78. Suspense thriller filmed in New Orleans including the famed Louisiana Superdome. Music by John Cacavas. Story by Barry Oringer and Bill Svanoe.
Producer William Frye
Company ABC Circle Films
Director Jerry Jameson
Art Director Bill Kenney

CAST

Mike Shelley	David Janssen
Lainie	Donna Mills
Joyce	Edie Adams
P. K. Jackson	Clifton Davis
Doug Collins	Peter Haskell
Dave Walecki	Ken Howard
Nancy Walecki	Susan Howard
Chip Green	Van Johnson
Sonny	Vonetta McGee
George Beldridge	Ed Nelson
McCauley	Tom Selleck
Faye Bonelli	Jane Wyatt
Brooks	Shelly Novak
Gail	Robin Mattson
Mooney	Marvin Fleming
Caretta	Les Josephson
Moses	Bubba Smith
Tony	Michael Pataki
Whitley	M. Emmet Walsh
Hennerson	Dick Butkus
Announcer	Charlie Jones

1351 The Superstars ABC
Program Type Limited Sports Series
90 minutes. Sundays. Series premiered in 1973 (with men only). Fifth season premiere: 1/8/78. Eleven programs pitting championship athletes against each other in competitions outside their specialties. "The Superstars" (male athletes—five programs): 1/8/78–1/29/78 plus two-part final 2/5/78 and 2/12/78. "The Women Superstars" (fourth season—one program): 2/19/78; "The Superteams" (fourth season—three programs): 2/26/78–3/12/78; "The World Superstars" (Second season—one program): 3/26/78.
Executive Producer Roone Arledge
Producers Chet Forte, Bob Goodrich
Company ABC Sports

Directors Larry Kamm, Roger Goodman
Host Keith Jackson, Andrea Kirby, Cathy Rigby Mason, Bruce Jenner
Expert Commentators Reggie Jackson, Bruce Jenner, Bill Russell

1352 Superstunt
The Big Event NBC
Program Type Documentary/Informational Special
2 hours. Premiere date: 11/17/77. Displays of Hollywood stunts.
Producers Bill Davis, Al Rogers
Company Bill Davis Productions, Inc. in association with Hollywood's "Stuntmen's Association" and NBC-TV
Director Bill Davis
Host Lee Marvin
Guest Stars Ernest Borgnine, James Caan, James Coburn, Robert Conrad, Angie Dickinson, Jane Fonda, James Garner, Buddy Hackett, Lee Majors, Burt Reynolds, Robert Wagner

Superwitch *See* The New Archies

Support Your Local Gunfighter *See* The CBS Tuesday Night Movies

1353 Sweathog Back-to-School Special
ABC
Program Type Comedy Special
30 minutes. Premiere date: 9/10/77. Repeat date: 8/24/78. The Sweathogs help Mr. Kotter recall (through flashbacks) those special moments of "fun" they've shared together.
Company Komack Company, Inc.

CAST

Gabe Kotter	Gabriel Kaplan
Julie Kotter	Marcia Strassman
Mr. Woodman	John Sylvester White
Juan Epstein	Robert Hegyes
Freddy Washington	Lawrence-Hilton Jacobs
Arnold Horshack	Ron Palillo
Vinnie Barbarino	John Travolta

1354 Sweden's Royal Command Circus
ABC
Program Type Music/Comedy/Variety Special
60 minutes. Premiere date: 5/21/78. Circus acts from all over the world gather in Copenhagen to perform live before an audience which includes King Karl Gustaf and Queen Silvia of Sweden.
Executive Producers Joseph Cates, Gilbert Cates
Producers Joseph Cates, Elizabeth Wennberg
Company Swedish Broadcasting Corporation and The Cates Brothers Company
Director Joseph Cates
Writer Frank Slocum
Host Hal Linden

1355 **Switch**   CBS
Program Type Crime Drama Series
60 minutes. Fridays/Mondays (as of 12/5/77).
Premiere date: 9/9/75. Third season premiere:
9/23/77. Ran until 1/16/78. Resumed as sum-
mer series Sunday, 6/25/78. Last show: 9/3/78.
Crime drama about a retired cop and an ex-con
man in private eye partnership. Created by Glen
A. Larson.
Executive Producer Jon Epstein
Producer Leigh Vance
Company Universal Television in association
  with Glen Larson Productions
Directors Various
Executive Story Consultant Larry Forrester
Writers Various
CAST
Pete Ryan .... Robert Wagner
Frank "Mac" MacBride .... Eddie Albert
Malcolm .... Charlie Callas
Maggie .... Sharon Gless
Revel .... Mindi Miller
Wang .... James Hong

1356 **Sybil**
The Big Event/NBC Monday Night at the
Movies   NBC
Program Type Dramatic Special
4 hours. Premiere dates: 11/14/76 and 11/15/76
(two hours each night). Repeat date: 3/6/78 and
3/7/78. Drama of a real woman with 16 person-
alities. Based on the book by Flora Rheta Schrei-
ber about the experiences of Dr. Cornelia B. Wil-
bur. Music by Leonard Rosenman; Lyrics by
Alan Bergman and Marilyn Bergman.
Executive Producer Peter Dunne, Philip Capice
Producer Jacqueline Babbin
Company Lorimar Productions, Inc. In associa-
  tion with NBC-TV
Director Daniel Petrie
Writer Stewart Stern
CAST
Dr. Cornelia B. Wilbur .... Joanne Woodward
Sybil .... Sally Field
Richard .... Brad Davis
Hattie .... Martine Bartlett
Frieda Dorsett .... Jane Hoffman
Dr. Quinoness .... Charles Lane
Grandma Dorsett .... Jessamine Milner
Willard Dorsett .... William Prince

1357 **Symbiosis**   PBS
Program Type Music/Dance Special
30 minutes. Premiere date: 1/17/78. Award-win-
ning ballet creates fantasy of man and computer.
Performed by San Diego Ballet Company.
Company KPBS-TV-TV/San Diego
Executive Producer Sarah Luft
Cinematographer Tom Karlo
Producer David Craven
Director David Craven
Choreographer Thor Sutowski

1358 **Szysznyk**   CBS
Program Type Comedy Series
30 minutes. Wednesdays. Premiere date: 8/1/77.
Season premiere: 12/7/78. Last show: 1/25/78.
Originally shown as summer series. Ex-Marine
sergeant is the playground supervisor at the
Northeast Community Center in Washington,
D.C. Created by Jim Mulligan and Ron Landry.
Music by Doug Gilmore.
Executive Producer Jerry Weintraub
Producers Rich Eustis, Michael Elias
Company Four's Company Productions
Directors Various
Writers Various
Costume Designer Bill Belew
Art Director Ken Johnson
CAST
Nick Szysznyk .... Ned Beatty
Ms. Harrison .... Olivia Cole
Leonard Kriegler .... Leonard Barr
Ralph .... Jarrod Johnson
Fortwengler .... Barry Miller
Tony La Placa .... Scott Colomby
Ray Gun .... Thomas Carter

T. R. Baskin *See* The CBS Wednesday
  Night Movies

1359 **Tabitha**   ABC
Program Type Comedy Series
30 minutes Saturdays/Fridays. Premiere date:
9/10/77. Last show: 8/27/78. Comedy about the
grown-up daughter of Samantha, the witch of
"Bewitched." Special effects by Robert Peterson.
Executive Producer Jerry Mayer
Producer Robert Stambler
Company Columbia Pictures Television
CAST
Tabitha .... Lisa Hartman
Paul .... Robert Urich
Marvin .... Mel Stewart
Adam .... David Ankrum
Aunt Minerva .... Karen Morrow

1360 **The Taiwan Dilemma**
CBS Reports   CBS
Program Type Documentary/Informational
  Special
Premiere date: 6/20/78. The situation in Taiwan
as the U.S. approaches full diplomatic relations
with the Peking government.
Executive Producer Howard Stringer
Producer Paul Greenberg
Company CBS News
Writer Paul Greenberg
Cinematographer Skip Brown
Researcher Susan D. Werbe

The Take *See* The ABC Sunday Night
  Movie

Take the Money and Run *See* The ABC Friday Night Movie

1361 The Tapestry

Visions   PBS
Program Type Dramatic Special
60 minutes. Premiere date: 12/30/76. Repeat date: 11/17/77 (Edited version. Shown originally with "The Circles.") A play about ambitious black women and the pressures to make them conform. Program made possible by grants from the Ford Foundation, the National Endowment for the Arts and the Corporation for Public Broadcasting.
Producer Barbara Schultz
Company KCET-TV/Los Angeles
Director Maya Angelou
Writer Alexis DeVeaux
Production Designer Ralph Holmes
CAST
Jet .... Gloria Jones Schultz
Axis .... Glynn Turman
Lavender .... Ebony Wright
Rev. Paradise .... Alvin Childress
Momma .... Ruth Beckford-Smith
Daddie/Man in Legal Office .... Raymond Allen
Sister Lott/Woman in Legal Office .... Lareyn Carole
Prof. Wane/Other Man .... Rai Tasco
Woman .... Tamu

1362 Tarantulas: The Deadly Cargo

The CBS Wednesday Night Movies   CBS
Program Type TV Movie
2 hours. Premiere date: 12/28/77. Drama about tarantulas loose in a Southwestern town. Spider wrangler is Warren Estes.
Executive Producer Alan Landsburg
Producer Paul Freeman
Company Alan Landsburg Productions
Director Stuart Hagmann
Writers Guerdon Trueblood, John Groves
Choreographer Robert Morrison
CAST
Bert Springer .... Claude Akins
Joe Harmon .... Charles Frank
Cindy Beck .... Deborah Winters
Chief Beasley .... Sandy McPeak
Mayor Douglas .... Bert Remsen
Doc Hodgins .... Pat Hingle
Buddy .... Tom Atkins
Fred .... Howard Hesseman
Rich Finley .... Charles Siebert
Sylvan .... John Harkins
Honey Lamb .... Noelle North
Gloria Beasley .... Penelope Windust
Frank .... Edwin Owens
Harry Weed .... Lanny Horn
H. L. Williams .... Jerome Guardino

1363 Tartuffe

Great Performances/Theatre in America   PBS
Program Type Dramatic Special
2 hours. Premiere date: 5/31/78. Play by Moliere about a 17th century con artist performed by New York's Circle in the Square Theater. Program made possible by a grant from Exxon Corporation with support from PBS stations.
Executive Producer Jac Venza
Producer Ann Blumenthal
Company WNET-TV/New York
Directors Stephen Porter, Kirk Browning
CAST
Tartuffe .... Donald Moffat
Orgon .... Stefan Gierach
Madame Pernelle ....Geraldine Fitzgerald
Elmire ....Tammy Grimes
Mariane ....Johanna Lesiter
Valere .... Victor Garber
Dorine .... Patricia Elliott
Damis ....Ray Wise
Cleante .... Peter Coffield

1364 Tattletales

                                                    CBS
Program Type Game/Audience Participation Special
30 minutes. Mondays–Fridays. Premiere date: 2/18/74. Continuous. Last show: 3/31/78. Three guest celebrity couples each week winning cash prizes divided among the studio audience.
Executive Producer Ira Skutch
Producer Paul Alter
Company Goodson-Todman Productions
Director Paul Alter
Host Bert Convy
Announcer Gene Wood

1365 Taxi

Hallmark Hall of Fame   NBC
Program Type Dramatic Special
60 minutes. Premiere date: 2/2/78. Original drama about a cab driver and his passenger.
Executive Producer Stan Parlan
Producer Joseph Hardy
Company Glen-Warren Production
Director Joseph Hardy
Writer Lanford Wilson
CAST
Passenger .... Eva Marie Saint
Taxi driver .... Martin Sheen

1366 The Ted Knight Show

                                                    CBS
Program Type Comedy Series
30 minutes. Saturdays. Premiere date: 4/8/78. Special broadcast: 10/26/77. Ted Knight stars as owner of New York City escort agency. Last show: 5/13/78. Created by Mark Rothman and Lowell Ganz.
Executive Producers Mark Rothman; Lowell Ganz; Ned Shankman
Producers Martin Cohan, David W. Duclon

The Ted Knight Show Continued
Directors Various
Writers Various
CAST
Roger Dennis .... Ted Knight
Burt Dennis .... Normann Burton
Winston Dennis ....Thomas Leopold
Dottie .... Iris Adrian
Graziella .... Cissy Colpitts
Honey .... Fawne Harriman
Irma .... Ellen Regan
Philadelphia .... Tanya Boyd
Cheryl ....Janice Kent
Joy .... Deborah Harmon
Hobart Nalvin .... Claude Stroud

1367   Telethon
The ABC Friday/Sunday Night Movie   ABC
Program Type TV Movie
2 hours. Premiere date: 11/6/77. Repeat date: 7/21/78. Drama set behind the scenes of a national fund-raising telethon in Las Vegas.
Producer Robert Lovenheim
Company ABC Circle Films
Director David Lowell Rich
Writer William Roberts
CAST
Mrs. Goodwin .... Polly Bergen
Matt Tallman .... Lloyd Bridges
Marty Rand .... Red Buttons
Charlie .... Edd "Kookie" Byrnes
Irv Berman .... Dick Clark
Elaine .... Janet Leigh
Arnold Shagan .... John Marley
Tom Galvin .... Kent McCord
Kim .... Eve Plumb
Roy Hansen ....David Selby
Fran ....Jill St. John
June .... Randi Oakes
Lorna .... Sheila Sullivan
Dave Burton .... Dave Burton
Jimmie Walker .... Jimmie Walker
Sugar Ray Robinson .... Sugar Ray Robinson
Poster Girl .... Dawn Rowan

1368   Tell Me My Name
GE Theater   CBS
90 minutes. Premiere date: 12/20/77. Story of a mother who is confronted by her illegitimate 19-year-old daughter. Based on the book by Mary Carter. Music composed and conducted by Hagood Hardy and Mickey Erbe.
Executive Producers David Susskind, Frederick Brogger
Producer Donald W. Reid
Company A Talent Associates Production
Director Delbert Mann
Writer Joanna Lee
Art Director Karen Bromley
CAST
Porter McPhail .... Arthur Hill
Emily McPhail .... Barbara Barrie
Uncle Tyler .... Barnard Hughes
Alexandra/Sarah .... Valerie Mahaffey

P.J. .... Glenn Zachar
Timmy .... Doug McKeon
Lucy ....Deborah Turnbull
Thurmond .... Murray Westgate
Catherine .... Dawn Greenhalgh

1369   The Tender Grass
Eternal Light   NBC
Program Type Religious/Cultural Special
30 minutes. Premiere date: 3/30/69. Repeat date: 4/16/78. Dramatic fable written by the late Morton Wishengrad about a man whose seven sons were born speechless.
Executive Producer Doris Ann
Producers Martin Hoade, Milton E. Krents
Company NBC Television Religious Programs Unit of NBC News with the Jewish Theological Seminary of America.
Director Martin Hoade
Narrator Marian Seldes
CAST
Shulamith .... Marian Seldes
Shalom .... Boris Tumarin
Additional Cast Jody Rocco, Norman Atkins, Nancy Franklin, Joseph Julian

Tennis See 1977 Transamerica Open Tennis Championships

1370   Terraces
NBC Movie of the Week/NBC World Premiere Movie   NBC
Program Type Dramatic Special
90 minutes. Premiere date: 6/27/77. Repeat date: 12/27/77. Drama surrounding residents who share adjoining terraces in a high-rise apartment building.
Executive Producer Charles Fries
Company Charles Fries Productions in association with NBC-TV
Director Lila Garrett
Writers Lila Garrett, George Kirgo
CAST
Dr. Roger Cabe .... Lloyd Bochner
Chalan Turner .... Julie Newmar
Gregg Loomis .... Bill Gerber
Julie Borden .... Kit McDonough
Beth Loomis ....Eliza Garrett
Alex Bengston .... James Phipps
Roberta Robbins .... Jane Dulo
Martin Robbins .... Arny Freeman
Dorothea Cabe .... Lola Albright
Steve ....Timothy Thomerson

Terror in the Wax Museum See The ABC Friday Night Movie

1371 Terrorism—The World at Bay PBS
Program Type Documentary/Informational
Special
2 hours. Premiere date: 3/21/78. Live, international satellite broadcast on terrorism.
Executive Producer Jim Karayn
Producer Don Fouser
Company WHYY-TV/Philadelphia
Director Alvin R. Mifelow
Host James Hoge
Interviewer Marciarose Shestack

**1372 Bob Hope—On the Road with
Bing** NBC
Program Type Music/Comedy/Variety Special
2 hours. Premiere date: 10/28/77. Tribute to
Bing Crosby.
Producer Howard W. Koch
Company Hope Enterprises
Director Howard W. Koch

**1373 Texaco Presents The Bob Hope
All-Star Comedy Special from Australia**
NBC
Program Type Music/Comedy/Variety Special
90 minutes. Premiere date: 4/15/78. First special
to originate from abroad since his 1972 tour of
South Vietnam.
Executive Producer Bob Hope
Producer Chris Bearde
Company Hope Enterprises
Director Dick McDonough
Writers Charles Lee, Gig Henry, David Letterman, Robert L. Mills, Chris Bearde
Consultant Norman Sullivan
Host Bob Hope
Guests Barbara Eden, Florence Henderson,
Charo, Kamahl

**1374 Texaco Presents the Bob Hope
All-Star Comedy Tribute to The Palace
Theatre** NBC
Program Type Music/Comedy/Variety Special
90 minutes. Premiere date: 1/8/78. Bob Hope
salutes vaudeville.
Executive Producer Bob Hope
Producer Sheldon Keller
Company Hope Enterprises
Director Dick McDonough
Writers Charles Lee, Gig Henry, Howard Albrecht, Sol Weinstein, Robert L. Mills, Sheldon Keller
Host Bob Hope
Guests George Burns, Sammy Davis, Jr., Eydie
Gorme, Carol Lawrence, Steve Lawrence,
Donny Osmond, Marie Osmond

**1375 Texaco Presents the Bob Hope
Christmas Special** NBC
Program Type Music/Comedy/Variety Special
60 minutes. Premiere date: 12/19/77.
Executive Producer Bob Hope
Producer Sheldon Keller
Company Hope Enterprises
Director Dick McDonough
Writers Charles Lee, Gig Henry, Howard Albrecht, Sol Weinstein, Robert L. Mills, Sheldon Keller
Host Bob Hope
Guests Mark Hamill, Perry Como, Olivia Newton-John, The Muppets, Associated Press All-American Football Team

**1376 Texaco Presents The Bob Hope
Comedy Special from Palm Springs** NBC
Program Type Music/Comedy/Variety Special
60 minutes. Premiere date: 2/13/78. Taped at
Riviera Hotel, Palm Springs, for the benefit of
the Eisenhower Medical Center.
Producer Bob Hope
Company Hope Enterprises
Director Dick McDonough
Host Bob Hope
Guests Phyllis Diller, Telly Savalas, Raquel
Welch, Andy Williams

1377 Thaddeus Rose and Eddie
The CBS Friday Night Movies   CBS
Program Type TV Movie
2 hours. Premiere date: 2/24/78. Drama of two
men in a Texas town. Filmed in Texas. Music by
Charles Bernstein.
Producers Dan Paulson; Rod Sheldon
Company CBS Television Network
Director Jack Starrett
Writer William D. Wittliff
CAST
Thaddeus Rose .... Johnny Cash
Crystal .... June Carter Cash
Eddie .... Bo Hopkins
Carlotta .... Diane Ladd
Alvin Karl .... James Hampton
Judge .... Nobel Willingham
Singer .... Clay Tanner
Vioreen .... Annabelle Weenick
Pablo .... Jesus Rosales Morales
Irene .... Sarah Norvell
Waiter .... Steve Schneider
First boy .... John Starrett Berry
Second boy .... Greg Gault
Third boy .... John O'Connor White

**1378 Thanksgiving Reunion with the
Partridge Family and My Three Sons**
ABC
Program Type Music/Comedy/Variety Special
60 minutes. Premiere date: 11/25/77. Two tele-

Thanksgiving Reunion with the Partridge Family and My Three Sons *Continued*
vision families reunite for an hour of singing, dancing, comedy and reminiscences with film clips from the shows. Special musical material by Billy Barnes.
Executive Producer Dick Clark
Producer Al Schwartz
Company dick clark teleshows, inc.
Director Perry Rosemond
Writers Bob Sand, Bo Kaprall
Musical Director Lenny Stack
Choreographer Ron Poindexter
Art Director Keaton Walker
Star David Cassidy
Hosts Fred MacMurray, Shirley Jones
Special Guest William Demarest
From "My Three Sons" Beverly Garland, Tim Considine, Stanley Livingston, Barry Livingston, Don Grady, Tina Cole, Meredith MacRae, Ronnie Troupe, and Tramp.
From "The Partridge Family" Danny Bonaduce, Suzanne Crough, Susan Dey.

1379   That Second Thing on ABC   ABC
Program Type Music/Comedy/Variety Special
60 minutes. Premiere date: 3/8/78. Sequel to "That Thing on ABC."
Executive Producers Bernie Kukoff, Jeff Harris
Company Boiney Stoones, Inc.
Director Tony Mordente
Writers Bo Kaprall, Bob Sand, Valri Bromfield, Terry Hart, Jim Brecher, Scot McGibbon
Stars Irv Burton, Judy Carter, Denny Evans, Shelley Long, Andrea Martin, Mandy Patinkin, Kim Thomerson, Paul Tracey, Deborah Zon

1380   That Thing on ABC   ABC
Program Type Music/Comedy/Variety Special
60 minutes. Premiere date: 1/4/78. A comedy variety special featuring a resident company of comedians recruited from all over the United States.
Executive Producers Bernie Kukoff, Jeff Harris
Company Boiney Stoones, Inc.
Director Tim Kiley
Writers Valri Bromfield, Ray Taylor, Allyn Warner, Bernie Kukoff, Jeff Harris
Stars Cheryl Ladd, John Ritter, Bill Bixby, Henny Youngman, John Cameron Swayze
Featuring Judy Carter, Denny Evans, Shelley Long, Andrea Martin, Mandy Patinkin, Will Porter, Paul Tracey, Marsha Warfield

That's Entertainment, Part 2 *See* CBS Special Movie Presentations

1381   That's Hollywood   Syndicated
Program Type Educational/Cultural Series
30 minutes. Premiere date: 9/14/77. Series based on film clips from past movies.
Executive Producer Jack Haley, Jr.
Producer Lawrence Einhorn
Company 20th Century-Fox TV
Writers Eytan Keller, Stu Bernstein
Narrator Tom Bosley

1382   Theater in America
Great Performances   PBS
Program Type Drama Series
Times vary (generally two hours). Wednesdays/Sunday. Premiere date: 1/23/74. Fifth series premiere: 11/23/77. Classic and contemporary plays performed by different American repertory companies. Plays shown during the 1977–78 season are: "All Over," "The Prince of Homburg," "School for Scandal," "Secret Service," "The Time of Your Life," and "Waiting for Godot." (*See* individual titles for credits.)

1383   The 36 Most Beautiful Girls in Texas   ABC
Program Type Music/Comedy/Variety Special
60 minutes. Premiere date: 9/24/78. The Dallas Cowboys Cheerleaders star in their own musical comedy.
Executive Producers Merrill Grant, John Hamlin
Producer Bob Wynn
Company A Grant-Case-McGrath Production in association with Mellodan Productions
Director Bob Wynn
Writer Bob Arnott
Choreographers Tom Hansen, Currie Pederson
Host Hal Linden
Cheerleaders' Director Suzanne Mitchell
Guest Stars Joey Travolta, Charles Nelson Reilly, Billy Crystal, Melinda Naud

1384   This Is My Son   NBC
Program Type Religious/Cultural Special
60 minutes. Premiere date: 6/19/77. Repeat date: 7/16/78. Drama about a family's struggle to adjust to their retarded child.
Producer Doris Ann
Company NBC Television Religious Programs Unit in association with the National Council of Churches
Director Lynwood King
Writer Allan Sloane
Costume Designer George Drew
Production Designer Leon Munier
Consultant Emily Perl Kingsley
CAST
Emily Kingston .... Carolee Campbell
Jay Kingston .... Don Gantry
Joe .... Glenn Zachaı

Jennifer .... Taryn Grimes
Doctor .... Maurice Copeland
Fathers .... Joel Colodner, Michael Sedgwick
Interns .... George Patterson, William Schultz
Nurse .... Elinor Mays

1385   Thomas A. Edison: The Old Man
PBS
Program Type Educational/Cultural Special
30 minutes. Premiere date: 9/5/77. Pictorial
biography of American genius Thomas A. Edison who was called "the old man" by his friends
and co-workers. Program made possible by a
grant from the Bureau of Education for the
Handicapped.
Company WNJT-TV/Trenton

1386   Thomas Hardy's Wessex Tales PBS
Program Type Limited Series
60 minutes. Premiere date: 7/3/78. 6-part short
story series.
Producer Irene Shubik
Company BBC and Time-Life Films

1387   Those Golden Years   PBS
Program Type Documentary/Informational
Special
2 hours. Premiere date: 12/13/77. Documentary
on what it is like to grow old in America as a
member of the working class poor. Filmed in
New York City in 1975 by Swedish filmmakers
Lars Ulvenstam and Tomas Dillen. Program
made possible by a grant from the Corporation
for Public Broadcasting.
Company WNET-TV/New York
Cinematographer Anders Ribbsjoe

1388   Thracian Gold   PBS
Program Type Documentary/Informational
Special
30 minutes. Premiere date: 4/15/78. An opulent
presentation of archeological treasures recently
unearthed in the People's Republic of Bulgaria.
Producer Margaret MacLeod
Company WGBH-TV/Boston with Museum of
Fine Arts, Boston
Narrator Alexander Scourby

1389   Three Artists in the Northwest PBS
Program Type Documentary/Informational
Special
30 minutes. Premiere date: 3/1/77. Season
premiere: 9/28/77. The words and visions of
painter Guy Anderson, sculptor George
Tsutakawa and poet Theodore Roethke featuring
the music of Alan Hovhaness. Roethke poetry
read by Roberta Byrd Barr. Program made possible by grants from the Washington State Arts

Commission, the National Endowment for the
Arts, the Members of Nine and the Corporation
for Public Broadcasting.
Producer Jean Walkinshaw
Company KCTS-TV/Seattle
Cinematographer Wayne Sourbeer

Three Days of the Condor *See* CBS
Special Movie Presentations

Three Men in a Boat *See* PBS Movie
Theater

The Three Musketeers *See* CBS Special
Movie Presentations

1390   Three on a Date
The ABC Friday Night Movie   ABC
Program Type TV Movie
2 hours. Premiere date: 2/17/78. Repeat date:
8/11/78. Comedy-romance depicts the adven-
tures of four couples and their young chaperone
on a Hawaiian holiday. From a book by Stepha-
nie Buffington. Music by George Aliceson Tip-
ton.
Executive Producers Ronald Jacobs, Danny
Thomas
Producer David Shapiro
Company ABC Circle Films
Director Bill Bixby
Writers Michael Norell, Stanley Ralph Ross,
Dale McRaven
CAST
Marge .... June Allyson
Angela .... Loni Anderson
Andrew .... Ray Bolger
Donald .... John Byner
Eve .... Didi Conn
Leonard .... Gary Crosby
Emcee .... Geoff Edwards
Joan .... Carol Lawrence
Valerie ....Meredith MacRae
Bob .... Rick Nelson
Roger .... Patrick Wayne
Stephanie .... Forbesy Russell

1391   Three on Three   CBS
Program Type Sports Series
30 minutes. Premiere date: 4/23/78. CBS Sports'
version of halfcourt basketball which includes a
current NBA star, a past NBA star and a show
business celebrity on each team. Shown seven
consecutive Sundays, last show of season:
6/4/78.
Company CBS Sports
Director Tony Verna
Announcer Gary Bender
Referees Ed Rush, Darell Garretson

1392 Three's Company   ABC
Program Type Comedy Series
30 minutes. Tuesdays. Premiere date: 3/24/77.
Second season premiere: 9/13/77. Comedy
about two women sharing their Santa Monica,
Calif. apartment with a man. Based on the
Thames (England) television program "Man
About the House" created by Johnnie Mortimer;
and Brian Cooke. Developed by Don Nicholl;
Michael Ross and Bernie West. Theme music by
Joe Raposo; lyrics by Don Nicholl; sung by Ray
Charles and Julia Rinker.
Producers Don Nicholl, Michael Ross, Bernie
West
Company The NRW Company in association
with TTC Productions, Inc.
Director Bill Hobin
Executive Story Consultants Paul Wayne,
George Burditt
Writers Various
Animation Director Don Roberts
CAST
Jack Tripper .... John Ritter
Janet Wood .... Joyce DeWitt
Chrissy Snow .... Suzanne Somers
Helen Roper .... Audra Lindley
Stanley Roper .... Norman Fell

1393 Thunder   NBC
Program Type Children's Series
30 minutes. Saturdays. Premiere date: 9/10/77.
Action-adventure about black stallion of mys-
terious origin. Created by Irving Cummings and
Charles Marion. Title changed to "Super Horse
Starring Thunder" 11/12/77 and back to "Thun-
der" 12/10/77.
Producers Irving Cummings; Charles Marion
Company Marcum Productions for NBC-TV
Directors Sig Newfeld, Jr., William Beaudine, Jr.
Writers Various
CAST
Bill .... Klint Ritchie
Ann .... Melissa Converse
Cindy .... Melora Hardin
Willie Wilson .... Justin Randi

Thunderbolt and Lightfoot *See* The ABC
Sunday Night Movie

1394 Time and the Cities   NBC
Program Type Documentary/Informational
Special
60 minutes. Premiere date: 7/14/74. Repeat
date: 8/27/78. In-depth study of why cities and
civilizations rise and fall. Filmed at the sites of
eight ancient cities in Turkey. Photography by
Joseph Vadala.
Producer Doris Ann
Company NBC Television Religious Programs

Unit in association with the Southern Baptist
Radio and Television Commission
Director Joseph Vadala
Writer Philip Scharper

1395 The Time of Your Life
Great Performances   PBS
Program Type Dramatic Special
Two hours. Premiere date: 3/76. Repeat date:
9/6/78. 1939 comedy performed by The Acting
Company of John Houseman. Prologue read by
William Saroyan. Program made possible by
grants from Exxon Corporation, The Ford Foun-
dation, PBS stations, National Endowment for
the Arts and Corporation for Public Broadcast-
ing.
Executive Producer Jac Venza
Producer Lindsay Law
Company WNET-TV/New York
Directors Jack O'Brien, Kirk Browning
Writer William Saroyan
Host Hal Holbrook
CAST
Dudley .... Robert Bacigalupi
Harry .... Brooks Baldwin
Lorene/Sidekick .... Glynis Bell
Killer .... Cynthia Dickason
Society Gentleman .... Peter Dvorsky
Wesley .... Gerald Gutierrez
Elsie .... Sandra Halperin
Blick .... James Harper
Newsboy .... Elaine Hausman
Nick .... Benjamin Hendrickson
McCarthy .... Kevin Kline
Kitty Duval .... Patti LuPone
Sailor .... Anderson Matthews
Society Lady .... Mary-Jane Negro
Arab .... Richard Ooms
Mary L. .... Mary Lou Rosato
Kit Carson .... David Schramm
Tom .... Norman Snow
Krupp .... Roy K. Stevens
Joe .... Nicolas Surovy
Drunkard .... Michael Tolaydo
Willie .... Sam Tsoutsouvas

1396 The Tiny Tree
Bell System Family Theatre   NBC
Program Type Animated Film Special
30 minutes. Premiere date: 12/14/75. Season
premiere: 12/18/77. Created by Chuck Couch.
Theme songs "To Love and Be Loved" and
"When Autumn Comes" by Johnny Marks sung
by Roberta Flack. Characters designed by Louis
Schmitt. Story development by Bob Ogle and
Lewis Marshall.
Executive Producers David H. DePatie, Friz Fre-
leng
Producer Chuck Couch
Company DePatie-Freleng Enterprises, Inc.
Director Chuck Couch
Music Supervisor Dean Elliott

VOICES

Squire Badger ....Buddy Ebsen
Hawk ....Allan Melvin
Turtle ....Paul Winchel
Lady Bird/Little Girl ....Janet Waldo
Boy Bunny/Girl Raccoon .... Stephen Manley
Groundhog/Father Bird/
Beaver/Mole ....Frank Welker

1397 To Kill a Cop

The Big Event/NBC Monday Night at the
Movies/NBC World Premiere Movie   NBC
Program Type Dramatic Special
4 hours. Premiere date: 4/10/78 and 4/11/78.
Drama about two police officers whose relation-
ship extends beyond working hours.
Executive Producer David Gerber
Producer James H. Brown
Company David Gerber Production in associa-
tion with Columbia Pictures Television and
NBC-TV
Director Gary Nelson
Film Editor Harry Kaye, Donald Rode

CAST

Chief Detective Earl Eischied .... Joe Don Baker
Everett Walker .... Lou Gossett
Police Commissioner .... Patrick O'Neal
Delehanty .... Desi Arnaz, Jr.
Agnes .... Christine Belford
Deputy O'Connor .... Alan Fudge
Betty .... Joyce Van Patten
Finnerty .... Alan Oppenheimer
Charles .... Nathan George
Gleason ....Scott Brady
Florence ....Diana Muldaur
Fitzgerald .... Ken Swofford
Paula .... Eartha Kitt
Cornworth .... George DiCenzo
Hoyt .... Rosey Grier
Klopfman .... Milton Selzer
Rolfe .... Robert Hooks

1398 To Say the Least   NBC

Program Type Game/Audience Participation
Series
30 minutes. Mondays–Fridays. Premiere date:
10/3/77. Last show: 4/21/78. Game show fea-
turing celebrities and audience contestants, pits
two teams—men vs women—in contests to re-
duce words to a minimum and try to keep each
other from guessing answers. Music by Stan
Worth. Talent coordinators Liz Fertig and Ida
Mae McKenzie.
Producer Robert Noah
Company Heatter-Quigley Productions
Director Jerome Shaw
Writers Barbara Allyn, Joe Hoffman, Michael
Rudin
Art Director Ed Flesh
Host Tom Kennedy

1399 Today   NBC

Program Type News Magazine Series
2 hours. Monday–Friday mornings. Premiere
date: 1/14/52. Continuous. Live program of
news, weather reports, sports results, interviews,
discussions, reviews and occasional special enter-
tainment. Regular features: "Critic's Corner,"
"Family Doctor," consumer reports, "What's
Hot," "Living," and "Washington on the Spot."
Executive Producer Paul Friedman
Producers Douglas P. Sinsel, Ron Steinman as of
8/15/78. Michael A. Krauss (as of 4/78).
Company NBC News
Directors Marvin D. Einhorn, James W. Gaines
Host Tom Brokaw
Anchor Floyd Kalber
Regulars Gene Shalit, Jane Pauley, Betty Fur-
ness, Dr. Art Ulene, Eric Burns, Jack Perkins,
Bob Abernethy
Weather/Sports Reporter Lew Wood, Bob Ryan
(as of 4/78).

1400 Tom and Joann   CBS

Program Type Comedy Special
60 minutes. Premiere date: 7/5/78. Pilot about
family relationships shaken by an amicable di-
vorce. Music by Hagood Hardy.
Executive Producer David Susskind
Producers Frederick Brogger, Diana Kerew
Company Time-Life Television
Director Delbert Mann
Writer Loring Mandel

CAST

Joann ....Elizabeth Ashley
Tom ....Joel Fabiani
Amy .... Jennifer Cooke
T. C. .... Colin McKenna
Gabe ....David Ackroyd
Lou .... Bibi Besch
Kenny ....Tom Okon
Beth .... Marie McCann
Helene ....Brenda Donohue
Norman ....Louis Del Grande

1401 Tom Wolfe's Los Angeles   PBS

Program Type Comedy Special
60 minutes. Premiere date: 1/10/77. Season
premiere: 9/25/77. Author turns his unique per-
ceptions on Los Angeles and wraps up the inter-
esting lives of seven people. Presented by WETA-
TV/Washington, DC, Corporation for Public
Broadcasting, the Ford Foundation and the Na-
tional Endowment for the Arts.
Producers Eugene A. Aleinikoff, Richard O.
Moore
Company PTV Producion, Inc.
Writer Tom Wolfe
Helicopter pilot Pancho Petty

1402 **Tomorrow**   NBC
Program Type Talk/Service/Variety Series
60 minutes. Tuesday–Friday mornings (1–2
a.m.). Premiere date: 10/15/73. Continuous.
Early-morning talk show with guests covering a
broad range of topics. Show originated in Bur-
bank, Calif., went to New York City 12/2/74
and returned to Burbank 6/6/77.
Producers Pamela Burke, Bruce McKay
Company NBC Television Network Production
Director George Paul, Bruce McKay (as of
   12/77)
Art Director Scott Ritenour
Host Tom Snyder

1403 **The Tonight Show Starring Johnny
Carson**   NBC
Program Type Talk/Service/Variety Series
90 minutes. Mondays–Fridays. Premiere date:
12/27/54. Continuous. Johnny Carson became
host 10/1/62. Two hour 15th Anniversary Spe-
cial: 9/30/77. 4,000th show: 4/12/78. Late-night
entertainment program. Guest hosts each Mon-
day.
Producer Fred de Cordova
Company NBC Television Network
Director Bobby Quinn
Writing Supervisor Hal Goodman
Musical Director Doc Severinsen
Host Johnny Carson
Announcer Ed McMahon
Assistant Music Conductor Tommy Newsom

1404 **The Tony Awards**   CBS
Program Type Parades/Pageants/Awards
Special
90 minutes. Live coverage of the 32nd annual
Tony Awards presented by the American The-
atre Wing on 6/4/78 from the Schubert Theatre
in New York City.
Executive Producer Alexander H. Cohen
Producer Hildy Parks
Director Clark Jones
Writer Hildy Parks
Musical Director Elliot Lawrence
Presenters/Performers Edward Asner, Lauren
   Bacall, Mikhail Baryshnikov, Carol Channing,
   Bonnie Franklin, Robert Guillaume, Julie
   Harris, Helen Hayes, Gene Kelly, Linda La-
   vin, Jack Lemmon, Hal Linden, Liza Minnelli,
   Roy Scheider, Dick Van Patten

1405 **The Tony Randall Show**   CBS
Program Type Comedy Series
30 minutes. Saturdays. Premiere date: 9/23/76.
Second season premiere: 9/24/77. Last show
3/25/78. Comedy about a widowed Philadelphia
judge with two children. Each episode entitled
"Case: . . ." Created by Tom Patchett and Jay

Tarses. Music by Pat Williams. Last regular
show on ABC: 3/10/77. Went to CBS for the
1977–78 season.
Producers Tom Patchett, Jay Tarses
Company An MTM Enterprises Production
Directors Various
Writers Various
                        CAST
Judge Walter Franklin .... Tony Randall
Jack Terwilliger .... Barney Martin
Miss Janet Reubner .... Allyn Ann McLerie
Roberta (Bobby) Franklin .... Penny Peyser
Oliver Wendell Franklin .... Brad Savage
Mrs. Bonnie McClellan .... Rachel Roberts
Wyatt Franklin .... Hans Conried

1406 **Top Secret**
The Big Event/NBC World Premiere Movie
                                         NBC
Program Type TV Movie
2 hours. Premiere date: 6/4/78. Drama about a
special agent called to Rome to locate 120
pounds of potentially destructive plutonium.
Filmed in Italy.
Executive Producer Sheldon Leonard
Company Jemmin Inc. production in association
   with NBC-TV
Director Paul Leaf
Writer David Levinson
                        CAST
Aaron Strickland .... Bill Cosby
McGee .... Tracy Reed
Carl Vitale ....Sheldon Leonard
Judith Strick .... Gloria Foster
Gino .... Paolo Turco
Murphy .... George Brenlin
Rosa Tattagia .... Marisa Merlini
Brigitte .... Francesca DeSapio
Tomas ....Leonard Treviglio
Pietro ....Luciano Bartoli
Christian .... Bryan Rostran
Zeeger .... Craig Hill
Macaferri .... Walter Williams
Sgt. Kwitney ....Nat Bush

1407 **Tour En L'Air**   PBS
Program Type Music/Dance Special
60 minutes. Premiere date: 10/11/77. A pair of
complementary National Film Board of Canada
productions—"Tour En L'Air," a documentary
depicting the complex relationship of Canadian
ballet dancers David and Anna-Marie Holmes,
and "Ballet Adagio," a filmed performance by
the couple.
Company National Film Board of Canada
Choreographers A. Meserer, Norman McLaren
Cinematographer Grant Munro

1408 **Tournament of Champions**   ABC
Program Type Sports Special
Live coverage of professional golf's Tournament

of Champions at Carlsbad, California 4/15/78 and 4/16/78 at the LaCosta Country Club.
Executive Producer Roone Arledge
Producer Bob Goodrich
Company ABC Sports
Directors Jim Jennett, Terry Jastrow
Commentator Keith Jackson
Expert Commentators Dave Marr, Bill Flemming, Bob Rosburg, Jim Lampley

Tournament of Roses Parade *See* Pasadena Tournament of Roses Parade/CBS Tournament of Roses Parade

1409 Tournament Players Championship Golf Tourney   ABC
Program Type Sports Special
Live coverage from the Sawgrass Golf Course in Jacksonville, Florida, 4/15–16/78.
Executive Producer Roone Arledge
Producer Bob Goodrich
Company ABC Sports
Directors Jim Jennett, Terry Jastrow
Anchor Keith Jackson
Expert Commentators Dave Marr, Peter Alliss, Bob Rosburg, Bill Flemming

1410 Track and Field, Wrestling, Volleyball: The NCAA Champions   ABC
Program Type Sports Special
2 hours. 6/24/78. NCAA Championship competitions. Coverage includes "Up Close and Personal" reports of several of the key figures.
Executive Producer Roone Arledge
Producer Terry O'Neill
Company ABC Sports
Directors Brice Weisman, Lou Volpicelli, Craig Janoff
Host Keith Jackson
Reporters Keith Jackson, Bill Flemming, Jim Lampley, Ken Kraft, Bruce Jenner
Expert Commentators Marty Liquori, Ken Kraft, Chris Marlow

1411 Trailblazers of Modern Dance
Dance in America/Great Performances   PBS
Program Type Music/Dance Special
60 minutes. Premiere date: 6/22/77. Repeat date: 9/9/78. The development of modern dance —from the turn-of-the-century through the 1930s. Program includes two reconstructions of Isadora Duncan's "Scriabin Etudes" danced by Annabelle Gibson, "Five Brahms Waltzes in the Manner of Isadora Duncan" choreographed and introduced by Sir Frederick Ashton and danced by Lynn Seymour, "Japanese Spear Dance" choreographed by Ted Shawn and danced by Clif

da Raita and "Soaring" choreographed by Doris Humphrey and danced by the Trisler Danscompany. Program made possible by grants from Exxon Corporation, the National Endowment for the Arts and the Corporation for Public Broadcasting.
Executive Producer Jac Venza
Producer Emile Ardolino
Company WNET-TV/New York
Director Merrill Brockway
Choreographers Isadora Duncan, Martha Graham, Ruth St. Denis, Doris Humphrey, Ted Shawn, Frederick Ashton
Narrator Michael Tolan
Voice of Isadora Duncan Rosemary Harris

The Train Robbers *See* The CBS Wednesday Night Movies

1412 Transamerica Open Tennis Championships   PBS
Program Type Sports Special
Semi-finals and finals live coverage for four hours 10/1/77 and four hours on 10/2/77 of tennis matches at The Cow Palace, San Francisco.
Producer Jim Scalem
Company KQED-TV/San Francisco
Announcers Bud Collins, Donald Dell

1413 Transformations
Opera Theater   PBS
Program Type Music/Dance Special
90 minutes. Premiere date: 8/14/78. Opera by Conrad Susa with text by Anne Sexton performed by the Minnesota Opera Company. Program made possible by grants from Public Television Stations, The Jerome Foundation, The Surdna Foundation, The National Opera Institute, the Martha Baird Rockefeller Foundation, and The Nate B. and Frances Spingold Foundation. David Griffiths is series producer.
Producers Elizabeth Davis, Cyrus Bharucha
Company WNET-TV/New York and KTCA-TV/Minneapolis
CAST
Anne Sexton .... Barbara Brandt
Additional Cast Marsha Hunter, Janis Hardy, Michael Riley, Vern Sutton, William Wahman

1414 Treasure
National Geographic Special   PBS
Program Type Documentary/Informational Special
60 minutes. Premiere date: 12/7/76. Repeat dates: 5/30/78, 5/31/78. The story of Mel Fisher's search for the lost Spanish galleon *Atocha* sunk off the Florida Keys on Sept. 6, 1622. Program

Treasure *Continued*
made possible by a grant from Gulf Oil Corporation.
Executive Producer Dennis B. Kane, Thomas Skinner
Producer Nicolás Noxon
Company The National Geographic Society and WQED-TV/Pittsburgh
Director Nicolas Noxon
Writer Nicolas Noxon
Host E. G. Marshall
Narrator Alexander Scourby

1415   The Treasures of Ireland   CBS
Program Type Educational/Cultural Special
60 minutes. Premiere date: 10/30/77. Repeat date: 3/26/78.
Producer Pamela Ilott
Company CBS News
Writer Brian O'Doherty
Narrator Brian O'Doherty

1416   The Treasures of Tutankhamun   PBS
Program Type Documentary/Informational Special
30 minutes. Premiere date: 11/1/77. Repeat date: 11/4/77. Documentary on the tomb of young King Tut and the 20th century discovery that brought it to the attention of the world. Program made possible by grants from the National Endowment for the Humanities and Exxon.
Executive Producer Donald Knox
Producer Valerie Gentile
Company WTTW-TV/Chicago, the Field Museum of Natural History and the Oriental Institute of the University of Chicago

1417   The Trial of Lee Harvey Oswald
ABC Friday/Sunday Night Movie   ABC
Program Type Dramatic Special
4 hours. Two hours each 9/30/77 and 10/2/77. Dramatizes the story behind the man accused of assassinating John F. Kennedy. Music by Fred Karlin.
Executive Producer Charles Fries
Producer Richard Freed
Company Charles Fries Productions, Inc.
Director David Greene
Writer Robert E. Thompson
Art Director Joel Schiller
CAST
Anson "Kip" Roberts .... Ben Gazzara
Matthew Arnold Weldon .... Lorne Greene
Jan Holder ....:... Frances Lee McCain
Ewbank .... Lawrence Pressman
Malvin Johnson .... Charlie Robinson
Blandings .... George Wyner

Marina Oswald .... Mo Malone
Lee Harvey Oswald .... John Pleshette

1418   The Trial of the Moke
Great Performances   PBS
Program Type Dramatic Special
90 minutes. Premiere date: 5/3/78. Play by Daniel Stein about the career and court martial of Henry O. Flipper, the first black man to graduate from West Point. Program made possible by a grant from Exxon Corporation. Performed by the Milwaukee Repertory Theater.
Producer Ken Campbell
Company WNET-TV/New York and WQLN-TV/Erie
Director Stan Lathan
CAST
Flipper .... Franklin Seales
Col. William Shafter .... Robert Burr
Additional Cast Thalmus Rasulala, Alfre Woodard, Samuel Jackson

1419   A Tribute to 'Mr. Television'
Milton Berle   NBC
Program Type Music/Comedy/Variety Special
60 minutes. Premiere date: 3/26/78.
Executive Producer Jerry Frank
Producers Jerry Frank, Bill Carruthers
Company The Jerry Frank Company
Director Bill Carruthers
Writer Marty Farrell
Stars Lucille Ball, Joey Bishop, George Carlin, Johnny Carson, Angie Dickinson, Kirk Douglas, Bob Hope, Gabriel Kaplan, Gene Kelly, Kermit the Frog, Donny Osmond, Marie Osmond, Gregory Peck, Carl Reiner, Don Rickles, Frank Sinatra, Marlo Thomas, Flip Wilson

1420   A Tribute to the America's Cup   PBS
Program Type Music/Dance Special
60 minutes. Premiere date: 9/12/77. A concert tribute to the America's Cup competitors. Part of the 1977 Newport Music Festival held in Fort Adams, Rhode Island.
Executive Producers John Robert Curtin, Mark Malkovich
Producers Ray Fass, Peter Frid
Company WSBE-TV/Providence
Directors Ray Fass, Peter Frid
Conductor Ulf Bjorlin
Guest Performer Sven Bertil Taube

1421   Trouble in Coal Country
NBC Reports   NBC
Program Type News Special
60 minutes. Premiere date: 12/20/77. Examination of task America faces in trying to make coal

the major energy source, and the problems this effort is creating for miners, the coal industry and environmentalists.
Producer Fred Flamenhaft
Company NBC News
Reporter Douglas Kiker

1422 Trouble in Tahiti
Opera Theater   PBS
Program Type Music/Dance Special
60 minutes. Premiere date: 5/4/76. Repeat date: 9/4/78. Television version of the jazz-based one-act opera by Leonard Bernstein featuring the London Symphonic Wind Band. Program made possible by grants from the Ford Foundation, the Corporation for Public Broadcasting and Public Television Stations and presented by WNET-TV/New York.
Executive Producer Humphrey Burton
Coordinating Producers Linda Krisel, David Griffiths
Company Amberson Video, Inc. and London Weekend Television
Director Bill Hays
Conductor Leonard Bernstein
CAST
Sam .... Julian Patrick
Dinah .... Nancy Williams
Greek Chorus .... Antonia Butler, Michael Clarke, Mark Brown

1423 Trouble River
ABC Children's Novel for Television/ABC Weekend Specials   ABC
Program Type Children's Special
60 minutes. Shown in two parts: 11/12/77 and 11/26/77. Repeat dates: 4/1/78 and 4/8/78. Based on a story by Betsy Byars. A young boy and his grandmother escape renegades by riding a makeshift raft down a river. Music composed by Glenn Paxton. Filmed in Bend, Oregon.
Producer Martin Tahse
Company A Martin Tahse Production
Director Roger Flint
Writer Larry Bischof
Costume Designer Carole M. Carter
Art Director Ray Markham
CAST
Grandma .... Nora Denney
Dewey .... Michael Le Clair
Indian ....Geno Silva
Mr. Dargan .... Mike Howden
Mr. Martin .... Hal England
Mrs. Martin .... Jay W. MacIntosh

1424 True Grit
The ABC Friday Night Movie   ABC
Program Type TV Movie
2 hours. Premiere date: 5/19/78. Western drama featuring Rooster Cogburn, first portrayed by John Wayne in the 1969 motion picture. Music

by Earle Hagen. Filmed near Canon City, Colorado.
Producer Sandor Stern
Company Paramount Television
Director Richard Heffron
Writer Sandor Stern
Art Director Arch Bacon
Film Editor Jerry Young
CAST
Rooster Cogburn .... Warren Oates
Mattie .... Lisa Pelikan
Annie .... Lee Meriwether
Joshua ....James Stephens
Christopher ....Jeff Osterhage
Daniel .... Lee Harcourt Montgomery
Sheriff .... Ramon Bieri
Clerk .... Jack Fletcher
Rollins .... Parley Baer
Skorby .... Lee De Broux
Chaka ....Fred Cook
Harrison .... Redmond Gleeson

1425 Turnabout   PBS
Program Type Talk/Service/Variety Series
30 minutes. Premiere date: 2/4/78. Series on the world of American women.
Executive Producer Martha Glessing
Producer Roxanne Russell
Company KQED-TV/San Francisco
Director Louise Lo
Host Gerri Lange

1426 Tut: The Boy King   NBC
Program Type Documentary/Informational Special
60 minutes. Premiere date: 7/27/77. Repeat date: 8/3/78. The art treasures from the tomb of Tutankhamun. Taped at the National Gallery of Art in Washington, D.C. Music composed by Robert Maxwell.
Executive Producer George A. Heinemann
Producer Joseph F. Callo
Director Sidney Smith
Writer W. W. Lewis
Conductor Robert Maxwell
Art Director Norman Davidson
Narrator Orson Welles

1427 TV on Trial   PBS
Program Type Documentary/Informational Special
2 hours. Premiere date: 5/23/78. Repeat date: 8/15/78. Documentary featuring highlights of the Florida murder trial of 15 year-old Ronney Zamora.
Executive Producer Shep Morgan
Producer Don Fouser
Company WPBT-TV/Miami

1428   TV: The Fabulous '50s   NBC
Program Type Music/Comedy/Variety Special
90 minutes. Premiere date: 3/5/78. A nostalgic
look at some of the TV shows of the 1950s.
Executive Producer Henry Jaffee
Producers David Lawrence, Draper Lewis
Company Henry Jaffee Enterprises, Inc. in asso-
ciation with Twentieth Century-Fox Studios
Director Jonathan Lucas
Writers David Lawrence, Draper Lewis
Hosts Lucille Ball, David Janssen, Michael Lan-
don, Mary Martin, Dinah Shore, Red Skelton

1429   TVTV Looks at the Oscars
Documentary Showcase   PBS
Program Type Documentary/Informational
Special
60 minutes. Premiere date: 3/18/77. A humor-
ous look behind the scenes of the 1976 Academy
Awards presentation.
Producers Wendy Apple, David Axelrod, Paul
Goldsmith, Hudson Marquez, Tom Morey,
Allen Rucker, Michael Shamberg, Megan Wil-
liams
Company TVTV and KCET-TV/Los Angeles
Directors Wendy Apple, David Axelrod, Paul
Goldsmith, Hudson Marquez, Tom Morey,
Allen Rucker, Michael Shamberg, Megan Wil-
liams
CAST
Judy Beasley ....Lily Tomlin

1430   'Twas the Night Before Christmas
ABC
Program Type Comedy Special
60 minutes. Premiere date: 12/7/77. A comedy
drama about Christmas.
Executive Producers Raymond Katz; Sandy Gal-
lin
Producers Joe Layton; Ken Welch; Mitzi Welch
Company A Hoysyl Production in association
with Layton/Welch Productions
Director Tim Kiley
Writers Dick Clair, Jenna McMahon
Musical Director Velton Ray Bunch
Choreographer Jim Bates
Costume Designer Ret Turner
Art Director Charles Lisanby
CAST
Clark Cosgrove .... Paul Lynde
Nellie Cosgrove .... Anne Meara
Edmund Butler .... Foster Brooks
Elvira Butler ....Martha Raye
Mildred Cosgrove .... Alice Ghostley
Heinrich Kotzebue ....Howard Morris
Nathaniel Terwilliger .... George Gobel
Sarah Cosgrove .... Susan Page
Nancy Cosgrove ....Tiffany Ann Francis
Mary Beth Cosgrove .... Rachel Jacobs
Clarkie Dosgrove .... Sparky Marcus
Elias Cosgrove .... Tommy Crebbs
Santa Claus .... Joe Giamalva

1431   'Twas the Night Before Christmas
CBS
Program Type Animated Film Special
30 minutes. Premiere date: 12/8/74. Repeat
date: 12/12/77. Adapted from "A Visit From St.
Nicholas" by Clement Moore Music by Maury
Laws; Jules Bass; Artist: Paul Cohen, Jr.
Producers Arthur Rankin, Jr., Jules Bass
Company Rankin-Bass Productions
Directors Arthur Rankin, Jr., Jules Bass
Writer Jerome Coopersmith
Narrator Joel Grey
VOICES
Albert Mouse ....Tammy Grimes
Mayor of Junctionville ....John McGiver
Father Mouse .... George Gobel
Additional Voices Patricia Bright, Alan Swift, Robert
McFadden, Christine Winter, Scott Firestone

1432   The $20,000 Pyramid   ABC
Program Type Game/Audience Participation
Series
30 minutes. Mondays–Fridays. Premiere date
(on CBS): 3/26/73. Moved to ABC 5/6/74.
Continuous. Name (and prizes) changed from
"The $10,000 Pyramid" 1/19/76. Two celebri-
ties and two contestants team up to test their
word power.
Executive Producer Bob Stewart
Producer Anne Marie Schmitt
Company A Bob Stewart Production
Director Mike Gargiulo
Host Dick Clark

1433   20/20   ABC
Program Type News Magazine Series
60 minutes. Premiere date: 6/6/78. Broadcast
edition of a news magazine in the traditional
sense with a wide range of interests and diverse
elements. Harold Hayes and Robert Hughes
hosted the premiere show. "20/20" theme music
lyrics by Jon Silberman.
Executive Producer Bob Shanks
Senior Editorial Producer Harold Hayes
Field Producers Aram Boyajian, Dan Cooper,
John McBride, Donovan Moore, Marcel
Ophuls, Ene Riisna, Dennis Sullivan, Charles
C. Thompson II, Anthony Van Witsen, Alan
R. Weisman
Company ABC News
Director Jorn Winther
Writers Brock Brower, Edward Tivnan
Film Editors Peter Altschuler, Dina Boogard,
Sharon Kaufman, Gerry Klein, Bernie Stone,
Rob Wallace
Host Hugh Downs
Investigative Reporters Hugh Aynesworth, Low-
ell Bergman, Barbara Newman
Correspondents David Marash, Sander Vanocur,

Sylvia Chase, Dr. Carl Sagan, Thomas Hoving
Special Reports Geraldo Rivera

Twilight's Last Gleaming *See* The CBS
Tuesday Night Movies

1434   The Two-Five
The ABC Friday Night Movie   ABC
Program Type TV Movie
90 minutes. Premiere date: 4/14/78. Two police-
men resort to anonymous police work in setting
up a major narcotics arrest.
Executive Producer Robert A. Cinader
Producers Gian R. Grimaldi, Hannah Shearer
Company Universal Studios
Director Bruce Kessler
Writers Robert A. Cinader, Joseph Polizzi
CAST
Charlie ....Don Johnson
Frank .... Joe Bennett
Malloy .... George Murdock
Carter .... John Crawford
Dale .... Carlene Watkins
Vinnie .... Michael Durrell
Angel .... Tara Buckman
Waldo .... Marty Zagon
Menoir .... Jacques Aubuchon
Chief .... Richard O'Brien
Ralston .... Sandy McPeak
Bandit .... Henry Olek

1435   Uncle Tim Wants You!   CBS
Program Type Music/Comedy/Variety Special
60 minutes. Premiere date: 9/17/77. A salute to
the U.S. Armed Forces. Special musical material
by Artie Malvin.
Producer Joe Hamilton
Company Noway, Inc.
Director Dave Powers
Writers Bill Richmond, Gene Perret, Roger
Beatty, Tim Conway, Jonathan Winters
Musical Director Peter Matz
Choreographer George Foster
Costume Designer Bob Mackie
Art Director Paul Barnes
Star Tim Conway
Guest Cast Jonathan Winters, Bernadette Peters,
the Marquis Chimps, Bob Holt, Chuck Blore,
Brad Trumbull

1436   Uncommon Women and Others
Great Performances/Theatre in America   PBS
Program Type Dramatic Special
90 minutes. Premiere date: 5/24/78. Play by
Wendy Wasserstein performed by The Phoenix
Theatre about graduates of an exclusive women's
college who meet seven years later to evaluate
their lives.
Executive Producer Jac Venza
Producer Phyllis Geller

Company WNET-TV/New York
Directors Steven Robman, Merrily Mossman
Narrator Alexander Scourby
CAST
Kate .... Jill Eikenberry
Rita .... Swoozie Kurtz
Holly .... Alma Cuervo
Muffet .... Ellen Parker
Samantha .... Ann McDonough
Leilah .... Meryl Streep
Susie ....Cynthia Herman
Carter .... Anna Levine
Mrs. Plumm ....Josephine Nichols

1437   Union Maids   PBS
Program Type Documentary/Informational
Special
60 minutes. Premiere date: 11/21/77. Repeat
date: 1/13/78. Documentary on three active
members of the Chicago rank and file labor
movement in the thirties. Based on "Rank and
File," by Alice and Staughton Lynd.
Company WNET-TV/New York
Filmmakers Julia Reichert, Miles Mogulescu,
James Klein

1438   U.N. Day Concert (1977)   PBS
Program Type Music/Dance Special
90 minutes. Premiere date: 10/24/76. Repeat
date: 10/25/77. Annual concert honoring the
founding of the United Nations from the U.N.
General Assembly Hall. Music performed by the
Philadelphia Orchestra. Program made possible
by grants from the Corporation for Public
Broadcasting and IBM Corporation.
Company United Nations Television in cooper-
ation with WNET-TV/New York
Conductor Eugene Ormandy
Guest Pianist Andre Watts

1439   US Against the World II   ABC
Program Type Sports Special
2 hours. Premiere date: 9/9/78. United States
team and the World team participate in second
annual athletic event at Magic Mountain amuse-
ment park and at College of the Canyons, Va-
lencia, Calif. Special event horse race filmed at
Del Mar, Calif.
Executive Producer Howard Katz
Producers Carolyn Raskin, Craig Tennis
Company Trans World International Production
in association with NBC Television Network
Director Jim Cross
Hosts Gabriel Kaplan, Ed McMahon, Ted
Knight
World Team: William Shatner, Bo Svenson,
Rich Little, LeVar Burton, Britt Ekland, Vic-
toria Principal, Jane Seymour, Fionnuala
Flanagan, Dudley Moore, Oleg Cassini, Sivi
Aberg, Paul Nicholas

US Against the World II *Continued*
US Team: Erik Estrada, Dan Haggerty, Scott
Baio, Dick Clark, Dick Van Patten, Jimmie
Walker, Cloris Leachman, Melissa Gilbert,
Valerie Bertinelli, Kristy McNichol, Joyce De-
Witt, Gary Burghoff

**1440 U.S. Amateur Boxing
Championships**   ABC
Program Type Sports Special
Coverage of U.S. Amateur Boxing Champion-
ships from Biloxi, Mississippi, 4/23/78.
Executive Producer Roone Arledge
Producer Ned Steckel
Company ABC Sports
Director Craig Janoff
Announcer Keith Jackson

1441 USAC Texas 200 Auto Race CBS
Program Type Sports Special
2 hours. Live coverage of United States Auto
Club race from Texas World Speedway in Col-
lege Station, Texas 8/6/78.
Company CBS Sports
Director Bernie Hoffman
Announcers Ken Squier, Dan Gurney

**1442 United States Boxing Team vs. the
World in Amateur Boxing**   ABC
Program Type Sports Series
60 minutes. Sundays. Premiere date: 1/8/78.
Competitions between the U.S.A. team orga-
nized by the Amateur Athletic Union of the U.S.
and national teams from the Soviet Union; Cuba;
Yugoslavia; Rumania; and Ireland. Satellite cov-
erage of the finals shown 5/21/78 from Belgrade,
Yugoslavia.
Executive Producer Roone Arledge
Producer Ned Steckel
Company ABC Sports
Director Craig Janoff
Announcer Keith Jackson

1443 U.S. Clay Courts Championships
                                   CBS
Program Type Sports Special
Same day coverage of 68th annual tennis cham-
pionships 8/13/78.
Producer Perry Smith
Company CBS Sports
Director Bob Dailey
Announcers Tony Trabert, Rick Barry

**1444 USGA Girls and Boys Junior
Championships**   ABC
Program Type Sports Special
Highlights of Junior Championships featuring

top young American golfers 8/20/78 from the
Wilmington Country Club in Wilmington, Dela-
ware.
Executive Producer Roone Arledge
Producer Bob Goodrich
Company ABC Sports
Director Jim Jennett
Host Chris Schenkel
Expert Commentator Rhonda Glenn

1445 U.S. Grand Prix West   CBS
Program Type Sports Special
2 hours. Live coverage of auto race from Long
Beach, Calif. 4/2/78.
Company CBS Sports
Director Bernie Hoffman
Announcer Ken Squier
Commentators David Hobbs, Bobby Unser
Expert Analyst Brock Yates

**1446 U.S. Men's Amateur Golf
Championship**   ABC
Program Type Sports Special
Same-day coverage of amateur golf tournament
from Plainfield Country Club in Plainfield, New
Jersey 9/3/78.
Executive Producer Roone Arledge
Producer Bob Goodrich
Company ABC Sports
Director Jim Jennett
Announcer Jim McKay
Expert Commentators Dave Marr, Bob Rosburg

**1447 U.S. National Men's Indoor Tennis
Championships**   CBS
Program Type Sports Special
Same-day coverage of finals of the 77th annual
Tennis Championships 3/5/78 from the Racquet
Club of Memphis (Tenn.)
Producer Perry Smith
Company CBS Sports
Announcer Pat Summerall

**1448 United States National Table
Tennis Championship Finals**   PBS
Program Type Sports Special
4 hours. 7/16/78. Taped coverage of competition
in the men's and women's singles and doubles
games played July 2 from the Myriad Convention Center in Oklahoma City. Program made
possible by a grant from the Kerr Foundation.
Executive Producer Bob Allen
Company Oklahoma Educational Television Authority
Director Jim Rankin
Announcer John Brooks

1449 U.S. Open Golf Championship
ABC
Program Type Sports Special
Most extensive live coverage of a golf tournament ever presented in the United States from the Cherry Hills Country Club in Englewood, Colorado 6/15–18/78.
Executive Producer Roone Arledge
Producers Chuck Howard, Bob Goodrich
Company ABC Sports
Directors Jim Jennett, Terry Jastrow, Andy Sidaris
Commentators Jim McKay, Keith Jackson
Expert Commentators Peter Alliss, Dave Marr, Bill Flemming, Bob Rosburg

1450 U.S. Professional Tennis Championships
PBS
Program Type Sports Special
Live coverage of the semi-finals and finals from Longwood Cricket Club in Chestnut Hill, Massachusetts 8/27/78 and 8/28/78. Made possible by a grant from Cullinane Corporation.
Company WGBH-TV/Boston
Commentators Bud Collins, Donald Dell

1451 U.S. Women's Open Golf Championship
ABC
Program Type Sports Special
Live coverage of the final two rounds from the Country Club of Indianapolis 7/22/78 and 7/23/78 of the 33rd annual U.S. Women's Open.
Executive Producer Roone Arledge
Producer Bob Goodrich
Company ABC Sports
Director Jim Jennett
Commentators Jim McKay, Peter Alliss
Expert Commentators Dave Marr, Bill Flemming, Bob Rosburg

1452 The Unwanted
PBS
Program Type Documentary/Informational Special
60 minutes. Premiere date: 6/20/78. Documentary about illegal Mexican aliens.
Producer Jose Luis Ruis
Company KCET-TV/Los Angeles
Director Jose Luis Ruis
Writer Frank del Olmo

Up the Sandbox *See* The CBS Wednesday Night Movies

Uptown Saturday Night *See* The CBS Wednesday Night Movies

1453 Valery and Galina Panov
In Performance at Wolftrap
PBS
Program Type Music/Dance Special
60 minutes. Premiere date: 11/17/75. Repeat date: 9/21/78. Five ballet selections danced by Galina Panov and Valery Panov. Music by the Filene Center Orchestra. Performed at the Wolf Trap Farm Park in Arlington, Va. Program made possible by a grant from Atlantic Richfield Company.
Executive Producer David Prowitt
Producer Ruth Leon
Company WETA-TV/Washington, D.C.
Director Stan Lathan
Conductor Seymour Lipkin
Hosts Beverly Sills, David Prowitt
Executive-in-Charge Jim Karayn

Vanishing Point *See* CBS Special Movie Presentations

1454 Vanishing Wilderness
ABC
Program Type Documentary/Informational Special
2 hours. Premiere date: 5/28/78. Oregon's Rogue River and fur seals on the Pribilof Islands of Alaska are part of this film which was five years in the making.
Producer Arthur R. Dubs
Company Pacific International Enterprises, Inc. Production
Director Heinz Seilmann
Narrator Rex Allen

1455 Variety '77—The Year in Entertainment
CBS
Program Type Music/Comedy/Variety Special
90 minutes. Premiere date: 1/9/78. Special featuring the top entertainment stories and names of the year, as recorded in the pages of the entertainment weekly, *Variety*. Film sequences produced by Marshall Flaum.
Executive Producer Jack Watson
Producer Ernest Chambers
Company Ernest Chambers Productions
Director Stan Harris
Writers William Box, Ernest Chambers
Musical Director Nelson Riddle
Art Director Rene Lagler
Segment Hosts Valerie Perrine (Movies), Alan King (Nightclubs and Concerts), Dionne Warwick (Music), Telly Savalas (Television), Sada Thompson (Theater and the Performing Arts)
Personalities Represented Visually Steve Martin, Penny Marshall, Cindy Williams, Henry Winkler, Ron Howard, Yuri Kuklachov, Kenny Rogers, Ben Vereen, LeVar Burton, Georg Stanford Brown, Olivia Cole, Lou Gossett, The Sex Pistols, Andy Kauffman, Joan Craw-

Variety '77—The Year in Entertainment
Continued
ford, Judd Hirsch, Anita Gillette, Barry Manilow, Farrah Fawcett-Majors, Peter Frampton, Alicia Alonso, Bette Davis, Totie Fields, Mae West, Leopold Stokowski, Elvis Presley, Bing Crosby, Ethel Waters, Rochester, Sebastian Cabot, Guy Lombardo, Maria Callas, Zero Mostel, Andy Devine, Alfred Lunt, Groucho Marx, Charlie Chaplin, Mary Tyler Moore, Jane Fonda, Vanessa Redgrave, Shirley MacLaine, Anne Bancroft, Marsha Mason, Diane Keaton, Arnold Schwartzenegger, Rose Royce, Mikhail Baryshnikov, Virginia Wade, Pele, Steve Cauthen, Reggie Jackson, Tom La Sorda.

1456   Vega$
The ABC Summer Movie/ABC Movie Special
ABC
Program Type TV Movie
90 minutes. Premiere date: 4/25/78. Repeat date 8/24/78. Search for a runaway teenager turns into a murder investigation. Music by Dominic Frontiere.
Executive Producers Aaron Spelling, Douglas S. Cramer
Supervising Producer E. Duke Vincent
Company Aaron Spelling Productions
Director Richard Lang
Writer Michael Mann
CAST
Dan Tanna ....Robert Urich
Loretta Ochs ....June Allyson
Bernie Roth ....Tony Curtis
Nate DeStefano ....Michael Lerner
Tom Cirko ....Red Buttons
Harlon Two Leaf ....Will Sampson
Marilyn ....Elissa Leeds
Beatrice ....Phyllis Davis
Costigian ....Chick Vennera
Larry ....Colby Chester
Merle Ochs ....Jack Kelly
Angie ....Judy Landers
Charlene ....Diane Parkinson
Hugh ....John Quade
Julie .... Katherine Hickland
Adamek ....Jason Wingreen
Rosie .... Scatman Crothers

1457   The Verdi Requiem
In Performance at Wolf Trap
PBS
Program Type Music/Dance Special
90 minutes. Premiere date: 12/15/75. Repeat date: 6/3/78. The National Symphony Orchestra and University of Maryland Chorus in a performance of the "Requiem" by Giuseppe Verdi at the Wolf Trap Farm Park in Arlington, Va. Program made possible by a grant from the Atlantic Richfield Company.
Executive Producer David Prowitt
Producer Ruth Leon

Company WETA-TV/Washington, D.C.
Director Jack Sameth
Conductor Julius Rudel
Hosts Beverly Sills, David Prowitt
Executive-in-Charge Jim Karayn
Guest Soloists Rachel Mathes, Gwendolyn Killebrew, Ermano Mauro, Samuel Ramey

1458   Verna: U.S.O. Girl
Great Performances
PBS
Program Type Dramatic Special
90 minutes. Premiere date: 1/25/78. Based on short story by Paul Gallico about a young Chicago dancer whose dreams of stardom are hampered only by a complete lack of talent. Program made possible by a grant from Exxon Corporation and PBS stations.
Producers Ronald F. Maxwell, Jac Venza
Company WNET-TV/New York
Director Ronald F. Maxwell
Writer Albert Innaurato
CAST
Verna .... Sissy Spacek
Maureen .... Sally Kellerman
Eddie .... Howard Da Silva
Walter .... William Hurt

1459   Very Good Friends
ABC Afterschool Specials
ABC
Program Type Children's Special
60 minutes. Premiere date: 4/6/77. Repeat date: 1/11/78. Drama of a teenager coping with the death of her younger sister. Based on the novel "Beat the Turtle Drum" by Constance Greene.
Producer Martin Tahse
Company Martin Tahse Productions, Inc.
Director Richard Bennett
Writer Arthur Heinemann
Film Editor Vince Humphrey
CAST
Kate .... Melissa Sue Anderson
Joss .... Katy Kurtzman
Father .... William H. Bassett
Mother .... Pamela Nelson
Tootie .... Sparky Marcus
Miss Pemberthy .... Anne Seymour
Essig ....William Lanteau
Mrs. Essig .... Montana Smoyer
Harry ....Joshua Davis

1460   Vietnam: Picking Up the Pieces
PBS
Program Type Documentary/Informational Special
60 minutes. Premiere date: 4/11/78. Documentary of Vietnam since the communist takeover at the end of the war in April 1975, by Jon Alpert and associates Keiko Tsuno and Karen Ranucci.
Executive Producer David Loxton
Producers Jon Alpert, Keiko Tsuno

Company Downtown Community TV Center and TV Laboratory at WNET-TV/New York
Writers Jon Alpert, Keiko Tsuno

Vigilante Force *See* The CBS Wednesday Night Movies

1461 Villa Alegre PBS
Program Type Children's Series
30 minutes. Monday–Friday mornings. Premiere date: 9/23/74. Third season premiere: 9/19/77. Repeats 6/19/78. Spanish/English show set in Villa Alegre (Happy Village) stressing themes of human relations, food and nutrition, the natural environment, energy and man-made objects. Series funded by grants from the U.S. Department of Health, Education and Welfare Department of Education and the Exxon U.S.A. Foundation.
Executive Producer Claudio Guzman
Producer Larry Gottlieb
Company Bilingual Childrens Television, Inc.
Director Charles Ed Rickey
Head Writer Barbara Chain
Writers Ken Clark, John Figueroa, Richard Kletter, Alex Nogales, Eyvind Rodriguez
Musical Director Dr. Moises Rodriguez
Production Designer Michael Baugh
Regulars Nono Arsu, Linda Dangcil, Sam Edwards, Maria Grimm, Darryl Henriquez, Julio Medina, Federico Roberto, Wilfredo H. Rodriquez, Hal Smith, Catana Tully, Carmen Zapata

1462 Violent Crossroads CBS
Program Type Religious/Cultural Special
Two 30 minute shows on consecutive Sundays: 1/22/78 and 1/29/78. Originally presented 9/28/64 and 10/5/69. Two-part series examining the history of the Middle East, particularly Palestine.
Executive Producer Pamela Ilott
Producers Dr. George Crothers, Ted Holmes
Company CBS News
Director Neil Smith
Narrators Keith Charles, Nicolas Coster

Virgin Spring *See* PBS Movie Theater

1463 VISA PBS
Program Type Miscellaneous Series
60 minutes. Sundays. Premiere date: 7/2/78. Series created by Nam June Paik as an exploration of foreign cultures in non-crisis situations. Video artists of diverse backgrounds record their wide-ranging global impressions as traditional artists. Taped locations include Pamplona, Spain, Solomon Islands, Paris, Moscow, New York and Siena, Italy. Contributors are Bill and Esti Mar-

pet, Russell Connor, Don Foresta, Dimitri Devyatkin, Bill Viola, John Sanborn, Kit Fitzgerald. Programs included in the series are "Running with the Bulls" shown 7/2/78, "To Siena with Love" shown 7/9/78, "Paris a la Carte" shown 7/16/78, "Memories of the Ancestors: The Solomon Islands" shown 7/23/78, and "Media Shuttle: New York/Moscow Express" shown 7/30/78.
Company WNET-TV/New York

1464 Visions PBS
Program Type Drama Series
90 minutes/2 hours. Sundays and Thursdays. Premiere date: 10/21/76. Second season premiere: 10/2/77. Weekly series of original television dramas. Programs shown during the 1977–78 season are: "Alambrista!" "All I Could See from Where I Stood," "The Dancing Bear," "Freeman," "The Gardener's Son," "Iowa," "Life Among the Lowly," "Liza's Pioneer Diary," "Nanook Taxi," "Over-Under, Sideways-Down," "Pennsylvania Lynch," "The Phantom of the Open Hearth," "Pleasantville," "Prison Game," "A Secret Space," "Tapestry," "War Widow," and "You Can Run But You Can't Hide." (*See* individual titles for credits.)
Executive Producer Barbara Schultz
Company KCET-TV/Los Angeles

1465 Vitalis/U.S. Olympic Invitational Track and Field Meet NBC
Program Type Sports Special
90 minutes. Premiere date: 2/4/78. The tenth annual Track and Field Meet from New York City's Madison Square Garden.
Producer Mike Weisman
Company NBC Sports
Director Ken Fouts
Announcers Charlie Jones, Fred Thompson, Frank Shorter

1466 The Volga
National Geographic Special PBS
Program Type Documentary/Informational Special
60 minutes. Premiere date: 3/8/77. Repeat date: 7/11/78. Film documentary of life along the Volga River through the heart of Russia. Filmed aboard the cruise ship *Lenin.* Program produced with the cooperation of Novosti Television, Moscow, and the captain and crew of the *Lenin,* Volga Passenger Lines. Funded by a grant from Gulf Oil Corporation.
Executive Producers Dennis B. Kane, Thomas Skinner
Producer Irwin Rosten
Company National Geographic Society and WQED-TV/Pittsburgh

The Volga *Continued*
Director Irwin Rosten
Writer Irwin Rosten
Host E. G. Marshall
Narrator Jack Palance

1467   Voyage of the Hokule'a
National Geographic Special   PBS
Program Type Documentary/Informational
Special
90 minutes. Premiere date: 1/18/77. Repeat
date: 7/25/78. Documentary recounting the re-
production and 3,000-mile voyage of modern
Hawaiians from Hawaii to Tahiti and back in a
double-hulled canoe re-enacting a feat of ancient
Polynesia. Program made possible by a grant
from Gulf Oil Corporation.
Executive Producers Dennis B. Kane, Thomas
Skinner
Producer Dale Bell
Company The National Geographic Society and
WQED-TV/Pittsburgh
Writer Theodore Strauss
Host E. G. Marshall
Narrator E. G. Marshall

W. C. Fields and Me *See* NBC Saturday
Night at the Movies

W. W. and the Dixie Dancekings *See*
The ABC Friday Night Movie

1468   Waiting for Godot
Theater in America/Great Performances   PBS
Program Type Dramatic Special
2-1/2 hours. Premiere date: 6/29/77. Repeat
date: 7/26/78. The Los Angeles Actors' Theatre
production of the 1953 tragicomedy by Samuel
Beckett. Program made possible by grants from
Exxon Corporation, the Corporation for Public
Broadcasting, the Ford Foundation and Public
Television Stations.
Executive Producer Jac Venza
Producer Ken Campbell
Company WNET-TV/New York
Directors Gwen Arner, Charles S. Dubin
Writer Samuel Beckett
CAST
Vladimir/Didi .... Dana Elcar
Estragon/Gogo .... Donald Moffat
Pozzo .... Ralph Waite
Lucky .... Bruce French

1469   Walker Cup Golf Match   ABC
Program Type Sports Special
30 minutes. Premiere date: 9/4/77. Gold tournament with golfers from United States versus

those from Great Britain and Ireland at Shin-
necock Hills, Long Island, NY.
Company ABC Sports

Walking Tall *See* The ABC Sunday
Night Movie

1470   Wall Street Week   PBS
Program Type Educational/Cultural Series
30 minutes. Fridays. Premiere date: 1/7/72.
Continuous. Theme "Twelve Bars for TWX" by
Donald Swartz. Weekly guests and panel of stock
market experts analyze economic trends and de-
velopments. Series made possible by grants from
the Corporation for Public Broadcasting, the
Ford Foundation and Public Television Stations.
Executive Producer Anne Traux Darlington
Producer John H. Davis
Company Maryland Center for Public Broad-
casting
Director George Beneman
Host/Moderator Louis Rukeyser

1471   The Waltons   CBS
Program Type Drama Series
60 minutes. Thursdays. Premiere date: 9/14/72.
Sixth season premiere: 9/15/77. Special two-
hour episodes: 11/3/77, 12/29/77, 2/16/78,
3/16/78. Family drama set in Walton's Moun-
tain, VA. during the 1930s depression. Created
by Earl Hamner and based on his novel and the
television special "The Homecoming." Standard
sign-off: the Walton's bedroom lights go off as
they bid each other goodnight. Theme music by
Jerry Goldsmith.
Executive Producers Lee Rich, Earl Hamner
Producer Andy White
Company Lorimar Productions
Directors Various
Executive Story Consultant Earl Hamner
Writers Various
Narrator Earl Hamner
CAST
John .... Ralph Waite
Olivia .... Michael Learned
Grandma .... Ellen Corby
Grandpa .... Will Geer
Mary Ellen .... Judy Norton-Taylor
Erin .... Mary McDonough
Jason .... Jon Walmsley
Ben .... Eric Scott
Jim-Bob .... David Harper
Elizabeth .... Kami Cotler
Ike Godsey .... Joe Conley
Corabeth .... Ronnie Claire Edwards
Curtis Willard .... Tom Bower
Emily Baldwin .... Mary Jackson
Mamie Baldwin .... Helen Kleeb

The War Between the Men and Women
See NBC Monday Night at the Movies

1472 The War Between the Tates
NBC Monday/Saturday Night at the Movies
Program Type TV Movie
2 hours. Premiere date: 6/13/77. Repeat date: 7/1/78. Comedy-drama of a marriage threatened by marital infidelity. Based on the novel by Alison Lurie. Music by John Barry. Filmed in Toronto, Canada.
Executive Producer David Susskind
Producer Frederick Brogger
Company Talent Associates Ltd. in association with NBC-TV
Director Lee Phillips
Writer Barbara Turner
Art Director Earl Preston
CAST
Brian Tate .... Richard Crenna
Erica Tate .... Elizabeth Ashley
Danielle .... Ann Wedgeworth
Wendy .... Annette O'Toole
Sanford Finkelstein .... Granville Van Dusen
Mathilda .... Laura Patrick
Jeffrey .... Shawn Campbell
Leonard .... Colin Fox
Roo .... Julie Philips
Celia .... Mina Badiyi

1473 The War Widow
Visions   PBS
Program Type Dramatic Special
90 minutes. Premiere date: 10/28/76. Repeat date: 1/22/78. An original television play dramatizing the relationship between two women during World War I. Program made possible by grants from the Ford Foundation, the National Endowment for the Arts and the Corporation for Public Broadcasting.
Producer Barbara Schultz
Company KCET-TV/Los Angeles
Director Paul Bogart
Writer Harvey Perr
Costume Designer Sandra Stewart
Production Designer Ralph Holmes
CAST
Amy .... Pamela Bellwood
Jenny .... Frances Lee McCain
Sarah .... Katharine Bard
Emily .... Maxine Stuart
Kate .... Barbara Cason
Annie .... Nan Martin
Beth .... Stephanie Retsek
VOICES
Leonard .... Tim Matheson

A Warm December *See* CBS Special Movie Presentations

1474 Washington Behind Closed Doors
ABC Novel for Television   ABC
Program Type Limited Series
10-1/2 hours. Premiere date: 9/6–10/77. Based, in part, on John Ehrlichman's novel, "The Company." Created by David W. Rintels. Music for Parts I, II, III, V and VI by Dominic Frontiere. Music for Part IV by Richard Markowitz; theme by Dominic Frontiere. Filmed on location in Washington, DC, in and around Los Angeles, and at Paramount Studio.
Executive Producer Stanley Kallis
Supervising Producers Eric Bercovici, David W. Rintels
Producer Norman Powell
Associate Producer Frank Cardea
Company A Stanley Kallis, David W. Rintels, Eric Bercovici Production in association with Paramount Television
Director Gary Nelson
Writers Eric Bercovici, David W. Rintels
Production Designer Jack DeShields
Art Director James Claytor
Set Decorator Barbara Krieger
Cinematographers Joseph Biroc, Jack Swain
Film Editors Gerald J. Wilson, Harry Kaye, Arthur Hilton
Technical Advisors Ronand J. Ostrow, Robert L. Jackson
CAST
Walter Turlock .... Phillip R. Allen
Alex Coffee .... Michael Anderson, Jr.
Bass .... Madison Arnold
Adam Gardiner .... Tony Bill
Jack Atherton .... Linden Chiles
Eli McGinn .... Peter Coffield
Elmer Morse .... Thayer David
Mrs. Monckton .... June Dayton
Kathy Ferris .... Diana Ewing
Jennie Jamison .... Meg Foster
Tibbitts .... Rick Gates
Brewster Perry .... George Gaynes
Carl Tessler .... Harold Gould
Esker Scott Anderson .... Andy Griffith
Jimmy Bird .... Joseph Hacker
Mrs. Anderson .... Danna Hansen
Lars Haglund .... Skip Homeier
Myron Dunn .... John Houseman
Dorothy Kemp .... Jean Cameron Howell
Ashton .... John Kerr
Anne Marie Lowman .... Mary LaRoche
Tucker Tallford .... John Lehne
Clifford Ryan .... Charles MacCauley
Allison .... Frank Marth
Paul Stoner Gardiner .... Frances Lee McCain
Bob Bailey .... Barry Nelson
Linda Martin .... Lois Nettleton
Simon Cappell .... Alan Oppenheimer
Wanda Elliott .... Lara Parker
Sally Whalen .... Stefanie Powers
Joe Wisnovsky .... Barry Primus
Hank Ferris .... Nicholas Pryor
Bennett Lowman .... John Randolph
Al Donnally .... James Ray
Richard Monckton .... Jason Robards

Washington Behind Closed Doors
Continued

William Martin	Cliff Robertson
Sid Gold	Fred Sadoff
Gus	J. Jay Saunders
Roger Castle	David Selby
Saraceni	Borah Silver
Peter Ozymandias	Joseph Sirola
Patti	Karen Smith Bercovici
Frank Flaherty	Robert Vaughn

1475 Washington Week in Review   PBS
Program Type Public Affairs Series
30 minutes. Fridays. Premiere date: 2/22/67. Continuous. Regular and guest reporters discuss the top national and international stories of the week. Series funded by grants from the Corporation for Public Broadcasting, the Ford Foundation and Public Television Stations.
Producer Elvera Ruby
Company WETA-TV/Washington, D.C.
Director Jim Eddins
Moderator Paul Duke
Regulars Neil McNeil, Charles Corddry

1476 Watch Your Mouth   PBS
Program Type Educational/Cultural Series
30 minutes. Premiere date: 4/8/78. Series of 10 programs addresses problems of language skills and communication for teenagers roughly between ages 14–17. Developed and designed by Ellis B. Haizlip. Program made possible by a grant from U.S. Dept. of Health, Education and Welfare.
Executive Producer Ellis B. Haizlip
Producers Alonzo Brown, Jr., Carlos De Jesus, Anna Horsford
Company WNET-TV/Thirteen, New York
Writers Bill Gunn, Ilunga Adell, Osa Iyaun, Michael Griffin, Gregory Robinson, Chiz Schultz
Curriculum Advisor Vivian C. Jackson
Consultants Dr. Milton Baxter, Dr. Richard Wright, Dr. Alberto Rey
Guest Artists Ruby Dee, Stephanie Mills, Sarah Dash, Alfred Drake, Frances Foster, Paul Roebling, Jr., Gretchen Wyler
CAST

Raymond Geeter	Joseph Morton

The Way We Were See The ABC Sunday Night Movie

1477 The Weather Machine   PBS
Program Type Documentary/Informational Special
2 hours. Premiere date: 2/24/75. Repeat date: 1/7/78. Special on climate and climate control. Program made possible by a grant from Champion International Corporation.

Company WNET/New York
Writer Nigel Calder
Correspondent David Prowitt

1478 Weekend   NBC
Program Type News Magazine Series
90 minutes. Monthly (the first Saturday each month). Premiere date: 10/19/74. Fourth season premiere: 10/1/77. Late-night television magazine with three or more topics each edition. Created by Reuven Frank.
Executive Producer Reuven Frank
Producers Various
Company NBC News
Director Gerald Polikoff
Head Writer Lloyd Dobyns
Anchor Lloyd Dobyns

1479 Welcome Back, Kotter   ABC
Program Type Comedy Series
30 minutes. Thursdays. Premiere date: 9/9/75. Third season premiere: 9/15/77. Comedy about a teacher assigned to his old high school in Brooklyn to teach the "Sweathogs." Series created by Gabriel Kaplan and Alan Sack; developed for television by Peter Meyerson. Music by John B. Sebastian.
Executive Producer James Komack
Supervising Producer Peter Meyerson
Producer Nick Arnold
Company The Komack Company, Inc. and Wolper Productions
Directors Various
Writers Various
CAST

Gabe Kotter	Gabriel Kaplan
Julie Kotter	Marcia Strassman
Mr. Woodman	John Sylvester White
Juan Epstein	Robert Hegyes
Freddie (Boom Boom) Washington	Lawrence-Hilton Jacobs
Arnold Horshack	Ron Palillo
Vinnie Barbarino	John Travolta

1480 Welfare   PBS
Program Type Documentary/Informational Special
3 hours. Season premiere: 6/5/78. Documentary on the operations of the New York City welfare system.
Producer Frederick Wiseman
Company WNET-TV/New York
Director Frederick Wiseman

1481 Wendy's Tennis Classic   PBS
Program Type Sports Special
3 hours. 8/13/78. Live coverage from the Murifield Village Country Club near Columbus, Ohio.

Program made possible by a grant from the Pepsi Cola Company.
Executive Producer Greg Harney
Company WGBH-TV/Boston
Commentators Bud Collins, Donald Dell

1482 West Berlin Town Meeting CBS
Program Type News Special
Live coverage of President Carter's participation in a West Berlin Town Meeting at Congress Hall 7/15/78.
Executive Producer Russ Bensley
Company CBS News
Anchor Bob Schieffer

West Side Story *See* The CBS Tuesday Night Movies

1483 Westchester Classic CBS
Program Type Sports Special
Live and taped coverage of the final rounds of the $300,000 Westchester Classic from the Westchester Country Club in Rye, NY 8/19/78 and 8/20/78.
Producer Frank Chirkinian
Company CBS Television Network Sports
Directors Bob Dailey, Frank Chirkinian
Commentators Vin Scully, Pat Summerall, Jack Whitaker, Ben Wright, Rick Barry, Frank Glieber, Ken Venturi

1484 Western Open CBS
Program Type Sports Special
Live and taped coverage of the final rounds of the 75th Open from the Butler National Golf Club, Oak Brook, Ill. 7/1/78 and 7/2/78.
Executive Producer Frank Chirkinian
Company CBS Television Network Sports
Directors Bob Dailey, Frank Chirkinian
Commentators Vin Scully, Pat Summerall, Jack Whitaker, Frank Glieber, Ben Wright, Ken Venturi

1485 We've Got Each Other CBS
Program Type Comedy Series
30 minutes. Saturdays. Premiere date: 10/7/77. Last show: 1/7/78. Plain-looking married couple reverses roles.
Executive Producers Tom Patchett, Jay Tarses
Producer Jack Burns
Company MTM Enterprises, Inc.
Directors Various
Writers Various
CAST
Stuart Hibbard .... Oliver Clark
Judy Hibbard .... Beverly Archer
Damon Jerome .... Tom Poston
Dee Dee .... Joan Van Ark

Donna .... Ren Woods
Ken Redford .... Martin Kove

1486 What a Nightmare, Charlie Brown CBS
Program Type Animated Film Special
30 minutes. Premiere date: 2/23/78. Written and created by Charles M. Schulz. Music by Ed Bogas. "Linus and Lucy Theme" by Vince Guaraldi.
Executive Producer Lee Mendelson
Producer Bill Mendelson
Company Lee Mendolson-Bill Melendez Productions, in cooperation with United Features Syndicate, Inc. and Charles M. Schulz Creative Associates
Directors Phil Roman, Bill Melendez
VOICES
Charlie Brown .... Liam Martin
Snoopy .... Bill Melendez

1487 What Katy Did
Once Upon a Classic PBS
Program Type Drama Series
30 minutes. Premiere date: 1/5/78. 6-part series about a 19th century 15-year-old, by Susan Coolidge. Presented by WQED-TV/Pittsburgh and McDonald's Local Restaurants Assn.
Executive Producer Jay Rayvid
Producer Barry Letts
Company Time-Life Television/BBC-TV
Director Julia Smith
Host Bill Bixby
CAST
Katy Carr .... Claire Walker
Aunt Izzie .... Thomasine Heiner
Dr. Carr. .... Ed Bishop
Clover Carr .... Julia Lewis
Elsie Carr .... Virginia Fiol
Dorothy Carr .... Scott Kunz
Cousin Helen .... Toria Fuller
Lily Page .... Caroline Hinton
Rose Red .... Kate Lock
Bella .... Jane Slaughter
Miss Jane .... Delia Paton

1488 What Really Happened to the Class of '65 NBC
Program Type Drama Series
60 minutes. Thursdays. Premiere date: 12/8/77. Telecast through 3/9/78. Resumed with special-2-hour telecast: 5/25/78. Last show of series: 7/27/78. Series based on non-fiction book by Michael Medved and David Wallechinsky.
Executive Producer Richard Irving
Director Harry Falk
Company Pan Arts Prods. and Universal TV
Writers Various
Directors Various
Narrator Tony Bill

1489 What's a Museum for, Anyway?
The CBS Festival of Lively Arts for Young
People   CBS
Program Type Children's Special
60 minutes. Premiere date: 2/5/78. Introduction
into the treasures found in the National Gallery
and in other museums throughout the country.
Special appearances by Joan Mondale, J. Carter
Brown, and Soupy Sales.
Executive Producers Robert Stolfi, Lester Gott-
lieb
Producer Burt Shevelove
Company Stolfi-Gottlieb Associates
Director Sid Smith
Writer Thomas Baum
Host Gabriel Kaplan

1490 What's Cooking   PBS
Program Type Miscellaneous Series
30 minutes. Wednesdays. Premiere date:
1/21/76. Series repeated: 6/7/78 and 9/6/78.
13-week low cost, high nutrition cooking series.
Producer Lynn Lonker
Company WHYY-TV/Wilmington-Philadel-
phia
Director Doug Bailey
Host LeDeva Davis

1491 What's Happened to Cambodia
                                                CBS
Program Type News Special
60 minutes. Premiere date: 6/7/78. First exten-
sive look at Cambodia since the revolution.
Executive Producer Leslie Midgley
Senior Producer Ernest Leiser
Producers Phyllis Bosworth, Brian Ellis
Company CBS News
Film Editor Patricia O'Gorman
Anchor Ed Bradley
Researcher Angela Le Juge

1492 What's Happening!!   ABC
Program Type Comedy Series
30 minutes. Thursdays/Saturdays. (from
1/21/78 to 4/13/78.) Premiere date: 8/5/76 (as
a four-week summer series). Second season
premiere: 9/22/78. Series about three high-spir-
ited black teenagers, their families and their
friends. Music by Henry Mancini.
Executive Producers Bud Yorkin, Saul Turtel-
taub; Bernie Orenstein
Producer Lloyd Schwartz
Company TOY Productions
Director Mark Warren
Writers Various
                     CAST
Roger "Raj" Thomas .... Ernest Thomas
Dwayne .... Haywood Nelson
Rerun .... Fred Berry
Mrs. Thomas .... Mabel King

Dee Thomas .... Danielle Spencer
Shirley .... Shirley Hemphill

1493 What's Happening to the Family?
                                                NBC
Program Type Religious/Cultural Special
30 minutes. Premiere date: 6/11/78. The Rev.
Donald Brusius, Family Life Director of the Lutheran Church-Missouri Synod, discusses his
views on the changing role of the family today
with NBC News correspondent Betty Rollin.
Producer Doris Ann
Director Robert Priaulx

1494 What's Up Doc?   ABC
Program Type Comedy Special
30 minutes. Premiere date: 5/27/78. Pilot for TV
series from movie of the same name.
Executive Producer Hal Kanter
Producer Michael Norell
Company Warner Bros. Television
Director E. W. Swackhamer
                     CAST
Howard .... Barry Van Dyke
Claudia .... Caroline McWilliams
Urban Wyatt .... Don Porter
Amanda Wyatt .... Neva Patterson
Fabian Leek .... Jeffrey Kramer

1495 Wheel of Fortune   NBC
Program Type Game/Audience Participation
Series
30 minutes. Mondays–Fridays. Premiere date:
1/6/75. Continuous. Word-gambling game for
cash and merchandise.
Producer Nancy Jones
Company A Merv Griffin Production in associa-
tion with NBC-TV
Director Jeff Goldstein
Hosts Chuck Woolery, Susan Stafford
Announcer Charlie O'Connell

1496 Wheels
The Big Event/NBC Monday Night at the
Movies   NBC
Program Type Limited Series
10 hours. 5/7–15/78. Dramatization of the Ar-
thur Hailey novel about the automobile industry.
Teleplay by Millard Lampell and Hank Searls.
Executive Producer Roy Huggins
Producer Robert F. O'Neill
Company Universal Studios with NBC-TV
Director Jerry London
                     CAST
Adam Trenton .... Rock Hudson
Erica Trenton .... Lee Remick
Barbara Lipton .... Blair Brown
Greg Trenton .... Howard McGillin
Peter Flodenhale .... John Beck
Lowell Baxter .... Ralph Bellamy

Rusty Horton ....Gerald S. O'Loughlin
Smokey ....Anthony Franciosa
Teresa ....Adele Mara
Wingate ....Fred Williamson
Merv Rucks ....John Durren
Val ....Debi Richter
Hub Hewitson .... Tim O'Connor
Ursula ....Jessica Walter
Rollie Knight .... Harold Sylvester
Kirk Trenton .... James Carroll Jordan
Parkland .... Johnny Crawford
Newkirk .... Al White
Emerson Vale .... Anthony Costello
Al Holleb .... Ray Singer
Jody Horton ....Lisa Eilbacher
Dr. Patterson .... David Spielberg
Sir Phillip .... James Booth

1497 When Every Day Was the Fourth of July

The Big Event   NBC
Program Type Dramatic Special
2 hours. Premiere date: 3/12/78. An attorney
faces strong hostility when he defends a local
handyman.
Producer Dan Curtis
Company Dan Curtis Production
Director Dan Curtis
Writer Lee Hutson
                          CAST
Ed Cooper .... Dean Jones
Millie Cooper .... Louise Sorel
Daniel Cooper ....Chris Petersen
Sarah Cooper .... Katy Kurtzman
Prosecutor Antonelli .... Harris Yulin
The Snow Man .... Geoffrey Lewis
Officer Doyle ....Scott Brady
Mrs. Najarian .... Ronnie Claire Edwards
Herman Grasser .... Ben Piazza
Judge Wheeler .... Henry Wilcoxon
Red Doyle ....Eric Shea
Mr. Najarian .... Michael Pataki

1498 Where Have All the People Gone?

Tuesday Movie of the Week   ABC
Program Type TV Movie
90 minutes. Premiere date: 10/8/74. Season
premiere: 11/22/77. Based on a story by Lewis
John Carlino.
Executive Producer Charles Fries
Producer Gerald I. Isenberg
Company Jozak Company, Alpine Productions
and Metromedia Producers Corporation in as-
sociation with NBC-TV
Director John Llewellyn Moxey
Writers Lewis John Carlino, Sandor Stern
                          CAST
Steven Anders .... Peter Graves
Jenny ....Verna Bloom
David Anders ....George O'Hanlon, Jr.
Deborah Anders .... Kathleen Quinlan
Michael .... Michael-James Wixted
Guide .... Nobel Willingham

1499 Where the Twisted Laurel Grows

PBS
Program Type Music/Dance Special
30 minutes. Premiere date: 6/4/78. Concert
taped at Marshall University, Huntington, West
Virginia. Performers are Lelly May Ledford; The
Red Clay Ramblers; and Tommy Jarrell. Pro-
gram made possible in part by a grant from the
Rockefeller Foundation.
Company WMUL-TV/Huntington, West Vir-
ginia

1500 Wherever We Lodge

NBC News Special   NBC
Program Type Religious/Cultural Special
60 minutes. Premiere date: 11/27/77. Documen-
tary of examples of hope and promise for solu-
tions to the worldwide problem of housing.
Executive Producer Doris Ann
Company NBC Television Religious Programs
Unit
Director Joseph Vadala
Writer Philip Scharper
Narrator Hugh Downs

1501 White Bear

Festival '78   PBS
Program Type Documentary/Informational
Special
60 minutes. Premiere date: 3/15/78. Documen-
tary on a Russian family that travels to Siberia
for five months of research on polar bears.
Company Soviet Television
Director Yari Ledin

White Lightning *See* The CBS Friday
  Night Movies

White Line Fever *See* The ABC Sunday
  Night Movie

1502 Whitewater, PA   PBS
Program Type Documentary/Informational
Special
30 minutes. Premiere date: 1/4/78. Explores the
sport of whitewater paddling and the variety of
whitewater sports available on Pennsylvania's
rivers and streams.
Company WPSX-TV/Clearfield

1503 Who Built This Place?   PBS
Program Type Documentary/Informational
Special
30 minutes. Premiere date: 4/23/74. Repeat
date: 8/6/78. The politics of landmark architecture in a comedy film using animation, historical
photographs and newsfilm. Filmed on location in

Who Built This Place? *Continued*
San Francisco, Boston, Atlanta and Dallas. Ragtime music composed by Paul Alan Levi and played by Helena Humann. Program partially funded by a grant from the National Endowment for the Arts.
Producer Samuel Hudson
Company KERA-TV/Dallas-Fort Worth
Directors Samuel Hudson, Ken Harrison
Cinematographer Kenneth Harrison
Film Editor Kenneth Harrison
Commentator Helena Humann

Who Is Harry Kellerman, and Why Is He Saying Those Terrible Things About Me? *See* NBC Movie of the Week

1504   Who Knows One?: The National Theatre of the Deaf Celebrates the Passover Seder   PBS
Program Type Religious/Cultural Special
30 minutes. Premiere date: 4/5/77. Repeat date: 4/20/78. Highlights of a seder held by the National Theatre of the Deaf in sign language, speech and song. Captioned for the hearing-impaired at WGBH-TV/Boston. Program made possible by grants from the National Theatre of the Deaf and the Bureau of Education for the Handicapped.
Producer Lucy Winslow
Company WGBH-TV/Boston and the National Theatre of the Deaf
Director David Atwood

1505   Who's Minding the Bank?
CBS Reports   CBS
Program Type Documentary/Informational Special
Premiere date: 3/7/78. Report on banking and its state and federal regulatory agencies.
Executive Producer Howard Stringer
Producer Steve Singer
Company CBS News
Writer Steve Singer
Cinematographer Larry Mitchell
Film Editor Joseph Fackovec
Researcher Susan D. Werbe
Reporter Bill Moyers

Wide World of Sports *See* ABC's Wide World of Sports

1506   Wild About Harry
Comedy Time   NBC
Program Type Comedy Special
30 minutes. Premiere date: 5/26/78. Pilot about a 45-year-old architect and a 20-year-old girl. Based on British TV series, "Second Time Around."
Producers George Eckstein, Leonard B. Stern
Company Universal Television
Director Robert Moore
Writer Richard Waring
CAST
Harry .... Efrem Zimbalist, Jr.
Vickie Knowles .... Andrea Howard
Don .... Bernie Kopell
Maggie .... Elaine Giftos
Delia .... Reva Rose
Jennie .... Stephanie Zimbalist
Sophie .... Ruth Manning
Sheila Marshall .... Gloria Strock
Larry Marshall .... George Sperdakos
Frank Knowles .... Dick Yarmy
Molly Knowles .... Emmaline Henry
Grace Baxter .... Queenie Smith
Pam .... Ruth Price

1507   Wild and Wooly
The ABC Monday Night Movie   ABC
Program Type TV Movie
2 hours. Premiere date: 2/20/78. Three women find romance, excitement and danger in the early 1900s in the last days of the Old West. Music by Charles Bernstein. Women's wardrobe by Nolan Miller.
Executive Producers Aaron Spelling, Douglas S. Cramer
Supervising Producer E. Duke Vincent
Producer Earl W. Wallace
Company An Aaron Spelling Production
Director Philip Leacock
Writer Earl W. Wallace
Art Directors Howard Kunin, Dennis Duckwell
CAST
Lacey .... Chris De Lisle
Liz .... Susan Bigelow
Shiloh .... Elyssa Davalos
Delaney Burke .... Doug McClure
Teddy Roosevelt .... David Doyle
Warden .... Vic Morrow
Otis Bergen .... Ross Martin
Tobias Singleton .... Paul Burke
Jessica .... Sherry Bain
Sean .... Charles Siebert
Megan .... Jessica Walter
Burgie .... Med Flory
Will .... Mark Withers
Demas Scott .... Robert J. Wilkie
Mark Hannah .... Kenneth Toby
Percy .... Eugene Butler
Sophie .... Joan Crosby
O'Rourke .... Wayne Grace
McHenry .... Jim Lough
Foreman .... Bill Smillie

1508   Wild Kingdom   Syndicated
Program Type Science/Nature Series
30 minutes. Weekly. Show premiered in 1962.

Season premiere: 9/77. Oldest of the animal documentary shows.
Producer Don Meier
Associate Producers Warren Garst, Richard Reinauer, Lorena Meier
Company Don Meier Productions, Inc.
Distributor Mutual of Omaha
Director Don Meier
Host Marlin Perkins

1509 Wild, Wild World of Animals
Syndicated
Program Type Science/Nature Series
30 minutes. Weekly. Premiere date: 9/73. Fifth Season Premiere: 9/77. Animals in their natural habitats fighting for survival.
Producer Jonathan Donald
Company Time-Life Television Productions
Narrator William Conrad

1510 Wilder and Wilder   CBS
Program Type Comedy Special
30 minutes. Premiere date: 8/26/78. Pilot about a married television writing team.
Executive Producer Mark Carliner
Producers Austin Kalish, Irma Kalish
Company Mark Carliner Productions, Inc./Viacom Enterprises
Director Peter H. Hunt
Writers Austin Kalish, Irma Kalish
CAST
Sam Wilder .... Greg Mullavey
Steffi Wilder ....Meredith MacRae
Jason .... T. K. Carter
Roger Bacon ....Lonnie Shorr
Al Meredith ....Louis Criscoulo
Tina Chambers ....Susan Lanier
Phil Crawford .... Warren Burton
Joel ....Vaughn Armstrong

1511 Wilder, Wilder   PBS
Program Type Dramatic Special
30 minutes. Premiere date: 8/30/78. Four plays by Thornton Wilder. Program made possible by grants from Univ. of Wisconsin Graduate School, Friends of Channel 21, Inc., Wisconsin ETV Network, and Wisconsin Arts Board.
Producer Rudi Goldman
Company University of Wisconsin-Extension Telecommunications Center
Director Rudi Goldman

1512 The Wilds of Ten Thousand Islands   CBS
Program Type Dramatic Special
60 minutes. Premiere date: 2/24/78 Adventure drama about a contemporary family living and working in western Florida. Animal trainers are

Bill Vergis, Brenda Watt, Lisa Debedts, and Chris Moorehouse.
Executive Producers Lee Rich, Philip Capice
Producer Andy White
Company Lorimar Productions, Inc.
Director Charles S. Dubin
Writers Andy White, Paul West
CAST
Dr. Jeff Wild .... Chris Robinson
Dr. Barbara Wild .... Julie Gregg
Clara Mooney .... Rachel Roberts
Sara Wild .... Mary Ellen McKeon
Tim Wild .... Charles Aiken
Fred Osceola ....John Kauffman
Orville .... John Ashton
Miss Kathy .... Monica Gayle

1513 Willa Cather's America   PBS
Program Type Documentary/Informational Special
60 minutes. Premiere date: 5/9/78. Documentary portrait of novelist Willa Cather by Richard Schickel.
Producer Richard Schickel
Company WNET-TV/New York
Narrator Hal Holbrook
Cather's Voice Gena Rowlands

1514 Williamson Disaster   PBS
Program Type Documentary/Informational Special
30 minutes. Premiere date: 7/5/78. Documentary on the aftermath of West Virginia flood disaster.
Producer Pegg Cerniglia
Company WSWP-TV/Berkley, West Virginia
Host Pegg Cerniglia
Commentators Robert Byrd, Jennings Randolph, Nick Joe Rahall

Willy Wonka and the Chocolate Factory
See NBC Movie of the Week

1515 Wilma
NBC World Premiere Movie/NBC Monday Night at the Movies   NBC
Program Type TV Movie
2 hours. Premiere date: 12/19/77. Movie about the career of Wilma Rudolph. Filmed in Tennessee.
Executive Producer Cappy Petrash Greenspan
Producer Bud Greenspan
Company Cappy Production in association with NBC-TV
Director Bud Greenspan
Writer Bud Greenspan
CAST
Wilma .... Shirley Jo Finney
Blanche Rudolph .... Cicely Tyson
Ed Rudolph ....Joe Seneca

Wilma *Continued*

Ed Temple ....Jason Bernard
Robert Eldridge .... Denzel Washington, Jr.
Coach Gray .... Charles Blackwell
Mae Faggs .... Paulette Pearson
Pappy Marshall .... Dury Cox
Martha Hudson .... Andrea Frierson
Dr. Gordon .... Norman Matlock
Tootie ....Stacey Green
Dr. Williams .... Roger Askew
The Principal .... J. Franklin Taylor

1516   Wimbledon   NBC
Program Type Sports Special
10-1/2 hours. Tape-delayed satellite coverage of
early-round and finals matches in the 101st
Wimbledon Tennis Championships from the All-
England Lawn Tennis and Croquet Club outside
London 7/1/78–7/8/78.
Executive Producer Don Ohlmeyer
Producers Ted Nathanson, Geoff Mason
Company NBC Sports
Director Ted Nathanson
Commentators Jim Simpson, Bud Collins, John
   Newcombe, Hilary Hilton

The Wind and The Lion *See* NBC
   Monday Night at the Movies

1517   Windows, Doors & Keyholes NBC
Program Type Comedy Special
60 minutes. Premiere date: 5/16/78. Adult
comedy pilot.
Executive Producer Leonard B. Stern
Producer Arne Sultan
Company Heyday Productions and Universal
   TV
Director Leonard B. Stern
Writers Arne Sultan, Earl Barret, Bill Dana,
   Leonard B. Stern
Actors Telly Savalas, Lindsay Wagner, John
   Schuck, Bill Dana, Hamilton Camp, Peter
   Palmer, Pat Cronin, Esther Sunderland, Ly-
   man Ward, Candy Ann Brown, Ceil Cabot,
   Robert Doyle, MacIntyre Dixon, Dee Dee
   Rescher, Linda Redford, Joy Garrett, Hilary
   Beane, Trisha Hart, Mickey Deems

1518   The Winged Colt
ABC Children's Novel for Television/ABC
Weekend Specials   ABC
Program Type Children's Special
90 minutes. Premiere date: 9/10/77. Shown
three consecutive weekends: 9/10, 9/17,
9/24/77. Repeat dates: 2/11/, 2/18, 2/25/78.
Based on a novel by Betsy Byars. Music by
Tommy Leonetti. Special photo effects by Phil
Kellison. The story of how a former movie stunt-
man and his greenhorn nephew become the own-
ers of a mysterious colt born with wings. Tele-
play by Jim Inman.
Executive Producer Robert Chenault
Producer Tom Armistead
Company An ABC Circle Film
Director Larry Elikann
Cinematographer Otto Nemenz
Colt Trainer Al Yanks
Dog Trainer Lou Schumacher
                        CAST
Uncle Coot .... Slim Pickens
Mrs. Minney ....Jane Withers
Charles .... Ike Eisenmann
Mr. Minney ....Frank Cady
Hiram the Hermit ....Keenan Wynn

1519   Winner Take All   CBS
Program Type TV Movie
60 minutes. Premiere date: 4/1/77. Season
premiere: 8/18/78. Crime drama pilot about a
police lieutenant and a free-lance insurance in-
vestigator. Music by John Elizalde.
Executive Producer Quinn Martin
Supervising Producer Russell Stoneham
Producer John Wilder
Company Quinn Martin Productions
Director Robert Day
Writer Cliff Gould
Art Director Herman Zimmerman
                        CAST
Charlie Quigley ....Michael Murphy
Allison Nash .... Joanna Pettet
E. P. Woodhouse ....Clive Revill
Mo Rellis .... Mark Gordon
Hiram Yerby .... David Huddleston
Maria von Alsburg ....Signe Hasso
Solange Dupree ....Martine Beswick
Room Clerk .... John Fiedler
Clarence Woo .... James Hong
Claude Villemont .... Alain Patrick
Mae Burt ....Dorothy Meyer
Swenson .... Loni Anderson
Hank .... James McCallion
Maitre D' .... Maurice Marsac
Waiter ....Roger Etienne
Herbie .... Bob Delegall
Fireman .... Dave Cass
Hood .... Frank Michael Liu
Second Hood .... Byron Chung
Third Hood .... Ken Endoso
Doyle ....Stephen Farr
Officer .... Phil Adams

1520   The Winners   CBS
Program Type Children's Series
30 minutes. Premiere date: 10/13/77. Dramatic
specials for young people broadcast the second
Thursday of each month. Stories demonstrate
how young people can reach their goals despite
personal and physical obstacles. Shows seen during the 1977–78 season are: "The Cruise of the
Courageous," "I Can!," "Journey Together,"

"Mobile Maidens," and "You Gotta Start Somewhere." (*See* individual titles for credits.)

1521 Winnie the Pooh and the Honey Tree NBC
Program Type Animated Film Special
30 minutes. Premiere date: 3/10/70. Repeat date: 11/25/77. Pooh develops a weight problem from eating too much honey and also has difficulty staying away from angry bees near the honey tree. Based on the stories by A. A. Milne.
Company Walt Disney Production
Director Wolfgang Reitherman
Writers Larry Clemmons, Xavier Atencio, Vance Gerry, Ralph Wright, Ken Anderson, Dick Lucas
VOICES
Pooh .... Sterling Holloway
Eeyore .... Ralph Wright
Owl .... Hal Smith
Christopher Robin .... Bruce Reitherman
Kanga .... Barbara Luddy
Roo .... Clint Howard
Rabbit .... Junius Matthews
Gopher .... Howard Morris

With Six You Get Eggroll *See* NBC Monday Night at the Movies

1522 With This Ring
The ABC Friday Night Movie ABC
Program Type TV Movie
2 hours. Premiere date: 5/5/78. As wedding dates rapidly approach, engaged couples and their families are involved in emotional crises. Music by George Aliceson Tipton.
Executive Producer Gerald W. Abrams
Producer Bruce J. Sallan
Company The Jozak Company in association with Paramount Television
Director James Sheldon
Writer Terence Mulcahy
Film Editor Jerry Dronsky
CAST
Peter .... Tony Bill
Edward .... Tom Bosley
Dolores .... Diana Canova
Viola .... Barbara Cason
Jilly .... Joyce DeWitt
Gen. Albert Harris .... John Forsythe
Tom .... Scott Hylands
James .... Donny Most
Alvin .... Dick Van Patten
Evelyn .... *...Betty White
Kate .... Deborah White
Dirk .... Peter Jason
Neil .... Harry Moses
Claude .... Marty Zagon
Bill .... Charles Thomas Murphy
Lenny .... Howard George
Mr. Pheeb .... Darrell Zwerling
Lisa .... Mary Frances Crosby

The Wizard of Oz *See* CBS Special Movie Presentations

1523 The Wolfman Jack Show Syndicated
Program Type Music/Comedy/Variety Series
30 minutes. Premiere date: 10/1/77. Wolfman Jack introducing acts, singing and playing skits.
Company Howl Productions, CBC
Directors Mark Warren, Donald Davis
Writers Mort Scharfman, Brad Hammond
Host Wolfman Jack

1524 Woman of Valor NBC
Program Type Religious/Cultural Special
60 minutes. Premiere date: 3/20/77. Repeat date: 7/30/78. Drama about Jewish settlers in New York City in the late 18th century based on a work by Morton Wishengrad.
Executive Producer Doris Ann
Producer Martin Hoade
Company NBC Television Religious Programs Unit in association with the Jewish Theological Seminary of America
Director Martin Hoade
Writer Virginia Mazer
CAST
Jessy Judah .... Carol Teitel
Walter Judah .... Donald Warfield

Womantime and Co. *See* Turnabout

1525 Women's Intercollegiate Invitational Gymnastics PBS
Program Type Sports Special
60 minutes. Premiere date: 7/9/78. Repeat date: 7/15/78. Top female gymnasts compete in Salt Lake City.
Company KUED-TV/Salt Lake City, Utah
Commentator Cathy Rigby

1526 The Wonderful World of Disney NBC
Program Type Children's Series
60 minutes. Sundays. Premiere date: 9/24/61. Seventeenth Season Premiere: 9/18/77. The longest-running prime-time program on television. Anthology series of nature stories, adventures, cartoons, dramas and comedies—some made for television and others originally released as theatrical features by Disney Studios. Several two-hour shows presented during the 1977–78 season.
Executive Producer Ron Miller
Producers Various
Company Walt Disney Productions in association with NBC-TV
Directors Various
Writers Various

1527 Word Grabbers   Syndicated
Program Type Game/Audience Participation
Series
30 minutes. Premiere date: 9/77. Fast-paced
game show with host Art James.
Executive Producer J. Reginald Dunlap
Producer Ron Greenberg
Company Show Biz, Inc.
Director Arthur Forrest

1528 World   PBS
Program Type Documentary/Informational
Series
60 minutes. Premiere date: 2/2/78. 13-part series
of international documentaries focusing on the
political, economic and social forces behind
global events. Series made possible by grants
from the Corporation for Public Broadcasting,
Polaroid Corporation, the Charles E. Merrill
Trust, the Ford Foundation, the German Mar-
shall Fund of the United States and the Charles
Stewart Mott Foundation.
Executive Producer David Fanning
Company WGBH-TV/Boston
Commentators John Chancellor, Joseph Angotti

1529 The World Beyond   CBS
Program Type Dramatic Special
60 minutes. Premiere date: 1/27/78. Supernatu-
ral drama about a sports writer brought back
from the brink of death, filmed in Canada. Music
composed and conducted by Fred Karlin.
Created and written by Art Wallace.
Executive Producer David Suskind
Producer Frederick Brogger
Company Time-Life Films, Inc.
Director Nel Black
CAST
Paul Taylor .... Granville Van Dusen
Marian Faber .... Jo-Beth Williams
Andy Borchard .... Barnard Hughes
Frank Faber .... Richard Fitzpatrick
Sam Barker .... Jan Van Evera

**1530 World Heavyweight
Championship-Muhammad Ali vs. Earnie
Shavers**   NBC
Program Type Sports Special
2 hours. Live coverage of World Heavyweight
Champion Muhammad Ali and Earnie Shavers
from Madison Square Garden, New York,
9/29/77. On the same program: non-title Light-
weight bout between Alexis Arguello and Jerome
Artis; non-title Lightheavyweight bout between
Mike Rossman and Gary Summerhayes.
Producers Ted Nathanson, Jim Marooney
Company NBC Sports
Director Ted Nathanson
Commentator Ken Norton

Sportscasters Joe Garagiola, Dick Enberg, Larry
Merchant

**1531 World Heavyweight Championship
—Muhammad Ali vs. Leon Spinks**   CBS
Program Type Sports Special
Live coverage of World Heavyweight Title Bout
from the Las Vegas Hilton between Muhammad
Ali and Leon Spinks 2/15/78. On the same pro-
gram: Featherweight title between Danny Lopez
and David Kotey, and Light Heavyweights Mi-
chael Spinks and Tom Bethea
Producer Frank Chirkinian
Company CBS Sports
Director Frank Chirkinian
Hosts Brent Musburger, Tim Ryan
Expert Analysts Dr. Ferdi Pacheco, Angelo
Dundee, Gil Clancy
Commentator Jack Whitaker

**1532 The World Invitational Racquets
Championship**   CBS
Program Type Sports Special
60 minutes. Premiere date: 6/11/78. Taped high-
lights of the World Racquets Championship
Tournament from San Diego, CA.
Company CBS Television Network Sports
Director Perry Smith
Commentators Tony Trabert, Pat Summerall

**1533 The World Invitational Tennis
Classic**   ABC
Program Type Sports Series
90 minutes. 5/14/78. 11-week series of taped ten-
nis matches from Sea Pines Plantation on Hilton
Head Island, South Carolina.
Executive Producer Roone Arledge
Hosts Chris Schenkel, Andrea Kirby, Pancho
Gonzalez

1534 The World of Charlie Company
    CBS
Program Type News Special
60 minutes. Premiere date: 1/17/78. Report on
the veterans of Vietnam and Cambodia, the foot
soldiers of Charlie Company.
Executive Producer Leslie Midgley
Senior Producer Ernest Leiser
Producer Bernard Birnbaum
Cinematographers Robert Gaff, Keith Kulin,
Cynthia Lund, Huxley H. Galbraith, Jr., Cal
Marlin, George Christian, John Smith, Louis
Ledford
Videotape Editors Robert Reingold, Al Rausch
Researcher Margaret Erschler
Reporter Bruce Morton

1535 **The World of Franklin and Jefferson**   PBS
Program Type Documentary/Informational Special
30 minutes. Premiere date: 5/10/77. Repeat date: 11/4/77. A mixed-media look at 18th century America and the accomplishments of Benjamin Franklin and Thomas Jefferson. Music by Elmer Bernstein. Program made possible by a grant from the IBM Corporation.
Producers Charles Eames, Ray Eames
Company KCET-TV/Los Angeles and the Office of Charles and Ray Eames for the American Revolution Bicentennial Administration
Narrators Orson Welles, Nina Foch

1536 **World Series**   ABC
Program Type Sports Special
Live coverage of the 1977 World Series between the Los Angeles Dodgers and the New York Yankees 10/11/77–10/18/77.
Executive Producer Roone Arledge
Producer Chuck Howard
Company ABC Sports
Director Chet Forte
Announcers Keith Jackson, Tom Seaver, Howard Cosell
Commentators Bill White, Ross Porter

1537 **The World Series of Auto Racing**   ABC
Program Type Limited Sports Series
60 minutes. Premiere date: 1/14/78. International Race of Champions (a series of four match races with identically prepared cars) 1/14/78 from Michigan International Speedway; 1/28/78 and 2/11/78 from Riverside International Raceway; and 2/25/78 from Daytona International Speedway.
Executive Producer Roone Arledge
Producer Ned Steckel
Company ABC Sports
Director Larry Kamm
Sportscasters Jim McKay, Al Michaels
Expert Commentators Chris Economaki, Jackie Stewart

1538 **The World Series of Jazz**
In Performance at Wolf Trap   PBS
Program Type Music/Dance Special
60 minutes. Premiere date: 10/25/76. Repeat date: 8/12/78. Three jazz artists in concert with their own groups at the Wolf Trap Farm Park for the Performing Arts in Arlington, Va.: Earl "Fatha" Hines with Marva Josie and Eddie Graham; Rudy Rutherford and Harley White; Dizzy Gillespie with Rodney Jones; Earl May and Mickey Roker; Billy Eckstine and his 14-piece

orchestra. Program made possible by a grant from the Atlantic Richfield Company.
Producers David Prowitt, Ruth Leon
Company WETA-TV/Washington, DC
Director Stan Lathan
Conductor Bobby Tucker

1539 **World Skate Challenge**   CBS
Program Type Sports Special
60 minutes. Taped coverage of competition between two teams of world and Olympic class ice skating stars 3/19/78 from Omni International in Atlanta, Georgia.
Producer Perry Smith
Company CBS Sports
Director Bob Dailey
Announcer Brent Musburger
Expert Commentator Gary Visconti

1540 **World Team Tennis All-Star Match**   ABC
Program Type Sports Special
2 hours. 7/14/78. Live coverage from the Hilton Pavilion in Las Vegas.
Executive Producer Roone Arledge
Producer Dick Buffinton
Director Craig Janoff
Hosts Chris Schenkel, Cheryl Tiegs

1541 **The World Turned Upside Down**
Ourstory   PBS
Program Type Dramatic Special
30 minutes. Premiere date: 11/4/75. Repeat date: 10/10/77. Story of slave who spied on the British in order to win his freedom. Music by Benjamin Lees. Filmed in part at Richmondtown Restoration, Richmondtown, Staten Island, N.Y. Special effects by Ed Drohan. Funded by a grant from the National Endowment for the Humanities.
Executive Producer Don Fouser
Producer Ron Finley
Company WNET-TV/New York
Director Ron Finley
Writer Beverly Cross
Costume Designer John Boxer
Art Director Stephen Hendrickson
Host Bill Moyers
CAST
Armistead .... David Harris
Lafayette .... Richard Brestoff
Abercrombie .... Michael Ebert
Stevens .... Frank Raiter
Cornwallis .... Louis Turenne
Rush .... Saylor Creswell
Hessian Major .... Kenneth Tigar

1542   The World's Largest Indoor Country Music Show   NBC
Program Type Music/Dance Special
2 hours. Premiere date: 4/5/78. Reprises of performances which resulted in 1978 Grammy Awards. 100 entertainers, including stars of Nashville's Grand Ole Opry. Taped during a concert at the Silverdome, Pontiac, Michigan, 3/5/78.
Executive Producer Jim Fitzgerald
Producers Rudy Callicutt, Jim Fitzgerald
Director Vincent Scarza
Hosts Kenny Rogers, Dottie West

1543   Yabba Dabba Doo! The Happy World of Hanna-Barbera   CBS
Program Type Animated Film Special
2 hours. Premiere date: 11/24/77. Retrospective animation special saluting 20-year partnership of William Hanna and Joseph Barbera. Special art work by Iwao Takamoto. Director of photography: Dennis Dalzell.
Executive Producers Joseph Barbera, William Hanna
Producer Marshall Flaum
Director Marshall Flaum
Writer Marshall Flaum
Film Editor B. Lovitt
Hosts Gene Kelly, Cloris Leachman, Jonathan Winters
Special Guest Lorne Greene

1544   The Year in Golf—1978   NBC
Program Type Sports Special
30 minutes. Premiere date: 8/13/78. Comprehensive look at this year's PGA Tour.
Company TWI Production

1545   The Year Without a Santa Claus   ABC
Program Type Animated Film Special
60 minutes. Premiere date: 12/10/74. Repeat date: 12/9/77. Animated special using dimensional stop-motion photography. Based on the book by Phyllis McGinley. Music by Maury Laws; lyrics by Jules Bass.
Producers Arthur Rankin, Jr., Jules Bass
Company Rankin/Bass Productions
Directors Arthur Rankin, Jr., Jules Bass
Writer William Keenan
VOICES
Mrs. Santa (Narrator) .... Shirley Booth
Santa Claus ....Mickey Rooney
Snowmiser .... Dick Shawn
Heatmiser .... George S. Irving
Jingle Bells .... Robert McFadden
Jangle Bells .... Bradley Bolke
Mother Nature ....Rhoda Mann
Ignatius Thistlewhite ....Colin Duffy
Mr. Thistlewhite .... Ron Marshall

"Blue Christmas" Girl .... Christine Winter
Additional Voices The Wee Winter Singers

1546   The Yeomen of the Guard
Opera Theater   PBS
Program Type Music/Dance Special
2 hours. Premiere date: 7/17/78. Operetta by Gilbert and Sullivan with the New Philharmonia Orchestra and featuring The Ambrosian Opera Chorus led by Chorus Master John McCarthy. Program made possible by public television stations with additional support from The Nate B. and Frances Spingold Foundation.
Producer Cedric Messina
Company BBC and WNET-TV/New York
Director John Gorrie
Conductor David Lloyd-Jones
CAST
Elsie Maynard .... Valerie Masterson
Dame Carruthers .... Elizabeth Bainbridge
Colonel Fairfax .... David Hillman
Jack Point .... Derek Hammond-Stroud
Sergeant Meryll .... Bryan Drake
Phoebe Meryll .... Janet Hughes

1547   You Can Beat City Hall
CBS Reports   CBS
Program Type Documentary/Informational Special
Premiere date: 6/20/78. Report on a one-man campaign to reform Laredo, Texas.
Executive Producer Howard Stringer
Producer Roger Sims
Company CBS News
Writers Bill Moyers, Roger Sims
Cinematographer Lou Kidd

1548   You Can Run But You Can't Hide
Visions   PBS
Program Type Dramatic Special
90 minutes. Premiere date: 11/13/77. Original drama by Brother Jonathan of the Order of St. Francis about a troubled Vietnam veteran.
Executive Producer Barbara Schultz
Producer Barbara Schultz
Company KCET-TV/Los Angeles
Director Rick Bennewitz
CAST
Tom LaPorta .... Tom La Grua
Papa LaPorta .... Robert Symonds
Mama LaPorta .... Angela Clarke
Neil LaPorta .... Tony Schwab
Terry LaPorta .... Jenny Maybrook
Elaine .... Deborah White
Dolan .... Joe Stern
Scooter .... Douglas Grant
Mikey .... Michael Arkin
Jimmy .... Jimmy Justice
Haila .... Haila Strauss
Boyle .... Phillip Baker Hall
Stevie .... George Tyne

Bartender .... Joseph Borcia
Dr. Maurillo ....Jason Wingreen

You Can't Steal Love *See* The ABC Friday Night Movie

1549 You Gotta Start Somewhere
The Winners   CBS
Program Type Children's Special
30 minutes. Premiere date: 12/8/77. True story of an 11-year-old Sioux Indian boy who established a special school for Indian children in Rapid City, South Dakota. Music by Richard LaSalle.
Producer Bob Birnbaum
Company D'Angelo/Bullock/Allen Productions
Director William P. D'Angelo
Writers Lois and Arnold Peyser
CAST
Philip Gilbert ....Panchito Gomez
Madonna Gilbert ....Dimitra Arliss
Ted Means .... Van Williams
Mr. Painter .... Parley Bear
Mr. Smith .... Bill Quinn
Howard ....David Yanez
Keith ....Eric Greene
Arnold .... Danny Agrella

1550 You Put Music in My Life   NBC
Program Type Music/Dance Special
60 minutes. Premiere date: 5/11/78. Mac Davis special whose theme is a live concert from rehearsals to the actual performance.
Executive Producers Sandy Gallin, Raymond Katz
Producers Art Fisher, Mike Post
Company Cauchemar Productions
Director Art Fisher
Writers Paul Pumpian, Ed Hider, Rod Warren
Host Mac Davis
Guests Art Carney, Donna Summer, KC and the Sunshine Band

1551 The Young and the Restless   CBS
Program Type Daytime Drama Series
30 minutes. Mondays–Fridays. Premiere date: 3/26/73. Continuous. Created by William J. Bell and Lee Phillip Bell. Story about the Brooks and Foster families in Genoa City, USA. "Theme from the Young and the Restless," by Barry De Vorzon and Perry Botkin. Cast Listed alphabetically.
Executive Producer John Conboy
Producer Patricia Wenig
Company Columbia Pictures Television
Directors Dick Dunlap, Bill Glenn
Head Writer William J. Bell
Writers Kay Alden, Elizabeth Harrower
Art Director Tom Trimble
Set Decorator Brock Broughton

Announcer Bern Beanett
CAST
Lorie Brooks Prentiss .... Jaime Lyn Bauer
Stuart Brooks .... Robert Colbert
Kay Chancellor .... Jeanne Cooper
Jill Foster .... Brenda Dickson
Larry Larkin .... Gary Giem
Snapper Foster .... David Hasselhoff
Greg Foster .... Wings Hauser
Nikki Reed .... Erica Hope
Brock Reynolds .... Beau Kayzer
Derek Thurston ....Joe La Due
Dr. Casey Reed .... Roberta Leighton
Lucas Prentiss .... Tom Ligon
Leslie Brooks .... Victoria Mallory
Liz Foster ....Julianna McCarthy
Lance Prentiss .... John McCook
Carol Jones .... Patty Minter
Vanessa Prentiss .... K. T. Stevens
Linda Larkin .... Susan Walden

1552 Young Dan'l Boone   CBS
Program Type Drama Series
60 minutes Mondays. Premiere: 9/12/77. Daring explorations of Boone when he was a young man. "Young Dan'l Boone" theme by Earle Hagen
Executive Producer Ernie Frankel
Producer Jimmy Sangster
Company Frankel Productions in association with 20th Century-Fox Television
Directors Various
Writers Various
CAST
Daniel Boone .... Rick Moses
Rebecca Bryan .... Devon Ericson
Peter Dawes .... John Joseph Thomas
Hawk ....Ji-Tu Cumbuka
Tsiskwa .... Eloy Phil Casados

1553 Young Joe, The Forgotten Kennedy
The ABC Friday/Sunday Night Movie   ABC
Program Type TV Movie
2 hours. Premiere date: 9/18/77. Repeat date: 6/30/78. Drama focusing on the eldest Kennedy brother. Based on "The Lost Prince: Young Joe, the Forgotten Kennedy," by Hank Searls.
Producer William McCutchen
Company ABC Circle Films
Director Richard T. Heffron
Writer M. Charles Cohen
Film Editor Ronald J. Fagan
CAST
Joseph Kennedy, Jr. ....Peter Strauss
Vanessa Hunt .... Barbara Parkins
Joseph Kennedy, Sr. .... Stephen Elliott
Kathleen Kennedy ....Darleen Carr
Delaney ....Simon Oakland
Mike Krasna .... Asher Brauner
Joe, Jr. (age 14) .... Lance Kerwin
Simpson .... Peter Fox
Ray Pierce ....Steve Kanaly
Willy .... Robert Englund
Rose Kennedy .... Gloria Stroock

Young Joe, The Forgotten Kennedy
Continued

Elinor	Tara Talboy
Hank Riggs	Ben Fuhrman
Commander Devril	James Sikking
Greenway	Ken Swofford
Anderson	Lawrason Driscoll
Jack Kennedy	Sam Chew
Ted Kennedy	Patrick Laborteaux
Bob Kennedy	Shane Kerwin
Jean Kennedy	Margie Zech
Rosemary Kennedy	Dristin Larkin
Eunice Kennedy	Rosanne Covy
Pat Kennedy	Deirdre Berthrong
Melody Lane	Kim O'Brien
Billy Harrington	Michael Irving
English Major	Gardner Hayes

1554 The Young Pioneers ABC
Program Type Western Series
60 minutes. Sundays. Premiere date: 4/2/78 (two hours). Last show: 4/16/78. A young couple build a life in the newly opened Dakota Territory in the 1870s. Based upon "The Young Pioneers" books, by Rose Wilder Lane. Developed for television by Blanche Hanalis. Originally produced for television by Ed Friendly. Music by Dominic Frontiere. Filmed entirely in Arizona.
Executive Producers Lee Rich, Earl Hamner
Producer Robert L. Jacks
Company A Lorimar Production in association with Amanda Productions, Inc.
Directors Various
Writers Various
CAST
Molly Beaton	Linda Purl
David Beaton	Roger Kern
Dan Gray	Robert Hayes
Mr. Peters	Robert Donner
Nettie	Mare Winningham
Flora	Michelle Stacy
Charlie	Jeff Cotler

1555 The Young Sentinels NBC
Program Type Animated Film Series
30 minutes. Saturdays. Premiere: 9/10/77. Retitled "The Space Sentinels" as of 11/19/77. Animated adventure series about three teenagers. Music and sound effects by Horta-Mahana Corp.
Executive Producers Lou Scheimer; Norm Prescott
Producer Don Christensen
Company Filmation Studios
Additional Voices Dee Timberlake, George DiCenzo, Evan Kim, Ross Hagen

1556 Your Place or Mine? CBS
Program Type Comedy Special
30 minutes. Premiere date: 5/27/78. Pilot about a Manhattan freelance writer who swaps homes with an editorial assistant from Long Island.
Executive Producer Bob Ellison

Producers David Lloyd, Dale McRaven
Company MTM Enterprises, Inc.
Director Jim Burrows
Writers Bob Ellison, David Lloyd
CAST
Kelly Barnes	Jane Actman
Jeff Burrell	Stuart Gillard
Ernie Barnes	Peter Hobbs
Frances Barnes	Alice Hirson
Mrs. Hicks	Elizabeth Kerr
Harold	George Pentecost
Linda Hiller	Judy Graubart
Carol	Elizabeth Halliday
Voice of Mr. Weinberg	Martin Garner

1557 Your Turn: Letters to CBS News CBS
Program Type News Series
30 minutes. Premiere date: 2/5/78. Viewer response broadcasts once every two months.
Executive Producer Joel Heller
Producers Anne Chambers, Leslie Waring Flynn
Company CBS News
Director Vern Diamond
Film Editor Jonathan Powell
Host Sharron Lovejoy

1558 You're a Good Sport, Charlie Brown CBS
Program Type Animated Film Special
30 minutes. Premiere date: 10/28/75. Repeat date: 1/23/78. Based on the "Peanuts" comic strip by Charles M. Schulz. Music by Vince Guaraldi.
Executive Producer Lee Mendelson
Producer Bill Melendez
Company Lee Mendelson-Bill Melendez Production in cooperation with United Feature Syndicate, Inc., and Charles M. Schulz Creative Associates
Director Phil Roman
Writer Charles M. Schulz
Musical Director Vince Guaraldi
Music Supervisor John Scott Trotter
VOICES
Charlie Brown	Duncan Watson
Linus	Liam Martin
Peppermint Patty	Stuart Brotman
Sally	Gail M. Davis
Marcie	Jimmy Ahrens
Lucy	Melanie Kohn

1559 You're a Poet and Don't Know It! ... The Poetry Power Hour
The CBS Festival of Lively Arts for Young People CBS
Program Type Children's Special
60 minutes. Premiere date: 11/14/76. Repeat date: 1/2/78. Recitations, dramatizations and discussions of 200 years of American poetry.

Executive Producers Lester Gottlieb; Robert Stolfi
Producer Burt Shevelove
Director John Desmond
Writer Thomas Baum
Costume Designer Leslie Renfield
Scenic Designer J. Newton White
Stars Frank Converse, Blythe Danner, Rosemary Harris, Leonard Nimoy, Tom Seaver, Jack Weston
Children Kelly Jordan, John McCurry, Gladys Moore, David Moskin, Julie Newman, Tony Perez, David Stambough

1560 You're Not a Hero Until You're Sung   PBS
Program Type Public Affairs Special
90 minutes. Premiere date: 9/3/78. Explores the American hero in myth and media. Program made possible by a grant from Levi Strauss and Company with additional funding from Friends of Channel 10, Inc. Filmed at Sun Valley, Idaho.
Executive Producer Elmo Sackett
Producers Dean Davies, Sterling Johnson
Company KBGL-TV/Pocatello
Panelists Julian Bond, Lindsay Wagner, Rob Reiner, Timothy Leary, Penny Marshall, William Kunstler, Roger Mosley, Doe Mayer

1561 Youth Unemployment: A Question of Survival   PBS
Program Type Public Affairs Special
60 minutes. Premiere date: 6/4/78. Documentary on jobless young people.
Executive Producer Joan Konner
Producer Patricia Sides
Company WNET-TV/New York
Correspondent Charlayne Hunter-Gault

1562 Yukon Passage
National Geographic Special   PBS
Program Type Documentary/Informational Special
60 minutes. Premiere date: 12/5/77. Story of how four young men traveled the Yukon wilderness in the manner of the old gold prospectors. Program made possible by a grant from Gulf Oil Corporation.
Producer James Lipscomb
Company WQED-TV/Pittsburgh
Director James Lipscomb
Host E. G. Marshall
Narrator James Stewart
Participants Keith Tryck (surveyor), Bob Clark (photographer), Paul Crews (professional skier), Jerry Wallace (logger).

1563 Ziegfeld: The Man and His Women
The Big Event/NBC World Premiere Movie   NBC
Program Type TV Movie
2 hours. Premiere date: 5/21/78. Musical drama about the legendary showman who built his Ziegfeld Follies around beautiful women.
Executive Producer M. J. (Mike) Frankovich
Company Columbia Pictures Television in association with Frankovich Productions and NBC-TV
Director Buzz Kulik
Writer Joanna Lee
Choreographer Miriam Nelson
Costume Designer Grady Hunt
Production Designer John DeCuir
Art Director John DeCuir
Set Decorator Richard C. Goddard
Cinematographer Gerald Perry Finnerman
Film Editor Leslie L. Green
CAST

Flo Ziegfeld	Paul Shenar
Lillian Lorraine	Valerie Perrine
Anna Held	Barbara Parkins
Billie Burke	Samantha Eggar
Marilyn Miller	Pamela Peadon
Dr. Ziegfeld	David Opatoshu
Charles Frohman	Nehemiah Persoff
Nora Bayes	Inga Swenson
Abe Erlanger	Cliff Norton
Will Rogers	Gene McLaughlin
Eddie Cantor	Richard Shea
Fanny Brice	Catherine Jacoby
Bert Williams	David Downing

1564 Zoom   PBS
Program Type Children's Special
30 minutes. Monday–Friday afternoons. Premiere date: 10/1/72. Sixth season premiere: 11/7/77. Magazine-format series produced for, by, and about youngsters 8–12 years old. Regular features: ZOOMgames and ZOOMbarrels, ZOOMplays, ZOOMraps, ZOOMphenomenon, ZOOMgoody, ZOOMguests, ZOOMdo, ZOO-Mailroom. New feature, cinema ZOOM, added 1977–78 season. Monday through Thrusday programs captioned for the hearing-impaired by WGBH-TV/Boston. Series made possible by grants from the Corporation for Public Broadcasting, the Ford Foundation, Public Television Stations, General Foods Corporation and the U.S. Bureau of Education for the Handicapped.
Executive Producer Terri Payne Francis
Producer Bob Glover
Company WGBH-TV/Boston
Director Richard Heller
Musical Director Newton Wayland
Scenic Designer Clint Heitman

Zorro *See* The CBS Friday Night Movies

1565   Zubin Mehta and the Los Angeles Philharmonic
Great Performances   PBS
Program Type Music/Dance Special
60 minutes. Premiere date: 2/8/78. Zubin Mehta
conducts the Los Angeles Philharmonic Orches-
tra in "Concerto in B Flat Major for Bassoon and
Orchestra" by Wolfgang Amedeus Mozart and
"Concerto for Orchestra" by B. Bartok in a pro-
gram taped at the Dorothy Chandler Pavilion of
the Los Angeles Music Center. Soloist for the
Mozart Concerto is David Briedenthal. Program
made possible by a grant from Exxon and local
PBS stations.
Executive Producers Klaus Hallig, Jac Venza
Producer David Griffiths
Company Unitel for WNET-TV/New York
Director Kirk Browning

1566   Zubin Mehta, The New York Philharmonic and Shirley Verrett
Live from Lincoln Center/Great Performances
                                                    PBS
Program Type Music/Dance Special
2 hours. Premiere date: 9/24/77. Zubin Mehta
conducts the New York Philharmonic Orchestra
in a live concert featuring soloist Shirley Verrett.
Program made possible by grants from Exxon,
CPB, and National Endowment for the Arts.
Producer John Goberman
Company Lincoln Center with WNET-TV/New
   York
Director Kirk Browning
Host Dick Cavett
Musical Director Zubin Mehta

Who's Who in TV 1977-1978